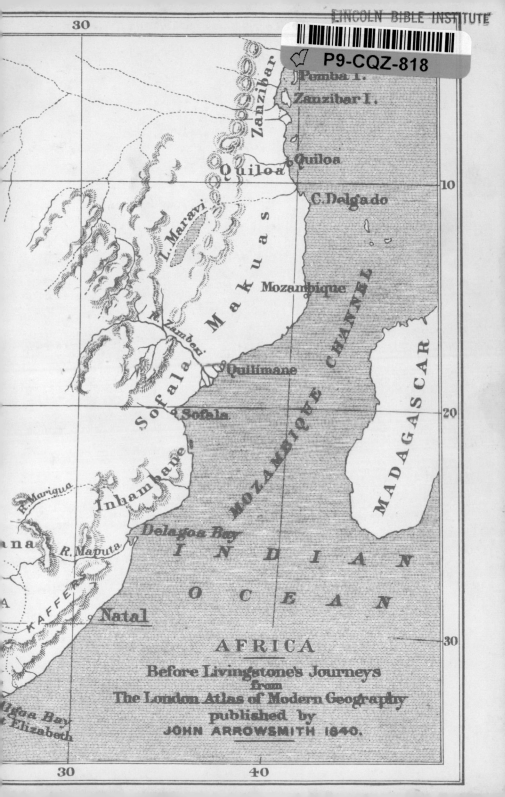

30

Zanzibar

Pemba I.

Zanzibar I.

Quiloa

Quiloa

C. Delgado

10

L. Maravi

M a k u a s

Mozambique

R. Zambezi

MADAGASCAR

MOZAMBIQUE CHANNEL

Quilimane

S o f a l a

20

Sofala

Inhambane

R. Marigua

Delagoa Bay

R. Maputa

I N D I A N

KAFFERS

O C E A N

Natal

30

ana

A

Algoa Bay
Pt. Elizabeth

AFRICA

Before Livingstone's Journeys
from
The London Atlas of Modern Geography
published by
JOHN ARROWSMITH 1840.

30

40

DAVID LIVINGSTONE:
HIS LIFE AND LETTERS

DAVID LIVINGSTONE
(1864)

Annan, Glasgow

DAVID LIVINGSTONE:
HIS LIFE AND LETTERS

by

GEORGE SEAVER

HARPER & BROTHERS · PUBLISHERS · NEW YORK

DAVID LIVINGSTONE: HIS LIFE AND HIS LETTERS

Copyright © 1957 by George Seaver

Printed in the United States of America
All rights in this book are reserved

Library of Congress catalog card number: 57-9884

CONTENTS

CONTENTS

ILLUSTRATIONS

MAPS

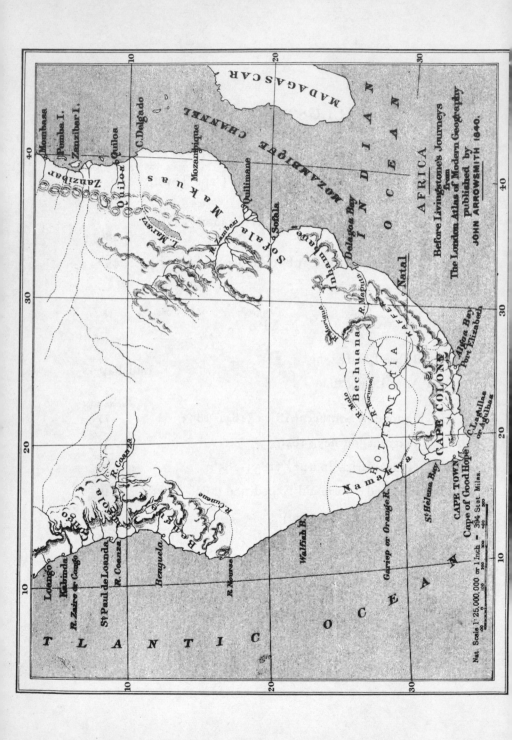

MADAGASCAR

MOZAMBIQUE CHANNEL

INDIAN OCEAN

AFRICA

Before Livingstone's Journeys
from
The London Atlas of Modern Geography
published by
JOHN ARROWSMITH 1840.

Mombasa
Pemba I.
Zanzibar I.
Zanzibar
Quiloa
Quiloa
C.Delgado

Makuas

Mozambique
Quillimane
R.Zambezi
Sofala
Sofala
Sena

Delagoa Bay
R.Maputa
Natal

L.Mar avi

Inhambane

Bechuana
R.Molo
R.Kuruman
HOTTENTOTIA
KAFFERS

Namakwa
Gariep or Orange R.

Algoa Bay
Port Elizabeth

CAPE COLONY

C.l'Agulhas
or Agulhas

St Helena Bay
CAPE TOWN
Cape of Good Hope

Walfisch R.

R.Nourse

R.Cunene

Benguela
R.Coanza

R.Coanza

St Paul de Loanda

Congo
R.Zaire or Congo
Mal inda
Loango

A T L A N T I C   O C E A N

Nat. Scale 1:25,000,000 or 1 Inch = 394 Stat. Miles.

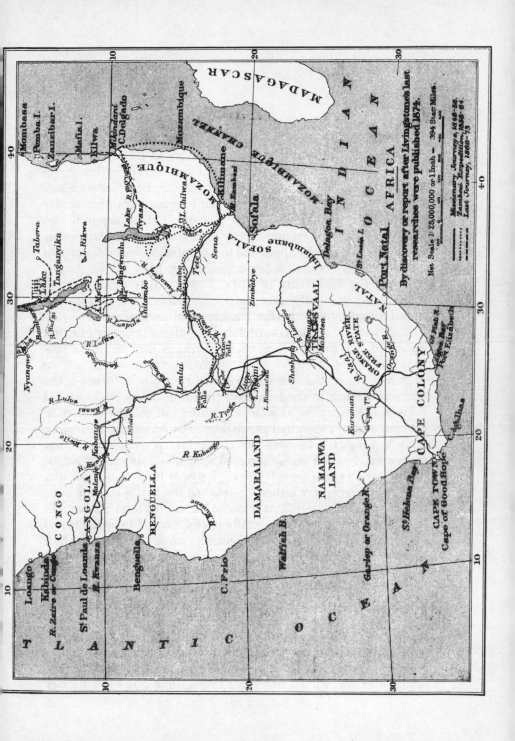

AFRICA

By discovery or report after Livingstone's last
researches were published 1874.

Nat. Scale 1:25,000,000 or 1 inch = 394 Stat. Miles.

Missionary Journeys, 1840-56.
Zambesi Expedition, 1858-64.
Last Journey, 1866-73.

PREFACE

THE aim of this book has been as far as possible to allow the subject of it to tell his own story in his own way, for a man's personality speaks out more truly in his direct utterance than by means of any paraphrase, however succinct. Drastically reduced from its original length it has of necessity excluded much that is of great interest, both substantial and subsidiary. The literature upon Livingstone is already enormous. A bibliography appended to Campbell's biography (1929) enumerates 87 books. A list compiled by Miss M. E. Appleyard for the University of Cape Town (1947) numbers 198. Since then, especially since the recent publication of a host of unpublished letters, the list has mounted considerably.

And yet no single comprehensive Life of Livingstone has appeared, for the sufficient reason perhaps that his ideal biographer would need to be a doctor, a naturalist in all its branches, an ethnologist of the Bantu race, an historian of the political science in the formative period of South and Central African colonization, as well as a student of the psychology of religion and of individual psychology. For he would be dealing with a subject who was an evangelist, physician, colonial statesman, linguist and anthropologist, geographer and scientist, as well as one for whom religion was the *leit-motiv* of life.

Of the biographies hitherto published the first is still the best, namely Blaikie's (1880), as it is also the most authoritative. He had access to material, especially in the form of private letters, some part of which has only recently come to light. He had also the advantage of personal converse with Livingstone's surviving contemporaries. But his book suffers from the defect of being uncritical. An aura of hagiography also beclouds the studies of his successors—except those few, having pro-Boer sympathies, whose estimate of Livingstone is distorted. But neither the one nor the other does justice to his subject; for a figure glimpsed through the refracted mists of sentiment is no more true to life than one whose portrayal is warped by prejudice. On the whole, however, Livingstone has been luckier than several of his great contemporaries. He escaped the brilliant but virulent pen of Lytton Strachey whose caricatures of some Eminent Victorians set the vogue for future less-gifted belittlers of human greatness. There is indeed a play which bears his name, with a celebrated actor in the title rôle, which is such a flagrant travesty of its original as to lack even the merit of a caricature.

The habit of biography is productive of one valuable discipline at least: it fosters in the conscience of him who essays it a habit of veracity. For it is required of a biographer above all else that he be found faithful; and such a requisite demands constant vigilance. Dead men cannot defend themselves; they cannot contradict or answer back. Not seldom in this task the present chronicler has caught himself up on the verge of perpetrating some factual misstatement or even some erroneous judgment, which further research or reflection corrected just in time. But he has been almost shocked that there was no hand to arrest him, no voice to say "Not so!"

Arising out of this it is the duty of a biographer to present all the many aspects of his subject's character without partiality, inviting comprehension but not seeking to compel it unduly. For this reason there will be found in this book the maximum of presentation and the minimum of interpretation. Its compilation has resembled that of fitting together the scattered pieces of a mosaic, gathered with some difficulty from various sources far and near, in the hope that the resultant pattern will present at least the lineaments of a recognizable portrait.

In collecting the materials for his task the writer has some good friends to thank, and chiefly the following: the Reverend Dr. J. I. Macnair who read through the first seventeen chapters and offered valuable comments, before his lamented death at an advanced age in 1955; any attempt to perpetuate Livingstone's memory is inseparable from the name of Macnair. Professor J. P. R. Wallis, the distinguished editor of contemporary records, performed the same kind office and generously lent the typescripts of his edition of the Zambesi Journals and Letters from the mass of recently found documents, of which their publication is of necessity an abridgment. To Dr. Hubert Wilson, the explorer's grandson, heartfelt thanks are due for the use of personal letters hitherto unpublished, and especially for his friendly co-operation both by correspondence and conversation. Another friend of former years, Professor Frank Debenham, whose recent study of Livingstone as geographer is the work of a specialist, has kindly allowed the reproduction of valuable maps of his own making. Last but not least Miss Fletcher, Librarian of the London Missionary Society, not only gave the writer the freedom of the Library but herself typed many manuscripts in its archives for his use, and never failed to respond to a request for information.

His thanks are also due to the late Earl of Clarendon for permission to consult and quote from the Clarendon Correspondence in the Bodleian Library; to Mr. H. V. Hiller, Custodian of the Central African Archives, for the loan of micro-films of all the Livingstone–Bruce Collection; to Dr. J. Desmond Clark, Curator of the Rhodes–Livingstone Museum, for the loan of copies of all the Livingstone documents in his custody; to the Keeper of the Rhodes House Library for access to the Waller Papers; to the Warden of the Livingstone Memorial for free use of the Library there; to the Curator of the Museum in High Barnet for an unpublished photograph of Livingstone, and to Miss Fletcher again for two others; and finally to the Reverend Cecil Northcott of the Lutterworth Press, who first suggested and then sponsored this undertaking.

Chapter One

ANTECEDENTS AND UPBRINGING
1813–1836

"I soon resolved to devote my life to the alleviation of human misery."

To a child of the nineteenth century thought was free and the world was wide. It was an age of emancipation, of liberalism and individualism. Before the close even of its second decade the war that had ravaged Europe for more than twenty years was over. Britain, having "saved herself by her exertions and Europe by her example" (she had done so before in 1588, she would do so again in 1940) was already leading the van in the march of the nations. Though not indeed crippled and destitute as they were, having been saved from the scathe of invasion by her "defensive moat", she was nevertheless impoverished. But partly by her quickness to seize opportunity, partly by her native resilience, she was already riding the crest of the industrial revolution. And even for the humblest of her sons there were opportunities, not only for acquiring wealth, but also for winning renown in almost any field of strenuous activity: there was, for example, an entire continent the interior of which had never been explored.

Never since the days of Elizabeth was there such scope for men of practical idealism and individual enterprise; nor has any age produced so many illustrious names in the realms of thought, of culture, or of action. Men were conscious of a sense of far horizons; their minds were awake to the dawn of a new renaissance. To us who watched its sunset, and then the splendour of its afterglow, these signs then seemed the presage of a yet more glorious morrow; but now, as we view them in retrospect, they were the portent of more than forty years of storm and tempest, the ruin of which is not yet spent.

It lacked only two years for that decisive battle to be fought and won, which would determine the fortunes of Europe for a century, when on 19 March 1813 David Livingstone opened his eyes upon a world in which the balance might yet swing either way.

He came of a hardy stock of poor crofters whose forebears had for generations wrested a meagre subsistence from the rocky soil of one of two small islands, Ulva, off the western coast of Mull. The other is Iona and thence, according to a Gaelic tradition, the clan of Mac an Leigh—"sons of the physician" (anglicized no doubt to an equivalent of Leighs-ton and corrupted in pronunciation)—had peopled the western Highlands from the time of St. Columba and one may suppose that it would have given him a passing whimsical pleasure to indulge the fancy that the noble art of healing was, even if remotely, in his blood.

One of his earliest memories was that of listening entranced to his grandfather's tales of bygone days, but of these there was only one which he thought worth recording. It was the precept bequeathed by a nameless worthy of their line to his children on his death-bed in the form of a motto which "ran in our blood": *Be Honest.*

His grandfather, Neil Livingston, certainly practised it and his trustworthiness earned him in old age a comfortable pension from the Blantyre cotton factory. He had also, said his grandson, a sense of the value of education, and never grudged the price of a school-book to any of his children. Of these there were seven—five sons and two daughters. All his sons served as sailors or soldiers in the Napoleonic Wars, except the youngest, Neil.

Neil Livingston the younger was born in 1788 and began life as a clerk in the cotton-factory which had been taken over in 1792 by James Monteith, "who maintained its kindly traditions". But he was soon apprenticed by his father to David Hunter (an old friend who like himself had been an impecunious crofter) in the tailoring department of the firm. The firm subsidized the education of its apprentices in the local school, and Neil's sons later had the benefit of the same privilege, a boon for which one of them at least never ceased to be grateful.

The Hunters were staunch Covenanters of Lowland breed, and of antecedents as humble as the Livingstons. As a result of this connection Neil Livingston married David Hunter's daughter Agnes in 1810, and their second son was christened after him. Much has been made by some of his admirers of the blend in him of Highland Celt with Lowland Scot: the adventurousness, imagination, and intrepidity of the one; the dauntlessness, sturdy independence, and indomitable resolution of the other; but, apart from the fact that such distinctions in racial temperament are somewhat arbitrary, it seems unnecessary to invoke heredity to account for their combination in a unique personality.

A sedentary occupation would appear to have been uncongenial to the younger Neil, for he soon resigned it to become an itinerant tea-vendor and incidentally a colporteur of religious tracts. There was evidently something of the rover in him, and something of the missionary. On his journeys as a commercial traveller, "though too conscientious ever to become rich" (says his son), he combined business with religious zeal. He brought up his family in the tenets of the established Kirk, but afterwards left it for an independent congregational conventicle of stricter discipline in Hamilton, where for the last twenty years of his life he held office as deacon. He altered the spelling of his name by the addition of a final *e* about the year 1855, since when the spelling was regularly adopted by his family.

> Of quick temper and of a tender heart, by his kindliness of manner and winning ways he made the heartstrings of his children twine around him as firmly as if he had possessed, and could have bestowed upon them, every worldly advantage. . . .

David revered the memory of his mother equally well. "My earliest recollection of her recalls a picture so often seen among the Scottish poor—that of the anxious housewife striving to make both ends meet." He delighted in recalling stories of her youth that she had told him by the home fireside. She had too all the native independence of her race. It was a three miles' walk to the little chapel in Hamilton for the family on Sunday, "and it was the friendly custom of those who resided near to entertain them and others who came from a distance", but it was related of Mrs. Livingston that "she would never accept more hospitality than a kettle of boiling water for tea and seats at table for her family group"; she had brought their lunch with her. The meal over, she would console herself with a few whiffs from her clay "cutty" pipe.[1]

Husband and wife had removed temporarily to Glasgow soon after their marriage, and in that city their eldest son John was born. But in preparation for the birth of their second child, Agnes returned to her parents' little home in Shuttle Row, Blantyre, where she herself had been born, and which has since become one of the most frequented places of pilgrimage in the British Isles. David was the second son of a family which grew to comprise five sons (two of whom died young) and two daughters. But as these two sons died in infancy, there was a gap of six years between David and his sister Janet; then came Charles and Agnes. It is a curious fact that his father was also one of a family of five sons and two daughters, as was also his father-in-law, Robert Moffat.

That little home was one of twenty-four "single kitchens" in the top flat of a three-storied tenement building for factory workers, situated on a high bank of the Clyde, overlooking the factory and the river beneath, and beyond them the higher bank with its grove of oaks and ash-trees bordering the Bothwell estate. Each of these rooms is of dimensions fourteen feet by ten: sufficient accommodation for one family for all purposes—living, cooking, sleeping. It contains recesses for two large beds: one for the parents, the other for the children. The bedsteads stand high enough for the stowage of truckle-beds beneath them; these could be pulled out at night if required, in which case nearly all the floor-space would be occupied. To us to-day life in such conditions would be considered unlivable, but it was the accustomed lot of factory-hands a century ago and better far than the cribbed "but an' ben" of the crofter in the open fields: the hardship to them was not in confined quarters but in the drudgery of long hours and scant pay. And yet with all its disadvantages "the management was paternal", and Blantyre was in its day a model village. Nor, in the case of the Livingstone family, were the conditions as bad as might appear, since John and David when in their 'teens were lodged with their grandparents in a neighbouring cottage.

Little now remains of the long line of factory buildings by the river, and nothing of the once populous dwellinghouses on the high ground above them—save only Shuttle Row. For more than two hundred years it was a scene of human and mechanical activity. But now the smoke is gone, the wheels are dumb, and the landscape of that sylvan riverside may be said to have reverted to the look of idyllic tranquillity that it wore before industry defaced it in 1785. The forty acres that contained this once humming hive of industry are now a grass-grown playing-field for children, in itself a spacious and wholesome part of the Livingstone Memorial; whilst the large twenty-four-roomed tenement in a small corner of which he was born, together with the long annexe of two-storied buildings extending from it, is converted into a museum, a library, and a shrine worthy in all respects, especially in their simplicity and completeness, of the memory of the man they are designed to honour.

Parental discipline in David's home was strict and was taken as a matter of course by the family, and on one occasion by himself too literally, though with characteristic fortitude and good humour.

> He seems from his earliest childhood to have been of a calm, self-reliant nature. It was his father's habit to lock the door at dusk, by which time all the children were expected to be in the house. One evening David had infringed this rule, and when he reached the door it was barred. He made no cry nor disturbance, but, having procured a piece of bread, sat down contentedly to pass the night on the doorstep.[2]

"On the doorstep" must however be considered a misapprehension on the part of the recounter of this story. The door at the bottom of the outside spiral stone stairway would not be locked, nor would it have been his father's province as one inmate of that section of the tenement to lock it at dusk. He locked his own door at the top of the flat, and it must have been in the corner of the wood-floored threshold outside it that David passed the night.

At the age of ten he was put into the cotton-factory as a piecer. His task was to walk back and forth between the reels of the whirring spinning-jenny and tie the broken threads. Having purchased a Latin Grammar with part of his first week's wages he placed the book on a portion of the frame, and memorized sentence by sentence as he passed to and fro. "I thus kept up a pretty constant study undisturbed by the roar of the machinery. To this part of my education I owe my present power of completely abstracting the mind from surrounding noises, so as to read and write with perfect comfort amidst the play of children or near the dancing and songs of savages." His hours were from 6 a.m. to 8 p.m., with intervals for breakfast and dinner. But with the close of the day's work his real work was just beginning—at least from the age of thirteen when the local schoolmaster, Mr. McSkimming, opened an evening class for Latin. "I pursued the study of that language for many years afterwards, with unabated ardour, at an evening school, which met between the hours of eight and ten." One wonders how he managed to get any supper, for it is certain that he was as punctual as he could be. Perhaps he took a "piece" with him in his pocket. But even then his ardour was unsatisfied. "The dictionary part of my labours was followed up till twelve o'clock, or later, if my mother did not interfere by jumping up and snatching the book out of my hands." And he had to be up—and at work—at 6 a.m.! There has been many a poor Scottish student who has shown a similar grit (such as by reading under a street lamp for lack of light at home), but a display of such will-power in a lad's early 'teens is surely something phenomenal.

The threading was itself light work and there would be periods of leisure. We are told that he "left no loose threads", but may take leave to doubt it. We cannot think that a lad of initiative and imagination would take kindly to such a monotonous task. We are also told that "the mill girls got great fun out of pitching bobbins at the book and trying to knock it off the frame". This is much more probable.

But it was not with him a case of all work and no play, even though the playtime was itself an education. He had a passion for natural history in all its branches, and especially for botany. On holidays and on long summer evenings together with his brothers he would scour the burns and braes in search of wildflowers, ferns and mosses; scrambling down the quarries for shells and fossils (in local parlance "bits o' flo'ers an' bits o' stanes an' sic like trash")—but chiefly collecting "simples", to identify them in an early guide-book to the plants of Lanarkshire.

Or it might be fishing. What boy has any respect for the sanctity of game? It was related by his sisters that once, fishing for trout, he hooked a salmon and could not bear the thought of relinquishing such a prize. So he slipped it down a leg of his brother Charles' trousers and they made for home, thereby "creating no little sympathy for the boy, as he passed through the village with his sadly swollen leg!"

Dr. Macnair has preserved the reminiscence of an old inhabitant which picturesquely points the contrast between the two brothers: "Oh aye, I kent the Livingstane laddies— Dauvid and Chairlie—weel. And there was a queer differ atween them. If they was walkin' along a road and cam' tae a puddle, Chairlie wud walk roon, but Dauvid—he'd stamp stracht through."

Sir Harry Johnston recorded that, on enquiring of an old acquaintance in Blantyre what sort of a person David was in his 'teens, was answered: "Dr. Livingstone was no thocht to be a by-ordinar' [extraordinary] laddie; just a sulky, quiet, feckless sort o' boy." ("Sulky" is Scotch for shy or taciturn.) And Dr. Macnair has illustrated the meaning of "feckless" by the remark of a farmer who employed him sometimes as a small boy to herd his cattle: "I didna' think muckle o' that David Livingston when he worked wi' me. He was aye lyin' on his belly readin' a book."

At eighteen he was promoted to be a spinner. "The toil", he says, "was excessively severe on a slim, loose-jointed lad, but it was well paid for": it enabled him later to support himself while attending lectures in medicine and divinity. It probably also gave him a little more leisure, since he now began the devouring study of solid books. One of these was "that extraordinary old work on astrological medicine, Culpeper's *Herbal* —and I believe I got as far into that abyss of fantasies as my author said he dared to lead me".

Scientific works and books of travel were his special delight: in the latter his father encouraged him, but not in the former. As for theology, he had an instinctive distaste for "dry doctrinal reading" and his father's "last application of the rod" was occasioned by his refusal to peruse a book of this kind. Instead he studied the works of Dr. Thomas Dick on natural philosophy, which confirmed his belief—not shared by his father and elders —that science was not hostile to religion. (Neither the statements nor the conclusions of this somewhat naïve philosophy of nature could bear the test of later criticism. The researches of Darwin had not yet invaded the strongholds of dogmatic theology.)

He was about twenty years of age when he read these books which reinforced his instinctive conviction that the God of nature and revelation were one, and soon afterwards there occurred in him an interior illumination which had the practical effect of determining his destiny. With characteristic reticence and deliberate restraint he adverts to this in the brief personal memoir which prefaces his *Travels*. The passage is so important that it must be quoted in full. (The italics are not his.)

> Great pains had been taken by my parents to instil the doctrines of Christianity into my mind, and I had no difficulty in understanding the *theory* of our free salvation by the atonement of our Saviour, but it was only about this time that I really began to feel the necessity and value of a *personal application* of the provisions of that atonement to my own case. The change was like what may be supposed would take place were it possible to cure a case of 'colour blindness.' The perfect freeness with which the pardon of all our guilt is offered in God's book drew forth feelings of *affectionate love* to Him who bought us with his blood, and a sense of *deep obligation* to Him for His mercy has influenced, in some small measure, my conduct ever since. *But I shall not again refer to the inner spiritual life which I believe then began, nor do I intend to specify with any prominence the evangelistic labours to which the love of Christ has since impelled me:* this book will speak not so much of what has been done, as of *what still remains to be performed* before the gospel can be said to be preached to all nations.
>
> In the glow of love which Christianity inspires, I soon resolved *to devote my life to the alleviation of human misery* . . . and therefore set myself to obtain a medical education, in order to be qualified for that enterprise.

In the first place it is necessary to notice the extreme simplicity of his faith. It was a faith which became ever simpler and also more personal as his life progressed, so as ultimately to require no doctrinal formulation. He was never a theologian nor had he any desire to be; he would have recoiled as much from the complexities and subtleties of dogma as he did from sentimental religious phraseology. It matters not at all that the "theory" of the Atonement which he accepted from his parents was that of the voluntary vicarious sacrifice of Christ which the Scottish Church derived from Calvin; for him, it was the personal experience of redemption that mattered, and this experience was the practical expression of that conceptual theory. But the experience of redeeming love thus freely given demanded from him a personal application, a practical response, something to touch the well-springs of action and determine the course of his future conduct. It came to him with the force of an inner obligation: the giving of himself and of his life to Christ, which is the service of love in action. For he would never know Christ fully as his Redeemer until in some way—"in some small measure" (the words are startling in their humility)—he could begin to participate in the self-same act of redemption. The compelling motive behind this resolve was compassion, which is the root impulse of the Christian ethic; large areas of the world were still unredeemed and in the bondage of sin and suffering; he would therefore devote his life to the alleviation of human misery. But concrete performance is more than abstract precept; he would therefore strive, in seeking to rescue the souls, also to heal the bodies of the afflicted.

His convictions thus settled, young Livingston applied for communicant membership of the Independent Church at Hamilton in which his father held the office of deacon. But his father, "doubtless from considerations of propriety", left to his colleagues the question of David's fitness for admission. Even then the grave and cautious elders, we are told, "dooted if Dauvit were soun'" and appointed two of their number to give him further instruction "in the doctrines". The man chiefly responsible for this tuition was a veteran named Arthur Anderson, between whom and his young probationer there developed a close personal friendship based on mutual respect. Week by week for five months David tramped from Blantyre to Hamilton, for the benefit of instruction and prayer with this elder, before the latter felt justified in recommending him for solemn public reception as a communicant. But as yet he had no thought of himself volunteering as a missionary. Feeling "that the salvation of men ought to be the chief desire and aim of every Christian" he had resolved to give to the cause of missions "all that he might earn beyond what was required for his subsistence". But in 1834 he was attracted by an Appeal to the Churches in Britain and America for qualified medical missionaries in China where the need was great. It came from Dr. Charles Gützlaff, "whose noble faith and dauntless enterprise, aided by his medical skill, pressing into China over

obstacles apparently insurmountable" fired Livingstone with
the ideal of what a missionary should be and attracted him to
the country where Gützlaff laboured. Thenceforth, "his efforts
were constantly directed towards that object without any fluc-
tuation". (The idea of Medical Missions was at that time
something new; and it was in connection with evangelism in
China that they originated.)

He confided his resolve to no one but his parents and the
minister of his church, the Rev. John Moir. His father was at
first opposed to it but, when convinced of the entire disinter-
estedness of the motive that underlay it, he withdrew his
objection and sought to further his son's project by every means
possible. His means were scant, but David's idea was to finance
his own training without imposing on his father's strained
resources, and to pay for his expenses during the winter sessions
by continuing to work as a factory hand during the summer.
Twenty years later, in his personal memoir, he says: "I never
received a farthing of aid from anyone. . . . " But in reply to a
question by the London Mission authorities about his occupation and its relation to his academic work, he wrote (in 1838),
"A brother similarly employed [John] gives a little assistance
in college fees. The brother has a family to support." The
apparent discrepancy is explainable if, as is almost certainly the
case, he regarded this assistance as a loan and repaid it as soon
as he could. It was a time-honoured custom in the households
of the Scottish poor for an elder brother to help a younger
towards the cost of college fees; and David later helped his
brother Charles towards his passage to America. Similarly it
was not unusual for a student to work in the summer to maintain himself at college in the winter. But to make these earnings
tide over two separate academic courses must have entailed the
utmost frugality and self-denial. He never regretted it, but was
thankful for it.

> Looking back now on that life of toil, I cannot but feel thankful that it
> formed such a material part of my early education; and, were it possible,
> I should like to begin life over again in the same lowly style, and to pass
> through the same hardy training.

And later still, it was with profound sincerity that on the
stone which he placed over his parents' grave in Hamilton he

caused to be inscribed these words (deliberately substituting a matter-of-fact headline in place of the conventional phrasing customary on such epitaphs, and rejecting a suggestion to change "and" of the last line into "but")—

TO SHOW THE RESTING PLACE OF
NEIL LIVINGSTONE
AND AGNES HUNTER HIS WIFE,
AND TO EXPRESS THE THANKFULNESS TO GOD
OF THEIR CHILDREN
JOHN, DAVID, JANET, CHARLES, AND AGNES,
FOR POOR AND PIOUS PARENTS.

Chapter Two

GLASGOW AND LONDON
1836–1840

*"Fire, water, or stone-wall would not stop Livingstone in
the fulfilment of any recognized duty."*

EARLY on a cold morning in the late autumn of 1836 Neil
Livingston and his son trudged through the snow eight
miles from Blantyre to Glasgow. It was probably not for
the first time; it was certainly not for the last. Armed with a
list of lodgings they searched all day for one within their means,
till at length they found one in Rotten Row at the rent of two
shillings a week. Next morning David began to attend his
classes, in Greek and Divinity, Chemistry and Medicine, and
wrote to friends at home that he felt lonely without his father,
but "I must put a stout heart to a stey brae". Soon afterwards,
finding his landlady untrustworthy, he changed his lodging for
another in the High Street where at half-a-crown a week he
was "very comfortable".

The immensity of his subsequent physical exertions has perhaps thrown into the shade his almost equal intellectual energy.
His first book is entitled *Missionary Travels and Researches in
South Africa*, and the scientific researches are as important as
the geographical feat. At the age of 23 his mind was already
trained by a thorough grounding in mathematics and in Latin,
together with the rudiments of Greek; he knew his Bible from
beginning to end; his scientific reading had given him an
initial grasp of the subjects required for *materia medica* (though
these of course were elementary as compared with later standards). And besides possessing the moral qualities without which
the acquisition of any kind of knowledge is impossible, he had
an eager interest in everything about him, an instinct for
accuracy and exactitude, a quick apprehension, a retentive
memory.

Dr. Ralph Wardlaw, one of the most active protagonists in

24

Scotland for the abolition of slavery, was Principal of the Congregational College; Livingstone had already read his book on Infant Baptism, and now attended his lectures in Divinity and joined his church. Dr. Thomas Graham was Professor of Chemistry, Andrew Buchanan of Medicine, James Thomson (the father of two very eminent scientists) of Mathematics. Livingstone entertained for Wardlaw, both as a man and a teacher, the highest regard; whilst Buchanan became a life-long friend. But there was another of his teachers with whom a friendship, begun in the laboratory and at the carpenter's bench, may be said to have outlasted death. This was the Professor of Chemistry's assistant, James Young. He first taught Livingstone "the use of his hands" and how to turn a lathe; and with three other pupils, James and William Thomson (Lord Kelvin), and Lyon (Lord) Playfair, initiated him into the mechanics and uses of a new type of galvanic battery. Young spoke of Livingstone as "the best man he ever knew, who had more than any other of true filial trust in God,' more of the spirit of Christ, more of integrity, purity, and simplicity of character, and of self-denying love for his fellow-men". Livingstone named after him a river which he supposed to be one of the sources of the Nile, and would often speak with admiration of Young's achievements as the inventor of distilling paraffin-oil from shale—"filling houses with a clear white light at a fraction of the cost of the smoky article which it displaced".

He completed his first session at Glasgow in April 1837, and returned to his home and the cotton factory for the "vacation". It was then that he was obliged to borrow a little money from his brother John to tide him over the second session. It was then also that a suggestion was made to him, by his old friend Arthur Anderson, of offering himself as a candidate for the foreign mission field to the London Missionary Society which alone among such societies had "the distinction of being entirely unsectarian". This accorded with Livingstone's own ideas of what a missionary society should be; but it cut across his long-cherished dream of work in China.

The first approach to the London Missionary Society was made on his behalf, on 12 August 1837, by the Minister at Hamilton, the Rev. John Moir. This recommendation, hitherto

25

unpublished, though somewhat colourless, is of interest as Livingstone's first introduction to the outside world.[1]

It was followed by a direct application from himself on 5 September of the same year, before returning to Glasgow for his second and final session. Not till the following January did he receive a reply. This took the form of a series of seventeen searching questions to which the candidate appended his answers. Two are of uncommon interest. In reply to the question: "What do you apprehend are the proper duties of a Christian missionary?"—he wrote:

> His duties chiefly are, I apprehend, to endeavour by every means in his power to make known the Gospel by preaching, exhortation, conversation, instruction of the young; improving, so far as in his power, the temporal condition of those among whom he labours, by introducing the arts and sciences of civilization, and doing everything in his power to commend Christianity to their hearts and consciences.

The other question related to marriage, and his reply to it is "sweeping".

> Unmarried; under no engagement relating to marriage, never made proposals of marriage, nor conducted myself so to any woman as to cause her to suspect that I intended anything relating to marriage; and, so far as my present wishes are concerned, I should prefer going out unmarried, that I might be without that care which the concerns of a family necessarily induce, and give myself wholly to the work.

In the light of subsequent events one may wonder whether he would not have been wiser to adhere to this self-denying ordinance.

It transpired that these answers were not read to the Committee of Directors of the Mission till 23 July, and since no reply from them was forthcoming it would appear that when home again in the spring of 1838 he must have discussed matters with his father, who then, without his knowledge, wrote a long and carefully-worded letter to the Foreign Secretary of the Society. This letter was printed for the first time in Campbell's *Livingstone*. It throws much light on the characters both of father and son. In it we learn (what he never mentioned) that he was top of his class in Latin as long as it existed; that he preferred to rise very early and walk to Glasgow for lectures rather than accept the offer of a lift and be late; that he had refused the offer of a teaching post with a good salary. It reveals also the sincerity of his father's trust in divine guidance, and the purity of motive which led him to withdraw all objections to his son's application. Dr. Campbell thinks that this letter may have helped to influence the Directors in the applicant's favour, and it is indeed more than probable.[2]

Whether as a result of this letter or not, Livingstone was invited to meet the Directors in London on 13 August, was interviewed and examined, again examined on the 20th, accepted on probation, and assigned to the tutelage of the Rev. Richard Cecil at Chipping Ongar in Essex for three months.

We gain a much fuller picture of him from impressions of contemporaries at Ongar and in London than in Glasgow.

The first of these comes from the Rev. Walter Inglis, who subsequently joined him in Kuruman but first met him by chance on the steamship from Leith to London.

> Livingstone stood middle-sized, firm upon his feet, light in the under-trunk, round and full in the chest. I have to admit he was 'no bonny'. His face wore at all times the strongly marked lines of potent will. I never recollect of him relaxing into the abandon of youthful frolic or play. I would by no means imply sourness of temper. It was the strength of a resolute man of work. . . . I only recollect of him playing one practical joke. A man came with a ripe boil that only required to be lanced. He gave the boil an honest skelp with a book. He had a grin, for dry Scotch humour he actually possessed. . . .
>
> Livingstone went with his whole soul into medical studies. His energy must have been very great. In company with a young man that was finishing his medical studies, for months they slept only two or three hours a night.[3]

The fullest of these reminiscences however are those of his life-long friend, the Rev. Joseph Moore, afterwards a missionary in Tahiti. He says that they first met on the day of their arrival, a Saturday, at 57 Aldersgate Street, the boarding-house for young missionary students kept by Mrs. Sewell. The one from Scotland, the other from the South of England, they were both strangers in the great city. On Sunday they attended three places of worship, one of which was St. Paul's. On Monday they passed their first examination.

> On Tuesday we went to Westminster Abbey. Who that had seen those two young men passing from monument to monument could have

divined that one day one of them would be buried with a nation's—
rather, with the civilized world's—lament, in that sacred shrine? . . .
I grew daily more attached to him. If I were asked why, I should be
rather at a loss to reply. There was a truly indescribable charm about
him which, with all his rather ungainly ways and by no means winning
face, attracted almost everyone. . . .
He won those who came near him by a kind of spell. There happened
to be in the boarding house at that time a young M.D., a saddler from
Hants., and a bookseller from Scotland. To this hour they all speak of
him in rapturous terms.[4]

What, it may be asked, was the secret of that indescribable
charm? In appearance he was unprepossessing, in manner
somewhat uncouth. These outward defects may have been redeemed to some extent by less obvious qualities: transparent
sincerity and simplicity, robust and wholesome commonsense,
a shrewd and pawky humour, a comradely and optimistic temper that was probably infectious. But they still leave the charm
unexplained, for there was never any outward grace about him.
Perhaps this, from Mr. J. S. Cook who also spent three months
with him at Ongar, comes nearest in understanding:

He was so kind and gentle in word and deed to all about him that all
loved him. He had always words of sympathy at command, and was
ready to perform acts of sympathy for those who were suffering.[5]

Having passed both their preliminary examinations the two
young friends were sent to Ongar for further instruction in
classics and divinity. The little house in which they lodged now
bears a commemorative inscription. Here they read Greek and
began the rudiments of Hebrew; but it must be doubted
whether Livingstone ever had time to attain much more knowledge of the former than would enable him to read the New
Testament in the original, and certainly not enough of the
latter to make the time spent on it worth while (despite the fact
that we find him later on, in a note-book, trying to find Semitic
roots for some Sechuana words).—"Every day we took walks
and visited all the spots of interest in the neighbourhood,
among them the country churchyard which was the burial
place of John Locke." Moore then related an episode the details of which are not quite correct; the first part of his account
is therefore somewhat emended.

One foggy November morning, at three o'clock, Livingstone set out from Ongar to walk to London, to transact some business for his eldest brother who had begun to deal in lace. It was about twenty-seven miles to the house he sought. In the darkness of the morning he fell into a ditch, smearing his clothes, and not improving his appearance for smart business purposes. He spent the whole day in going about in London from shop to shop, greatly increasing his fatigue. He then set out on foot to return to Ongar. Just out of London, near Edmonton, a lady had been thrown out of a gig. She lay stunned on the road. Livingstone immediately went to her, helped to carry her into a house close by, and having examined her found no bones broken, and recommending a doctor to be called, resumed his weary tramp. Weary and footsore, when he reached Stanford Rivers he missed his way, and finding after some time that he was wrong, he felt so dead-beat that he was inclined to lie down and sleep; but finding a directing-post he climbed it, and by the light of the stars deciphered enough to know his whereabouts. About twelve that Saturday night he reached Ongar, white as a sheet, and so tired that he could hardly utter a word. I gave him a basin of bread and milk, and I am not exaggerating when I say I put him to bed. He fell asleep at once, and did not awake till noon had passed on Sunday.

Any comment upon this would be superfluous and banal, except to say that Moore never knew, or else had forgotten, that his friend had fallen into a ditch and that he had tramped about London all day.

Their tutor does not seem to have been wise in teaching them the art of homiletics. They were required to submit to him written sermons and then, after correction, to memorize them and deliver them for the edification of village congregations.

Livingstone prepared one, and one Sunday the minister of Stanford Rivers, where the celebrated Isaac Taylor resided, having fallen sick after the morning service, Livingstone was sent for to preach in the evening. He took his text, read it out very deliberately, and then—then his sermon had fled! Midnight darkness came upon him, and he abruptly said: "Friends, I have forgotten all I had to say," and hurrying out of the pulpit, he left the chapel. He never became a preacher, and in the first letter I received from him from Elizabethtown in Africa he says, "I am a very poor preacher, having a bad delivery, and some of them said if they knew I had to preach again they would not enter the chapel. . . . "

Each student at Ongar had also to conduct family worship in rotation. I was much impressed by the fact that Livingstone never prayed without the petition that we might imitate Christ in all His inimitable perfections.

In due course Mr. Cecil sent in his report, which was unfavourable. Livingstone's long hesitations in conducting public prayer, and his utter failure in the pulpit, were unpardonable.

When a decision was about to be given against him, however, a member of the Board pleaded for an extension of his probation. "I sailed in the same boat," says Moore, "and was also sent back to Ongar as a naughty boy."

> At last we had so improved that both were fully accepted. Livingstone went to London to pursue his medical studies, and I went to Cheshunt College. A day or two after reaching College I sent to Livingstone, asking him to purchase a second-hand carpet for my room. He was quite scandalised at such an exhibition of effeminacy, and positively refused to gratify my wish.

Nine years later Livingstone, writing to his old friend from Africa, said: "Of all those I have met since we parted, I have seen no one I can compare to you for sincere, hearty friendship." Livingstone's family used to speak of them as Jonathan and David.

Mr. Cecil's final report on this somewhat problematical pupil, dated 26 January 1839, is as follows:

> Mr. Livingstone gives me pleasure in some important respects. The objection I mentioned, his heaviness of manner, united as it is with a rusticity, not likely to be removed, still strikes me as having importance, but he has sense and quiet vigour; his temper is good and his character substantial, so that I do not like the thought of his being rejected. Add to his stock of knowledge and then I trust he will prove after all an instrument worth having—a diligent, staunch, single-hearted labourer. If the decision were now coming on I should say accept him.[6]

The Committee forthwith acted on this advice and Livingstone was "fully admitted under the patronage of the Society". On July 8 he was also permitted at his own request to continue residence at Ongar until the beginning of the following year. It should be added that the caution of the Society in selecting candidates is greatly to its credit. The tide of the Evangelical Revival was then at full flood; the "romance" of work in the mission-field had captured public imagination, and any young man who responded to its call was likely to be regarded as something of a hero.

There is one other reminiscence from Ongar, and it contains a distinctively graphic touch. It comes from the Rev. Isaac Taylor, LL.D., who became as celebrated a philologist as his father had been a religious philosopher.

I well remember as a boy taking country rambles with Livingstone when he was staying at Ongar. Mr. Cecil had several missionary students, but Livingstone was the only one whose personality made any impression on my boyish imagination. I might sum up my impression of him in two words—Simplicity and Resolution. Now, after nearly forty years, I remember his step, the characteristic forward tread, firm, simple, resolute, neither fast nor slow, no hurry and no dawdle, but which evidently meant—getting there.[7]

.   .   .   .   .

It was early in 1839 that he first met his future father-in-law, and subsequent interviews determined his life's course.

Having occasion to call at the boarding-house for young missionaries in Aldersgate Street, Robert Moffat interested them in his story, and especially one of them "who would sometimes come quietly and ask me a question or two, and was always desirous to know where I was to speak in public".

By and by he asked me whether I thought he would do for Africa. I said I believed he would, if he would not go to an old station, but would advance to unoccupied ground, specifying the vast plain to the north, where I had sometimes seen, in the morning sun, the smoke of a thousand villages, where no missionary had ever been. At last Livingstone said: "What is the use of my waiting for the end of this abominable opium war? I will go at once to Africa." The Directors concurred, and Africa became his sphere.[8]

Livingstone recognized a man when he saw one, and this long-bearded veteran moreover was a Scot—as in fact were the majority of the L.M.S. personnel at this time. And—"the smoke of a thousand villages": there was magic in the phrase, and the lure of adventure in the picture, enough to capture the imagination of a young, ardent, yet sober-minded idealist. How could he guess that it was a grossly romantic exaggeration! From that day he never looked back. Africa was his goal.

But apparently the Directors did. His sisters in later years had a distinct recollection that the Directors at this time were intending him for the West Indies, and that he "remonstrated with them" on the grounds that, the British settlements in those islands being well supplied with qualified doctors, his two years' medical study would be time wasted. This recollection is confirmed by a somewhat long-winded letter from Livingstone to the Secretary, since found in the Society's archives, and quoted in full in Campbell's *Livingstone*. "It is of interest as illustrating his habitual attitude to the Society. Here in one of his earliest communications he shows the same respect without servility, the same boldness without discourtesy, and the same independent thinking which marked all his dealings with official bodies."⁹ The letter is dated from Ongar on 2 July 1839, and shows that Livingstone's intimation of their wish that "I should be employed in the West Indies in preference to South Africa" had just come to him verbally from the Rev. R. Cecil. He recalls at some length that, as a result of earnest prayer for divine direction, it appeared to be God's will that he should obtain a medical education with a view to service as a missionary. Settling in the West Indies, he feels, is too much like the ministry at home.

His final request is for more time for education: such as he has at present he feels to be insufficient for the task before him: "the more I contemplate the magnitude of the work, the greater does the necessity for good preparation for it appear to be. . . . I hope it will not be supposed from anything I have said that I at all mean to dictate to the Directors, but . . . "

What can the Directors have made of this dour, self-opinionated young man, rustic in demeanour, abrupt in speech and thick in his utterance, yet with such obvious sincerity and earnestness, with those bright and steady eyes, that pertinacious underlip, that chin with its stubborn crumple? Who among them could have foreseen the immense reserves of will-power and endurance, the force and fire that were in him?

But his letter had the desired effect, and he returned to London for further medical study on 2 January 1840. He had at this time what he afterwards described as a "mania" for medicine, and had no desire other than to qualify as a lay medical-missionary.

He had already begun to attend the Silver Street Chapel in Falcon Square, of which Dr. Bennett, then one of London's leading preachers, was the minister, and whose son—afterwards Sir J. Risdon Bennett, M.D., LL.D., F.R.S., President of the Royal College of Surgeons—was physician to the Aldersgate Street Dispensary and lecturer in pathology at the Charing Cross Hospital. He obtained for Livingstone free admission to hospital practice, lectures, and dispensary, as well as to the ophthalmic hospital in Moorfields.

"The brilliant and cultured physician discerned in the plain unpolished student from the north a character of rare worth and a mental grasp much above the ordinary." Years later he wrote:

> I entertained towards him a sincere affection, and had the highest admiration for his endowments, both of mind and heart, and of his pure and noble devotion of all his powers to the highest purposes of life. One could not fail to be impressed with his simple, loving, Christian spirit, and the combined modest, unassuming, and self-reliant character of the man.
>
> He placed himself under my guidance in reference to his medical studies, and I was struck with the amount of knowledge he had already acquired of those subjects which constitute the foundation of medical science. He had, however, little or no acquaintance with the practical departments of medicine, and had had no opportunities of studying the nature and aspects of disease. Of these deficiencies he was quite aware, and felt the importance of acquiring as much practical knowledge as possible during his stay in London. . . .[10]

Bennett appears to have been one of the few who recognized, thus early, promise of the remarkable intellectual vigour of which his young pupil afterwards gave proof.

In July 1840 Livingstone was himself taken seriously ill from overwork, with congestion of the lungs and liver, and was shipped aboard a steamer for home. His friend Moore "found him so weak that he could scarcely walk on board, and parted from him in tears, fearing that he had only a few days to live". But the voyage and the home-visit restored him, and the next month he was again hard at work in London.

During his last months in London it appears that Livingstone, together with his future colleague William Ross, had prosecuted further acquaintance with Robert and Mary Moffat. In a letter dated 25 November Mrs. Moffat, in writing to her old friend Robert Hamilton who with Rogers Edwards was holding the fort in Kuruman, to congratulate them on this forthcoming accession to their numbers, said: "I am sure you will enjoy their company, both being Scotchmen and plain in their manners. Of Mr. Ross we have seen the most, and the more we saw of him the better we liked him." It is added that with motherly advice she had tried to persuade Livingstone to get married as his colleague was, but in vain.[11]

By a coincidence Professor Graham had left Glasgow to occupy the Chair of Chemistry in University College, London, the first term in which Livingstone began his course there. In this way he met Graham's new assistant in the laboratory, Dr. George Wilson, afterwards Professor of Technology in Edinburgh. "In the simplicity and purity of their character, and in their devotion to science, not only for its own sake, but as a department of the kingdom of God, they were brothers indeed." Livingstone afterwards collected all he could find in Africa worthy of a place in the Edinburgh Museum of Science and Art, of which his friend was the first Director. And when Wilson received a copy of *Missionary Travels* in 1857 he wrote to its author: " . . . Meanwhile may your name be propitious; in all your long and weary journeys may the *Living* half of your title outweigh the other; till after long and blessed labours, the white *stone* is given you in the happy land."[12]

In all the toils and tribulations of his journeys, and in all the preoccupations of constant business in the intervals between them, Livingstone was never too weary or too busy to forget a friend. Nor did he ever forget a promise. A striking example of this is afforded by his friendship with Professor (Sir Richard) Owen, whose lectures on Comparative Anatomy he attended in the Hunterian Museum. When bidding him good-bye, Livingstone promised to send him any unusual organic specimen that he might find. Sixteen years passed and, as none reached him, Owen grew sceptical. He did not know that Livingstone had sent him several specimens which, with his journals and other treasures, sank off Madeira in 1856. What was his amazement to find the explorer at his door one day in 1857 bearing in his hands the tusk of an elephant with a spiral curve. Little wonder that he should have referred to this feat again and again in public and in private as a proof of Livingstone's inflexible adherence to his word. At the Farewell Festival in 1858 he said: "You may recall the difficulties of the progress of the weary sick traveller on the bullock's back. Every pound weight was of moment; but Livingstone said, 'Owen shall have this tusk', and he placed it in my hands in London."[13] The tusk is now among the relics in the Blantyre Memorial Museum.

Throughout his whole life Livingstone never failed to keep his old friendships in repair. He was a prolific and indefatigable correspondent, and he too liked to be remembered. Whatever sentiments of a contrary kind he may have provoked in later life when in the stress of toils and conflicts, there can be no doubt that in unclouded youth he had a genius for friendship. At Ongar he had opportunities for social contacts outside his own circle, and among these were the members of a county family named Prentice at Stowmarket, in Suffolk. With the two sons of this household, both of whom were preparing for missionary work, as well as with their father, he maintained a correspondence for many years. Another was with the family of Mr. Charles Ridley of Felstead in Essex, who were friends of the Prentice family—and concerning whom more is to be told.

His most intimate and trusted friend in London was a fellow-student who was also a fellow-Scot, afterwards a missionary in India, the Rev. D. G. Watt. To him most of all, during the sixteen years of his first sojourn in Africa, Livingstone "poured forth his views and feelings unreservedly in lengthy epistles", and these show the growth of his mind in relation to the missionary problem as a whole.

Watt afterwards recalled his friend's mode of discussion as a student. "He showed great simplicity of view, along with a certain roughness or bluntness of manner; great kindliness, and yet great persistence in holding to his own ideas."

That these encomiums were made after the subject of them had become a figure of world renown is a fact that does nothing to detract from their veracity. They are confirmed by the testimony of another young contemporary, Alexander Macmillan, afterwards head of the publishing firm, who was frequently in their company, and who wrote:

> I can recall nothing that would enable me to say that he made any special impression on my mind as regards the mental aspect of his character. But that the great characteristics to which he owed in after life his great eminence were recognized at that time I cannot doubt; these being resolute courage, singular purity and loftiness of aim, and an exquisite modesty of mind. . . . I have heard it said of him, "Fire, water, stone-wall—would not stop Livingstone in the fulfilment of any recognized duty."[14]

His habitual reticence on the subject of his most sacred feelings has been remarked. This reticence deepened with the years; but there is one letter of this period which must be quoted in part, since it reveals the keynote of the faith that sustained him, through every kind of disappointment, disillusion, frustration and eventual disaster, to the end of his life. It is dated 5 May 1839 and was written to his elder sister, who had obtained a post as teacher. Its emphasis is upon what is called in theology "the divine initiative". Had he been conversant with the literature of Christian mysticism he could have expressed the aspiration of its thought in a single sentence: *To be to the Eternal Goodness as a man's hands are to a man.*

Let us seek—and with the conviction that we cannot do without it—that all selfishness be extirpated, pride banished, unbelief driven from the mind, every idol dethroned, and everything hostile to holiness and opposed to the divine will crucified; that "holiness to the Lord" may be engraven on the heart, and evermore characterize our whole conduct. This is what we ought to strive after; this is the way to be happy; this is what our Saviour loves—entire surrender of the heart. May He enable us by His Spirit to persevere till we attain it! All comes from Him, the disposition to ask as well as the blessing itself. . . . If you have the willing mind, [your labour] is accepted; nothing else is accepted if that be wanting. God desires that. He can do all the rest. After all, He is the sole agent, for "the willing mind" comes alone from Him. This is comforting, for when we think of the feebleness and littleness of all we do, we might despair of having our services accepted, were we not assured that it is not these God looks to, except in so far as they are indication of the state of the heart.[15]

His political views were moderate. Though a man of the people and proud of it, he was never professedly a Radical. And, though a true-hearted patriot who loved the history and traditions of his country, he was not a Nationalist. When away and alone in the heart of Africa he loved to repeat and to hum the air of Burns' lyric with the refrain "A man's a man for a' that". Yet he also felt kindly towards the neighbouring gentry of Blantyre, especially Lord Douglas, who opened his parks to the public.

. . . The poorest among us could stroll at pleasure over the ancient domains of Bothwell, and other spots hallowed by the venerable associations of which our schoolbooks and local traditions made us well aware; and few of us could view the dear memorials of the past without feeling that these carefully-kept monuments were our own. . . . And whilst foreigners imagine that we want the spirit only to overturn capitalists and aristocracy, we are content to respect our laws till we can change them, and hate those stupid revolutions which might sweep away time-honoured institutions, dear alike to rich and poor.[16]

Yet again, though no Radical, he was a typical child of the century one of whose watchwords was Progress and another Expansion. He shared his father's hopes and beliefs in "the good time coming" for the under-privileged, and hailed every fresh invention and discovery as another milestone in the direction of social and economic welfare. In this as in other respects he was not only abreast of his times but in advance of them. For him, all that was wholesome in "the arts and sciences of civilization" was part and parcel of Christianity itself. He could not possibly foresee the devilish uses to which they would be put a century later.

He had already bidden farewell to his parents on what they supposed to be his last visit home in July 1840, when it was suggested that the possession of a diploma from the medical and surgical Faculty in Glasgow would be of service to him. So in November he returned in haste to qualify, and here his native obstinacy was nearly his undoing.

Having finished the medical curriculum and presented a thesis on a subject which required the use of the stethoscope for its diagnosis, I unwittingly procured for myself an examination rather more severe and prolonged than usual among examining bodies. The reason was, that between me and the examiners a slight difference of opinion existed as to whether this instrument could do what was asserted. The wiser plan would have been to have no opinion of my own. However, I was admitted a Licentiate of the Faculty of Physicians and Surgeons. It was with unfeigned delight I became a member of a profession which is pre-eminently devoted to practical benevolence, and which with unwearied energy pursues from age to age its endeavours to lessen human woe.[17]

With the diploma in his pocket he set out for home the same evening. He had only that one night to spend with his parents. There was so much to say and the hours were so precious that he proposed they should sit up all night. But his mother would not hear of this. She had often packed him off to bed at midnight when he was a boy; she would do it again now. Only a fragment remains of that last conversation. "I remember my father and him," wrote a sister, "talking over the prospect of Christian Missions. They agreed that the time would come when rich men and great men would think it an honour to support whole stations of missionaries, instead of spending their money on hounds and horses." Next morning, 17 November, the whole family were awake and astir, as often before, at

37

five o'clock. His mother made coffee. At his father's request he read from Scripture, choosing the 121st and 135th Psalms, and prayed. Farewells were said, and then for the last time father and son tramped the familiar road to Glasgow, to catch the packet steamer for Liverpool. On the Broomielaw Quay they said good-bye.

Almost exactly sixteen years later when on his way home, and looking forward to nothing so much as another family reunion, he heard in Cairo of his father's death. The old man had lived long enough to hear from Cape Town the tumult of acclaim that greeted his son's tremendous achievement, and had earnestly hoped to be spared long enough to see once again that son of whom he was so proud.

"You wished so much to see David," said one of his daughters as his life was ebbing away.

"Aye, very much, very much; but the will of the Lord be done," was the reply. Then after an interval of silence:

"But I think I'll know whatever is worth knowing about him. When you see him, tell him I think so."

Chapter Three

RIO DE JANEIRO AND KURUMAN
1840–1841

"My life will perhaps be spent as profitably as a pioneer as in any other way."

ON 20 November 1840 Livingstone was ordained in Albion Chapel, London Wall, "by solemn prayer and the imposition of hands". The ceremony meant little to him—he would as lief have gone out as a lay-missionary—but the prayers, no doubt, meant much.

His fellow-ordinand was William Ross, formerly a schoolmaster, eleven years his senior and recently married, a member of the United Secession Church of Scotland (Presbyterian). They were (said Inglis) "an ill-assorted pair". And Livingstone, in a letter to his friend George Drummond from the Cape, commented: "My colleague is a secession man and has a good deal of 'Act and Testimony' in his composition, but I am determined to live in peace and goodwill. I won't quarrel on any account, and may God give me wisdom to conduct myself aright. I see it is of great importance that missionaries should be united. . . ." On 8 December they embarked, together with Mrs. Ross, on the sailing ship *George* (Captain Donaldson), bound for the Cape and Port Elizabeth.

During this voyage Livingstone (who had already some knowledge of astronomy) set himself to learn the art of navigation, and in this he received valuable help from the Captain who "was very obliging to me, and gave me all the information respecting the use of the quadrant in his power, frequently sitting up till twelve o'clock at night for the purpose of taking lunar observations with me". How thoroughly he mastered this difficult art is shown by the use he made of it twenty-five years later when he piloted—and engineered—his own steamer, *a lake-steamer*, across the Indian Ocean from Quilimane. But Sundays on board the *George* were not times of spiritual refreshment. "The Captain is a well-informed shrewd Scotchman, but no Christian. He rigged out the Church on Sundays, and we had service; but I being a poor preacher, and the chaplain addressing them all as Christians already, no moral influence was exerted, and had there been [any such] on the Sabbath, it would have been neutralized by the week-day conduct."

A storm split the foremast of the vessel in the Atlantic and the Captain was obliged to make for Rio de Janeiro to refit. Livingstone was unaffected by the prevailing malady and contrived to write long letters to his friends, especially Thomas Prentice and his fiancée Catherine Ridley, which are published in Chamberlin's collection.[1] They are characteristic of his interest in the welfare of his friends, of his concern for the spread of the gospel, and also of his sardonic sense of humour. In one of them there is an aside connected with his immunity from sea-sickness which is decorously omitted from this letter by the editor, but which the present chronicler finds irresistible. He speaks of the malady as a "dolorous predicament to be in, and a really melancholy spectacle to behold"—"I pitied but could not cure". But there was one case in which he did neither. "Ross had rashly quoted to me the text, 'Two are better than one' just before. . . . The only cruelty I was guilty of was quoting the same text to him when both he and his spouse were turning their stomachs inside out into one basin."[2]

Arrived at Rio he went ashore alone, since no one else would venture out under the rays of a vertical sun, and plunged into the Brazilian forest and took a shower-bath under a waterfall. "That, with a flesh-brush and perhaps a pair of horsehair gloves," he told Prentice, "will do more towards the preservation of your health than all the drugs in my medicine-chest." Seeking a cottage to purchase fruit, he was attacked by three dogs, "but having a good stick in my hand I soon convinced them that I was not a member of the Peace Society.".

He then relates at length the wonderfully kind reception given him by these cottagers. They invited him to share their dinner, and the husband produced some kind of liquor which he declined, and asked for "aqua"—a word which they being Portuguese could understand. They refused any remuneration though he offered it in their own coin, so that he could only give their children a few English coppers as a memento. (The incident is of interest as Livingstone's first encounter with people of a foreign race and of alien speech, and illustrates his remarkable faculty of establishing cordial relations with them at first sight.) The husband had seemed surprised that an Englishman should refuse alcohol, since British seamen when ashore continually got drunk and quarrelsome, and were then robbed and stabbed. "The sailors of all other countries behave themselves like men, except ours and the Americans."

> I saw a case of this kind in the Misericordia Hospital. He was lying in a fit of raging delirium, secured by a strait-jacket, and the blood still flowing from his wound. . . . My heart warmed to my countryman. I sat on the edge of his bed and vainly endeavoured to lead his mind into a train of thought. . . . I turned away with a heavy heart, for I knew from the nature and position of the wound that he could not—with his system impregnated with alcohol—survive another night. O how much need have the Christians of Britain to exert themselves on behalf of seamen!

That need has been fully met since his day by the establishment in 1856 of the Institute of Missions to Seamen, an entirely undenominational mission, and a haven of refuge for seamen of every race and creed in foreign ports. This incident, it may be added, is also anticipative in another sense than the former, as Livingstone's first direct contact with human callousness, which in a huger and more evil shape he was to witness so often in the Dark Continent. He has one other experience to relate to Prentice concerning rowdy seamen, when he took upon himself a duty that was not without danger.

> I went into two public houses where a great many seamen lodge, and gave tracts to one to take on board to his shipmates who, he said, were all drunkards. An American seaman who stood by requested one or two but added, "Remember we are not all drunkards." I said, "It did not matter what we were if we were Christians." He got into a rage and asked if I thought he was a robber or a thief or a murderer. "Am I not as good a Christian as you are?" As I did not wish to argue with him and about twenty around, some of them drunk and swearing, I gave him some tracts explanatory of what true Christianity is and told him they would inform him better.

Writing to Watt in a more jocular vein, he sums up his impressions of churchmanship in Rio:

> It is certainly the finest place I ever saw. Everything delighted me except men. Even the 'Church Establishment' there [Roman Catholic] is beautiful, they really do the thing in style. If ever I join an Establishment it won't be either of the poor degenerate 'sisters' at home [Church

of England and Church of Scotland], but the good 'mother' herself in Brazil. . . . Tracts and Bibles are circulated, and some effects might be expected were a most injurious influence not exercised by European visitors. These only disgrace themselves and the religion they profess by drunkenness. All other vices are common in Rio. When will the beams of Divine Light dispel the darkness of this beautiful Empire?[3]

As with his relations with people, so too with his contacts with places, once his interest in them was seized it was abiding, and even when new ones came crowding in upon his mind it took a long time for them to displace the old. Writing to his father on 13 July 1842 about the increasing success of the mission work in Kuruman and its neighbourhood he says: "I have good news too from Rio de Janeiro. The Bibles that have been distributed are beginning to cause a stir."[4]

From another letter we glean that Livingstone, in addition to his nightly lessons on navigation, was also during this voyage of fourteen months' duration teaching himself the rudiments of the Sechuana language as well as Dutch.

Arrived at Cape Town on 14 March 1841, he and the Ross's were for some time the guests of Dr. and Mrs. Philip, and his first impression of his host was confirmed by closer acquaintance.

> I find the doctor a very amiable man although I came out prejudiced against him, for many complaints are made against him by some missionaries. He does not however appear so bad to us as he is represented at home. I hope we shall get on comfortably together. He claims no superiority over us. I was always determined not to submit to any bishop, and am therefore happy to know that he does not wish to domineer.

.   .   .   .   .

The fluid and formative period of South Africa's early troubled history was still in the making at the time of Livingstone's arrival at the Cape. On a lease from the Zulus, Natal had been partly occupied by British colonists in 1836; but in the following year it was annexed without resistance by Boers from Drakensburg in their Great Trek northwards. An appeal from the natives against oppression by these *voortrekkers* led to the re-occupation of Durban by a British force in May, 1842; and two years later, despite Boer resistance, Natal was annexed by the British Government. With these events and with others incidental to them the work of Christian missions had been intimately concerned, and that they were moulded for ultimate good rather than ill is due almost entirely to the efforts of one man. This was John Philip, whose inflexible zeal and unflinching courage had secured emancipation of the Hottentots from slavery in 1828, and the first Charter of Justice in the Colony. At the risk of his life (which was twice attempted) he had toured the northern territory during the Kaffir War of 1834 with a view to a just peace. He was the first to open the eyes of the British public to the evils of negro exploitation. He was never a missionary but for 25 years held the fort as Agent of the L.M.S. in Cape Town. Being himself of an autocratic temper he did not see eye to eye with his young contemporary Moffat, who also had a mind of his own.

"Moffat did not always approve of Philip's 'political activities', and Philip did not share Moffat's desire to see the Mission extend into the interior."[5]

This unfortunately is an understatement of the differences that existed between these two good men. "The ideological differences between them soon became tinged with personal animosity. . . ."

There were no doubt "faults on both sides"—and these can always be discerned in retrospect. It is clear that Livingstone, a shrewd and critical observer living close to these events, whilst agreeing with each of them against the other in the points wherein they differed, had a greater respect for the character of Philip than of Moffat. And his estimate of the value of Philip's services was confirmed by one who cannot be considered a partisan, namely, Moffat's son.

> It would be difficult to measure the good that has resulted from the work of Dr. Philip. Perhaps a test of the depth and reality of the influence he exerted is to be found in the fact that for many years he was the best-hated man in the Colony—hated, that is, by those who were not the friends of the natives. . . . He united a clear and scholarly mind with a will as firm as the granite of his native land, and he fought the battle of the native races at heavy odds. Now that the tide has turned, and that there is a strong Colonial party standing where Dr. Philip once stood, all but alone save for a few trusty friends, some men may have forgotten what he did.[6]

At the time of Livingstone's arrival Philip, now an old man, was still acting as financial agent to the Mission and was also responsible for its administration and discipline. His strictness in these matters occasioned resentment among some who were disposed to regard missionary work in the Colony as equivalent to a comfortable "cure of souls" at home. Livingstone threw himself whole-heartedly on to the side of his superior and in doing so incurred a full measure of the same unpopularity. He was shocked and his indignation was aroused by the laxity, the bickering, the inconsistency between profession and practice that he saw around him; and he gave no uncertain vent to his feelings in a long letter to his old tutor Richard Cecil before leaving the Colony. It was published in full in the *Congregationalist* for October 1925 and is valuable as the appraisal at first hand of an impartial observer of a critical situation in the affairs of the L.M.S. Incidentally it corrects a statement made in Blaikie's *Life* that Livingstone was offered the position of deputizing in Dr. Philip's church, but declined it. Here, an extract must suffice.

> The Doctor is at present in trouble with the church which he has been the means of raising, and has been induced to give up his charge as pastor over it. He has never been able to make pastoral visits in consequence of his connection with the Society, and the active part he has taken in securing the rights of the Coloured people. . . . It is really exceedingly painful to think of a Church of Christ in the deplorable state in which they are at present. From whatever cause it has arisen, it is a house divided against itself. The members have no confidence with each other, none with their pastor, and apparently none in the authority and presence of Christ. . . . I wonder he bears it so meekly, for the most insolent and violent of his enemies have been raised by him from indigence to comparative affluence. Several of them came to the Colony with scarcely a shilling in their pockets. He took them by the hand and assisted them both by his purse, his advice and influence. . . . They asked my companion, Mr. Ross, to remain as candidate. I wish with all my heart they had got him; they would have then found themselves out of the frying pan into the fire. They don't deserve a good pastor. I don't see anything will do for them but dissolution, and being remodelled. I was *honoured* by them with the character of being heterodox in my sentiments. A charge to that effect was preferred against me to the Doctor by one party, whilst another requested the notes of my sermons, expressing a determination to act more than they had done on the principle I had inculcated. My theme was on the necessity of adopting the benevolence of the Son of God as the governing principle of our conduct. No objection was made to this, but the manner in which I put some of the points connected with this assured the indignation of the worthies, who seem much more fearful of heterodoxy in sentiment than of heterodoxy in practice. . . .[7]

The affectionate regard of Dr. Philip's loyal young supporter was returned by him. Many years later when Livingstone's exhausting physical exertions in the Zambesi valley were considered in some quarters as unnecessary, and well-meaning advisers were counselling life on a settled station, he remembered a story which his old friend had told him "with great glee", and retailed it in a letter to his mother.

> When a young minister in Aberdeen, he visited an old woman in affliction, and began to talk very fair to her on the duty of resignation—trusting—hoping and all the rest of it, when the old woman looked up into his face and said, "Puir thing, ye ken naething aboot it."[8]

On 16 April Dr. Philip despatched his young brethren, Ross and Livingstone, by the *George* to Port Elizabeth to await the ox-wagons for their journey north, and wrote to the Directors "with typical Scots caution":

> They seem worthy men. I have endeavoured to impress upon their minds that the first and perhaps the most important thing they will have to do in this country will be to make peace, and to live in peace with their brethren.

Events were to justify the wisdom of this advice and also the difficulty of profiting by it.

His departure from Port Elizabeth was delayed for yet another month, during which he visited a settlement of Hottentots at Hankey, and the mission station, and wrote to his parents: "My expectations have been far exceeded. Everything I witnessed surpassed my hopes, and if this one station is a fair sample of the whole, the statements of the missionaries with regard to their success are far within the mark."[9]

His ten weeks' journey by the lumbering ox-wagon, of 530 miles over very rough ground rising in a series of steep terraces to a plateau of 3,000 feet above the sea, though slow was sometimes exciting. It would seem at least to have had the practical value of acquainting a novice with the recalcitrant habits of the veldt oxen and the uncomfortable proximity of their long, backward-sloping horns. Beginning a long letter to Watt, dated 7 July 1841, he says:

> I like travelling very much indeed, there is so much freedom connected with our African manners. We pitch our tent, make our fire, etc., wherever we choose, walk, ride, or shoot as our inclination leads us; but there

is one great drawback, we can't study or read when we please. I feel this very much, and I have made but little progress in the language (can speak a little Dutch), but I long for the time when I shall be able to give my undivided attention to it and thus be furnished with the means of making known the Gospel.

This long letter contains the fullest and frankest account of the missionary-political situation as he saw it and he lets himself go in no measured terms. It is quoted in Sir H. Johnston's biography (4½ pages of close type), but mention of names was tactfully withheld at a time when controversial matters were still a live issue.[10] The burden of his complaint is "the most disgraceful" tension prevailing between missionaries north and south of the Orange River, and also amongst themselves on each side of it. Though he has not in the least changed his own views in favour of thorough-going independency, yet he would prefer the despotism of a man like Philip (were he still in his prime) to the "committee-ocracy" of Moffat and others. "I do not avow myself a friend or partisan of either; but I certainly feel attached to the principles of the liberal rather than the illiberal party."

The letter continues with a reference to rumours of the existence of a great fresh-water lake (Ngami) at a distance of two months' journey northwards by ox-wagon; of the rivalry between French and British missionaries to be the first to discover it; and of a private gift of £400 to Moffat in England towards the cost of an expedition. Here is a first hint of the dreams of a born solitary explorer.

> If they give your humble servant a month or two to acquire the colloquial language they may spare themselves the pains of being first in at the death. I can acquire the language while travelling, without this ponderous vehicle, as well as by remaining at Kuruman—perhaps better, for I shall live as they do and mix constantly with them and I can obtain information respecting the population at the same time.

His thoughts stray even further. There is some talk about Abyssinia as a sphere for missionary endeavour. What does his friend think of that? Let him look at the map and he will see far beyond us "very populous country". He would cost the Society nothing if he were absent for six or seven years.

> If I should never return perhaps my life will be as profitably spent as a forerunner as in any other way. Whatever way my life can be spent best

to promote the glory of our gracious God I feel desirous to adopt it. I shall wait anxiously for your opinion and advice. To you alone I have disclosed it. I should like to hear from you frequently as I have confidence in your judgment more than in that of many others.

He arrived at Kuruman on 31 July after ten weeks' journey, "so pleasant that I never got tired of it", and continues his story in a letter to Prentice.

Two of these weeks were spent in visiting no less than six mission stations en route. At the last of these, Griqua Town, he stayed several days doctoring the pastor and his child who were sick. "We were much gratified by a little intercourse with the brethren there. They are excellent men and have been very successful in their labours," and at Graaf Reinet, "the prettiest town in all Africa", there are two Christians "worth going a hundred miles to meet"—namely Mr. and Mrs. Murray. As for Kuruman, it is a pretty spot though now, in winter, it lacks its charms. The church is the largest he has seen on any mission station, its stone-built walls "resembling those of a battery". But the native population is surprisingly sparse. The gardens are excellent, and the whole station has been made what it is by "the almost slave-drudgery of the missionaries". It is an oasis in a desert without relief save for stunted scraggy bushes, many of which are "armed with thorns villainously sharp and strong".

Some words of advice and affectionate thoughts: "Don't forget a good gun and how to shoot it. Also some carpentry— with tools. How is Catherine? You did not write to me at Christmas. How can I write you long letters when you serve me so?" The letter ends with a singular and prophetic sentence which concludes more than one letter of this period: "Remember me before the throne of Grace that I may be kept faithful unto death."[11]

But he does not do justice to the Mission at Kuruman. It stands indeed (next to his translation of the Bible) as the greatest monument to Moffat's industry and practical genius. The church, a spacious and solid but well-ventilated structure of dried brick with a high-pitched gable; the low wide-eaved dwelling houses, flanked with long verandahs; the neat and tidy compound of native huts—all embowered with fruit-trees and flowering shrubs; the fenced and irrigated garden filled with

47

every kind of fruit and flower and vegetable that the red soil could yield; the smithying-forge, the carpentry-shed, the other workshops, the stockaded cattle-pen—all these together had the air of prosperity and comfort of a southern farm; and yet, as has been truly said, "It would be hard to find in modern Africa any place so remote as Kuruman was at that time."

There are points in two other letters of the same date (4th August) which must be noticed. One of these, to Mrs. Philip, contains his first allusion to the subject of free trade between black men and white which, in view of his subsequent strenuous advocacy of it as an essential part of missionary endeavour, is of unusual interest:

> I find the brethren are opposed to everything having the least relation to trading. I shall follow their example, although I was made to believe by the good folks at the Bay [Algoa] that goods were absolutely necessary for getting along. I won't even give goods instead of money (which is all I ever intended), if the cause is to be in any way injured by it.[12]

The other is to an old friend in Hamilton, Henry Drummond, who later set up business as a lace manufacturer in Glasgow and provided Livingstone and his family with clothing. Its emphasis is on the necessity for a thorough knowledge of the native language and idiom, and the paramount importance of Native Agency in propagating the gospel to the natives themselves.

> I intend (D.V.) to remain here about two months for the purpose of acquiring a little of the colloquial language, and then with the hope of fully mastering the whole, I shall proceed to the Northward and live excluded from all European society. . . . We have people here who have come several hundreds of miles from the interior. This nomadic life is very favourable to the spread of the Gospel, although it is opposed to the spread of civilization. Ought the Churches at home not to take advantage of their news-telling propensities? . . . Native agency (I am fully convinced), although it has many evils connected with it, is the only thing that can evangelize the world.[13]

For Livingstone, the policy of Expansion was bound up with the necessity for Native Agency. Not concentration, but decentralization, was the need. In the Colony and also beyond the Orange River it seemed to him that there were not too few labourers in the vineyard, but too many. These should disperse far and wide into regions hitherto untouched.

48

In 1838 Moffat had completed the first draft of his translation of the New Testament and at the end of it set off with his wife and daughter to England in order to supervise its publication. As previously related, force of circumstances detained him and it was not until 1843 that he returned to Kuruman. Livingstone's instructions were to remain at Kuruman till Moffat's return, but at the same time "to turn his attention to the formation of a new station further north, awaiting more specific instructions". Northward of Kuruman lay the fringes of the vast Kalahari Desert, a trackless wilderness that had never been explored. It will be seen that Livingstone was not slow to take advantage of the second part of these instructions.

His ideas on mission policy are further unfolded in a laboriously constructed letter to the Rev. J. J. Freeman, assistant to Tidman, dated 23 September, on the eve of his departure. For the rest, he shows by careful statistics the paucity of the population near Kuruman, which is nomadic, compared with that a hundred miles north where it is settled. He and Rogers Edwards propose to take with them two of the best qualified native Christians and leave them as teachers in some promising locality, and if necessary to subsidize the maintenance of one of them from his own salary (£75 per annum as a bachelor). He hopes by this journey himself to become better acquainted with the habits of the people and "to slip more readily into their mode of thinking which is essentially different from ours". He is thankful to note that medical treatment has already proved effective in winning their confidence, and that an unsuccessful case has not impaired it. "The work is urgent, souls are perishing"—what more efficient introduction can there be for future missionaries than preparation (however imperfect) by native teachers?[14] The fatalistic belief that souls were actually perishing because the gospel had not yet reached them, was one which he only gradually outgrew.

This circuitous journey of three months' duration and 700 miles extent was never more than 250 miles directly north. Yet as he tells John Arundel, Home Secretary to the Mission, "this is farther in that direction than any missionaries have yet been. In one case the people had not before seen a white face and in some others only one—that of an enterprising trader [Wilson] who has frequently penetrated far beyond

anyone else." It took the travellers through the Bakwain country
and to the village of Chonuane where their chief Sechele with
his tribe was then living. Here they were well received, less
however from a desire on the part of the tribe to be converted
than from the hope of being protected by white men from the
raids of Mosilikatse, the fierce and dreaded Matabele maraud-
er. It was whilst returning from this journey that Livingstone
made his first contact with the custom of forced child-marriage
by the "bride-price". A little girl of twelve fled to his wagon
for refuge and crouched beneath it. He gave her food and protection. But presently an armed man appeared to reclaim her,
whereupon she sobbed violently. Pomare, a native teacher
from Kuruman and a chief's son, barred his way. The child
slipped off the beads with which she was loaded to make her
more attractive and gave them to the man. "I afterwards took
measures for hiding her, and if fifty men had come they would
not have got her."

For Blaikie, the little maid is a symbol of Africa, and the
incident a miniature of Livingstone's life.

On returning to Kuruman he wrote, 2 December, two letters
of importance. One is to T. L. Prentice. "Although I have not
as yet heard a syllable from you I proceed immediately to
write to you again"—the reason being to acquaint his friend
with the facts, as he now knows them. First, the climate: it is
dry and salubrious, "but I should be unfaithful to you if I did
not let you know that the summer months (with the wind
from the north) are very generally distressing, painfully so to
females". Then as to mission work: the success is really not
so great as has been represented.

> Don't expect to find chiefs friendly to missionaries. In general they are
> hostile, and when friendly it is generally for the purpose of 'milking'
> them. . . . In fact they have nearly encompassed us. Don't imagine I am
> sorry for it. I love to see their arms encompassing us for it will force us
> towards the dark Interior; if no other motive impels us this will.

He feels obliged to mention differences amongst the missionaries themselves, and he does so with a youthful tolerance
which unhappily proved to be premature.

> Quarrels somehow or other arose between the Griqua Town mission-
> aries and the Kuruman ones, and at different times there have been

squabbles and bickerings. You must not think I speak disrespectfully or censoriously of anyone. They are all excellent men. I have a great regard for them all and their wives too are excellent characters. You must work uphill and work hard too, and get no thanks for it. . . . There are encouragements too but these I need not mention. . . . It is pleasant work and if I had only more of the heavenly motives within, no life can be compared to it.

The other letter is to the Rev. Mr. McRobert, then Congregational minister in Hamilton. It is a matter for surprise that this letter has not hitherto been reproduced. From the point of view of the writer it was productive, as will be seen later, of an immediate result; but in the long view it contains the germ of an idea which was novel and original, and which has long since been the accepted practice: the idea namely that churches and chapels at home should make themselves responsible for the support of a particular mission, *their own* mission overseas. The simile which Livingstone uses to enforce his point is itself striking.

> When new Islands are discovered by voyagers, it is their custom to take possession of them in the name of their monarch. Now we can take possession of these tribes in a far nobler sense—in the name of the Lord. Every church almost might take a tribe under its own care, for if we can place two native teachers in any of their towns, they being able to keep school and preach in their own simple affectionate manner the message of mercy, as much will be effected in the first few years as can be expected from the labours of any two Europeans.

He goes on to explain how difficult it is to disabuse the native mind of the idea that Christianity is no more than one of "the white man's customs"; and how much more readily it is accepted when proclaimed by one of their own people. Then "their minds are brought more directly in contact with the Truth, and they are not diverted away from the subject by the peculiar strangeness which always clings to foreigners in every country". He contrasts the teachability and tractability of the unsophisticated tribes in the far interior with the perversity and hostility of those who have been contaminated by contact with Europeans, who, among other things, "have brought disease, but no remedies, either for body or mind".

He says the wage offered to a native agent, £10 per annum, though insufficient is gratefully received; that he will himself defray the cost of taking them to their destinations, each journey costing £6; that he has been living hard, and will continue to do so with this purpose. He begs for collections for the support of another native teacher, and asks pardon for making this request—as the natives say, "My heart was speaking".[15]

It was the dream of the imperialist Cecil Rhodes a generation later that the uncolonized portion of the map of South Africa, from the Cape to the Zambesi, should be painted red for Britain. It was the dream of the missionary David Livingstone thus early that the whole continent should be painted white for Christ.

On returning to Kuruman he wrote, 22 December, to Dr. Risdon Bennett a description of the terrain, and of the watermelons and esculent roots that grow below the arid soil. Some of these are powerfully astringent. There is also a bitter plant which the Bushmen use for poisoning their arrows. "I made a decoction and tasted it; it caused a burning sensation on the tongue and roof of the mouth with a sense of stopping in the nostrils. When however I added a little acetic acid to the decoction it made it quite bland. Would I be justified in trying this in a case of rheumatism?" Patients now come to him from a distance of 130 miles, and when travelling his wagon was quite besieged.[16]

On the same date, in letters officially to Freeman and more personally to Arundel, he is yet more emphatic on the subject of Native Agency. He can speak now with first-hand experience of "their warm affectionate manner of dealing with their fellow-countrymen, and of their capability to bring the truth itself before their minds, entirely divested of that peculiar strangeness which cleaves to foreigners". If only the Directors will allow their employment to be put "into vigorous operation" conversions may be expected to increase "in compound ratio, and regions not yet explored by Europeans will soon be supplied with the Bread of Life". It would also be an economy in man-power and in actual expense. Then too on the subject of Expansion: the adjoining tribes are averse to evangelization, their minds having been poisoned against it by Griqua hunters who were also introducing among them diseases (venereal) previously unknown, whilst the ravages of Mosilikatse were keeping the whole country in alarm. But from this hostility and these turmoils the tribes to the north were as yet immune. It is only a matter of time, however, before these injurious influences reach them also. It is therefore essential that the sphere of operations be moved from Kuruman to locations *in the interior* without loss of time; and he begs leave to draw the attention of the Directors to a tribe called the Bakhatla, whose location is the best he has seen. . . . "I state this with diffidence because it is in direct variance with the opinions expressed in my written instructions" . . . but he awaits their reply "with much anxiety".[17]

What can the Directors have made of these letters, cumbrous in expression yet confident in tone, the writer of which they remembered as a gauche unobtrusive student concerning whose fitness for the ministry they had entertained grave doubts, but who now after barely five months in the field of action held such very positive and decided views? Was it possible that his tone, besides being assured, was also becoming peremptory? that in fact he was even presuming to direct the Directors?

Chapter Four

PRELIMINARY JOURNEYS
1842–1843

*"I shall proceed to the northward and live excluded from all
European society."*

IN fulfilment of a promise made to the Bakwena and other
tribes Livingstone set forth again on 10 February 1842,
alone save for the company of two native converts and two
native drivers. His object, as he reported to Freeman, was twofold: by releasing himself for six months from the pressure of
medical work at Kuruman, to acquire fluency in Sechuana, and
to engage in direct evangelism with the help of native agents.

On 21 March he wrote to his father: "Janet may be pleased
to learn that I am become a poet, or rather a poetaster, in
Sechuana"—having translated some English hymns into that
language, and composed others on themes which she might
versify and Agnes set to music.

After twelve days' travel through unfrequented desert (the
eastern fringes of the Kalahari) he reached the valley of the
Bakhatla, an inviting situation, and thence proceeded a hundred
miles to the village of Lepelole in the country of the friendly
Bakwena. Here he met Bubi, a principal chief and one of "the
most sensible" he had met with, who supplied him with milk
and his men with food, refusing payment, and cheerfully co-
operated in establishing a school. "Although the wagon
attracted crowds of visitors daily, we did not miss a single
article."

On 14 April he addressed a long epistle to his confidential
friend Watt, then in Benares, from "the Tropic of Capricorn,
in the Bakwain country".

In the opinion of the Directors, no one but Mr. Moffat is to
be credited with any common sense, and therefore no definite
move from Kuruman is to be undertaken until his arrival,
which is now delayed till the end of the year.

54

But I did not come to Africa to be suspended on the tail of anyone, and what is of infinitely more importance as a motive to immediate action, souls are perishing while I have no power to point them to the Cross.

I could not settle down at Kuruman, saying with the worthy whom the worthiest of worthies in Bloomfield Street appointed my companion, "Perhaps the time for the people of the interior has not yet come. . . . " Because I could not wait for Mr. M., nor yet for the "time", I am here . . . opening up the way for the settlement of native teachers with the tribes who have not before been seen by any missionary.[1]

At the same time he wrote at length to Mr. Thomas Prentice of Stowmarket, the father of his two friends, expressing some anxiety lest they may be discouraged when they see things as they really are in Bechuanaland.

I fear that he [Thomas] will take a more pensive view than I do. . . . I have far too much levity in my composition. . . . It will be a sacrifice to him. I believe it is to most, and almost wish it were to me, to sober me down a little.

But if they come out at all they should come as far north as the Tropic of Capricorn at least, . . . for unless the new missionaries go forward they will not have work equal to what they might find in thousands of villages in England. And to Manning Prentice:

Here I could build Thomas a house for a few lbs. of beads, and would certainly begin if I knew his intentions, but I have not had a single line from him. . . . It would be well for Thomas if he were ordained or had his A.M. You can't conceive how much heartburning there has been on this subject. . . . Both you and Thomas must feel yourselves thoroughly independent. . . . I do not attach any importance to ordination. I only wish all had been ordained; it would have prevented some from despising others who remain here without that ceremony having been performed on them. . . . [2]

These and other epistolary exercises were however interludes in more strenuous manual work, and this is of great interest and importance in that it illustrates, better than any explanation could, Livingstone's instinctive comprehension of primitive intelligence, by means of which he was able to win from the very outset and almost effortlessly an ascendency over the people of Central Africa wherever he might go, and which colleagues who had lived among them for many years might envy but could not emulate. The fact that he, still a novice and not yet perfect in the dialect, could induce a chief to set his satellites to hard manual labour for "rain-making" is remarkable enough; but that he could jolly the professional rain-maker to the same task—for the sheer fun of the thing, though the laugh would be against the rain-maker in the end—is quite extraordinary; and yet, by anyone who has knowledge of the African it is also quite understandable.

[To Watt. April 14]: The doctor and the rainmaker among these people are one and the same person. As I did not like to be behind my professional brethren, I declared I could make rain too, not however by enchantments like them, but by leading out their river for irrigation. The idea pleased mightily, and to work we went *instanter*. Even the chief's own doctor is at it, and works like a good fellow, laughing heartily at the cunning of the 'foreigner' who can make rain so. We have only one spade, and this is without a handle; and yet by means of sticks sharpened to a point we have performed all the digging of a pretty long canal [between four and five hundred feet in length, three in width and four in depth—he tells Freeman]. The earth was lifted out in 'gowpens' and carried to the huge dam we have built, in karosses, tortoise-shells, or wooden bowls. We intended nothing of the ornamental in it, but when we came to a huge stone we were forced to search for a way round it. The consequence is, it has assumed a beautifully serpentine appearance. This is, I believe, the first instance in which Bechuanas have been got to work without wages.[3] [To Freeman: They showed surprising industry and perseverance, and although the dam was twice swept away by floods and I was unable, in consequence of getting both legs and arms severely sunburned, to stimulate them by my example, they did not seem in any way discouraged but laboured on to the end.][4]

He goes on to explain that he has adopted an entirely different method of approach from that of his older colleagues, but which produced the desired effect: he does not ask the natives to do anything; he tells them what to do and shows them how to do it.

[To Watt.] It was with the utmost difficulty that the earlier missionaries got them to do anything. The missionaries solicited their permission to do what they did, and this was the very way to make them show off their airs, for they are so disobliging: I am trying a different plan with them. I make my presence with any of them a favour, and when they show any impudence I threaten to leave them, and if they don't amend I put my threat into execution. By a bold, free course among them I have not had the least difficulty in managing the most fierce. They are in one sense fierce, in another the greatest cowards in the world. A kick would, I am persuaded, quell the courage of the bravest of them.

[To Manning Prentice.] They begin now to understand that I am not to be imposed upon. The other day the Chief came and begged something. I answered, "Bubi, you know I hate beggars." He disappeared in an instant. Some natives from a tribe about 100 miles south of this came on a visit while the dam was in progress and told the people that they ought to demand payment for that work. Next day when they began to be tired they told me what the strangers had said, adding that the missionaries at Kuruman always gave payment, and they did not mean to work without. I told them it was all kindness in me to show them how to do such a work, and instead of me paying them they ought to pay me, but as they were discontented we should stop it instantly. I left them immediately. They felt sorry they had proceeded so far and came begging I should not cease to shew them how to work; the Chief himself joining them, saying I must not think of leaving them alone—it was just their foolishness. Perhaps these little incidents will let you see what sort of people you will have to deal with. It is not so much the present as the future we have to look to. We must stimulate them to industry; giving —without making them feel that they have earned what they receive— has a very bad effect. It makes them covetous and does not tend to advance their civilization. This is the effect of all these clothes sent out by kind friends in England. . . .

A trader can do more for mere civilization han a missionary; the missionaries deny this but it is to me quite apparent.[5]

All this and more besides, too long to quote, goes to show how far removed his ideas were, as to *method*, from the accepted evangelistic ideas of his day.

After spending a month with the Bakwena, he proceeded slowly north again through the fringes of the desert with both his teachers (one, Pomore, being sick with fever) towards the country of the Bamangwato; but the sand proving too heavy for the oxen he was obliged to leave the wagon and perform the last part of the journey, between forty and fifty miles, on foot. This, however, was no cause for regret, since the chief Sekomi (father of the famous chief Khama who was then a youth) "was evidently pleased that I had thrown myself on his bounty without the least appearance of distrust"; and was not only most generous and friendly but also willing to be instructed. On the other hand, the people of his village, who were numerous (600 huts), were "sunk into the very lowest state of both mental and moral degradation, so much so indeed that it must be difficult or rather impossible for Christians at home to realize an accurate notion of the gross darkness that shrouds their minds". The country was infested with lions, and such careful precautions were taken when leaving the shelter of the village even in daytime that Livingstone at first believed them unnecessary.

[To Freeman.] But the earnestness with which the Chief remonstrated with me for going a few hundred yards from the town unattended, and the circumstance that he always sent an attendant if at any time he saw me going out afterwards, together with the fact that a woman was actually devoured in her garden during my visit (I had frequently walked past it), fully convinced me that there are good grounds for their fears. . . .

[To Watt.] It was most affecting to hear the cries of the orphan children of this woman. During the whole day after her death the surrounding rocks and valleys rang and re-echoed with their bitter cries. I frequently thought, as I listened to the loud sobs, painfully indicative of the sorrows of those who have no hope, that if some of our churches could have heard their sad wailings, it would have awakened the firm resolution to do more for the heathen than they have done.

He remained among the Bamangwato for a fortnight endeavouring, but apparently without success, to enlighten their hearts and minds. "The name of God conveys no more to their understanding than the idea of superiority. I was every day shocked by being addressed by that title." Sekomi himself was at least aware of a conscience, and propounded "a new theory of regeneration" which Livingstone was "unable to work out".

[To Watt.] On one occasion Sekomi, having sat by me in the hut for some time in deep thought, at length addressing me by a pompous title said, "I wish you would change my heart. Give me medicine to change it, for it is proud, proud and angry, angry always." I lifted up the Testament and was about to tell him of the only way in which the heart can be changed, but he interrupted me by saying, "Nay, I wish to have it changed by medicine, to drink and have it changed at once, for it is very proud and very uneasy, and continually angry with someone." He then rose and went away.[6]

On leaving Sekomi he was provided with thirty attendants to conduct him safely back to his wagon with presents for himself and his men. Four of this escort, including an underchief, were instructed to continue with him till he returned to Kuruman "and bring back a faithful report of all the wonderful things I had told him".

In order to reach the Bakaa tribe he by-passed the basaltic hills of the same name, at a point within only ten days' journey of Lake Ngami and, as he says in his *Travels*, "I might then have discovered that lake, had discovery alone been my object." He was still on foot and was joined by some members, apparently, of the Bakaa.

> Some of my companions who had recently joined us, and did not know that I understood a little of their speech, were overheard by me discussing my appearance and powers: "He is not strong, he is quite slim, and only appears stout because he puts himself into those bags [trousers]; he will soon knock up." This caused my Highland blood to rise, and made me despise the fatigue of keeping them all at the top of their speed for days together, and until I heard them expressing proper opinions of my pedestrian powers.[7]

And though he does not mention the fact except by inference and in passing, he had already penetrated farther north than any other white man had yet done and survived to tell the tale. Two European traders had preceded him, of whom one had perished from fever and the other, with three of his native companions, had been poisoned by the Bakaa; a fourth they had strangled. The Bakaa tribe had "a bad name", even among their savage neighbours, for treachery and cruelty. Livingstone's perfectly fearless and unceremonious approach to these murderers is consistent with his behaviour in yet more dangerous situations.

Except for the chief and his attendants all fled from him at first, but when a dish of porridge (mealie-meal) was produced and he partook of it without distrust they returned: he then lay down to sleep in their presence, and they flocked round in considerable numbers. He stayed among them for a few days, rebuked them for blood-guiltiness and preached the gospel, and when he left them the chief sent his son and an escort to conduct him safely on his way to the Makalaka.

His visit to the Makalaka though brief was of unexpected interest. This tribe, the smallest of those he had encountered, proved to be but one among five of a people of considerable numbers called the *Mashona*, whose language and customs differed from those of the Bechuana, who manufactured cotton cloth, iron and copper, and fought with guns instead of assegai. "These they obtain from the Portuguese on the eastern coast and . . . I am inclined to believe they procure them in exchange for slaves." This was indeed a new and more important discovery than he could be aware of.[8]

Whilst staying at Bubi's village again on the return journey he was visited by a deputation from a neighbouring chief, Sebehwe, "the bravest of all the Bechuanas" who, having been betrayed by cowardly allies, had retired with his people into the Kalahari from whence he, alone of them all, had successfully counter-attacked Mosilikatse's raiders and driven them from his borders. Sebehwe desired to know whether it was now safe for him to return. Livingstone replied that if he did so he would be exposed to attack from Mahura, chief of those among the Batlapi near Kuruman who were unconverted and were now armed with guns. Sebehwe, however, having been visited by some of the Baltapi who were converts, disregarded this advice with disastrous results.

These involved a minor tribal massacre the savagery of which, though he did not witness it, left a lasting impression on Livingstone's mind. It was indeed but one of countless such barbarities as were afflicting the dark continent at the time and had afflicted it from time immemorial: a reflection which is sufficient answer to the sceptic who scouts the necessity for Christian missions to the heathen with the query, "Why not leave them alone?" or the Pax Britannica with, "What are we doing there?" To Tidman he describes the depravity of these tribes as "sub-natural" and far below the level of ordinary sinners. "It almost makes us believe we have not got humanity to deal with."

He returned to Kuruman at the end of June 1842, having travelled a thousand miles in all by wagon and on foot, and wrote his report to Freeman on 3 July. He remarks that his address to the Bakaa was the first he had delivered without reading it: "I felt more freedom than I had anticipated, but I have an immense amount of labour still before me ere I can call myself a master of Sechuana." He is also applying himself to the kindred dialect of the Batlapi.

This was followed by another letter on 18 July. The theme of it is the "magnitude of difference" to be noticed between the morals of Bechuanas converted in the neighbourhood of Kuruman and "the depths of degradation" from which they have been raised, and in which the unconverted tribes in the interior are still sunk. It is a striking and forcible proof that "the Gospel has lost none of its pristine efficacy".

I can the more freely bear testimony to the mighty effects which have and do still follow the faithful and devoted labours of my elder brethren in this place, as my instrumentality has in no way contributed to the result. And from my knowledge of the character of Messrs. Hamilton and Edwards I believe, in their communications to the Directors they must always have kept considerably within what they might have told of the progress of the cause of Christ through their instrumentality. . . I pray to be enabled to walk with humility and zeal in their footsteps. May the same power which supported them ever uphold and cause me to be faithful.[9]

He has special praise for the work of Mrs. Edwards in the infant school. "It shows what an amount of influence may be exerted over a country by the devotion of a single individual"; and the intelligent expression on the features of these children, which is visible even to strangers, "would almost lead one to suppose that they belonged to another species". The Church too "is in a most flourishing condition—not stand-still, but making headway against the world"; in proof of which, one of his drivers to whom he paid eighteen dollars in wages immediately returned twelve as his subscription to the mission.[10]

Such an unsolicited testimonial to the work of his predecessors—one of whom was nearly old enough to be his grandfather and the other eighteen years his senior, and both men of long experience and proved worth—may appear somewhat gratuitous from the pen of a newcomer to the field, even though neither of them was a professional man, whilst he was both a qualified doctor and a clergyman. But certainly nothing of patronage was intended: only an expression of unfeigned thankfulness and an earnest desire to render justice where it was due. And these words of humble appreciation of his fellow-labourers have a pathetic interest in view of what was to befall in his relations with one of them.

There ensued a period of prolonged "suspense" for Livingstone, coinciding with an outbreak of sporadic raids by the Matabele among the tribes in the interior, during which no native drivers could be persuaded to venture beyond Kuruman. He therefore spent eight months of itinerant preaching in the neighbourhood, healing the sick, familiarizing himself with the habits and speech of the Batlapi, assisting his colleagues in building an out-station, in preparing the printing-press, and in the routine work of the Mission. Besides himself there were now on the station: old Mr. Hamilton, Mr. and Mrs. Edwards, Mr. and Mrs. Ross, whilst Mr. and Mrs. Moffat and two qualified recruits, W. Ashton and W. Inglis (both married) were shortly expected. This seemed to Livingstone a prodigal waste of manpower in a sparsely populated locality where the majority of natives were already converts, when the need was so urgent elsewhere, and though it was known that there would be some redistribution on Moffat's return this event was becoming unduly protracted. He was impatient for dispersal and wrote to Tidman bluntly: "Here, there is no scope for more than two missionaries at most."

That he was both conscientious and successful in his medical work is evident from long letters to Dr. Risdon Bennett, to whom he recounts his prescriptions and treatments of various cases, and frequently asks for advice. His practice in midwifery had both humorous and pathetic aspects. Native women in confinement were shy of the presence of male doctors. He therefore reserved himself for only the most difficult cases. A case of twins occurred in which the ointments of all the native doctors proved unavailing. A few seconds of the white man's art sufficed to afford the necessary relief for the mother, and to procure for the doctor "great fame in a department in which I could lay no claim to merit".

But he never from the outset regarded his medical work as other than of secondary importance in comparison with his work directly as a missionary; and he was now beginning increasingly to feel that the demands of the former were encroaching unduly upon the needs of the latter. This acute sense of conflict of duties, and a knowledge of where his real obligation lay, is strikingly expressed in a letter to Cecil.

I did not at first intend to give up all attention to medicine and the treatment of disease, but now I feel it to be my duty to have as little to do with it as possible. I shall attend to none but severe cases in future, and my reasons for this determination are I think good. The spiritual amelioration of the people is the object for which I came, but I cannot expect God to advance this by my instrumentality if much of my time is spent in mere temporal amelioration. And I know that if I gave much attention to medicine and medical studies, something like a sort of *mania* which seized me soon after I began the study of anatomy would increase, and I fear would gain so much power over me as to make me perhaps a very good doctor, but a useless drone of a missionary. I feel the self-denial this requires very much, but it is the only real sacrifice I have been called upon to make, and I shall try to make it willingly.[11]

This attitude of Livingstone towards his profession strikes one of his biographers as "curious". There can be no doubt that he had a natural aptitude as well as enthusiasm for medicine and that, had he concentrated on it, he might have made "a very good doctor". But in letters to his Directors, of earlier date than this, in referring to the welfare of the negroes we find him emphasizing—as even more urgent than the healing of their mortal bodies—"the salvation of their immortal souls". And the letter above-quoted marks a turning-point in his career. Henceforth he became less of a doctor as he became more of a missionary; just as later he was to become less of a missionary as he became more of an explorer. And yet through all his manifold activities it was a missionary he felt himself to be in heart and mind and soul, and as a missionary first and last that he wished to be known.

Not until 21 February 1843 had "the commotion in the interior" subsided sufficiently to allay the qualms of the native drivers and to set the ox-wagon again in motion. Twelve days' journey northwards (200 miles) brought them to Sebehwe's village. Livingstone's first concern was to disabuse the chief's mind of the mistaken notion that Batlapi converts had treacherously provoked Mahura against him and caused the slaughter of his people. In fact, these converts had disobeyed their chief Mahura's command to open fire. The explanation was accepted, and the next day being Sunday the chief ordered that "no one should do anything but pray to God and listen to the words of the foreigner".

Within but a few hours' distance of Sebehwe's village lay the country of the Bakhatla, the most populous tribe of any in the interior, whose soil was fertile and whose people were industrious not only as agriculturalists but as manufacturers in iron. This had always seemed to Livingstone the most suitable locality for a new mission station, and he now asked the chief whether he would be welcome if he came as the missionary. The chief held up his hands and said: "O, I shall dance for joy if you do. I shall collect all my people to hoe for you a garden, and you will get more sweet reed and corn than myself"—an effusion prompted less by a desire for spiritual enlightenment than for material benefit.[12] No instructions from his Directors on the subject having yet been received, Livingstone could only reply that "I would inform my Christian friends in England of his desires for a missionary". And in fact it was in this very place —Mabotsa—that he established his first mission station less than six months later.

On his first journey with Edwards two years previously he had made acquaintance with Sechele, paramount chief of the Bakwena, at his village Chonuane; but on his second journey he had incurred this chief's displeasure by remaining in Bakwena territory for a month with Bubi, his subordinate, and whom, moreover, Sechele regarded as a rebel. For this reason, Sechele had warned some Batlapi converts that he would do their missionary a mischief should he ever attempt to pass through his country again. Neither then nor later did Livingstone take the slightest notice of a threat. From Sebehwe's village he proceeded directly to Chonuane, a five days' journey to find instead of hostility an unexpectedly friendly welcome. Sechele's only child was sick, and the child of his under-chief reduced to a skeleton through dysentery; he treated them both successfully "and Sechele did not seem able to speak a single angry word".[13]

In his *Travels* Livingstone introduces this chief to his readers thus: "I was from the first struck by his intelligence, and by the marked manner in which we both felt drawn to each other. As this remarkable man has not only embraced Christianity, but expounds its doctrines to his people, I will here give a brief sketch of his career." This he proceeds to do in a digression of five pages. Sechele proved to be incomparably the best black friend that Livingstone ever knew. Livingstone was himself an unusual exception to men of European blood, in that he never felt conscious in Africa of the colour-bar; Sechele was unusual in his comprehension of European modes of thought. But the existence of a natural affinity between a white man and a black, recognized by each of them from the first as mutual, is something that escapes the bounds of ethnic psychology. And on Sechele's side it stood the test of many a strain imposed by his white friend's rigorist demands in matters of faith and morals.

In his first instruction he was required, for example, to believe that "all who die unforgiven are lost forever", and a terrible picture of the Great Assize portrayed for him in the graphic language of the Seer of Patmos. On enquiring whether these facts had been known to his preceptor's forefathers, and having been answered in the affirmative, it is little wonder that the bewildered chief responded: "You startle me—these words make all my bones to shake—I have no more strength in me: but my forefathers were living at the same time as yours, and how is it that they did not send them word about these terrible things sooner? They all passed away into darkness without knowing whither they were going?"—"I thought immediately", says Livingstone in a letter to Tidman, "of the guilt of the Church, but did not confess." In his *Travels* he recounts part of his impromptu answer, apparently quite oblivious of the fact that it is no answer at all. "I got out of the difficulty by explaining the geographical barriers in the North, and the gradual spread of knowledge from the South, to which we first had access by means of ships; and I expressed my belief that, as Christ had said, the whole world would yet be enlightened by the Gospel."

The fact that Livingstone should have recorded this conversation without comment as late as 1856 and after the experiences of his first Great Journey is sufficient to show how deeply and stubbornly ingrained in him were the grim doctrines of his upbringing. They were, of course, the accepted currency of evangelical discourse of his time, and none of his fellow-missionaries would have dreamed of disputing them. They believed without question that the souls of the heathen were in danger of perishing eternally unless converted; hence the sense of urgency with which they, and Livingstone especially, pursued their vocation : indeed we find him writing to Tidman in 1848 : "I have never been able to contemplate the condition especially of the old without a painful foreboding that our entreaties and warnings would only render their doom the more terrible. . ." since they ascribed their longevity to witchcraft "and it would be folly to think of another Saviour now."[14] There is no explicit evidence to show that Livingstone ever disavowed such a grim doctrine of conditional salvation; nevertheless it is clear that, even as early as his first Great Journey, acts of spontaneous kindness and self-sacrifice on the part of his pagan retinue frequently evoked his surprise and

admiration ; whilst on his Last Journeys, when concern for the
spiritual (no less than the temporal) welfare of the negro was
the constant theme of his thoughts, he is altogether silent on
the subject of penalties hereafter.

The outcome of this his first conversation with Sechele was
more enlivening than the topic which prompted it.

> Pointing to the great Kalahari desert, he said: "You can never cross
> that country to the tribes beyond; it is utterly impossible even for us
> black men, except in certain seasons, when more than the usual supply
> of rain falls and an extraordinary growth of water-melons follows. Even
> we who know the country would certainly perish without them." Re-
> asserting my belief in the words of Christ, we parted; and it will be seen
> further on that Sechele himself assisted me in crossing that desert which
> had previously proved an insurmountable barrier to so many adventurers.

During his stay, several women refugees who had escaped
from captivity after Mosilikatse's latest raid found temporary
asylum at Sechele's before returning to their respective tribes.
Reduced almost to skeletons from prolonged exposure and
semi-starvation, their wretched plight evoked no slightest sign
or sound of sympathy from the men who listened to their tale
of woe. "Truly heathenism has no bowels of compassion."
But their tale, though it had no effect on the Bakwena, "had a
powerful effect on the people of my wagon. I could not prevail
upon them to go an inch farther, for to go any nearer the
Matabele than they were seemed like rushing into the jaws of
death. Their very hearts seemed ready to die within them."

> [To Tidman.] I was thus reduced to the necessity of either giving up
> my tour and returning, or going forward on ox-back. I chose the latter,
> and although it has some inconveniences, it possesses some advantages
> over the wagon.[15]
> [To R. Bennett.] I think I see you smile at the idea of such a convey-
> ance. It is rough travelling, as you can conceive. The skin is so loose that
> there is no getting one's greatcoat, which has to serve for both saddle and
> blanket, to stick on. And then the long horns in front, with which he can
> give one a punch in the abdomen if he likes, make us sit as bolt upright
> as dragoons. In this manner I travelled more than 400 miles.[16]

This novel and precarious method of transport, which he
put to a first trial now on the level surface of the desert, he was
to adopt again in far more difficult and dangerous circumstances when travelling up the rocky bed of the Zambesi.

By this means he was now enabled to visit villages in the desert which no wagon could approach and where no white man had ever been. These were the dwellings of the Bakalahari, a poor and primitive race, who lived as far as possible from the tribes that would enslave them and therefore far from water. "They were more attentive to my instruction than any other tribe, which made me feel much interested in them. . . . By far the happiest portion of my journey was, when sitting by their fires and listening to their traditionary tales, I could intermingle the story of the Cross with their conversation." They slaked their thirst on the juices of no less than forty varieties of roots, and thirty of fruits, which the desert provided. Their women had also an ingenious, if to us repulsive, method of extracting water from below the sand by suction through a reed and storing it in ostrich egg-shells. Livingstone, who was never squeamish but often thirsty, would frequently accept with thankfulness a draught of this "precious fluid" produced from he knew not where. [17]

But their staple diet was locusts and wild honey, concerning which Livingstone has some quaint observations to make to his Directors.

[To Tidman.] Perhaps I may be excused if I mention the physiological effects of the Baptist's food: the former is excessively constipating and the latter has quite the opposite tendency. The locusts pounded and mixed with honey are as good if not better than shrimps at home. It is not probable that he confined himself to that diet. If, however, locusts and wild honey were as plentiful in the wilderness of Judaea as they are now in the desert of the Da-kalahari, he would have had very little difficulty in finding a constant supply. During a period of twelve months I saw no fewer than nineteen swarms of locusts, and yet no particular damage was done to the crops of the natives in consequence, and had I myself attended all the calls of the 'honey bird' I should never have been without a sufficiency of honey.

[To Dr. Bennett.] The locusts taste just like the vegetables on which they subsist, generally like the soft juicy parts of a stalk of wheat. . . . We find the honey by means of a bird, the skin of which I shall send you. They call us by a peculiar kind of chirping, and following it we very seldom are disappointed. I have followed them four or five miles, and when hungry was sure of finding a meal at the spot she pointed out.

On this journey, accompanied by three Bakwena guides, he revisited the Bamangwato, Bakaa, and Makalaka, all of whom "live on the summit of a range of lofty black basaltic rocks" and the latter within two days of the dreaded Matabele; but the caverns in these rocks provided an impregnable defence. He found the ill-famed Bakaa less hospitable than ever, for having been accused (though not by him) of poisoning one of his black companions the year before, they now refused to give him any food, "so we had to feast for two days on the delectable things we saw in our dreams". The remark, thus casually thrown out, occurs in a personal letter to Dr. Risdon Bennett. So also does the sequel, and it is characteristic of his stoical and almost contemptuous indifference to privation, danger, or pain.

[To Dr. Bennett.] This low diet had a good effect on me, for when descending their lofty rocks, after having addressed them, I felt so much interested in the questions they were putting concerning what they had heard, that I forgot for a moment where I was going, and then feeling as if about to fall, made a violent effort to save myself. But though I succeeded, I struck my hand with so much violence on a sharp angle as produced a compound fracture of the finger-bone. The Testament served as a rest between which and the rock my finger was injured, and a very good splint was made of a piece of reed. The fasting, I suppose, prevented irritative fever, and although I did not rest a day on account of it, it was about to heal kindly. But one night a lion began to roar tremendously and very near to the bush at which we were all fast asleep. It was nearer than from your room in the dispensary to the open street. My ox leapt in among us. My poor Bakwains shrieked for fear, and I, half awake and stupid, seized a pistol with the disabled hand and fired at the monster, but the rebound rebroke my finger. When we got him driven away the poor Bakwains seeing the blood running, said, "You have hurt yourself but you have redeemed us. Henceforth we shall swear by you." (Poor creatures, I wished they had felt gratitude for the blood that was shed for their precious souls.)* The second fracture was worse than the first, but as I can bear a little pain pretty well, it did not hinder me as much as I expected. It prevented my obtaining provisions by my gun, and the whole party being entirely dependent on it, we should have been put to shift had it not been for the kindness of the Bakalahari. They generously gave us what food they had, and although some of it is absolutely indi-

* These words are omitted from the text in the published collection of his letters, no doubt from motives of delicacy. But they should be retained, since their omission renders the incident, for the narrator himself, pointless. He would obviously not have thought it worth relating for its own sake. Moreover, such and similar expressions of evangelical fervour are of frequent occurrence in Livingstone's early letters and, however repugnant to our habits of thought and feeling to-day, they represent an important element in his own, and therefore are essential to our understanding of the whole man.

gestible, and undergoes no alteration by being subjected to the action of the stomach, I never enjoyed better health. . . .

I slept during my oxback journey for three weeks and four days on the sand with only my great coat over me and a little grass under, and yet I never once caught cold.[18]

This last observation is made in testimony, not to his own capacity to endure hardship, but to the salubrity of the climate.

His companion on part of these journeys—400 miles on foot —had been an unconverted native youth named Sehamy, to whom he had often "spoken" and with whom he had often prayed; and with whom he had often endured thirst and who was "my bedfellow behind many a bush". He had been the leader of the party and had "anticipated my every want". Six months later Livingstone heard that he had died of fever. The news of this caused him great agony of mind, and more than a year later we find him referring to it in a letter, 17 September 1844, written to a school in Southampton which had sent him £15 to the support of a native teacher.[19] At the time his grief expressed itself in a lamentation which reveals the depth and intensity of his passion for souls, and the sense of his own inadequacy for his task as an evangelist.

> Poor Sehamy, where art thou now? Where lodges thy soul tonight? Didst thou think of what I told thee as thou turnedst from side to side in distress? I could now do anything for thee. I could weep for thy soul. But now nothing can be done. Thy fate is fixed. Oh, am I guilty of the blood of thy soul, my poor dear Sehamy? If so, how shall I look on thee in the judgment? But I told thee of a Saviour; didst thou think of Him, and did He lead thee through the dark valley? Did He comfort as only He can? Help me, O Lord Jesus, to be faithful to everyone. Remember me, and let me not be guilty of the blood of souls. . . . [20]

Let who will smile at the naïveté of such words, they cannot forbear to salute the tenderness of affection and solicitude, the sense of responsibility and personal unworthiness, of the heart that uttered them. There was never any self-satisfaction or complacency in Livingstone. Like his great predecessor in the missionary field he never counted himself to have attained, but knew that he was always pressing on towards a mark for the prize of his high calling. He had been storing his mind on these lonely journeys with familiar lines of human pathos in the poetry of Coleridge and of contemporary poets such as Hood and Tennyson, and of Longfellow, Whittier, and Lowell in

America; as well as with the spiritual wisdom of the Christian Fathers—Augustine, and Bernard whose hymn *Jesu, dulcis memoria* "rings in my ears as I wander across the wide, wide wilderness, and makes me wish I was more like them".[21]

He had proved himself to his own satisfaction to be a hardy traveller with a constitution equal to great exertions and prolonged strain. But how the Directors would regard his activities, and whether they would listen to his reiterated requests to establish a permanent station in the far interior, was still for him a matter of doubt. They must have been aware from his frequent solicitations, no less than from his restless proceedings, that they were dealing with a very unusual type of missionary. Their reply to his letters of July 1842, so long and so impatiently awaited by him, is dated 29 January 1843, and came to hand at last six months later. It ran as follows:

It affords us unfeigned pleasure to express our entire approval of the measures you have pursued, and our grateful satisfaction at the vigour, perseverance and fidelity with which they were prosecuted. Nor do we hesitate to state our cordial concurrence in your sentiments as to the desirableness of expanding the permanent operations of the Society among the tribes to whom your attention has been directed. It is on this principle we have appointed the Brethren by whom Mr. Moffat is accompanied on his return to Africa, and we trust arrangements will be made at an early period towards carrying these views into effect.

We refrain from entering, on the present occasion, into any enlarged detail on the important subject of native agency in reply to your communications, as you will have ample opportunity, in your official capacity as a member of the District Committee, of explaining and advocating your views or proposing any specific measures which you may deem desirable, and you may rest satisfied that the recommendations of the Committee, in support of such views and proposition, will always meet our ready and cordial consideration, inasmuch as we highly appreciate your exertions and cherish an earnest desire to respond to your solicitudes and encourage your efforts on behalf of the native tribes.[22]

Chapter Five

MABOTSA: MAULED BY A LION
1843–1844

"I will go anywhere, provided it be—forward."

"WITH feelings of irrepressible delight I hail the decision of the Directors that we go forward to the dark interior."

With these words Livingstone welcomed the sanction of the Directors to his own proposal, by him so long and eagerly awaited, by them so long and cautiously withheld. It was however sugar to a pill, or rather two, which were hard to swallow: their refusal of direct sanction as yet to the employment of native teachers; and their reference of this and other specific measures to the deliberations of a local committee. But he was now in a position to reinforce his advocacy of the first by informing them of his receipt by the same mail as their letter of the gift of £12, already collected by Mrs. McRobert for the support of a native teacher, together with the promise of two other such sums for the same purpose.[1]

Rumours of the projected appointment of a local committee, proposed to the Directors by Moffat while in England to offset the sole authority of Dr. Philip, had already reached Cape Town and Livingstone had long since been aware of it. Moffat had in fact confided it to him in London. He thus expressed his views upon it to his friend George Drummond in the South Seas: "A committee is to be, *alias* a presbitery: this is as much against the grain with me as a bishopric. But if it will advance the cause I won't spend time quarrelling."[2] And thus to the Directors in no uncertain terms:

I only know of two of the brethren, Messrs. Moffat and Ross, at all desirous of its establishment. This and the fact that the others will join simply because such is the expressed rule of the Directors, seem to augur ill for its prosperity. . . . I however endeavour to repress my private feelings on the subject, and I do so with the hope that the measure may

71

be productive of all the advantage to the cause which a well conducted combination is calculated to effect. But the Directors will not, I trust, consider me guilty of any impropriety if, when yielding to a prompt compliance with their wish, I feel constrained to add I must reserve to myself the power of withdrawing from that committee if at any future time I feel that to be my duty.[3]

His letter continues with an even bolder criticism of the policy of the Mission. A conviction, he says, has been forced upon him both by his own personal inspection of the field which is more extensive than any hitherto undertaken by any-one else, either missionary or trader, and also by the corrobora-tion of all others who have investigated the subject according to their opportunities, that—

> A much larger share of the benevolence of the Church and of mission-ary exertion is directed into this country than the amount of population, as compared with other countries, and the success attending those efforts, seem to call for. . . . In England, I was led to believe that the population of the interior was dense, and now since I have come to this country I have conversed with many, both of our Society and of the French, and none of them would reckon up the number of 30,000 Bechuanas.

He then proceeds to detailed statistics, covering several pages of close writing, being careful as always to underestimate his case rather than to exaggerate, and concludes:

> In view of these facts, and the confirmation of them I have received from both French and English brethren, computing the population much below what I have stated, I confess I feel grieved to hear of the arrival of new missionaries. Nor am I the only one who deplores their appoint-ment to this country. Again and again have I been pained at heart to hear the question put: Where will these new brethren find fields of labour in this country?—because I know that in India or China there are fields large enough for all their energies. . . .
> This consideration makes me earnestly call the attention of the Direc-tors to statistics. . . . If these were actually returned—and there would be very little difficulty in doing so—it might, perhaps, be found that there is not a country better supplied with missionaries in the world, and that, in proportion to the number of agents compared to the amount of population, the success may be inferior to that of most other countries.[4]

Insubordinate sentiments, these, from one who was yet among the most junior recruits in the field, even though they were prefaced by the statement that he felt "tremblingly alive to the responsibility" incurred by expressing them to the

Directors. Nor were they the only persons who were aware that Livingstone was assertive and opinionated: his colleagues on the station were too; and so was Dr. Philip. The latter, as it happened, had visited Kuruman during Livingstone's recent absence in the interior and had left him a friendly message "not to think of building his house on the crater of a volcano", adding that Mosilikatse was ready "to pounce on any white man and spill his blood". With reference to this well-meant warning Livingstone wrote to a friend:

> I believed these reports too when I left this [Kuruman], but found to my surprise that the Bamangwato are eight days north of the Bakwena, and that Mosilikatse is at least fourteen days north of them. Seeing then that the Doctor, from having been misinformed, is about to oppose the Gospel being carried into the interior, I intend to go on without his sanction. Besides, he does not point out any place where I can be useful. In fact he cannot, for the country behind is overstocked with missionaries. . . . 5

Philip had in fact, in the previous year, officially opposed Livingstone's proposal to go north; but the Directors had supported it by a resolution of the Board, 9 January 1843, a copy of which was transmitted to Philip.6 As to the strength of Mosilikatse in the distant territory into which he had been driven by the Boers, the only information available was that contained in Moffat's book, concerning which Livingstone wrote curtly and disrespectfully (but truly) to George Drummond: "You will see numerals in that book, for instance, the immense armies of Mosilikatse. Cut off a few cyphers always, and then you will have the truth."

His letter continues with an interesting self-impression:

> The Doctor stated to some of the brethren that he thought I was ambitious. I really am ambitious to preach beyond another man's lines; but I suppose he meant the wrong kind of ambition. I don't feel in the least displeased with him. I am only determined to go on and do all I can, while able, for the poor degraded people in the north.

He could not but have been conscious, even at this stage, of possessing capacities far exceeding those of any of his colleagues, a will for achievement beyond their comprehension; and foresight far beyond the horizon of any of his superiors. And yet, though scornful of advice and convinced always of the

73

soundness of his own decisions, he was capable of sincere self-depreciation:

> I feel the necessity more than ever of active devotedness to the Redeemer's cause. I don't feel anything we usually call sacrifices at home to be such. There is so much to counter-balance them that they really don't deserve the name, and I am in a great deal more danger from levity than from melancholy; indeed it sometimes makes me blame myself severely. . . . I wish my mind were more deeply affected by the condition of those who are perishing in this heathen land. I am sorry to say I don't feel half as concerned for them as I ought.[7]

Reference has been made to his scepticism of some statements in Moffat's *Missionary Researches*. Therein also, Moffat had emphatically denied the existence among the Bechuanas of any religious beliefs: God, conscience, and a future life. In a letter of 24 February from Motito to the Rev. Adolphe Mabille of the French Mission in Basutoland, who was a student of primitive beliefs, Livingstone asks: "What do *you* say?" He quotes a fragment of folklore he had heard from a Mochuana which seemed to point to the existence among these people of "an ancient creed". This makes him dubious of Moffat's assertion that "they had no conscience until it was formed by the missionaries". It also points to a distinct belief in some kind of God and in survival after death. He is open to correction but feels that the question requires more investigation than has been given to it. Dr. Smith, who in his book *Robert Moffat* devotes an illuminating chapter to Bantu folklore, is inclined to the view that Livingstone with his three years' experience in the field was nearer the truth than Moffat with his twenty.[8] He would certainly be supported by two modern authorities, Willoughby and Schwartz.

In accordance with his instructions Livingstone was still impatiently waiting "in suspense and daily expectation" for the arrival of Moffat and his party, who had reached Cape Town in April 1843, before pushing north-eastwards to a better site among the friendly Bakhatla. "No one out of this country", he wrote to the Directors, "can imagine how grievously slow everything in it moves except time. But it cannot be otherwise so long as the heavy Dutch wagon and tedious pack-ox are the only permanent conveyances." At the end of July came tidings from Moffat that he would be detained for two or three months longer near the coast (at Bethelsdorp), to await the arrival of their baggage in a slower ship. (In fact it was not till February 1844 that his party reached Kuruman.) But he had sent word that the Directors "would have no objection to Mr. Edwards removing to the Interior". Accordingly Livingstone consulted his colleagues. They agreed that further delay would involve the unhealthy task of building on a new site during the hot weather which would commence in October, or else would oblige them to postpone it till the following year.

> I concluded that it would be proper to proceed immediately and erect a hut on the spot selected near the Bakhatla. And in this decision I was cordially joined by the brethren Hamilton and Edwards. The latter indeed resolved to accompany me, and I feel happy in being able to state that on account of his superior knowledge of the use of tools, he was a much more efficient agent in the labour that ensued than I was.

Edwards also lent Livingstone his wagon, Ross having borrowed Livingstone's to go to the Cape and assist the Moffat Party.[9]

The site selected, Mabotsa, was some 220 miles distant from Kuruman, approximately coincident with that of Mafeking to-day. Geographically and climatically it was far more suitable for a mission station than the wilderness of Kuruman. Well-wooded and well-watered, it lay at the foot of picturesque hills rich in iron ore. "A lovelier spot you never saw." The people were both numerous and industrious in agriculture and smelting: "it is the Sheffield of the interior". It was a menagerie also of wild game and, in consequence, of lions.

Starting at the end of the first week in August the two missionaries fell into company with a party of three big-game hunters who, Livingstone wrote to Tidman, "were totally unlike some others of the same class, for they behaved with great propriety before the natives, and towards us with the greatest kindness". And to his parents: "Captain Steele, of the Coldstream Guards, is the politest of the three, well versed in the Classics, and possessed of much general knowledge."

Livingstone never sought the society of those who were "above his station"—it was rather they who sought his. Being themselves men of gentle birth and chivalrous traditions, it is evident that these three sportsmen recognized in him a good companion and instinctively discerned, beneath his rough and unpolished husk, grain that was sound to the core. They must have liked the way in which with quiet, dogged, Scotch tenacity he maintained his views against theirs: his literal interpretation of the Fourth Commandment, for example, and his abhorrence of killing wild animals except for necessity. He bluntly called their sport "itinerant butchery". (In this latter respect he was almost a century in advance of his times.) They must have recognized in him a man of intelligence and good nature, but one with whom no liberties were to be taken; one who in times of crisis, hardship or hazard, could show that he had nerves as sound as theirs—perhaps sounder. Amongst themselves they referred to him half-affectionately, half-banteringly, as 'the little man', but never in his presence. And if they subscribed to the definition of a gentleman as "one who never gives offence unless he intends to", then this tough little Scot conformed to their standard and they accepted him as one of themselves. Arrived at Mabotsa, they took an interest in his selection of a site for his mission, agreed that it was the best, and went their ways. Livingstone wrote on 1 September to Mrs. McRobert concerning the "dreadfully degraded state" of the tribes:

> Their condition is such that I fear to do with your teacher what I earnestly desire. I wish to place him with another tribe than that with which we have commenced, in order that, when he is favoured to be the means of converting souls, his success may stand out distinct from ours. . . . He is at present with us and is invaluable. I cannot speak too highly of the spirit he has shown.[10]

He little knew that, were it not for the courage and loyalty of this faithful convert, Mebalwe, his own career would have been cut short within a few months' time.

The missionaries were cordially, even eagerly, welcomed by the chief Moseealele and his people. The presence of white men amongst them was a guarantee of security against attack by marauders, and it also held the hope of desirable gifts such as guns and beads. No persuasion was required to induce them to remove their entire village to a neighbouring valley with a more abundant supply of water, since that same situation had been in their minds for some time. Accordingly, Livingstone drew up a formal agreement, dated 28 August 1843, in the name of the London Missionary Society, signed by himself and

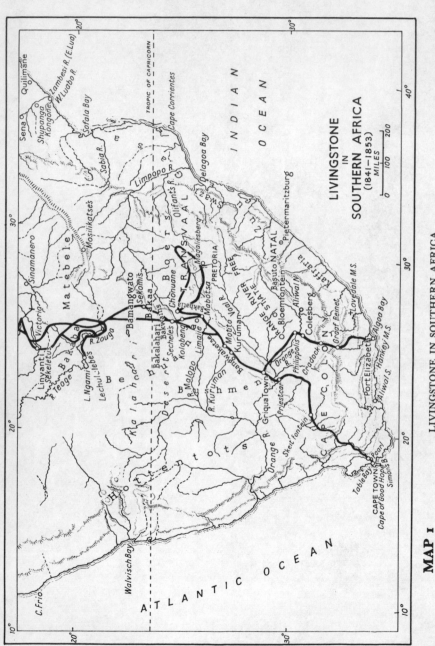

MAP 1   LIVINGSTONE IN SOUTHERN AFRICA

(1841–1853)

This map was prepared by Stanford for the original edition of Blaikie's

Edwards of the one part, and attested by marks opposite the names of Moseealele's underchiefs and counsellors of the other part, whereby the chief allots to the former that parcel of his land which is bounded, etc. (the bounds are clearly defined), with streams, wood and pasturage thereon, in exchange for a gun, some powder, lead and beads, in perpetuity. This he solemnly declaimed in Sechuana before the chief and an assembly of all his people, and gained their unanimous consent. In forwarding this document to Tidman he apologized for its apparent "foolishness" but explained that the natives recognized it as binding, and that a similar formality had been adopted by Mr. Moffat in securing the lands at Lattakoo (Kuruman). He was grateful for the assistance of Edwards, who was a much better builder than himself; they were proceeding with the erection of a hut of dimensions 50 feet by 18 feet. He had explained the objects of the mission to all the people, and had only met with one objection: prohibition of polygamy. (As will be seen, Livingstone was himself beginning to be troubled in mind concerning this rigorous prerequisite for the admission of negro converts to Church membership.) Nevertheless:

> We explained that our province was not to compel but to teach the commands of God, to entreat and warn. But should men refuse to obey God, guilt would be incurred before Him and He will requite it.

As to his future companion at Mabotsa, "I should prefer from a variety of considerations one of the younger, especially Inglis, to any of the older brethren " This wish coincides with a peremptory missive to the man of his preference who had just arrived with Mr. Moffat in the Cape: "Come on, Inglis; we must go north, and far, too. Let us have the spirit of the apostle Paul, not to build on another man's foundation."

His letter to Tidman of this date (30 October 1843) also contains the famous phrase which heads this chapter: "Though I should be delighted to consider [this place] the centre of my sphere of labour, I shall try to hold myself in readiness to go anywhere *provided it be forward.*"

For the next three months he was hard at work with Edwards constructing the large hut and digging a watercourse, and by the end of December these tasks were well on the way to completion. It has been assumed that during this period there occurred the famous incident of his encounter with the lion, as a result of which he was "laid aside", according to Edwards, for three months. But it is known that in January he rode on horseback from Kuruman to the Vaal River, a distance of 150 miles, to meet Moffat and his party proceeding north—concerning which meeting Moffat wrote to the Directors somewhat sententiously: "Such a visitant as Mr. Livingston in the wild wilderness was to us a most refreshing circumstance. Few can conceive the hallowed feeling his presence gave."[11]

But the *date* of the lion-incident does not appear in any published record. Blaikie is vague about it and subsequent biographers, aware that it occurred during the building operations at Mabotsa, have assumed a date sometime before his ride in January, one of them adding—"his arm still probably in a sling". But on this supposition the date of the lion-incident would have to be placed very early in November (after his last letter to the Directors on 30 October), thus reducing his three months' convalescence to barely two; and Livingstone himself be credited, on partial recovery from his wounds, with performing a feat which would be physically impossible even to a man of his magnificent constitution. It would also leave Moffat's silence respecting any injury to his unexpected visitor inexplicable.

The difficulties of reconciling the sequence of events before the lion-incident with those after it, led the present writer to request the Librarian of the L.M.S. to seek for any document in its archives which would fix its date. Miss Fletcher's search resulted in her unearthing again the letter which Moffat wrote to the Directors on his return to Kuruman. It is dated on the 24th February, and he had just completed it for dispatch when news came from Mabotsa which caused him to add a hurried postscript, briefly describing the accident which was so nearly a fatality, and ending with the words: "The event transpired on the 16th of February."

Livingstone always professed a contempt for the king of beasts: "Nothing I have ever heard of the lion would lead me to attribute to it either the noble or the ferocious character ascribed to it." Nor did his personal encounter at Mabotsa cause him to alter that opinion. For him it was "an occurrence which, but for the importunities of friends, I meant to have kept in store to tell my children when in my dotage".

Lions were infesting the cattle-pens of Mabotsa, even in open day. So unusual an occurrence gave rise to the belief among the Bakhatla that they were bewitched and hence to a fear of attacking them, even though they knew that if one were killed the whole troop would disperse. At the next opportunity Livingstone went with them to encourage them to attack. He had fired both barrels and was in the act of reloading when he heard a shout.

> Starting, and looking half round, I saw the lion just in the act of springing upon me. I was upon a little height; he caught my shoulder as he sprang, and we both came to the ground below together. Growling horribly close to my ear, he shook me as a terrier dog does a rat. The shock produced a stupor similar to that which seems to be felt by a mouse after the first shake of the cat. It caused a sort of dreaminess, in which there was no sense of pain, nor feeling of terror. . . . The shake annihilated fear, and allowed no sense of horror in looking round at the beast. The peculiar state is probably produced in all animals killed by the carnivora; and if so, is a merciful provision by our benevolent Creator for lessening the pain of death. Turning round to relieve myself of the weight, as he had one paw on the back of my head, I saw his eyes directed to Mebalwe, who was trying to shoot him at a distance of ten or fifteen yards. His gun, a flint one, missed fire in both barrels; the lion immediately left me and attacking Mebalwe, bit his thigh. Another man, whose life I had saved before, after he had been tossed by a buffalo, attempted to spear the lion while he was biting Mebalwe. He left Mebalwe and caught this man by the shoulder, but at that moment the bullets he had received took effect, and he fell down dead. . . . I had on a tartan jacket on the occasion, and I believe that it wiped off all the virus from the teeth that pierced the flesh, for my two companions in this affray have both suffered from the peculiar pains, while I have escaped with only the inconvenience of a false joint in my limb. The man whose shoulder was wounded showed me his wound [when it had] actually burst forth afresh on the same month of the following year. This curious point deserves the attention of inquirers.[12]

When asked what thoughts were passing through his mind during these critical moments, he would reply with a twinkle, and probably with complete truth: "I was wondering what part of me he would eat first."

The first thing one notices in this narration is its remarkable detachment: he writes as though he were describing an experience which befell someone else. Then too one notices his scientific interest: the shock produced a stupor; his jacket wiped off the virus from the teeth. He escaped with only the inconvenience of a false joint in his shoulder. Of the effects of this "inconvenience" and of the agony of pain that he endured for many weeks, he says not a word.

For this we have only the testimony of Edwards, who apparently did his best under Livingstone's own directions—to lance the flesh and set the splintered bone—all without an anaesthetic—and wrote to the L.M.S., "His sufferings were dreadful." Inglis says that he starved himself until he was certain that the inflammation had subsided. But Livingstone, who had frequently praised Edwards' skill in the use of tools, never so much as mentioned (in any letter extant) his colleague's surgical aid, or even explains how the compound fracture was mended. Nor does Edwards enlighten us: his letter continues—that he had finished all the building unaided save for native assistance, "but had to be in hourly attendance on Mr. Livingston for three months"—a statement which with regard to hours must be considered a manifest exaggeration; and also with regard to months, since we find Livingstone writing to his parents *from Kuruman* on 27 April. This allows an outside limit of less than two and a half months, inclusive of time for travel, from the date of his mauling at Mabotsa. We find him again writing on 28 May 1845 to a friend and former fellow-student, Robert Newton Hayward in Edinburgh, Surgeon R.N., as follows:

> . . . I was without medical assistance, without house, and had very few attentions save *what the poor black fellows about me* could give. . . . They put up one of their own little huts to shelter me from the sun, and, though that was so far good, I often dreamed that I was in London and saw Dr. Bennet coming to put up my arm properly. . . . I had begun to build my house before I was perfectly well, and a partial false joint in the upper third of the humerus is the result. . . . People in general condemn me for going near the lions, but they don't know that we live among them. Others say it was because the lion killed my sheep, but I had not one single sheep to kill. . . . [13] [A characteristically caustic touch.]

Dr. Campbell may be right in surmising that "the spirit in which the service was rendered may have had something to do with this silence on the part of the beneficiary". But it may be wondered whether the service itself was such as to render any acknowledgment necessary.

A permanent result of the inconvenience for Livingstone was that he could never again raise his left arm above his shoulder, nor support the barrel of his gun steadily with his left hand. The gun was an old-fashioned muzzle-loader carrying a solid bullet $\frac{3}{4}$ inch in diameter, much heavier than the modern elephant gun, and requiring to be re-loaded after every shot. This fact makes his future exploits with big game the more remarkable. He fired from the left shoulder, sighting his target with his left eye.

He would himself have preferred complete reticence on the subject. But Moffat's immediate disclosure to the Directors of his injury left him no choice than to write to them himself in explanation of his temporary incapacity. This he did in a belated letter of 9 June when he was back at work in Mabotsa. In it he makes no reference to the actual occurrence but begins abruptly:

> The Lord having in tender mercy restored me to my wonted health I have much cause for gratitude in being able again to communicate with you. The affliction from which I have been raised was both painful and protracted, as the wounds discharging profusely prevented the union of the fragments into which the bone was broken; and these having been seldom properly secured, every motion of the body produced a grating irritation which reacted on the wounds. But through the mercy of our Heavenly Father the whole has healed well beyond my most sanguine expectations, and the bone is perfectly straight and firm. . . .

At the same time he takes occasion to praise the courageous behaviour of Mebalwe and thereby to reinforce his plea for native agency:

> . . . In endeavouring to save my life he nearly lost his own, for he was caught and wounded severely, but both before being laid aside and since his recovery he has shown great willingness to be useful. The cheerful manner in which he engages with us in manual labour on the station, and his affectionate addresses to his countrymen, are truly gratifying. Mr. Edwards took him to some of the neighbouring villages recently in order to introduce him to his work; and I intend to depart tomorrow for the same purpose. . . . It would be an *immense advantage* to the cause if we had many such agents.[14]

As the date of this letter shows, the speed of his own recovery was little short of miraculous. He could not but be aware that his family would get wind of what had happened and had previously written thus to his father on 27th April:

> . . . The lion bit me on the arm so as to break the bone. It is now nearly well, however, feeling weak only from having been confined to one position so long; and I ought to praise Him who delivered me from so great a danger. I hope I shall never forget His mercy. You need not be sorry for me, for long before this reaches you it will be quite as strong as ever it was. Gratitude is the only feeling we ought to have in remembering the event. Do not mention this to anyone. I do not like to be talked about.[15]

In April Livingstone had recovered sufficiently to be moved to Kuruman, where he arrived in time for an annual meeting of the Committee. Its proceedings were disturbed by the presence of Inglis who was not a member, but who wished to remain as a spectator. To this Livingstone objected as it was out of order, and there was private business to be discussed. His motion was agreed to unanimously and the spectator was desired to withdraw. This incident, communicated in a private letter of Livingstone to his parents on 27th April, is significant in view of the future relations of Inglis with the Society and its missionaries. The letter continues with some vehemence to say, in effect, that this newcomer was a conceited pedant, a mischief-maker and scandal-monger, a critic of everything and everybody, and that not a single member of the Committee would associate with him.[16] This estimate, harsh as it seems, is borne out by a careful perusal of the *Memoirs* of Walter Inglis, in which it appears that during the whole of his nine years in Africa, Edwards was his sole associate.

As has been told, Livingstone had been attracted to Inglis in their student days. There was much in common between them: detestation of slavery, forthrightness, "Scotchness", agreement in matters of faith, and both of them were cast in a rugged mould. But there were differences: the interests of Inglis, though not informed by sound education, were academic; those of Livingstone, whose general fund of knowledge was much wider, were nothing if not practical. "Mr. Livingston, you are all physics," Inglis had said in a student debate. "I am all metaphysics."

It does not appear that the two ever saw each other again.

Unaccepted at Mabotsa, Inglis was sent to work among the Baharutsi tribe—with what success is not recorded—where he was soon joined by Edwards, till both were expelled from the country by the Boers for their courageous stand against slavery. This was in 1852 when Livingstone, who had made himself even more obnoxious to the Boers than they, suffered a worse fate at Kolobeng. Edwards (ordained in 1845) remained in the Colony in charge of a small church at Port Elizabeth where he died in old age in 1876. Inglis removed to Philippolis and worked for some months among the Griquas till, the Society having no further use for his services, he returned to England in 1855, joined the Presbyterian Church and sailed for Canada, where he gained the reputation in three several pastorates, among Scottish colonists, of a vigorous and original preacher, and died at Ayr in 1884. From his *Memoirs*, written and edited by a staunch admirer, one gains the impression of an abrupt, explosive, and somewhat self-centred character. But his good qualities shine through his defects. There is no doubt that he was better fitted as a minister to his own countrymen than as a missionary to the heathen.

Meanwhile, Ross, the third of his colleagues with whom Livingstone could not agree, had been sent in January 1844 to commence a mission at Taung, some 200 miles east of Kuruman and only 25 from Inglis's post. His wife died two years later at Motito, and Livingstone wrote (to Watt) with scant sympathy: "Poor Mrs. Ross is dead of dysentery—a great loss to her husband and children, but to no one else." In 1855, owing to tribal disturbances, Ross removed to Lekatlong (80 miles south-east of Kuruman) where he died at his post in 1863. Mrs. Moffat wrote of him: "He had been a hard-working plodding man in evangelistic work."

To return to Inglis. The year before his death he delivered to the Mechanics' Institute in Ayr a lecture on David Livingstone. In it there appears no trace of resentment; on the contrary, it is eloquent of generous and genuine admiration. Some extracts from it, dealing with their youthful friendship, have already been quoted here: there are others (in the lecture itself and in a covering letter to the chairman) which throw sidelights on some of the missionary personnel in Kuruman and at the same time reveal the indiscretion of their author.

Livingstone and Ross were an ill-assorted pair. It is a great mistake to yoke a fiery young colt with a strong steady ox. . . . Neither Moffat nor Livingstone could bear a yoke-fellow. They were created with ambition to work alone. . . . Ross was an ardent admirer of Mr. Moffat. Livingstone, feeling the throbbings of young life in him, scandalized Mr. Ross by the prophetic declaration that if he lived he would far excel Mr. Moffat as a traveller. This at the time was the utterance of a conceited young man. I have often thought of the remarkable fulfilment of this youthful banter.

Chapter Six

MARRIAGE: MABOTSA AND CHONUANE
1844–1847

"I screwed up my courage to put a question beneath one of the fruit-trees. . . ."

THE exchange of rough quarters and hard pain for home-comforts and the warmth of home-affection must have been pure refreshment to Livingstone. And the presence of this "romantic invalid" in the Moffats' household must have touched the heart of Mary, then just twenty-three years old. She no doubt ministered to his necessities, and he in turn was deeply moved by her gentle, steadfast character. In October of the previous year, whilst building the large hut with Edwards at Mabotsa, he had written to his friend Watt:

> There's no outlet for me when I begin to think of getting married but that of sending home an advertisement to the *Evangelical Magazine*, and if I get very old, it must be for some decent sort of widow. In the meantime I am too busy to think of anything of the kind.[1]

But now in July of 1844:

> After nearly four years of African life as a bachelor, I screwed up my courage to put a question beneath one of the fruit-trees [in Kuruman], the result of which was that I became united in marriage to Mr. Moffat's eldest daughter Mary. Having been born in the country and being expert in household matters, she was always the best spoke in the wheel at home; and, on two occasions, when I took her to Lake Ngami and far beyond, she endured more than some who have written large books of travels.[2]

And in his next letter to Watt he says, in a similar strain of light-hearted raillery:

> We once thought nearly alike in respect of celibacy; we now seem to be assimilated in our views respecting matrimony. I have put your floating ideas to the test. Don't be faint-hearted, laugh at a rebuff, and as soon as you can convince her you are sincere you are 'done for'. They are

suspicious at first, convince them of your sincerity—no matter by what
means—and any means duly executed will do, except hanging yourself.
And all comes right *instanter*. That's my advice, and I hope by this time
you are as far in the scrape as myself. . . . Ah, I should like to be just
one evening in Mrs. Sewell's with you all. How the good little woman
would laugh to see me a sober married man.[3]

And to George Drummond:

Your welcome and excellent letter found me in my monkish cell a few
days ago as happy as any of your domesticated animals, and (*mirabile
dictu*) just on the eve of becoming one myself. But I cannot leave the
bachelor life without a sigh. . . . Let Moore, dear good fellow, know of
my marriage. It will comfort all your hearts to know that I am become
as great a fool as any of you. . . . In love! words, yea thoughts, fail—so
I leave it to your imagination and recollection. . . . [4]

Nor was his description of his bride at all flattering: "Not
romantic but a matter-of-fact lady, a little, thick, black-haired
girl, sturdy, and all that I want". He might have added
that she was also possessed of refinement, delicacy, and tact;
qualities which he lacked. From other sources we glean
the impression that she had also the defects of these: that
she had little practical capacity, except for house-keeping,
no money sense, and was in everything dependent upon
him. It must be remembered that she happened to be
the first young woman that he had met since he had left
England. "He felt," said Inglis, "that he needed a wife."
There can have been nothing in the least "romantic" about
their courtship, if such it can be called. It was with evident
soberness that they plighted troth, and with soberness that they
settled down to live together.

There is something almost inhuman about Livingstone's
announcement of his engagement to his Directors. He begins
by recommending that the subscription of £15 from the Sunday School in Southampton had better be placed at present in
the general funds of the Society, and then continues without a
break:

Various considerations connected with this new sphere of labour . . .
having led me to the conclusion that it is my duty to enter into the
marriage relation, I have made the necessary arrangements for union
with Mary, the eldest daughter of Mr. Moffat, in the beginning of
January, 1845. It was not without much serious consideration and earnest
prayer, and, if I have not)t deceived mysulf, I was in some measure
guided by a desire that the Divine glory might be promoted in my

increased usefulness. I hope this will be considered a sufficient notification of the change contemplated and that it will meet with the approbation of the Directors.

He hastens to add: "I may mention that I do not regret having come out single"—but considers this an advantage to younger men, "to acquire the language and become acclimatized". Indeed in some cases a much longer period would be advantageous. "But where there is an almost total deprivation of European society, long delay would be improper."[5]

"She is all that I want." If he ever noticed her deficiencies, he turned a blind eye to them: her goodness of heart made up for all. But did he ever for his part seriously consider, it may be wondered, whether he was all that she wanted?

There is no doubt that Livingstone, had he not been at heart a rover, would have been well satisfied with the comparative tranquillity of home-life on a mission station. He appreciated and even delighted in the cleanliness and comfort of a well-ordered home. Soon after their marriage he wrote to his mother: "Only yesterday I said to my wife, when I thought of the nice clean bed I enjoy now, 'You put me in mind of my mother; she was always particular about our beds and linen.' I have had rough times before."[6] He had been a good son and a good brother; he had in him the makings of a good husband and a good father. He had both a natural domestic sense and a practical aptitude for home-craft. But the call of the wild and the call of the hearth-side and the home-acre strike notes that are hard to harmonize.

Mary would herself have answered the question with a loyal and courageous Yes—and that despite his frequent and prolonged absences, despite the exacting strains imposed upon her by journeys with him that were beyond her strength. But there must have been others, and especially her parents, who would have answered otherwise. For anyone who would walk with Livingstone must keep his pace, or at least keep pace with him, or else—fall out. She could not keep his pace—what woman could? But she kept step, she did not fall out, she dropped in the track.

By all who knew them, whether in their three homes in Africa or in the security of their brief reunion in England, their marriage was regarded as "ideal". It is true that there was

87

never a cloud between them, never a cross word—nothing but the completest understanding and concord. But the epithet, of time-honoured but too frequent usage, must be deemed an overstatement unless it be qualified by saying that their love for one another, strong and true as it was, was ideal—not so much in the sense of temperamental affinity—as rather in the fact that it was subordinated by each of them to the Love of God and the doing of His will, which lifted their human love and themselves with it to a higher point of unity than would have otherwise been possible.

This deeply religious tone is apparent in his first letter to his future bride, written from Motito on 1st August, when he was en route to Mabotsa to build their future home. She is to ask her father to order some necessary household things, and to write to Colesburg for their marriage-licence—if her father does not get it, they would license themselves! The letter ends:

> And now, my dearest, farewell. May God bless you! Let your affection be towards Him much more than towards me: and kept by His mighty power and grace, I hope I shall never give you cause to regret that you have given me a part. Whatever friendship we feel towards each other let us always look to Jesus as our common friend and guide, and may He shield you with His everlasting arms from every evil.[7]

There is no doubt whatever that Mary accepted him as her husband in the same spirit.

Back again at Mabotsa he set to work with a will on building their future home, of dimensions 52 feet by 20 feet externally and with walls a foot thick, a little larger than her home at Kuruman, but more air space was necessary in the hotter climate. He had begun with stone and had got breast-high, but was forced to continue with mud on account of an accident. He had instinctively caught a falling stone with his left hand and the jolt was so severe that it nearly broke his arm again. "It swelled up again and I fevered so much I was glad of a fire, although the weather was quite warm. I expected bursting and discharge, but Baba* bound it up nicely, and a few days' rest put all to rights"—and now he is progressing with the

* This native convert from Kuruman was killed by a rhinoceros in October 1846. "Unprovoked, it rushed on him and ripped him up." (Chamberlin, no. 25.)

walls at the rate of a foot a day, and soon will be ready to begin on the roof. "Mr. E's finger is the cause in part of my having no aid from him, but all will come right at last."

> It is pretty hard work, and almost enough to drive love out of my head, but it is not situated there; it is in my heart, and won't come out unless you behave so as to quench it! . . .
> You must excuse soiled paper, my hands won't wash clean after dabbling mud all day. And although the above does not contain evidence of it, you are as dear to me as ever, and will be as long as our lives are spared.

This was on 12th September. The house was nearly finished and the windows were in; if Mary's mother "thinks there are too many she can just let me know. I can build them all up in two days and let the light come down the chimney, if that would please." The time of their separation is becoming "beautifully less". He has begun a school for little native children [who, he tells the Southampton Sunday School, were "tremblingly and tearfully fearful at first"].

> . . . I had a great objection to school-keeping but I find that, as in almost everything else I set myself to as a matter of duty, I soon became enamoured of it. . . .
> If I can get them on a little, I shall translate some of your infant-school hymns into Sechuana rhyme, and you may yet, if you have time, teach them the tunes to them. I, poor mortal, am as mute as a fish in regard to singing, and Mr. Inglis says I have not a bit of imagination.

He sends his kindest salutation to Mary's mother, and his love to her sister Annie. "She must not be vexed with herself that she was not more frank to me. If she is now pleased all is right. I have sisters and I know all of you have your failings, but I won't love you less for these. . . ." "And now I must again, my dear, dear Mary, bid you good-bye." He is still her "most affectionate and confiding lover—D. Livingston".[8] It is improbable that he ever permitted himself to address her in more endearing terms than these. And neither to her, nor to his parents and sisters, nor to his children afterwards did he ever subscribe himself otherwise—whether D. or David, the surname is never omitted. (Students of calligraphy should note the formidable drooping dunt in the curl that ends the D.: it butts out from the capital letter like the lowered head of a bull.) He never addressed his wife or any other near relation more fondly than as "Dear . . ." It is only to near friends such as Watt or Drummond that he allows himself the use of a superlative. His father-in-law and other colleagues are addressed as "Dear Brother"; a Director of the Mission as "My Dear Sir" or "Dear Friend". To them all, as to his nearest and dearest, he ends "Yours affectionately". In letters to friends he frequently refers to his wife jocosely as "my rib". This deliberate absence of sentiment, so pronounced in Livingstone, was common among the pioneer missionaries at that time. Mrs. Moffat for example, who greatly admired her son-in-law, writes to him—"My dear Livingston".

They were married on 2 January 1845 in the old church that still stands in Kuruman. No formal register was kept, and the marriage was recorded in Moffat's handwriting in the minute-book of the Church.[9] Hence the generally accepted notion that it was he who performed the ceremony. But it appears from a notice in the *South African Commercial Advertiser* on 17 May of that year that the Rev. Prosper Lemue, then a well-known member of the Paris Evangelical Society, was the officiating minister.

By what seemed a happy coincidence, the word *mabotsa* means "marriage-feast", but neither then nor thereafter can their life together be considered as an idyll of connubial bliss. At first all went well. Mary took over the infant school and her husband went to work with zest. He now conceived the station as another Kuruman "whence the beams of divine light might radiate far and wide into regions to the north that were in gross darkness. . . . I have now the happy prospect before me of real missionary work. All that has preceded had been preparatory."

The superstitions of the Bakhatla extended to the belief that witchcraft was necessary for the smelting of iron-ore. Livingstone, with his insatiable thirst for scientific knowledge of every kind, had added the discovery of minerals to his study of the geology; he had indeed collected duplicate specimens of every species of rock on the high veldt for despatch to Professor Buckland. He now commenced a course of "lectures" to his unenlightened audience on the theme of divine creation and natural law, with a view to "giving them a general knowledge of the simplicity of substance" and thereby weaning them from their trust in magic. This brought him into collision with the local witch-doctor who was also (it was a season of drought) the rain-maker.

He is most insignificant in appearance. Of low stature, his hair twisted or plaited like that of a female, the numerous wrinkles around his eyelids nearly obscure the white of his small cunning eyes; wide nostrils, and irregular teeth. His body was without ornament and his kaross filthy, yet some of the most intelligent among the Bakhatla were literally afraid of him.

Livingstone, having first privately rebuked the magician for the folly and wickedness of his course, soon found himself accused in public of withholding the rain. He then repeated to the chief what he had said to the rain-maker, adding that he was sorry to see his friends deceived by an impostor. Being then gravely informed that the latter could not only produce rain but also kill people with lightning, Livingstone besought him to put his powers to the proof, offering himself as the victim. The challenge being disregarded he then offered himself as a pupil to the rain-maker, who agreed upon payment in advance of the fee of an ox.

I offered three if he would only exhibit his power by collecting the clouds during the time we were sitting. He excused himself by saying that he must first go and dig medicines, but promised to bring the clouds in our presence in a few days. But though I placed the whole of my wagon-oxen at his disposal he declined to have me for a pupil when I stipulated that he should make some little difference between his rain and the 'rain from heaven'—such as causing it to rain on my garden one day and on none of the others, or on all the other gardens and not on mine. But the people were afraid of exasperating him, for several called out, "We have done with him", evidently anxious that I should not proceed to provoke him.

Nevertheless Livingstone continued to press his attack, and once when the "rain-maker" made a great smoke for the purpose of "healing the clouds" he pointed out that whilst it was drifting one way the clouds were drifting in another, whereupon "many laughed outright". But not even so could he induce them to abandon their superstitious fears of the witch-doctor.[10]

He might perhaps have done better had he continued to employ the weapon of ridicule, since this is a much more effective method of persuasion with the native than any appeals to reason. Instead, however, we find him recording an elaborate argument with a rain-maker, in the form of a duologue, the purpose of which is to show that it is better to wait patiently for God to send the rain than expect Him to produce it with the aid of magical spells.

Nevertheless, the impression left from a perusal of this document upon an impartial reader is that it is the magician rather than the missionary who has the better of the argument, and that the magician shows a surprising amount of logical acumen. And a specialist in Bantu rite and culture, discerning beneath their magical practices a genuinely religious instinct, has written:

> Livingstone, like his contemporaries, regarded the rain-rites as a farrago of inept magic; but he was courteous in his method of approach to the 'rain-doctors', and scrupulously fair in reporting what he understood to be their claims. They claimed, he said, that it was God alone who made the rain and they prayed to God by means of these 'medicines'. He was misled by their ambiguous use of the term *modimo*, which may be applied to any divinity.[11] [The word is also spelt *morimo*.]

But it is clear from other references in his *Travels* that Livingstone understood the ambiguity in its usage very well.

Belief in divine intervention in response to prayers for rain is almost universal, despite the fact that it is contradicted by universal human experience. Livingstone was no Elijah, nor did he pretend to be. He was to suffer much from prolonged droughts, and even more from prolonged rains, but there is no evidence that he ever prayed for "fair weather" or that he encouraged others to do so. Whatever the weather conditions might be, he accepted them as sent by God and therefore God's will. And his advice to the natives was the eminently sensible and truly moral one: namely, to select a site near a good river, dig a canal, and lead off the water to irrigate their gardens.

But troubles soon began, and they must be ascribed chiefly to his own making. They are of interest as indicative of a dominant trait in his character: he could not brook opposition; and when opposition came it both surprised him and annoyed him. He had long been cherishing the plan of a training seminary for native converts. To this end he prepared a paper for submission to the Committee at its next meeting in May, 1845. That it was forthwith rejected must have been due not to its demerits—since it was later officially proposed by Moffat himself to the Directors and adopted—but to the man by whom it was presented. There can be no doubt that by this time Livingstone was becoming somewhat of a thorn in the flesh of his colleagues. Dr. Philip had opined that he was ambitious; is it any wonder that *they* found him impatient, assertive, and even aggressive? They were not to be dictated to, and they would let him know it. Livingstone saw his mistake, but too late. If he had left the proposal to his seniors it would have been carried without opposition. The reaction upon him was bitter disappointment at the miscarriage of his plan. He felt, as he told the Directors much later in response to their enquiry on the subject, that by his premature action he "had retarded instead of furthering this most important mode of spreading the Gospel. This conviction caused me months of bitter grief—every time the subject arose in my mind I felt a pang."[12] But it was also a shock to his personal pride. To Watt he confided on 23rd May:

> You ask if I am immersed in the quarrels of the missionaries here. Yes. What a shame, you reply; and so do I, but thus it is. I had a row with my father-in-law in the Committee about a seminary for native teachers. I proposed it, but all the old gents opposed it, and we did not spare each other, but we are good friends notwithstanding. I was very sorry afterwards that I had spoken as bitterly as I did. . . . I could have carried the motion, for I had all the younger missionaries on my side, but I saw that it would have died a natural death. So I withdrew the paper altogether and will not again bring it forward. If the old gents don't of themselves commence an institution it won't succeed. It did not appear in the Minutes for that reason. . . . This is private. I tell you my sorrows, although I have a wife.[13]

A letter to his mother of 14 May (apparently while in Kuruman for the Committee meeting) throws an interesting sidelight on his impressions of Moffat and on the jealousy of some of his colleagues:

> I cannot perceive that the attentions paid to my father-in-law at home have spoiled him. He is, of course, not the same man he formerly must have been, for he now knows the standing he has among the friends of Christ at home. But the plaudits he received have had a bad effect, though not on his mind, yet on that of his fellow-labourers. If one man is praised, others think this is more than is deserved, and that they too ought to have a share. . . .

Some boots sent to him from home were too large, but the sender would be pleased to know that they "are worn by a much better man—Mr. Moffat".

But now he found himself suddenly embroiled in another and more serious quarrel, "which was not of my making"; this was the final breach with his elder colleague Rogers Edwards. "We parted in apparent harmony when I went to get married, and when I returned a storm burst on my head such as I never had before." Edwards' charges against Livingstone are set forth in detail and answered by him with complete candour in a letter of some 7,000 words to the Directors. It is a tedious rigmarole and must have sorely tried the patience of its readers. Nor was its despatch necessary, since Edwards subsequently withdrew his accusation and it was never sent. Reduced to their simplest terms his charges were: that Livingstone had chosen Mabotsa on his own initiative and without consultation with anyone; that he had engaged Mebalwe privately and for private ends; that he had removed a ban to communion which Edwards had imposed for disciplinary reasons upon Mebalwe's wife; that he had usurped Edwards' authority over an under-chief in digging the watercourse; that he had in fact from the outset of their partnership wished "to drive things all his own way"; and finally that he, Edwards, strongly resented being made "a mere appendix to this young man". Livingstone ends his long letter with the words: "The degradation involved in answering these childish charges is more harmful than any sacrifice I have yet been called to."[14]

That the specific charges were trivial, and were either without foundation or due to misapprehension, there is no doubt. Nor is there any doubt that Edwards was a somewhat peevish character, "prone to take offence and magnify trifles". According to Livingstone, who wrote to Watt "in bitter grief" about the whole affair, he was "a fiery old gent". It is quite clear from Livingstone's own account that grievances had been rankling in Edwards' mind for many months and they now suddenly erupted like fire from a volcano. It is equally clear from hints in his letters that, since the lion-incident, Livingstone had set little store on Edwards' usefulness.

But the gravamen of the whole indictment lies in the last words, and it is unanswerable. It points to the radical defect of a strong character. His grandson Dr. H. F. Wilson has put it succinctly to this chronicler: "He could see black and white, but he had no notion of a grey." This uncompromising outlook was doubtless a factor which goes far to explain the secret of his moral strength, enabling him to ride rough-shod over the susceptibilities and frailties of lesser men, but it also accounts for his own prejudices and misjudgments.

The upshot of this unhappy division was however productive of an important change. Perceiving that further co-operation was impossible, and wishing to avoid any appearance of scandal in the sight of the heathen, Livingstone proposed in Committee to vacate Mabotsa, frankly stating his reasons. This proposal was at first "uproariously opposed" by Ross, Inglis, and Edwards himself, on the ground that it was "informal" (i.e. without sanction from headquarters); but on Livingstone's offer to surrender to Edwards the station and the house which he had toiled so hard to build, and to establish another farther north at Chonuane at his own expense, the latter now came forward to say—with curious inconsistency that, had he known such to have been Livingstone's intention, he would never have brought any charges against him.[15] Livingstone's chief regret was in relinquishing the garden which, following the example and instruction of his father-in-law, he had cultivated with care.

Mabotsa did not flourish after the Livingstones left it.

> [To Watt. 8th June 1846.] Inglis is snug in my house at Mabotsa. Fear he will not do much good. Edwards ploughed my beautiful garden and Inglis that of Mebalwe. . . . I like a garden but Paradise will make amends for all our sorrows here.
>
> [To B. Pyne. Dec. 1846.] Inglis was expelled from Mabotsa by the natives. Edwards had to give them a large present to be allowed to remain. They wish us back.[16]

Receipt of an answer to his request for sanction to remove to Chonuane could not be expected from the Directors for a twelve-month at least. In fact a year elapsed before they even replied to it, and their letter is a model of discretion and good sense.

In general we find the Directors in London much more sympathetic to Livingstone's aims and ideas than the local Committee at Kuruman. They were much more ready than the latter to support his plea for native agents and a native seminary.

Livingstone had been disappointed by the result of his work among the Bakhatla: "They have not the smallest love for the Gospel of Jesus. . . . It appears to them as that which, if not carefully guarded against, will seduce them and destroy their much-loved domestic institutions." Yet now to his amazement he found that, on 17 October, when inspanning his wagon for removal, they came forward with many entreaties that he would stay, even offering to build him a new house with their own hands if only he would not leave them.

Chonuane, some forty miles north of Mabotsa, was then the residence of his old friend Sechele, chief of the Bakwena. Meanwhile, the amiable but ill-starred Bubi, whose acquaintance he had cultivated four years before, had died tragically.

> In August last Bubi, having received some gunpowder in a present from Sechele, and conceiving that coming from such a quarter it must be bewitched, he endeavoured to dissolve the charm by holding some medicines, in a state of combustion, over it. But his incantations were interrupted by an explosion which inflicted so much injury as subsequently to cause his death. Poor Bubi being dreadfully scorched sent messengers off to Mabotsa immediately to entreat assistance. . . . [17]

But Livingstone was then at Chonuane and by the time the message reached him it was too late. Rather than submit to the rule of Khake, Bubi's successor, many of his principal men escaped to Sechele who then, according to native custom, was obliged to demand their goods and dependants. This demand would normally have occasioned a fight, but Sechele had given his word to the missionary that he would avoid bloodshed. His pacific attitude induced many others from Bubi's village to join him; they were soon followed by Khake and the remainder, and Sechele thus became paramount chief of the entire tribe. Nothing could better illustrate the contrast between Livingstone's influence with the natives and his lack of it with his colleagues.

Sechele was a unique example of a negro endowed with intelligence far above that of his people.

> He acquired the alphabet on the first day of my residence at Chonuane. He set himself to read with such close application that, from being comparatively thin, the effect of having been fond of the chase, he became

quite corpulent from want of exercise. . . . He was by no means an ordinary specimen of the people, for I never went into the town but I was pressed to hear him read some chapter of the Bible. Isaiah was a great favourite with him. . . . "He was a fine man, that Isaiah; he knew how to speak." Sechele invariably offered me something to eat on every occasion of my visiting him.

Seeing me anxious that his people should believe the words of Christ, he once said, "Do you imagine these people will ever believe by your merely talking to them? I can make them do nothing except by thrashing them; and if you like, I shall call my head-men and with our litupa (whips of rhinoceros hide) we will soon make them all believe together."

Livingstone, who was aware of the power of what is now called "group-consciousness" in the psychology of primitive man, was himself in favour of the idea of mass-conversion— but not by these means. His decided disagreement with Sechele in this matter was a cause for genuine bewilderment on the part of the chief "who considered they ought to be only too happy to embrace Christianity at his command".

Sechele, on succeeding to the chiefdom, had become the principal "rain-maker" (by the simple process of exterminating his rivals in the craft), and this prerogative was one which he found hardest of all to relinquish. But when at the beginning of 1847 Livingstone asked him whether he intended to make rain this year he replied, "You will never see me at that work again." Sechele's uncle was however less amenable to instruction. "We like you," he remonstrated, "as well as if you had been born amongst us. You are the only white man we can become familiar with, but we wish you would give up that everlasting preaching and praying. We cannot become familiar with that at all. You see, we never get rain, while those tribes that never pray get plenty."[22]

Livingstone's wounded arm had been troubling him, and a letter to Dr. Bennett dated 26 December 1845 from Chonuane contains some remarks on this subject and others of scientific interest.

When only partially recovered I had to begin the erection of my house and received a jerk in lifting (sic) a stone has led to a false joint in my left humerus. I often think of putting a seton through it but never have been able to plan a six weeks' leisure. It is not however a great hindrance, even in heavy work; the chief inconvenience is the want of power to steady the arm when extended; the fissure is oblique and being situated in the upper third of the bone seems to run into the socket. The point of the bone . . .

97

starts out when my arm is extended and the hand in the supine position, and appears as if it would burst through the skin. But the biceps being situated internally to it, I could easily put the needle through. I can use the adze and hammer and lift heavy weights notwithstanding, and if I try the seton I shall let you know how it succeeds.[18]

He mentions the extreme rarity of pulmonary complaints in the dry bracing climate of the veldt, and indeed of other diseases in general. These included lunacy.

I have heard it remarked that in certain climates, injurious effects are produced by exposure to the influence of the moon in sleep. Nothing of the sort is known here. I have myself slept for weeks on the bare ground and often looked up to the beautifully clear orb until I have fallen asleep. Yet I have felt nothing in consequence nor have I heard the natives ascribe anything to her baneful rays.

In reply to a letter from his friend asking why he had not sought surgical aid for his wound he wrote again in 1848:

It would have taken at least three months to reach Cape Town, and more than six months to return, so that was my reason for not journeying to Cape Town for medical assistance. Instead I have now fitted a screw to my arm, so as to produce pressure between the ends of the bones. It is now nearly as useful as the other, only more unsteady. I shoot with a heavy rifle, but with the left eye, and the right arm extended, just as well as I did before the injury. I lately shot an enormous buffalo at about twenty paces from our door. Many shots were fired as he rushed through the village at full speed down to us, but mine went through his heart. . . . I had a great horror of snakes, but usage, not courage, makes me care little for them now. We killed one eight feet three inches long near our house a few months ago, another of six feet more recently, and one evening, when returning from a prayer meeting, I put a lantern on to a box, saw a cobra moving at my feet. Had I seen this in England I would have been petrified; but men are so wisely constituted that the mind as well as the body readily acclimatizes.

In *Travels* he recalls another similar escape:-

In making the door for our Mabotsa house, I happened to leave a small hole at the corner below. Early one morning a man came to call for some article I had promised. I at once went to the door and, it being dark, trod on a serpent. The moment I felt the cold scaly skin twine round a part of my leg my latent instinct was roused, and I jumped up higher than I ever did before, or hope to do again, shaking the reptile off in the leap. I probably trod on it near the head, and so prevented it biting me, but did not stop to examine.

In July of 1846 Livingstone undertook two journeys eastward of the station, of eight months' duration in all, with a view
to finding localities in which to place his two native teachers.
Whilst still engaged in building another house at Chonuane,
he had received two messages from that quarter: one from a
chief named Mokhatla who desired Paul as a teacher; the
other from the Boer Commandant (he must have been Gert
Krieger: not Kruger—later President—as Campbell erroneously states) who had lately arrived there with emigrants from
the south, requesting an explanation of his intentions and inti-
mating that they were about to deprive Sechele of his firearms.
Accordingly, as soon as the house was made habitable for his
wife, he proceeded eastwards with Paul. They found across the
Marikoe river a numerous population, and a proportionate
absence of big game. Mokhatla proved to be the chief of a large
section of the Bakhatla tribe, of which that in the Mabotsa area
was a mere fragment. He was expert in drawing copper wire,
in iron and woodwork, and in manufacturing ornaments;
besides which he had a good name with all the surrounding
tribes. He repeated his desire for the services of Paul but with
the reservation that, for his own peace and safety, agreement
must first be reached with the Boers who now considered themselves masters of this territory. Proceeding further eastwards
and crossing the head-waters of the Limpopo (400 yards in
breadth and called "the mother of rivers") Livingstone found
a large tribe of the Bakwena whose chief Mamogale was "a
most friendly man and shewed me the scars on his back, of
stripes which had been inflicted by those who consider themselves masters of his country". No less than eleven villages, all
of which acknowledged him as their chief, could be seen in the
plain below his town. "Everywhere we were received with
kindness and confidence."

The Commandant lived near to this tribe, and being a well informed
man we found no difficulty in persuading him that an attempt to disarm
the Bakwains would break up our mission, and that he ought to delay the
execution of the orders of the Council until I should lay the whole matter
before it. This I did by letter and likewise stated my intention of introducing the gospel amongst the eastern tribes by means of native agents.

On returning to Chonuane they built a school in less than
two months and set systematic instruction into operation under

Paul and his son Isaac. Then, accompanied by his wife and their infant son—named Robert Moffat after his grandfather (there is no record of the date of his birth)—together with Mebalwe, they went eastwards again through the villages of another considerable tribe, the Bamosetla; thence across the Limpopo again to an even denser district of the Bagalaka who spun cotton with a rude spindle and distaff, were rich in cattle, could smelt iron and other ores and produce an alloy of copper and tin. But the people received them with fear, mistaking them for Boers.

> If either Mrs. L. or myself made any movement towards them, a general rush backwards and treading over each other occurred. Mebalwe was better able to quiet their fears and held many conversations on revealed truth. Very little can be effected in one visit. . . . We preached several times but there was far more palaverish ceremoniousness than we could relish. The chief, though not more than 20 years of age, had 48 wives and 20 children.

These tribes were more numerous than any he had seen hitherto, "but all living in enmity—hated and hating one another—and plagued by the Boers". On returning westwards he again visited the Boers and, confining himself to their own statements, reported as follows:

> They have taken possession of nearly all the fountains, and the natives in the country live only by sufferance. . . . Labour is exacted as an equivalent for being allowed to live in the land of their forefathers. In this system of unrequited labour all the emigrants, from the Commandant downwards, unanimously agree. In other ways of maltreatment they are not so unanimous. The better-disposed lament the evils they witness. But the absence or laxity of law leaves the natives open to the infliction of inexpressible wrongs. . . . [He then records a massacre in which three tribes were compelled to form 'a living bulwark' against one tribe, in front of one hundred mounted Boers.]
>
> On the side of the oppressor there is power; the black man may yet obtain a knowledge of that power and then it may appear that the emigrants have industriously sowed the seeds of some future Caffre War. The lawless alone may now be guilty but vengeance may be wreaked on both good and bad, as is now the case in the Colony.

Such, in barest outline, is the gist of his report to the Directors on a crowded series of events.[19] It may be supplemented by a brief letter written in December, 1846, from the banks of the Moretele when nearing home, to a friend in Ongar, Mr. Benjamin Pyne.

The natives say the times are worse for us than when Mosilikatse was here, "for now we have no one to whom we can appeal". An old Boer appropriates as many fountains and the lands adjacent to it, as he has sons. They enter the villages, take corn, etc., at pleasure and pay nothing, drive off cattle, slaughter sheep and commit other enormities. . . .

The Boers to whom I have spoken all admit bad treatment, but none admit themselves guilty of it. One told me to-night, "As well teach baboons". I proposed a trial of reading and writing between one of these baboons and himself, and he soon drew in his horns.[20]

He tells also of domestic affairs. Little Robert had been very ill on the journey but was now mercifully restored. His wife when faced with the prospect of recrossing the Limpopo in flood had burst into tears (can it be wondered at, with a sick infant in her arms?). "Our supplies will be all gone long before we reach home, but a kind Providence will provide. . . . We have lost our crop of corn this year. Building and itinerary prevented our giving it the attention it needed and buffaloes ate it for us." A postscript is dated from Kuruman, 20 March 1847. His wife is expecting another baby. "We came here to attend a Committee meeting and now must remain six weeks, waiting the arrival of a little stranger. It is now two years since we were here last. Very happy to see our old friends again." This, their second child, was christened Agnes.

All this while Livingstone had been assiduous in adding to his collection of specimens, hitherto rare—of rocks, bulbs, seeds, roots, nuts, insects and skins—for transmission when opportunity afforded to Professors Owen and Buckland in sealed boxes and jars of spirit. Hearing that a box containing rock-fragments and fossils had been lost on the railway in England, he wrote with characteristic good humour: "The thief thought the box contained bullion, no doubt. You may think of one of the faces in *Punch* as that of the scoundrel when he found in the box a lot of 'chucky-stones'."[21] [*Punch* was a great favourite with him.]

He was also reading as much and often as he could: the current periodicals of theology and medicine, and whatever other books of educational value he could beg to be sent from England—including a new translation of Josephus by Dr. Isaac Taylor, an old friend of Ongar days.

[To Watt.] I can read in journeying, but little at home. Building, gardening, cobbling, doctoring, tinkering, carpentering, gun-mending, farriering, wagon-mending, preaching, schooling, lecturing on physics according to my means, besides a chair in divinity to a class of three, fill up my time.[22]

[To Mr. Charles Whish in Glasgow.] As I write now my hands have the same aching sensation I had when spinning. My mind is often so exhausted in sympathy with the body I cannot write on the evenings, and this is the only time I have.[23]

[To H. Drummond.] I often, in reading some of the periodicals which reach us, afar from the din of war and strife of tongues, exult in the glorious prospects which God is working out for our world in this nineteenth century. But never yet has a wish crossed my mind to return homewards. *All my desires tend forwards, to the North.* Why, we have a world before us here. We have no missionary beyond this—all is dark.[24]

His salary as a married man was now £100 a year, but of this he had already spent much in the maintenance of native teachers when on travel, and in supplying his medicine-chest. Prices of household goods in the Colony were doubled and even trebled before they reached him. "We are more than 200 miles from the nearest trader, and every time we are compelled to go near his vile shop we feel as if going to get the marrow sucked out of our bones." His colleagues in Kuruman made no scruple of going down to Grahamstown or even Algoa Bay periodically for a year's supplies; but he had stuck to his post without intermission for six years, exposing himself to privations and hardships of which none of them had any comprehension. Denying himself very often the bare necessities, and his wife not seldom the reasonable comforts of life, he had accomplished three or four days' work to most men's one; and this without injury—as yet—to his magnificent physique, though not without a heavy toll upon his material resources. It is little wonder that he ends his letter of ten extra large foolscap pages to his Directors, dated 17 March 1847, on this note:

I have spent every farthing I have in the world—worked hard and fared hard—and am not ashamed to say that I am in debt £29 for building expenses. . . . But for the assistance of the native teachers I could not have succeeded with so little expense to the Society. . . . If in consistency with your financial plans, may I be favoured with £5 or £10 for medicines? . . . I have spent more than £30 of my salary in this way. . . .

And again on 1 November 1848:

[At Chonuane] when our corn was done we were fairly obliged to go to Kuruman for supplies. I can bear what other Europeans would consider hunger and thirst without any inconvenience, but when we arrived —to hear the old women who had seen my wife depart about two years before, exclaiming at the door, "Bless me! how lean she is! Has he starved her? Is there no food in the country to which he has been?" etc.—this was more than I could well bear.[25]

The above-quoted letter to Watt contains other sentences worthy of quotation:

Here I live with the people, they are collected in groups ready to our hand, and as soon as I can leave them under native instruction—Forward I go. . . . A crying evil—that of missionaries leaving their posts for six, nine, or twelve months at one time. If you meet me down in the colony before eight years are expired you may shoot me. . . . A small fly [tsetse] will put a stop to travelling far north with wagons or horses. . . . Who will penetrate through Africa?

Chapter Seven

KOLOBENG: FIRST PHASE
1847–1850

"I am Jack-of-all-trades and my wife is Maid-of-all-work."

THE removal to Chonuane had been precipitate: Livingstone's choice of it had been determined by his friendship with the chief rather than by its practical suitability. But increasing drought had depleted its water supply which was "scanty and bad", and had rendered maintenance of cattle and cultivation of corn impossible. He had no difficulty in persuading Sechele—"who declared that he would cleave to us wherever we went"—to move his entire village to a better site forty miles north-west on the river Kolobeng which drained a mass of hills eastwards. Thither he moved with Mebalwe in August 1847, leaving Paul and others with Mrs. Livingstone and her two little children for a few weeks at Chonuane.

> Mary feels her situation among the ruins a little dreary and no wonder, for she writes me yesterday that the lions are resuming possession and walk around our house at night. Kolobeng means 'haunt of the wild boar' but it seems to have been the haunt of everything wild. Hyaenas abound exceedingly, buffaloes in immense herds, and zebras quite tame in the thickly wooded country. Elephants too have left their traces. . . .

His wife rejoined him with the rest of the company at the end of September, by which time temporary huts of poles and reeds were built—for the first time square in shape; and Sechele had volunteered to erect a school. "I desire," said he, "that you be at no expense whatever. I wish to build a house for God who is the defence of my town. I shall call upon all the people to cut wood, etc. It will be my work." He proposed also a division between them of skilled and unskilled labour for further building, irrigation, and cultivation of crops. Livingstone's sole concern now was for the conversion of these "immortal souls that are still in darkness. We earnestly pray for this. Everything else goes on as well as we could wish; indeed better than we could have expected." All this he communicated in a letter (30 September) to his young brother-in-law, John Smith Moffat, then aged nineteen, with notes for his use on the grammar and phonetics of Sechuana.[1]

The building operations continued for nearly eleven months: a period for Mary of considerable discomfort in a draughty, dusty, fly-infested hut, and for her husband of hard manual labour.

Once he found himself dangling from a beam by his weak arm. Another time he had a fall from the roof. A third time he cut himself severely with an axe. Working on the roof in the sun, his lips got all scabbed and broken. If he mentions such things to Dr. Bennett or other friend, it is either in the way of illustrating some medical point, or to explain how he had never found time to take the latitude of his station till he was stopped working by one of these accidents.[2]

He had intended an early itinerary to other tribes eastwards but was prevented by an appeal for help from "a mad sort of Scotchman" [Gordon Cumming] who, "having wandered past us elephant-shooting lost all his cattle from the bite of a small fly" [tsetse], which obliged Livingstone to send all his oxen to his assistance. (Cumming later publicly acknowledged that this service had probably saved his life.[3]) Hardly had they returned when repairs to a breach in the dam at Kolobeng caused further delay. Not until February was he able to start and thus to recruit his strength after these toils and injuries. Sechele conveyed him 50 miles on the way but was obliged to return in order to receive a party of strangers, and presented him on parting with four gallons of porridge and two servants to act in his stead.[4]

Though actual conversions were not as yet evident, after six months he could tell Watt while en route (13 February 1848), that meetings were far better attended than at Mabotsa and "we have endeavoured to carry on systematic instruction at the same time, but have felt it very hard pressure on our energies".

The daily routine: up with the sun, family worship, breakfast, school, then manual work as required—ploughing, sowing, smythying, and every other sort. Mary busy all the morning with culinary and other work; a rest of two hours after dinner; then she goes to the infant school with an attendance of from 60 to 80. Manual work for him again till 5 o'clock; then lessons in the town and talk to such as are disposed to listen. The cows are milked; then a meeting, followed by a prayer meeting in Sechele's house, which brings him home about 8.30 too tired for any mental exertion. "I do not enumerate these duties by way of telling you how much we do, but to let you know a cause of sorrow I have that so little of my time is devoted to real missionary work."[5]

When the school house was finished he applied to the Committee for permission to purchase a bell to call the people to divine service, "and it was with joy we mounted it". Formerly a bell-man had been appointed for this office—a tall, gaunt fellow.

> Up he jumped on a sort of platform and shouted at the top of his voice, "Knock that woman down over there! Strike her, she is putting on her pot! Do you see that one hiding herself? Give her a good blow. There she is—see, see, knock her down!" All the women ran to the place of meeting in no time, for each thought herself the one meant. But, though a most efficient bell-man, we did not like to employ him.[6]

Sechele, with a sacrifice to his own interests which Livingstone at the time did not fully appreciate, "continued to profess to his people his full conviction of the truth of Christianity; and in all discussions on the subject he took that side, acting at the same time in an upright manner in all the relations of life".

The conversion and subsequent baptism of Sechele is of importance in that it raises an acutely debatable problem (then as now) in the ethics of Christian missions. The full admission of this enlightened chief to church membership was delayed for three years on account of his very natural reluctance "to get rid of his superfluous wives, without appearing ungrateful to their parents who had done so much for him in his adversity". (This refers to the murder of his father and his deprivation of the succession, till he was forcibly reinstated by the paramount chief of the Makololo, Sebituane, of whom more later.) It was accentuated by the fact that these wives were converts themselves, whilst his principal wife was the reverse.

Livingstone was himself evidently not without misgivings on the question, and in a letter to Watt admitted that he was not clear whether he ought to refuse baptism to a polygamist. As will be seen, Sechele's eventual disposal of his wives and admission to baptism caused a kind of mutiny among his people.

At last, on 4 July 1848, the house was ready for occupation and Livingstone could say with pardonable pride, "In the case of three large houses erected by myself at different times, every stick and brick had to be put square by my own right hand." He does not mention the unserviceability of his left.

As he says in his *Travels*: "We came nearly up to what may be considered as indispensable in the accomplishments of a missionary family in Central Africa, namely, the husband to be jack-of-all-trades without doors, and the wife to be maid-of-all-work within." They made their own candles, their own soap from the ashes of the plant *salsola*, their own butter in a jar serving as a churn. They ground their own meal and baked the bread (as others have done since) in ant-mud covered with hot ashes; once they were reduced to living on bran, which had to be thrice ground. When in want of meat they subsisted on a large species of caterpillar, or on locusts roast and pounded into a meal. With a fastidiousness unusual with him Livingstone remarks: "Boiled they are disagreeable; but when they are roasted I should much prefer locusts to shrimps, though I would avoid both if possible." But the chief delicacy, when procurable, was an enormous frog (*Pyxicephalus adspersus*) which croaks *before* the coming of a shower: "I found that these musicians could be merry on nothing else but the prospect of rain." They made their holes in the roots of bushes across which, as they seldom emerge, a large spider weaves its web: "the frog is thus furnished with a window and screen gratis". He adds whimsically: "As it is nearly as large as a chicken, it would no doubt tend to perpetuate the present alliance, if we made it a gift to France."

His clothes of fustian were by this time worn out (his wife made her own); and in June he wrote to his friend Henry Drummond for two moleskin jackets and trousers "that will stand washing—the strongest you can furnish". The colour does not matter but common drab would be preferred. Flannel shirts such as sailors use; cloth caps also as worn in the navy. He encloses a sample of the material for the jackets—"we use it on Sabbaths, although green".

On 1 October 1848 the chief Sechele, having put away his 'superfluous' wives, was baptized. In reporting this to the Directors a month later there can be little doubt that

Livingstone minimized both the seriousness of the situation and the shock to himself of its result.

> An event which excited more open enmity than any other, was the profession of faith and subsequent reception of the chief into the church. . . . Many of the spectators were in tears of sorrow for the loss of their rain-maker, or of grief at seeing some of the ties of relationship to him completely broken. . . .[7]

This seems to do less than justice to the heroism of the chief in making such a renunciation, or to the feelings of compassion—even the misgivings—with which the missionary accepted it. The chief who had been regarded with veneration by his people was now a renegade among them; the betrayer of all their ancestral institutions.

Sechele was in fact the earliest and most conspicuous example in Africa of a far-sighted chief who cultivated friendship with the Europeans, and who sought initiation into their religious customs and beliefs because he recognized in them the source of a strength and stability superior to his own. He lived to old age through a period of transition and upheaval in the history of his race, and, perhaps more than any other chief of his times, deserves to be regarded as their representative. It is significant that a former Resident Commissioner of the Bechuanaland Protectorate, Mr. Sillery, whose study of the native races of South Africa in general and of the Bakwena in particular is the most informed and comprehensive that has been written, should entitle it *Sechele: The Story of an African Chief*; and should end it with the judicious comment that he is remembered not as Livingstone's first convert, nor as the reigning chief when the Protectorate was declared, but as the man who made his people great.

Sechele's temporary lapse from discipline, which may in itself be regarded as meritorious rather than culpable, occurred a few months after his baptism. In March or April 1849 it was discovered that he had cohabited with one of his former wives "whom, in consequence of her having a young child and no parents, he had found impossible to send away with the others. He at once confessed his sin, and added as an excuse that, having been accustomed to her he had not felt as if he were sinning by going to another man's wife." But despite much penitence and entreaty, Livingstone cut him off from communion and allowed him only "to remain as a spectator of the ordinance"—apparently for two years.

Instances of Livingstone's scorn of danger in the face of duty were related by Moffat. A party of big-game hunters, travelling by ox-wagon through a wood some ten miles distant from Kolobeng, were charged by a black rhinoceros which drove its horn into the driver inflicting a frightful abdominal wound. A messenger arrived with this news, having run all the way. The wood was known to be a haunt of dangerous beasts. Livingstone, not to be dissuaded by the remonstrances of friends, mounted a horse and rode alone through the night to the scene, to find the driver dead and the wagon deserted, and then rode home. He underwent a similar peril on another occasion to attend a sick child, through country which was infested by lions.[8] His own sole reference to the latter incident appears in a report to the R.G.S. of later date, but with no mention of lions. He had been examining some fossils in the bed of an ancient river with a view to ascertaining its probable age, "when he was called off by express to the child of another missionary, and galloped a hundred miles to find him in his grave".[9]

"I have felt," he wrote at this time, "more than ever lately that the great object of our exertions ought to be conversion." What, it may be asked, was the theme of his teaching?—It followed the well-worn path trodden by the missionaries of his day, for which perhaps "dramatized theology" might be an appropriate description. Creation; the Fall of Man; Redemption and the Means of Grace; Sanctification; Resurrection; the Day of Judgment; Eternal Life. With this must have been interspersed of course an outline of the history of the Chosen People. What, it may be wondered, can the untutored sons of Ham have made of all this—reinforced, as the message of Salvation was, by the threat of eternal retribution on rejection and disobedience? Livingstone's heart was too large to allow the motive of fear to predominate in his teaching. He shows in a letter to his father, 5 July 1848, that he fully realized from his own experience where the true emphasis lay:

For a long time I felt much depressed after preaching the unsearchable riches of Christ to apparently insensible hearts; but now I like to dwell on the Love of the great Mediator, for it always warms my own heart.

and I know the gospel is the power of God—the great means which He employs for the regeneration of our ruined world.

And again in his Journal—though this comes later:

Jesus came not to judge—κρίνω—condemn judicially, or execute vengeance on anyone. His was a message of peace and love. He shall not strive nor cry neither shall his voice be heard in the streets. Missionaries ought to follow his example. . . .

But to return to his life at Kolobeng.

He was frequently annoyed by the pilfering of goods in transit on the British railways, and on 18 January 1849 wrote to his father-in-law:

Most of our boxes which come to us from England are opened and usually lightened of their contents. You will perhaps remember one in which Sechele's cloak was. It contained, on leaving Glasgow, a parcel of surgical instruments which I ordered and of course paid for. One of these was a valuable cupping apparatus. . . .

The box which you kindly packed for us and despatched to Glasgow has, we hear, been gutted by the Custom-House thieves, and only a very few plain karosses left in it. . . .

Can you give me any information how these annoyances may be prevented? Or must we submit to it as one of the crooked things of this life, which Solomon says cannot be made straight?[10]

As though his labours in other directions were not sufficient, he was deeply engrossed in linguistic studies and wrote to Watt:

I have been hatching a grammar of the Sechuana language. It is different in structure from any other except the ancient Egyptian. Most of the changes are effected by means of prefixes and affixes, the radical remaining unchanged. Attempts have been made to form grammars, but all have gone on the principle of establishing a resemblance between Sechuana and Latin-and-Greek: mine is on the principle of analyzing it without reference to any others. . . .

Can his friend ascertain the cost of printing a few copies of the size of a small tract; would he correct the proofs? Will he examine catalogues for any dictionary of ancient Egyptian of, say, two or three pounds?

Professor Vater has written on it, but I do not know what dictionary he consulted. One Tattam has written a Coptic grammar; perhaps that has a vocabulary. I see Tattam advertised in John Russell Smith, 4 Old Compton Street, Soho, London—'Tattam, H., *Lexicon Egyptiaco-Latinum e veteribus Linguae Egyptiacae monumentis*; thick, 8vo, bds., 10s., Oxf. 1835'. Will you purchase the above for me?[11]

"Nothing is heard, however, of the plan till 1859, when he had thirty copies printed for the use of the members of the Zambesi Expedition. The book was lost sight of till recently, and now only four copies are known to exist" (Macnair).

Concerning this, Dr. A. N. Tucker, Professor of Bantu in the London School of Oriental Languages, wrote in December 1936:

> It is a great pity that the Analysis had not a wider circulation at the time of publication, as Livingstone's method of presenting his material would have been a great inspiration to all grammarians in all parts of Africa. It is possible that, had the work been well known at the time, it would have given a great impetus to a movement away from the conventional classical grammar, that is only now making serious progress in the realm of African linguistics.[12]

From Kolobeng he wrote to Tidman on 26 May 1849 that a severe drought in the previous year had necessitated daily excursions, even on the Sabbath, for the villagers to seek food —a fact to be deplored but not censured. The population to be fed was augmented by a host of Bakaan refugees from predatory raids by the Bamangwato, 150 miles distant. So intense was the heat during this long period of drought that a thermometer buried three inches below the soil registered 133°; and beetles exposed to the light died in a few seconds. So dry was the air that needles lying out of doors for months did not rust. In scraps retrieved from the subsequent wreck of his journals by the Boers, he appears tempted to wonder whether this drought may be due to malign influence:

> November 1848. Long for rains. Everything languishes during the intense heat; and successive droughts having only occurred since the gospel came to the Bakwains, I fear the effect will be detrimental. There is abundance of rain all around us. . . . Has Satan power over the course of the winds and clouds? . . . O Devil! prince of the power of the air, art thou hindering us? Greater is He who is for us than all who can be against us. I intend to proceed with Paul to Mokhatla's. . . . May God Almighty bless the poor unworthy effort!

Our information for what follows is derived from a letter to Tidman hitherto unpublished, now deposited in the Central African archives. It is of some historical interest as recording Livingstone's first encounter with the notorious Boer Commandant, Hendrik Potgieter, who was subsequently styled "the Founder of the Dutch Republic" in the Transvaal. He died in 1853, having been ousted from his command by his yet more notorious rival, Andries Pretorius, who gave his name to Pretoria, and died in the same year.

The chief Mokhatla had expressly desired a teacher, and his village was the centre of a populous tribe in the region of the Cashan mountains to the east of Chonuane. But a section of the Boers had recently crossed the Vaal River and now occupied the whole of this territory, which they called Magaliesberg.

> They felt aggrieved by their supposed losses in the emancipation of their Hottentot slaves, and determined to erect themselves into a republic, in which they might pursue without molestation the "proper treatment of the blacks". It is almost needless to add that the 'proper treatment' has always contained in it the essential element of slavery, namely, compulsory unpaid labour.

Mosilikatse had been expelled from this territory by the Caffre chief Dingaan, and a glad welcome was given to the Boers by the oppressed Bechuana tribes who regarded them as white men and deliverers; but they soon found that the contrary was the case, and said that "Mosilikatse was cruel to his enemies, and kind to those he conquered; but the Boers destroyed their enemies and made slaves of their friends".

This was the situation when Livingstone and his few black friends arrived in this territory, though he was unaware at the time of the reason for the presence of Boers in it. He went by invitation on December 16 to the Commandant Potgieter's residence, where, despite professed friendship, he sensed an undercurrent of hostility. On his bluntly informing the Commandant that he intended not merely an itinerant mission, but a permanent station, the latter threatened to raid the tribe. "I told him if he hindered the Gospel the blood of these people would be required at his hand. He became excited at this." Potgieter affirmed that the missionary intended to arm the Bakhatla and seize this territory for the British. When Livingstone emphatically denied any such intention, "he offered no further impediment if I would promise to teach the natives that Boers were a *superior* race to themselves".

Without making any such promise, Livingstone went next day to meet the Rev. Dr. Robertson of Swellendam who was friendly. "Boers very violently opposed". Thence to Pilanies where he had large and attentive audiences.

> On the way back Paul and I looked for a ford in a dry river. Found we had got a she black rhinoceros between us and the wagon, which was only twenty yards off. She had calved during the night—a little red beast like a dog. She charged the wagon, split a spoke and felloe with her horn and then left. Paul and I jumped into a rut, as the guns were in the wagon.

The black rhinoceros is one of the most dangerous of the wild beasts in Africa, and a dam that has calved still more so. But such an incident was for Livingstone no more than a trifling inconvenience—not worth recording save in a fragment of his Journal.

Returning to the village without further parley, Livingstone began to build a school, but hearing that a deputation from the Dutch Reformed Church had come within forty miles of it, and believing "that the Boers would be won over to forebearance by their own ministers", he went to meet them only to find that he had been preceded by Potgieter and his sub-commandants, "who were now all flattery towards my person and objects, and requested only one month's delay prior to the removal of all obstacles to our permanent settlement". Though loth to make this concession Livingstone was persuaded by his teachers to agree, and returned to Kolobeng in January—only to find that Potgieter had meanwhile written to Kuruman demanding his recall. "Their blandness before their own ministers was a feint to get me out of the way." He was "tickled" to read also that they had imputed his withdrawal from the village to cowardice: "But I have no intention of deserting my post now, any more than I had then." He had supplied Sechele with five guns for protection and also with a cooking-pot; the Boers had now multiplied the former by a hundred, and transformed the latter into a cannon. This strange and perverted belief of theirs was, however, salutary in that it "had restrained them from attempting to slaughter the Bechuana as they had done to several other defenceless tribes". Hence, when questioned by them on this matter, he had declined to discuss it. He had unintentionally become acquainted recently with the Commandant Pretorius on whose head (he now learnt) the British Government had placed £2,000, so that his appearance amongst the Boers might have been mistaken for that of a Government spy. Seeing that the East is now closed to missionaries by the opposition of the Boers, he feels it imperative that he should turn northwards "to extend the gospel to all the surrounding tribes".

While returning home he heard that the Rev. J. J. Freeman, Home Secretary to the L.M.S., was on his way up from the Cape visiting all the mission stations as far as Kuruman, whereupon he wrote earnestly inviting him to visit Kolobeng:

> ... for when you have visited the Colonial stations you have only visited one end of the chain, and as your advice at home will probably vitally affect the onward movement of the whole, you ought for your own satisfaction to see the other end.

Mr. Freeman contrived a short visit to Kolobeng at the tail end of the year, a visit which his frugal hosts found pleasant and refreshing. On 9 January 1850 Livingstone wrote a long letter to his guest then departing from the Cape, of which the main emphases are two. The first is expressed in a sentence: "I feel strongly drawn towards the North." Reasons: Preoccupation of these regions by missionaries is the only remedy against further annexation by the Boers. The North would provide an outlet for evangelism in case of rejection by other tribes to whom the white man was no stranger, or who desired the missionary only for the temporal benefits he brings. The second emphasis is on the importance of a thorough mastery of native languages, without which all missionary endeavour is fruitless. "I cannot help earnestly coveting the privilege of introducing the Gospel into a new people . . . to reduce their language to writing and perhaps translate the scriptures into it. . . . Perhaps it arises from ambition, but it is not of an ignoble sort." As for the Sechuana translations, it is better for the present to leave these in Mr. Moffat's hands: "he excels us all in critical knowledge of the language". The attempts of the Dutch missionaries are worthless in comparison. He ends by suggesting that a triennial visit from a Director "might be as efficient as a committee or superintendent".[13]

But to Watt he confided that Freeman's visit, though pleasant to him and his wife, was productive of little positive good to the mission at large, since the Director was quite persuaded of the soundness of Dr. Philip's views "which are—that the missions must be kept up as they were in the beginning, are now, and evermore shall be". In two letters of seven closely-written pages of foolscap he expounds carefully to his friend the "conservative" policy of the former, and cogently argues the merits of his own "radical" policy—expansion and decentralization. He explains the whole position of missionary enterprise from the point of view of the Directors, of Dr. Philip, of the missionaries in the field of all denominations, with a grasp of detail, a wealth of illustration, and withal a moderation and understanding—and all with a view to elucidating what will be to the best practical advantage of the cause they all have at heart—which mark the prevision of the future missionary-statesman.[14]

In April 1849 Mary had presented her husband with their third child, who in memory of his friend of former days was named Thomas Steele. Some time before this he had written to Steele suggesting a trip in the direction of Lake Ngami. Steele was unable to go, but passed on the suggestion to their mutual friend Mr. Oswell, and together with him to Mr. Mungo Murray.

Chapter Eight

DISCOVERY OF LAKE NGAMI
1849

*"I love him with true affection, and I believe he does the same
to me; and yet we never show it."*

WILLIAM COTTON OSWELL, whose athletic prowess, brains, good looks and generous nature had made him *facile princeps* among his contemporaries at Arnold's Rugby, and for seven years "the *beau ideal* of a civilian" in the Honourable East India Company, being prostrated with fever in its service, had in 1844 embarked for South Africa in search of restored health and fresh adventure. There in abundant measure he found both, and in two years established a reputation for intrepidity in big-game hunting which has probably never been surpassed. He was as good a scholar as sportsman: with a sound knowledge of political science and kindred subjects he was also proficient in Sanscrit, could converse with natives in Tamil, Persian and Arabic, besides being fluent in French; and at the end of a long day's hunt would beguile the evening, if he lacked company, in rendering favourite passages from Shakespeare or Milton into Greek iambics and Latin elegaics. But greater than either his mental or physical endowments were his moral qualities. An aristocrat to his finger-tips, unspoiled by popularity or wealth and utterly devoid of personal ambition, he was magnanimous almost to a fault. His biography, written with filial love and admiration by his son and introduced by Sir Francis Galton, is indeed the record of "a brave and blameless life".

In company with Mr. Mungo Murray he had reached Kuruman early in June 1845, and thus wrote home:

> We stayed a short time at the station of that grand old patriarch of missionaries, Mr. Moffat, where we received all the kindly hospitality, attention and advice possible from him and Mrs. Moffat—verily the two best friends travellers ever came across. I shall never forget their affectionate courtesy, their beautifully ordered household, and their earnest

desire to help us on in every way. He advised us to go to Livingstone—220 miles or so to the northward, and obtain from him guides and counsel for our further wanderings.

He describes the scenery as "most desolate—a burnt, barren, interminable plain, literally without a bush", till, arriving at the Bakhatla, "the country changed its character entirely. Fine ranges of hills, well wooded and watered, close you in on every side, and the scenery is strikingly like some parts of India".

> After staying two days with Mr. Livingstone, *the best, most intelligent and most modest of the missionaries,* . . . we certainly revelled for three months in the finest climate, the finest shooting, and anything but tame scenery.

He visited, as Livingstone had done before him, the country of the Bawangketsi, the Bamangwato, and the Bakaa, with a sufficiency of hair-breadth adventures among each, and returning to Mabotsa "to shake the dear old Doctor and Mrs. Livingstone by the hand" went down to the Cape to refit for another expedition in the following year—which, with Captain Frank Vardon as his companion, proved even more strenuous and exciting than the former.

The first letter "of a correspondence which continued with singular fidelity and increasing affection till his death" was written by Livingstone to Oswell, who was then again in India in June of 1847. Its main purpose was to correct an error in Oswell's chart of the course of the Limpopo river, which he had accidentally detected when journeying twelve days eastwards of Chonuane. Oswell's compass must have been affected by magnetic attraction from iron oxide in the hills. The letter continues with similar items of geographical interest and personal news such as must have kindled in his friend's memory a desire to revisit the country; and a last request, "Do remember and write soon"—with one sentence on a serious note: "Allow me, my dear sir, to recommend the Atonement of Christ as the only ground of peace and happiness in death."[1]

It was not until the end of 1848 that Oswell again could reach the Cape. He then began preparations for another expedition on a grand scale and, equipped with 20 horses, 80 oxen, two wagons, and a year's supplies for three men and eight servants, inspanned from Port Elizabeth in the middle of

February, and arrived at Colesberg five weeks later. Here for a month he awaited Murray. At the end of May the cavalcade reached Kolobeng, where it was joined by Livingstone, an adventurous trader named Wilson and a party of some thirty Bakwena. The start for the "farthest north" was made on 1 June 1849.

The existence of a large lake far to the northward had long been known from native reports; but its existence beyond latitude 23° was a matter for surmise. In 1834 an expedition under Dr. Andrew Smith, the largest and best equipped that had ever left Cape Town, had reached that latitude, but the waterless desert beyond it had compelled their return. Later, Captain Sir James Alexander, with the official and generous support of the Geographical Society, had similarly tried and failed. The chief Sechele, as has been told, had warned Livingstone of the impossibility, even for natives accustomed to such travel, of crossing that corner of the Kalahari unless in a season of exceptional rain; and now Sekomi, in returning to him seventeen oxen which had been driven into his compound by a hyaena, did so with a message: "Where are you going? You will be killed by the sun and thirst, and then all the white men will blame me for not saving you." Sekomi, indeed, had an ulterior reason for not wishing the expedition success; he feared that it would ruin his monopoly of ivory. Livingstone replied by sending him a handsome present, with the promise that "if he allowed the Bakalahari to keep their wells open for us, we would repeat the gift on our return". He also assured the chief's messengers that "the white men would attribute our deaths to our own stupidity, as we did not intend to allow our companions and guide to return until they had put us into our graves". The principal guide was in fact a fugitive from Sekomi's tribe, named Ramotobi; a circumstance still less conducive to the chief's goodwill. He sent two other men, ostensibly as additional guides, to spread a report among the natives to the north that the object of the white men's expedition was plunder: one of these died of fever on the journey, with the result that the natives, seeing his death as a judgment, became friendly and helpful.

Livingstone's account of this notable journey is contained in letters written from the banks of the Zouga to Tidman and (much more fully) to Captain Steele, both of which, but slightly edited, were immediately sent to the *Journal* of the R.G.S. for publication. They are severely factual and objective; the latter encloses a sketch of the route, plotted with the aid of Steele's "beautiful sextant", which exhibits its author's skill and accuracy as a surveyor.[3]

Of his two companions, Murray apparently wrote nothing; whilst Oswell's contribution is limited to a belated letter to his uncle Benjamin Cotton, and another to Captain Vardon. The latter was reproduced in the *Journal* of the R.G.S. immediately after Livingstone's report and also in his biography.[2] It is much the fuller and more graphic of the two, and to it we must look for details of human interest. Oswell, unlike Livingstone, was a deplorably bad correspondent, and one who cared nothing for fame, but everything for sport, travel, and adventure for their own sake. Sir Francis Galton in his preface to Oswell's biography rightly draws attention to this. But he overstates the case in asserting that Oswell, the more experienced traveller, was the real leader of the expedition; though admitting the value of Livingstone's knowledge of the native languages (which Oswell and Murray lacked) and of the natives' personal affection for him. In the first place one cannot imagine Livingstone allowing himself to be led by anyone, not even by so great a friend as Oswell, and indeed subsequent events prove the reverse to have been actually the case. And in the second place, his knowledge of the natives and their speech was not only invaluable but indispensable; nor was he less experienced as a traveller. The truth is that the expedition would have been impossible without the princely financial assistance of both Oswell and Murray: for the rest, these three great-hearted travellers relied on each other and on each other's capacities. It should be added that Galton was himself a scientific explorer of high repute in South-West Africa; and also that he tried, but in vain, to reach Lake Ngami the year after their discovery of it.

The whole party assembled at a water called Shokuan, a few miles north of Kolobeng, and inspanned on 2nd June. On the third day they reached Serotle, which Oswell regarded as "the portal of the desert": it was the last watering-place for 70 miles, and in coming even thus far they had been without water for three days. Here sandy hollows, the vestiges of ancient river-beds, were dug into with care to prevent the water-pockets they concealed from seeping through the harder stratum of sand beneath. The water thus uncovered proved sufficient for the horses, but not for the oxen which were led back 25 miles to Lebotani for refreshment, whilst the hollows slowly filled against their return. Proceeding after ten days' delay, and travelling only for a few hours after sunrise and towards sunset (the heat of full day, even in mid-winter, being too severe for the oxen), they made no more than six miles in one day, and the next night reached a little clump of camel-thorn trees called Mokelani. The scrub which the weary oxen chewed was so dry that it crumbled to dust in the hand. The sameness of the landscape now began to deceive even the guides. Ramotobi announced that at this rate of progress they could never reach the next water. At this point Oswell confessed that, "though no one, I really think, would have turned back for any consideration, I felt considerable anxiety". It was decided that Murray with the guide and the horses should go ahead and prospect for water, the oxen following at a slower pace. Thus they "hardly crawled" eight miles. But the guide had lost his way and Murray very rightly called a halt. The other natives then spread out to reconnoitre for a small marsh of which they had been informed, and soon found it; the oxen which had been considered as all but exhausted were re-yoked, and two miles' struggle brought them to this oasis. Here they were given a Sunday's rest. (Livingstone himself would never travel on a Sunday, unless forced by necessity.)

For four days after this they fared well since they were following a subterranean river-bed, and on the fourth day reached the first surface water on their whole journey. Continuing in the same course they came upon a large but dried-up marsh surrounded by withered grass, and here the guide again wandered. Now having been for two full days without water, they would have been in sore straits had not Oswell caught sight of a Bushwoman (whom in the blinding glare he first mistook for a lion) escaping through the grass, and galloped off in pursuit. Terrified by apparent capture, she was calmed by Livingstone's assurance of their goodwill, which was backed by the present of a piece of meat and a bunch of beads, and was induced to lead them for eight miles to a spring which lay

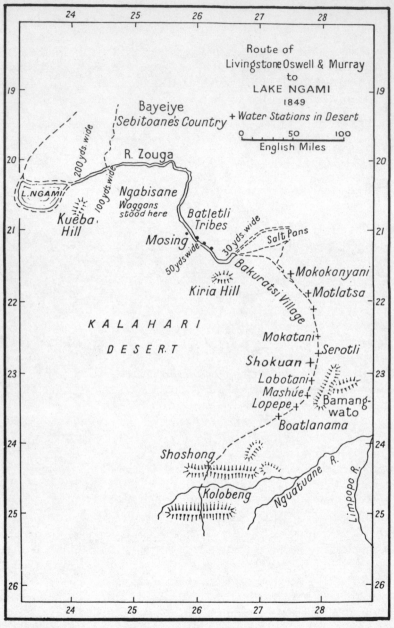

MAP 2   LAKE NGAMI JOURNEY
(1849)

The route to Lake Ngami taken in 1849 by Living-
.stone with his friends Cotton Oswell and Mungo
Murray from the mission station at Kolobeng—his first
major journey into unknown country.

in a very different direction from that which they had been following. Here a thick belt of mopane trees concealed what lay beyond, but having penetrated it they came suddenly in view of what appeared to be a vast sheet of water.

> Oswell threw his hat up in the air at the sight, and shouted out a huzza which made the poor Bushwoman and the Bakwains think him mad. I was a little behind him, and was as completely deceived by it as he. . . . The mirage on these salinas was marvellous. It is never, I believe, seen in perfection except over such saline incrustations. . . . the loose cattle, the horses, dogs, and even the Hottentots ran off towards the deceitful pools.[3]

They had now progressed with the utmost difficulty and in danger, on at least three occasions, of death from prolonged thirst, a distance of 300 miles from Kolobeng; they little guessed that they had yet another 300 miles to go. They had slaked their thirst, white men and black, oxen, horses, and dogs together, at the same scant pools. But from now, July 4th, the worst of their troubles were ended. For on that date they came in sight of a veritable river which was both broad and deep—the Zouga, with a cluster of inhabited huts on its farthest bank. This welcome sight prompted Oswell to try and urge his horse through a drift, but he got his horse bogged and nearly lost it. Livingstone and two Bakwena succeeded in wading across beside a fishing-weir. "The water was clear as crystal, and very cold. . . . The keen cold air from the water increased our appetites amazingly." They interrogated the villagers, who proved friendly, and informed them that the river flowed *out of* the Ngami. "This news gladdened our hearts, for we now felt certain of reaching our goal." It was at this point, however, that Sekomi's two pretended guides joined them, and after a friendly conversation proceeded ahead to circulate the report "that our object was to plunder all the tribes living on the river and lake"—with the fortunately abortive result which has been mentioned.

Following the course of the river for 96 miles and being informed by the dwellers on its banks that they had still a long way to go, they left at a village the bulk of their retinue and all the oxen and wagons but one (Oswell's which was the lightest) with the freshest team, in order to recruit the strength of the remainder for the home journey, while "we made a push for it". They found the banks populated by a peace-loving tribe who lived mainly in their primitive canoes which they regarded "as the Arab does his steed", and whose pacifist attitude subjected them to intermittent raids which they never attempted to repel. "They are thus the Quakers of the body politic in Africa". Their language was totally different from Sechuana. "Of 300 words which I collected only 21 had any resemblance to it. Some words have a click." Livingstone soon found that the Zouga was connected with other rivers flowing into it from the north, of which the Tamanakle was the largest, and enquired whence it came. "Oh, from a country full of rivers—so many that no one can tell their number—and full of large trees!" This confirmed statements that he had heard from natives who had been with Sebituane, far to the north-east, and his reflections upon it are characteristic of his whole attitude to exploration, which for him was merely a means to an end.

> The prospect of a highway capable of being traversed by boats to an entirely unexplored and very populous region, grew from that time forward stronger and stronger in my mind; so much so that, when we came to the lake, the actual discovery seemed of but little importance. . . .[4]

After twelve "hard days' work" they arrived, on 1 August, 1849, in sight of "an unbounded sheet of water". They had hit the Lake at its north-east extremity. It proved to be shallow: "I saw a native punting his canoe over seven or eight miles off the shore; it can never therefore be of much value as a commercial highway." He computed its level above the sea at 2,100 feet—approximately half that of Kolobeng, from whence its distance, measured by trocheameter, was 600 miles. Livingstone's main object after reaching the Lake had been to visit Sebituane, the paramount chief of the Makololo 200 miles distant, and to that end he applied to the young distrustful chief on the river for guides and canoes. On being refused, he tried very hard to construct a raft, "but the wood was worm-eaten and would not bear the weight of a single person". He tried again, working for many hours in the water, unaware that it was infested with crocodiles, but fortunately without success. Then, as he stood waist-deep in the water, searching with fixed gaze the opposite bank which was only some 50 or 60 yards distant, he seriously contemplated swimming across—"for most sorely do I dislike to be beat".[5] It was only the thought that "my appearance there in a state of nudity would be unbecoming in a missionary" that caused him to abandon the idea. Thereupon Oswell, impressed with his persistence, offered to bring up a boat from the Cape the following year and finance another expedition. Their return journey is not recorded; apparently it was accomplished with a comparative mitigation of the extreme hardships they and their beasts of burden had experienced on the outward journey. These can only be appreciated by an imaginative perusal of Oswell's narrative.

The exploit brought its performers immediate fame, of which however only one of them reaped any advantage. As the surveyor and scientist of the expedition Livingstone was awarded half the annual royal grant for geographical discovery, and the Society's Gold Medal, and wrote playfully to his parents:

> The Royal Geographical Society have awarded twenty-five guineas for the discovery of the lake. It is from the Queen. You must be very loyal, all of you. Next time she comes your way, shout till you are hoarse. Oh you Radicals, don't be thinking it came out of your pockets! Long live Victoria![6]

Straitened though his family circumstances were, he spent this gift on the purchase of a watch for observing the occultation of stars by the moon, to fix latitudes.[7] But the discovery of the Lake itself was, as he surmised, one of little importance. It proved indeed to be a corroboration of his view that South Africa as a whole was then, as it still is, in process of gradual desiccation. The vast sheet of water which was visible a century ago is now a meadow. Among their zoological discoveries were those of the *lechwe* antelope and of the straight-horned rhinoceros.

More important by far to two of the explorers than their discovery of the Lake was their discovery of each other. Time and time again, publicly in his reports to the R.G.S. and the L.M.S. and privately in his Journals, Livingstone testifies his admiration of his friend's "unselfishness, desperate courage, and nobility of character", and constantly expresses grateful recognition for "his disinterested kindness and unstinted generosity" without which he could never have accomplished the objects of his journeys at this time. Years later, when in England for the last time, he wrote to their mutual friend Mr. W. F. Webb of Newstead Abbey:

> I have been reading *Tom Brown's Schooldays*—a capital book [the author of which, Thomas Hughes, Q.C., was to be one of his own biographers]. Dr. Arnold was a man something better than his weight in gold. You know Oswell was one of his Rugby boys. One could see his training in always doing what was brave, true, and right. [And again] I love him with true affection, and I believe he does the same to me; and yet we never show it.[8]

Probably no one has better discerned than Oswell the essential element in Livingstone's character: "his unagressive obstinacy".

> One trait in his character was, to do whatever he had set his mind on. In an Englishman we might, I think, have called the phase obstinacy, but with Livingstone it was 'Scottishness'. It was not the *sic volo sic jubeo* of imperiousness, but a quiet determination to carry out his own views in his own way, without feeling himself bound to give a reason or explanation further than that he intended to do so-and-so. This was an immense help to him, for it made him supremely self-reliant. He was the Fabius of African travel—*vicit cunctando* might well be his epitaph. I have sat seven weeks with him on the bank of a swamp, because he was unwilling to run counter to the wishes of the people. I pressed him to move on with the horses; no active opposition would have been offered, but he would not wound the prejudices of the natives—and he was right. With his quiet endurance and entire lack of fussiness and excitability, content to wait and let patience have her perfect work, he was eminently the *justum et tenacem propositi virum* on whom man or elements could make little impression—yet strangely withal very enthusiastic. This nature fitted him for the successful traveller and trustworthy companion. His inner man and noble aspirations belong to the histories of his life. We were the firmest of friends, both a trifle obstinate, but we generally agreed to differ, and in all matters concerning the natives I of course waived my crude opinions to his matured judgment. . . .
>
> He was pre-eminently a *Man*—patient, all-enduring under hardships, content to win his way by inches, but never swerving from it; gentle, kindly, brotherly to the children of the land; absolutely unruffled amidst danger and difficulty, and well satisfied to see but one step in advance. If ever a man carried out the Scriptural injunction to take no thought for the morrow, that man was David Livingstone.[9]

Chapter Nine

TOWARDS THE ZAMBESI
1850–1851

"God had an only Son, and He was a missionary and a physician. A poor, poor imitation of Him I am, or wish to be."

I T must be reiterated that in establishing his mission at Kolobeng, Livingstone had from the outset envisaged it as a permanent station, a northerly Kuruman, a centre or focus from which to propagate the gospel by means of native teachers *eastwards*, where the country was more populous than any he had seen, gradually extending thence as far as the east coast where the Limpopo flows into Delagoa Bay. ("Itineracy is good," he wrote, "if you have a permanent sphere—a focus.") Two causes frustrated this plan: one, the obstruction of the emigrant Boers who were occupying the territory, since called the Transvaal; the other, the increasing drought which was now rendering his station uninhabitable. Not only the tributaries of the Kolobeng but the river itself was drying up, and in many cases the very "eyes" of the fountains were closing. Eastwards therefore the way was barred by the hostility of man, westwards by that of nature the Kalahari Desert; southwards by a surplus of missionaries. It was the combination of these circumstances that compelled Livingstone to look to the unexplored north, where his own natural inclinations lay. While it is true that "he did not seek this line, it was forced upon him", it is also true that the north had for long been in the back of his mind; and even if he had succeeded in making Kolobeng a permanent station he would, sooner or later, quite certainly have gone prospecting thither with a view to establishing yet more northerly stations in the heart of the continent. And he looked to the north with greater confidence because the centre of it comprised the empire of the great paramount chief Sebituane, of whom he had heard much from Sechele. His second attempt to reach this chief was however both imprudent and unsuccessful.

Oswell, true to his promise, had purchased a boat and transported it by ox-wagon from the Cape to Kolobeng, but it was so warped by exposure to the sun on the long journey as to be unserviceable. He found also on his arrival in May that Livingstone had left a month before, and "had, perhaps rather unwisely, taken his wife and children with him". (In his *Travels* Livingstone says: "Some mistake had happened in the arrangement with Mr. Oswell"; certainly April, the beginning of winter, would have been the month in which to start if a long absence were intended.) Oswell therefore went off big-game hunting in the hope of meeting the Livingstones on their return. Whilst doing so and when he had almost run out of lead, he fell in with another big-game hunter, Mr. W. F. Webb, and exchanged greetings. Next day this sportsman sent him several bars of the metal "more valuable than gold in Central Africa", refusing Oswell's offer of three pairs of elephants' tusks in exchange for it. This was the beginning of a life-long friendship in which, as will be seen, Livingstone was included.

The Livingstones left Kolobeng on 26 April 1850. Their cavalcade comprised themselves and their children, Mebalwe and twenty Bakwena. They were obliged to travel somewhat east of their former route because Sekomi, chief of the Bamangwato, had caused the water-holes, which had been uncovered with so much labour at Serotli, to be filled in. Their route thus lay directly through the town of this chief, who asked, "Why had I avoided him in our former journeys?" Livingstone: "Because I knew you did not wish me to go to the Lake, and I did not want to quarrel with you." Sekomi (in native idiom): "Well, you have me there."[1] Livingstone always had a soft spot in his heart for this wily chief and said of him later: "He has a bad name, but is not so black as he is painted." On this occasion he was suffering from an indolent abscess in the pit of the stomach, and so "he was glad to see us".

The northern bank of the Zouga was reached with difficulty. Trees had to be felled for the progress of the wagons; a report of tsetse-fly on the banks of the Tamanakle obliged them to recross the river. When near the Lake they learned that a party of English hunters were ill with malaria, so they travelled with haste some 60 miles out of their course to render assistance. All recovered under their care; among them were the trader Wilson and Mr. Edwards' son. But to their grief one had already died: this was the young artist Alfred Rider who had come to make a sketch of the Lake immediately after its discovery. His unfinished sketch, made just before his death, is reproduced in Livingstone's *Travels*. It shows Livingstone and his family clad in mid-Victorian dress—figures that look strangely incongruous in the sub-tropical setting.

In crossing the Zouga and ascending the northern bank "I stumbled on a native grave, for the first time since I came into the country"; it was that of a Bushman, and above it were placed some grass and bushes, an old tortoise-shell used as a dish and a stick used in digging roots.

A little farther on we came upon an old man quite naked and hopelessly diseased. He informed us that he had been deserted a few days before us by his daughters, that he suffered much from thirst, for though lying under the large trees which line the banks of the river he could not crawl down for water. Having supplied him with a covering and some food, we offered to carry him to the next village. "O," said he, "if they saw me they would flee from me." Socialism has but sorry fruits among these unsophisticated specimens of humanity.[2]

At last they reached the Lake, the level of which had fallen three feet since the previous year: "the children took to playing in it as ducklings do". Their presence and that of his wife, he says, inspired the natives with confidence and promoted tender feelings and kind relations. Lechulatebe, the formerly suspicious young chief, set eyes on Livingstone's gun "which I had received as a present from Lieutenant Arkwright, after setting his collar-bone, and also the broken thigh of one of his servants. It must have cost him £25". In exchange for this, Lechulatebe said that he would give him everything he wished, including food and protection for his wife and children while he went on (on ox-back) to Sebituane. (This proposal was by no means so horrifying as may appear: it is one which could be accepted with perfect safety, then as now, among the primitive races of Central Africa.) Despite the value of the gift, both for its usefulness and as a personal memento of the giver—"I handed it to him at once. It is of great importance [he told Watt] to gain the confidence of these fellows in the beginning."

But now an outbreak of fever occurred, which attacked the two elder children and others of the party so severely that a return home became urgent. It was clear that the region of the Lake was not habitable for Europeans. Livingstone left the gun with the young chief, telling him that he could fulfil his part of the bargain next year. To the Directors he wrote:

> That which inspires more fear than anything else in the Lake country is mosquitoes. They are dreadful. Their bite is more venomous than anywhere else, at least so it is said by those who had been in India, New South Wales, and Brazil. They are really painful and the pain continues for several days—sleep is out of the question when you come to a den of them. I could not touch a square half-inch on the bodies of the children unbitten after a single night's exposure.[3]

This is indeed a terrible picture of the results of the scourge, and Livingstone did not exaggerate. Neither he nor anyone else at that time connected malarial fever with mosquitoes, though he does observe that fever seems most often prevalent where they abound. (The shores of the Ngami were of course no more than a glorified swamp.) The use of quinine as an antidote, extracted by Jesuit priests in the 17th century in Peru from the bark of the *cinchone* and imported into other tropical countries in 1820, had for some time been in use in South Africa and Livingstone compounded his own pills with it, of which a vital ingredient was calomel.

Oswell, after two months' sport, hearing that the Livingstones were within fifty miles of him, hastened to meet them and escorted them on their homeward way as long as he could be useful to them. "He brought supplies for us from the Colony, and returned a bill for £40 which was to have been spent on purchasing them."

But there was a yet more urgent reason—though he does not so much as mention it—which necessitated his wife's immediate return from the Lake. It seems incredible that Livingstone should have taken her with him on this journey or have undertaken it at all. On their return to Kolobeng in August she was delivered of her fourth child—a girl. The tragic sequel is announced to Mr. Benjamin Pyne of Ongar on 4 December from Kuruman in terms which are devoid of any self-reproaches and seem to render his conduct even less pardonable.

I can only write a few lines to you now. Mrs. Livingstone had a paralytic attack a short time after her confinement—the right side of her face becoming motionless. The motor power has been restored, but the pain continually recurs and affects the right side and leg. Our little Elizabeth Pyne took the sickness which was prevailing amongst the Bakwains, and bearing up under it for a fortnight was taken to see the King in His beauty and the blessed land. Hers is the first grave marked as such in the country.[4]

To his parents he wrote on the same date:

Our last child, a sweet little girl with blue eyes, was taken from us to join the company of the redeemed, through the merits of Him of whom she never heard. . . . We could not apply remedies to one so young, except the simplest. She uttered a piercing cry, and then went away to see the King in His beauty. . . .[5]

And in his Journal: "It was the first death in our family, but just as likely to have happened had we remained at home, and we have now one of our number in heaven." It is difficult to read these sentiments thus expressed without distaste; yet they were deeply and sincerely felt.

He had even been discussing with Mary—presumably before the birth of the child—plans for another attempt to reach Sebituane in the following year; since in a letter to Watt dated 18 August we find: "My wife, poor soul I pity her, proposed to let me go for that time [namely a year] while she remains at Kolobeng." As will be seen, Mary changed her mind and insisted upon accompanying him, but her courage in doing so does nothing to extenuate her husband's lack of consideration.

Her recurrent paralysis caused him grave concern and, had she been fit to travel, he would have taken her to the Cape for treatment. But she recuperated with rest at Kuruman, at least temporarily. Meanwhile his thickened uvula was causing him acute trouble with a swelling of the tonsils, and had a journey to the Cape been possible he would have taken the opportunity to have it excised.

He tried to persuade his father-in-law to perform the operation and, under his directions, Dr. Moffat went so far as to take a pair of scissors for the purpose; but his courage, so well tried in other fields, was not equal to the performance of such a surgical operation.[6]

A digression is necessary here upon the relations that existed between Livingstone and his father-in-law. "Perhaps," says a student of their times, "Livingstone and Moffat agreed better than any other two men in the field."[7] One good reason for this may be that each possessed, and discerned in the other, the indefinable quality of greatness. Moffat was a man of guileless disposition and transparent goodness. Shy and diffident in youth, he had become in manhood a vigorous, arresting and somewhat overwhelming personality. A sanguine optimist, he was prone to exaggerate. A child at heart, he had all a child's love of appreciation: in other words, he was somewhat vain. Accustomed for so long to dominate the missionary scene, he tended to see himself in the centre of the picture, round whom everything and everybody revolved. This tendency had a smothering effect on his colleagues, none of whom could tolerate his company for very long; and even Ashton, the most amenable and self-effacing of them all, rebelled at last and left him. His wife, a woman of fine intelligence and character, as devoted to him as he to her, was the power behind the scenes in their household, and her influence went far to fostering this tendency. It had a similar effect upon his family (of ten) who grew up with a sense of inferiority. The three eldest daughters had escaped from the shelter of this benevolent despotism for three years' education in Cape Town, but had been drawn into its orbit again during the family's long furlough in England, when Mary was emerging from girlhood into womanhood. But there was nothing of the *poseur*, nothing of the romanticist, in Livingstone, nor was there anything of the child: he had matured young. He had an instinct for truth, for reality, for exactitude in thought and speech, which Moffat lacked. He was also, and for this reason, in spite of all his assertiveness, fundamentally modest—as Moffat was not. And he could afford to do with Moffat what others could not; he could afford quite genially to chaff him. Yet he must have admired his father-in-law's unaffected piety and genuine devotion; he must have loved him for his simplicity of character and human loving-kindness. And, beside the gift of his daughter, he owed him much. More than any man Moffat had sponsored, in face of much opposition, his schemes for advanced mission stations; and it was Moffat only and above all men whom he earnestly desired as companion on his first great journey. Moreover he regarded Moffat's unremitting labours on the translation of the Bible into Sechuana not only with admiration but with concern for its effects upon his health, and its final completion as an achievement beyond praise. These facts are to be borne in mind when considering the unhappy disagreement between them at the outset of Livingstone's third journey to the north.

It turns on his determination to take his wife and children with him again, and this in the face of her parents' strong remonstrances and despite the disastrous experiences of the previous journey. This action has been more seriously criticized than any other in the course of his career, especially since this journey, though successful in its issue, was attended with more pains and greater risks than the other. For this reason, the matter must be given a closer examination than it has yet received.

The correspondence between Livingstone and the Moffats has not been preserved but Blaikie, who read it, has recorded that Mrs. Moffat wrote twice—

Remonstrating in the strongest terms against his plan of taking his wife with him: reminding him of the death of the child, and other sad occurrences of the last year; and, in the name of everything that was just, kind, and even decent, beseeching him to abandon an arrangement which all the world would condemn.

This appeal proving ineffective she wrote again

—Informing him that much prayer had been offered that, if the arrangements were not in accordance with Christian propriety, he might in great mercy be prevented by some dispensation of Providence from carrying them out.[8]

Livingstone copied these extracts into his Journal with the comment: "They show in what light our efforts are regarded by those who, as much as we do, desire that the Gospel may be preached to all nations." And several months later, in reporting to Tidman on the results of both journeys, he wrote: " . . . The death of the child and the complaint [illness] of the mother have both been charged to my account, and I have been asked if 'the loss of one child, etc., etc., was not enough to satisfy me.' This and other severe expressions have been used even by those whom I esteem."[9]

There is no doubt that the Moffats were right in their remonstrances and that these were justified by results. But on

Livingstone's side something may be said in partial extenuation. He was not by nature impetuous; his courses of action, like his walk, were methodical and marked by deliberation. But the speed of his life and its intensity were such that sometimes his decisions appeared to be precipitate when in fact they were premeditated. Not only his body but his mind worked faster and went farther than the average.

In the present circumstances he could not leave Mary in Kolobeng. It was, as he knew, threatened by a raid from the Boers at any time; and the continued drought threatened also the speedy removal of the whole of Sechele's tribe. For these reasons he had provided for "an absence of a twelve-month", with the hope too of establishing yet another permanent settlement in the hills of Sebituane's country which he knew abounded with water and would be out of reach of the Boers. He could not send his wife and family to England, or even to the Cape; he had no resources for maintaining them in civilization. What were the alternatives? The only and at first sight obvious one was Kuruman, but against this, says Blaikie discreetly, since he was writing during the Moffats' lifetime, "there were invincible objections". We may be reasonably sure that he would never have taken Mary without her consent, and further that her consent in this case was equivalent to her own expressed wish. There is only one possible inference to be drawn from this: Mary could no longer feel happy in her parents' home; she would be subject to their whims and treated as she had always been from childhood—as a child; but she was a child no longer, she was a wife and a mother. And her husband was a human being with a sense of humour, a freedom-loving fellow-mortal, and she loved him. There is yet another consideration which should not be overlooked: by the time they left Kolobeng in April she must have known, and he must also, that she was again with child. Her husband had always been her doctor in her travails; is it likely that she would desire the services of another man?

If it be said, in reply to this attempt to justify Livingstone's conduct, that it only lends weight to the argument that he should never have undertaken the journey at all, there is no answer but one. It is true that, judged by any normal standards of matrimonial responsibility, his conduct must be deemed indefensible; but he had a faith in the Providence of God which, though to us it may seem fanatical, inspired all his aims and without which he would never have attempted, much less could have accomplished, what he did. This faith included trust in divine providence for the welfare of his wife and children. He sought the will of God in constant prayer; then, by the use of his mother-wit, "he was most careful to scan all the providential indications that might throw light on the divine Will". Many of these "indications" at this time are minutely enumerated by Blaikie. Finally, and in the most general terms, it must be recognized that to a soul on fire as his was with the flame of a sacred mission—to bring light to them that sit in darkness and in the shadow of death—all lesser loves must be subordinated to the Love of God and the proclamation of the gospel, and if that mission entailed hardship, illness, or even final disaster for his nearest and dearest, had not the Master himself said, "He that loveth . . . wife and children more than me is not worthy of me"?

The truth is, that criticism of Livingstone's conduct in this particular involves a general criticism of his whole career, and raises the inevitable question: ought this man ever to have married? In the view of the present writer the answer would be emphatically No, were it not qualified by the consideration that this man like others (and more than most, with his masculinity) was a creature of flesh and blood with a man's emotions that required satisfaction and fulfilment. We are presented here with an abstract dilemma, but to him it must have been a very real and concrete one. For this journey was to prove the crux of his career. It forced upon him the realization that his aims as an active missionary and his duties as a husband were two things incompatible, and that one or other must be sacrificed. Even now, as we see from a letter to Tidman, 24 August 1850, his thoughts were turning in the direction of a goal that must have seemed to others beyond possibility: "We must have a passage to the sea on either the Eastern or Western coasts. I have hitherto been afraid to broach the project on which my perhaps dreamy imagination dwells. But . . . without promising anything I mean to follow a useful motto in many circumstances and *try again*." This is one of the most informative and interesting of all his letters of this period, especially so for the natural historian and the ethnologist. He appends to it a note on the political situation. The Boers had lately sent an order to Sechele to stop all English travellers and traders proceeding to the North, but he had advised Sechele to take no notice of it.[10]

When a few days out, he wrote to Tidman, and the words are charged with a significance of which the recipient knew nothing:

> It is a venture to take wife and children into a country where fever—African fever—prevails. But who that believes in Jesus would refuse to make a venture for such a Captain? A parent's heart alone can feel as I do when I look at my little ones and ask, shall I return with this or that one alive? However, we are His and wish to have no interests apart from those of His kingdom and glory. May He bless us and make us blessings even unto death.[11]

> [To his father.] I am a missionary, heart and soul. God had an only Son, and He was a missionary and a physician. A poor, poor, imitation of Him I am, or wish to be. In this service I hope to live, in it I wish to die.[12]

Starting towards the end of April, 1851, Oswell was again "the good genius" of the party. He had gone ahead with guides to open up the water-holes as far as Nchokotsa. Leaving Lake Ngami on the left, the whole party struck northwards by an untried route.

They left Nchokotsa on 27 May and crossed the dry bed of the Zouga some 15 miles N.N.E. of it: "Road hard—country terribly scorched." In traversing a salt-pan (100 miles long and 15 broad) two days later, the wagon-wheels sank through the hard crust to their naves: "The latitude might have been taken on its horizon as well as upon the sea."

On 3 June the party reached a veritable spring and the country east of it was called the "links", as of a chain of springs, "which become full in seasons when no rain falls . . . probably due to percolation from the river system in the country beyond". Here they found many families of Bushmen. "What a wonderful people the Bushmen are! Always merry and laughing and never telling lies wantonly like the Bechuana." One of these, Shobo, consented to be their guide through the wastes that lay to the north, but gave them no hope of water in less than a month. Now began the most difficult part of the whole journey. They entered a 20-miles belt of heavy sand and thick bush. "The axes were kept going constantly, and the course cut through was so winding we could scarcely ever see the front oxen." They emerged at length upon a vast plain of low thorny scrub. "Not a bird or insect enlivened the landscape. It was without exception the most uninviting prospect I ever beheld." Shobo, with a good-natured smile, confessed entire ignorance of their whereabouts, curled himself up like a dog in the sand, and went to sleep. Three days later he vanished altogether.

They had been thirsty before, but now began the real perils of their journey. On 11 June they were reduced to the last drops in the water-bottles. The oxen were terribly fatigued and thirsty: "we never saw them so distressed". At last they observed some birds and soon afterwards came upon the spoor of rhinoceros—an animal which never lives far from water. They unyoked the oxen which set off at a hard trot and did not stop till they reached the Mababe, which flows out of the Tamanakle. Meanwhile Oswell and Livingstone remained with the mother and children by the wagons.

> The supply of water in the wagons had been wasted by one of our servants, and by the afternoon only a small portion remained for the children. The idea of their perishing before our eyes was terrible. It would almost have been of a relief to me to have been reproached with being the entire cause of the catastrophe, but not one syllable of upbraiding was uttered by their mother, though the tearful eye told of the agony within. In the afternoon, to our inexpressible relief, some of our men returned with a supply of that fluid of which we had never before felt the true value.[13]

On their arrival at the Mababe the following day Shobo suddenly reappeared at the head of a party "and commanded the whole of our cavalcade to stop, and to bring forth fire and tobacco, while he coolly sat down and smoked his pipe. It was such an inimitably natural way of showing off that we all stopped to admire the acting, and, though he had previously left us in the lurch, we all liked Shobo, a fine specimen of that wonderful tribe, the Bushmen."

Next day (13 June) they came to a lake-dwelling on piles, on the borders of a marsh where the Mababe terminates. They were now within the realms of Sebituane.

> The country was totally different from anything I knew or could have fancied. . . . It is for hundreds of miles intersected with numerous rivers

and branches of rivers coming out of these and returning into them again.*

This region was of course infested with swarms of mosquitoes which even the indigenous lake-dwellers dreaded, and kept smoky fires burning beneath their huts by night. Oswell and he proceeded 30 miles down the river in a canoe propelled by "five rare good rowers"; the speed, after travelling by wagons, seemed to them "like that of boat races at home". On 18 June they reached the Chobe river and found themselves for the first time among tsetse, the insect which was now to become "a perfect pest to us". Livingstone's observations of the habits of this fly and of its effects on cattle are probably the first ever made. He exposed his hand to the bite of one of them and watched its body turn crimson till, gorged to repletion, it flew away. They kept all their cattle in the reeds by day, in the hope of their being thus protected from the fly. Two days later they were met by an emissary of Sebituane who informed them that the chief was awaiting them on an island 30 miles away, having come himself more than 400 miles to meet them. He had despatched parties to search for them along the Zouga, with considerable presents to the chiefs, desiring them to render the white men all possible assistance and furnish them with guides.

They left Mrs. Livingstone and the children with the wagons on the south bank of the river, and on 21 June, paddling briskly downstream, reached their destination. Livingstone described the chief as "a cool, collected, wiry man of about forty-five, decidedly the best specimen of a native chief I ever met". Oswell's description is fuller and more graphic.

> Presently this really great Chief and man came to meet us, shy and ill at ease. We held out our hands in the accustomed way of true Britons, and I was surprised to see that his mother-wit gave him immediate insight into what was expected of him, and the friendly meaning of our salutation. . . .

* Professor Debenham writes thus of Livingstone: "He had an extraordinary understanding of the whole river system, which he achieved by constant questioning of the inhabitants, added to a real sense of hydrology. There can be little doubt that it was these early journeys in a thirsty land that made him so 'river-wise' and 'water-conscious' for the rest of his life. So ingrained was this feeling for water that in his future journeys he hardly ever crossed a stream without mentioning its size and direction in his notes."

Livingstone entered at once into conversation with him; but throughout that day and the next a sad, half-scared look never faded from his face. . . . But the reality of our coming, with all its possibilities and advantages, seemed to flit through the man's mind as a vision. He killed an ox for us and treated us right royally; he was by far and away the best Kaffir I ever saw. Beloved of the Makololo, he was the fastest runner and best fighter among them; just, though stern, with a wonderful power of attaching men to himself, he was a gentleman in thought and manner. He had allotted to us a bright clean *kotla* for eating and sleeping in, and after supper we lay down on the grass which had been cut for our beds by the thoughtful attention of the Chief.

In the dead of night he paid us a visit alone, and sat down very quietly and mournfully at our fire. Livingstone and I woke up and greeted him, and then he dreamily recounted the history of his life, his wars, escapes, successes and conquests, and the far-distant wandering in his raids. By the fire's glow and flicker among the reeds, with that tall dark earnest speaker and his keenly-attentive listeners, it has always appeared to me one of the most weird scenes I ever saw. With subdued manner and voice Sebituane went on through the live-long night till near the dawn, in low tones only occasionally interrupted by a question from Livingstone. . . .[14]

Instances of their chief's personal bravery in battle, and of his summary way of dealing with deserters, were related to the white men by his followers.

But when during their stay a woman, an attendant of one of his wives who had deserted him, was recaptured in a dreadful plight and brought in to share the same fate as her mistress, Livingstone interceded on her behalf. Sebituane then said, "Shall I kill her after you prayed for her?—Oh no."

Observing that many of his followers wore cheap clothes of European manufacture though their country lay from 1,500 to 1,800 miles from the coast, they were at a loss to account for this, till on the chief's explanation they found that they had reached the southern limit of the slave-trade. This was news to Livingstone of the most momentous consequence.

On the second day Sebituane expressed a wish to be introduced to the white lady, and remarked on arrival at the wagons that their cattle had been bitten by the fly and would certainly die, but begged them not to trouble themselves, "for I have plenty more, and I will give you as many as you need".

This frank and cordial goodwill, added to the strong character and intelligence of the chief, held out high hopes for the prospect of civilization and commerce in the very heart of Africa. "It is impossible," wrote Livingstone, "to overstate the importance we attached to Sebituane"—when suddenly, on 6 July, he succumbed to pneumonia, set up by inflammation from an old spear-wound in his chest.

> I saw his danger but, being a stranger, I feared to treat him medically, lest in the event of his death I should be blamed by his people. . . . On the Sunday afternoon in which he died, when our usual religious service was over, I visited him with my little boy Robert. "Come near," said Sebituane, "and see if I am any longer a man. I am done." He was thus sensible of the dangerous nature of his disease, so I ventured to assent, and added a single sentence regarding hope after death. . . . After sitting with him some time, and commending him to the mercy of God, I rose to depart, when the dying chieftain, raising himself up a little from his prone position, called a servant and said, "Take Robert to Maunku (one of his wives) and tell her to give him some milk." These were the last words of Sebituane.[15]

The same evening his people removed him towards Linyanti, but when still on the way, beside a clump of date bushes where Livingstone and Oswell stood, he expired in his canoe. "I never felt so grieved," wrote Livingstone, "at the death of a black man before." According to native custom he was buried in his cattle-pen, the cattle being driven over and round the grave till it was quite obliterated. Livingstone addressed the people and advised them to hold together and support the heir. "They received our condolences very kindly and took our advice in good part. 'Do not leave us; though Sebituane is gone his children remain, and you must treat them as you would have treated him.'"

Livingstone then broke forth in his Journal into one of those impassioned soliloquies which recall his lament on the death of the unconverted youth Sehamy years before:

> Poor Sebituane! my heart bleeds for thee, and what would I not do for thee now that nothing can be done! Where art thou now? I will weep for thee till the day of my death. Little didst thou think, when in the visit of the white men thou sawest the long-cherished desire of years accomplished, that the sentence of death had gone forth. Thou thoughtest that thou shouldst procure a weapon from the white man which would be a shield from the attacks of the fierce Matabele, but a more deadly dart than theirs was aimed at thee; and though thou couldst well ward off a dart—none better—thou didst not see that of the King of Terrors. I will weep for thee, my brother, and I would cast forth my sorrows in despair for thy condition, but I know thou wilt receive no injustice whither thou art gone. Shall not the judge of all the earth do right? I

leave thee to Him. Alas, alas, Sebituane! I might have said more to him. God forgive me, free me from blood-guiltiness. If I had said more of death I might have been suspected of having foreseen the event and being guilty of bewitching him. I might have recommended Jesus and His great atonement more. It is however very difficult to break through the great crust of ignorance which envelops their minds. . . .

I do not wonder at the Roman Catholics praying for the dead. If I could believe as they do I would pray for them too. . . .[16]

Chapter Ten

FROM THE ZAMBESI TO THE CAPE
1851–1852

"Providence seems to call me to the regions beyond."

THE death of Sebituane rendered it necessary for the travellers to await permission to proceed northwards from his successor, a daughter, and her reply involved five weeks' delay. Their objective was now a great river, of which the chief had told them, called Sesheke. Oswell had planned to return to England early in 1852, but was persuaded by Livingstone to stay on and share with him its discovery. Whilst waiting they drew up several maps of the Linyanti district with its vast system of interconnected waterways and swamps, from their own observations and from native reports: one of these is appended to Oswell's biography and is surprisingly accurate. In a private letter written long afterwards to the Rev. Dr. Blaikie, Oswell reveals the fact that it was here and now that his friend first determined upon finding a route through Central Africa to the Atlantic. It provides an interesting sidelight on his habitual taciturnity.

> He had a way of repeating his intentions baldly and without any explanation. After we had been lying some time on the Chobe river he suddenly announced his intention of going down to the west coast. We were about 1,800 miles off it. To my reiterated objection that it would be impossible—"I'm going down. I mean to go down" was the only answer. . . . Not till long afterwards did I realise that he was speaking of a future intention just then born.[1]

On 31 July they received a favourable reply from Sebituane's daughter, and leaving Mary and the children at Chobe camp proceeded north-eastwards on horseback, partly through dense jungle swamps, swimming their horses through the rivers, a distance of 100 miles. On August 4 they reached the southern bank of the Sesheke which proved to be none other than the upper reaches of the Zambesi: "a most important point, for that river was not previously known to exist there". They were transported with joy at the sight and Livingstone wrote to his brother Charles, "It is the first *river* I ever saw". The water happened to be so rough that they had difficulty in procuring a canoe, but at length an old man appeared and ferried them across to the town of Sesheke where, "as we were the very first white men the inhabitants had ever seen, we were visited by prodigious numbers". They were told of rapids above the river, and of a cataract called *Mosioatunya*—"smoke which sounds"—below. It was now late afternoon and they had eaten nothing since the previous night (and then only two biscuits apiece), but must wait perforce till the people had satiated their curiosity in gazing upon them. At length they were regaled by a sickly-looking man and a drunken lady, and soon afterwards returned to the other side to sleep with their horses. "The waves were running so high, it was only by great persuasion I could induce the people to paddle us back."

Livingstone spent many hours in making exhaustive enquiries into the nature and extent of the slave-trade. He was told—and accepted as truth—that it had only commenced in the previous year, with a tribe to the west called the Mambari (half-caste Portuguese), who sold guns, baize, calico and other clothing, in exchange for boys of about fourteen years of age—one gun, one boy. Two hundred boys, captured in raids, had already been sold. Sebituane had himself confessed that he needed the guns as a protection against attacks by the Matabele, and had offered—though in vain—to purchase them with cattle or ivory. "But for the unwillingness of Lechulatebe to allow us to pass, we should have been with Sebituane in time to have prevented the slave-traffic from commencing at all. The Makololo declare that they never heard of people being bought and sold till then, and disliked it, but the desire to possess the guns prevailed. . . . I have never known in Africa an instance of a parent selling his own offspring."[2]

These conversations were sufficient to convince Livingstone where his path of duty lay henceforward. It was to put an end to the slave-traffic by introducing legitimate trade along the highway of the Zambesi. With this project Oswell cordially agreed, but to achieve it some preliminary exploration would be necessary.

Our plan was that I should remain in pursuit of my objects as a missionary, while Mr. Oswell explored the Zambesi to the east. For such an undertaking I know none better qualified than my friend Mr. Oswell. He has courage and prudence equal to any emergency, and possesses that qualification moreover so essential in a traveller, of gaining the confidence of the natives while maintaining the dignity of a gentleman.[3]

But Oswell found the immense marshes and the prevalence of the tsetse insuperable barriers to a speedy advance; and Livingstone for a good reason was anxious to rejoin his wife without undue delay. Moreover they were still some days distant from the late chief's daughter, without whose permission nothing could be definitely settled. Both recognized the possibility of ultimate success, and it was with great reluctance that they abandoned the project for this year. The Makololo were equally reluctant to see them go. They offered to make for them a garden, and to fulfil Sebituane's promise to supply them with cattle. Consideration of the latter point provokes an interesting digression in Livingstone's Journal on Christian ethics. It begins with the question: "Is it right to receive them? They have probably been stolen", and ends with the quotation, "Whatsoever is sold in the shambles, that eat."[4]

He was well aware of the insalubrity of the Linyanti district for European settlement: the low-lying swamps were a death-trap for all but the most hardened; the healthier hilly regions were exposed to invasion by Mosilikatse and his Matabele. He was forced to the conclusion that the hopes on which he had set such store must be abandoned: he could nowhere find a residence for his family. Moreover the problem of their future education was causing him concern. They were growing up with a knowledge of the native languages, and he could not subject them to the demoralizing influence of filthy conversation and filthy manners. And yet he knew that his own immediate and pressing duty was here—here in the heart of Africa—where the needs and the risks were greatest. He was driven by circumstances to a conflict of loyalties such as he had never experienced before, nor ever would again. He had, we are told, no secrets from his friend, and "at night over the camp-fire poured into his most sympathetic ears his ambitions, his troubles, his anxieties". Oswell's contribution to these discussions would appear to be that, if Livingstone intended to return to Linyanti for a prolonged stay (and this seemed necessary), then his wife and family must return to civilization.

Inspanning their oxen on the southern bank of the Chobe, which was free from tsetse, on August 13 they lengthened their homeward journey for the sake of water by travelling westward along a tributary of the Tamanakle to the river itself and thence to its junction with the Zouga, where on September 15 Mary gave birth to her fifth child, named William Oswell in compliment to their "brave and generous friend" (but the boy was called by his nickname "Zouga"). Here too Oswell's letter has a curious reminiscence:

> Again on the Zouga I found him determinedly set on remaining in a grassless locality for eight days. After several fruitless objections eliciting the same obstinate replies, "I'm going to stay", Oswell said. "Come, out with it! What's the matter?" "Oh, nothing. . . . Mrs. L. had a little son last night." So I waited eight days very willingly, but I had a deal of trouble to get the reason out of him.[5]

The circumstances preceding and attending this event were similar to those which Mary had undergone only a little more than a year before, and with disastrous consequences. An attempt has been made above to explain, though not to justify, Livingstone's conduct in this matter; but nothing can be said to extenuate the gratuitous insolence with which he wrote to his father-in-law in announcing the event:

> What you say about difference of opinion is true. In my past life I have always managed to think for myself, and act accordingly. I have occasionally met with people who took it on themselves to act for me, and they have offered their thoughts with an emphatic 'I think'; but I have generally excused them on the score of being a little soft-headed in believing they could think both for me and themselves.[6]

There is no record to tell whether he ever apologized for these words. And they are all the more blameworthy from the fact that his wife, again as a result of her confinement, was afflicted with a recurrence of the partial paralysis which had beset her before. This at any rate alarmed him and increased his anxiety to get her to the Cape as soon as possible.

But more than eight days' cessation from travel were evidently necessary, since on October 1 he wrote to Tidman from the banks of the Zouga a letter which gives the first indication of maturing plans:

You will see by the accompanying sketch what an immense region God in His Providence has opened up. If we can enter in and form a settlement we shall be able in the course of a very few years to put a stop to the slave-trade in that quarter. . . . If I were to follow my own inclinations, they would lead me to settle down quietly with the Bakwains or some other small tribe and devote some of my time to my children. But Providence seems to call me to the regions beyond.[7]

They were still on the Zouga when he wrote again on the 17th at greater length a letter which is virtually a repetition and an extension of the first. His object in journeying to the Zambesi was not merely with a view to discovery, but to effect a settlement in the hilly country, "and though to some extent unsuccessful, I think I erred on the right side in attempting much". He doubts whether the erection of "comfortable establishments" is the best way of propagating Christianity, since the tribes are generally nomadic:

... and though I have undergone much fatigue and manual labour in rearing three such, I would cheerfully undergo much more if it should prove a sanatorium for more unhealthy districts.

After giving a very detailed description of the nature of the country and the condition of the tribes inhabiting it, he states his conviction that it should be made a highway to and from the coast, either east or west, for the spread of Christian civilization and legitimate commerce.

The tokens of Divine care which have already bestowed, and a full conviction that I am in the path of duty, induce me to offer myself for this service. . . . Nothing but a strong conviction that the step will tend to the Glory of Christ would make me orphanize my children. Even now my bowels yearn over them—they will forget me. But I hope when the day of trial comes I shall not be found a more sorry soldier than those who served an earthly sovereign. Should you not feel yourselves justified in incurring the expense of their support in England, I shall feel called upon to renounce the hope of carrying the gospel into that country. . . . But stay, I am not sure, so powerfully convinced am I that it is the will of our Lord I should, I will go—no matter who opposes. But from you I expect nothing but encouragement. . . .[8]

He was asking much from the Directors, but he was offering more than had ever been heard of by them or any other Missionary Society.

It was on this journey that Livingstone met William Frederick Webb, the third of the big-game hunters who was to prove a life-long friend. Hearing of Webb's serious illness some distance from Kolobeng, he set off at once in search of him and brought him to Kolobeng for recuperation: "he was thus the last of the Livingstones' white visitors, and one of the few who saw the Doctor surrounded by his family in the only real home he ever possessed".[9]

On arrival at Kolobeng from Lake Ngami they found the station deserted. Sechele and his tribe had removed, as indeed they expected, to a water some ten miles distant, named Limaue, where native corn could be grown. Next day however he arrived to greet them and presented them with an ox—a valuable gift for the continuance of the long journey south.

It had been agreed that a general halt of a few days should be made at Kolobeng, and it was a surprise and a disappointment to the Livingstones that Oswell, without vouchsafing any explanation of his change of mind, expressed his intention of pushing on immediately alone.[10] His intention became apparent later, when they reached the Cape. Meanwhile Livingstone wrote to Tidman:

> But for the disinterested kindness of Mr. Oswell we could not have come down to the Cape. He presented supplies for last year's journey worth £40, for that to Sebituane upwards of £20, also a wagon worth £55.

But he had been obliged to purchase another wagon, new wagon sails, and several oxen, besides paying off extra drivers. In the result, he had spent the whole of this year's salary and more than half that for 1853. "We have used no delicacies of any kind besides tea and coffee. I have been a teetotaller for 20 years." Neither did he ever smoke.

With Livingstone's departure from Kolobeng ends the first stage of his career, that is, as an itinerant missionary among the Bechuana in the waterless regions of the high veldt. For eleven years he had undergone more physical hardship than had fallen to the lot of any pioneer, and this without damage to his constitution. There is an entry in his Journal for June 12 of this year which deserves comment:

> No one knows the value of water till he is deprived of it. We never need any spirits to qualify it or prevent an immense draught of it doing us harm. I have drunk water swarming with insects, thick with mud and putrid from rhinoceros urine and buffaloes' dung, and no stinted draughts of it either, yet never felt any inconvenience from it.

His grandson, Dr. Hubert F. Wilson, M.C., who as an officer in the R.A.M.C. served in Africa during the first great war, wrote in reply to a query on this point from the present writer:

> Did he boil his water?—To this I would say, probably No—not at this stage, though he did so towards the end of his last journey: the germs (to kill which succeeding travellers boiled water, as you and I did) were not then discovered, nor was their existence as a cause of disease suspected. My reading of his life suggests that he traded on his sound healthy constitution and got away with it, until in the end a dysenteric type of disorder carried him off.

An answer to the question how he escaped sunstroke is of course simpler, pith-helmets having been discarded in the tropics since 1930 without injurious results. "The Livingstone peaked cap was the nautical cap which he would see used alike in temperate and tropical climates," says his grandson. But there is another question which admits of no ready reply: how did he escape sleeping-sickness, and not only so, but why (though he frequently mentions the ravages of the *tsetse morsitans* among domesticated animals) does he never once record, in all the fly-infested areas he traversed, a single instance of the fatal effects of the *tsetse trypanosoma* to man? The present writer, and of course others, have seen whole villages in the Zambesi and Loangwa valleys decimated and even exterminated by the disease. Are we to suppose that the *trypanosoma* type of tsetse was inactive in Livingstone's day? Or did he possibly mistake its more deadly infection for that of chronic malaria, which, so prevalent in the region of lakes and swamps infested with the *anopheles* mosquito, he dreaded for his family and called "African fever"? To use his own words in another connection, "This curious point deserves the attention of enquirers".

During a short halt at Kuruman he had been gravely concerned about his father-in-law's health, which had suffered severely from his intense application to sedentary work, and on arrival at the Cape wrote to Tidman on March 17: "My opinion expressed to him with sufficient earnestness, was that he ought to lay aside his translation and seek the re-establishment of his health on the sea coast." But Moffat's finances did not permit of this, and his son-in-law takes occasion to chide the Directors for their "injustice" towards him in the matter of salary. They had charged the expense of his son John's voyage to Mr. Moffat's account, which, in the case of one of their own sons, "would have been charged to the general funds" (!). The salary of the "Apostle of the Bechuana" is considerably less than that of any missionary in the Colony.[11] Sufficiently curt language to a Director!

The Livingstones reached Cape Town on 16 March 1852, after six months' travel from the Chobe river, to find that their benefactor had placed a further large sum to their credit. To make the gift more easy of acceptance Oswell offered it with the remark that it was merely profit on the sale of ivory from the Livingstones' estate! "He assisted me in every possible way. May God reward him!" "The best friend we had in Africa", wrote Livingstone again and again.

His wife and their four children sailed from the Cape on 23 April. It was a moment of heart-break for them all. He found some relief in writing to them by every mail. The first letter is dated 5 May and sent by the mail-steamer which would anticipate their arrival in England.

> My dearest Mary—How I miss you now, and the dear children! My heart yearns incessantly over you. How many thoughts of the past crowd into my mind! I feel as if I would treat you all more tenderly and lovingly than ever. . . . I never show my feelings; but I can say truly, my dearest, that I loved you when I married you, and the longer I lived with you, I loved you the better. . . .[12]

He had now had his troublesome uvula cut out, and began to preach in English before his throat was healed, feeling at first as nervous in doing so as he had felt at Ongar.

> [To Moffat.] What a little thing is sufficient to bring down to old-wifeishness such a rough tyke as I consider myself! Poor proud human nature is a great fool after all.

Livingstone lodged with the Society's new Agent, the Rev. William Thompson and his family, during his stay in Cape Town. He had formerly been a missionary in South India and, returning to England to be married in 1840 to a daughter of the Rev. Dr. Wardlaw, had met Livingstone at Mrs. Sewell's boarding-house in Aldersgate Street. He was now to prove one of his staunchest allies and most loyal friends.

To him Livingstone related the true story of "Sechele's Cooking-Pot" and Thompson requested him to commit it to writing. When next year a Boer named Kotse accused Livingstone in *The Cape Town Mail* of having provided natives with ammunition, Thompson replied on 23 April 1853 that "this most unjust reflection on the character of that enterprising missionary makes it necessary to lay this paper before the public."[13]

Another friend was Thomas Maclear, the Astronomer Royal. "Having publicly invited anyone to make observations on certain stars, he engaged to observe them simultaneously and make calculations." Livingstone now took the opportunity to seek advice and further tuition in the art of navigation from this friendly and enthusiastic astronomer, with results that were momentous for geography.

He sorely needed these friendships, for his stay at the Cape was fraught, not only with the sorrow of parting from his wife and children, but also with much anxiety and trouble. The latest Kaffir War, of twenty months' duration, was still in progress and he made no secret of where his sympathies and antipathies lay.

On 1 June he began to write a paper for publication in the *London Gazette* and in the *Morning Herald*. But it expanded into something the size of a pamphlet and apparently was never sent. It is a scathing indictment of the injustice and inconsistency of British officialdom in the Cape, the full facts of which, he avers, cannot be known to the British Government and people at home. This paper, now deposited in the Central African Archives, is worthy of being reproduced in its entirety; some passages may be quoted here.

> We are no advocates for war but we would prefer perpetual war to perpetual slavery. No nation ever secured liberty without fighting for it. And every nation on earth worthy of freedom is ready to shed its blood in its defence. We sympathise with the Caffres; we side with the weak against the strong. Savages they are, but surely deserving of Independence seeing they have fought right gallantly for it for upwards of twenty months. . . . It has been termed the Hottentot Rebellion. A great deal of stuff has been said and written about the *sin* of such rebellion. Of course when unsuccessful it is a sin. When attended with success it is lofty patriotism. . . . But whether sin or patriotism, rebellion is invariably *prima facie* evidence of bad government.

While in Cape Town, Livingstone continued his correspondence with Tidman, from whom he received replies when on his northward journey. These letters reveal aspects of a rugged character chequered with light and shade—the latter showing somewhat like seams of clay in the rifts of a granite boulder.

On April 14 1852, Tidman had written confirming the Directors' approval of Livingstone's plan for a two years' sojourn in Sebituane's country, but they were decided that he should not attempt the journey *alone*, and suggested Mr. Ashton as a suitable companion. To this Livingstone replied sarcastically that "they might as well send the Lieutenant-Governor as Mr. Ashton". The only suitable companion for him would be Mr. Moffat, but that is impossible. He adds: "I am not given to despondency. I enjoy a perpetual flow of good spirits."

He had concluded a previous letter with a denigration of his former colleagues, of whom he could never think but in terms of disparagement. "You will see no success in that region so long as Inglis and Edwards are your missionaries. . . ."

Tidman's reply to these mordant effusions is, though ponderous in style, a model of discretion and restraint. The Directors' views as to the desirability of a companion remain unchanged, but they commend him with all sympathy and affection to the gracious Providence of God. They regret the tone of his animadversions against Messrs. Inglis and Edwards, and would remind him that *ex parte* representations are little calculated to promote the cause of equity. With regard to his previous remarks alleging inequalities in the allowances to missionaries, this by implication involves a charge of mismanagement on the part of the Directors, but a person viewing an object from an isolated aspect is liable to misinterpret measures applied to a wide scale. They are however aware that some of these demand attention and will seek to apply the proper remedy.[14]

Livingstone received this very moderate and conciliatory letter when northward-bound from Kuruman, and at once put upon it what seems nothing less than a perverse and deliberate misconstruction.

Taking the last paragraph of Tidman's letter first, he says that it does not affect his own remarks on the relative expenditure on missions in the Colony and those beyond it, since these were based on data published over a series of years and cannot be affected by "our mode of viewing them". Then follows this piece of downright impertinence.

> Having full reliance on the purity of motive which influences and controls the general administration of the Directors, I imagined that their attention might be drawn to certain inequalities without impugning their integrity, and even now, if we push aside for a little the very laudable touchiness on the subject of management, my remarks may be viewed as implying no more than want of faith in their omniscience.

As to his unfavourable comments upon some of his brethren, he had been enjoined by the Society's letter of instructions to present statements from time to time on the course of events and opinions relative to the spread of Christianity.

> But when winding up my connection with that part of the country it seemed natural and proper to obey the positive injunction of the Directors and give a general view of the causes of the failure of the mission in the Kolobeng district.[15]

It does little to extenuate the sarcastic tone of this tirade to add that Livingstone was probably right in his views both of the expenditure and of the personnel of the Mission, and that these were shared in principle, though not expressed so forcibly, by Moffat. The Directors, sober virtuous citizens in far-off London, could hardly view the situation in the same perspective as those on active service in the field, but, if lacking in perspicacity, they at least possessed good manners and they do not appear to have replied to this communication. Perhaps the difference may be expressed by saying that whereas the outlook of some of the missionaries was parochial, and that of the Directors was provincial, Livingstone's was continental.

He had intended to leave the Cape a week after Mary's departure, but was detained for six weeks longer by the difficulty of securing supplies. "Never surely before or since did a traveller prepare for a plunge into the unknown with resources so small." He was so distrusted by the authorities for his sympathy with the negroes that they would hardly sell him powder and shot, or even percussion-caps. To Moffat he wrote that he was cordially hated and perhaps might be pulled up; his father-in-law must not be surprised if he saw him abused in the newspapers. "At the last moment a troublesome country postmaster, to whom he had complained of an overcharge on

Two unpublished miniatures taken at Cape Town, April 1852

By permission, London Missionary Society

postage, threatened an action against him for defamation of character, and rather than be further detained, deep in debt though he was, Livingstone had to pay him a considerable sum"[16]—actually £13. Penniless, bereaved, and almost friendless, regarded with suspicion and dislike by his own countrymen and with hatred by the Boers, it must have been with relief that he said farewell to the Cape. When he returned to it six years later he was acclaimed by all as a national hero.

Meanwhile his pen had not been idle: Papers on the geography of South Africa; on the philology of the Bantu races, and on their religious beliefs; articles on Christian missions for the *British Quarterly Review*, and on the Boers for the *British Banner*, besides those already mentioned on the Hottentot War. "But the editorial cold-shoulder was beyond even his power of endurance, and he laid aside his pen in a kind of disgust." Five years later reputable English periodicals were offering him £100 for a single article.

Chapter Eleven

THE WRECK OF KOLOBENG
1852

"I will go—no matter who opposes."

AT long last on 8 June 1852 Livingstone—"with his wagon loaded to double the usual weight from his good nature in taking everybody's packages"—pulled out from the Cape. He had arranged with a mercantile friend, Mr. H. E. Rutherfoord, to assist a native trader, George Fleming, in introducing lawful traffic into the Linyanti district. Fleming joined him later at Kuruman. Meanwhile he was accompanied by two Kuruman converts—"than whom I never saw better servants anywhere"; two Bakwain men; and two girls from Kolobeng who had come as nurses with the children to the Cape.

> Wagon-travelling in Africa has been so often described, that I need say no more than that it is a prolonged system of picnicking, excellent for the health, and agreeable to those who are not over fastidious about trifles, and who delight in being in the open air.[1]

In contrast to the mood of despondency that marked his long detention at the Cape, his lively letters to Thompson en route read like those of a boy setting forth on a holiday. His cares were all behind him now, and though the journey proved a chapter of accidents and mishaps, these seem only to have added to the fun of it all. His first stop was at Paarl, where he bought a horse of the Rev. George Barker, and wrote on the 9th:

> I reached this yesterday evening without falling into mischief once, although I had no one to take care of me! . . . Gave an address—which shows how very firmly I can hold to my resolution of not speaking again till I get back to my own country. . . . I hope a sense of gratitude for your disinterested friendship will never be effaced from my heart. Many

152

thanks to Miss Thompson for her kind attentions to a poor forlorn widower from the Sesheke—and love to all the children.[2]

From Skeit Fontein he forwarded "the fulmination of the Commandant Potgieter", who, he heard, had gone to a tribunal. This reminded him that when his Bakwains heard of it they had instantly summoned a *Picho* "and resolved unanimously to defend their missionary with their blood. On my objecting to their exposing their lives on my account, they replied that whatever was done to me was done to them."

Had Potgieter come he would have met a very different reception from any he ever had before. . . . His fighting has been a series of cold-blooded murders. . . .

The wagon is however enormously heavy. This loading is one of those things I shall do but once in my life. We had to pass through a bad defile and hired a span from a Boer to take us through. He took us into it, but his large fat oxen could not move it farther. I inspanned our meagre beasts and they walked out with it at once. The Boer then left us in disgust and, when we had got fairly through, wanted payment, but this I declined. I shall feel glad when I deliver the articles to their owners. The woodwork of the wheels cracks from the enormous strain. There now, take a lesson by my folly. . . .[3]

Thompson had given him some advice about the management of oxen.

I tried your plan on one ox, and he became a beauty and so tame. All the Boers wanted to exchange him, and, poor fellow, he was drowned in the Orange River. Three fell into a muddy place on a Saturday evening. We all worked the whole night trying to get them out of the sloughy bank, and as morning dawned the finest of the whole lot expired. You may guess how eagerly we toiled when I mention that when daylight appeared I thought it was only about twelve o'clock.

Worse, if possible, was to come. Soon after crossing the river at Priestcar,

The enormous weight told on one of the wheels and down came the elegant Dutch vehicle, the South African coach and ten, on to its marrow bones. Mr. Hughes kindly lent me a wheel, and by the assistance of himself and some of my old patients I managed to crawl to this place [Kuruman]. I was sometimes vexed with myself for having loaded up so much, but when I reached the places where I could off-load it gave me sincere pleasure to hand the goods to the owners.

He had reached Kuruman on 27 August—the very day, though he did not know it then, that the Boers encamped before Kolobeng. He was joined at Kuruman on 6 September by George Fleming and on the same day wrote to Thompson.

> Edwards has left his station and the people of Mabotsa have come over to Sechele. The Boers are reported by an individual who came here two days ago to be encamped at Mabotsa. They contemplate rooting out Sechele, and wait only till two or three of their party return from the Lake. . . . They may find it more difficult to subdue Sechele than they dream of. But their plan is to secure the whole country to themselves and prevent traders and travellers from going beyond them. . . .

He seems however to dismiss this rumour lightly. He is more interested in his own good fortune in breathing again the pure air of the desert instead of the "effluvia" of the Cape, and exchanging the artificialities of civilization for a simple life. "I could not breathe freely till I got over the Orange River."[4]

But a fortnight later, on 20 September, he added a post-script: "You will see by Mr. Moffat's to you the doings of Dr. Robertson's dearly beloved brethren. I mourn over my books and medicines, instruments, etc. Please say nothing about my losses. . . . Many thanks for the Psalter and other books—doubly precious now."

The wreck of Kolobeng is a signpost indicative of a period of transition in South African history. One of Livingstone's biographers, looking forward from the event, sees it as "one facet of the colour-problem that is the cause of so much of the unrest of the world".

> It is impossible to conceive his having taken any other stand than that which he took. A born fighter, raised in the Scots tradition of freedom . . . it was inevitable that he should espouse the cause of the African with all the impetuosity of his Highland nature. This he did, however, from no dislike of the Dutch. Far from that, while criticising their attitude towards the 'sons of Ham', he liked and admired the farmers in the settled parts of the country, especially the older men. Both in their theology and in their general outlook on life, they reminded him of his father.
> It was with the younger hot-heads who formed the spear-head of the northern drang that he clashed.[5]

Another, looking backward from the event, sees it as the inevitable consequence of the British authorities' refusal to heed the warning of John Philip ten years before. "It had been mainly owing to Philip's agitation that in 1843 the Trekkers had been brought under control in Natal" and no discrimination allowed there in law between black and white. But this policy had not been followed up and enforced in the new emigrant Boer settlement in the Transvaal. It was British weakness in this matter that "led ultimately to the tragedy of Kolobeng".

Livingstone was no pacifist though patient in the extreme in his dealings with armed or hostile parties or individuals. He believed in the moral use of physical force to restrain the predatory and homicidal proclivities of the unruly and malevolent among whom his lot was cast. . . . There is no doubt that he would have coerced the Boers by British military force if he could . . . and it is not too much to say that had his advice been followed at this period, much subsequent trouble and bloodshed would have been saved in South Africa.[6]

Since the immediate causes of the tragedy have been a matter of debate from time to time ever since its occurrence, it is worthwhile to devote some space to Livingstone's own several accounts of what occurred. Though to some extent they overlap, they view the matter from different aspects—both personal and political.

[To his wife, 20 September 1852.] Along with this I send you a long letter; this I write in order to give you the latest news. The Boers gutted our house at Kolobeng; they brought four wagons down and took away sofa, table, bed, all the crockery, your desk (I hope it had nothing in it— have you the letters?), smashed the wooden chairs, took away the iron ones, tore out the leaves of all the books, and scattered them in front of the house, smashed the bottles containing medicines, windows, oven-door, took away the smith-bellows, anvil, all the tools—in fact everything worth taking: three corn-mills, a bag of coffee for which I paid six pounds, and lots of coffee, tea, and sugar, which the gentlemen who went to the north left; took all our cattle and Paul's and Mebalwe's. They then went up to Limaue, went to church morning and afternoon, and heard Mebalwe preach! After the second service they told Sechele that they had come to fight, because he allowed Englishmen to proceed to the North, though they had repeatedly ordered him not to do so. He replied that he was a man of peace, that he could not molest Englishmen, because they had never done him any harm, and always treated him well. In the morning they commenced firing on the town with swivels, and set fire to it. The heat forced some of the women to flee, the men to huddle together on the small hill in the middle of the town; the smoke prevented them seeing the Boers, and the cannon killed many, sixty (60) Bakwains. The Boers then came near to kill and destroy them all, but the Bakwains killed thirty-five (35), and many horses. They fought the whole day, but the Boers could not dislodge them. They stopped firing in the evening, and then the Bakwains retired on account of having no water. The above sixty are not all men; women and children are among the slain. The Boers were 600, and they had 700 natives with them. All the corn is burned. Parties went out and burned Bangwaketse town, and swept off all the cattle. All the Bakhatla cattle gone. Neither Bangwaketse nor Bakhatla fired a shot. All the corn burned of the whole three tribes. Everything edible is taken from them. How will they live? They told Sechele that the Queen had given off the land to them, and henceforth they were the masters—had abolished chieftainship. . . . I wonder what the Peace Society would do with these worthies?[7]

[To Watt.] I am lightened by the Boers of property worth upwards of £300. I shall move all the more lightly to the new region. . . . Think of a big fat Boeress drinking coffee out of my kettle and then throwing her tallow corporiety on my sofa, or keeping her needles in my wife's writing-desk. Ugh! . . . The Boers are very anxious to get my head, they are mad with rage against me because my people fought bravely. It was I, they think, who taught them to shoot Boers. Fancy your reverend friend teaching the young idea how to shoot Boers! As I have still some use for my head I will keep it out of their way till they are out of the way. Then Hurrah for the North![8]

[To Thompson.] Enclosed you will perceive a letter which I have ventured to address to the Lieutenant Governor. . . . My reason for troubling you is that you may exercise your judgment on whether it ought to be delivered at all. From it, and Mr. Moffat's letter, you will have a pretty clear idea of the doings of Dr. Robertson's converts. . . .

They went the whole hog—attended Church on Sunday hearing Mebalwe preach, and then made the parson flee for his life on Monday. He ran the gauntlet—some of them calling out when they saw him with clothes on, "Here is the chief!"—and then the bullets whistled over, behind and before him. He seems to have become rather terrified—ran through the midst of the Boers so fast that his feet were dreadfully bruised. He has lost all he had: 7 head of cattle, and his furniture, etc. His house was burned by these *Christians*. . . . Some fine young men whom I knew and loved, have fallen. My heart is sore when I think of them. Sechele had two bullets through his hat and a third through his coat sleeve. The Boers have lost one of their principal men. . . .

The destruction of my property is a fortunate thing for me. There is not a native in the country but knows on whose side I am. The Boers in plundering my house often expressed great regret that they had not got a hold of me. "But we shall catch him yet," said they. How good God's providence is to me! I was detained in Cape Town till I fretted, and then again on the way up. . . . [9]

[To Tidman.] . . . Had I been able to travel as quickly as my desires dictated I should have been at Kolobeng at the very time of the attack. . . . It is necessary to distinguish between the Colonial Boers of Dutch extraction who are usually called Boers, and those in the Interior of the same name whose independence has lately been acknowledged by the Government. The latter are the dregs of the Colonial population.

. . . If they had made any use of my books and medicines I could have forgiven them; but tearing, smashing, and burning them was beyond measure galling.[10]

His formal protest to the Lieutenant-Governor, which contains the completest account of the whole affair, is printed in full in Campbell's *Livingstone*. By way of a jocular postscript to this he wrote to Tidman:

My property having been destroyed in express violation of the Treaty I can scarcely expect any compensation, but I thought the more noise we made the less likely would they be to do the same thing over again. But the more I become acquainted with the present Governor, Sir George Cathcart's, feelings, the less hope I have of the least favour being shown to anything in the shape of either missionary or Hottentot. Indeed, it would be unspeakably pleasing to Sir George to hang us all on one gibbet. He will never forgive the Hottentots for completely foiling him in the war, nor us missionaries because our belief that the Hottentots have souls has turned out true.[11]

In *Travels* he wrote an indictment of the Boers' treatment of the natives, which is all the more trenchant for its studied restraint, appealing to the Commandant Krieger for confirmation of its truth. He rejects with ridicule "the credit of having taught the tribe to kill Boers". With regard to his personal losses he adds:

The books of a good library—my solace in our solitude—were not taken away, but handfuls of the leaves were torn out and scattered over the place. My stock of medicines was smashed; and all our furniture and clothing carried off and sold at public auction to pay the expenses of the foray.

I do not mention these things by way of making a pitiful wail over my losses, nor in order to excite commiseration; for though I do feel sorry for the loss of lexicons, dictionaries, etc., which had been the companions of my boyhood, yet, after all, the plundering only set me free for my expedition to the north, and I have never since had a moment's concern for anything I left behind. *The Boers resolved to shut up the interior, and I determined to open the country; and we shall see who have been most successful in resolution—they or I.*[12]

But the tale would be incomplete without the testimony of Sechele whose wife brought a letter from him to Moffat in Kuruman a fortnight afterwards. "She had hidden herself in a cleft of a rock, over which a number of Boers were firing. Her infant began to cry, and, terrified that this should attract the notice of the men, the muzzles of whose guns appeared at every discharge over her head, she took off her armlets as playthings to quieten the child." The letter, literally translated, read as follows:

> Friend of my heart's love, and of all the confidence of my heart, I am Sechele: I am undone by the Boers who attacked me, though I had no guilt with them. They demanded that I should be in their kingdom, and I refused; they demanded that I should prevent English and Griquas from passing (northwards). I replied, These are my friends, and I can prevent no one (of them). They came on Saturday, and I besought them not to fight on Sunday, and they assented. They began on Monday morning at twilight, and fired with all their might, and burned the town with fire, and scattered us. They killed sixty of my people, and captured women and children and men. And the mother of Baleriling (a former wife of Sechele) they also took prisoner. They took all the cattle and all the goods of the Bakwains; and the house of Livingstone they plundered, taking away all his goods. The number of wagons they had was eighty-five, and a cannon; and after they had stolen my own wagon and that of Macabe, then the number of their wagons (counting the cannon as one) was eighty-eight. All the goods of the hunters (certain English gentlemen hunting and exploring in the north) were burned in the town; and of the Boers were killed twenty-eight. Yes, my beloved friend, now my wife goes to see the children, and Kobus Hae will convey her to you.
>
> I am SECHELE, the son of Mochoasele.[13]

To this Livingstone adds with pardonable sarcasm:

> Very soon after Pretorius had sent the marauding party against Kolobeng, he was called away to the tribunal of infinite justice. His policy is justified by the Boers generally from the instructions given to the Jewish warriors in Deuteronomy, xx, 10–14. Hence, when he died, the obituary notice ended with "Blessed are the dead who die in the Lord".

Sechele (probably on Moffat's advice) went at once to Bloemfontein and laid his grievance before the British Resident, who forwarded it to Sir George Cathcart, the Governor at the Cape. Livingstone's letter was supported by a complaint from the L.M.S. to the Secretary of State, who desired Cathcart to report. But Cathcart was inimical to missionaries and antipathetic to native rights, and he had in hand a trump card to play. By the terms of the Sand River Convention the British Government had limited its own jurisdiction only so far as to the Vaal River, and had vaguely ceded to the Boer emigrants the right "to manage their own affairs" beyond it without interference. He could therefore, without instituting any judicial enquiry, write to the British Resident:

> You will be pleased to acquaint the Chief Sechele that, although I am unacquainted with the circumstances which may have led to hostilities between his people and the Trans-Vaal emigrants, and cannot attempt to judge their relative merits, I sincerely lament his recent losses; but my military command does not extend beyond the Vaal, without special orders from home, and that, although this matter shall be referred, I cannot hold out any hope to him that H.M. Government will authorize any armed intervention between powers situated beyond the Vaal. . . .

Livingstone received an even dustier answer. "His losses and inconveniences do not, in my view, amount to more than the ordinary occurrences incidental to a state of war, or to which those who live in remote regions beyond Her Majesty's dominions must frequently be liable."[14] It is certain, however, that had the affair occurred during the rule of Cathcart's predecessor, Sir Harry Smith, whose sympathies and policy were the reverse of his, it would have met with a very different reaction. Not until 1884, and after many vacillations in policy, was Bechuanaland declared a British Protectorate, and then only by resort to force of arms.

Such are the facts concerning the raid and the method in which it was conducted, and no historian with Boer sympathies has ventured to gainsay any of them, nor can any person with feelings of decency deny that it was barbarous and abominable. The question in dispute is whether an attack of any sort on the Bakwena people, or on Livingstone's property or person, was justified. One nationalist historian of the Transvaal attempted a somewhat shamefaced defence on the ground that the raid was a reprisal for some atrocities perpetrated by the Bakwena against the invaders, but without adducing a shred of evidence for such.

> Dr. Livingstone was a strong partisan of the Bantu, and did his utmost to oppose the claim of the immigrant farmers to dominion over the clan with which he was living, so that his statements are those of an advocate rather than those of a judge. He represented Sechele as wholly in the right, and the farmers as wholly in the wrong: but any impartial writer who examines Sechele's own account of the matter, as given by himself personally to the Governor in Capetown, must come to a different conclusion.

Wars cannot be carried on without cruelty, but in these contests acts were sometimes performed which exceeded the limit regarded as permissible by civilized nations. . . .[15]

It happened that among the raiders was a young field-cornet, then aged twenty-seven, named Paul Kruger. He took part in it as a commandant. He was twice in danger. A ball from a Boer gun rebounding from a rock struck him senseless for a time; and another from a Bakwain ripped open his jacket. His *Memoirs* were edited for publication in 1902 by a clergyman, the Rev. Dr. A. Schowalter, who quotes from them as follows:

. . . Sechele was protecting another Kaffir chief, called Moselele,* who had committed several murders in the South African Republic, and refused to deliver him up. . . . A commando under Chief Commandant Scholtz with myself as deputy commandant, was sent to punish him. . . .

After hostilities were concluded, Commandant Scholtz sent up to the house of Livingstone, the English missionary, which was not far from the Kaffir town. Here Theunis Pretorius found a complete workshop for repairing guns, a quantity of materials of war which Livingstone was storing for Sechele. This was a breach of the Sand River Convention of 1852, which laid down that neither arms nor ammunition should be supplied to the Kaffirs, and that they should not be permitted to provide either for themselves. Scholtz accordingly confiscated the missionary's arsenal, and in consequence the Boers were abused by Livingstone throughout the length and breadth of England, and slandered in every possible way as enemies of the missionaries and cruel persecutors of the blacks. As a matter of fact, the Boers were neither opposed to the mission nor enemies of the natives. . . .[16]

Many years after the event, however, the question was raised again in conversation with Kruger by one who, as a soldier and statesman and in all else, was of far greater stature than he or indeed than any South African ever born. In an address delivered in Edinburgh in 1929 General Smuts said:

I once took the opportunity to discuss the matter with President Kruger, and his explanation of the differences which arose between the Boers and Livingstone was, that Gordon Cumming—another of your errant countrymen—had supplied the border tribes with rifles and ammunition in exchange for ivory; and the Boers, finding the natives armed, concluded erroneously that Livingstone had done so, and treated him accordingly.[17]

* This was the Bakhatla chief who had given Livingstone land for his former mission station at Mabotsa. But neither he nor Sechele were, properly speaking, Kaffirs (that is, Zulus).

This must be considered final. There is no foundation whatever in the assertion which has sometimes been made that Livingstone was guilty of "arming the natives". Agar-Hamilton's book *The Policy of the Voortrekkers*, which in other respects deserves to rank as a classic of the period it reviews, is marred by the inference it draws and advances as an argument from evidence which is in itself inconsistent, that Livingstone was in fact a deliberate "gun-runner."

Nevertheless there is an aspect of the affair in respect of which he cannot be held wholly inculpable, and it may be ascribed partly to his sardonic sense of humour. It will be remembered that when asked by Potgieter whether the Bakwena did actually possess five hundred guns and a cannon, as was reported, he refused to answer—supposing to himself that this fantastic rumour would have a dampening effect on the Boers' predatory designs.

Further, it is difficult to exonerate him from the charge of withholding, subsequently, knowledge of the fact that Sechele and his people were actually much better armed than with five guns: how else account for the fusillade that greeted the Boer raid and killed 35 of their number? His house at Kolobeng had become a hospitable rendezvous for many British hunters and traders (such as Cumming, Chapman, Macabe and others) who had used it for the best part of four years as their base south and north of "the missionaries' road" or alternatively "the hunters' road"—that open highway to the north which the Boers were bent on closing. There can be little doubt that Sechele had bought guns and powder from them in exchange for ivory and other goods; and not only from them but also (as Livingstone distinctly states in his letter to the Governor) from the Boers themselves. By this means he must have acquired quite a small armoury. This supposition would go far to explain the somewhat cryptic sentences in Livingstone's letters to Thompson: "Had Potgieter come he would have met a very different reception from any he ever had before. . . They may find it more difficult to subdue Sechele than they dream of."

As to the destruction of Livingstone's house, an outrage of which he was not himself a witness: there is reason to doubt whether this was officially sponsored by the Boer commando.

Both Scholtz and Kruger admitted that a patrol did "visit" the mission, but not until after the raid was over, and that they found in it "a complete workshop for repairing guns and a quantity of materials of war"; and Scholtz adds that it had been already broken open and that only arms and tools were removed. Mr. Sillery, after carefully weighing this and other evidence, is disposed to conclude "that Sechele entered the house before the raid and removed some guns; that a Boer patrol visited it after the battle and took away the contents of the workshop; and that a good deal of damage was done by 'some person or persons unknown'. Some furniture and household goods may well have been taken by the Boers." Against this it must be said that Livingstone never mentioned any guns in the list of his personal losses, for the obvious reason that he had taken all he possessed—a smooth-bore rifle and a shot-gun— with him on his journey to the Cape and back; that Sechele therefore neither would nor could have broken into his house to abstract them; that the damage done to his property was obviously of a deliberate and malicious character and would never have been perpetrated by the natives among whom he had no enemies. Who then but the Boers—though probably an irresponsible gang of hot-heads (as Mr. Sillery himself suggests) —can have been guilty?

"Your fathers stoned the prophets and ye build their sepulchres." This august saying has been fulfilled in the case of Livingstone. In 1939 the Rev. J. H. L. Burns, a missionary in Bechuanaland, wrote to the Rev. J. I. Macnair as follows:

> The ruins of Livingstone's house at *Mobotsa* (now Maanwane) is concealed by a cluster of trees. General Smuts caused a fence to be put round them, in order, as he said, to make some reparation for the Boers' treatment of Livingstone. It is in the Transvaal.
>
> His house at *Chonuane* had been built of sun-dried bricks; all that remains of it is a heap of mud on a European farm known as 'Sechele's Oude Stadt'. The Union Government has taken over the site as a National Monument. It is in the Transvaal.
>
> The house at *Kolobeng* has stone foundations and sun-dried brick walls. A few feet of brick remained at one corner. It is in the Bechuanaland Protectorate. The site is uninhabited. For many years it has been protected by a fence, with another stronger one round the little graveyard, put up by the Protectorate Government.

When proceeding northwards in December, Livingstone met

Sechele at Motito. The outraged chief announced that he was going to London to lay his grievance before the Queen. Livingstone well knew that the Cape authorities would refuse him permission to sail and tried in vain to dissuade him. "He had abstained from all acts of retaliation lest the English should be offended. . . . When at Sechele's town I took down the names of 124 children who had been stolen from that tribe alone. Many of them I could identify as having been in the Mission School." Livingstone was also very averse to the exhibition of the chief as a prize convert. "I have always been opposed to exhibiting real or supposed converts prize-cattle fashion. Whatever he may be now, I have not the shadow of a doubt that during the two and three-quarter years before his admission he was sincere and most consistent." Sechele made his way to the Cape where he was stopped and obliged to return home. Livingstone's last word on his black friend is as follows:

> On his return he adopted a mode of punishment which he had seen in the Colony, namely, making criminals work on the public roads. And he has since, I am informed, made himself the missionary to his own people. . . . Great numbers of the tribes, formerly living under the Boers, have taken refuge under his sway and he is now in greater power than he was before the attack on Kolobeng.[18]

The panic produced throughout the country as a result of the raid was such that Livingstone's delay of a fortnight at Kuruman for repairs to the wheel was protracted to three months, owing to the impossibility of engaging drivers to continue the journey. Meanwhile he "sketched out" a Sechuana grammar, wrote natural history notes, and continued his article on the Kaffir War. He was distressed about the health of his father-in-law who had declined the Society's offer of a holiday on the coast.

> [To Thompson, 12 October.] Tell me some of your trials and how you manage to overcome. It is something to overcome oneself. . . . You possess a great deal more prudence that I ever did or ever will get hold of. . . . When I think of it [the grammar], it grows on me and seems the work of a lifetime, and I suspect mine will not be a long one. . . .
>
> Yet that you may not think me entirely destitute of prudence, I may mention that I have remained here more than a month after my wheel was repaired, waiting till the Boers have got out of my way. They intend, it is reported, to send a party on horseback after me, and if I will not

come back they must kill me. I intend to lighten the wagons of as much food as possible and everything else except bare necessaries, and then we shall have a run. . . .

Last Sunday I preached 3 times and did not feel the pain I have had for some time, so you need not think anything more about it. . . .[19]

[To Tidman, 2 November.] I have especial reason for gratitude in the kind consideration shown towards the case of Mr. Moffat. Every variety of treatment we have either seen, heard or read of, has been tried, but hitherto without the smallest effect on the complaint. Sudden pressure on one side of the head having been observed to make some little difference in the constant loud ringing sound within, I recommended iodine on the supposition that the symptoms might have been caused by hypertrophy of one of the cerebral membranes, but there is not as yet the slightest benefit from its employment. The thorough manner in which he applies himself to the translation involves a large amount of mental toil. Incessant attempts to make the Sechuana harmonise with the Hebrew render the undertaking nearly the same as learning the latter language and translating too. The various uses of each Hebrew word are ascertained and uniformity in the use of the Sechuana attempted. Assistance in this is drawn from the Dutch, German, French and English translations and also from a number of commentaries. Complete cessation from this severe toil is almost the only means which remain to be tried for his recovery. . . . His own inclination, if he could tear himself away from translation, would perhaps lead him to visit his old friend Mosilikatse— that chief having sent him lately a pressing invitation.[20]

But Moffat refused to relinquish his labours. Not till May 1854 did he travel north to make a heroic though unsuccessful attempt to reach Livingstone then journeying down the Zambesi. And not till early in 1857 did he finish his great task. He lived to the age of 88, a venerable figure deservedly honoured.

In his *Travels* Livingstone, by a lapse of memory, states that he finally left Kuruman on 20 November; but in fact he wrote from that place on the 24th to Thompson: "Am sorry to say I am still here in durance vile, but matters are in a fair way now . . . and I think I shall be off positively before the next moon." During this long stay he must have put together notes on many topics which he afterwards incorporated in the first chapter of his *Travels*. His minute observations on natural history are too long and too numerous to be quoted, though they make most fascinating reading. There is one, however, on the physical structure of the Kalahari Desert which must be mentioned. He shows that it is due to the direction of the prevailing easterly wind, and compares it with a similar phenomenon on Table

Mountain. This original excursus reveals him as a meteorologist of unusual ability for his time, as well as a writer of the first rank on scientific subjects.[21]

Moffat's translation of the Bible was an achievement which filled him with enthusiastic admiration, and led him to speculate on the future of mission-work in general. These reflections are evidence of a liberality in outlook transcending denominational differences, and show him to have been far in advance of his own times, or ours.

> We believe Christianity to be divine, and equal to all it has to perform; then let the good seed be widely sown and, no matter to what sect the converts may belong, the harvest will be glorious. Let nothing that I have said be interpreted as indicative of feelings inimical to any body of Christians, for I never as a missionary felt myself to be either Presbyterian, Episcopalian, or Independent, or called upon in any way to love one denomination less than another. . . .[22]

Chapter Twelve

FROM THE CAPE TO THE ZAMBESI
1852–1853

"Who will penetrate through Africa?"

NOT until December could Livingstone find three drivers willing to risk a journey north, and his coloured companion George Fleming found three more. "Our servants were the worst possible specimens of those who imbibe the vices without the virtues of Europeans, but we had no choice and were glad to get away on any terms." The start was made on 14 December 1852.

He had greatly desired to revisit the ruins of Kolobeng and especially the grave of his little daughter Elizabeth, but, hearing that some Boers were in the vicinity and eager to waylay him, he skirted the edge of the Kalahari westward in order to give them a wide berth. Hereabouts he was pleased to meet "that energetic traveller" Mr. J. Macabe returning from Lake Ngami after having discovered a new and shorter route thither, and having been imprisoned by the Boers pending payment of a fine because he had published in the Cape papers a sketch of his route through *their* country. His companion Mahar, mistaken by the Baralongs for a Boer, had been shot by them. Another traveller, Captain Shelley, having lost his way and reached Kuruman shirtless and blackened by exposure, had been mistaken by Mrs. Moffat for a Griqua.

Arrived at Sechele's ruined town on 31 December, Livingstone found that some of the chief's young men had seized four Boer wagons in retaliation. The Boers, fearing that this might be a signal for guerilla war, sent a deputation to ask for peace! This was refused unless they restored Sechele's children whom the commandant Scholz had appropriated as domestic slaves. Livingstone was present when one little boy, scarred with burns from having been allowed to roll into a fire, was returned to his weeping mother; the rest of the children were subsequently taken in and cared for by the Moffats.

> The Boers knew from experience that adult captives may as well be left alone, for escape is so easy in a wild country that no fugitive slave-law can come into operation; they therefore adopt the system of seizing only the youngest children, in order that these may forget their parents and remain in perpetual bondage.

From the Bakwain country he wrote on 12 January an order for books to Mr. John Snow of Paternoster Row, to replace in part his loss. These are chiefly medical but they include also the latest books on Natural History, *Uncle Tom's Cabin*, Bunsen's *History of Egypt*, the new edition of Gesenius' Hebrew Lexicon, the *Septuagint*, and Bloomfield's Supplement to his Greek New Testament. His tone is characteristically curt.

> The last parcel of books came to hand in a damaged condition in consequence of having been done up in regular dish-clout fashion. . . . I had imagined that the natives of Paternoster Row knew better than to send books abroad wrapped only in a bit of brown paper, without the teaching of a missionary   Please attend to this and if you don't, should I be cut off by the fever, you will never get a farthing from my executors and indeed would not deserve it.[1]

He spent a fortnight with the Bakwena people and was loth to leave them. He had lived among them so long and knew their speech and customs so intimately that he had always felt their welfare as his own, and they had felt the same for him. Now he could do nothing for them but try and comfort their distress. "I have much affection for them," he wrote in his Journal, "and though I pass from them I do not relinquish the hope that they will yet turn to Him to whose mercy and love they have often been invited. The seed of the living Word will not perish." And again: "We cannot accuse them of ingratitude; in fact, we shall remember their kindness to us as long as we live."

Leaving the Bakwena on 15 January 1853, Livingstone and his party reached the wells of Boatlanama on the 21st to find them for the first time empty, so pushed on to some clear water, and thence to his old friends the primitive and impoverished Bakalahari.

> The Bakalahari, who live at Moklatsa wells, have always been very friendly to us, and listen attentively to instruction conveyed to them in

their own tongue . . . but, when we kneel down and address an unseen Being, the position and the act often appear to them so ridiculous that they cannot refrain from bursting into uncontrollable laughter. After a few services they get over this tendency. I was once present when a missionary attempted to sing among a wild heathen tribe of Bechuanas, who had no music in their composition; the effect on the risible faculties of the audience was such that tears actually ran down their cheeks. . . .

If asked then, what effect the preaching of the Gospel has at the commencement on such individuals, I am unable to tell, except that some have confessed long afterwards that they then first began to pray in secret. . . .

Leaving Moklatsa on 8 February they made for Nchokotsa, but found the water bitter and the whole country parched. Here they dug several wells and waited perforce some days for the water to fill them sufficiently for the oxen to slake their thirst. Herds of game then gathered near, looking wistfully at the pools, and thus exposing themselves to death from bullets.

It is wanton cruelty to take advantage of the necessities of these poor animals. . . . In desperation they come slowly up to drink in spite of danger—"I must drink, though I die". . . . I could not order my men to do what I would not do myself; but, though I tried to justify myself on the plea of necessity, I could not adopt this mode of hunting.[2]

At Unku they exchanged the dreary prospect round Nchokotsa for "a delightful scene, all the ponds full of water, and the birds twittering joyfully", and on 1 March entered the fringe of what is now known as the Rhodesian bush. This required the constant application of the axe; and on the 10th they were brought to a stand by fever, the whole party being prostrated one after another except Livingstone and a Bakwain lad. "He managed the oxen, while I attended the patients and occasionally went out with the Bushmen to get a zebra or a buffalo, so as to induce them to remain with us." This sickness held them up in the bush for more than a week; on the 18th he wrote:

One of the people went about fifty yards from the wagon last night, fell down in a swoon, and remained so the whole night. The rain poured down on him and he felt nothing. In searching for him this morning my driver, himself ill, came on him and thought him dead. You may be sure I felt glad when I roused him from his protracted swoon.[3]

Here for the first time Livingstone had leisure to profit by the instructions of "my kind teacher, Mr. Maclear, that eminent astronomer and frank friendly man"—and calculated several longitudes from lunar distances.

He had so many and absorbing interests that any one of them would have sufficed for the study of a lifetime. It must have been this experience of sickness in the camp which prompted the following reflections in his Journal:

> I would like to devote a portion of my life to the discovery of a remedy for that terrible disease, the African fever. I would go into the parts where it prevails most, and try to discover if the natives have a remedy for it. I must make many enquiries of the river people in this quarter. What an unspeakable mercy it is to be permitted to engage in this most holy and honourable work! What an infinity of lots in the world are poor, miserable, and degraded compared with mine! I might have been a common soldier, a day-labourer, a factory operative, a mechanic, instead of a missionary. If my faculties had been left to run riot or waste as those of so many young men, I should now have been used up, a dotard, as many of my school-fellows are. I am respected by the natives, their kind expressions often make me ashamed, and they are sincere. So much deference and favour manifested without any effort on my part to secure it comes from the Author of every good gift. I acknowledge the mercies of the Great God with devout and reverential gratitude.[4]

Unfortunately, in this case, his patients were unworthy of either his attention or solicitude. They were, as he says later in his Journal, "the very dregs of the people of Kuruman".

> It was with difficulty I could get them to do half their duties; perpetually threatening to turn. I had to submit to almost anything which lazy, dirty, greedy servants can invent to annoy or destroy. . . .
> I wished to get rid of these, the first which I have been unable by kind treatment to manage; but some of them had been weakened by fever, and I allowed them to remain till their strength was renewed. The first use these worthies made of their strength was whoredom.[5]

On the 19th the oxen, scared by a hyaena in the night, bolted away into the bush; the Bakwain lad went after them, found them late in the following afternoon, stood by them all night, and returned with them next morning—"as I was setting off in search of him. It is wonderful how he managed without a compass, in such a country, to find his way home at all, bringing about forty oxen with him." As soon as the sick could travel they moved slowly forward again, improvising beds in the wagons for the worst cases and nursing them as they went; the convalescents behaving like refractory children, added to which the leading oxen's harness became frequently entangled with trees. Then, to avoid tsetse, a new path must be hewn through the bush; "but notwithstanding an immense amount of toil, my health continued good".

> We were however rewarded in lat. 18° with a sight we had not enjoyed the year before, namely, large patches of grape-bearing vines. There they stood before my eyes; but the sight was so entirely unexpected that I stood some time gazing at the clusters of grapes with which they were loaded, with no more thought of plucking them than if I had been beholding them in a dream.

Here Livingstone discovered a new species of the ant-lion, whose habits he describes minutely; and made sketches of the leaves of new types of the papilionaceous family which he observed among the multifarious forms of trees in the ever-thickening bush. By the end of March the trader Fleming, who had hitherto assisted in driving his own wagon, knocked up.

> As I could not drive two wagons I shared with him the remaining water, half a caskful, and went on, with the intention of coming back for him as soon as we could reach the next pool.
> Heavy rain now commenced; I was employed the whole day in cutting down trees, and every stroke of the axe brought down a thick shower on my back, which in the hard work was very refreshing, as the water found its way down into my shoes.

He remarks on the large number and variety of big game in this region and of their singular fearlessness in the presence of man; and on the increasing beauty of the scenery as they advanced.

> It being Sunday all was peace and, from the circumstances in which our party was placed, we could not but reflect on that second stage of our existence which we hope will lead us into scenes of perfect beauty. If pardoned in that free way the Bible promises, death will be a glorious thing; but to be consigned to wait for the Judgment-day, with nothing else to ponder on but sins we would rather forget, is a cheerless prospect.

The farther they advanced the ranker became the vegetation and the more waterlogged the whole country after a season of excessive rains. Watercourses had become rivers, the bottoms of which were pitted with holes made by wading elephants. "In these the oxen floundered desperately, so that the wagon-wheel broke, compelling us to work up to the breast in water for three hours and a half; yet I suffered no harm."

They at length arrived at the Sanshureh river which flowed out of the Chobe and, being in flood, "presented an impassable barrier". Livingstone took a Bushman with him to explore its banks to the west: "we waded a long way among the reeds in water breast deep". Then to the east with similar ill-success "till my Bushmen friends became quite tired of the work" and after some days, in spite of presents, slipped away by night. He then took one of the strongest of his still weak companions, provisions and a blanket, and crossed the river in a pontoon (the gift of Captains Codrington and Webb); and by dint of splashing and wading penetrated 20 miles westwards till they were halted by "a wall of reeds".

> Having shot a lechwe and made a glorious fire, we got a good cup of tea and had a comfortable night. While collecting wood that evening, I found a bird's nest consisting of live leaves sewn together with threads of the spider's web. Nothing could exceed the airiness of this pretty contrivance; the threads had been pushed through small punctures and thickened to resemble a knot.

Next morning Livingstone, by climbing the highest trees, descried a broad sheet of the veritable Chobe River, dotted with islands, but flanked with the same impenetrable belt of reeds. To reach it, reeds were not the only obstacle: "a peculiar serrated grass, which at certain angles cut the hand like a razor, was mingled with the reed, and the climbing convolvulus, with stalks which felt as strong as whipcord, bound the mass together". With their legs in the cool water, and perspiration steaming from their bodies in the stifling airless heat of this growth—leaning their weight with all their strength against the stubborn stalks till they bent enough to allow passage—"after some hours' toil" they reached an island.

> Here we met an old friend, the bramble-bush. My strong moleskins were quite worn through at the knees, and the leather trousers of my companion were torn and his legs bleeding. Tearing my handkerchief in two I tied the pieces round my knees, and then encountered another difficulty. We were still forty or fifty yards from the clear water, and now we were opposed by great masses of papyrus, which are like palms in miniature, eight or ten feet high, and an inch and a half in diameter.

These were also laced together by convolvulus, and would have proved impenetrable, had they not found the track of a hippopotamus, and so eager was Livingstone to follow it to the clear water that, when he did so, "I stepped in and found it took me at once up to the neck". Returning "nearly worn out" and carrying the pontoon, they proceeded up the bank of the Chobe to the junction of the Sanshureh, then down the bank, climbing trees for a view of nothing but reeds. "This was a hard day's work", and finding a deserted hut, horrible in its decay, "we were fain to crawl beneath its shelter"—from mosquitoes and the cold night dew. Here their unseen companions were water-snakes and otters and a hippopotamus: "curious birds, too, jerked and wriggled among these reedy masses, and we heard human-like voices and unearthly sounds, with splash, guggle, jopp, as if rare fun were going on in their uncouth haunts".

After a cold damp night they set forth again with the dawn, leaving the pontoon by the hut. Hereabouts were several unusually high ant-hills, and from the top of one of these Livingstone discovered an inlet to the Chobe. Returning for the pontoon they launched out into the river, and were nearly capsized by a hippopotamus. They paddled from midday to sunset and were preparing for a supperless night in their float when, just before darkness fell, they perceived a village of the Makololo on an island. The headman and his people remembered Livingstone and welcomed him with jubilation: "He has dropped among us from the clouds, yet came riding on the back of a hippopotamus! We thought no one could cross the Chobe without our knowledge, but here he drops among us like a bird!"

Next day a flotilla of canoes crossed the flooded lands to collect the rest of the party and transport them and the wagons, which were dissembled and mounted on canoes lashed together, to safety on the further bank. During Livingstone's absence, however, the cattle had been allowed to wander into a patch of fly-infested scrub, whereby he lost ten fine large oxen which cost him between £25 and £30.[6]

Such in brief are the high-lights in what was to the narrator an adventure of minor importance, a mere preliminary to a greater journey, but which to an ordinary traveller would have provided material enough for a book. They are interspersed for the most part almost casually in a chapter which is filled with observations of many other kinds. Only an imaginative reader, and only one with some experience of similar travel in the jungle, can even faintly apprehend—between the lines of this dry factual narrative—the sheer physical exertion, to say nothing of the moral resolution, that such a performance must have entailed.

His *Travels*, however, which were for the public eye, are descriptive only of scenes and circumstances in which the adverse features are minimized. It is to his private Journals that we must look for a revelation of the inner man. And these self-communings and heart-searchings evince a depth and intensity of religious feeling which, to those who know Livingstone only from his published writings as also to those who thought they knew him in the flesh, must make him appear almost a stranger. With all his temperamental optimism and with all his trust in Providence, he was never under any illusions about the danger of his undertaking and its possible, even probable, termination in disaster; and to a man of such phenomenal vitality as he possessed, the proximity of death was a familiar theme for reflection; indeed, the thought of it and of speculation concerning continued existence in another sphere were never absent from his mind. Thus, when anticipating a much earlier departure from Kuruman than eventuated, he had written in his Journal for 28 September 1852 words which soar from half-mournful meditations upon the future state to a sublime crescendo of renewed self-dedication in the service of Love while yet there is time.

Am I on my way to die in Sebituane's country? Have I seen the end of my wife and children?—the breaking up of all connections with earth, leaving this fair and beautiful world, and knowing so little of it? I am only learning the alphabet of it yet, and entering on an untried state of existence. Following Him who has entered before me into the clouds, the veil, is a serious prospect. Do we begin again in our new existence to learn much from experience, or have we full powers? My soul, whither wilt thou emigrate? Where wilt thou lodge the first night after leaving this body? Will an angel soothe thy flutterings? for sadly flurried wilt thou be in entering upon eternity. Oh, if Jesus speak one work of peace, that will establish in thy breast an everlasting calm! O Jesus, fill me with Thy love now, and I beseech Thee accept me, and use me a little for Thy glory. I have done nothing for Thee yet, and I would like to do something. O do, do, I beseech Thee, accept me and my service, and take Thou all the glory. . . .

On 23 January, when among the simple Bakalahari in the desert, his Journal has the pathetic entry: "I think much of my poor children." Again on 4 February, when all his party were prostrated with malaria, his previous thoughts on death recur and even find an echo later in his *Travels*:

> I am spared in health, while all the company have been attacked by the fever. If God has accepted my service, then my life is charmed till my work is done. And though I pass through many dangers unscathed while working the work given me to do, when that is finished, some simple thing will give me my quietus. Death is a glorious event to one going to Jesus. Whither does the soul wing its way? What does it see first? There is something sublime in passing into the second stage of our immortal lives if washed from our sins. But oh! to be consigned to ponder over all our sins with memories excited, every scene of our lives held up as a mirror before our eyes, and we looking at them and waiting for the day of Judgment!

When these trials were surmounted and the wheels slowly turning northwards again, he wrote on 17 February in noble words vindicating the justness of his endeavour:

> It is not the encountering of difficulties and dangers in obedience to the promptings of the inward spiritual life, which constitutes tempting of God and Providence; but the acting without faith, proceeding on our errands with no previous convictions of duty, and no prayer for aid and direction.

The last of these entries to be quoted, made on 22 May, the day before he reached Linyanti and was already safe among his Makololo friends, begins with a magnificent declaration of the purpose of his life and ends with a prayer which is unconsciously prophetic of his death.

> I will place no value on anything I have or may possess, except in relation to the kingdom of Christ. If anything will advance the interests of that kingdom, it shall be given away or kept, only as by giving or keeping of it I shall most promote the glory of Him to whom I owe all my hopes in time and eternity. May grace and strength sufficient to enable me to adhere faithfully to this resolution be imparted to me, so that in truth, not in name only, all my interests and those of my children may be identified with His cause. . . . I will try and remember always to approach God in secret with as much reverence in speech, posture, and behaviour as in public. Help me, Thou who knowest my frame and pitiest as a father his children.[7]

.   .   .   .   .

The whole population of Linyanti, some six or seven thousand souls, turned out to welcome the travellers as they entered the town in their huts borne on moving wheels—a phenomenon which they had never witnessed before. The court herald after performing some preliminary antics roared out in adulatory shouts, "Don't I see the white man? Don't I see the comrade of Sebituane? Don't I see the father of Sekeletu?—We want sleep. Give your son sleep, my lord." (Sleep meaning protection from raids by the Matabele.)

"It is remarkable," Livingstone comments, "how anxious for peace those who have been fighting all their lives appear to be."

The Makololo had set aside a garden for him and planted maize in readiness for his return, so that he might have his own crop of corn; and the women were now pounding it into fine meal. "God has touched their hearts," he wrote in his Journal. "I have used no undue influence. Kindness shown has been appreciated here, while much greater kindness shown to tribes in the south has resulted in the belief that we missionaries must be fools."

There had been a change in the chieftainship, Sebituane's daughter having resigned in favour of her young brother Sekeletu. He, being afraid of his half-brother Mpepe who was a rival, had strongly urged his sister to retain it whilst he himself led the Makololo in war. But she, embarrassed by the number of husbands she would have to maintain in that position and preferring to have her own home and children like other women, after three days' public debate stood up in the assembly and addressed her brother with a gush of tears: "I have been a chief only because my father wished it. You, Sekeletu, must be chief and build up your father's house."[8]

The young chief was only eighteen years of age; but "there was nothing weak or childish in his conduct or conversation"; and though he had neither his father's presence, character nor ability, yet his respect for the missionary and professions of friendship were genuine. Actuated partly by expectations of miraculous benefits and partly out of regard for his father's wishes, he placed everything at the missionary's disposal— land, labour, and provisions in abundance. When Livingstone proposed to examine the country northwards to the Zambesi for a healthy locality, Sekeletu at once volunteered to accompany him. But the project was postponed by the fact that, within a week of his arrival at Linyanti, Livingstone was *for the first time* stricken with fever. He attributed this "to a sudden change in his habits from great exertion to comparative inactivity", coincident with the commencement of the cold season.

> Anxious to ascertain whether the natives possessed the knowledge of any remedy of which we were ignorant, I requested the assistance of one of Sekeletu's doctors. . . . I fondly hoped that they had a more potent remedy than our own medicines afford; but after being stewed in their vapour-baths, smoked like a red-herring over green twigs, and charmed *secundum artem*, I concluded that I could cure the fever more quickly than they can. . . .
>
> There is a good deal in not "giving in" to this disease. He who is low-spirited, and apt to despond at every attack, will die sooner than the man who is not of such a melancholic nature.[9]

He was fond of quoting the text in *Proverbs*: "A merry heart doeth good like medicine."

As soon as he had shaken the fever off he proceeded northwards on ox-back with Sekeletu and his following, but when sixty miles on the way they encountered Mpepe. This claimant to the chieftainship had not abandoned his ambition; he had for some time been in league with the slave-owning Mambari, a large party of whom had come to Linyanti when Livingstone was, as he says, floundering in the marshes of the Chobe. Hearing that the white man was near, the Mambari precipitately fled to the protection of Mpepe, who, aware that the white man would favour Sekeletu, conspired with the Mambari and agreed to kill his young brother at the first opportunity. It now happened that they and the white man unexpectedly met, but when Sekeletu who was in advance saw that Mpepe was armed with a small axe he fled to the nearest village, where he was soon joined by Livingstone and then by Mpepe.

> I happened to sit between the two in the hut where they met; being tired with riding all day in the sun, I soon asked Sekeletu where I should sleep and he replied, "Come, I will show you." As we rose together I unconsciously covered Sekeletu's body with mine, and saved him from the blow of the assassin. I knew nothing of the plot, but remarked that all Mpepe's men kept hold of their arms—a thing quite unusual in the presence of a chief; and when Sekeletu showed me the hut in which I was to spend the night, he said to me, "That man wishes to kill me."

Retribution was as cunning as it was swift. Two of Sekeletu's men went to the fire at which Mpepe was sitting and one of them offered him snuff. As he held out his hand it was seized by this man, and his other seized by the second; they then led him out a mile from the village and speared him. This was the common mode of executing a criminal. Mpepe's men fled to the Barotse tribe; the country was so disturbed by the occurrence that it was thought advisable to return to Linyanti.[10]

Ever since his arrival Livingstone had been pressed by the young chief to name some object or other that he specially desired—anything at all, whether in his town or outside it—so that he might show his affection by presenting it. But this request Livingstone steadily put aside, explaining that "my only object was to elevate him and his people to be Christians"—though not in the manner which they anticipated. "The idea seemed universal that, with a missionary, some great indefinite good had arrived. . . . 'Jesus had not loved their forefathers, hence their present degradation. He had loved the white men and given them all the wonderful things they now possess. And as I had come to teach them to pray to Jesus, and to pray for them, their wants would soon be all supplied.'" Livingstone therefore first offered to teach Sekeletu to shoot and also to read. But Sekeletu replied that "he did not wish to learn to read the Book, for he was afraid it might change his heart and make him content with only one wife, like Sechele". When Livingstone assured him that nothing was required but his own voluntary decision on the matter, Sekeletu answered, "No, no; he wanted to have five wives at least." As a result of this conversation Livingstone characteristically adds: "I liked the frankness of Sekeletu; for nothing is so wearying to the spirit as talking to those who agree with everything advanced." But one day Sekeletu laid twelve elephants' tusks by the wagon in his absence, so that he had no opportunity of refusing them. "He then came and begged me so earnestly to accept them that I felt at a loss how to act." Eventually, when departing, "I requested him to leave orders that if any traders came, my ivory must be used as well as his own. By this means no offence was given."[11]

Livingstone's considered view on the question whether missionaries should engage in trading with the natives (by barter, of course, money being valueless) was, that while it was lawful it was not expedient. Unfortunately George Fleming's commercial efforts, though honest, were not successful; he returned to the Cape, however, with a load of ivory which more than compensated him for the expense of such a long journey.[12]

Livingstone was anxious to pursue his interrupted journey north without delay.

But Sekeletu objected first that he had not yet had a satisfactory look at me. He must see me longer. Then he could not think of letting me go alone. He must accompany me and see that no evil befell me. This required considerable preparations, during which I offered to teach the people to read. Long and profound were the deliberations over this. They are never in a hurry in Africa.

At length Sekeletu's father-in-law and step-father were appointed to learn this art "in order that their experience might serve as a beacon to others". They mastered it with wonderful rapidity.[13]

To all who have not acquired it the knowledge of letters is quite unfathomable; there is naught like it within the compass of their observation. . . . It seems to them supernatural that we see in a book things taking place, or having occurred at a distance.

The white man's letters were not the only mystery; his looking-glass was another. This was a special source of attraction to the women, who came frequently to ask for it.

And the remarks they made—while I was engaged in reading and apparently not attending to them—on first seeing themselves therein, were amusingly ridiculous. "Is that me?"—"What a big mouth I have!"—"My ears are big as pumpkin-leaves."—"I have no chin at all." Or, "I would have been pretty, but am spoiled by these high cheekbones."—"See how my head shoots up in the middle!" laughing vociferously all the time at their own jokes. They readily perceive any defect in each other, and give nicknames accordingly. One man came alone to have a quiet gaze at his own features once, when he thought I was asleep; after twisting his mouth in various directions, he remarked to himself, "People say I am ugly, and how very ugly I am indeed!"[14]

During five weeks of enforced delay at Linyanti, Livingstone instituted public religious services on Sundays in the *kotla*. This open space held "associations unfavourable to solemnity", since half-an-hour beforehand it had been the scene of barbaric dancing. But he did not oppose the custom. "It is always unwise to hurt their feelings of independence. Much greater influence will be gained by studying how you may induce them to act aright, with the impression that they are doing it of their own free will." His custom was to read a portion of Scripture and follow it with an explanatory address, short enough to prevent weariness or lack of attention. The summons was made by the court-herald, who acted as beadle, and the congregation usually numbered between five and seven hundred. The necessity of raising his voice to address so many in the open air delayed the recovery of what he called his "clergyman's throat". The services were often concluded with diversions of a lighter kind, and "at the risk of appearing frivolous to some" he tells how the women, who always behaved with decorum, were disconcerted when the time came for prayer.

> When all knelt down, many of those who had children, in following the example of the rest, bent over their little ones; the children, in danger of being crushed to death, set up a simultaneous yell, which so tickled the whole assembly that there was often a subdued titter, to be turned into a hearty laugh as soon as they heard Amen.[15]

He was also assiduous in doctoring their sick, though never without the consent of their own doctors; and he thus restricted himself to the severer cases only, "lest they should be offended at my taking their practice out of their hands". As among his old friends the Bakwena, so now among his new friends the Makololo, "we always found medical knowledge an important aid in convincing the people that we were really anxious for their welfare. . . . Medical aid is most valuable in young missions; this is not the case to the same extent in old missions, where the people have learned to look upon relief as a right."

But Livingstone never concealed from himself or from the public that the effects of his missionary labours were for the most part superficial. He found it impossible to disabuse the minds of his barbaric audience of the notion that his religion was one of some other kind of medicine, and could only be made effective by charms and enchantments.[16]

Perhaps his sermons produced a more lasting impression

than he supposed. Dr. Macnair quotes a Scottish missionary, famous in his day, as writing in 1884:

> Although thirty years have elapsed since Livingstone first visited the Barotse valley and more than twenty years since he was last seen there, yet the remembrance of him—his ways, his words, his physique—is as fresh as yesterday. Many of the older men had whole sermons of his by heart. One old blind man, at my request, gave me one of Livingstone's sermons. He got up and went through it bravely, spoken in a high authoritative voice.[17]

He was constantly enforcing on Sekeletu and his companions the duty of living peaceably with their neighbours. Lechulatebe, the foolish and irresponsible young chief to the south, having become possessed of fire-arms, had thought fit to abstract from a neighbouring tribe some tribute which belonged of right to Sekeletu, and had in various ways manifested joy at the death of his father. Livingstone sent him a message advising him to abandon this course, "because, though Sebituane were dead, the arms he had fought with were still alive and strong". At the same time he persuaded Sekeletu to exchange presents with Lechulatebe. Sekeletu sent ten cows, in return for which Lechulatebe sent back the same number of sheep instead of their equivalent of sixty or seventy. Despite these provocations "I prevailed on the Makololo to keep the peace during my stay, but could easily see that public opinion was well against it."[18]

All this while he had been anxiously awaiting permission to resume and extend his interrupted journey north-westwards along the Zambesi to the Barotse tribe, amongst whom he still hoped to find a suitable location for a mission. "But Sekeletu does not like to part with me at all." On Livingstone persisting —"He says he will take me with him." But first he must consult those who had opposed the journey. At length on 16 June he definitely gave consent and began to muster his retinue for departure in the following week. "It is certain" (wrote Livingstone in his Journal) "that I am to be permitted to go. Thanks be to God for influencing their hearts!"[19]

The retinue numbered some 160 young men and under-chiefs, and as the long procession wound its tortuous way in single file along the bush-paths, it was pleasant to look back at the bright-coloured garments and headgear adorned with waving plumes of black ostrich feathers, or the white ends of ox-tails, or caps of lions' manes; the various head-borne loads; the shields, and the swinging clubs of short rhinoceros-horn. Livingstone had lent Sekeletu his old horse, and his young attendants vied with each other as they ran in attempts to mount and ride, without saddle or bridle, the lumbering oxen from whose backs they slid and tumbled to the huge amusement of their fellows. Thus they reached the Zambesi at a village above Sesheke where the river was very wide, and several days were spent in collecting canoes from the Makalaka villagers from far and near, whilst Livingstone went north to examine the country and shoot game "in order to assist in the support of our large party". This was a form of "sport" which he always disliked intensely, "but the Makololo shot so badly that, in order to save my powder, I was obliged to go myself".

The canoes being at length assembled he was given the choice of the entire fleet and selected the best, with six paddlers, while Sekeletu took the largest, with ten. The pages of his *Travels* become descriptive of the beauty of the river scenery, "and I took pleasure in looking at lands which had never been seen by a European before". He devotes much space also to the fauna and flora, and the habits and industries of the natives on the islands and the banks. But he is oppressed by the lack of any historical background in a people whose knowledge of the past extends no farther than to the days of their grandfathers, and also by the dearth of geological records. "One never expects to find a grave nor a stone of remembrance set up in Africa; the very rocks are illiterate, they contain so few fossils." Having surmounted the thirty-foot drop of the Gonye falls by carrying the canoes for a mile by land, they reached the country of the Barotse to which Mpepe's followers had fled, and here Livingstone was compelled to witness a horrible scene—their execution by being tossed into the river.

> When I remonstrated against human blood being shed in this off-hand way, the counsellors justified their acts by the evidence, and calmly added, "You see we are still Boers; we are not yet taught."

Here too was the stockade which the slave-owning Mambari had erected for their protection and that of their chained victims against attack. The Makololo proposed to attack them at once (though they were armed with a few muskets), and drive them from the country. But Livingstone, dreading the result of hostilities, strongly urged the strategic difficulties of such a course. They then proposed to starve them out. "Hunger is strong enough for that," said an under-chief; "a very great fellow is he." But Livingstone, knowing that the chief sufferers would be the poor slaves, interceded on their behalf, with the result that they were spared "and allowed to depart in peace".

Arrived at Nariele, the Barotse capital, artificially constructed on a mound by a chief who added to this and other accomplishments a remarkable gift for taming wild animals, they stayed several days; and Livingstone found a ridge some distance from it, called Katongo, which from its elevation he thought might be suitable for a settlement, but was informed "that no part of this region is exempt from fever". He therefore left Sekeletu—who provided him with a mixed retinue of Makololo and Makalaka men, besides his rowers and a herald ("that I might enter his villages with befitting dignity")—and pushed on to the confluence of the Leeba with the Leeambye* and beyond it to the region of Lobale. The herald's customary proclamation was *Tau e tona*—"(Here comes) the great lion!"—but his mispronunciation of the word *tau* (lion) was so like *sau* (sow) "that I could not receive the honour with becoming gravity and had to entreat him, much to the annoyance of my party, to be silent". Another objection was more serious, and it exemplifies Livingstone's moral force among tribes with whom he was not familiar. They came upon a number of people from the Lobale region, hunting hippopotami.

> They fled precipitately as soon as they saw the Makololo, leaving their canoes and all their utensils and clothing. My own Makalaka, who were accustomed to plunder wherever they went, rushed after them like furies, totally regardless of my shouting. As this proceeding would have destroyed my character entirely at Lobale, I took my stand on a commanding position as they returned, and forced them to lay down all the plunder on a sandbank, and leave it there for its lawful owners.

At this point he was compelled to conclude that no healthy

* Lat. 14° 10′ 52″ S., Long. 23° 35′ 40″ E. Leeba is the name which Livingstone gives to the upper reaches, and Leeambye to the extreme upper reaches, of the same great river which is now known as the Zambesi throughout its entire length.

location, even as far north as this, could be found. The Lobale region proved to be an extensive swamp. He had thus, he says, a fair excuse for coming home with the sad news that "the door was shut". "But believing that it was my duty to devote some portion of my life to these (to me at least) very confiding and affectionate Makololo, I resolved to follow out the second part of my plan, though I had failed in accomplishing the first." This was to prospect a little farther for a route to the coast. He had with him an old Portuguese map which showed a river called Coanza as rising in the centre of the Continent and flowing westward to the sea; and gauged that by ascending the Leeba for two or three degrees of latitude he would be within reach of the Coanza. With his paddlers he forthwith proceeded some 44 miles of latitude up the winding river (upwards of 50 geographical miles) in a single day—only to find that Coanza was nowhere near its position on the map. The country abounded in big game, especially buffaloes, elands, and lions. Having slept the night on a sandbank, they fell in with a party of Arabs from Zanzibar with whom they shared their cooking-pot; and then without loss of time paddled down the Leeba and into the Leeambye, rejoining Sekeletu at his mother's town, and thence without pause to Sesheke and Linyanti.

It had for long been Livingstone's hope, as is apparent from his many letters home on the subject, to find among the unsophisticated natives to the north a people unspoiled by such injurious influences as those to which the Bechuana and others were exposed by contact with the vices of civilization. In this too he was disappointed. The "noble savage" of Rousseau's fancy did not exist—at least in Central Africa. His account of this preliminary journey in his *Travels* closes with words which must be taken as marking the close of an epoch in his experience, and of his career as a missionary whose aim hitherto had been the conversion of souls. Henceforth he felt himself called to be a preparer of the way for others.

> I had been, during a nine weeks' tour, in closer contact with heathenism than I had ever been before; and though all, including the chief, were as kind and attentive to me as possible . . . yet to endure the dancing, roaring, and singing, the jesting, anecdotes, grumbling, quarrelling, and murdering of these children of nature, seemed more like a severe penance that anything I had before met with in the course of my

missionary duties. I took thence a more intense disgust at heathenism than I had before, and formed a greatly elevated opinion of the latent effects of missions in the south, among tribes which are reported to have been as savage as the Makololo. The indirect benefits, which to a casual observer lie beneath the surface and are inappreciable, in reference to the probable wide diffusion of Christianity at some future time, are worth all the money and labour that have been expended to produce them.[20]

His Journal records time and again his sense of utter weariness from the tumultuous din, the frenzied dancing, the wanton disregard of human life or human feelings; and, more concretely, the scenes which he witnessed but was powerless to prevent, of revolting savagery and the dreadful callousness with which the aged and the very young were treated. "Occasionally he would think of other scenes of travel; if a friend, for example, were going to Palestine, he would say how gladly he would kiss the dust that had been trod by the Man of Sorrows."[21]

But mental distress was not his only affliction on this journey. The other was extreme physical debility: seven attacks of malaria in nine weeks. Only those who have succumbed even to a moderate bout of this disease can know that nothing short of dire necessity would induce them to any form of exertion. Only they can faintly appreciate the strength of will required to keep moving day by day under the stress of recurrent attacks, in sweltering heat and human stench, gripping with his knees the back of an ox, or staggering along on foot, or swaying in a hollowed tree-trunk on the water—urged on by no necessity but the inner compulsion of a dauntless spirit. Added to this, his worst attack must have occurred at or about the time when he was dealing wrathfully with the refractory Makalaka.

[To Tidman.] I never had a touch of fever till my employment became sedentary here. I have had eight attacks since. The last when going north to Nariele was very severe, being accompanied with a large loss of florid blood. It thinned me much. But on no occasion did I lay by. Fits of vertigo, probably from exhaustion, troubled me for some time. Everything seemed to rush to the left, and I had to lay hold on something to prevent a fall. These induced me to give up collecting Barotse words and other materials for a Dictionary.[22]

"On no occasion did I lay by." The character of the man is revealed in that terse sentence.

It was in this condition of health that, immediately after his return to Linyanti early in September, he began to make preparations for a renewed assault upon the interior "as soon as the cooling influence of the rains should be felt in November". He could have arranged with the Mambari to accompany them on the route towards the nearest port on the west coast, St. Philip de Benguela, but this was already defiled by the slave-traffic and therefore "I proposed to find out another line of march". Sekeletu at his request sent out scouting parties to ascertain if any belt of country to the west was free from tsetse, but the search proved fruitless. He had been informed that many English lived at Loanda and "the prospect of meeting with countrymen seemed to over-balance the toils of the longer march".

Many *pichos* were held to deliberate on the steps proposed. When at length twenty-seven porters were appointed to attend him on the way, one old diviner who was a "noted croaker" said "Where is he taking you to? This white man is throwing you away. Your garments already smell of blood." But the general voice was in his favour. Of this little band, collected from an assortment of Zambesi tribes, only two were Makololo; but for convenience he referred to them generically by that name. Considering his recent illnesses Sekeletu's people thought it almost certain that he would die, and that in that event they would be blamed by the white men for allowing him to go away into "an unknown, unhealthy country of enemies". To meet this objection and absolve them from any blame he deposited with Sekeletu his Journal up to date, for transmission to Mr. Moffat by the next trader going south. He left also in their care his wagon and remaining goods.

During these weeks of preparation he preached twice on Sundays (sometimes to as many as a thousand people), taught them to read and to shoot, wrote many letters—to his wife, children, parents and friends, and confided deeper reflections to his Journal. Those who think of Livingstone as primarily an explorer, enticed into the wilderness by the lure of adventure or by the ambition of geographical and scientific discovery, would do well to read and ponder these latter or such extracts as have been committed to print. They show that he was under no illusions about the nature of his undertaking or of its possible, even probable, outcome. The ambition of discovery was there, but only as a secondary consideration; the primary motive was nothing more, nor less, than a simple sense of duty. The experience, he well knew, would be an indefinite prolongation of the "penance" he had already undergone.

[From his Journal. 27 August.]—The more intimately I become acquainted with barbarians, the more disgusting does heathenism become. It is inconceivably vile. They are always boasting of their fierceness, yet dare not visit another tribe for fear of being killed. . . . They bestow honours and flattering titles on me in confusing profusion . . . and food without any recompense, out of pure kindness. They need a healer. May God enable me to be such to them!

[13 October.] Missionaries ought to cultivate a taste for the beautiful. We are necessarily compelled to contemplate much moral impurity and degradation. We are so often doomed to disappointment. We are apt to become either callous or melancholy, or, if preserved from these, the constant strain on the sensibilities is likely to injure the bodily health. . . . See the green earth and the blue sky, the lofty mountain and the verdant valley, the glorious orbs of day and night, the starry canopy with all its celestial splendour, the graceful flowers so chaste in form and perfect in colouring. . . .
We must feel that there is a Governor among the nations who will bring all His plans with respect to our human family to a glorious consummation. He who stays his mind on his ever-present, ever-energetic God, will not fret himself because of evil-doers. He that believeth shall not make haste.

[To his Father. 30 September.] You see what they make of the gospel [some friends who had advised his settling somewhere and converting people by every sermon], and my conversation in it, in which my inmost heart yearned for their conversion. . . . The conversion of a few, however valuable their souls may be, cannot be put into the scale against the knowledge of the truth spread over the whole country.

[To his Father. 8 November.] . . . May God in mercy permit me to do something for the cause of Christ in these dark places of the earth! May He accept my children for His service, and sanctify them for it! My blessing on my wife. May God comfort her. If my watch comes back after I am cut off, it belongs to Agnes. If my sextant, it is Robert's. The Paris medal to Thomas. Double-barrelled gun to Zouga.—Be a Father to the fatherless, and a husband to the widow, for Jesus' sake.

To the Directors he wrote: "Can the love of Christ not carry the missionary where the slave-trade carries the trader?"— And to his brother-in-law Robert Moffat: "I shall open a path into the interior, or perish."[23]

Chapter Thirteen

FIRST GREAT JOURNEY: LOANDA

1853-1854

"I shall open a path into the interior, or perish."

LIVINGSTONE and his party of twenty-seven natives left Linyanti on 11 November 1853. Sekeletu lent him his own canoe and escorted him to the Chobe, where he embarked from the same island upon which he and Oswell had first met Sebituane two years before.

His equipment was as follows: three muskets for his party, a rifle, revolver, and a double-barrelled smooth-bore for himself; a few biscuits, a few pounds of tea and sugar, twenty of coffee, and twenty of beads for currency; a tin canister fifteen inches square containing clothes for civilization; another of the same size for medicines; a bag for spare clothing on the way; a third case for books, and a fourth for a magic lantern (the gift of Mr. Murray); a small gypsy tent, a sheepskin mantle for a blanket, and a horse-rug for a bed. His sextant, artificial horizon, and chronometer (the gifts of Colonel Steele), thermometer and compasses, were carried separately. His ammunition was distributed throughout the whole luggage. These articles represented in fact the whole of his worldly possessions, except the wagon left at Linyanti. As he said, "the Boers had lightened me of the trouble of making a will".

> As I had always found that the art of successful travel consisted in taking as few 'impedimenta' as possible, and not forgetting to carry my wits about me, the outfit was rather spare, and intended to be still more so when we should come to leave the canoes. Some would consider it injudicious to adopt this plan, but I had a secret conviction that, if I did not succeed, it would not be for lack of the 'nicknacks' advertised as indispensable for travellers, but from want of 'pluck', or because a large array of baggage excited the cupidity of the tribes through whose country we wished to pass.[1]

The Rev. W. A. Elliott, a missionary of the L.M.S. at Inyati from 1877 to 1892, contrasts Livingstone's equipment with that of Stanley when he went in search of him on his last journey in 1871.

> Stanley was accompanied by two white men, 23 native soldiers, 160 porters, 27 donkeys and one cart, bearing 6 tons of cloth, beads, wire, provisions, utensils, boats, instruments, medicines, and "every conceivable article". The party was armed with 39 guns and revolvers. Livingstone covered some 3,000 miles of mostly new ground; Stanley's route, 1,600 miles, was partly known. The contrast is made not in depreciation of Stanley, but in appreciation of Livingstone.[2]

Sir Harry Johnston, writing in 1891, remarked that had Livingstone travelled with that reasonable amount of comfort which would provide a bed and a rain-tight tent and even a moderate supply of what were even then thought necessaries, "he would have completed his great scheme of geographical discovery and would have been alive now in the enjoyment of honours and competence, as are several of his old companions." To this he adds that Livingstone none the less was very far from recommending a shabby and careless method of equipment and personal appearance. He always endeavoured to be both neat and clean, and to maintain a distinctly European mode of life.[3] In his own words: "I feel certain that the lessons of cleanliness rigidly instilled by my mother in childhood helped me to maintain that respect which these people entertain for European ways."

Not until he was about to start did he become aware of a theft of his goods perpetrated by the ruffians he had brought with him from Kuruman.

> [From his Journal.] I was compelled to order them home with full wages. They would not go nor would they take their wages, they would remain, eating up my stores. When they did go, the package containing my stock of ammunition and prepared medicines was stolen by one of them. This has crippled me badly and I feel the loss of the medicines severely.

It was not however the lack of material but of intellectual resources that he himself regretted most. Only a few days after setting out he wrote in his Journal:

> I feel the want of books in this journey more than anything else.   A Sechuana Pentateuch, a lined journal, Thomson's Tables, a Nautical Almanack, and a Bible, constitute my stock. The last constitutes my chief

resource; but the want of other mental pabulum is felt severely. There is little to interest in the conversation of the people. Loud disputes often about the women, and angry altercations in which the same string of abuse is used, are more frequent than anything else.[4]

This Journal, it has been remarked, "was probably the most wonderful thing of the kind ever taken on such a journey". The advantage of keeping a systematic record had been suggested to him by Tidman in the postscript of a letter dated 1 March 1851, as being of more value than the "vague and general impressions conveyed in a hastily written letter".[5] The criticism was not without justification. Livingstone's letters were for the most part ill-composed and ill-written; untidy, and in a large hand. His Journal is the opposite of this: it is written with meticulous care in beautiful script. (Students of calligraphy would be interested to compare his handwriting with his father's. The latter is also that of an educated man; but while his style is pointed, long, and sloping, that of his son is rounded. But in spite of this difference in style, there is a pronounced similarity in the formation of the letters, namely an *openness*—of the kind which is supposed to signify the possession of candour.) The Journal is a strongly-bound quarto volume of more than 800 pages, with lock and key. His custom was to jot down his observations in small notebooks, and extend them in the Journal when detained by rain or other causes. As Blaikie has well said:

> The writing is so neat and clear that it might almost be taken for lithograph. Occasionally there is a page with letters beginning to sprawl, as if one of those times had come when he tells us that he could neither think nor speak, nor tell anyone's name—possibly not even his own, if he had been asked for it.[6]

Besides the Journal, he must also have acquired at Loanda a vast store of writing-paper; the large sheets covered with figures calculated from astronomical observations, for despatch to Sir Thomas Maclear, were said by him when collected to fill a tin trunk.

Early rains having fallen, it was now possible to navigate the Chobe, but its course was so tortuous that some of the party preferred to walk between the bends, at one point traversing in six hours a distance which the canoes, at double their speed, took twelve hours to accomplish. Within a week they had reached the main river and on the 19th were again in Sesheke. Here Livingstone on his previous visit had introduced the system of punishing crime by the exaction of manual labour, instead of a fine—or of torture till it was paid. He now gave many public addresses to the people under the welcome shade of a camel-thorn tree, and found his audience both numerous and attentive, though he was partially recovering from another severe attack of fever, and the exertion of loud speaking again inflamed his throat. He was too weak to "supply the camp with flesh"—but he was well supplied by the chief with honey, milk, and meal; and by nature with various kinds of wild fruit. "We all felt great lassitude in travelling. The atmosphere is oppressive both in cloud and sunshine. The evaporation from the river must be excessively great."

On 30 November they were again at the Gonye Falls: "viewed from the mass of rock which overhangs them, the scenery was the loveliest I had seen". The river-dwellers there were "a merry set of mortals—a feeble joke sets them off into fits of laughter". They were importunate with requests for the magic lantern and, "as it is a good means of conveying instruction, I willingly complied". At Nameta's village, on the edge of the Barotse valley, the people were suspicious because of recent raids by the Makololo. These had been carried out, in defiance of Sekeletu's orders, by his uncle Mpololo. A little further on they heard that another foray was impending, "but I sent forward orders to disband the party immediately". Mpololo himself was found in the town of Sekeletu's mother who heartily concurred with the winged words which Livingstone had addressed him. She even suggested that the prisoners taken in the raid should be restored. "Her good sense appeared in other respects besides." Mpololo was amenable to correction, and desired that the matter be laid before the underchiefs at Nariele, the Barotse capital. Arrived there on 9 December, Livingstone caused a *picho* to be summoned, at which "Mpololo took all the guilt upon himself before the people, and delivered up a captive child whom his wife had in her possession; others followed his example till we procured the release of five of the prisoners." The incident is noteworthy as the first act of liberation in which Livingstone took a direct part.

The rains began in earnest at Nariele but, though refreshing, they did not lessen the oppressive heat of the Zambesi valley; and here Livingstone was stricken again with fever "which caused excessive languor". From this place he sent back Sekeletu's canoe, and, furnished with others by Mpololo as well as with eight riding oxen and seven for slaughter, departed "amidst an abundance of good wishes". Arrived at Libonta on 17 December the party was detained for some days by collecting produce which Sekeletu had ordered for presentation to the Balonda chiefs, and also by the sickness of some of the party and of the villagers who required medical assistance. Here Livingstone demanded the restitution of the rest of the captives taken in the Makololo raid, bringing their number up to nineteen. The country beyond this was uninhabited as far as Lunda, a village owned by two of the chief wives of Sebituane, who provided him with an ox and other food in abundance.

> The same kindness was manifested by all who could afford to give anything; and as I glance over their deeds of generosity recorded in my journal, my heart glows with gratitude to them, and I hope and pray that God may spare me to make them some return.

When some forty miles above Libonta he sent eleven of the freed captives some distance westward to their homes, and perforce waited for their escort's return. Quantities of wild game and herds of antelopes of various species wandered near, unsuspicious of the close proximity of human beasts of prey. "It was grievous to shoot these lovely creatures, they were so tame. . . . If we had been starving I could have slaughtered them with as little hesitation as I should cut off a patient's leg; but I felt a doubt, and the antelopes got the better of it." He lay in the grass watching them so long that his men, thinking him ill, came up and frightened them away. He reflects on the superior tenacity of life in the nervous organisms of creatures adapted for an amphibious existence over those of others, and the fact that a bullet through the heart will not always cause instant death. His men were continually begging him for "gun-medicine", and he only wished that he could give it to them; "for, having but little of the hunting *furore* in my composition, I always preferred eating the game to killing it". Instead, he tried to teach them how to shoot, but they would soon have spent all the ammunition: "I was thus obliged to do all the shooting myself ever afterwards"—while the men searched for fruit.

On 27 December, a Sunday, they were again at the confluence of the Leeba with the Leeambye.* The scene was one of indescribable beauty.

> All of us rise early to enjoy the luscious balmy air of the morning. We then have worship; but amidst all the beauty and loveliness with which we are surrounded, there is still a want in the soul in viewing one's poor companions, and hearing bitter impure words jarring on the ear in the perfection of the scenes of nature, and a longing that both their hearts and ours might be brought into harmony with the great Father of Spirits.

At this point he writes, "I shall not often advert to their depravity"; and in a striking passage (which Campbell quotes in full) compares his self-detachment from their revolting habits with that of a physician in the slums who seeks to alleviate and cure human misery and sin "without remaining longer in the filth than is necessary to his work".

Here he sent some remaining captives—two little boys, a girl, a young man, and two older women—eastwards to Masiko, the Barotse chief who had succeeded Santaru, with an admonitory message that "I was sorry to find that Santaru had not borne a wiser son. Santaru had loved to govern men, but Masiko wanted to govern wild beasts only, as he sold his people to the Mambari"—and that if Masiko desired a fuller explanation of his views he had better send a sensible man to talk with him at the first town of the Balonda.

He discourses at length on the flora of the Barotse valley, the soil of which is most fertile and if ploughed would yield a prolific crop of grain. The crocodiles in the Leeambye were more numerous and more savage than he had seen elsewhere. In remembering them and other dangerous beasts—such as the buffalo and the black rhinoceros—he writes: "In many cases, not referred to in this book, I feel more horror now in thinking of the dangers I have run than I did at the time of their occurrence."

* See footnote p. 182.

He was now outside the domains of Sekeletu and diplomatic negotiations became more than ever necessary. His party had entered the territory of the Balonda who were suspicious of the warlike Makololo. The village of their nearest chief, a young female named Manenko, lay some miles away to the east, and Livingstone sent her a message explaining his intentions. After waiting two days a reply was returned, with a basket of manioc-roots, that he must stay where he was till she should vist him. This was soon followed by a message, of typically feminine caprice, that he must come to her!—"After four days of rains and negotiations, I declined going at all and proceeded up the river."

On 1 January 1854 "we had heavy rains almost every day, indeed the rainy season had fairly set in"—so much so that for a fortnight he could get no single observation either for latitude or longitude. On the 6th they came near to the village of Nyamoana, who was Manenko's mother, and sister of the paramount chief Shinte. Here a court was convened to meet the stranger with due ceremony, a spokesman from either side acting as interpreter. On Livingstone's perceiving that his message of peace and goodwill was being misinterpreted and confused with local politics, he intervened to correct it; and, the meeting having ended, he gained their confidence by showing them his hair and the skin of his chest and comparing it with theirs. He also produced his watch and pocket compass, objects which were always regarded with wonder, but Nyamoana could not be induced by her husband so much as to come near them.

Livingstone wished to continue his journey upstream without delay, but Nyamoana was anxious to provide him with an escort to her brother; and when he explained the advantage of water-carriage, she replied that her brother did not live beside the river, and moreover there was a cataract higher upstream. She was afraid too that the Balobale people, ignorant of the object of his party, "would kill us". To Livingstone's assurance that he had been so often threatened with death if he visited a new tribe that he was now more afraid of killing some-one than of being killed, she rejoined that, though the Balobale would not kill him, they would certainly kill the Makololo. "This produced considerable effect on my companions", and the discussion had reached a critical stage when it was interrupted—and clinched—by the arrival of Manenko herself upon the scene.

Manenko was a tall strapping woman of about twenty, distinguished by a profusion of ornaments and medicines hung about her person. Her body was smeared all over with a mixture of fat and red ochre, as a protection against the weather; a necessary precaution, for, like most of the Balonda ladies, she was otherwise in a state of frightful nudity. This was not from want of clothing, for, being a chief, she might have been as well clad as any of her subjects, but from her peculiar ideas of elegance in dress.

She and her husband listened for some time attentively to the white man's arguments in favour of river-transport and of cementing a bond of friendship between the Balonda and Makololo; after which he, acting as spokesman, commenced an oration explaining their arrival and during pauses in the delivery picked up a little sand and rubbed it on his chest and arms—a polite mode of salutation. Having ended he rose and strutted about, displaying the copper rings with which his ankles were adorned. Manenko then spoke. She was quite decided in adopting the policy of friendship with the Makololo, and to cement the bond proposed that Kolimbota, the spokesman of Livingstone's party, should immediately take a wife from among the Balonda. "Kolimbota, I found, thought favourably of the proposition, and it afterwards led to his desertion from us." But Manenko was equally decided in agreeing with her mother's views concerning the best method of travel and announced that she intended to accompany the white man's party to her uncle herself.

On the evening of the same day an imposing embassy arrived from Masiko with large presents. Through his under-chiefs who came in force, he expressed his delight at the return of the captives, and at the proposal of peace and alliance with the Makololo. In return Livingstone presented them with an ox, which Sekeletu had given him for his own party; this reduced their provisions to a few manioc-roots and a small loaf of maize. The deputation from Masiko was equally destitute, yet all were so rejoiced at the upshot of this meeting that they resolved to spend a day together; and "after pleasant hungry converse by day, we regaled our friends with the magic lantern by night", and then erected their sheds in Nyamoana's village. Whilst doing so, Manenko fell upon their friends from Masiko with her tongue "in a way that left no doubt in our minds but that she is a most accomplished scold". Her grievance was concerning a cloth which she had sent to Masiko and which he had returned, since it had the appearance of having been bewitched.

She advanced and receded in true oratorical style, belabouring her own servants as well for allowing the offence, and, as usual in more civilized feminine lectures, she leaned over the objects of her ire, and screamed forth all their faults and failings ever since they were born, and her despair at ever seeing them become better. Masiko's people followed the plan of receiving this torrent of abuse in silence, and, as neither we nor they had anything to eat, we parted until next morning.

Manenko provided them with some more manioc-roots in the morning, and repeated her intention of conveying their baggage to her uncle's town. Unwilling to encounter a scolding from "this black Mrs. Caudle" Livingstone ordered his men to pack their goods; but she then announced that they must wait for the arrival of her porters the next day. "Being on low disagreeable diet I felt annoyed at this further delay, and ordered the packages to be put into the canoes"; but Manenko was not to be circumvented in this way; she came forward with her people and seized the luggage, "declaring that she would carry it in spite of me".

My men succumbed sooner to this petticoat government than I felt inclined to do, and left me no power; and, being unwilling to encounter her tongue, I was moving off to the canoes when she gave me a kind explanation and, with her hand on my shoulder, put on a motherly look, saying, "Now my little man, just do as the rest have done." My feelings of annoyance of course vanished, and I went to try and get some meat.

In this however he was unsuccessful, his gun misfired when he had sighted a zebra and the herd made off. He was also suffering, and had been for days previously, from attacks of intermittent fever. The start was made next day, 11 January, led at a quick pace by the athletic young virago in a heavy drizzling mist which soon turned to drenching rain, "and on our Amazon went, in the very lightest marching order, and at a pace that few of the men could keep up with". Livingstone, riding beside her on an ox, asked why she wore no protection against the rain, and was told that it was unbecoming in a chief to appear effeminate and that she should set an example in bearing hardship. But all were glad when she at last proposed a halt and the erection of four shelters for the night. The downpour was of a ferocity that Livingstone had never known in the south and it held them up for two days. Manenko herself went out to forage for her guest and returned with no more than five heads of maize. The forests became ever more dense as they moved on; they were in fact passing out of the stunted Rhodesian bush into the great tropical forest of West Equatorial Africa. Livingstone was subsisting on a diet of "a little tapioca", conserving his scanty stock of meal "for worse times". The rains with which he was constantly drenched had, however, done some good; they had produced vast mushrooms in the spongy soil, many of them very large "and very good, even when eaten raw".

> The deep gloom contrasted strongly with the shadeless glare of the Kalahari, which had left an indelible impression on my memory. Though drenched day by day at this time, it was long before I could believe that we were getting too much of a good thing. Nor could I look at water being thrown away without a slight quick impression flitting across the mind that we were guilty of wasting it.

The Balonda were superstitious in the use of spells to a degree unknown among the Bechuanas or any southern tribes, besides which Livingstone found among them for the first time in his experience the worship of idols. These by the use of charms could be made to hear and give responses. When Manenko insisted on sending forward messengers to apprise her uncle of their coming and on waiting for their return, Livingstone, who had fever "and found it very difficult to exercise patience with her whims", asked why this was necessary seeing that the idols could inform her uncle just as well. To this she replied in native idiom, "It's only my idea". She then ground some meal for him with her own hands, and told him she had begged the corn for it from a village, with an air as though to say, "I know how to manage, don't I?"

On Sunday, 15 January, they received a favourable reply from Shinte by messengers with a present of manioc and dried fishes, and went forward to the next village. "They behaved with reverence at our religious services. This will appear important, if the reader remembers the almost total want of prayer and reverence we encountered in the south." Next day, which "for a wonder was fair", they entered Shinte's populous town at a time "when Manenko thought the sun was high enough for us to make a lucky entrance"; and were greeted first by a crowd of fully armed men "who ran towards us as if they would eat us up"; and next by two native Portuguese traders and many of their Mambari accomplices who had a gang of female slaves in a chain hoeing the ground of their encampment. "They are not men," exclaimed his Makololo, "who treat their children so!"

On the 17th they were honoured with a grand reception in the *kotla*. Shinte, seated on a kind of throne under a banian tree, was first saluted with a fusillade, drums and trumpets, and the obeisance with ashes of the headmen of each tribe. Livingstone had retreated to the shade of another tree some distance off and was followed by his men. "Then came the soldiers all armed to the teeth, running and shouting towards us with their swords drawn, and their faces screwed up so as to appear as savage as possible, for the purpose, I thought, of trying whether they could not make us take to our heels. As we did not, they turned round towards Shinte and saluted him, then retired." This was followed by a variety of the "curious caperings" customary at *pichos*, after which Manenko's husband as spokesman delivered a theatrical oration before Shinte in praise of the white man and in explanation of his journey. Then a party of musicians paraded the *kotla*, and after nine speakers had concluded their orations Shinte stood up and so did all the people. "He had maintained true African dignity of manner all the while, but my people remarked that he scarcely ever took his eyes off me for a moment."

Livingstone was awakened that night by a message from Shinte desiring an immediate visit. As he was in the sweating stage of fever and the path led through a wet valley, he declined. When Kolimbota, who knew their customs best, expostulated, Livingstone replied that "he hated the words of night and deeds of darkness, and that he was neither a hyaena nor a witch". He expressed himself ready at ten o'clock the next morning and was forthwith conducted to the chief's court, the walls of which were woven rods "all very neat and high. Many trees stood within the enclosure and afforded a grateful shade." Shinte soon came: an elderly man, of frank and open countenance, and evidently in good humour. He had expected yesterday, he said, that "a man who came from the gods would have approached and talked to him". Livingstone replied that such had been his own intention, but when his men saw the formidable preparations he yielded to their suggestion to keep a respectful distance first. "His remark confirmed my previous belief that a frank, open, fearless manner is the most winning of all with these Africans." Livingstone then unfolded the objects of his mission: the return of captives; the opening up of the country for trade; the Bible as a word from heaven; his desire for the tribes to live in peace; "and to all that I advanced the old gentleman clapped his hands in approbation", his company following suit. When asked whether he had ever seen a white man before, he replied never—only Mambari and native Portuguese. Livingstone then presented him with an ox, to his great delight; and advised him to begin a trade in cattle with the Makololo, an idea which pleased him.

> During this time Manenko had been extremely busy with all her people in getting up a very pretty hut and courtyard to be, as she said, her residence always when white men were brought by her along the same path. When she heard that we had given an ox to her uncle, she came forward to us with the air of one wronged, and explained that "This white man belonged to her; she had brought him here, and therefore the ox was hers, not Shinte's." She ordered her men to bring it, got it slaughtered by them, and presented her uncle with a leg only. Shinte did not seem at all annoyed at the occurrence.

Livingstone does not relate his farewell with this bossy but good-natured maiden; yet one cannot but be faintly and remotely reminded, *mutatis mutandis*, of the encounter of the much-enduring Odysseus with the white-armed Nausicaa and of his introduction by her to the shadowy halls of her father the great-hearted Alcinous. At any rate it formed one of the lighter, brighter episodes of a journey in which such were all too few.

On the 19th he was again awakened at an early hour whilst copiously perspiring after the thirst of a raging fever, and again declined the summons. After a few hours he went, and violent action of the heart did not predispose him to be patient when

informed that Shinte could not be found. Hardly had he returned to bed when another message was received: "Shinte
wished to say all he had to tell me at once." This was too
tempting an offer, so he went; Shinte had a fowl ready in his
hand to present, also a basket of manioc-meal and a calabash
of mead. Remarking on Livingstone's constantly recurrent
fever, he said that this would prove the only possible hindrance
to his journey since he would supply men who knew all the
paths. In reply to an enquiry what he would recommend for
the fever, he advised plenty of mead: "as it gets in, it will drive
the fever out". Since it was strong, Livingstone suspected that
he liked the remedy himself, though he had no fever. Shinte
said that he had always been friends with Sebituane, and
therefore felt towards Sekeletu as a father to a son; and if a
son asked a favour, the father must give it. He was much
pleased with Sekeletu's presents of clarified butter and fat, and
proposed to detain Kolimbota as the bearer of presents in
return. He offered Livingstone a little slave-girl to be his child
and bring him water, and on his refusal offered him another
who was a head taller. Livingstone thanked him for the kind
thought and proceeded to explain at length the reasons for his
abhorrence of any kind of slavery.

Shinte was most anxious to see the pictures of the magic
lantern, but Livingstone had by this time such violent action
of the heart and such a buzzing in the ears that he could not
show them for some days. The exhibition was attended by the
principal men and a bevy of court beauties.

> The first picture exhibited was Abraham about to slaughter his son
> Isaac; it was drawn as large as life, and the uplifted knife was in the act
> of striking the lad. The Balonda men remarked that the picture was
> much more like a god than the things of wood or clay they worshipped.
> I explained that this man was the first of a race to whom God had given
> the Bible we now held, and that among his children our Saviour ap-
> peared. The ladies listened with silent awe; but when I moved the slide,
> the uplifted dagger moving towards them, they thought it was to be
> sheathed in their bodies instead of Isaac's. "Mother! mother!" all
> shouted at once, and off they rushed helter-skelter, tumbling pell-mell
> over each other, and over the little idol-huts and tobacco-bushes; we
> could not get one of them back again. Shinte, however, sat bravely through
> the whole, and afterwards examined the instrument with interest.

Livingstone always added an explanation of its powers, "so

that no one should imagine there was aught supernatural in it". People would come long distances to see it. "It was the only mode of instruction," he adds dryly, "I was ever asked to repeat."

Rain was again frequent and heavy; in spite of constant care his guns and surgical instruments were rusty, clothing mildewed, shoes mouldy, his little tent so rotten and perforated that he covered his head with his blanket when he lay down. The temperature dropped with startling suddenness; Manenko's husband who had been sent for guides returned without them, dead drunk; Shinte himself was busy preparing meal for the journey. Livingstone chafed at the delay: "one cannot get away quickly from these chiefs".

> As the last proof of friendship Shinte came into my tent, though it could scarcely contain more than one person, looked at all the curiosities . . . with the greatest interest; then closing the tent, so that none of his own people might see the extravagance of which he was about to be guilty, he drew out from his clothing a string of beads, and the end of a conical shell which is considered, in regions far from the sea, of as great value as the Lord Mayor's badge is in London. He hung it round my neck and said, "There, now you *have* a proof of my friendship."

At their last interview on 26 January he appointed as principal guide among others an elderly man, Intemese, with orders to remain with the white man till he reached the sea; supplied eight additional bearers; and provided the party with food for the way; and after remarking that "no one could say we had been driven away from his town, he gave a most hearty salutation, and we parted with the wish that God might bless him."

On 22 January, his last Sunday at Shinte's town, Livingstone had written in his Journal words which deserve to be repeated here, since they reflect his view of the missionary scene in the interior of Africa in its relation to the progress of missionary enterprise as a whole, and his own religious toleration and lack of any kind of ecclesiastical partisanship. He constantly compares his own and his colleagues' efforts to the planting of seeds of which they will never see the fruits; or to stars whose light will fade when the dawn breaks; or to little stones cut out of a mountain that will one day help to build a temple.

This age presents one great fact in the Providence of God: missions are sent forth to all quarters of the world—missions not of one section of the Church, but of all sections, and from nearly all Christian nations. It seems very unfair to judge the success of these by the number of conversions which have followed. These are rather proofs of the missions being of the right sort. They show the direction of the stream which is set in motion by Him who rules the nations, and is destined to overflow the world. The fact which ought to stimulate us above all others is, not that we have contributed to the conversion of a few souls, however valuable these may be, but that we are diffusing a knowledge of Christianity throughout the world. The number of conversions in India is but a poor criterion of the success which has followed the missionaries there. The general knowledge is the criterion; and there, as well as in other lands where missionaries in the midst of masses of heathenism seem like voices crying in the wilderness—Reformers before the Reformation—future missionaries will see conversions following every sermon. We prepare the way for them. May they not forget the pioneers who worked in the thick gloom with few rays to cheer except such as flow from faith in God's promises! We work for a glorious future which we are not destined to see —the golden age which has not been, but yet will be. . . .

For this time we work; may God accept our imperfect service!

The next stage of the journey—to Katema's town—was attended by some incidents of a pleasant, others of an unpleasant nature. Their staple food was as before manioc-porridge, which when boiled had "the consistency of starch and the flavour of diseased potatoes: and no matter how much one may eat, two hours afterwards he is as hungry as ever." But occasionally a generous chief would vary this unpalatable diet with the meal of maize, or even a few fowls, or fish. Progress was often impeded by the delay in forwarding messages and awaiting the replies. Livingstone was impressed with the punctiliousness in etiquette of the Balonda as compared with the Makololo, as well as by their more elaborate superstitions. Above Cazembe's village they crossed the river (which he still called the Leeba) with difficulty, though here it was only a hundred yards wide; and here he had the satisfaction of taking astronomical observations. But heavy rains persisted. "Again and again did I take out the instruments and, just as all was right, the stars would be suddenly obscured. . . . Five out of six days we had this pouring rain, at or near break of day, for months altogether." His tent was already beginning to be worn to shreds. On 1 February one of the guide's men was found to have stolen a fowl from the tent, an offence which

greatly angered the Makololo; fortunately the confusion of
Intemese, when the crime was detected, provoked much
laughter. But it was the first instance of the kind that Livingstone had met with, north or south. The night-rains were such
that their sleeping-places were flooded from below, so that
from now on they dug a furrow round each booth and slept
on mounds raised above it. The Makololo were always cheerful,
whether wet or hungry, and never afraid of work. On the 7th
they camped in the village of Katema's half-brother, where
Intemese (as instructed by Shinte) was loud in protestations of
their good credentials and behaviour, but himself refused to
move on the next day. "We packed up and went on without
him. We did not absolutely need him, but he was useful in
preventing the inhabitants of secluded villages from betaking
themselves to flight. We wished to be on good terms with all,
and therefore put up with our guide's peccadilloes." He caught
them up the day after. Their next host, Mozinkwa, was "a
most intelligent and friendly man"—whilst his children "were
the finest negro family I ever saw". He and his one wife had
cultivated a garden, hedged with live banian round the neat
huts of their compound, with various useful crops, and shaded
the whole with hand-planted trees. They were most hospitable
to the white man and his party. But, alas, when Livingstone
passed that way again the wife was in her grave, and the trees,
garden, and huts were left—by native custom on the death of
a favourite wife—in ruins. "This renders any permanent village
in the country impossible." After leaving Mozinkwa's "hospitable mansion" on the 10th, they were led next day by the
wiles of Intemese to the abode of Katema's father-in-law,
Quendende.

> This fine old man was so very polite, that we did not regret being
> obliged to spend Sunday at his village. He expressed his pleasure at
> having a share in the honour of the visit as well as Katema; though it
> seemed to me that the conferring of that pleasure required something like
> a good stock of impudence—in leading twenty-seven men through the
> country without the means of purchasing food.

Here Livingstone held as usual a religious service, and spoke
on the central theme of Christianity: "the fact, than which
none more striking can be mentioned, that the Son of God

came down from heaven to die for us. If this fails to interest them, nothing else will succeed." Quendende himself, though stricken in years, accompanied the travellers to Katema's town where a similar formal presentation was made as at Shinte's. The chief was liberal with gifts of food. "He seemed in good spirits, laughing heartily several times. This is a good sign, for a man who shakes his sides with mirth is seldom difficult to deal with." But his government was lax and he had little control over his people. Here for the first time Livingstone found himself in difficulties with the language: "it is a misery to speak through an interpreter, as I was now forced to do". He presented the chief with gifts of European make, and pleased him by showing him how to milk his cows. His men formed many friendships with Katema's people, but none of them would be enlisted as porters, even at their chief's orders. The day before leaving, Livingstone was again seized with fever when for the first time in his experience a cold wind was blowing from the north.

> [From his Journal.] Sunday, 19th. Sick all Sunday and unable to move. Several of the people were ill, too, so that I could do nothing but roll from side to side in my miserable little tent, in which, with all the shade we could give it, the thermometer stood upwards of 90°, though this was the beginning of winter.
>
> Amidst all the beauty and loveliness with which I am surrounded, there is still a feeling of want in the soul—as if something more were needed to bathe the soul in bliss than the sight of the perfection in working, and goodness in planning, of the great Father of our spirits. I need to be purified—fitted for the eternal, to which my soul stretches away in ever-returning longings. I need to be made more like my blessed Saviour, to serve my God with all my powers. Look upon me, Spirit of the living God, and supply all Thou seeest lacking.

He was up and on the move again next day notwithstanding, and was cheered by the sight and song of canaries; and after progressing some seven miles came round the "small end" of Lake Dilolo. "If it be thought strange that I should pass so near the broad end without looking at it, it must be remembered that I had eaten nothing for two whole days, and, instead of sleep, employed the night in incessant drinking of water."

Having been bitten on the forehead by a spider while half-asleep he is led to discourse on the habits and anatomy of several species of these creatures, and then on those of ants. On the 24th they had crossed the almost level waterlogged plain, at an elevation of about four thousand feet, which Livingstone correctly conjectured to be the watershed between the Zambesi and the Congo; and now as they progressed westward the tribes became more unfriendly and avaricious as well as "more bloodily superstitious". It was evident that frequent traffic with the Portuguese slave-dealers had demoralized them.

> This trade causes bloodshed; for when a poor family is selected as the victims, it is necessary to get rid of the older members of it, because they are supposed to be able to give annoyance to the chief afterwards by means of enchantments. The belief in the power of charms for good or evil produces not only honesty, but a great amount of gentle dealing. The powerful are often restrained in their despotism, from a fear that the weak and helpless may injure them by their medical knowledge. They have many fears.

Barter, also, now took the place of friendly exchange of gifts, and sometimes tricks were devised in order to extort fines. At Kabinje's village they were refused a guide to Kangenke's unless he was sent back when within sight of the latter. On the 27th they had reached Kangenke who promptly furnished guides without demur, but secretly caused a knife to be dropped near Livingstone's camp and a watch to be kept. When his party had reached the ford of the Kasai (a main tributary of the Congo) and half of their number were across it, the charge was made that one of his men had stolen a knife. Certain of their honesty, Livingstone angrily desired the luggage to be searched; the unlucky lad who had taken the bait then came forward and confessed it. But the owner now demanded the payment of a fine. An offer of beads was scornfully rejected, and the lad was compelled to part with a precious shell similar to Shinte's gift, worn round the neck. Livingstone, in charge of his party, always followed the custom of being the last to cross a river; had he not submitted to the demand he would have been seized as a hostage.

He camped three miles from the next village, Katende's. The chief sent word next day desiring an interview. It was raining when Livingstone arrived and a long time was spent in a hut, giving and receiving messages from the invisible chief who was reported to be very corpulent, and who demanded either a man, a tusk, beads, copper-wire, or a shell. "My men were as much astonished as myself at the demand for payment for leave to pass, and the almost entire neglect of the rules of hospitality." Unable to comply, he took his leave and walked back to his camp through the rain. But one of the chief's men suggested that a shirt might be acceptable; whereupon Livingstone selected the worst and despatched it with an invitation to Katende to come himself for more clothing if he wanted it, adding that "when I reached my own chief naked, and was asked what I had done with my clothes, I should be obliged to confess that I had left them with Katende". The shirt however was accepted, and guides and food provided for the following day. His bluff had succeeded where the timidity of many passing traders, who yielded to exorbitant demands, had failed. Again, when tribute was vociferously demanded from one of his men by one of Katende's on the pretext of an alleged affront—the man having jocularly addressed him by the name of a Barotse friend whom he resembled—Livingstone told his Makololo to make no reply whatever. When the man returned and suggested the exchange of a small gift instead, and still no notice was taken, he departed somewhat crestfallen. But on crossing a rude bridge over a stream beyond the village and being unexpectedly confronted at the other end by a negro who demanded a fee on the ground that the right of way and the bridge were his, Livingstone was for a moment nonplussed by this reminder of civilization. "I stood for a few seconds, looking at our bold toll-keeper, when one of my men took off three copper-bracelets, which paid for the whole party." The toll-keeper was however better than he seemed, for he immediately went to his garden and produced some tobacco-leaves as a present. When they were well away from any villages and had reached a junction of three paths, Katende's guides sat down and announced that unless they were immediately presented with some cloth they would not show the travellers which path to take. Livingstone was in favour of proceeding without them and taking his chance of the route with the aid of his compass, but one of his men asked leave to present his own cloth which, when the guides saw, they took with shouts of acceptance. Their route now took them through a network of tributary streams, some of them chin-deep and others with dangerously rapid currents; or through saturated bogs in which they waded thigh-deep. "We had not met with a stone since leaving Shinte's." Their oxen were swum across the streams, the men holding on by their tails. On one of these occasions Livingstone was parted from his ox in midstream, so struck out for the opposite bank alone.

> My poor fellows were dreadfully alarmed when they saw me parted from the cattle, and about twenty of them made a simultaneous rush into the water for my rescue, and just as I reached the opposite bank one seized my arm and another threw his about my body. When I stood up, it was most gratifying to see them all struggling towards me. Some had leaped off the bridge, and allowed their cloaks to float down the stream. Part of my goods, abandoned in the hurry, were brought up from the bottom after I was safe. Great was the pleasure expressed when they found that I could swim like themselves, without the aid of a tail, and I did and do feel grateful to these poor heathens for the promptitude with which they dashed in to save, as they thought, my life. I found my clothes cumbersome in the water; they could swim quicker from being naked. They swim like dogs, not frog-fashion as we do.

Whilst he was drying himself afterwards by turning round and round before a fire, he was pleased to hear them say, "We can all swim; who carried the white man across the river but himself?"

On 4 March they came to the outskirts of the territory of the Chiboque who proved the fiercest and most implacable people yet encountered. Arrived at Njambi's village with all their provisions spent, and intending to pass a quiet Sunday, Livingstone ordered a riding-ox to be slaughtered and sent him the hump and ribs as customary tribute. The chief returned thanks and the promise of food. But next day he sent an impudent message, with a very little meal, demanding either a man, an ox, a gun, powder, cloth or a shell. To this Livingstone replied with a reasonable but firm refusal. Some of the Chiboque were heard to remark, "They have only five guns." At noon on Sunday his camp was surrounded by Njambi's men armed with swords and guns aimed at the white man. His own men seized their javelins and stood on the defensive. Livingstone's calm deliberation in this crisis is impressive.

> I sat on my camp-stool, with my double-barrelled gun across my knees, and invited the chief to be seated also. When he and his counsellors had sat down on the ground in front of me, I asked what crime we had committed that he had come armed in that way.

The reply was that one of his men had in spitting allowed some spittle to fall on a Chiboque, and this offence must be settled by the fine of a man, ox, or gun. The man being questioned admitted the offence, which was accidental and had occurred while he was making the offended party the present of some meat. Livingstone then said in reply to the demand for a man, "that my men might as well give me, as I give one of them, for we were all free men".—A gun, then. This also Livingstone refused, saying that he did not wish to assist them in their evident intention to plunder him.

> This they denied, saying that they wanted the customary tribute only. I asked what right they had to demand payment for leave to tread on the ground of God, our common Father? If we trod on their gardens we would pay but not for marching on land which was still God's and not theirs. They did not attempt to controvert this, because it is in accordance with their own ideas, but reverted again to the pretended crime of the saliva.

At this point his men entreated him to give something; and on his asking the chief if he really thought this trivial accident culpable, and being answered in the affirmative, he gave him one of his shirts. But the young Chiboque were still dissatisfied and began shouting and brandishing their swords. Thereupon the innocent Makololo offender begged him to offer something else. Livingstone offered some beads, but the counsellors now objected; then a handkerchief, but the more he yielded, the more they demanded and the more threatening their behaviour became.

> One young man made a charge at my head from behind, but I quickly brought round the muzzle of my gun to his mouth and he retreated. I pointed him out to the chief, and he ordered him to retire a little. I felt anxious to avoid the effusion of blood; and though sure of being able with my Makololo, who had been drilled by Sebituane, to drive off twice the number of our assailants, though now a large body and well armed with spears, swords, arrows, and guns, I strove to avoid actual collision. My men were quite unprepared for this exhibition, but behaved with admirable coolness. The chief and counsellors, by accepting my invitation to be seated, had placed themselves in a trap; for my men very quietly surrounded them, and made them feel that there was no chance of escaping their spears.
>
> I then said that, as one thing after another had failed to satisfy them, it was evident *they* wanted to fight, while *we* only wanted to pass peaceably through the country; that they must begin first and bear the guilt before God: we would not fight till they had struck the first blow. I then sat

silent for some time. It was rather trying for me, because I knew that the Chiboque would aim at the white man first; but I was careful not to appear flurried, and having four barrels ready for instant action, looked quietly at the savage scene around.

He noticed, he says, that "the Chiboque countenance, by no means handsome, is not improved by their practice of filing the teeth". This quiet observation bespeaks a long moment of tension. It was broken at last by the Chiboque. "You come among us in a new way, and say you are quite friendly: how can we know it unless you give us some food, and you take some of ours?" Urged by his men he gave them an ox, and received in return the same evening a very small basket of meal, and two or three pounds' weight of the same ox!

It was impossible to avoid a laugh at the coolness of the generous creatures. I was truly thankful nevertheless that, though resolved to die rather than deliver up one of our number as a slave, we had so far gained our point as to be allowed to pass on without shedding human blood.

We had proceeded on the principles of peace and conciliation, and the foregoing treatment shows in what light our conduct was viewed; in fact, we were taken for interlopers trying to cheat the revenue of the tribe. They had been accustomed to get a slave or two from every slave-trader who passed them, and now that we had disputed the right, they viewed the infringement on what they considered lawfully due, with most virtuous indignation.

This experience however was enough to convince him of the unwisdom of following the direct slave-route to the coast; he therefore struck northwards through soggy ground and in heavy rain towards the Portuguese settlement of Cassange. But from now on troubles, so far from diminishing, thickened about him. His clothes were seldom dry and his fever, which had been intermittent, became almost chronic. This was to him a source of much regret, he says, in that it induced a confusion of mind which prevented him, on one rare cloudless night, after some hours' trial, from obtaining a lunar observation of which he could be quite confident. But he still made notes on the flora. Commenting on Livingstone's almost reckless disregard of either his comfort or his health at this stage of the journey, Sir Harry Johnston, himself a seasoned African traveller, wrote:

He had to cross streams or rivers daily, and on these occasions was always wetted up to his thighs, if not up to his neck. It never seems to have occurred to him to change and dry his clothes; he either attempted to dry himself by walking on through the blazing sun, or he did not even make the attempt, but sat down or remained stationary in his wet clothes whenever he had occasion to wait for his men or to stop for any purpose on the line of march. Is it surprising under these conditions that he was attacked by fever? Is it not rather surprising that he lived through such experiences at all?[7]

Once his ox 'Sinbad'—which had a softer back but a much more intractable temper than the others—ran so low below a hanging climber in the forest that he was swept off and fell on the crown of his head; "and he never allowed an opportunity of this kind to pass without trying to inflict a kick, as if I neither had, nor deserved, his love".

The nadir of his misfortunes appeared to be reached on Saturday, 11 March, when an attempt at mutiny was made. Some of his men (not Makololo) had been grumbling about his distribution of beads. He had given them to a few men to purchase a little food for a hasty march to a village before slaughtering a tired ox to give them all for a feast and a rest on Sunday. He explained this to them, patiently, and then sank into a stupor which rendered him oblivious of everything. He awoke next morning to a terrible din, and requested them twice by a message to be more quiet, as the noise pained him. No attention being paid, he put out his head and repeated the request—to be answered by an impudent laugh. They thought him now too weak to exercise control.

> Knowing that discipline would be at an end if this mutiny were not quelled, and that our lives depended on vigorously upholding authority, I seized a double-barrelled pistol and darted forth from the domicile, looking, I suppose, so savage as to put them to precipitate flight. As some remained within hearing, I told them that I must maintain discipline, though at the expense of some of their limbs; so long as we travelled together they must remember that I was master, and not they. There being but little room to doubt my determination, they immediately became very obedient, and never afterwards gave me any trouble, or imagined that they had any right to my property.

A striking proof of their changed demeanour was afforded the next day. They had progressed some miles when the severity of Livingstone's fever compelled a halt. He again sank into a state of partial coma, and awoke in the night to find the camp fenced in with a stockade before which his men armed with spears had mounted guard. They were surrounded with Chiboque who reiterated the now familiar demand for a man, an ox, a gun, or a tusk. He interviewed them in the morning and found them civil; they offered three pigs as "tokens of goodwill", in exchange for which he presented a razor, two bunches of beads, and twelve copper rings which his men contributed. Unable to move from excessive giddiness he remained there till the following evening, when the deputation returned from their chief with the same demand as before. Realizing that refusal would provoke bloodshed Livingstone was about to give a tired riding-ox, when the chief mutineer of the day before posted himself in the gateway and declared that he would rather die than see his master imposed upon. Livingstone ordered him to be removed, and told his men that he esteemed one of their lives of more value than all the oxen, and that nothing would ever induce him to fight except the protection of their lives and liberties. Next day the deputation returned with thirty yards of calico, an axe and two hoes; they also made a pretence of restoring the copper rings which, they said, their chief did not require but which they nevertheless took back themselves. Rains prevented further progress until Thursday, when messengers appeared from the chief with the news that he had punished those who had appropriated the copper rings and also part of the cloth which he had sent. Livingstone's guides thought these were only the spies of a larger party, concealed in the forest farther on. They therefore prepared for defence by marching in a compact body and in torrential rain "through many miles of gloomy forest in gloomier silence", but were not molested. "I was too ill to care whether we were attacked or not." The air was so thick with vapour that sight was limited to a few yards, and when 'Sinbad' broke into a sudden gallop and the bridle broke, his rider was again dismounted backwards on the crown of his head, this time with the added injury of a kick on the thigh. "I felt none the worse for this rough treatment, but would not recommend it to others as a palliative for fever!" He was now reduced "almost to a skeleton". His riding-blanket remained wet beneath him even in the heat of the sun and caused extensive abrasion of the skin. "To this inconvenience was now added the chafing of my projecting bones on the hard bed." In the

day-time he was never dry: even the bridges over the innumer-
able streams to be forded were submerged. At one of these
they were met by another Chiboque band who refused them
further passage. Livingstone ordered his men to proceed, "but
our enemies spread themselves out in front of us with loud
cries"—some running off to their village for guns and arrows.
Livingstone then told his men to ground their baggage at the
edge of the forest, cut down some saplings quickly and fence
it and themselves with a screen, but—though he knew them to
be more than a match for their assailants—to do nothing
unless actually attacked.

> I then dismounted and, advancing a little towards our principal oppo-
> nent, showed him how easily I could kill him, but pointed upwards
> saying "I fear God." He did the same, placing his hand on his heart,
> pointing upwards and saying, "I fear to kill; but come to our village:
> come—do come." At this juncture the old headman, Ionga Panza, a
> venerable negro, came up, and I invited him and all to be seated, that
> we might talk the matter over.

It was the same story: the accustomed tribute, exacted from
slave-traders, was demanded from every chance passer-by;
and Livingstone is led to reflect at some length on the economic
causes and effects of this iniquitous system. At the same time
he calmly took a geographical bearing on the old headman's
village. With him alone he could have dealt well enough; but
negotiations were complicated and in the end frustrated by
Kangenke's guides who now turned traitors and were abetted
by some Bangala traders. "During these exciting scenes I
always forgot my fever, but a terrible sense of sinking came
back with the feeling of safety." The upshot was the beginning
of a scrimmage which he could prevent only by offering all his
beads and shirts, and his men all their ornaments. "It was,"
he says in his Journal, "a day of torture. After talking nearly
the whole day we gave the old chief an ox, but he would not
take it, but another"—this in exchange for some yams, a goat,
fowl and meat. His men were now so thoroughly disheartened
by the whole affair that some of them proposed to leave him
and return home.

> The prospect of being obliged to return when just on the threshold of
> the Portuguese settlements distressed me exceedingly. After using all my
> powers of persuasion, I declared to them that if they returned I would

go on alone, and went into my little tent with the mind directed to Him who hears the sighing of the soul; and was soon followed by the head of Mohorisi, saying—"We will never leave you. Do not be disheartened. Wherever you lead we will follow. Our remarks were made only on account of the injustice of these people." Others followed, and with the most artless simplicity of manner told me to be comforted.—"They were all my children; they knew no one but Sekeletu and me, and they would die for me. . . . "

A little before this he had committed to his Journal words charged with the intensity of his feelings at this moment: a spontaneous heart-cry—not, be it noted, for his own safety (he never prayed for that)—but only for the furtherance of his enterprise and the salvation of heathen Africa.

. . . All I can say has no effect. I can only look up to God to influence their minds, that the enterprise fail not . . . for what else can be done for this miserable land I do not see. It is shut. O Almighty God, help, help! and leave not this wretched people to the slave-dealer and Satan. The people have done well hitherto, I see God's good influence in it. Hope He has left only for a little season. No land needs the gospel more than this miserable portion. I hope I am not to be left to fail in introducing it.

This experience, which was perhaps the worst but not the last in a series of tribulations, had the salutary effect of cementing the bond between Livingstone and his men so that it was henceforth equal to any strain. And it had a happy sequel. It transpired that the first of the two oxen which was proffered had been rejected on the supposition that, because it had lost part of its tail, the remnant had been bewitched with "medicine"—and "some mirth was excited by my proposing to raise a similar objection to all the oxen we still had in our possession. The remaining four soon presented a singular shortness of their caudal extremities . . . and we were no more troubled by the demand for an ox!" He now caused another to be slaughtered, that his men might not be seen fasting while the Chiboque were feasting.

He got away from this village of robbers on 24 March, but not before the venerable but inexorable headman had deprived him of the talismanic shell, Shinte's parting gift, as payment in advance for guides. He was "strongly averse to this", but yielded to the entreaties of his men. Having crossed a stream in a bark canoe (the only one of its kind he ever saw), and being charged dues thrice over for the passage, they were shortly

afterwards deserted by the "guides". Livingstone had expected
this when he paid for them in advance at the request of the
Makololo, "who were rather ignorant of the world". To his
relief they now said that they would do without guides altogether. They spent the next Sunday at a village on the banks
of the Quilo, a beautiful glen; "but fever took away much of
the joy of life, and rendered me very weak and always glad to
recline". The headman, a civil, lively old man, offered no
objections to their progress; but rains and fever impeded it.
On the 30th they came to a sudden descent from the high land,
so steep that Livingstone was obliged to dismount. But he was
now so weak that he could not walk unaided and had to be led
and supported by his companions. "It was annoying to feel
myself so helpless, for I never liked to see a man, either sick or
well, giving in effeminately." Below them lay the valley of the
Quango, a hundred miles in breadth; the scene was magnificent
and reminded him on a much magnified scale of the vale of the
Clyde viewed from the heights above Langside. Stricken as he
was with fever, to which dysentery was now added, he made
detailed notes on the geology of this region.

On Sunday, 2 April, their hunger was severe from having
subsisted for days on nothing but manioc; so they slaughtered
another ox. The Bashinje tribesmen refused to sell them any
food in exchange for the few poor ornaments they had left.
Their chief Sansawe sent the usual formal demand for a man,
an ox, or a tusk. The Bashinje even demanded some of the
flesh of the slain ox, and being refused said, "You may as well
give it, for we shall take all after we have killed you to-morrow."
After arguing all day with different parties sent by Sansawe,
the chief appeared himself—"a quite young man, and of a
rather pleasing countenance"; but Livingstone was informed
by traders that a display of force was often necessary to get
past him. Since he seemed amicable, Livingstone at his request
showed him his hair and skin, "which seemed to strike him
with wonder". To entertain him further and to win his confidence, he produced his watch and pocket compass, but Sansawe then desired him to desist as he was afraid of these marvels.
On being invited to witness a magic lantern display, he resorted
to the use of charms "to dispel any kindly feelings he might
have had", and then asked leave to go; but had gone only a

little way when he returned a message that "if we did not add a red jacket and a man to our gift of a few copper rings and a few pounds of meat, we must return by the way we had come". To this Livingstone returned answer that he would certainly go forward next day, whatever the outcome. "Hunger has a powerful effect on the temper", he remarks; and having suffered considerably from it of late "we were all rather soured in our feelings". But a good meal put a fighting spirit into his followers, and all were prepared to cut their way through if necessary. When day dawned in a drizzle of rain they were astir and set off, passing close to the village; and no sign of opposition appeared.

On 4 April they were on the banks of the Quango, a broad river and very deep. It was said to abound in venomous water-snakes, and all the villages were situated far from its banks. Livingstone was anxious to cross it without delay, so as to be within reach of the Portuguese, and he begged some of the villagers, who were Bashinje, for the loan of canoes. This brought out the local chief, another youth, with the usual demand for a man, an ox, or a gun. Livingstone had now nothing left to offer but his blanket, and this he would not part with in advance. He told his men to go at once to the bank, some two miles distant, and first of all secure possession of canoes; but they demurred, fearing to be attacked while crossing. They stripped off the last of their copper rings and offered them, but the chief was still importunate in his demand for a man. "He thought, as others did, that my men were slaves."

As I resisted the proposal to deliver up my blanket until they had placed us on the western bank, this chief continued to worry us with his demands till I was tired. My little tent was now in tatters, and having a wider hole behind than the door in front, I tried in vain to lie down out of sight of our persecutors. We were on a reedy flat, and could not follow our usual plan of a small stockade, in which we had time to think over and concoct our plans.

It was whilst he was in this extremity—perhaps the severest of all, and happily it proved to be the last—that a young half-caste Portuguese sergeant of militia named Cypriano di Abreu appeared on the scene. He had come across the Quango in search of bees'-wax; and he now reinforced Livingstone's persuasions to his men to move on towards the river in spite of the chief. They had moved off a little way when they were pursued by a scattered hail of bullets from the Bashinje, but disregarded it and walked quietly on. Cypriano himself arranged matters with the ferrymen, and the whole party was soon landed scatheless on the opposite bank. "Happily all our difficulties with the border tribes were at an end." But though he was now free from long weeks of continual anxiety and semi-starvation, his bouts of fever were unabated.

They reached the dwelling of Cypriano after dark and for the first night could rest with a feeling of safety. Next morning they were supplied with a generous provision of pumpkins and maize, and Livingstone with a meal of nuts, fruit and honey. "I felt sincerely grateful for this magnificent breakfast." Their good host slaughtered an ox for their needs and "quite bared his garden" to provide grain for four or five days' journey, and never hinted at payment.

Rains detained them till April 10, but after three days' hard travelling through high wet grass they reached Cassange where they received equal hospitality from the Commandant, Senhor de Silva Rega. An officer on his staff, Captain Neves, made Livingstone stay in his own house. "Next day this generous man arrayed me in decent clothing, and continued during the whole period of my stay to treat me as if he had been my brother. . . . He not only attended to my wants, but also furnished food for my famishing party free of charge." During his stay here he was an interested spectator of the Portuguese celebration of Easter Day (16 April). Here too he was able to dispose of Sekeletu's ivory, and with one tusk procured sufficient calico and baize to clothe his entire party; with another, enough calico to pay his way to the coast; and the two remaining were sold for money wherewith to purchase a horse for Sekeletu at Loanda. The Commandant offered him a negro corporal as a guard to Ambaca. But now once again his men proposed to leave him; they had been told that when they reached the coast they would be taken aboard ship, fattened and eaten, as the white men were cannibals. When at last reassured on this point, they said again that they would follow wherever he led the way. The Commandant then gave them an ox, and invited Livingstone to a farewell dinner. The merchants of Cassange gave him letters of introduction to their friends in Loanda and, on 21 April, accompanied the party some distance on their way.

They had yet 300 miles to go. The black corporal though useful was not immune from some of the vices imbibed from contact with unlawful traffic, such as secretly obtaining his own commission on the purchases made. "A land of slaves is a bad school even for the free," is Livingstone's comment; "and I was sorry to find less truthfulness and honesty in him than in my own people." But in other respects he did his duty and, when Livingstone returned to Cassange, "I was glad to see that he had been promoted to sergeant-major".

Heavy rains continued by day, drenching the long grass, and at night the evaporation from the ground was such as to cloud the inside of the glass of his instruments and prevent him from taking an astronomical observation. But his Journal throughout this last lap is filled with other observations—ethnological, geological, botanical. Pitsane (his personal attendant) and another of his men were violently attacked by fever, and as for himself: "The vertigo produced by frequent fevers made it as much as I could do to·stick on the ox." Whilst in this condition and in fording a river, 'Sinbad' plunged into a deep hole "and so soused me that I was obliged to move on to dry my clothing, without calling on the Europeans who live on the bank. This I regretted, for all the Portuguese were very kind, and like the Boers placed in similar circumstances, feel it a slight to be passed without a word of salutation."

They were again most kindly received by the Commandant of Ambaca, Senhor Arsenio de Carpo, who spoke a little English.

He recommended wine for my debility, and here I took the first glass of that beverage I had taken in Africa. I felt much refreshed, and could then realise and meditate on the weakening effects of the fever. They were curious even to myself. . . . Often, on getting up in the mornings, I found my clothing as wet from perspiration as if it had been dipped in water. In vain had I tried to learn or collect words of the Bunda, or dialect spoken in Angola. I forgot the days of the week and the names of my companions and, had I been asked, I probably could not have told my own. The complaint itself occupied many of my thoughts. One day I supposed that I had got the true theory of it, and would certainly cure the next attack whether in myself or my companions, but some new symptoms would appear, and scatter all the fine speculations which had sprung up with extraordinary fertility in one department of my brain.

Here he was bitten on the foot by a tick—for the first time in a European house; the effects are dangerous and may even prove fatal when the poison reaches the abdomen; but he suffered nothing worse than an itch in the foot for a week.

On 12 May they left Ambaca, provided with bread and meat and with two militia-men as guides; and stopping at noon for shelter from the sun in the house of Senhor Mellot, Livingstone was regaled with a fowl and a glass of wine "which prevented the violent fit of shivering I expected that afternoon. The universal hospitality of the Portuguese was most gratifying, as it was quite unexpected. And even now as I copy my journal, I remember it all with a glow of gratitude." He spent the 14th, a Sunday, at Cabinda and there wrote his first letter to the Cape. It was to his friend Thompson and begins: "I am not very far from Loanda and as I shall have very little time in writing there, because my purse is light and followers numerous and hungry, I give you a few particulars now. We have had a most tedious journey from the land of the Leeambye. . . ." The particulars are indeed few, and the "tediousness" enlivened in reminiscence. For example:

> . . . At last instead of gifts of food we were offered knocks on the head. The Chiboque, for instance, are the most outrageous blackguards. We came upon them as quiet as Quakers, and were spending Sunday on Peace Society principles, when a whole tribe surrounded us fully armed. . . . Then we all got angry, chafed in mind, and hungry, and replied angrily to their demands. Sometimes I was furious and would have fought, but my companions were more pacific. At other times they were on the bloody key and I was quakerish, and we rose up by night and passed our enemies, expecting an assault in every thicket and glen. And after all I thank God sincerely in that He prevented us from shedding human blood.[8]

From Ambaca to Golungo Alto his pen is busy with descriptions of scenery so beautiful that "I forgot my fever". And arrived there, "We were most kindly received by the Commandant, Lieutenant Antonio Canto y Castro, a young gentleman whose whole subsequent conduct will ever make me regard him with great affection." Leaving him on the 24th they passed through forests of gigantic timber and then a flourishing coffee-estate, and then along the river Senza. Though now so near his desired haven his physical trials were far from over.

The banks are infested by myriads of the most ferocious mosquitoes I ever met. Not one of our party could get a snatch of sleep. I was taken into the house of a Portuguese, but was soon glad to make my escape and lie across the path on the lee side of the fire, where the smoke blew over my body. My host wondered at my want of taste, and I at his want of feeling, for to our astonishment he and the other inhabitants had actually become used to what was at least equal to a nail through the heel of one's boot, or the tooth-ache.

As they were now approaching the sea his faithful followers again showed signs of alarm. Would any of them be kidnapped? —He replied that he was as ignorant of Loanda as they were, and that they could return if they wished; but that "nothing will happen to you but what happens to myself. We have stood by each other hitherto, and will do so to the last." On their first sight of the boundless ocean they looked upon it with awe. They had always believed what "the ancients" had told them, namely that the world had no end; but all at once the world said to them, "I am finished; there is no more of me!"

By this time Livingstone was afflicted with chronic dysentery in addition to fever, so that he could not remain on his ox for more than ten minutes at a time; and as he at long last descended the slope towards the city of Loanda on 31 May 1854, a broken wreck of a man in body, he was also, he says, labouring under great depression of mind. He had been told that in a population of twelve thousand souls there was but one Englishman, whose name was Mr. Edmund Gabriel. Would he be good-natured, or "one of those crusty mortals one would rather not meet at all?"

His doubts on this point were allayed by circumstantial evidence, his immediate appreciation of which is in keeping with the wholesomeness of his own nature.

When we entered his porch I was delighted to see a number of flowers cultivated carefully, and inferred from this circumstance that he was, what I soon discovered him to be, a real whole-hearted Englishman. Seeing me ill, he benevolently offered me his bed. Never shall I forget the luxuriant pleasure I enjoyed in feeling myself again on a good English couch, after six months' sleeping on the ground. I was soon asleep; and Mr. Gabriel, coming in almost immediately, rejoiced at the soundness of my repose.

Chapter Fourteen

FIRST GREAT JOURNEY: LINYANTI
1854-1855

*"I will place no value on anything I have or may possess,
except in relation to the kingdom of Christ."*

JUDGED by any standard of comparison with subsequent feats
of exploration, the first stage of Livingstone's transcontinental journey, taken by itself alone, must be held to
surpass them, and this for several reasons. It was the first of its
kind and the precursor of many in the same field; it was undertaken with scarcely any preparation and with totally inadequate provision or equipment; it was prosecuted through
tropical rain and in the face of hostile opposition; it was accomplished single-handed and without either the material or
moral support of any official body. He was a sick man even
before he started, was half-starved and fever-stricken throughout, and when at last in safety nearly died. Despite obscuring
cloud and frequent ague he charted his route with an accuracy
which has astonished his successors, whilst the wealth and
variety of his scientific observations still hold their own place
in the history of travel. Other explorers, especially in this century, both in the torrid and frigid zones have endured hardships and privations of equal severity, but none have suffered
and overcome such a concentration of adverse circumstances.
And whereas their journeys were ends in themselves, his was
merely incidental to an aim beyond scientific or geographical
discovery. Only a reader with sympathetic discernment and
insight can be in a position to share in imagination the toils
and conflicts of this journey, as he reads between the lines of
the narrator's terse factual chronicle, or begin to assess the
demands made upon the mental, moral, and physical stamina
required for its performance.

After a fortnight's rest under the kind and unremitting care
of Mr. Gabriel, aided soon after by the attentions of a British

219

naval surgeon of the *Polyphemus*, and the "exhilarating presence" of the ships' officers, he felt sufficiently restored to return the courteous call of the Roman Catholic Bishop of Angola (who was then acting Governor of the province)— accompanied by his men all arrayed in robes of striped cotton and red caps presented by Mr. Gabriel. He also visited the officers and men of the three British cruisers that had come to port—*Polyphemus*, *Pluto* and *Philomel*—actually for the purpose of blockading it against the Portuguese slave-traffic. The smell of brine and tar, the sight of snowy sails and oaken hulls afloat on the sparkling water, the sound of hearty British voices and the creaking of tackle, the thought of whither they would soon be bound—these must have stirred in him acute feelings of heart-hunger and homesickness. He had been brought up to believe that the ships of the Navy were "floating hells" (as indeed most of them were, before Nelson); his visits aboard these vessels now caused him to revise that opinion entirely. One of the hopes upon which he had stayed himself during his long lonely journey was that news from his wife and family, from whom he had had no word for two years—not even of their safe arrival in England—might be awaiting him at Loanda. He was counting on the doubtful possibility that Mary would have received from the Cape news of his intended destination by the time he reached it. But of letters there were none. Instead, there was the free offer of an almost immediate passage home—either aboard the *Polyphemus* via St. Helena, or direct by the mail-packet *Forerunner* by which he was sending his letters, reports and maps. The situation has been well, if imaginatively, described by Basil Mathews in a little book on Livingstone for boys.

"You are ill," said the Captain of the vessel when he landed and saw Livingstone's worn limbs and fever-stricken body. "You have worked and travelled without rest for fourteen years. All Britain will cheer to see you. Come home with us and rest—and see your wife and your daughter and your sons again." . . .

He looked at his Makololo companions who had risked life again and again and lived with him through all the perils of the path-finding journey. He had brought them fifteen hundred miles from their homes. They had called him their 'father'. They could not return alone. . . . [1]

All that he says himself on the subject is: "It would be

altogether impossible for my men to return alone. I therefore resolved to decline the tempting offers of my naval friends." But it may be doubted whether he ever allowed the idea of acceptance so much as to cross his mind: he was in honour bound to lead his Makololo back to their homes, and had already determined, as he says, to follow the Zambesi from Linyanti to the coast. Nevertheless, it was this refusal to abandon his men which stirred public enthusiasm when he returned to England, even more than his achievements as an explorer.

Though he does not mention it in his book, his letters tell that he was several times again prostrated with fever after this premature and partial recovery. He was in fact more ill than he was willing to confess. These attacks, which were even more debilitating than those he had suffered on the march, delayed him in Loanda for nearly four months, and he admits in his *Travels* that early in August "I suffered a relapse which reduced me to a mere skeleton", and to Thompson on the 14th, "I nearly marched off from the land of the living"—adding with characteristic optimism, "will start on my return on the 20th currt".[2] (To his brother Charles he wrote from Golungo Alto on 8 November, "Bad health and good hope [of letters from home] kept me a month longer than was absolutely necessary at Loanda".) Complete rest was imperative for recuperation, but he employed his time of convalescence instead in writing letters to his family and friends, and in preparing his reports for the R.G.S. and L.M.S., though he was sometimes too weak to write and availed himself of his kind host's offer to act as amanuensis.

> The unwearied attentions of this good Englishman from his first welcome to me when, a weary, dejected and worn-down stranger, I arrived at his residence, and his whole subsequent conduct, will be held in lively remembrance by me to my dying day.

When able to walk he cultivated his acquaintance with the Portuguese authorities, chiefly with a view to ascertaining the effectiveness upon them and the Lisbon Government of the British suppression of the slave-trade; made notes on the commerce, census, merchandise, harbour-dues and other aspects of life in the city; and took his men sight-seeing. The deference and generosity with which he was treated by his own countrymen and by the Portuguese greatly enhanced his prestige among his simple followers, and when taken aboard a ship-of-war, and informed that the jolly sailors who fraternized with them had been sent there by the Queen of England to prevent the buying and selling of black men, their fears were allayed completely. The size of the ship amazed them. "It is not a canoe at all: it is a town." The sailors' deck they named the Kotla; and then, as a climax to their description of this great ark, added, "and what sort of a town is it that you must climb up into with a rope?"

He took them also to a service of High Mass in the Cathedral, but the gorgeous ritual, frequent genuflections, burning of incense, and the manifest irreverence of the singers—"did not convey to the minds of my men the idea of adoration. I overheard them in talking to each other remark that 'they had seen the white men charming their demons'; a phrase identical with one they had used when seeing the Balonda beating drums before their idols."

With the friendly and liberal-minded bishop, however, Livingstone got on very well. After a formal reception in the hall of the Palace at which he gave the Makololo the freedom of the city during their stay, he discussed amicably with Livingstone their differences in matters of faith. He was entirely in sympathy with Livingstone's aims to promote legitimate commerce between the coast and the interior, to which he promised his own co-operation; and also with Livingstone's desire for native education, having himself established schools in Loanda. "His whole conversation and conduct showed him to be a man of great benevolence and kindness of heart." And before they left Loanda this good bishop expressed these qualities in a practical way. He provided all the Makololo with blue and red suits of clothing, caps and cotton blankets, and sent for Sekeletu with other gifts the present of a horse, saddled and bridled, and the complete uniform of a Portuguese colonel!

Livingstone, with his high sense of the importance of self-discipline in the practice of self-devotion, was himself always a Puritan at heart, and therefore had a sympathetic regard for Christian asceticism wherever found. For this reason he welcomed the services that the Roman Catholic missions were rendering to the natives in Africa, especially those of the Jesuits. Where the *head* lay, in matters of creed or cult, mattered little to him so long as the *heart* was right. Profession was nothing, conduct and performance everything. But with all the breadth and tolerance of his religious outlook he had his reservations. "He could not away with the sight of men of intelligence kissing the toe of an image of the Virgin, and taking part in services in which they did not, and could not, believe."[3]

In consequence of his severe relapse he was unable to "attend to his men for a considerable time" (actually six weeks); but on recovery was thankful to find freedom from the lassitude which had previously succeeded these attacks, by which he judged that his system was now free of the infection. He was also pleased to find that his men had established for themselves "a brisk trade in firewood" as well as a good name in the city; and that they had been further well remunerated, as they delightedly told him, by employment which Mr. Gabriel had procured for them in unloading freighters "of stones that burn, for a moon and a half".

Nothing, he felt, could exceed the kindness of the British Consul and of the Portuguese authorities and merchants to himself and to his men. The latter had supplied him with handsome specimens of all their wares for barter on the route, and with two donkeys (which are immune to infection from the tsetse) for the purpose of introducing their breed into the interior; stocks of cotton, ammunition, and beads, and a musket for each man. The Makololo had by their earnings amassed so many goods that the bishop furnished the party with twenty additional carriers, besides orders for supplies everywhere throughout Angola, and letters of introduction to Portuguese officials on the east coast. The seamen aboard the *Polyphemus* had made for Livingstone a stout canvas tent: a welcome change from the miserable perforated little covering he had used on his outward journey. It was therefore a cheerful and confident company that embarked on 20 September 1854 with the cordial good wishes of all sections of the people of Loanda for a detour round the coast to the mouth of the River Bengo, and thence upstream to the native town of Icollo.

> We were accompanied thus far by our generous host Mr. Gabriel, who, by his unwearying attentions to myself, and liberality in supporting my men, had become endeared to all our hearts. My men were strongly

impressed by a sense of his goodness, and often spoke of him in terms of admiration all the way to Linyanti.

Some months later Mr. Gabriel, in acknowledging receipt of a missive from the Directors of the L.M.S., took occasion to write:

> Dr. Livingstone, after the noble objects he has achieved, most assuredly wants no testimony from me. I consult, therefore, the impulse of my own mind alone, when I declare that in no respect was my intercourse more gratifying than of observing his *earnest, active, and unwearied solicitude for the advancement of Christianity*. . . . It is indeed fortunate for that sacred cause, and highly honourable to [your] Society, *when qualities and dispositions like his are employed in propagating its blessings among men*. . . . I fervently pray that the kind Providence, which has hitherto carried him through so many perils and hardships, may guide him safely to his present journey's end.[4]

The warmth of his reception by the Portuguese authorities and merchants had surprised him the more, since they knew him to be an open opponent of slavery. In a postscript of a letter to Tidman, marked *private*, he says shrewdly: "I may remark that the Portuguese in Africa have a good character for polite hospitality, but I came amongst them in a peculiar manner. I came out from behind them. It would, I suspect, be a different story if a missionary had come to Loanda and wished to go in from thence."[5] His Journal at this time and for some time after abounds in expressions of gratitude for all the spontaneous kindness and ready help he had received at their hands, and also for the sincerity of their desire to comply with British regulations for the suppression of the slave-traffic. But in the margins against the latter are a profusion of large question-marks inserted when he came to realize that his confidence had been misplaced.

> But it was only gradually that his detestation of the system as a whole found vent in unrestrained language . . . and it was not until his denunciations of Portuguese connivance at the barbarities of the slave trade with Zanzibar reached Europe in 1860 that their friendly attitude changed to one of resentment and opposition.[6]

To his brother Charles he wrote a cogent argument in favour of the proved practical value of a display of armed force off the coast to prevent the sale or exportation of slaves, in contradiction to the theoretical pacific views of a Professor of Political Economy in America: adducing the fact among others that whereas in 1837 (prior to the Treaty with Portugal for suppression of the trade) Mr. Gabriel had counted 39 slave-ships in the harbour, none now dare appear at all or engage in the traffic except by stealth. A new system had since been instituted whereby conscripts, called carriers or *carregadores*, were recruited for compulsory labour from native chiefs, but a law for its abolition had lately been enacted, though there was little hope at present of its being carried into effect.[7]

At Icollo he visited a large sugar factory worked by a multitude of slaves; it compared unfavourably with those which he saw later in the Mauritius run on a free-labour system. Cotton-spinning and weaving were everywhere in evidence in the villages throughout Angola, and the method resembled exactly that practised by the ancient Egyptians. He was impressed by the fertility of the soil, the luxuriance of the vegetation, and the beauty of the scenery in the province; and having contributed papers to a newspaper in Loanda urging the superior economic advantages of agriculture to slavery, he felt it a duty to visit some large coffee-plantations in the district of Cazengo. Here he was ordered more coffee than he could take or needed, and wrote to his wife: "It is the best in the world. One spoonful makes it stronger than three did of what we used. It is found wild on the mountains"; and to his brother, "All that it requires is to have the ground partially cleared and the fruit dried and sorted. I encouraged them to persevere." Thence by canoe with the Commandant of Cazengo down the river Lucalla, the banks of which bore large crops of maize, manioc, tobacco and country produce, to Massangano and the ruins there of a famous old iron-foundry, still in use for the smelting of ore. The district was also well adapted for the cultivation of sugar and rice; there were the remains of a canal; the flat lands would be suitable for railway-transport, and so forth; Livingstone's observations of the commercial potentialities of the whole region are acute and detailed.

Returning to Golungo Alto he found several of his men sick with fever and lame with cracked feet caused by the hard dry soil. "They had always been accustomed to moisture in their own well-watered land." Whilst waiting for their recovery he

225

visited, in company with his old friend Lieutenant Canto y Castro, the deserted monasteries nearby which were still kept in good repair: "I would fain have learned something of the former occupants, but even the graves of the good men stand without any record; their resting-places are however carefully tended. But turning to the people we soon recognize their memorials in the great numbers who can both read and write." Soon after this Lieutenant Canto was stricken with fever so severely as to be for some time unconscious and "it afforded me much pleasure to attend him in his sickness, who had been so kind to me in mine". His domestic establishment of which Livingstone now took charge consisted, like others, of slaves and these he now detected in making away with their master's eatables in a shameless fashion. In such households visitors are provided with keys to their rooms. "At Kolobeng we never locked our doors by night or day for months together; but there slavery is unknown." He nursed his sick host until completely restored and employed his spare time, as always, in writing letters.

[To his Wife. 25 October.] It occurs to me, my dearest Mary, that if I send you a note from different parts on the way through this colony, some of them will surely reach you; and if they carry any of the affection I bear to you in their composition, they will not fail to comfort you. . . . I remained a short time longer in Loanda than was actually required to set me on my legs, in longing expectation of a letter from you. None came, but should any come up to the beginning of November, it will come after me by post to Cassange. . . .

Give my love to all the children. . . . How happy I shall be to meet them and you again! I hope a letter from you may be waiting for me at Zambesi. Love to all the children. How tall is Zouga? Accept the assurance of unabated love.[8]

[To his Brother. 8 November.] The ship of the Commodore called the *Scourge* has gone up to Fernando-Po for the mails. She is much behind her time and we cannot guess the cause of her detention. But when she comes, my last hopes of hearing from friends will have to expire. I go away into the region where there are no mails to cheer the weary wanderer. . . .

He also exchanged several letters with Mr. Gabriel, who was an ornithologist, on the subject of rare birds and made further notes for his own researches on flora, fishes, and insects. About this time Sekeletu's horse took sick and eventually died, though it had been carefully protected against tsetse; and it was not till 14 December that "we left the hospitable residence of Mr. Canto with a deep sense of his kindness to us all".

The early rains had now fallen and thus it was again during the rainy season—the most unhealthy time of the year—that Livingstone started on the second stage of his journey. To allow for the recovery of his men the days' marches were at first undertaken slowly. At Ambaca he received the valuable gift of ten head of oxen from Mr. Schut of Loanda, and thence made a detour to the south to visit the famous rocks of Pungo Andongo, and to inspect the vegetable products of that place of which he had everywhere heard glowing accounts. He found that these were not exaggerated and that they referred to the activity of one man, Colonel Pires, who was the wealthiest merchant-prince in Angola and "whose slaves appeared more like free servants than any I had elsewhere seen". Livingstone made a careful study of the mixed geological structure of the gigantic pillars which once, in primaeval ages, "had withstood the surges of the ocean". At a village nearby he bought a pair of stout leather thigh-boots for 5.8d.—the equivalent of a pound weight of ivory, or half the price of a boy-slave. While the guest of this princely magnate, he heard of the loss of the *Forerunner* off Madeira with every soul on board save one, and all his despatches, maps, and Journal. Had he accepted the offer of a berth, he soberly reflects at the end of his *Travels*, he would doubtless have shared the fate of his papers. "I felt so glad that my friend Lieutenant Bedingfeld, to whose care I had committed them, had not shared a similar fate, that I was at once reconciled to that labour of rewriting"—a feat comparable, in the estimation of Thomas Hughes, with Carlyle's in reproducing the first volume of his *French Revolution* after its use by a housemaid for lighting fires. He completed this task while enjoying Colonel Pires' hospitality by the end of the year, and also whilst ministering to the sick, and on New Year's Day 1855 once again said farewell to civilization.

Travelling along the right bank of the Coanza he struck into his former route at the village of Malange and was soon within sight of the magnificent panorama of the Quango valley near Cassange. Here he was the victim of an attack by one of the tiniest yet most pugnacious of all insects in Africa, the red ant.

My attention being taken up in viewing the distant landscape, I accidentally stepped upon one of their nests. Not an instant seemed to elapse before a simultaneous attack was made on various unprotected parts, up the trousers from below, and on my neck and breast above. The bites of these furies were like sparks of fire, and there was no retreat. I jumped about for a second or two, then in desperation tore off all my clothing; and rubbed and picked them off seriatim as quickly as possible. Ugh! they would make the most lethargic mortal look alive. Fortunately no one observed this rencontre, or word might have been taken back to the village that I had become mad. . . . It is really astonishing how such small bodies can contain so large an amount of ill-nature.[9]

At the invitation of Captain Neves he stayed for a month at Cassange to complete the reproduction of his lost papers and maps for despatch by the fortnightly mail to Loanda; and it was whilst engaged in this task that he received a packet of the latest *Times* newspapers containing accounts of the Crimean War (in which his friend Colonel Steele was serving with distinction) "up to the terrible charge of the light cavalry. The intense anxiety I felt to hear more may be imagined by every true patriot; but I was forced to brood on in silent thought, and utter my poor prayers for friends who perchance were now no more, until I reached the other side of the continent."

He learned also that two native traders with Portuguese names had (in 1806–11*) actually made a return journey from Cassange to Mozambique—the only instance of such a journey on record. To this he adds significantly: "No European ever accomplished it, though this fact has lately been quoted as if the men had been *Portuguese*."

From Colonel Pires' residence he had written to Mr. Gabriel on 5 January a letter of enormous length which he continued from Cassange between the 18th and 23rd. It is filled with news of personal interest to the recipient and with notes of the geology of the rocks of Pungo Andonga even more detailed than those published in his *Travels*. "It would take a week to collect all the varieties of rock in the conglomerate." He sends his friend a packet of specimens of these, as well as of the seeds and bulbs of many rare plants and flowers. The country abounds not only with wild coffee and many kinds of fruit-trees, but also with wild vines in profusion.

* Not 1815 as he states in *Travels*.

I have a lot of experiments in my head for them. I sit on my ox and think, till the sun permits neither thinking nor travelling. I could never keep an umbrella up without risk of a tumble. Sinbad has the same aversion to my reading *Punch*. If he carries me back to the Zambesi I must write his biography and get the Poet Laureate Tennyson to make an epitaph for him.

The Portuguese maps of Angola are inaccurate: some places being more than a hundred miles out of position. "I often take ten distances, straining my eyes to the utmost for each, the seconds' stop in the watch assisting much, and then take the mean of distances and times." Colonel Steele had been commended in Lord Raglan's despatches.

I suppose it will ensure further promotion. He wrote to me several times in this strain: "If you require anything be sure and tell me, for I wish to serve you with my purse. I really mean what I say." I never needed to make a call for his assistance, but his generous offers made and makes my heart warm to him, and I pray God to be his shield. . . . Lord Raglan is a wrothy old stumper—I beg his pardon for calling him so, though no one ever heard his name before. If Sir Charles [Napier] had said less before, less would have been said about him now. But poor old fellow, he will catch it in England. Be sure and send me *Punch* on the subject.

He encloses a letter for despatch to Lord Clarendon, but only if his friend approves. "Either for him or for your kitchen fire. . . . I might make some small improvements if·I wrote a copy but I really have not time. . . . I repeat again, if the letter is not a proper one—and my impressions are that it is not—do commit it to the flames." He wrote also to Sir Roderick Murchison, enclosing an 'ideal section' of South Central Africa. "If he does not cry out, 'My dear fellow, no more of your nonsense'—he will be less clever than I take him to be." (This sketch, delineated with the assistance of the Geological Survey, afterwards formed a valuable feature in his *Travels*.)

He had had trouble with the *Corregadores* who complained of their rations, though he had been instructed to give them nothing.

I reduced their allowance one half every time they grumbled; this is one of the odd things one meets with throughout Africa—generosity is looked upon as weakness. The Empaccaserros took French leave of me at Malange during the night, thus going two or three days' march instead of as many or more months.

DAVID LIVINGSTONE

He had met a negro Canon of the Roman Catholic Church with a high-sounding Portuguese name and title, who informed him that there were thirteen churches in the Congo, but no priests! The letter ends:

Our correspondence has afforded me unmixed pleasure; and I have an equal amount of pain knowing now that this is the end of it. It is doubtful whether we shall ever meet again in this world. But I pray to our heavenly Father that we may meet in joy before Him in a better land. I remember telling you how I might do in England if by God's good providence I should reach it. The country explored is unfit for a European family. I might live to do good in it, but it would be subjecting those whom God has committed to my care to an extended orphanage. On their account I would, if a situation under Govt. could be fairly obtained, accept of it. But it would be a pang, and on their account alone. "He that careth not for his own and especially them of his own house hath denied the faith and is worse than an infidel" (St. Paul). For I always, since I knew the value of Christianity, wished to spend my life in propagating its blessings among men. I have the same desire now undiminished, but to leave my family to the tender mercies of a charitable institution—some of whose members have a sort of spite at my success in exploration—seems hard. I can only hope that He who has helped and guided me hitherto will be with me still. Into His everlasting care I commend you as your most affectionate friend, David Livingston.[10]

These words are as revealing as any Livingstone ever wrote in his inevitable realization of the dual and divided claims upon his allegiance; they show where his own inclinations lay, corresponding as they did with his sense of a higher duty; and they foreshadow his future rôle as an agent of the Government.

From Cassange he wrote to Maclear on 24 January (and it appears to be his sole mention of the fact): " . . . We have had a great deal of sickness in Angola. Intermittent fever perpetually. Last night I had three hours' of teeth-chattering and breathing hard as if running up hill. . . ."[11]

Captain Neves was busy in preparing a valuable present for Matiamvo, paramount chief of the Balonda, to be sent in charge of a Pombeiro, Senhor Pascoal, and Livingstone was himself strongly inclined to visit this chief who, he heard, had threatened to punish the Chiboque for their behaviour to him. But Matiamvo's town lay well off his route and since his Makololo did not of their own accord suggest this long detour he refrained from proposing it. "When I can get the natives to agree in the propriety of any step, they go to the end of the

230

affair without a murmur. I speak to them and treat them as rational beings and generally get on well with them in consequence." He decided however to accompany the Pombeiros as far as Cabango.

Descending the Quango valley, he reflected on the vast potential natural resources of Angola which, if in British possession, would yield as much or more raw material than an equal extent of cotton-growing country in America. "A railway from Loanda to this valley would secure the trade of most of the interior of South Central Africa." But he was oppressed by thoughts of the superstitious terrors, the dread of ghosts, the tyranny of witchcraft, the ordeals by poison which caused hundreds of deaths annually.

> How painful is the contrast between this inward gloom and the brightness of the outer world, between the undefined terrors of the spirit and the peace and beauty that pervades the scenes around us. . . . I have often thought, in travelling through this land, that it presents pictures of beauty which angels might enjoy. How often have I beheld, in still mornings, scenes the very essence of beauty, and all bathed in a quiet air of delicious warmth! Yet the occasional soft motion imparted a pleasing sensation of coolness as of a fan. Green grassy meadows, the cattle feeding, the goats browsing, the kids skipping, the groups of herd-boys with miniature bows, arrows, and spears; the women wending their way to the river with watering-pots poised jauntily on their heads; men sewing under the shady banians; and old grey-headed fathers sitting on the ground, with staff in hand, listening to the morning gossip, while others carry trees or branches to repair their hedges; and all this, flooded with the bright African sunshine, and the birds singing among the branches before the heat of the day has become intense, form pictures which can never be forgotten.[12]

The village of the young half-caste sergeant Cypriano, his first helper on the outward journey, was reached on 28 February. "He acted with his wonted kindness," though after the recent death of a relative he had spent more than his patrimony on funeral orgies and was also deeply in debt from drink. "The funeral rites are half-festive, half-mourning, partaking somewhat of the character of an Irish wake. There is nothing more heartrending than their death-wails." The exorbitant ferrymen demanded thirty yards of calico for a passage of the river, but received six thankfully.

The weather had so far been favourable for astronomical work, but the rainy season was now setting in.

We now had rain every day, and the sky seldom presented that cloud-less aspect and clear blue, so common in the dry lands of the south. The heavens are often overcast by large white motionless masses, which stand for hours in the same position, and the intervening spaces are filled with a milk-and-water-looking haze. Notwithstanding, I obtained good obser-vations for the longitude of this important point on both sides of the Quango.

The local chief Sansawe now ran out to meet him "with wonderful urbanity", but before leaving said that he would return that evening to receive his dues. "I replied that, as he had treated us sö scurvily, even forbidding his people to sell us any food, if he did not bring a fowl and some eggs, as part of his duty as a chief, he should receive no present from me." Returning later, Sansawe visited the Pombeiros first and from them received large gifts of powder, calico, and even brandy; he then went with a present of two cocks to Livingstone, who treated him to a lecture on the impolicy of his behaviour and concluded by denying his right to any payment at all. To all this Sansawe meekly agreed: "and then I gave him, as a token of friendship, a pannikin of coarse powder, two iron spoons, and two yards of coarse printed calico". And though the Pom-beiros produced yet other gifts the next day, Livingstone gave nothing more. He realized that the practice of extortion was simply a system of blackmail levied by petty chiefs on slave-traders.

Finding the pace of the Pombeiros too slow he parted from Senhor Pascoal and pushed on towards Cabango, requesting him to take back some letters which he would leave for him on the way. But in what proved a fortunate event, Senhor Pascal soon overtook him.

On 16 March, Livingstone was again stricken with malaria. He disregarded this, though it continued intermittently for five weeks and on the 20th wrote to Mary without mentioning it:

> I long for the time when I shall see you again. I hope in God's mercy for that pleasure. How are my dear ones? I have not seen any equal to them since I put them on board ship. My brave little dears! I only hope God will show us mercy and make them good too. . . .
> I work at the interior languages when I have a little time, and also at Portuguese, which I like from being so much like Latin. Indeed, when I came to understand much that was said from its similarity to that tongue,

and when I interlarded my attempts at Portuguese with Latin, or spoke it entirely, they understood me very well. The negro language is not so easy, but I take a spell at it every day I can. It is of the same family as the Sechuana. . . .

On the 19th the malaria "changed into an extremely severe attack of rheumatic fever".

This was brought on by being obliged to sleep on an extensive plain covered with water. The rain poured down incessantly, but we formed our beds by dragging up the earth into oblong mounds somewhat like graves in a country churchyard, and then placing grass upon them. The rain continuing to deluge us, we were unable to leave for two days, but as soon as it became fair we continued our march. The heavy dew upon the high grass was so cold as to cause shivering, and I was forced to lie by for eight days, tossing and groaning with violent pain in the head. This was the most severe attack I had endured. It made me quite unfit to move, or even know what was passing outside my little tent. . . . After many days I began to recover and wished to move on, but my men objected to the attempt on account of my weakness.

Whilst he was in this extremity a quarrel took place in the village where he lay, when the headman was struck in the beard by one of the Makololo. Atonement for the affront was duly paid—a gun and some lengths of calico, but more and yet more was demanded. The sequel to this episode must be given verbatim.

As their courage usually rises with success, I resolved to yield no more and departed. In passing through a forest in the country beyond, we were startled by a body of men rushing after us. They began by knocking down the burdens of the hindermost of my men, and several shots were fired. I fortunately had a six-barrelled revolver [the gift of Captain Need of the *Linnet*]. Taking this in my hand, and forgetting fever, I staggered quickly along the path with two or three of my men, and fortunately encountered the chief. The sight of six barrels gaping into his stomach, with my own ghastly visage looking daggers into his face, seemed to produce an instant revolution in his martial feelings, for he cried out, "Oh! I have only come to speak to you, and wish peace only." Mashauana had hold of him by the hand, and found him shaking. We examined his gun and found that it had been discharged. Both parties crowded up to their chiefs. One of the opposite party coming too near, one of mine drove him back with a battle-axe. The enemy protested their amicable intentions, and my men asserted the fact of having the goods knocked down as evidence of the contrary. Without waiting long I requested all to sit down, and Pitsane, placing his hand on the revolver, somewhat allayed their fears. I then said to the chief, "If you have come with

peaceable intentions, we have no other; go away home to your village."
He replied, "I am afraid lest you shoot me in the back." I rejoined, "If
I wanted to kill you, I could shoot you in the face as well." Mosantu
called out to me, "That's only a Makalaka trick; don't give him your
back." But I said, "Tell him to observe that I am not afraid of him,"
and turning, mounted my ox. There was not much danger in the fire
that was opened at first, there being so many trees. The enemy probably
expected that the sudden attack would make us forsake our goods, and
allow them to plunder with ease. The villagers were no doubt pleased
with being allowed to retire unscathed, and we were also glad to have
got away without having shed a drop of blood, or having compromised
ourselves for any future visit. . . .

I do not mention this little skirmish as a very frightful affair. The negro
character in these parts, and in Angola, is essentially cowardly, except
when influenced by success. . . . They are by no means equal to the
Cape Caffres in any respect whatever.

For all that, it must have been a close call, though not so
close as the last of such "skirmishes" as he was to engage in—
and that too without ever once firing a shot in self-defence—
before the end of his journey. Half dead with physical debility
as he must have felt, his mind and will were dominant to the
situation. Only a man with nerves of steel could have surmounted this crisis and situations yet to come that were even
more critical.

He was so weak and deaf from fever that he could only progress at the rate of seven miles a day and was glad of the company of Senhor Pascoal, whose thieving carriers were a nuisance
even to him. "It was pitiable to observe the worrying life he
led. There was the greatest contrast possible between the conduct of his people and that of my faithful Makololo." Studying
carefully the features of the country and the course of the rivers
which formed the watershed of the Congo and Zambesi, and
making patient enquiries as he went, it was at this time that
he began to form the opinion, which became a certainty when
he reached Lake Dilolo, that the interior of South Central
Africa is a shallow basin fed by numerous tributaries of these
rivers from their sources in the slightly more elevated surrounding ridges. Exactly the same conclusion had been reached, he
was soon to find somewhat to his chagrin, by Sir Roderick
Murchison in his study in London from a geological map
furnished by Mr. A. Bain and from other sources including
Livingstone's own reports of the region of Lake Ngami. This

brilliant geographer had made it the subject of his Presidential Address to the R.G.S. in 1852. Thus "he had forestalled me by three years, though I had been working hard through jungle, marsh, and fever, and, since the light first dawned on my mind at Dilolo, had been cherishing the pleasing delusion that I should be the first to suggest the idea."

With great difficulty he reached Cabango early in May and was prostrated there for "some days". His route had lain mostly through forest. On the 18th he wrote to Maclear, enclosing an elaborate map of the Quango and several sheets of trigonometrical calculations which he had completed on 7 April:

> I cannot give the route thus far. Nearly blind from a blow in the eye by a branch in riding through the forest. I have given the Quango and will add others. Had a terrific attack of rheumatic fever from sleeping some days on a plain on which the water was flowing ankle deep. We had trenches round our berths but I had 25 days of it and am now very weak, having lost time besides. There was no help for it. We got soaked by going on, and sodden if we stood still.

His stay at Cabango was extended by endeavouring "though with much pain" to draw a sketch of the country thus far for transmission to Loanda, and also by "the fond expectation" of receiving letters and newspapers from "my good angel" Mr. Gabriel. He still had a keen desire to visit Matiamvo, partly from motives of policy and partly to examine the river system farther to the east; but long and frequent delays caused by sickness in himself and his men had depleted their stock of goods for barter, "and we had not found mendicity so pleasant on our way to the north as to induce us to return to it". Leaving Cabango on 21 May with a guide who deserted him next day, he found the country populous with villages separated from each other by dense jungle-grass, and the people, who had never seen a white man before, fearful at first but afterwards friendly.

> Even the dogs ran away with their tails between their legs, as if they had seen a lion. The women peer from behind the walls till he comes near them, and then hastily dash into the house. When a little child meets you in the street, he sets up a scream at the apparition, and conveys the impression that he is not far from going into fits.

On 2 June he reached Kawawa's village, where funeral obsequies were in progress and drums beat all night "with the regularity of engine-thumps". The next day Livingstone held "agreeable intercourse" with the chief, witnessed a court-case for alleged murder of the deceased by witchcraft, and in the evening showed his magic-lantern slides with which all were delighted except Kawawa. "He showed symptoms of dread, and several times started up as if to run away but was prevented by the crowd behind." The next morning as Livingstone was preparing to start, he came with an altered demeanour and the demand for an ox, a gun and a robe—"though nothing could have exceeded his civilities the day before". But Kawawa had inspected the white man's camp and had heard of the success of the Chiboque's extortions. He now threatened to prevent Livingstone's passage across the Kasai unless this tribute were forthcoming.

> I replied that the goods were my property and not his; that I would never have it said that a white man had paid tribute to a black; and that I would cross the Kasai in spite of him. He ordered his·people to arm themselves, and when some of my men saw them rushing for their bows, arrows, and spears, they became somewhat panic-stricken. I ordered them to move away, and not to fire unless Kawawe's people struck the first blow. I took the lead and expected them all to follow, as they had usually done, but many of my men remained behind. When I knew this, I jumped off the ox and made a rush to them with my revolver in my hand. Kawawa ran away amongst his people, and they turned their backs too. I shouted to my men to take up their luggage and march; some did so with alacrity, feeling that they had disobeyed orders by remaining; but one of them refused, and was preparing to fire at Kawawa, until I gave him a punch on the head with the pistol, and made him go too. I felt here, as elsewhere, that subordination must be maintained at all risks. We all moved into the forest, the people of Kawawa standing about a hundred yards off, gazing, but not firing a shot or an arrow. It is extremely unpleasant to part with these chieftains thus, after spending a day or two in the most amicable discourse, and in a part where the people are generally civil.

But Kawawa was not a good specimen of his class. He had desired of the white man among other gifts "a book by which he might see the state of Matiamvo's heart towards him, and which would forewarn him, should Matiamvo ever resolve to cut off his head". Nor were his apprehensions in this regard altogether groundless, so Livingstone was informed.

He was not however to be baulked of his supposed rights so easily, for when Livingstone and his party reached the north bank of the Kasai it was to find themselves forestalled by Kawawa's orders to the ferrymen to refuse them a passage unless the goods demanded were forthcoming—and a man besides. The canoes were taken away before their eyes. But Pitsane, gazing with apparent indifference on the wide river, carefully marked where they were concealed among the reeds on the further bank; and when it was dark, swam across and abstracted one of them. By this means the whole party were transported in the night.

> In the morning Kawawa's people appeared on the opposite heights and could scarcely believe their eyes when they saw us prepared to start away to the south. At last one of them called out, "Ah! ye are bad." To which Pitsane and his companions retorted, "Ah! ye are good; and we thank you for the loan of your canoe."

Punctilious as ever in all his dealings with native chiefs and in respect for their customs, and jealous for the honour and good name of the white men who sojourned among them, Livingstone was careful to explain this occurrence to Katema and other chiefs south of the Kasai, who all agreed that his conduct was justifiable and that Matiamvo would approve it.

Beyond the Kasai the character of the country changed to a vast expanse of level plains which, on his outward journey, had been flooded. These were now carpeted with a small flower of every shade either of yellow or of blue. Birds of many varieties abounded, as well as dragonflies and butterflies, and numbers of caterpillars mounted the stalks of grass, "though this was winter". The soul of the born nature-lover, not less than the curiosity of the naturalist, was excited by the profusion of wild life around him—as thus:

> Another beautiful plant attracted my attention so strongly that I dismounted to examine it; to my great delight I found it to be an old home acquaintance, a species of *Deoscua*, closely resembling our own sun-dew; the flower stalk never attains a height of more than two or three inches, and the leaves are covered with reddish hairs, each of which has a drop of clammy fluid at its tip, making the whole appear as if spangled over with small diamonds. I noticed it first in the morning, and imagined the appearance was caused by the sun shining on drops of dew, but, as it continued to maintain its brilliancy during the heat of the day, I proceeded to investigate the cause of its beauty, and found that the points of

the hairs exuded pure liquid in, apparently, capsules of clear glutinous matter. This is intended to entrap insects which, dying on the leaf, probably yield nutriment to the plant.

Here, on the second day across the plains, Livingstone suffered his twenty-seventh attack of fever in a place where there was no surface water. "To allay my burning thirst" his men dug with sticks a few feet below the surface. Next day he went on and on 8 June forded the Lotembwa and struck into his former route near Lake Dilolo. He was astonished to find that the river flowed out of the lake in two directions, west and south, and "I would have returned in order to examine more carefully this most interesting point but, having been chilled in crossing the Lotembwa, I was seized with vomiting of blood." It was here nevertheless and despite this condition, that Livingstone made his first and one of his most important geographical discoveries, namely "that this little lake Dilolo (only 4,000 feet above the sea), by giving a portion to the Kasai and another to the Zambesi, distributes its waters to the Atlantic and Indian Oceans".

I state the fact exactly as it opened itself to my own mind; for it was only now that I apprehended the true form of the river-systems and continent. . . . I was not then aware that anyone else had discovered the elevated trough-form of the centre of Africa.

I had observed that the old schistose rocks on the sides dipped in towards the centre of the country, and their strike nearly corresponded with the major axis of the continent; and also that where the later erupted trap-rocks had been spread out in tabular masses over the central plateau, they had borne angular fragments of the older rocks in their substance; but the partial generalization which these observations led to was—that great volcanic action had taken place in ancient times, somewhat in the same way as it does now, at distances of not more than three hundred miles from the sea, and that this igneous action, extending along both sides of the continent, had tilted up the lateral rocks in the manner they are now seen to lie. The greater energy and more extended range of igneous action, in those very remote periods when Africa was formed, embracing all its flanks, imparted to it its present very simple lateral outline. This was the length to which I had come.

The trap-rocks, which now constitute the "filling-up" of the great valley, were always a puzzle to me, till favoured with Sir Roderick Murchison's explanation of the original form of the continent, for then I could see clearly why these trap-rocks, which still lie in a perfectly horizontal position on extensive areas, held in their substance angular fragments, containing algae of the old schists, which form the bottom of the original lacustrine basin; the traps, in bursting through, had broken them off and preserved them. There are, besides, ranges of hills in the central parts, composed of clay and sandstone, schists, with the ripple mark distinct, in which no fossils appear; but as they are usually tilted away from the masses of horizontal trap, it is probable that they too were a portion of the original bottom, and fossils may yet be found in them.

To this he appended a footnote of extracts from the address of Sir Roderick Murchison, a man for whom he later formed an attachment resembling, it was said, that of a Highlander to his chief.

Apart from the intellectual stimulus imparted by this discovery, the sight of the Lake itself had an invigorating effect upon his spirits.

> Though labouring under fever, the sight of the blue waters, and the waves lashing the shore, had a most soothing influence on the mind after so much of lifeless, flat, and gloomy forest. The heart yearned for the vivid impressions which are always created by the sight of the broad expanse of the grand old ocean. That has life in it; but the flat uniformities over which we had roamed made me feel as if buried alive.

Moreover, the chief of the Lake was "a fat jolly fellow" who presented his men with some meal, and putrid buffalo's flesh as a sauce for their tasteless manioc.

On 14 June he reached Katema's district and was "thankful to see old familiar faces again". Next day the chief himself appeared with an abundance of good cheer for which he refused payment. Livingstone had promised him a cloak from Loanda, and this having been duly presented with other gifts, Katema added a cow and the services of an underchief to the Zambesi.

Leaving Katema's on the 19th they forded the Lake at its junction with the southern Lotembwa, waist-deep in water for a mile and a quarter through masses of tangled reeds. They found their pontoon where they had left it carefully preserved, but a mouse had gnawed a hole in it so that it was useless. Arrived at the end of the month at the town of "our old friend Shinte, we received a hearty welcome from this friendly old man and abundant provisions of the best he had". Shinte had postponed a *picho* of his councillors to deliberate on the solution of a dispute between Masiko and his elder brother Limboa, in which he was himself involved, until the arrival of Livingstone to arbitrate: his judgment in the matter was regarded by all three as final. He had brought with him from Angola a pot containing a little plantation of several kinds of fruit-trees and these he now planted in an enclosure for the future benefit of Shinte and his people. His men had also collected quantities of seeds which they distributed among their friends. On 6 July "we parted on the best possible terms with our friend Shinte" and went on to his sister Nyamoana, now a widow. From her Livingstone received the loan of five canoes, and his men having procured others, they proceeded down the Zambesi, some afloat and some ashore. At one point Livingstone was entreated to stop and attack some buffaloes which were destroying the villagers' crop of manioc by night.

> We followed the footprints of a number of old bulls. They showed a great amount of cunning by selecting the densest parts of the very closely planted forests, to stand or recline in during the day. We came within six yards of them several times before we knew they were so near. We only heard them rush away among the crashing branches, catching only a glimpse of them. It was somewhat exciting to feel as we trod on the dry leaves with stealthy steps that, for anything we knew, we might next moment be charged by one of the most dangerous beasts of the forest. We threaded out their doublings for hours, drawn on by a keen craving for animal food, as we had been entirely without salt for upwards of two months, but never could get a shot.

Hereabouts the virulence of tsetse-bites at last proved fatal to the intractable old ox 'Sinbad' despite all efforts to protect him. He had carried his harassed rider from the Zambesi to Golungo Alto and back again "without losing any of his peculiarities. I wished to give the climax to his usefulness and allay our craving for animal food at the same time; but, my men having some compunction, we carried him to end his days in peace at Nariele."

Manenko being lame from a burnt foot was unable to travel but, on hearing of Livingstone's arrival some miles from her village, instantly despatched her loquacious husband with liberal supplies of food. On her behalf he solemnized a blood-pact with the Makololo, symbolizing a defensive alliance between them and the Balonda. (Livingstone himself once became similarly allied to a young woman by accident, when performing a surgical operation on her arm. Some blood from the incision squirted into his eye, whereon she remarked: "You were a friend before, now you are a blood-relation; and when you pass this way, always send me word, that I may cook for you.")

His energies were now directed towards pacification among the tribes and especially persuasion of the warlike Barotse to live at peace with themselves and their neighbours; as well as towards the study of wild life, including that of frogs, toads, and turtles. Though big game was abundant, "I had got quite out of the way of shooting and missed perpetually". (Recurrent fever would be quite enough to account for this.) Once when in pursuit of a zebra which he had wounded he suddenly observed a solitary buffalo coming towards him at a gallop.

> I glanced around, but the only tree on the plain was a hundred yards off and there was no escape elsewhere. I therefore cocked my rifle, with the intention of giving him a steady shot in the forehead when he should come within three or four yards of me. The thought flashed across my mind, "What if your gun misses fire?" I placed it to my shoulder as he came on at full speed, and that is tremendous. A small bush, and a bunch of grass fifteen yards off, made him swerve a little and exposed his shoulder. I just heard the ball crack there as I fell flat on my face. The pain must have made him renounce his purpose, for he bounded close past me into the water, where he was found dead. In expressing my thankfulness to God among my men, they were much offended with themselves for not being present to shield me from this danger.

On 27 July they reached Libonta "and were received with demonstrations of joy such as I had never witnessed before. . . . We were looked upon as men risen from the dead, for the most skilful of their diviners had pronounced us to have perished long ago." Having thanked them and briefly explained the causes of their long absence, Livingstone left the rôle of chief speaker to Pitsane who rose to the occasion and concluded a long and highly flattering speech by saying that "I had not only opened up a path for them to the other white men, but conciliated all the chiefs along the route". He was followed by two elders who, after replying in suitable terms, expressed their displeasure with the Makololo for their recent marauding expeditions, and besought him to admonish Sekeletu as his "child". Their presents were so liberal and spontaneous that Livingstone "felt ashamed that he could make them no return.

'It does not matter', they say. 'You have opened a path for us, and we shall have sleep'. Strangers from a distance come flocking to see me, and seldom come empty-handed. I distribute all presents among my men." It was the same in his progress all down the Barotse valley.

> The people were wonderfully kind. I felt and still feel most deeply grateful, and tried to benefit them in the only way I could, by imparting the knowledge of that Saviour who can comfort and supply them in time of need, and my prayer is that He may send His good Spirit to instruct them and lead them into His kingdom. Even now, I earnestly long to return and make some recompense to them for their kindness.
>
> Though we set out from Loanda with a considerable quantity of goods, hoping both to pay our way through the stingy Chiboque, and to make presents to the kind Balonda and still more generous Makololo, the many delays caused by sickness made us expend all our stock, and we returned as poor as when we set out. Yet no distrust was shown, and my poverty did not lessen my influence. They saw that I had been exerting myself for their benefit alone.

He had planted some palm-tree seeds from Angola in the riverside villages, and these began to sprout during his stay but were mostly devoured by the mice which swarmed in every hut. Leaving Libonta on 31 July he arrived at Nariele the next day and remained there over two Sundays.

> *August 5.* A large audience listened attentively to my address this morning, but it is impossible to indulge any hopes of such feeble efforts. God is merciful and will deal with them in justice and kindness. This constitutes a ground of hope. Poor degraded Africa! A permanent station among them might effect something in time, but a considerable time is necessary. Surely some will remember the ideas conveyed and pray to their merciful Father in their extremity, who would never have thought of Him but for our visit.

On 2 August he notes in his Journal: "Yesterday and today I have written 20 pages of geology from memory." The number of pages is actually thirty, and is no less than a detailed study of the rocks, land formations and water resources, all the way from the Orange River to the Zambesi.[13]

He found Mpololo as helpful as ever though in great affliction, his daughter and her new-born child having been brutally murdered. Many of the wives of his own men had remarried during their husbands' two years' absence and he spent much time in endeavouring to compose these domestic differences.

Though now so near the end of the second stage of his journey, his adventures were not over.

> I left Nariele on the 13th of August, and when proceeding along the shore at mid-day a hippopotamus struck the canoe with her forehead, lifting one half of it quite out of the water so as nearly to overturn it. The force of the butt she gave tilted Mashauana out into the river; the rest of us sprang to the shore, which was only about ten yards off. Glancing back, I saw her come to the surface a short way off and look to the canoe, as if to see if she had done much mischief. It was a female whose young one had been speared the day before. No damage was done, except wetting the person and goods. This is so unusual an occurrence, when the precaution is taken to coast along the shore, that my men exclaimed, "Is the beast mad?"

He was also stung occasionally by a species of hornet from their hanging-nests in the bushes. "Its sting, which it tries to inflict near the eye, is like a discharge of electricity. It produces momentary insensibility, and is followed by the most pungent pain." Arrived at Sesheke he found that the large packet of goods which had been consigned by Moffat to the care of the chief Mosilikatse had been faithfully delivered exactly a year before and kept in perfect safety in a hut on an island specially built for their protection.

It would seem that Livingstone regarded his adventures with big game as among the more frivolous incidents in his missionary travels and scientific researches, and that he was induced by his publisher to retail at least a few of them for the amusement of less seriously-minded readers. The following laconic entry from his Journal the day after his arrival at Sesheke does not appear in his book.

> Yesterday we came to a herd of elephants on an island, and having landed at 60 yards distance I shot one in the ear. The others fled, but he came to a stand at a short distance, and showed by a horizontal movement of his proboscis that he was writhing with pain. Another shot which happened to pierce the proboscis near the root made him advance again with a gruff snorting. This is the first elephant I have killed. I mean the tusks for my companions should they return to Loanda. A strong east wind prevails at this season of the year in these parts and will continue till the rains begin.

The entry runs on thus without a break. We are not told whether the wounded elephant charged or where it fell. The meteorological note seems of as much importance to the writer as the adventure.

Here too at Sesheke long-expected letters came to hand: from the Moffats and many friends, all of which had been despatched via the Cape and Kuruman; as well as a courteous letter from Sir Robert Murchison enclosing (for the recipient's information!) a copy of his Presidential Address to the R.G.S. on the true form of the African Continent; and the following from Maclear:

> *27 March, 1854.* It is both interesting and amusing to trace your improvement as an observer. Some of your early observations, as you remark, are rough, and the angles assigned to the objects misplaced in transcribing. *But upon the whole I do not hesitate to assert that no explorer on record has determined his path with the precision you have accomplished.* It is delightful to remark your cheerful tone midst so many difficulties, dangers and privations—your amusing anecdotes and happy knack of turning everything to the best account. This is an enviable gift, and the more enviable still when in union with the high sense of duty that has led you into the wilderness. May heaven continue to preserve and direct you!

> *11 August.* . . . I send you three Cape newspapers. . . . The third reports the annual meeting of the Society, where you will find that you were presented (on July 26) with the *Queen's Gold Medal*, which Dr. Tidman received for you. . . . But the compliment paid to you on this occasion, even including the Medal, falls far short in my opinion of the one which fell from the President on the receipt of your discoveries up the Zambesi. He said there was more sound geography in the last sheet of foolscap which contained the result of your observations than in many imposing volumes of high pretensions. . . . O may life be continued to you, my dear friend! You have accomplished more for the happiness of mankind than has been done by all the African travellers hitherto put together.[14]

He waited at Sesheke for a few days for the arrival of horses from Linyanti; his progress thither resembled a triumphant procession; he found his wagon perfectly intact; and his reception is best described in a letter to Maclear dated 12 September:

> We reached this two days ago and I have been incessantly worried ever since by salutations, enquiries and welcomes, by persons whose black physiognomy I really think I never saw before, but they all seem to believe that they are as closely related to me as every person named Campbell imagines he is to the Duke of Argyle.[15]

Chapter Fifteen

FIRST GREAT JOURNEY: QUILIMANE
1855–1856

"I view the end of the geographical feat as the beginning of the missionary enterprise. . . ."

MOFFAT, then in his sixtieth year, had pulled out from Kuruman for his third long journey by ox-wagon on 23 May 1854. His health was still impaired from prolonged application to his translation of the Bible; he had been importuned by repeated requests from his old friend Mosilikatse, the fierce warrior-chief of the Matabele, to visit him in his new and distant dominion; and there had been no tidings of Livingstone since his departure into the unknown interior. The time seemed opportune for the coincidence of three objectives: restoration of health by means of travel; direct propagation of the gospel among the heathen; and chiefly, contact if only remotely feasible with his errant son-in-law. Formerly it had been thought in Kuruman a simple matter to convey provisions and packages of every sort from thence to any place northwest; but now, with wars or the threat of them amongst hostile tribes, the delivery of so much as a letter was considered impossible. But, as he wrote to his wife from Sekhomi's town on 10 June: "This to me does not appear difficult. Many things appear so till they are attempted."

His travel-diary, which displays the invincible faith and moral force of the veteran pioneer, has since been published as the *Matabele Journals*. Suffice it that the packages and letters for Livingstone were faithfully conveyed by Mosilikatse's warriors to the south side of the Zambesi in September, near an island above the "Mosioatunya" Falls: but the Makololo, fearing that these packages were bewitched, refused to cross the river. The Matabele therefore deposited their loads on the southern bank, repeating that these were for Livingstone. (Only when their enemies had departed did the Makololo, after much divination, cross the river, take up the loads, place them on the island and cover them with a hut.)[1]

The provisions from Kuruman, though most of them (such as dried fruit) had perished from a year's lapse, were a welcome refreshment to the weary traveller; the newspapers, though nearly eighteen months out of date, were at least something to read; as for the letters: "A whirl of thoughts rushed through my mind as I opened them, but, thank God, I had no cause for sorrow."

Yet there was one cause for dire disappointment: among all his letters there was none from Mary. He was silent about this. By some mischance her letters never reached him; but the news of her welfare and that of the children, which came from London and from Hamilton, was good.

To the Moffats he wrote separately and at great length in response to their request for information about his journey and his future plans. His mother-in-law's letters to him, and his to her, evince the existence of a constant bond of understanding and mutual regard which was never shaken by past differences regarding his duties as her daughter's husband or by subsequent tragedy. She had expressed her own indignation at the criticism, current among some of his erstwhile colleagues in the south, that he was deserting his post in the mission-field by wandering about the continent; and he takes occasion in his reply to counter it by a scathing comment on "those so-called missionaries to the heathen, who never march into real heathen territory, and quiet their consciences by opposing their do-nothingism to my blundering do-somethingism!" To the further criticism that "the Bakwains, Bahurutse, and Bakhatla were not a whit better for all our labours" he replies more temperately. Good seed had been sown among them, but the husbandmen had need of much patience, and the harvest was sure.[2] Enlarging upon this in a letter to Thompson he admits their hostility to the gospel, but "though they refuse to bow in humility to the Divine law, the truths they have imbibed exert a most salutary influence on their morals" and in returning from the Makololo to them and to some of the people near Kuruman "I used to feel I had entered civilized life".[3]

On his arrival at Linyanti a grand *picho* was summoned to hear his companions' report of their journey, which lost nothing in the telling: they had "reached the end of the world". Livingstone then explained that none of the goods brought from Loanda were his property, but were tokens of goodwill from the Portuguese merchants to the Makololo with a view to opening commercial relations between them. These gifts were received with expressions of great satisfaction and delight, whilst their remarks concerning himself were so flattering "that I felt inclined to shut my eyes". (He used the same expression afterwards about his reception in London.) On Sunday he held a service of thanksgiving at which the appearance of Sekeletu, arrayed in his new colonel's uniform, "attracted more attention than the sermon". In due course he took the young chief aside. "I did not fail to reprove 'my child Sekeletu' for his marauding. This was not done in an angry manner, for no good is ever achieved by fierce denunciations. Motibe, his father-in-law, said to me 'Scold him much, but don't let others hear you!'"

There was no dearth of volunteers to accompany him to the east coast, and of others to proceed immediately to Loanda with loads of ivory. They would be followed, after some weeks for recuperation, by his former companions; and then it was hoped that convoys would proceed to and from the coast in continuous relays.

Sekeletu consulted him as to presents for despatch to the Governor and merchants at Loanda, and suggested a trader from Zanzibar named Syde ben Habib; but Livingstone, having little confidence in this Arab, advised that they be sent by the trustworthy Pitsane. Another *picho* was then called to discuss the advisability of removal of the entire tribe from Linyanti to the Barotse valley, so as to be nearer the market. The older men wisely objected to abandoning the line of defence afforded by the Chobe and Zambesi: and some of the younger to the prospect of footing it through rank grass in a country where "it never becomes cool". Sekeletu at last stood up and, addressing Livingstone directly, said:

I am perfectly satisfied as to the great advantages for trade of the path which you have opened, and think that we ought to go to the Barotse, but with whom am I to live there? If you were coming with us I would remove tomorrow; but when you return you will find me near to the spot on which you wish to dwell.

He spent much time in compiling his Journal and in writing letters for despatch by his "Arabian postman" who was leaving for Loanda at the end of September. Of these few have survived, but extracts from two letters to Thompson are of interest.

> I am very well pleased to see that you have lifted up your voice against certain iniquities. . . . Onward, my man. There are lots of good men and true in the Colony who sympathize with what is righteous and just. . . .
> I particularly wish to express my sympathy in the bereavement you have been called on to suffer in the departure of your most excellent father-in-law. I hear of it only now and as I have always regarded him with great affection, I think of his removal with unfeigned sorrow. Unquestionably he served God in his day and generation with rare abilities and unswerving devotion through good and bad report. When such are removed we feel somewhat nearer the grave. . . . I shall always revere his memory. . . .
> [With reference to missionary prospects in this region.] I feel perplexed on one point, viz., the insalubrity of the climate. It is no obstacle to myself personally. . . . And my better half would go as readily as anyone. But I am not clear on exposing my little ones without their own intelligent self-dedication. . . . . .
> The Word of the Living God has life and power. Few human hearts can withstand its force, and no hatred, however deep, can quench its power. I bless God from the bottom of my heart for allowing me to sow the good seed among the Bakwains. . . . You will probably live longer than I shall. Remember seed was sown among the people of Sechele. . . . Go on and fear nothing, my friend. . . .
> I get no letters from my wife, cannot account for it. Hope she has not come to the Cape. But you will take care of her no doubt.[4]

Livingstone had proposed the beginning of October for his departure, but Sekeletu protested. Then the 20th, but the heat and dust became intense. "Only wait," said he, "for the first shower, and then I will let you go." This seemed reasonable since the thermometer rose to 138° in the sun, 108° in the shade, and stood at 96° at sunset; yet Livingstone felt a qualm in subsisting so long on Sekeletu's bounty. It does not seem to have occurred to him for a moment that the boot was really on the other leg, seeing that he had dispensed among his companions, as if it were their right, all the gifts of oxen and ivory that he had received in abundance from the Barotse and from the Makololo themselves. When he did set forth on the third stage of his journey he would in fact have been as destitute as on the first, had not the young chief said to him: "The ivory I have is all your own. If you leave any in my country it will be your own fault."

Meanwhile he was thankful for the comparative solitude which this respite afforded, and wrote in his Journal: "Travelling from day to day among barbarians exerts a most benumbing effect on the religious feelings of the soul. One is refreshed in spirit by a few weeks' rest and reflection."

His report to Tidman, delayed for lack of time till 12 October, is of the size of a pamphlet dealing with a geographical survey of the entire region he had traversed and its prospects as a field for missionary expansion. Theoretically, he says, he would suggest as the healthier districts "the country about the forks of the Leeba and Leeambye or Kabompo, and rivers of the Bashukulompo" (that is, Shinte's country and the Kafue hills, of which latter he had hitherto only heard by report); and adds: "Unfortunately I must mar my report by saying . . . I can speak only for my wife and myself. *We will go, whoever remains behind.*"[5] This letter also forcibly reiterates his view in favour of the moral value of the wide-flung dispersal of the gospel, as against its concentration in small areas in the south; and his sense of the value of lawful commerce.

> If we call the actual amount of conversions the direct result of missions, and the wide diffusion of better principles the indirect, I have no hesitation in asserting that the latter are of infinitely more importance than the former. I do not undervalue the importance of the conversion and salvation of the most abject creature that breathes, it is of overwhelming worth to him personally; but viewing our work of wide sowing of the good seed relatively to the harvest which will be reaped when all our heads are low, there can, I think, be no comparison. . . .
>
> Commerce has the effect of speedily letting the tribes see their mutual dependence. It breaks up the sullen isolations of heathenism. It is so far good, but Christianity alone reaches the very centre of the wants of Africa and of the world. The Arabs are great in commerce, but few will say that they are as amiable as the uncivilized negroes in consequence. You will see I appreciate the effects of commerce much, but those of Christianity much more.

The start was made on 3 November. He was accompanied by Sekeletu and some two hundred men. The guide appointed was Sekwebu who had travelled both banks of the Zambesi and could speak the various dialects. "I found him to be a person of great prudence and sound judgment." He advised a route well to the north of the river above Sesheke, out of reach of tsetse and rocky ground, and also so as to cut the wide loop to the Zambesi where it bends north-eastwards. On the very first night they were overwhelmed by a thunderstorm of such violence as Livingstone had never before experienced. "Then came a pelting rain, which completed our confusion. . . . My clothing having gone on, I lay down on the cold ground expecting to spend a miserable night, but Sekeletu kindly covered me with his own blanket and lay uncovered himself." By this unselfish action on the part of a heathen he says he was "much affected"; and adds that if such men must perish by the advance of civilization "it is a pity". At Sesheke the young chief again provisioned him with necessities and luxuries (butter and honey), "and did everything in his power to make me comfortable for my journey".

From Sekote's Island, whence it was intended to strike off north-east from the river, he decided to visit the Mosioatunya Falls of which he had often heard. Soon, from a distance of five or six miles, he came in sight of five columns of spray which "appeared to mingle with the clouds"; nevertheless he was not prepared for the stupendous grandeur of what he saw. We should not know the date of this, his most spectacular discovery, but for an entry in his note-book which he omitted from his Journal: it was 17 November 1855. In his Journal he wrote: "We sailed swiftly (in a light canoe) down to an island situated at the middle and on the northern verge of the precipice over which the water pours. At one time we seemed to be going right to the gulph, but though I felt a little tremor I said nothing, believing I could face a difficulty as well as my guides." This island is in fact the only one, among several, which projects over the very lip of the Falls. He lay flat on the brink and gazed into the seething cauldron below him. The dry season of the year had only just ended, so that the water was low and his view was not obstructed by the density of spray which, after the rains, conceals everything—when too the island itself would have been inaccessible. "It had never been seen before by European eyes; but scenes so lovely must have been gazed upon by angels in their flight." In this he was mistaken, for the Falls had been marked in an old Portuguese map; no one hitherto, however, had ever attempted to survey or describe them. And Livingstone's description, though scientific and devoid of extravagance, has about it a flavour that is almost Ruskinesque. He notes how the shower of spray, falling outwards, condenses on the straight hedge of evergreen trees (now known as the Rain Forest) on the opposite lip of the fissure and drips down to their roots; and then how the cataract nearest him overhangs the rocks.

> From their roots a number of little rills run back into the gulph; but as they flow down the steep wall there, the column of vapour in its ascent licks them up clean off the rock, and away they mount again. They are constantly running down, but never reach the bottom. . . . On the left side of the island we have a good view of the mass of water which causes one of the columns of vapour to ascend, as it leaps quite clear of the rock, and forms a thick unbroken fleece all the way to the bottom. Its whiteness gave the idea of snow, a sight I had not seen for many a day. As it broke into (if I may use the term) pieces of water, all rushing on in the same direction, each gave off several rays of foam exactly as bits of steel, when burnt in oxygen gas, give off rays of sparks. The snow-white sheet seemed like myriads of small comets rushing on in one direction, each one of which left behind its nucleus rays of foam.

It must have been a cloudy day when he saw the Falls or he would certainly have noted the many miniature rainbows in the clouds of spray; but he records that sacrifices were offered by three Batoka to the "Barimo" upon this island, and adds: "The play of the double iris on the cloud, seen by them elsewhere only as the rainbow, may have led them to the idea that this was the abode of Deity." His estimate of the dimensions of the Falls is typical of his horror of exaggeration, as well as of his honesty and modesty. In his note-book he gives their full length as "not less than 600 yards" and their depth as 100 feet, but revised the former estimate in his Journal after another visit next day.

> I thought, and do still think, the river above the falls to be one thousand yards broad; but I am a poor judge of distances on water, for I showed a naval friend what I supposed to be four hundred yards in the bay of Loanda and, to my surprise, he pronounced it to be nine hundred. . . . In vain I tried to bring to my recollection the way I had been taught to measure a river, by taking an angle with the sextant. That I once knew it, and that it was easy, were all the lost ideas I could recall, and they only increased my vexation.

He tried to measure it with a line and the help of his men, but the line broke. Actually the length of the Falls is 1,900 yards, and its depth between 200 feet at one end and 350 feet at the other.

His surmise that the "crack" in the basaltic bed of the Zambesi at this point was seismic in origin, though mistaken, was a very natural one; the true explanation, that it is due to a fault in the crust, would have been at once apparent to him had an aerial view been possible, when he would have detected the surface prolongation of the fault westwards.

Next day he revisited the island and carefully selected a sheltered spot for the plantation of about a hundred peach and apricot stones, and a quantity of coffee-seed, and called it Garden Island. His previous patient attempts at this kind of cultivation had been frustrated by the negligence of man; now he feared the tread of hippopotami, and so "I bargained for a hedge with one of the Makololo, and, if he is faithful, I have great hopes of Mosioatunya's abilities as a nurseryman." This done, he cut his initials and the date on a tree: "the only time I have been guilty of this act of vandalism"; they were still faintly visible in 1880. He had long outgrown any trace of his youthful radicalism and in proof of his loyalty named this marvel of the natural world—"the most wonderful sight I had witnessed in Africa"—the Victoria Falls: "the only English name I have affixed to any part of the country". The gigantic statue of Livingstone that now looks across the chasm from its western end to the township opposite which bears his name may well, as Professor Debenham remarks, be threatened in time to come when the rushing water carves out a new gorge below it along the line of the surface fault.[6]

On 20 November Sekeletu and his retinue said farewell and returned, leaving Livingstone with a company of 114 men and large quantities of ivory. (It was in far less happy circumstances that they met again five years later.) His route led through the country of the Batoka, "a very degraded tribe", and much of the journeying was made by night to avoid the tsetse, but it was for a long time without any untoward incident. His Journal is happy; it abounds in natural history notes, describing with remarkable minuteness the habits of various ants and other insects; the conformation of the country; big game; rocks and trees and flowers—nothing escaped his eye. "I have never yet discovered any phenomenon in Africa," writes a scientist and explorer who has recently travelled over much of the same ground, "which had not been noted by Livingstone."

Having shot a large bull buffalo near the Kalomo he was charged by the herd at full gallop, but mounted an ant-hill and observed that the leader was an old cow with some twenty buffalo-birds on her withers. This leads him to a digression on their habits and those of the rhinoceros-birds, and then of the honey-guide. On 3 December they crossed the Kalomo and came upon the site of Sebituane's old home from which he had been ousted by the Matabele; it was now derelict but the healthy situation seemed promising for a settlement. Next day they reached a village where Livingstone made contact, too close to be pleasant, with a man possessed of what he curiously calls "prophetic frenzy".

> The headman came and spoke civilly, but when nearly dark the people of another village arrived and behaved very differently. They began by trying to spear a young man who had gone for water. Then they approached us, and one man came forward howling at the top of his voice in the most hideous manner; his eyes were shot out, his lips covered with foam, and every muscle of his frame quivered. He came near to me and, having a small battle-axe in his hand, alarmed my men lest he might do violence; but they were afraid to disobey my previous orders, and to follow their own inclination by knocking him on the head. I felt a little alarmed too, but would not show fear before my own people or strangers, and kept a sharp look-out on the little battle-axe. It seemed to me a case of ecstasy or prophetic frenzy, voluntarily produced. I felt it would be a sorry way to leave the world, to get my head chopped by a mad savage, though that perhaps would be preferable to hydrophobia or delirium tremens. Sekwebu took a spear in his hand as if to pierce a bit of leather, but in reality to plunge it into the man if he offered violence to me. After my courage had been sufficiently tested, I beckoned with the head to the civil headman to remove him, and he did so by drawing him aside. I would fain have felt his pulse, to ascertain whether the violent trembling were not feigned, but had not much inclination to go near the battle-axe again. There was, however, a flow of perspiration and the excitement continued fully half an hour, then gradually ceased. This paroxysm is the direct opposite of hypnotism.

Impressed by the value of all this region as a link in a chain of communication with the coast, at Monze's village he enquired of the chief, who had never seen a white man before, whether one such as himself would be acceptable as a teacher, and received an enthusiastic reply. His comment upon this, which is made with emphasis, shows the intuitive conviction of the Christian humanist—confirmed by personal experience—that in missions to the heathen example is better than precept, and ethics than dogma.

> The answer does not mean much more than what I know, by other means, to be the case—that a white man of *good sense* would be welcome and safe in these parts. By uprightness, and by laying himself out for the good of the people, he would be known all over the country as a *benefactor* of the race.

Having released a violent prisoner a week before, he was now met at the next village by this man with loud expressions of gratitude and a handsome present of corn and meal. "It is not often," he remarks, "that jail-birds turn out well." The scenery became more lovely as they proceeded, the soil more fertile, and the game more abundant. At the entrance to a beautiful valley on 14 December he shot a buffalo; it turned on him for a final charge; he ran to some rocks to find his retreat cut off by three elephants, but these made off; trying a long shot he brought one of them down. Numbers of villagers thronged to share the feast. "I was right glad to see the joy manifested at such an abundant supply of meat."

But the following day he was the horrified spectator of the slow slaughter with spears of a cow elephant and her calf. With his abhorrence of the wanton destruction of noble animals, which familiarity never lessened, he turned from the spectacle "with a feeling of sickness", and then qualifies his disgust by a typical self-criticism: "But it is right to add that I did not feel sick when my own blood was up the day before. We ought perhaps to judge those deeds more leniently in which we ourselves have no temptation to engage. Had I not previously been guilty of doing the very same thing, I might have prided myself on my superior humanity." From this he is led to discourse on the anatomy, diet, and other peculiarities of elephants, both African and Asiatic.

Semalembue, whose town was reached on 18 December, received them with true native courtesy and hospitality; and near it was another district where Sebituane had formerly

·lived. Here they crossed the Kafue and Livingstone was more than ever impressed with the suitability of the whole of this hilly region for settlement. The plains below were alive with big game peacefully grazing: "I wished that I had been able to take a photograph of the scene, so seldom beheld, and which is destined, as guns increase, to pass away from earth. . . . The number of animals was quite astonishing, and made me think that here I could realize an image of that time when Megatheria fed undisturbed in the primaeval forests." Beasts and birds were wonderfully tame. Hereabouts he brought down four geese with two shots, and "had I followed the wishes of my men, could have secured a meal of water-fowl for the whole party".

All this while he says that both he and his men enjoyed much better health than with a very much smaller party on the previous journeys. He attributes this to the fact that he no longer braved the drenching rains when on the march; that if wet, he caused shelters to be built and large fires to be made; that, to vary his own diet, he had taken wheat-flour and baked his own bread; and that the climate was in general healthier than in the west. Once he spent a night in a hollow baobab tree which could contain twenty men.

Semalembue accompanied the party through a deep gorge round a bend below high hills to a ford over the Kafue whence, crossing its tributary the Chiponga on 30 December, they continued along its north bank to a point eight miles beyond its confluence with the Zambesi, the sight of whose "goodly broad waters gladdened our hearts". But the hot steaminess of the air was oppressive. Here too were the first evidences of slave-trade and the first signs of hostility. An Italian had attacked several inhabited islands east of Tete and carried off many slaves and much ivory and had been killed in consequence; Livingstone was now suspected of being one of that race or else a Portuguese, until he showed his whiter skin and fairer hair. Even so, suspicions were not allayed and when at Mburuma's village he was threatened with attack. "His people never came near us, except in large bodies and fully armed. We had to order them to place their bows, arrows, and spears at a distance before entering our encampment." Mburuma, however, who never appeared himself, promised the loan of only two canoes and sent two men ostensibly as guides to the Loangwa, but actually with a view to dividing the party and attacking them.

This incident stands out as one of the most dramatic and critical in Livingstone's career; and the simplicity of his faith and the quality of his courage are nowhere better exhibited than in his behaviour in meeting it. His reference to it in *Travels* is brief and reticent; it is here supplemented by more intimate passages from his Journal.

January 14th. We reached the confluence of the Loangwa and the Zambesi, most thankful to God for His great mercies in helping us thus far. . . . I walked about some ruins I discovered, built of stone, and found the remains of a church, and on one side lay a broken bell, with the letters I.H.S. and a cross, but no date. Mburuma's guides had behaved so strangely that we were suspicious we might be attacked while crossing the Loangwa. We saw them collect in large numbers, and though they professed friendship they kept at a distance. They refused to lend us more canoes than two, though they have many.

Thank God for His mercies thus far. How soon may I be called upon to stand before him, my righteous Judge, I know not. O Jesus, grant me resignation to Thy will and reliance on Thy powerful hand. But wilt Thou permit me to plead for Africa? My family is Thine. They are in Thy hands.

It seems a pity that the important facts about two healthy ridges should not be known to Christendom. Thy will be done.

Evening. Felt some turmoil of spirit in view of having all my efforts for the welfare of this great region and its teeming population knocked on the head by savages to-morrow. But I read that Jesus came and said: "All power is given unto me in Heaven and earth. *Lo, I am with you always, even unto the end of the world.*" It is the word of a gentleman of the most sacred and strictest honour, and there's an end on't. I will not cross furtively by night, as I had intended. It would appear as flight, and should such a man as I flee?* Nay verily. I shall take observations for latitude and longitude to-night, though it be my last. I feel calm now, thank God.

15th. The natives of the surrounding country collected round us this morning, all armed. . . . Only one canoe was lent to us, though we saw two others tied to the bank. The part we crossed was about a mile from the confluence; it seemed upwards of half a mile in breadth. We passed all our goods first on to an island in the river, then the cattle and men; I, occupying the post of honour, being the last to enter the canoe. A number of the inhabitants stood armed all the time we were embarking. I showed them my watch, lens, and other things to keep them amused, until there remained only those who were to enter the canoe with me. I thanked them for their kindness, and wished them peace. After all, they

* The sentence is a quotation from Nehemiah vi, 11.

may have been influenced only by the intention to be ready in case I should play them some false trick, for they have reason to be distrustful of the whites.

The guides came over to bid us adieu, and we sat under a mango-tree, fifteen feet in circumference. I gave them some little presents for themselves, a handkerchief and a few beads, and they were highly pleased with a cloth of red baize for Mburuma, which Sekeletu had given me to purchase a canoe. We were thankful to part good friends.

His handwriting in the Journal on the eve of this crossing is, as Doctor Macnair has observed, clearer and firmer even than usual. And though he carried firearms, as his opponents did not, his silence on the subject would seem to indicate that had he used them, it would only have been in desperation as a last resort.

On the farther side of the Loangwa, at the point of its junction with the Zambesi, lay the ruins of the Portuguese settlement called Zumbo, abandoned fifty years before. The houses with wide verandahs and high walled courts, the fort, and the church at the angle, badly constructed by slave-labour and of soft sandstone, were all in a state of decay; but the situation was magnificent and "admirably well chosen as a site for commerce". The administration had, like all Portuguese settlements, been military, but the officers being poorly paid had been obliged to engage in trade. A later entry in Livingstone's Journal is worth quoting:

> The Governor (of Tete) says frankly that the cause of the decay of this Colony is undoubtedly the slave-trade, which withdrew the attention of the colonist from agriculture; and every other branch of industry— cotton, indigo, wheat, coffee, even gold—was neglected for the gambling gains of the hateful traffic. And the ill-will of the natives was engendered as well.

Zumbo was reoccupied by the Portuguese in 1862, largely on account of Livingstone's interest in it; but in 1891 when the frontiers between British and Portuguese territory were delineated, it would appear to have come more and more under British influence as did most of the other populous native villages on the north bank of the Zambesi.*

* When the present writer camped there in 1921 it was a large and flourishing native village. He was informed that the people generally preferred life on that side of the river where labour was voluntary, rather than on the other where it was forced.

The high rough tree-covered hills which had made progress difficult and slow from the Kafue region persisted beyond the Loangwa, and became denser with bush and more infested with tsetse which destroyed the riding oxen. One of the men was tossed by a buffalo and fell in a prone position, but without serious injury. Livingstone says that he "shampooed" him thoroughly, and within a week he was fit to hunt again. He looked with longing to the broad plains on the other side of the Zambesi; and when getting near to Mpende's village on the 17th was advised by a clothed negro from Tete to cross it at once, since that chief was hostile to white men. He tried in vain to procure canoes, but their owners feared the wrath of Mpende. A promise was made by one headman, but retracted. The villagers were, however, liberal with gifts of food. They toiled on slowly through beautiful country but in growing apprehension of the outcome of their march. His company of "sturdy vagabonds" were in a sorry state with their clothing dropping from them piecemeal, but they were "veterans in marauding" and boasted: "You have seen us with elephants, but you don't yet know what we can do with men."

January 23rd. This morning, at sunrise, a party of Mpende's people came close to our encampment, uttering strange cries and waving some bright red substance towards us. Then they lighted a fire with charms in it, and departed uttering the same hideous screams as before. This was intended to render us powerless, and probably also to frighten us. Ever since dawn parties of armed men have been seen collecting from all quarters, and numbers passed us while it was yet dark. Had we moved down the river at once it would have been considered an indication of fear or defiance, and so would a retreat. I therefore resolved to wait, trusting in Him who has the hearts of all men in His hands.

(*Addendum from his Journal.*)—To Thee, O God, we look. And oh! Thou who wast the Man of Sorrows for the sake of poor vile sinners, and didst not disdain the thief's petition, remember me and Thy cause in Africa. Soul and body, my family and Thy cause, I commit all to Thee. Hear, Lord, for Jesus' sake.

They evidently intended to attack us, for no friendly message was sent. . . . Other things also showed unmistakeable hostility. As we were now pretty certain of a skirmish I ordered an ox to be slaughtered, as this is a means which Sebituane employed for inspiring courage. I have no doubt that we should have been victorious; indeed, my men, who were far better acquainted with fighting than any of the people on the Zambesi, were rejoicing in the prospect of securing captives to carry the tusks for them.

258

Mpende's whole tribe was now assembled within half a mile of the intruders' encampment. Presently spies approached, but would answer no questions. Livingstone handed them a leg of the ox, desiring them to take it to Mpende.

After a considerable time of suspense two old men appeared and asked Livingstone who he was. He replied, "I am a Lekoa" (Englishman). They said, "We don't know that tribe. We suppose you are a Mozunga" (Portuguese). He showed them his hair and skin, whereupon they exclaimed, "Ah! you must be one of that tribe that loves the black men." They returned to their chief and there ensued another long debate, as a result of which Mpende was at last persuaded that this European belonged to the "friendly white tribe". Livingstone then sent Sekwebu to negotiate for the purchase of a canoe, the more necessary now since one of his men had become too ill to walk. Sekwebu conducted this conversation with adroit diplomacy, but even before he could finish his story Mpende interrupted. "That white man is truly one of our friends. See how he lets me know his afflictions!" Sekwebu: "Ah! if you knew him as well as we do, you would understand how highly he values your friendship; and as he is a stranger he trusts in you to direct him." Mpende: "Well, he ought to cross to the other side of the river, for the way to Tete is rougher and longer on this." Sekwebu: "But who will take us across if you do not?" Mpende: "Truly! I only wish you had come sooner."

> He did everything he could afterwards to aid us on our course, and our departure was as different as possible from our approach to his village. I was very much pleased to find the English name spoken of with such great respect so far from the coast, and most thankful that no collision occurred to damage its influence.

They ferried to an island in midstream that evening, and darkness had fallen before all were ashore; for precaution they slept in the canoes, and reached the opposite bank next morning. Livingstone sent back one of his two spoons and a shirt as a thank-offering to Mpende. Rains were continuous and held up progress for some days, and his tent was now so rotten as to be nearly useless. The sick member of his party, a Batoka, after a long illness "which I did not understand", died. Livingstone had had much difficulty in persuading his companions to carry him when his case became hopeless. This was the first casualty on the whole of his journey, but it was not to be the last. His Journal throughout is filled with medical notes which have never been published; if these were collected and annotated by a doctor they would make an interesting and perhaps valuable contribution to the study of tropical diseases.

He says that he felt "most sincerely thankful" to find himself on the south bank of the Zambesi; but, in the light of future events, his crossing it at this point must be considered a major disaster. Not until he reached Tete was he informed of the existence of a "small rapid" in the river, below the Chicova flats, and then wrote: "Had I known this previously, I would certainly not have left the river without examining it. It is called Kebrabasa, and is described as a number of rocks which jut out across the stream." But that he did not think seriously of it even then, is apparent from a letter to Tidman on the prospects of the navigability of the Zambesi as far as to the Victoria Falls: "the only two impediments I know of being one or two rapids (not cataracts), and the people in some parts who are robbers." He was in fact never nearer than fifty miles from these colossal rapids, having circled round them to the south; had he continued the northward route he would either have seen them or have been told that they formed an insuperable barrier to any river traffic. He had taken altitudes by the boiling point of water at almost every stage of his journey, as well as the rate of flow of the Zambesi wherever he touched it. Professor Debenham has drawn attention to an inexplicable miscalculation whereby he underestimated the 600 foot drop between the point where he crossed the Zambesi and the point where he joined it again at Tete.[7] But for this error he must have realized that the Kebrabasa Rapids could be by no means "small", and on his next expedition he would never have subjected himself and others to such desperate toil and danger in attacking them from below and above.

His Journal at this time is filled with natural history notes and other observations of many kinds: winds and weather; rivulets of running sand; fossil trees; rare insects and spiders; butterflies and song-birds, especially the strange nesting-habits of the *korwe*; native customs such as rain-charming and trial by ordeal; big game—"I once saw a white rhinoceros give a buffalo which was gazing intently at myself a poke in the chest, but it did not wound it, and seemed only a hint to get out of the way." It is not only the extraordinary variety and acuteness of his observations—especially of *minutiae*—but his patience in prosecuting them and the logic of his deductions therefrom, which so impress the reader.

There are similarities between the ending of this final stage of his journey with the ending of the first stage of it. On both he was in Portuguese territory, and on both in the routes of the slave-trade, exactions for tribute becoming more importunate as he neared civilization. On both he was at the end of his resources, both materially and bodily (though not so utterly exhausted on the last stage as on the first), and in each case was restored by the active sympathy of a friendly host. There were similarities too in the composition and shelving stratification of the rocks at each side of the continent (sandstone, mica, schist, calcareous tufa).

The last miles to Tete were drawn out not only by the exhaustion of the party but also by the attempt, not always successful, to circumvent villages by leaving the beaten track and thus avoid demands for tribute. At Monina's village on 20th February the plea of poverty was not accepted; there was a war-dance, a furious beating of drums, and a display of weapons including guns. "We sat and looked at them for some time and then, as it became dark, lay down, all ready to give them a warm reception. But an hour or two after dark the dance ceased and, as we saw no one approaching us, went to sleep." But there was one fatality. During the night one of Livingstone's best men, Monahin, wandered from the camp and was never seen again. "I felt his loss greatly, and spent three days in searching for him." When Livingstone informed Monina of this sad loss, the chief enjoined his people to aid in the search, expressed his sympathy and allowed the party to move on. The country abounded in lions and this poor fellow was probably the victim of one of them.

Despite his increasing physical weariness it must have been on the day after his departure from Monina's that Livingstone assembled his thoughts to write the long letter to the King of Portugal,[8] of which an excellent summary is given in Blaikie's *Life*.

The going was harder than ever; the feet tripped among wild-vine stems or slipped on rounded shingle and granite-gravel concealed under long grass—and this for many a weary mile, so that he wrote to Sir Roderick Murchison:

> Pedestrianism in such circumstances may be all very well for those whose obesity requires the process of Pressnitz, but for one who had become as thin as a lath the only discernible good was, it enabled an honest man to gain a vivid idea of the phrase "a Month on the Tread-mill".[9]

Their stock of food was now exhausted; for many days they had subsisted on roots and honey. On 2 March, when only eight miles from Tete, Livingstone could go no farther. He sent a message to the Commandant and the same night was roused from sleep by two officers and a company of soldiers with the materials for a civilized breakfast and a *machila* (slung hammock).

> My companions thought that we were captured by the armed men, and called me in alarm. When I understood their errand, and had partaken of a good breakfast, though I had just before been too tired to sleep, all my fatigue vanished. It was the most refreshing breakfast I ever partook of, and I walked the last eight miles without the least feeling of weariness, although the path was so rough that one of the officers remarked to me, "This is enough to tear a man's life out of him." The pleasure experienced in partaking of that breakfast was only equalled by the enjoyment of Mr. Gabriel's bed on my arrival at Loanda. It was also enhanced by the news that Sebastopol had fallen, and the war was finished.

At Tete he was persuaded by the hospitable Commandant, Major Sicard, to give himself a month for recovery from his "emaciated condition", and meanwhile he wrote a long and informative essay on the history, politics, products, and economics of the town, which appears as a chapter in his *Travels*. He also exchanged valuable medical and geographical notes with a kindred spirit, Senhor Candido, whose map of the river from Tete to Sena he inserted into his own. The Commandant provided the Makololo with clothing, lodged them in a house till they could erect their huts on a portion of ground which he gave them to cultivate, as well as freedom to hunt and purchase goods, pending Livingstone's return from England to take them home. "I was in a state of want myself and, though I pressed him to take payment in ivory for both myself and men, he refused all recompense. I shall ever remember his kindness with deep gratitude."

Tete is a notoriously malarial quarter and on the eve of his intended departure, 4 April, he was stricken with his first severe attack of fever since leaving Linyanti; the Commandant with most of his household were also laid low. "I intended," he wrote to Mr. Gabriel on that date, "on reaching Tete to move down the river in 3 or 4 days, but though I soon began to recover flesh I felt something wrong with the kidneys. . . . As Quilimane is reported very deadly and Major Sicard kindly advised me to remain with him till next month which is more salubrious, I thought it my duty to accede. . . . But Quilimane has such a bad name that I hope to get quickly past it."

His stock of quinine and other medicines were all but expended and there were none to be found in Tete. Some leaves of a tree were produced which were supposed to be those of the *cinchona*; Livingstone examined them and concluded that they were not, but were allied to it; he therefore made a decoction from the bark and this proved efficacious. He soon recovered himself, but Major Sicard and his little boy were confined much longer. "It afforded me pleasure to attend the invalids in their sickness, though I was unable to show a tithe of the gratitude I felt for the Commandant's increasing kindness." He made a careful sketch of the leaves of this tree and sent them for identification to Dr. J. D. Hooker of Kew Gardens (later a valued friend) who at once obliged and pronounced them to be "reputed powerful febrifuges, equal to the *cinchona* in their effects".

On 22 April, when all were recovered, he descended the Zambesi with Sekwebu and sixteen good paddlers from his own company, all liberally provisioned, and escorted by the Commandant's Lieutenant with orders that he should not be allowed to pay for anything all the way to the coast. He was also furnished with letters to four Portuguese gentlemen "from every one of whom I received disinterested kindness and I ought to speak well for ever of Portuguese hospitality". He was assiduous with his star-sights and other observations all the way. Arrived at Sena on the 27th he found its decayed condition ten times worse than that of Tete, which itself was "quite lamentable". All the Portuguese possessions were in a state of miserable decline. At Sena he had a recurrence of fever which was severe, but it did not prevent him from climbing a hill and taking its height, whence he could view the hilly country across the river (now spanned by the longest railway-bridge in the world) with which he was to become all too painfully familiar on his next expedition. Whilst laid up he endeavoured to practise another of his many novel experiments for self-help with characteristic equanimity; but it is only in his Journal that he deigns to mention it.

> A large species of bats abounds in all the houses here. Last night while unable to sleep on account of rapid pulse, skin sometimes hot and dry or bathed in perspiration, it was interesting to observe . . . that they often hover close to the face when the eyes are shut and produce a pleasant fanning sensation. I believed they were killing mosquitoes and had no objection to their familiarity. Having bared my thigh, I gave them a fair opportunity of playing the vampire, but they did nothing.

He was again "seized by a severe tertian fever" at Mazaro, but walked along the bank of the Matu for 15 miles through long grass and in torrid heat. "The pulse beat with amazing force, and felt as if thumping against the crown of the head. The stomach and spleen swelled enormously, giving me an appearance which I had been disposed to laugh at among the Portuguese." He was by this time evidently very ill and was at once provided by one of Major Sicard's friends with a launch to Quilimane. With a house in the stern, and anchored in midstream, "it gave me some rest from mosquitoes, which in the whole of the delta are something frightful". With eight of his followers who begged not to leave him, he reached Quilimane on 20 May 1856, almost to the day on which he had left Cape Town four years before.

There he was housed and befriended by the last of those to whom Sicard had commended him, Colonel Nunes, "one of the best men in the country"; and his extreme debility may be surmised by the bald statement that he requested his host, in case of his death, to sell Sekeletu's ivory and give the proceeds to his men. Letters awaited him, but none from his family; and his joy on reaching the coast was further sadly embittered by the news that the Commander, Lieutenant and five men of H.M. brigantine *Dart*, in coming to take him aboard, had been lost on the bar. "I never felt more poignant sorrow. It seemed as if it would have been easier for me to have died for them." But the Captain of H.M. brig *Frolic*, calling at the port in November, and twice later, had "most considerately" left for him some wine and an ounce of quinine: "These gifts made my heart overflow." It was the *Frolic* which called again six weeks later, and took him out to sea.

Amongst his large mail was a letter from Sir Roderick Murchison dated from London on 2 October 1855:

> ... You will long ago I trust have received the cordial thanks of all British Geographers for your unparalleled exertions and your successful accomplishment of the greatest triumph in geographical research which has been effected in our times. I rejoice that I was the individual in the Council of the R.G.S. who proposed that you should receive our first Gold Medal of the past session, and I need not say that the award was made by a cordial and unanimous vote.
>
> Permit me to thank you sincerely for having selected me as your correspondent in the absence of Colonel Steele, and to assure you that I shall consider myself as much honoured as I shall certainly be gratified by every fresh line which you may have leisure to write to me.
>
> Anxiously hoping that I may make your personal acquaintance and that you may return to us in health to receive the homage of all geographers. . . .

The above refers only to the journey to Loanda. On 23 May 1856 Sir Roderick wrote again from the Dingle Peninsula in Ireland; and though his letter did not come to hand till the recipient was home again, it may find a fitting place here.

> Your admirable (three) letters from the Interior and from Tete afforded me the sincerest gratification in acquainting me with the successful termination of your wonderful journey, and, as I hope, in good health notwithstanding your privations and sufferings. Your letters came into my hands at Cheltenham just as the British Association for the Advancement of Science was about to open its business, and I took especial care to bring their chief contents before the geographers and ethnologists who were present, whilst I prepared the abstract which was published in *The Times*. . . .
>
> I forbear from saying more than that *I thank you most heartily* for having made me your correspondent. I shall indeed have the liveliest pleasure in talking over your verification of my theoretical speculations on the ancient and modern outline of Africa, and in endeavouring to glean from you much of the knowledge you possess of the structure of the country. . . .
>
> I write from the S. Western extremity of Ireland where I am geologizing. . . .[10]

In this letter Sir Roderick suggests that Livingstone should publish an account of his Travels, and strongly recommends him to consider Mr. John Murray, "the great publisher". Mr. Murray had, however, himself written previously to Livingstone on 5 January 1856:

> I am quite willing to take upon myself the whole cost of publication—including engraving of maps, plates, and all other incidental expenses, bearing whatever risks there may be, and to give you two-thirds of the profits of every edition. My usual condition in such cases is to give one-half of the proceeds to the author,* but in your case I cede that in consideration of the probable interest of your work.[11]

As he stood on the deck and looked back to the low fever-infested delta of the Zambesi, his heart may well have been filled with elation. It might be, and indeed quite probably was, that others—Arab traders and half-caste Portuguese—had preceded him along much the same route years before, and he gives them credit for their achievements. But that was no matter. He had done something that had never been done before. He had not only traversed the continent, he had charted his route; he had not only unveiled Africa, he had revealed the African. He had discovered populated regions hitherto unknown, and had passed through and even placated tribes of hostile savages without firing a shot. He had opened up a highway from each end of the continent to the interior, thereby (so he fondly hoped) to introduce the wholesome flow of honest trade—the herald of civilization and Christianity—into the very heart of that dark continent. The humble cotton-spinner on the Clyde, the obscure missionary in the Kalahari, had become at one bound a figure of national fame. The presence of British men-of-war off the coast to pick him up was sufficient evidence of that.

Yet there is not a word in his letters that betrays the slightest hint of self-praise; rather, of self-depreciation. To Sir Roderick Murchison he wrote: "I do not feel so much elated by the prospect of accomplishing this feat. I feel most thankful to God for preserving my life, where so many—who by superior intelligence would have done more good—have been cut off. But it does not look as if I reached the goal. Viewed in relation to my

---

* An agreement of which contemporary publishers and authors may be interested to take note!

calling, the end of the geographical feat is only the beginning of the enterprise. . . ." And then, expanding on that last sentence, he continues as a fitting epilogue to his *Travels* with these noble and memorable words:

> I view the end of the geographical feat as the beginning of the missionary enterprise. I take the latter term in its most extended signification, and include every effort made for the amelioration of our race; the promotion of all those means by which God in His providence is working, and bringing all His dealings with man to a glorious consummation. Each man in his sphere, whether knowingly or unknowingly, is performing the will of our Father in heaven. Men of science, searching after hidden truths which when discovered will, like the electric telegraph, bind men more closely together—soldiers battling for right against tyranny—sailors rescuing the victims of oppression from the grasp of heartless men-stealers—merchants teaching the nations lessons of mutual dependence—and many others, as well as missionaries, all work in the same direction, and all efforts are overruled for one glorious end.[12]

Chapter Sixteen

FIRST VISIT HOME
1856–1858

"Gentlemen, . . . I beg to direct your attention to Africa."

LIVINGSTONE'S intention, expressed in a letter to Mr. Gabriel from Tete on 4 April, had been "to rest myself a month or two in England and come back to do some good in Africa before I die". And to Tidman from Quilimane on 23 May:

> It being absolutely necessary to get through this delta during either April, May, June or July, on account of its well-known insalubrity, and also because I have a number of Sekeletu's people waiting for me at Tete, my stay in England must be extremely short . . . too short, I fear, to allow of my being cured of disease of the spleen and kidneys which has shown itself in the fevers of the delta. . . . The sea voyage however may set me right.[1]

Of his Makololo, sixteen had come with him to Sena; eight returned to Tete, and eight had come down to Quilimane but had since gone back to join the others. Sekeletu had wished that all should accompany him to England, but Livingstone felt justified in taking only one, Sekwebu, "a sensible worthy heathen". He had no thought then that the "two months' rest" would extend to eighteen months of almost continuous activity.

How far he had moved from the comprehension of his home-folk in Hamilton appears in a letter to his parents from Quilimane on 1 June:

> Agnes remarks that I ought to have turned trader when I saw a good chance of gain at the Lake [Ngami]. I could turn trader now with a good prospect of gain. Do the wise people of Scotland really imagine that we are missionaries (living at what the Directors declare is a bare subsistence) because it would be impossible to better our worldly prospects by engaging in other enterprises? The majority of us could better our worldly prospects by abandoning missions altogether.[2]

268

He then instances the recent success of his brother-in-law, Robert Moffat, first in land-surveying and then in a good Government post, and concludes on his own account with decisive finality: "I still prefer poverty and mission service to riches and ease. It's my choice."

This was however but the prelude to a much more serious difference of opinion which caused him to view the prospect of homecoming with very mixed feelings. A few days before the *Frolic* sailed he received via Mozambique the duplicate of a letter from Tidman dated 24 August 1855, the original of which had been sent to the care of Mr. Gabriel to ensure his receipt of it at one side of the continent or the other. It was in reply to his despatches from Linyanti on 24 September and 8 November 1853, from Loanda on 4 July 1854, and from Cassange on 14 January 1855. It begins by expressing in truly Victorian style the Directors' admiration of his fortitude in prosecuting such a bold and hazardous enterprise, their prayerful solicitude for his personal safety, and the writer's own pleasure on receiving on his behalf the award of the Queen's Gold Medal from the President of the R.G.S. at the anniversary meeting in May 1855. It then continues:

The Directors, while yielding to none in their appreciation of the objects upon which, for some years past, your energies have been concentrated, or in admiration of the zeal, intrepidity, and success with which they have been carried out, are nevertheless restricted in their power of aiding plans connected only remotely with the spread of the Gospel. Of the important bearing of your researches upon the interests, not only of science, but of general humanity, we have the most entire confidence, and we would also cherish the hope and belief that they will ultimately tend to the diffusion of Christian truth among the populous but yet uncivilized tribes inhabiting the districts to which you have obtained access. But your reports make it sufficiently obvious that the nature of the country, the insalubrity of the climate, the prevalence of poisonous insects, and other adverse influences, constitute a very serious array of obstacles to missionary effort, and even were there a reasonable prospect of their being surmounted—and we by no means assume they are insurmountable—yet, in that event, the financial circumstances of the Society are not such as to afford any ground of hope that it would be in a position, within any definite period, to enter upon untried, remote, and difficult fields of labour. In view of these circumstances we should, independently of the pleasure of seeing you amongst us, regard your visit to England as affording a most favourable opportunity for conferring with you fully on your future plans. . . .

I have the pleasure to report that Mrs. Livingstone, whom I have seen within these few days, is, together with your children, in good health, but she is of course looking forward, with no little anxiety, to the termination of your long and perilous journey, and your reunion with your family.[3]

There is no doubt that this communication came to Livingstone as a severe shock. Previous reverses in his career such as friction with his colleagues at Kuruman, the hostility of his countrymen at the Cape, the sack of his house at Kolobeng— he could dismiss with a laugh and a shrug. But this was something new in his experience. It must have seemed to him that his life's purposes, to which he felt himself divinely called, were being frustrated by the very agency which God had appointed to fulfil them. As Professor Wallis says: "Livingstone was taken aback, but he faced a critical position stoutly" and his letter in reply is "Livingstone at his best: modest, respectful and straightforward".[4] Having announced his arrival at the port, and his pleasure on receiving a letter from Dr. Tidman after a silence of more than four years, he gives his news briefly and then proceeds as follows:

Accompanied by many kind expressions of approbation which I highly value on account of having emanated from a body of men whose sole object in undertaking the responsibility and labour of the direction, must have been a sincere desire to promote the interests of the kingdom of our Lord among the heathen, I find the intimation that the Directors are "restricted in their power of aiding plans connected only remotely with the spread of the gospel". And it is added also that even though certain very formidable obstacles should prove surmountable, "the financial circumstances of the Society are not such as to afford any ground of hope that it would be, within any definite period, in a position to enter upon untried, remote and difficult fields of labour".

If I am not mistaken, these statements imply a resolution on the part of the gentlemen now in the direction to devote the decreasing income of the Society committed to their charge to parts of the world of easy access and in which the missionaries may devote their entire time and energies to the dissemination of the truths of the gospel with reasonable hopes of speedy success. This, there can be no doubt, evinces a sincere desire to perform their duty faithfully to their constituents (to the heathen) and to our Lord and Master. Yet while still retaining that full conviction of the purity of their motives which no measure, adopted during the sixteen years of my connection with the Society, has for a moment disturbed, I feel constrained to view "the untried, remote and difficult fields" to which I humbly yet firmly believe God has directed my steps, with a resolution widely different from that which their words imply. As our aims and purposes will now appear in some degree divergent, on their part from a sort of paralysis caused by financial decay, and on mine from the simple continuance of an old determination to devote my life and my all to the services of Christ in whatever way He may lead me in Intertropical Africa, it seems natural, while yet without the remotest idea of support from another source, to give some of the reasons for differing with those with whom I have hitherto been so happily connected.

He then surveys his sixteen years of service in the Society during which he had undertaken no single journey without the Board's approval, and "is at a loss to understand the phraseology" of their letter. His own ends: "The difficulties are mentioned in no captious spirit, though—from being at a loss as to the precise meaning of the terms—I may appear to be querulous. I am not conscious of any diminution of the respect and affection with which I have always addressed you"—and he is as always "Yours affectionately".[5]

There is no doubt that he was genuinely nonplussed. "That same day, perplexity set him down to indite a second letter of even greater length" showing the reasonableness of his plans for a mission in the interior: the Barotse highlands were healthy; the Zambesi an excellent highway; the Makololo tractable; life and property safe; additional expense to the Society negligible or unnecessary; the Portuguese Governors (de Cunha and Lourenço Marques) trustworthy—and so forth. "At the same time, though he does not say so, his own mind was made up. With or without the Directors' support, he would return, and that speedily." This decision is made clear in a letter to Thompson on 8 August:

I had imagined in my simplicity that both my preaching, conversation, and travel were as nearly connected with the spread of the Gospel as the Boers would allow them to be. The plan of opening a path from either the East or West coast for the teeming population of the interior was submitted to their judgment and received their formal approbation. I have seven times been in peril of my life from savage men, while laboriously and without swerving pursuing that plan, and never doubted but that I was in the path of duty. . . . I will follow out the work in spite of the veto of the Board. If it is according to the Will of God, means will be provided from other quarters.[6]

But a little later, on 17 September, he wrote more soberly

from the Mauritius; after quoting Tidman's reference to the financial circumstances of the Society:

> As these statements are embalmed in some flattering sentences of approbation . . . I suppose it is intended to send me to some tried, near, and easy fields where I may wax fat and kick like Jeshurun. As the proposition to leave the untried, remote and difficult fields of labour (as they have been ever since our Saviour died for the poor sinners who inhabit them) involves my certain severance from the L.M.S. . . . I shall leave you without abuse of any sort. The Directors have always treated me well, and I shall remember you all with affection.[7]

Livingstone's failure to appreciate the point of view of the Directors is the less understandable since he was already acquainted with their financial straits and their large commitments in other fields than Africa. He had written to Mr. Gabriel on 27 June:

> The L.M.S. was last year £13,000 in debt, the income having fallen to about £54,000; and I am told by Dr. Tidman that it is not likely they can afford to begin a new mission in an unknown field, but much wish to confer with me on the subject. I think they may propose to send me to China as this proposal was once entertained since my arrival in Africa, and I see they cannot get suitable men for that inviting field. . . . But I have now no desire to leave this land. And if I cannot work for the good of this nation in connection with the same Society I shall leave it, and God will provide for my wants otherwise.[8]

The Society's deficit in 1855 was due to the fact that the Crimean War had drained all that the benevolent public could spare for the relief of misery and suffering; and yet in May of this same year the Directors had resolved "hereafter" to extend to the tribes whom Livingstone had visited "the blessings of salvation". By May 1856 the Society had by a great effort cleared the deficit and secured a balance of over £6,000. When in May 1857 Livingstone spoke at the annual meeting he was received "with overwhelming demonstrations of good-will, and the stimulus of his presence was so great as to create another forward movement of the Society's operations".[9]

It must be affirmed at this point that Livingstone was fundamentally possessed of natural good sense and sober judgment. All his writings, public and private, are proof of this. It is not that he magnified the importance of his vocation beyond that of others who were engaged in different fields of work for God elsewhere: his perspective was too wide and his sense of proportion was too true for any notions of personal superiority. It is simply that he identified himself with his vocation, and his vocation with what he conceived to be the Will of God. Therefore when his purposes were thwarted or obstructed his wrath was aroused: criticism or opposition brought out the crossgrain in him.

The present contretemps with his Directors provoked him to conclude his *Travels* with a retrospect, in the nature of an *apologia pro vita sua*, which is so characteristic of his implicit faith in providential guidance that no account of his career would be complete without it. Though to us his conclusions may seem to be no more than the offspring of an almost childlike credulity, none the less they were true for him.

If the reader remembers the way in which I was led, while teaching the Bakwains, to commence exploration, he will, I think, recognize the hand of Providence. Anterior to that, when Mr. Moffat began to give the Bible—the Magna Carta of all the rights and privileges of modern civilization—to the Bechuanas, Sebituane went north, and spread the language into which he was translating the sacred oracles in a new region larger than France. Sebituane, at the same time, rooted out hordes of bloody savages, among whom no white man could have gone without leaving his skull to ornament some village. He opened up the way for me—let us hope also for the Bible. Then again while I was labouring at Kolobeng, seeing only a small arc of the cycle of Providence, I could not understand it and felt inclined to ascribe our successive and prolonged droughts to the wicked one. But when forced by these, and the Boers, to become explorer, and open up a new country to the north rather than turn my face southward, where missionaries are not needed, the gracious Spirit of God influenced the minds of the heathen to regard me with favour, the Divine hand is again perceived. Then I turned away westwards, rather than in the opposite direction, chiefly from observing that some Portuguese, though influenced by the hope of a reward from their Government to cross the Continent, had been obliged to return from the east without accomplishing their object. Had I gone at first in the eastern direction, which the course of the great Leeambye seemed to invite, I should have come among the belligerents near Tete when the war was raging at its height instead of, as it happened, when all was over. And again, when enabled to reach Loanda, the resolution to do my duty by going back to Linyanti probably saved me from the fate of my papers in the *Forerunner* and then, last of all, this new country is partially opened to the sympathies of Christendom, and I find that Sechele himself has, though unbidden by man, been teaching his own people. In fact he has been doing all that I was prevented from doing, and I have been employed in exploring—a work I had no previous intention of performing. I think that I see the operation of the Unseen Hand in all this, and I humbly hope that it will still guide me to do good in my day and generation in Africa.[10]

Although he realized and frankly confessed, after an interview with the Directors, that he had misunderstood their intentions, nevertheless "The old love of independence, which I had so strongly before joining the Society, again returned . . . While I hope to continue the same cordial co-operation and friendship which have always characterized our intercourse, various reasons induce me to withdraw from pecuniary dependence on any Society." The fact is that, though there was never a more individualistic missionary Society in the field than the L.M.S., even it was not individualistic enough for Livingstone.

An agreeable surprise was the appearance at Quilimane on 10 July, two days before he sailed, of his coloured friend George Fleming who had been sent by Thompson with clothing, bedding, and other comforts for the voyage. Thompson had in fact done more. He had entered into an agreement with Fleming for a certain remuneration and subscribed it in the form of a Memorandum dated 3 June 1856 "to all whom it may concern" that he proceed in the *Frolic*, rendering all possible assistance to the Commander, to Quilimane to meet Dr. Livingstone, and thence—in the event of his non-arrival or of the lack of any certain intelligence of him—to proceed into the interior in quest of him, and if successful to accompany him to the coast and act under his direction. But, to provide for a possible contingency "the mere apprehension of which causes intense anxiety and pain", it is further stipulated that "should he receive the sad intelligence that Dr. Livingstone has fallen a victim to his arduous enterprise, he is to proceed to the place of his alleged death and procure the fullest and clearest particulars thereof, together with all his effects, but especially his *instruments*, his *chronometer*, and his *papers*. Recovery of his *papers* (doubly underlined) is of great importance, and in this the Portuguese Authorities will doubtless earnestly co-operate. The Commander of the *Frolic* has kindly taken charge of a sum of money (500 Spanish dollars and 50 Sovereigns) which he will disburse, deposit, or return according to his discretion." To this Thompson added a letter to the Governor of Quilimane gratefully recording the valuable assistance already rendered to Dr. Livingstone by the Portuguese Authorities, and requesting his aid to Mr. Fleming in his quest for him—a service which "will be appreciated not only by the Society which he represents and by men of Science and Philanthropy everywhere but also by the whole civilized world."[11]

The township of Quilimane lay twelve miles upstream from the harbour bay and the *Frolic* had anchored ten days before her presence was known there. But even after six weeks' rest Livingstone was only partially recovered from his fever. The weather was so rough that the Captain sent two boats, in case of accident, to convey him to the brig. "Poor Sekwebu, who was well acquainted with canoes, was terrified and when the breakers swept the deck cried piteously, 'Is this the way you go? Is this the way you go?'" Once aboard the brig, however, he became a favourite with both men and officers and acquired a smattering of English. As for Livingstone: "I felt myself at once at home in everything except my own mother-tongue. I seemed to know the language perfectly, but the words I wanted would not come at my call . . . and this made me feel sadly at a loss on board the *Frolic*." But the strain on poor Sekwebu's un-tutored mind increased and reached a climax off the Mauritius, and he became insane. Since he was violent the officers proposed to secure him in irons, but Livingstone objected and tried to soothe him. This had a temporary effect but in the end he leapt overboard and, though a good swimmer, pulled himself down by the chain cable, hand under hand. Nor was his body ever found.

This tragedy was the prelude to a series of misfortunes on his homeward way. He landed at the Mauritius on 12 August, intending to continue living aboard while the ship was in port, but a recurrence of fever and pain in the enlarged spleen prostrated him, so that he was the guest of the Governor, Major-General C. M. Hay, for several weeks. Yet even then he could not rest, as appears from a letter written much later to Tidman from his lodgings in Chelsea on 26 January 1857. He begs to be excused from further public speaking on account of the "disabling" condition of his throat.

A quarter of an hour's speaking in the open air always causes pain and loss of voice since, as well as before, the operation. I made a fair trial at the Mauritius for the purpose of raising a fund for a Sailors' Home there. Thousands of our men calling at that port annually are robbed and abused by every variety of bad character; but I found my deficiency still remaining.[12]

When at last recovered, he boarded the steamship *Candida*, and was nearly shipwrecked in the Red Sea. In Cairo he received letters telling of his father's death after a short illness in February. Tremendous seas between Malta and Tunis caused the breakage of the engine-shaft and the steamship *England* was within an ace of being driven upon the rocks; the passengers were eventually landed at Marseilles and he entrained for Paris and thence for Dover, where he landed on 9 December. But Mary was waiting at Southampton where his ship should have docked, and this involved for him a journey up to London and down again. Hence it must be that he gives the day of their reunion, the 12th, as the date when he was "once more in dear old England".

Blaikie, in his *Personal Life of David Livingstone*, wrote—within the lifetime of their contemporaries:

The years that had elapsed since Dr. Livingstone bade his wife farewell at Cape Town had been to her years of deep and often terrible anxiety. Letters were often lost, and none seem more frequently to have gone missing than those between him and her. A stranger in England, without a home, broken in health, with a family of four to care for, often without tidings of her husband for great stretches of time, and harassed with anxieties and apprehensions that sometimes proved too much for her faith, the strain on her was very great. Those who knew her in Africa when, "queen of the wagon" and full of life, she directed the arrangements and sustained the spirits of a whole party, would hardly have thought her the same person in England. When Livingstone had been longest unheard of, her heart sank altogether; but through prayer, tranquillity of mind returned, even before the arrival of any letter announcing his safety.[13]

A perusal of her letters to Dr. Tidman during these four years of suspense leave the reader with the painful impression that Blaikie's appraisal of her situation is an understatement. From them it appears that she was not only homeless and friendless but was often living on the edge of poverty in cheap lodgings: at first in Hamilton where the old Livingstones resided but proved unhelpful; afterwards in Manchester, Kendal, Epsom, but nowhere with any settled abode or peace of mind; that early in 1854 with recovered health she begged, almost in desperation, a passage to the Cape, but was either dissuaded by the Directors or changed her mind, which proved to be fortunate.

Was Mary difficult? From two strongly-worded letters of old Neil Livingstone in Hamilton to Tidman dated as far back as 24 June 1853, requesting information about the grandchildren, it appears that she was so.

> Mrs. L. does not write to us, nor are we anxious that she should, neither do we wish her to know that we are enquiring about them. Yet we do love the children much. . . .
>
> I addressed a note to you yesterday enquiring after our grandchildren, having no other way of getting any word about them, as their mother was pleased to forbid all communication with us no less than three different times. We received a note from her this morning which I enclose, but owing to her remarkably strange conduct ever since we became acquainted with her, we have resolved to have no more intercourse with her until there is evidence that she is a changed person. We are all sorry however for the poor boys, and if you and Mrs. L. can arrange matters we are quite willing to receive Robert and Thomas, put them to school and do all in our power for their spiritual and temporal welfare.[14]

Livingstone was of course unaware of her adversities and it is probable that he never knew—from her—the full extent of them; but the tail-end of his letter to her from Tunis, telling her the reasons of his further delay, can have been but cold comfort: "The Company will do everything in their power to forward us quickly and safely. I'm only sorry for your sake, but patience is a great virtue, you know. Captain Tregear has been six years away from his family, I only four and a half." As is the way of women for the most part, her love was her life and she had given her whole heart to him; and as is the way of men, his heart was given in the first place to his work and only in part to her. But it is to be hoped, and indeed may well be believed, that his greeting was warmer than his message, which contrasts very miserably with that which she had treasured and committed to writing for him. What these verses lack in poetic sense is more than supplemented by their pathos in the outpouring of womanly love:

A hundred thousand welcomes, and it's time for you to come
From the far land of the foreigner, to your country and your home.
Oh, long as we were parted, ever since you went away,
I never passed an easy night, or knew an easy day.

Do you think I would reproach you with the sorrows that I bore?
Since the sorrow is all over now I have you here once more,
And there's nothing but the gladness and the love within my heart,
And the hope so sweet and certain that again we'll never part.

.   .   .   .   .

A hundred thousand welcomes! how my heart is gushing o'er
With the love and joy and wonder thus to see your face once more.
How did I live without you these long long years of woe?
It seems as if 'twould kill me to be parted from you now.

You'll never part me, darling, there's a promise in your eye;
I may tend you while I'm living, you will watch me when I die;
And if death but kindly lead me to the blessed home on high,
What a hundred thousand welcomes will await you in the sky!

MARY.

A few days earlier her mother had been writing from Kuruman, in anticipation of this long-awaited reunion, a long letter of greeting. It breathes the spirit of an old-world piety: subdued thankfulness for present mercies and devout submission to providential guidance for their future, mingled with a mother's natural solicitude for their material welfare.

. . . Yet, my dear Mary, while we are yet in the flesh my heart will yearn over you. You are my own dear child, my first-born, and recent circumstances have had a tendency to make me feel still more tenderly towards you. . . . [And regarding "Mr. Livingston—your dear husband"] . . . Now with a little rest and relaxation, having youth on his side, he might regain all, but I cannot help fearing for him if he dashes at once into hardships again. He is certainly the wonder of his age, and with a little prudence as regards his health, the stores of information he now possesses might be turned to a mighty account for poor wretched Africa. . . .[15]

And there was this from Moffat to his son-in-law, expressed in his own hearty, manful, forthright fashion: "The honours awaiting you would be enough to make a score of light heads dizzy, but I have no fear of their affecting your upper storey. . ."

Moffat was right: from now on, with but a six months'

respite in which to write his book, Livingstone was the unwilling victim of his own renown.

The first public demonstration in his honour was made at Cape Town, but he was spared that. Sir George Grey, the new Governor and himself a traveller of repute, presided and said:

> I think no man of the present day is more deserving of honour than Dr. Livingstone—a man whom we, indeed, can hardly regard as belonging to any particular age or time, but who belongs rather to the whole Christian epoch, possessing all those great qualities of mind and that resolute desire at all risks to spread the Gospel, which we have been generally in the habit of attributing solely to those who lived in the first ages of the Christian era. Indeed, that man must be regarded as almost of apostolic character who, animated by a desire of performing his duty to his Maker and to his fellow-men, has performed journeys which we cannot but regard as altogether marvellous.
>
> The inhabitants of this Colony owe him a double debt—first for what he has accomplished, and secondly, and I think this is the greater debt of the two, for having shown us what great things may be accomplished by a man actuated by the purest and noblest motives. . . .

The Colonial Secretary, the Hon. R. W. Rawson, in moving a resolution "that his eminent services in the promotion of geographical and general science, which have earned for him the applause and gratitude of the civilized world, merit a special recognition from the inhabitants of this Colony", said: "I am convinced that Livingstone's name will live amongst the first heroes and the first benefactors of our race."

The Bishop of Cape Town stressed his influence in bringing the Spirit of Christ to bear upon regions hitherto afflicted by the twin blights of superstition and slavery. "No contribution to scientific knowledge can compare in beneficence with a blessing so inestimable."

But the finest as well as the most understanding appreciation of his missionary zeal came from his true friend Thompson, still the Society's agent at the Cape:

> I am in a position to express my earnest conviction, formed in long, intimate, unreserved communications with him, personally and by letter, that in the privations, sufferings, and dangers he has passed through during the last eight years, he has not been actuated by mere curiosity, or the love of adventure, or the thirst for applause, or by any other object, however laudable in itself, less than his avowed one as a messenger of Christian love from the Churches. Whilst so much has been achieved,

probably more than by any former explorer, Dr. Livingstone's journeys have been carried out unostentatiously, and at the greatest possible economy of means. If ever there was a man who, by realising the obligations of his sacred calling as a Christian missionary, and intelligently comprehending its object, sought to pursue it to a successful issue, such a man is Dr. Livingstone.

To show "the spirit in which he engages in his work" he then read the moving extract of Livingstone's last letter to him from Linyanti (above quoted) beginning, "I think I am in the way of duty". Amongst those present was Mr. Rutherfoord, the merchant whose projects Livingstone had sought to further among the Makololo. He described Livingstone as "one of the most honourable, benevolent, conscientious men I ever met with" and one who exercised his undoubted capacity in mercantile affairs never in his own interest but in that of others.

At the very time when he was engaged in such important duties and exposed to such difficulties, he found time to fulfil his promise to do what he could to save me from loss, to attend to a matter quite foreign to his usual avocations, and in which he had no personal interest; and by his energy and good sense, and self-denying exertions, to render the plan, if not perfectly successful, yet by no means a failure.

It was however Maclear's testimony to his achievements in accurate lunar observation which most of all impressed the assembly.

I never knew a man who, knowing scarcely anything of the method of making geographical observations, or laying down positions, became so soon an adept that he could take the complete lunar observation, and altitudes for time, within fifteen minutes. His observations of the course of the Zambesi, from Sesheke to its confluence with the Lonta, are the finest specimens of geographical observation I ever met with.

To give an idea of the laboriousness of this branch of his work: on an average each lunar distance consists of five partial observations, and there are 148 sets of distances, being 740 contacts—and there are two altitudes of each object before, and two after, which, together with altitudes for time, amount to 2,812 partial observations. But that is not the whole of his observations. Some of them entrusted to an Arab have not been received, and in reference to those transmitted he says, "I have taken others which I do not think it necessary to send". How completely all this stamps the impress of Livingstone on the interior of South Africa! ... I say, what this man has done is unprecedented. You could go to any point across the entire continent, along Livingstone's track, and feel certain of your position.[16]

Maclear's collection of Livingstone's astronomical papers alone are said to have filled a box which one man could carry with difficulty.

When, two and a half months later, the Cape newspapers came to hand, Livingstone wrote to his old friend:

> ... Many thanks for the kind things you said at the Cape Town meeting. Here they laud me till I shut my eyes, for only trying to do my duty. . . . I got the gold medal, as you predicted, and the freedom of the town of Hamilton, which insures me protection from the payment of jail fees if put in prison![17]

Hardly had he arrived in Southampton than he and Mary must return to London for a special meeting of the R.G.S. convened on 15 December to present him with its Gold Medal. Sir Roderick Murchison was in the chair and delivered a eulogium without precedent in the annals of the Society. "How much indeed," he ended, "must the influence of the British name be enhanced throughout Africa, when it has been promulgated that our missionary has thus kept his plighted word to the poor natives who so faithfully stood by him."

> On receiving the medal, Dr. Livingstone apologized for his rustiness in the use of his native tongue; said that he had only done his duty as a Christian missionary in opening up a part of Africa to the sympathy of Christendom; that Steele, Vardon, or Oswell [who were all present] might have done all that he had done; that as yet he was only buckling on his armour, and therefore in no condition to speak boastfully; and that the enterprise would never be complete till the slave-trade was abolished, and the whole country opened to commerce and Christianity.

His old tutor Professor Owen also paid tribute to the value of his contributions to zoology and palaeontology, no less flattering than the President's were to his services to the geography, geology, climatology and products of the countries he had traversed; and added his own admiration of "the moral qualities of the man who had taken such pains to keep his word". Oswell gracefully expressed the gratitude for the unbounded kindness and hospitality that he and Mrs. Livingstone had shown to travellers in the neighbourhood of their home. To crown the meeting, a message was read from Mr. Gabriel that the second party from Linyanti had reached Loanda with loads of ivory for sale, and had thus shown the practicability of the route.[18]

Next day he was due for his reception by the Directors of the L.M.S. in Freemasons' Hall. The chairman was the great philanthropist Lord Shaftesbury whose leadership in all good causes, especially in the establishment of Ragged Schools, Livingstone himself greatly admired. His theme was the value of the missionary's explorations to the cause of Christendom, and of his wife's co-operation with his efforts both actively in the field and in patient endurance during his long absence. He was followed by Tidman who sang his praises in much the same terms as when he had received the Gold Medal on his behalf. Livingstone was brief in his reply. He said that he was grateful for the kindness of the Directors with whom, for sixteen years, he had never had a word of difference and spoke of his own shortcomings as an evangelist. But he could not forbear from a hit at his erstwhile colleagues: he had been told that his explorations were "only a tempting of Providence, but such ridiculous assertions were only the utterances of the weaker brethren".[19]

A general meeting was arranged for 5 January 1857 in the Mansion House to consider the form of a testimonial from the City of London, but he escaped from the threat of further public meetings with the plea that he must visit his mother and sisters in Hamilton. Of this first visit there is no record save that on seeing his father's empty chair he burst into tears, and at family prayers that evening said with deep feeling, "We bless thee, O Lord, for our parents; we give thee thanks for the dead who has died in the Lord."[20]

Returning to London on the 21st, he was for some time the guest with Mary and the children of his old friend Dr. Risdon Bennett, and then took lodgings at 57 Sloan Street in Chelsea and wrote to Maclear: "I begin tomorrow to write my book, and as I have a large party of men (110) waiting for me at Tete, and I promised to join them in April, you will see I shall have enough to do to get over my work here before the end of the month." The words show his anxiety to fulfil his promise and his ignorance at the outset of the nature of his task. Its completion within six months is in fact a veritable *tour de force*. Written at such terrific speed it is of necessity an ill-constructed work, whole pages of it being transcribed almost verbatim from his Journal; but the style itself (to say nothing of the substance)

282

bears the impress of an intellect of tremendous vigour with a real talent for lucid and vivid description. The soundest appreciation of its quality is, by a curious irony, also the most recent. It comes from the pen of his latest biographer, Mr. Jack Simmons.

> The book is a clear and palpably honest account of one of the historic journeys of the world: satisfying in its fullness and the accuracy of its observation. The narrative, though there is a Victorian amplitude about it, is not prolix: it is often taut, sometimes exciting, and humorous too in an astringent Scots manner. For all the success it won at the time, and the permanent place it retains in the library of exploration, it may be questioned whether the literary merit of the book has ever been recognized quite as it deserves. Livingstone's biographers have usually been a little apologetic about it. In the official *Life*, speaking of this book, Blaikie thinks it right to explain that he had no time to plan, to shape, to organize; the architectural talent could not be brought into play. But the "architectural talent" would surely have been misplaced here. The book is a narrative, and Livingstone's simple instinct was perfectly sound, in leaving it as plain narrative and nothing more. The result is to give the reader an overpowering sense of the absolute truth of the story: that is why, in its workaday English, it is so life-like and often so moving. Even the occasional *longueurs* are in place, with unintended effect, serving to remind us of the tedium from which Livingstone himself suffered so much in travelling. Altogether, the *Missionary Travels* may fairly be claimed as one of the great books that we owe to un professional writers.[21]

That is well said, and it needed saying.

But at least, whilst engaged on his book, he could plead exemption from the tyranny of public appearances. All save one: this was the presentation in a gold casket of the Freedom of the City of London on 21 May. The Chamberlain, Sir John Key, Bart., said: "Your calling has led you to seek the honour of your country and the moral elevation of mankind by . . . preparing the way for that intercommunication and commerce between alienated races, the tendency of which is to make a corporate guild of all nations—to unite all the tribes of the earth in a bond of universal brotherhood."

The writing was done mostly in the Chelsea lodgings with the clamour of his children all about him, but he had schooled himself to the art of mental detachment as a boy in the Blantyre mill and as a man in the tumultuous din of African villages, so that this was no distraction but a joy. It was also subject to interruptions, especially in the first two months: meetings, interviews, visits by train and afoot, necessary correspondence.

The printing of a book of 687 pages, with many illustrations and maps, was almost as remarkable an achievement as the writing. Sent to the printers at the end of July, it was actually published on 10 November. It was an instantaneous success: 12,000 copies at a guinea each were issued for a first edition; but 13,800 were ordered in advance (10,000 by the London trade alone), so that a second edition was launched immediately. Seven editions followed in quick succession. The astonished author, for whom the task had been a penance of sheer drudgery, suddenly found himself the possessor of a small fortune which enabled him to provide for his widowed mother and even for the education of his family. With the bulk of the remainder of his profits he could equip his young brother-in-law, J. S. Moffat, for a missionary expedition to the Matabele early the following year. His personal frugality was unaffected by the accession of wealth: "he bestowed it freely and cheerfully wherever it seemed likely to do good."

Among the many reviews was one from the pen of Charles Dickens, who made it his editorial for *Household Words* on 23 January 1858. "The man with the soft heart and the smile in it", as another African traveller of note has described him, had an intense dislike for foreign missions. His praise of Livingstone is therefore all the more remarkable.

> I have been following a narrative of great dangers and trials, encountered in a good cause, by as honest and as courageous a man as ever lived. . . . The effect of it on me has been to lower my opinion of my own character in a most remarkable and most disastrous manner. I used to think I possessed the moral virtues of courage, patience, resolution and self-control . . . I find that [these] turn out to be nothing but plated goods . . . my self-esteem oozed out of me.
>
> Dr. Livingstone's sensible independence of all those mischievous sectarian influences which fetter so lamentably the exertions of so many good men; and his fearless recognition of the absolute necessity of associating every legitimate aid, which this world's wisdom can give, with the work of preaching the Gospel to heathen listeners, are merits without parallel in the previous history of Missionary Literature. . . .

During these six months of literary labour he had had little time for personal correspondence (though he exchanged frequent notes with Oswell)[22] and on the day of the publication of his book wrote to Maclear with a whimsical reference to astronomy: "You must ascribe my culpable silence to 'aberration'. I am out of my orbit, rather, and you must have patience till I come in again."

There were some who complained both of his book and of his speeches that they were more secular than evangelistic, and his reply to a lady in Carlisle who had written in this strain is characteristic of his whole attitude to his vocation:

> Nowhere have I appeared as anything else but a servant of God, who has simply followed the leadings of His hand. My views of what is *missionary* duty are not so contracted as those whose ideal is a dumpy sort of man with a Bible under his arm. I have laboured in bricks and mortar, at the forge and carpenter's bench, as well as in preaching and medical practice. I feel that I am "not my own". I am serving Christ when shooting a buffalo for my men, or taking an astronomical observation, or writing to one of His children who forget, during the little moment of penning a note, that charity which is eulogized as "thinking no evil"; and after by His help having got information, which I hope will lead to more abundant blessing being bestowed on Africa than heretofore, am I to hide the light under a bushel merely because some will consider it not sufficiently, or even at all, *missionary*? Knowing that some persons do believe that opening up a new country to the sympathies of Christendom was not a proper work for an agent of a Missionary Society to engage in, I now refrain from taking any salary from the Society with which I was connected; so no pecuniary loss is sustained by anyone.[23]

In the case of a man who loomed so large in the eyes of his contemporaries it is both disappointing and strange that there is little in their recollections to reveal his features clearly. We catch glimpses of him romping with his children in the Barnet woods, and delighting in the first signs of an English spring: "We saw daisies, primroses, hawthorns, robin-redbreasts—it was so pleasant." But of the details that help towards the delineation of a portrait, the sidelights, episodes, anecdotes, there are very few. We are left with the impression that Livingstone was outwardly an unimpressive personality, and that his natural shyness and reserve communicated itself even to those who loved and admired him. The best of all the reminiscences comes from the pen of a member of the family of Mr. Frederick Fitch with whom he stayed in Highbury.

> Dr. Livingstone was very simple and unpretending, and used to be annoyed when he was made a lion of. Once a well-known gentleman,

who was advertised to deliver a lecture next day, called on him to pump him for material. The Doctor sat rather quiet and, without being rude, treated the gentleman to monosyllabic answers. He could do that—could keep people at a distance when they wanted to make capital out of him. When the stranger had left, turning to my mother he would say, "I'll tell *you* anything you like to ask."

He never liked to walk in the streets for fear of being mobbed. Once he was mobbed in Regent Street, and did not know how he was to escape, till he saw a cab and took refuge in it. For the same reason it was painful for him to go to church. Once, being anxious to go with us, my father persuaded him that, as the seat at the top of our pew was under the gallery, he would not be seen. As soon as he entered he held down his head and kept it covered with his hands all the time, but the preacher somehow caught sight of him and rather unwisely, in his last prayer, adverted to him. This gave the people the knowledge that he was in the chapel, and after the service they came trooping towards him, even over the pews, in their anxiety to see him and shake hands.

Dr. Livingstone usually conducted our family worship. On Sunday mornings he always gave us the text for the day. His prayers were very simple and direct, just like a child asking his father for what he needed.

. . . Dr. and Mrs. Livingstone were much attached, and thoroughly understood each other. The Doctor was sportive and fond of a joke, and Mrs. Livingstone entered into his humour. . . . In society both were reserved and quiet. Neither of them cared for grandeur; it was a great trial to Dr. Livingstone to go to a grand dinner.

. . . He used to rise early; about seven he had a cup of tea or coffee, and then he set to work with his writing. He had not the appearance of a very strong man.[24]

No sooner was he free from his desk than he was in demand for lectures all over the country. And happily there is preserved one vivid touch which describes his manner and appearance on the platform. It comes from an unknown correspondent to the *Nonconformist* newspaper:

A foreign-looking person, plainly and rather carelessly dressed, of middle-height, bony frame, and Gaelic countenance, with short-cropped hair and moustachios, and generally plain exterior, rises to address the meeting. He appears to be about forty years of age. His face is deeply furrowed, and pretty well tanned. It indicates a man of quick and keen discernment, strong impulses, inflexible resolution, and habitual self-command. Unanimated, its most characteristic expression is that of severity; when excited, a varied expression of earnest and benevolent feeling, and remarkable enjoyment of the ludicrous in circumstances and character, passes over it. . . . When he speaks, you think him at first to be a Frenchman; but as he tells you a Scotch anecdote in true Glasgo-wegian dialect, you make up your mind that he must be, as his face

David Livingstone and his friend Wilbraham Taylor of Barnet
Unpublished photograph of a painting by an unknown
artist, 1857

By permission of the Curator, Barnet Library

indicates, a countryman from the north. His command of his mother-tongue being imperfect, he apologizes for his broken, hesitating speech, by informing you that he has not spoken your language for nearly sixteen years; and then he tells you, as but a modest yet earnest man can, concerning his travels. . . . His narrative is not very connected and his manner is awkward, excepting once when he justifies his enthusiasm, and once when he graphically describes the great cataract of Central Africa. He ends a speech of natural eloquence and witty simplicity by saying that he has "begun his work, and will carry it on". His broken thanks are drowned by the applause of the audience.[25]

But all this publicity was pain and grief to him. "I would really prefer," he told Murchison, "to follow the quiet example of Miss Nightingale, for that I do admire."

In August he went to Dublin to address a meeting of the British Association for the Advancement of Science and wrote to his wife on the 29th:

> I am very sorry now that I did not bring you with me, for all enquire after you, and your father's book is better known here than anywhere else I have been. . . . The Archbishop's daughters asked me if they could be any use in sending out needles, thread, etc., to your school. I of course said yes. They are devotedly missionary, and work hard in ragged schools, etc.

A member of the audience in Dublin wrote to a friend: "Dr. Livingstone's lecture I should like everybody to have heard. People say it was signally lacking in arrangement, but I have no nose for logic; I thought one just mounted his ox and went on behind him."[26]

In September he addressed the Chamber of Commerce in Manchester and was subjected to a barrage of questions concerning the raw materials and products of Central Africa. Here, too, the missionary was equal to the occasion. He had brought home some twenty-five new kinds of fruit; he told them of oils never heard of; dyes that were a secret to the natives; fibres for the manufacture of paper; sheep that were hairy but not fleeced; crops and metals of many kinds that were suitable for commerce. In the same month he was in Glasgow, where the University conferred on him the honorary degree of LL.D.; the Corporation presented him with the Freedom of the City in another gold box; and the Faculty of Physicians and Surgeons, of which he had been a humble licentiate, admitted him as an honorary Fellow. A testimonial from the City of £2,000 for his work had been raised by public subscription. To the United Presbyterians of Glasgow he spoke of mission work in Africa: saying that while at one time he had thought its results among the Bechuana were exaggerated, he had revised his opinion since his contact with heathenism "in all its unmitigated ferocity" in the interior. No one, he added, must expect gratitude for the performance of what was only a simple matter of duty in carrying the gospel to the heathen.

His reply to the welcome of the cotton-spinners of Scotland is the one in which he strikes the loftiest note, and it shows the consistency of his quest through life of the One Ideal, recalling as it does a memory of his old student-friend Moore that "he never prayed without the petition that we might imitate Christ in all His inimitable perfections". It shows also how fresh his sympathy still was with the sons of toil, and his respect for poverty and hard work. The life of toil was the lot of the majority of our race, and poverty was no reproach to any man. The Saviour of the world occupied the same humble position in which he and they had been born.

> My great object was to be like Him—to imitate Him as far as He could be imitated. We have not the power of working miracles, but we can do a little in the way of healing the sick, and I sought a medical education in order that I might be like Him. In Africa I have had hard work. I don't know that anyone in Africa despises a man who works hard. I find that all eminent men work hard. Eminent geologists, minera-logists, men of science in every department, if they attain eminence, work hard, and that both early and late. That is just what we did. . . . There is one thing in cotton-spinning which I always felt to be a privilege. We were confined through the whole day, but when we got out to the green fields, and could wander through the shady woods, and rove about the whole country, we enjoyed it immensely. We were prepared to admire. We were taught by our confinement to rejoice in the beauties of nature.

In the Hamilton Congregational Chapel where he had worshipped in his youth, his theme was the sinking of sectarian differences in the proclamation of the same gospel which all the churches shared: the principle, in short, that unity in diversity is always preferable to uniformity. The sense and sanity of this proposition was, it must be noted with regret, more commendable on the whole to the mid-Victorian era than it is to ours—though not so much perhaps to the "Wee Free" audience that he was addressing.

In going about we learn something, and it would be a shame to us if we did not; and we look back to our own country and view it as a whole, and many of the little feelings we had when immersed in our own denominations we lose, and we look to the whole body of Christians with affection. We rejoice to see them advancing. I believe that every Scotch Christian abroad rejoiced in his heart when he saw the Free Church come out boldly on principle, and I may say we rejoice very much when we see the Free Church and the United Presbyterian Church one, as they ought to be. . . . I am sure I look on the different denominations in Hamilton and in Britain with feelings of affection. I cannot say which I love most. I am quite certain I ought not to dislike any of them. Really, perhaps I may be considered a little heterodox; if I were living in this part of the country I could not pass one Evangelical Church in order to go to my own denomination beyond it. I still think that the different denominational peculiarities have, to a certain degree, a good effect in this country; but I think we ought to be much more careful lest we appear to our fellow-Christians unchristian, than to appear inconsistent with the denominational principles we profess. . . .

To the Blantyre factory-workers, by many of whom he was remembered, he spoke of the need for more trust between employers and employed. He reminded them that when the proprietors had wished to give every man his own garden, some had said that when the ground was cleared it would be taken from them again. That, he said, was nasty and suspicious. If masters were more trusted for their honest good intentions they would do more good. He disagreed with Mrs. Beecher Stowe's notion that factory-workers were slaves (somewhat unadvisedly perhaps: Lord Shaftesbury's latest Factory Act was only seven years in force). "Finally, he exhorted them cordially to accept God's offer to them of mercy in Christ, and give themselves wholly to Him. To bow down before God was not mean; it was manly. His one wish for them all was that they might have peace with God, and rejoice in the hope of eternal inheritance."

His remarks to the operatives, says Blaikie, show how sound and sagacious his views were on social problems, and how far in this sphere, as in others, he was in advance of his times.

The quickness and correctness with which he took up matters of public interest in Britain, mastered facts, and came to clear intelligent conclusions on them, was often the astonishment of his friends. It was as if, instead of being buried in Africa, he had been attending the club and reading the daily newspapers for years—this too while he was at work writing his book, and delivering speeches almost without end. . . .

It should be noted that he never lectured for money, though he might have done so with great pecuniary benefit.

He was indeed offered thirty guineas for a lecture at the Athenaeum and had thought of accepting this and of handing the sum to his old friends the cotton-spinners with a definite object:

> ... To fit up a room as a coffee-room on the plan of the French cafés, where men, women, and children may go, instead of to the whisky-shops. There are coffee-houses already, but I don't think there are any where they can laugh and talk and read papers just as they please. The sort I contemplate would suit poor young fellows who cannot have a comfortable fire at home. I have seen men dragged into drinking ways from having no comfort at home, and women also drawn to the dram-shop from the same cause.

"Don't you think," he wrote to a friend, "that something could be done by setting the persons I mention to do something for themselves?"

In Blantyre he had caught a cold, his first for sixteen years (though he had had slight recurrences of malaria in London), and by the time he reached Edinburgh at the end of September he was exhausted. There he received the Freedom of the City and addressed two other meetings. On the 27th he wrote to Sir Roderick Murchison that he was to go next to Leeds, Liverpool, and Birmingham, "and then farewell to public spouting forever. I am dead tired of it. The third meeting at Edinburgh quite knocked me up." Yet his speeches there, which he thought a failure, were mainly instrumental in sowing the seed which led afterwards to one of the greatest of his memorials: the foundation of the Presbyterian *Livingstonia Mission* in Nyasaland, with its headquarters at the capital named Blantyre after his birthplace.

He was not done yet however: the last two engagements, and the most important of all, were still to come. On 10 November he wrote to Maclear:

> I finish my public spouting next week at Oxford. It is really very time-killing, this lionizing, and I am sure you pity me in it. I hope to leave in January. Wonder if the Portuguese have fulfilled the intention of their Government in supporting my men. . . . I shall rejoice when I see you again in the quiet of the Observatory. It is more satisfactory to serve God in peace. May He give his grace and blessing to us all. I am rather

anxious to say something that will benefit the young men at Oxford. They made me a D.C.L. there!!![27]

But his reception at Oxford, enthusiastic as it was, was eclipsed by that at the sister University, where he arrived on 3 December 1857 as guest of the Rev. William Monk of St. John's College. Next morning he addressed a crowded gathering in the Senate House. Fifty years later, his appearance and the effect of his address were thus described by Mr. J. W. Clarke, then Registrar of the University:

> He appeared in company with the veteran Professor Sedgwick, Dr. Whewell, and other distinguished persons. In marked contrast to them, we saw a man of moderate height, very plainly dressed, his face tanned to a dark brown by long exposure to sun and wind, and furrowed by deep lines that spoke of anxiety, hardship, and disease, endured and overcome. I think I never saw any man whose appearance told its own tale as Livingstone's did.
>
> The lecture which followed, when the cheers which greeted his entrance had subsided enough to allow him to begin, was not a lecture in the ordinary sense of that word. It was a series of notes on the physical features of Africa; on its inhabitants; on their language; on the way to deal with them, and on the "open path for commerce and Christianity" which he had himself been permitted to make.
>
> His language, for which he apologized on the ground that for seventeen years he had spoken the native language of Africa, and had in consequence almost forgotten his own, was peculiar to himself. He used short, jerky sentences, expressive of thoughts which he could not arrange in set periods, but which he did not wish his hearers to lose. But the most carefully ordered speech would have been far less effective; and when he suddenly shouted, "*Do you carry on the work which I have begun. I leave it with you!*"—and sat down, there was silence for a few seconds, and then came a great explosion of cheering never surpassed in this building.[28]

The substance of the lecture, though plain and factual, was well adapted to hold the attention of his audience and was relieved by lighter touches, as when, in mentioning that the bite of the tsetse is fatal to domesticated animals, he added, "but not to men or donkeys": or again, in referring to the looks of native women, "They would be much handsomer if only they would let themselves alone—though unfortunately that is a failing by no means peculiar to African ladies." Only towards the close did he strike a serious note, and it is the only attempt he ever made at a peroration:

It is true that missionaries have difficulties to encounter; but what great enterprise was ever accomplished without difficulty? It is deplorable to think that one of the noblest of our missionary societies, the Church Missionary Society, is compelled to send to Germany for missionaries, whilst other societies are amply supplied. Let this stain be wiped off.— The sort of men who are wanted are such as I see before me: men of education, standing, enterprise, zeal, and piety. It is a mistake to suppose that *anyone*, as long as he is pious, will do for this office.

Then he broke off to revert to a favourite theme: the example of the old monks, the first teachers of Christian truth, who were men not only of piety but of ability and education. "The monasteries were the schools of Europe, and the monks were not ashamed to hold the plough."

I hope that many whom I now address will embrace that honourable career. Education has been given us from above for the purpose of bringing to the benighted the knowledge of a Saviour. If you knew the satisfaction of performing such a duty, as well as the gratitude to God which the missionary must always feel, in being chosen for so noble, so sacred a calling, you would have no hesitation in embracing it.

For my own part, I have never ceased to rejoice that God has appointed me to such an office. People talk of the sacrifices I have made in spending so much of my life in Africa. Can that be called a sacrifice which simply paid back, as a small part of a great debt which brings its own blest reward in healthful activity, the consciousness of doing good, peace of mind, and a bright hope of a glorious destiny hereafter? Away with the word in such a view, and away with the thought! It is emphatically no sacrifice. Of this we ought not to talk. . . . I would rather be a poor missionary than a poor curate.

He broke off again, with one of the abrupt turns of thought which were habitual with him, this time to mention the pleasure of a brief homecoming and to thank them for the welcome they had given him: "You can hardly tell how pleasant it is to see the blooming cheeks of young ladies before me, after an absence of sixteen years from such delightful objects of contemplation." And then, almost without a pause, came the final sentences ending in a shout which electrified his audience:

I beg to direct your attention to Africa. I know that in a few years I shall be cut off in that country, which is now open. Do not let it be shut again! I go back to Africa to try to make an open path for commerce and Christianity. *Do you carry on the work which I have begun. I Leave It With You!*[29]

The lecture, together with that which he delivered in the Town Hall next day, was published in full in a volume entitled *Dr. Livingstone's Cambridge Lectures*, edited by the Rev. W. Monk and prefaced at great length by Professor Sedgwick. It contains several Appendices, of which the most valuable are: an account of the formation of the *Universities Mission to Central Africa*; a brief digest of Livingstone's Analysis of Bechuana; and twenty of his letters of 1858/59 not published elsewhere. This book excited almost as much interest as his *Travels*. The direct result of his Cambridge Lectures was the formation of the Universities Mission in 1860, in which Oxford, Dublin and Durham joined.

In writing his thanks to his host in Cambridge, Livingstone said that he looked back on this visit as one of the most pleasant episodes of his life, and to his intercourse with such noble Christian men as Sedgwick and Whewell* and others as not the least important privilege he had enjoyed. "It is something inspiriting to remember that the eyes of such men are upon one's course. May blessings rest upon them all, and on the seat of learning which they adorn."[30] This letter is noteworthy as tacitly expressive of his insatiable thirst for knowledge of every kind; his liberality of outlook and the range of his interests; his modesty in the feeling, that never left him, that his own education was defective; his genuine admiration for men of learning and culture; and the fact that, hard campaigner and man of action as he was, he felt himself instinctively at home in their company.

One last academic distinction awaited him—the greatest of all. Early in 1858 he was elected a Fellow of the Royal Society, but had left England before the formal admission could be made, and consequently did not sign the Charter Book till 4 May 1865 when on his second visit home. The manner of his admission was exceptional. His Certificate was signed by the Earl of Carlisle, then Lord-Lieutenant of Ireland, with the addition P.R. (*pro Regina*); and all the other signatories signed

---

*Sedgwick, Professor of Geology for more than fifty years, was Vice-Master of Trinity and a Canon of Norwich. He collaborated closely with Sir Roderick Murchison. William Whewell was something of an intellectual phenomenon. Having graduated as Second Wrangler, he was appointed Professor, first of Mineralogy, and then of Moral Theology. He was also a D.D. and F.R.S., and Vice-Chancellor of the University.

with amplifications—a procedure which is said to be unique.[31]
On 13 February he was summoned to the Palace for a private
interview with the Queen. He appeared without ceremony and
in his usual attire: black coat, blue trousers, and peaked cap
with a stripe of gold. A Scottish correspondent of an American
newspaper is quoted by Blaikie as reporting that the Queen
conversed affably with him for an hour and a half.

> Dr. Livingstone told Her Majesty that he would now be able to say to
> the natives that he had seen his chief, his not having done so before
> having been a constant subject of surprise to the children of the African
> wilderness; that they were in the habit of enquiring whether his chief
> were wealthy; and that when he assured them that she was very wealthy,
> they would ask how many cows she had got, at which the Queen laughed
> heartily.[32]

The same evening he was invited to a farewell banquet in
Freemasons' Tavern attended by over 350 guests, including the
Duke of Argyll, the Earl of Shaftesbury and Earl Grey, Foreign
Ministers, Bishops, and a host of celebrities in almost every
sphere of public life. Sir Roderick Murchison presided and
touched the heart of his audience when he said:

> His keeping of his promise to his black servants by returning with them
> from Loanda to the heart of Africa, in spite of all the perils of the way,
> and all the attractions of England, thereby leaving for himself in that
> country a glorious name, and proving to the people of Africa what an
> English Christian is. . . .
> Notwithstanding eighteen months of laudation, so justly bestowed on
> him by all classes of his countrymen, and after receiving all the honours
> which the Universities and cities of our country could shower upon him,
> he is still the same honest, true-hearted David Livingstone as when he
> issued from the wilds of Africa.

The Duke of Argyll followed and recalled that Livingstone's
family was an Argyllshire one; that Ulva was the sister-isle of
Iona, and that as Iona had sent Columba with the gospel
message to the rude barbarians of Europe, "so this son of Ulva
had carried the same blessings to Africa and might be remembered perhaps, by millions of the human race, as the first
pioneer of civilization, and the first harbinger of the gospel".
The Bishop of Oxford dwelt on the unparalleled magnitude of
the debt which England owed to Africa in the suppression of
the slave-trade and urged the immediate prosecution of

Livingstone's plans for legitimate traffic in the heart of the continent. Professor Owen spoke of the great value of his services to zoological knowledge, whilst rating him for "destroying the moral character of the lion". Applause was loudest when Mrs. Livingstone's name was mentioned as her husband's companion on his forthcoming journey. When all had spoken Livingstone rose to reply.

> He was overwhelmed with the kindness he had experienced. He did not expect any speedy result from the expedition, but was sanguine as to its ultimate benefit. He thought they would get in the thin end of the wedge, and that it would be driven home by English energy and spirit. For himself, with all eyes resting on him, he felt under an obligation to do better than he had ever done.
>
> It was scarcely fair to ask a man to praise his own wife, but she had always been the main spoke in his wheel; able to work, and willing to endure; and right glad he was indeed to be accompanied by his guardian angel.[33]

If Philip was right in his opinion, now of distant days, that Livingstone was ambitious, his ambitions—in so far as they were personal—were now realized beyond all possible expectation; and Moffat's prediction that "honours would not make him dizzy" was equally fulfilled. He was on the crest of a tremendous wave of public enthusiasm which happily coincided with a wave of national prosperity. He was already a national hero. In the eyes of his countrymen nothing comparable with his achievements had occurred since Drake sailed round the world. His sudden disclosure of the resources, both human and material, of a portion of the globe hitherto unknown at a time when British enterprise was at its peak, was spectacular in the extreme; and henceforth Central Africa became a focus of national interest—political, mercantile, and missionary. There is no doubt whatever that had he died at this time he would have been buried in Westminster Abbey.

Chapter Seventeen

APPOINTMENT AS CONSUL
1857–1858

"The best friend I ever had—warm, true, abiding."

THERE is no record to be found in the minutes of the Board of Directors of the L.M.S., or of its Committee for South African missions or in any other of its archives, of Livingstone's resignation from the Society. One can only say that it must have been made some time before July 1857 when he made it public in his *Travels*. It may well have been held in suspense for some time when negotiations for Government service were being made on his behalf and could not be divulged till they were completed.

On 12 January 1857 the Directors convened a special meeting to welcome Livingstone and to confer with him on his proposals for the opening of two mission stations simultaneously among the Makololo and the Matabele, who had long been at enmity with each other. Some prudently enquired: how maintain a line of communication over nearly a thousand miles from Kuruman? Was such a sudden leap desirable? Would not an advance by stages be preferable? They resolved to appoint a committee to consider, in consultation with Livingstone, the best method of adopting his proposals.

The committee met on 22 January and "after mature deliberation" recommended that the two new mission stations be opened: that Robert Moffat and his wife be invited to "commence" the mission among the Matabele (if his health permitted), and that a missionary be appointed "to assist Dr. Livingstone in organizing" that among the Makololo. These resolutions were confirmed by the Board on the 26th. A further meeting was held on 10 February when a letter from Livingstone was read expressing "certain objections to what had been recorded". It has been surmised by Dr. Edwin Smith, who has carefully studied the records, that these referred to a sentence

296

in the minutes of the 12th, that "the success of the mission to the Makololo would be promoted by the residence of Dr. and Mrs. Livingstone among them"—since he had agreed only to assist in its organization and could not commit himself to a promise of immediate or direct co-operation. When this sentence was deleted he was brought into the room by Dr. Risdon Bennett and expressed his "entire concurrence" with the Board's resolutions. He also spoke at the May meetings of the Society,* and presumably he was still at that time officially in its employment.[1]

Dr. Campbell, the latest of Livingstone's biographers to deal with this subject, wrote:

> It has hitherto been taken for granted that Livingstone's withdrawal from the service of the L.M.S. and engaging in that of the British Government was due to the initiative of the latter. . . . That, in consequence of representations from various influential quarters the Foreign Secretary, the Earl of Clarendon, approached Livingstone on behalf of the Cabinet with the offer to send him out again with a special commission . . . to explore the region of the lower Zambesi.
> This belief is incorrect. It was Livingstone himself who took the first step in making the connection, as a copy of his letter to Lord Clarendon, dated May 22 1857, preserved in his private Journal, now reveals.[2]

Dr. Campbell's statement itself now stands in need of correction, since the whole of the Clarendon Correspondence has been made public. From this it appears that the first step (as Dr. Macnair rightly surmised) and indeed every subsequent step, was made neither by the Earl of Clarendon nor by Livingstone but by an intermediary—Sir Roderick Murchison —who happened to be a personal friend of both.

On the same night on which the public meeting in the Mansion House had been held, 5 January, Murchison wrote to Lord Clarendon reporting the substance of his own speech . . . "I ventured to say that I hoped you might make good use of the man who knows more African languages than any other European, and who seemed to have such a happy way of carrying on an intercourse with the natives along our frontiers. . . ."

---

* Dr. Campbell has remarked that one notable sentence in his speech on this occasion deserves to have emphasis: "I do not think better of the Africans for being black, because if I were not a missionary to them I believe I should be a missionary to the poor in London."

That he then urged Livingstone to write to Lord Clarendon himself is apparent from the fact that on 27 January he forwarded a letter from Livingstone to the Earl written the previous day, "which fully explains the large and enlightened views he wishes to carry out for the civilization of a vast portion of South Africa".

> This is the first occasion on which our country has had the means of testifying to the natives in the vast interior that they may trust *our word*, and the moral influence has been so spread by the conduct of this remarkable man that every means should be taken to confirm the impression. . . .
>
> Maclear, justly eulogizing the unparalleled researches of the man, expresses the earnest hope that the Crown may take some method of recognizing Livingstone. Seeing that Parliamentary labours are now to begin and that you will doubtless be soon immersed in an incessant whirl of active business, may I entreat you to let me bring him to you at the Foreign Office one day this week, when you can obtain from him any additional information you may require.

Faced with the task of composing a letter to a nobleman in high office, Livingstone becomes verbose. The salient passages of it however must be quoted. It is dated 26 January from 57 Sloan Street. He explains that his difference with the Directors of the L.M.S. was caused by "nothing of a disagreeable nature" between them, but by a divergence of view respecting the best mode of promulgating the gospel among the heathen in Central Africa. This discrepancy first became clear to him in their letter which he received at Quilimane "at a time when my intentions were conscientiously and fully formed of continuing to labour for the enlightenment of the Africans, and when an affection of the throat rendered much exertion in preaching impossible"—his intentions being "to devote a portion of my life to the special development of the commercial resources of the country drained by the Zambesi".

> It is a very great undertaking and involves a vast amount of toil. I cannot hold out the hope of instantaneous success. . . .
>
> In proposing this work to myself I must bear the imputation in the minds of some that I have forsaken missionary labour for the sake of "filthy lucre" but am fully convinced that viewing the subject on a large scale I should be performing a work which would effect a much larger amount of good than I could do by settling down for the remaining portion of my life with any one of the small tribes which are dotted over

the country. Legitimate commerce breaks up the isolation engendered by heathenism and the slave trade and surely if we take advantage of the very striking peculiarity of the African character (i.e. their fondness for barter and agriculture) we shall eventually bring this people within the sphere of Christian sympathy and the scope of missionary operations.

As Her Majesty's Government is most anxious to promote education at home, I suppose that connection with it would not imply giving up the character I already hold among the people of a Christian teacher. I am unable from the state of my throat to preach long in the open air, but would like at all times to assist and co-operate with those who do so. . . . Whatever position it may be deemed advisable for me to occupy, I hope the standing I at present hold as a missionary and the influence which I can exercise in that connection will not be kept out of view. . . .

Sir Roderick next conducted him to the Foreign Office for an interview with Clarendon, who was most sympathetic and desired him to submit a formal statement of his views and requirements in detail. To this Livingstone replied in a letter dated 19 March from 57 Sloan Street. The magnitude of the political implications of the scheme contrasts strikingly with the modesty of his own requests.

1. To make the Zambesi a path for commerce into the Interior and thus end the slave trade.
2. To take advantage of the agricultural habits and love of barter prevalent among the tribes and distribute cotton seeds to the native chiefs. (In this project he is supported by an association of merchants in Manchester.)
3. The Portuguese are in virtual possession of the outlets of the fertile countries on both sides of the continent. Angola is by far the best adapted for the growth of cotton. But there the Portuguese are firmly seated. In Eastern Africa, however, no vestige of their ancient authority remains and they would gladly co-operate in developing the resources of a fertile country from which they derive no benefit. Both countries, Britain and Portugal, could then go forward together.
4. He suggests that Prince Albert should interview the King of Portugal, his cousin.
5. He prefers to make a small beginning. To take out:
   2 or 3 cotton gins of the simplest construction (such as are used in the Niger valley).
   2 or 3 strong malleable iron ploughs.
   2 presses for extraction of oil from ground-nuts.
   2 small pairs of rollers for extracting juice from sugar cane. Portability is as necessary as efficiency.

"I have no wish," he wrote, "to attempt anything on a large scale at first, and would greatly prefer a small beginning with a

view to making greater efforts as the prospects might open out."
This sentiment, expressed again in other words in his letter of
2 May, should be borne in mind when considering the sequel.

His suggestion of royal aid in furtherance of a commercial
treaty with Portugal was not, as may appear, presumptuous, for
the Prince Consort had granted him a personal interview soon
after his arrival in England, and must have given serious consideration to Livingstone's proposal. It would appear however
that later the Prince Consort proposed as an alternative that
Livingstone himself should call at Lisbon on his way to the
Cape and promised him an introduction to the King. But the
prevalence of yellow fever in Lisbon prevented this.

The next step in the negotiations was again taken by Sir
Roderick Murchison, who prompted Livingstone to write again
to Clarendon on the question of his salary as a prospective
Consul. This is the letter to which Dr. Campbell referred and
which by a slip he dates 22 May. It is dated 2 May and is again
addressed from 57 Sloan Street. After recapitulating his aims
and showing that they will tend to the benefit of trade and the
enhancement of his country's good name in Africa, Livingstone
continues:

> Should your Lordship wish to aid me in my efforts, in adopting a line
> of policy which would give no offence to our allies the Portuguese, to
> support me in my enterprise, by appointing me an Agent of H.M. for
> the promotion of commerce and civilization with a view to the extinction
> of the slave trade—I beg to solicit such a salary as may be deemed suit-
> able. I do not intend to accept any gratuity from my former employers,
> the London Missionary Society.

Murchison, in a covering letter to this, which he specifically
says that he prompted Livingstone to write, suggests £500 p.a.
as a reasonable salary. It would appear that Clarendon's only
hesitation at this stage was due to a statesman's fear of offending
Portuguese susceptibilities by encroaching on their rights. This
would explain the purport of Murchison's next letter, dated
17 May.

> Prince Albert in a long conversation with him recommended the
> Doctor to take Lisbon on his way to South Africa, and there seeing the
> King to obtain more authenticity and privilege so that British and
> Portuguese interests might not clash.

The young King of Portugal being a good naturalist would certainly take a great interest in Livingstone and would, I doubt not, do everything to promote the success of this new expedition.

At the same time the objects, which the British Government may reasonably look to, are of a higher cast, i.e. the endeavour to introduce cotton and other products of essential use. . . . Portuguese power, based upon the slave-trade, has dwindled to zero. The once flourishing St. Paul de Loanda is declining rapidly.

Now Livingstone was never treated with suspicion by the Portuguese, but on the contrary with all civility and hospitality. He is therefore precisely the person who, by his profound acquaintance with the natives and their languages and his possession of the confidence of the Portuguese, may be the means of introducing British commerce to lands where fertility is sufficient to supply us with all those elements of our own manufacturing power for which we are now dependent on foreigners. Either England and her ally Portugal may be made *one* for this great object, or the latter country might readily part with her Colony of Quilimane and Tete, etc., useless to her, but which in our hands might be rendered a paradise of wealth.

Pardon this sally, written *currente calamo*, but with the fervid hope that the Chinese War will not so absorb your thoughts that Livingstone and the great good he may accomplish should be forgotten.[3]

The significance of the words "dependent on foreigners" would not be lost on the Foreign Secretary; for it was from the Southern States of America that cotton was imported to Britain, and this by slave labour. From a subsequent letter from Murchison to Lord Clarendon, 13 December, it appears that the latter had already written to Lisbon, and the Prince Consort personally to the King. The previous day Livingstone had attended a reception at the Prime Minister's house, where Lord Shaftesbury assured him of the country's support, and Lord Palmerston said to him privately: "We managed your affair very nicely. Had we waited till the usual time when Parliament should be asked, it would have been too late." Delay would have involved the loss of a season on the Zambesi, and the Foreign Office could probably settle the formalities with Lisbon by post. A day or two later Lord Shaftesbury confirmed that the visit to Lisbon would be unnecessary since the Portuguese Ambassador, Count de Lavradio (whom Livingstone had already met in London and with whom he was on friendly terms) would have returned from Lisbon before February. He had himself arranged matters with the Admiralty and Livingstone had only to go there on his authority for any requirements.

"He repeated, 'Just come here and tell me what you want, and I will give it you.' He was wonderfully kind."[4]

The "serene confidence" that both Palmerston and Clarendon showed in giving Livingstone *carte blanche* for his enterprise was, it has been pointed out, very remarkable. They were both men of the world, well-seasoned politicians, and neither was particularly susceptible to the missionary aspect of his work. Moreover, British policy at this time was averse to further colonial responsibilities.

> Yet, with this man they were trusting to so implicitly, they had very little to go upon except the record of his journeys and the impression he made on them in personal intercourse. There is the heart of it all—something that is beyond our recovery now. Livingstone owed his power over other men not to his charm of manner, but to the force and earnestness of his purpose. He was never a fluent speaker. He carried conviction, especially with such hard-headed men as these politicians, by mastery of his subject and single-minded determination. . . . His exposition of his policy was impressive and cogent; he so clearly knew what he was talking about.[5]
>
> Though the Zambesi Expedition was a Government expedition, its organization was more Livingstone's work than Government's. . . . It was a remarkable achievement if only in point of speed. . . . Two or three months were surely a record time for the improvisation—programme, personnel, equipment—of any such Government operation, and the officials concerned deserve their meed of praise. But . . . it was Livingstone who made the Expedition. The Expedition *was* Livingstone.[6]

Captain John Washington, the Admiralty's hydrographer and a keen enthusiast of African exploration, had submitted to Clarendon at the end of December an imposing list of names of naval officers and men, and of equipment on an elaborate scale; but Livingstone expressed himself as altogether averse to such proposals. Before the end of the first week in the New Year he outlined to Clarendon in a memorandum his requirements —a paddle-steamer of shallow draught, and an iron house for stores, both to be taken out in sections: and the number, qualifications, and even actual names of his "assistants".

1. As navigator—Commander Norman Bedingfeld (aged 34), who was personally known to him. (But he did not state that this officer had been twice reprimanded for insubordination, on one occasion dismissed from his ship, on charges of "contempt and quarrelsome conduct towards his superior officer".)

2. As practical mining geologist—Mr. Richard Thornton (aged 20), of the Government School of Mines, strongly supported by Sir Roderick Murchison.

3. As economic botanist—John Kirk, M.D., of Edinburgh (aged 25), strongly recommended by Sir William and Dr. J. D. Hooker of Kew. He had served in the Crimea.

4. As general assistant and "moral agent"—Mr. Charles Livingstone, his brother (aged 34). He had had experience of cotton in the States, and its manufacture.

5. As artist and storekeeper—Mr. Thomas Baines (aged 38), a member of the late North Australian Expedition (though upon this choice he had not yet fully made up his mind).

6. As ship's engineer with the necessary qualifications—none had yet presented himself. The vacancy was soon filled however by George Rae, of Blantyre.

7. Ten Kroomen, skilled in canoe work, to be engaged at Sierra Leone.

Of these only two were known to Livingstone previously: Bedingfeld from a cursory acquaintance at Loanda; and his brother whom he had not seen since the latter was a youth. They proved in the event to be his most mistaken choice.*

* It has hitherto been assumed that Livingstone was unaware of Bedingfeld's previous record in the Navy, and he has been criticized for lack of care in selecting this officer. But on general grounds it would seem incredible that the Admiralty could fail to have informed him, and this doubt is confirmed by the publication recently of his letters and despatches. On 6 August 1858 we find him writing to the Earl of Malmesbury: "I had no inclination to encounter a man who frequently boasted that, when formerly tried by court-martials, the newspapers took up his case". And on 10 September to Maclear: "It was against Washington's wish that I named him. I suffer for it now." It would therefore seem probable that Livingstone accepted Bedingfeld's offer for service in the friendly hope that it would help to re-establish his reputation. But what would predispose him still more favourably was the fact that Bedingfeld had been commended more than once by both Palmerston and Clarendon for his signal services in the suppression of the slave-trade off the West Coast. In the wreck of the *Forerunner* too, "his presence of mind was instrumental in saving many lives". He rose to the rank of Vice-Admiral, retiring at his own request in 1877, and died in 1894. (*Army and Navy Gazette* for 7 April 1894.)

Charles Livingstone had, on his brother David's advice and with his help financially, emigrated to America and entered a college at Oberlin where students supported themselves by manual work. To reach it—700 miles from New York—almost penniless and without begging once, he had shown considerable grit. In the third year he entered the theological course, became ordained and wrote frequently to his brother who was then at Kolobeng, asking support for his application for missionary service under the L.M.S. This David gave and suggested China rather than Africa in

The plan of operations was as follows:

The Expedition is to pass rapidly through the unhealthy area of the Lower Zambesi, deposit its heavy baggage at Tete, visit the leading chiefs above Tete, and proceed to the Kebrabasa Rapids "to discover whether the launch would be able to steam up there when the river is high". The iron house is then to be erected on a suitable site above the confluence of the Zambesi and the Kafue to serve as a central depôt. Further exploration is then to be undertaken towards the source of the Zambesi and up the rivers flowing into it from the north, "in order to ascertain whether the network of waters reported by the natives exists or not". Some members of the Expedition will be left at the central depôt to experiment in agriculture and give religious instruction. It is understood that the duration will be for two years, when the members will have the option of returning home.[7]

These plans have an important bearing, as will be seen, on another aspect of Livingstone's deliberations which, for obvious reasons, it was not necessary for him to disclose officially: namely, a rendezvous with the missionary party at Linyanti. They also preclude any thought of his own *residence* there. But the point to be observed here is the speed and the ease with which he expected to navigate the Zambesi to the Kebrabasa Rapids and beyond them.

"This seems a very estimable plan", noted Lord Clarendon and he at once requested Livingstone to reproduce it in a more detailed form to serve as his own official Instructions. "So Livingstone prepared a draft of his own instructions, submitted it to Lord Clarendon, and was duly presented with an almost *verbatim* copy of it." Was ever, it may be wondered, a Government Agent granted a freer hand?

The preparation of the equipment proceeded with equal despatch. £5,000 was voted by the Government for its purchase. The most important item, the paddle-steamer (christened the *Ma-Robert*—the native name for Mrs. Livingstone), was designed and constructed by Macgregor Laird of Birkenhead

case of his acceptance; but the L.M.S. could not accept a candidate without a personal interview. In 1850 Charles was pastor of a church in Lakeville, situated by a curious coincidence in Livingstone County, N.Y., at a stipend of £750 a year. Happening to have returned home in 1857 when his brother was preparing the Expedition, he sacrificed his cure in the States and volunteered to join it. His behaviour on the Expedition seems strangely out of keeping with his previous and also his subsequent career.

at the very moderate cost of £1,200. It was built of a new untried steel of only one-sixteenth of an inch thickness, of dimensions 75 feet long and 8 feet beam; of two-foot draught; rigged with two sails and awning-frames fore and aft; in three water-tight compartments; and was capable of carrying 36 men and ten to twelve tons freight. Her engine was twelve horse-power and her furnace was devised to burn wood. The design was approved by the Admiralty on 12 December, and on 5 February—within five weeks—she was tried on the Mersey under Bedingfeld's supervision, but not under that of Rae. The rest of the equipment was easily procured: preserved foods, medicines, instruments, and many rolls of cloth for barter with the natives.

There remained the political negotiations. The completest published account of these is contained in Professor Coupland's *Kirk on the Zambesi* in a chapter entitled "Livingstone's Lead". The barest international courtesy required that the Portuguese Government should be informed of the project and purposes of a British Expedition through territory which it claimed to possess but did not pretend to administer. Livingstone's friendly passages with the Portuguese Ambassador in London had paved the way; the Prince Consort's letters to King Pedro and Clarendon's to the Lisbon Government had followed. But the primary purpose of the Expedition—the destruction of the slave-trade—had been barely touched upon. Now, at Clarendon's request, a memorandum was drafted by Livingstone for transmission through the Foreign Office to the British Minister in Lisbon.

> In the Livingstone manner it went straight to the root of the question. . . . It baldly declared that the prospects of development and prosperity in Portuguese East Africa were blighted by the Slave Trade, and it boldly suggested that Portugal and Britain should act in concert to suppress it. . . . It insisted frankly, moreover, on the need for free trade. To give full effect to the policy of the two Governments, "the river ought to be declared a free pathway for all nations".

This gave the Portuguese Ministers furiously to think. "They had been uneasily expecting some communication of this kind from London." They knew that their colony had scarcely proved a model of colonial enterprise. The very fact of their sovereignty there might soon be questioned. The extent of their inland territories had never been definitely delimited. Not all the native races had ever formally acknowledged their rule.

> The first irruption, therefore, of a wandering British missionary into this particular area must have caused some little disquiet in official circles. . . . He was not, it seemed, merely an other-worldly evangelist, intent on nothing but conversions. He was a colonial politician, full of ideas about trade and settlement; and he was making a public scandal of the Slave Trade.

True, he could not charge the Portuguese Government itself with complicity in the Trade. It had issued repeated injunctions of prohibition, but these had proved ineffective; Governor after Governor had been dismissed, but still the infamous Trade somehow continued to exist.

> And this fact the impetuous explorer was not only certain to find out, but certain also to make trouble over. A new convulsion of the British conscience might easily result in the focussing of all Europe on Portuguese East Africa. Its stagnant condition would be disclosed. . . .
>
> The Portuguese, in fact, were in a dilemma from which there was no clear way way of escape. The British Government had to be permitted, it could scarcely be forbidden, to send its Expedition up the Zambesi.

Their only resource to cover their ·retreat lay in tactical manoeuvres. Assuring Lord Clarendon of all possible support to the Expedition, and of their immediate despatch of instructions to their Governors in Mozambique, Quilimane and Tete, to render every assistance to Dr. Livingstone and his companions, they expressed a desire that some Portuguese might accompany the Expedition. "It was doubtless realized in Lisbon that this suggestion was almost bound to be rejected . . . and rejected it was, with due politeness. But it had been an adroit move. Was it not a step to that 'combined effort' for which Livingstone himself had pleaded?"

On the next issue their attitude stiffened. Lord Clarendon had decided that Livingstone's consulate at Quilimane should include Sena and Tete, since this would enhance his standing with the Portuguese. But soon after the despatch of this commission to Lisbon, a telegram from the British Minister there reported that the Portuguese Government "were ready to grant it for Quilimane, which is open to foreign commerce, but not for Sena and Tete, which are not so yet".

Livingstone, who was at once informed of the hitch, had no doubt as to its meaning. "In reference to the refusal of the Portuguese Government to recognize the right of free intercourse up the Zambesi," he wrote to the Foreign Office, "I beg to suggest that it is very undesirable to admit the claim, as it involves the admission of their power over the independent tribes on its banks." And he suggested that no town or area should be specified in his Commission, but that he should be accredited to Sekeletu and other free tribes beyond the limits of Portuguese East Africa.

With the latter suggestion Lord Clarendon concurred, but thought it advisable to limit the consulate to Quilimane; and the new Commission was despatched to Lisbon, not without a sharp expression however of his own Government's "disappointment that the Portuguese Government should appear desirous to restrict commerce in regions about to be visited by Dr. Livingstone, instead of taking this opportunity to encourage and extend it".

But an important point had been raised by Livingstone's protest: namely, the exact limits of the Portuguese frontier. "I should like to know a little more clearly," was Lord Clarendon's pencil comment upon it, "his meaning respecting the limits of the Portuguese territory in order that we may place something on record about it with the Portuguese Government." Livingstone was ready at once with a detailed reply.

The Portuguese power in East Africa . . . resembles our own in China, with the important difference that the Portuguese are so few and weak that they can scarcely hold the few forts they possess. They have no authority on the south bank until we come to Sena. . . . The Portuguese inhabitants of Sena, about half a dozen in number, have several times paid tribute to the independent tribes adjacent. There is a hiatus again in their authority above Sena until we come to Tete, another village and fort. There is a stockade on the river below Tete which commands the river, and this is possessed by a native chieftain who has at different times waged war with the Portuguese. The north bank is under a chief who has also been at war with the Portuguese. . . .

Beyond that, from long. 30 W.—"we enter an immense extent of territory of which the Government of Portugal never had any cognizance".

But the Portuguese Government anticipated the Foreign Office by a public reassertion of its sovereignty over the Zambesi area and a definition of its extent by a decree promulgated at Lisbon on 4 February, directing that "the name of Zambesia shall be given in all official documents to all the territories to which the Crown of Portugal has a right in the valley of the Zambesi, from the mouths of that river to beyond the fortress of Zumbo"—that is, to its junction with the Loangwa. At the same time it authorized Livingstone "to carry all his goods up to Tete without paying any import duties and thence freely into the interior". It had certainly played its cards well.

Accordingly, on 8 February 1858, Livingstone was formally appointed "H.M. Consul at Quilimane for the Eastern Coast and independent districts of the interior, and commander of an expedition for exploring Eastern and Central Africa, for the promotion of Commerce and Civilization with a view to the extinction of the slave-trade".[8] Such at least were his official credentials. But at the back of his own mind was an undisclosed idea with far-reaching consequences. For it was to prove nothing less than the seed-thought of future colonial expansion in Central Africa. It is revealed in a very private letter to his friend Professor Sedgwick of Cambridge which has only recently come to light, appropriately enough, in the archives of the Rhodes-Livingstone Museum in Livingstone, Northern Rhodesia. This letter is quoted by Professor Debenham, who remarks: "It is therefore clear that Nyasaland owes its establishment as a Crown Colony, even more definitely than most historians suppose, to the dreams of David Livingstone." The salient sentences in the letter are these:

> That you may have a clear idea of my objects I may state that they have something more in them than meets the eye. They are not merely exploratory, for I go with the intention of benefitting both the African and my own countrymen.
>
> I take a practical mining geologist to. tell us of the mineral resources of the country—an economic botanist to give a full report of the vegetable productions—an artist to give the scenery—a naval officer to tell of the capacity of the river communication—and a moral agent to lay a Christian foundation for anything that may follow.
>
> All this ostensible machinery has for its ostensible object the development of African trade and the promotion of civilization, but I hope it may result in an English colony in the healthy highlands of Central Africa. (I have told it only to the Duke of Argyll) . . .
>
> In the course of time, say when my head is low, free labour on the African soil may render slave labour, which is notoriously dear labour, quite unprofitable.

One may note that he does not say, what is an obvious fact,

that he could have combined in his own person all the required qualifications—except that of the artist.

In examining the text of these negotiations (here very briefly summarized), and the major part which Livingstone was called upon to play in them, one knows not which to admire most: his perspicacity or his steadiness or his discretion or his modesty. What with these negotiations and his book, his lectures, his necessary movements from place to place, and preoccupations with preparations for his expedition during the last few weeks— it is little wonder that he had no time to spare for consultation with the missionary party to the Makololo.

Livingstone's severance from the L.M.S. was as much a shock to that Society as the cause which prompted it, their Secretary's ill-advised missive to the returning wanderer, had been to him. They had since then been "basking in the sunshine of his popularity" and were now as ready as the Foreign Office to give him a completely free hand in the pursuance of his plans for service in "untried, remote, and difficult fields of labour". It was a matter too of grave concern to others outside the pale of the organized churches, who feared that his resignation would damage his reputation as a Christian minister. Amongst the host of men who extended to him the right hand of fellow- ship during his brief home-visit were some distinguished members of the Society of Friends. Though himself neither quietist nor pacifist, he admired their principles and respected their convictions of the certainty of divine guidance through obedience to the Inner Light. Of these, Mr. J. Bevan Braith- waite of Lincoln's Inn was his most trusted counsellor, and his attempts to dissuade Livingstone from severing official con- nection with a recognized missionary society, preserved in Blaikie's *Life*, are worthy of reproduction.

> To dissolve thy connection with the missionary society would at once place thee before the public in an aspect wholly distinct from that in which thou art at present, and, what is yet more important, would in a greater or less degree, and, perhaps, very gradually and almost insen- sibly to thyself, turn the current of thy own thoughts and feelings away from those channels of usefulness and service, as a minister of the Gospel, with which I cannot doubt thy deepest interest and highest aspirations are inseparably associated.
>
> Thy heart is bound, as I truly believe, in its inmost depths to the service of Christ. This is the "one thing" which, through all, it is thy

desire to keep in view. And my fear has been lest the severing of thy connection with a recognized religious body should lead any to suppose that thy Christian interests were in the least weakened; or that thou wast now going forth with any lower aim than the advancement of the Redeemer's kingdom. Such a circumstance would be deeply to be regretted, for thy character is now, if I may so speak, not thy own, but the common property, in a certain sense, of British Christianity, and anything which tended to lower thy high standing would cast a reflection on the general cause.[9]

Livingstone's reply to this is not preserved, but if the general sense of it may be conjectured, it would be to the effect that he was careless of the world's praise or blame, and that the cause of Christianity could not be affected by so slight a thing as his reputation. Besides, he had made it perfectly clear to the Government that he intended to return to Africa as an accredited, though independent, missionary.

As has been shown above, the Directors of the L.M.S. had definitely decided in favour of missions to the Matabele and Makololo on 22 January 1857; but not till 4 April did they write to apprise Moffat and ascertain his views. Moffat received their letter on 6 July and wrote at once in reply. He expressed strong doubts as to the wisdom of the enterprise, preferring the idea of stepping-stones from Kuruman to the north; but he was intensely loyal to the Society and was ready to act on their instructions. (Indeed for him—in the opinion of his daughter-in-law Emily—"the Society was essential to his Christianity".) He therefore set out in his sixty-second year for a fourth visit to Mosilikatse of 700 miles, and was back in Kuruman by February 1858.

But not until January—exactly a year after the Directors' decision—were the new missionaries appointed. Upon this Dr. Smith writes:

> The delay was perhaps inevitable in view of the necessity to collect funds and obtain Mosilikatse's consent; but it had unfortunate consequences. It aroused suspicions that the Directors were but half-hearted in prosecuting the enterprise. Livingstone in particular chafed at the apparent lukewarmness and procrastination. His attitude can be understood if, as appears, he was kept in the dark. Apart from one single communication there is (so far as I can discover) no evidence that— although he had been invited to assist in the organization of the Makololo mission—he was ever consulted after the meeting on 10 February 1857.[10]

But neither, it must be added, does it appear that he offered any advice or took any interest in the proceedings. He was obviously too preoccupied with his own affairs.

The new missionaries were instructed by the Board to continue their studies until called upon for embarkation. One of those who had been accepted for the Matabele mission was John Smith Moffat, who had already completed his college course and was about to be married to a wife as eager-hearted for service as he. Livingstone had always liked his quiet, sensitive, thoughtful young brother-in-law, his previous letters to whom display an unusual freedom from reserve. He entertained also a high regard for John's gay and gallant young wife Emily, and had been present at their wedding on 12 March 1858 "addressing them afterwards, but, characteristically, in tones so low as to be almost inaudible to the reporters and the crowd that had thronged for a glimpse of the famous man".[11]

Now begins a correspondence which is as revealing of the character of the writer as any he ever wrote. The tone of the first, dated from 12 Kensington Palace Gardens on 14 January 1858, is curt and peremptory.

> I wrote you yesterday, but forgot to ask when you suppose you are going to start for Africa. Unfortunately I have been unable for some time to call at the Mission House or learn whether the new mission is to be occupied at all or not. . . .
>
> Are you youngsters dilly-dallying so that they cannot move you to go, or what is it? Is there an oligarchy impeding the wishes of the great body of the Directors? I certainly expected that men would have been on their way ere now. And if I might venture to advise you I would say, take your passage at once and send a note of it to the Mission House. . . .
>
> I hope to be off in the second week in February.[12]

This letter continues with matter-of-fact advice about the northward journey by wagon from the Cape. It is followed by a sudden decisive offer, characteristic of Livingstone's independence and generosity. Dated from 18 Hart Street, Bloomsbury Square, it begins abruptly:

> If you will go to the Makololo country and conscientiously do your duty as a missionary to them or to the Matabele, I shall most gladly pay you £500 down on Monday next and give you my waggon at Cape-Town. (It is a good, well-seasoned one, not so handsome as a new one, and was given me by Mr. Oswell.) This, with the hire of another, would secure you passage up the country comfortably, and then I engage to pay

you £150 per annum afterwards so long as I live. . . . I shall secure £300 to take you away if you wish to retire, in case of my death, by any bond you like. Now don't reject this because it is the proposal of one man. I meant to do good with my increased means and will secure the whole to you in any way a lawyer may direct. I avoided making any offer, but both Mary and I had the same thought; only as you had received education from the Society, we did not like to make the proposition. Now, however, as the conduct of the Directors is merely trifling and it involves trifling with the affections of your wife, the most sacred thing in the world, I make it in all seriousness and beg you will accept the offer. It will both aid me and the cause of Christ. If you like you need not say from whom you derive support. We shall not mention it, nor exercise any control over you in doing your duty. . . .[13]

A week later, the indenture was sent, agreed and signed. In a covering letter Livingstone repeated his disavowal of any wish "to assume the direction of your movements or to exercise a control over your arrangements". He wanted John and Emily to have as completely free a hand in their labours as he had always desired for himself.

Next comes a letter from the sanctum of the Foreign Office on the 20th. "As I am detained a little while here today I may just write what I have been unable to say *viva voce*." He has arranged with his bankers about the payment of the money, and has written to Dr. Tidman. He suggests, as a possible resting-place for Emily *en route*, a Griqua settlement at Boochap (60 miles E.S.E. of Kuruman), where there are a lot of un-collected fossil-bones in a mound. He encloses a map and description of the route. "You would accomplish a good service to science . . . if you send a lot with the matrix to Sir Roderick Murchison or Mr. Owen." (These were no doubt the fossils which he examined, but was prevented by medical duties from securing, as long ago as 1848.) Writing from 4 Athol Place, Glasgow, on 2 March he encloses a note from Dr. Tidman to himself in answer to his, that John may "understand the *animus* there". He points out that a distinction should be made "between the men now in power, with whom you cannot feel cordial, and the main body of the Directors in the country".[14] (Lovett in his centenary history of the L.M.S. describes Tidman as "very autocratic". He would resent Livingstone's masterful intervention no less than Livingstone would ignore his assumption of authority.)

Returning from his fourth visit to Mosilikatse in February

1858, Moffat heard that his daughter Mary was aboard the *Pearl* with her husband, and fearing that they might never see her again he and his wife travelled on from Kuruman in haste to the Cape only to find that the ship was three weeks late. On the way thither he had heard (as he wrote to Tidman two days before its arrival) the "perfectly confounding and very painful news" that his son-in-law had dissolved connection with the Society and, more afflicting still, that his own son John had followed his example. This, he wrote, would prejudice the other missionaries unfavourably in the eyes of Mosilikatse. Further, the proposal that they should undertake the immensely toilsome journey overland and through the fever-infested swamps of the Chobe—instead of awaiting Livingstone's opening of a navigable highway into the interior—seemed to him "the height of folly", and as such it would appear also in the eyes of the natives. Events were to prove the correctness of the veteran's apprehensions.

There is no record of his conversations with Livingstone at the Cape but they do not appear to have changed his views. He wrote again to Tidman on 20 July, pertinently enquiring: "What would happen to the missionaries and their wives if they reached Linyanti before Livingstone had been able to prepare the Makololo for their reception? Would the Makololo remove to higher ground without assurance from a source on which they can place the fullest reliance—i.e. from Livingstone or myself—that they would not be molested by the Matabele? It is a serious matter to recommend three missionaries and their wives to proceed at once to Linyanti. In summer this might prove fatal to some, if not all." His advice would have been that they should postpone their departure from England for a year, but that having now started they should remain in Bechuanaland till the removal of the Makololo to the new field was definitely ascertained.[15]

Nevertheless, despite his many misgivings, all of which were too tragically justified in the event, this loyal and greathearted man took steps immediately to convoy the party to Kuruman—whilst Livingstone went round the coast to Quilimane. Moffat never saw his son-in-law again. In 1874 he wrote to the *Sunday at Home* a brief memoir "from one who knew him long and loved him much".

With the exception of his own wife, no one could know Livingstone better than myself. Besides much personal intercourse we kept up a constant correspondence in which we mutually unbosomed our views and feelings on whatever occurred to us worthy of notice. . . .

His *forte* was not the affectation of the finer feelings, of exquisite sensibility, nor the sensational; it was the stern necessity of determined warfare against everything that would arrest the progress of the Gospel. His weapons were from the armoury of God; his panoply the omnipotence of Him who gave the commission "Go"—with the promise "Lo, I am with you". He was a man of strong faith. . . . He performed feats of daring which he never recorded, from a feeling that it was only what others could do, and perhaps better than himself. He would make any sacrifice or expose himself to any danger to save life or to be able to soothe the sorrowing heart.

His ruling passion was to live for suffering humanity.

He was characteristically humble. When I came down to Cape Town in 1858 to meet him, laden with honours and honorary degrees, he seemed more humble than ever. . . . He sacrified everything—home, Christian intercourse, lucrative prospects and earthly honours—for one grand object, to carry the Gospel of the Son of God to the heart of Africa.

Moffat ends this tribute with words which go far to explain that indefinable charm which Livingstone, despite all his surface roughnesses, is said to have possessed. He speaks of him as "one whose loving spirit could not but endear him to all". These words should be borne in mind, especially during the next phase of his career, in any critical estimate of his character.

It is not possible here to pursue the misfortunes of the ill-starred missionary party to the Makololo, though it forms one of the most tragic and heroic episodes in the annals of missionary endeavour. But the question must be posed: to what extent was Livingstone responsible for the disaster? Was there any undertaking on his part to meet the party at Linyanti and introduce them to Sekeletu? Lovett, the historian of the L.M.S., says distinctly Yes, but without adducing evidence.[16] Blaikie, arguing from silence, says No.[17] But Campbell maintains that Blaikie's denial goes beyond Livingstone's own admissions— made in a letter to Tidman after visiting the scene of the disaster in August 1860: "Having been unexpectedly detained in the lower parts of this river until May last . . . I was too late to render the aid which I had fondly hoped to afford."[18] To this Dr. Edwin Smith replies: "This is an expression of what he undoubtedly hoped to do; it is no admission that he failed to carry out a promise"—and he adds that, in the nature of things, a definite assignation was impossible on both sides.[19] The view of the present writer is that, though no definite promise was made—since none is mentioned either by Livingstone or by any of the missionaries themselves—it was nevertheless his original purpose to arrive at Linyanti before, or at the time, or very soon after they arrived there. The circumstances that prevented him were insuperable and totally unforeseen, as will appear subsequently. But there is no gainsaying the truth of Dr. Campbell's observation that "in the case of the Makololo mission he cannot be entirely acquitted from blame, as the enterprise had been undertaken in reliance upon his advice and co-operation".[20] And, as will be seen later, nothing would be more unjust than his own final comment on the cause of the tragedy.

He continued somehow to keep abreast of his personal correspondence. Many letters were written hastily while waiting at railway stations or in Government offices. Among them is one to his elder brother John who had settled long since at Listowel near the Niagara Falls as a respected and energetic farmer and storekeeper, and with whom he must have corresponded as frequently as with Charles and his other near relations. It is of interest not only because of its contents, but because it is one of the very few letters to this brother that appear to have been preserved.

18 February 1858.

My dear Brother,

I have been unable until this moment to write you on a very important point, to which I am happy to call your attention. A friend of mine, Mr. James Young, who was the assistant to the Professor of Chemistry at University College, London, when I was there, made a discovery by which he is able to extract oil from a peculiar kind of coal—this is named Paraffin, and it is simply gas in a fluid state. By a very simple lamp it burns like gas, and is so cheap that one gallon, which in London sells at 3/8, gives as much light as 22 lbs. of spermaceti candles. He has made a large fortune by it, and being a good man he wishes to do good and is very generous. I mentioned you as a suitable agent in Canada, and he is willing to employ you and give you such a percentage as will make you anxious to keep Niel at home instead of sending him abroad. He wants you to go into the thing without any doubt. It will return you an abundant income. He will supply all the materials, lamps, oil, vessels, etc., and you must lay yourself out for an immense sale by advertising it beforehand for next winter. Write to him: James Young, Esq., Sardinia Terrace, Glasgow, and tell him whether you are willing to engage in it. You will be able both to benefit yourself and him by entering into it heartily. Tell him freely all your affairs and what you will or can do. Can you devote your entire time suppose he sends you 10,000 lamps and some hundreds of tons of oil? Write at once. I shall be off in a week or ten days. I got a letter from our cousin John, and will send him a book, having the index, before I sail. Our launch was tried yesterday and gave from 8 to 10 knots an hour. We sail in the *Pearl*. She puts into the Zambesi, then we put our launch together, as she goes out in three pieces, and go up. I am Consul—£500 only—the Portuguese are favourable. If you still think of Africa for Niel I have not forgot my promise—you will hear from me. Charles gave up £750 a year on the West, he has £350 now.

Love to Sarah and all.

I was waiting at the Admiralty and found time for this. Write at once to yours

DAVID LIVINGSTONE[21]

Writing later to James Young, he said: "If I die at home I would lie beside you. My left arm goes to Professor Owen, mind. That is the will of David Livingstone."

His conduct of the Zambesi Expedition, both direct and indirect, was to be the subject of adverse criticism in many quarters. But through good report and ill there were men in high office—such as Palmerston and Clarendon—who never lost faith in him; and among them one whose faith and friendship were as steadfast when the Expedition was launched with enthusiastic hope as when it ended with failure. Sir Roderick Murchison's parting words to Livingstone on the eve of his embarkation were:

Accept my warmest acknowledgements for your last farewell note. Believe me, my dear friend, that no transaction in my somewhat long and very active life has so truly rewarded me as my intercourse with you, for from the beginning to the end it has been one continued bright gleam.[22]

And when Livingstone heard from Oswell of Sir Roderick's death in April 1872 (only a year before his own), he wrote in his Journal with profound emotion:

Alas! alas! this is the only time in my life I ever felt inclined to use the word, and it bespeaks a sore heart; the best friend I ever had—true, warm, and abiding—he loved me more than I deserved; he looks down on me still.[23]

Chapter Eighteen

ZAMBESI EXPEDITION: KEBRABASA RAPIDS
1858

"Men are drawbacks everywhere!"

LIVINGSTONE was not, as some suppose, a complex character. On the contrary he was, as his father-in-law said of him, "the man of 'one thing'—the temporal and eternal happiness of Africa's long-trodden-down sons and daughters". This single-mindedness, this consistency of purpose, gave to his character its fundamental integrity. But there was in him temperamentally (as there is in all of us to some degree) a combination of opposites. Some of his qualities, and these the most conspicuous, can be set down without qualification: absolute candour, dauntless courage, stubborn fortitude, inflexible pertinacity. But of some others it is impossible to affirm an attribute without at the same time qualifying it by its opposite. He was rough, but he was also gentle; a solitary, yet a lover of good fellowship; a peace-lover with a horror of bloodshed, but no pacifist; austere, but with a lively sense of fun; lacking all social graces, yet with an indefinable and unconscious charm; constitutionally cheerful, but on occasion morose; profoundly religious yet "sanely secular"; both realist and idealist, he combined the practical sagacity of the man of affairs with the other-worldliness of the visionary. These antitheses formed the warp and woof of his nature; they make intelligible the gleams and glooms in him—especially during this next phase of his life when the glooms were most apparent: his ruth and ruthlessness, his selflessness and selfwill, his modesty and assertiveness, patience and impatience, tolerance and intolerance. It was not until the last phase of his life that these conflicting strands were unified in a seamless weft which gave to his character its final integration.

His conduct of the Zambesi Expedition reveals him in his most unattractive light and convicts him of complete failure as a leader. But in admitting his incapacity in this rôle it must be remembered that this man was, both by nature and in principle, above all else an individualist. As his letters show, he embarked upon a Government-sponsored expedition with some misgiving. He had been "edged into it" almost without his volition and certainly against his better judgment. He would far rather have chosen to go out again alone and pursue his explorations with the help only of his faithful Makololo. The man who could never work harmoniously in a team, and had no instinct for co-operation, was called upon to assume the leadership of a team. Ill at ease with himself, he found himself out of terms with his fellows, whom he could never bring himself to regard as colleagues but only as subordinates. Is it any wonder that, in so far as management was concerned, he proved a failure?

Of this double strain in him, his embarrassment and discomfiture amongst his fellows and his equanimity and infinite patience with the children of nature, no one has written better or with more understanding than Sir Reginald Coupland.

. . . The strength of will, the power of endurance, with which he drove himself on to his goal, not merely at intervals of brief intense endurance, but month after month and year after year, were beyond the range of ordinary men. . . .

It was partly, perhaps, this very strength of will that made Livingstone less successful in his dealings with white men than with black. Though the friendships he made were intimate and lasting, he was slow to make them. As often happens with strong men and sometimes hampers their success, he lacked the capacity for co-operation. In a conflict of wills he could not easily give or take. He was as impatient with the follies of white men as he was patient with those of the black. There was no touch of arrogance in his self-confidence; in the deepest sense he was a humble man; but his personality was too original, too individual, for him to work smoothly in a system, to be anything but restive in harness. And even with his friends he could be very obstinate. . . .

There was a hardness, too, in Livingstone, not of feeling—he was sensitive, affectionate, a man of strong emotion under the still surface—but of bearing. He lacked altogether the lighter social graces, the natural *camaraderie* which makes its possessor at home with all sorts of his fellow men. He was awkward, brusque, inarticulate and, as if he realized these failings, self-conscious sometimes among white men as he never was among black. . . . Drawing his strength from within himself, he could do without the praise or encouragement, even without the society, of others. Nature in fact had made him, at least as far as his own race was concerned, a lonely man. And it was his not uncongenial fate to live the greater part of his adult life with no white man to companion him, and to die at last with no white man by his side.[1]

On 12 March 1858 after some incidental delays the screw-steamer *Pearl*, lent by the Colonial Office, put out from Liverpool having on board the *Ma-Robert* in three sections, all the members of the Expedition, Mrs. Livingstone and her six-year-old son Oswell. On the 18th "when all had recovered from sea-sickness" Livingstone formally read the Instructions from the Foreign Office to his staff (who were unaware that he had drafted them), and during the next two days wrote out his own specific instructions to each member "in order to avoid confusion and collision, making each independent in his own sphere". But these included a general definition of their *moral* duties, with special stress on treatment of the natives and on respect for animals:

> . . . Setting an example of consistent moral conduct to all . . . treating them with kindness, relieving their wants; teaching them to make experiments in agriculture, explaining to them the more simple arts, imparting to them religious instruction as far as they are capable of receiving it, and inculcating peace and good-will to each other.
> . . . I would earnestly impress on every member of the expedition a sacred regard to life, and never to destroy it unless some good end is to be answered by its extinction; the wanton waste of animal life which I have witnessed . . . makes me anxious that this expedition should not be guilty of similar abominations.
> . . . The chiefs of tribes and leading men ought always to be treated with respect, and nothing should be done to weaken their authority. Any present of food should be accepted frankly, as it is impolitic to allow the ancient custom of feeding strangers to go into disuse. We come among them as members of a superior race and servants of a Government that desires to elevate the more degraded portions of the human family. We are adherents of a benign, holy religion, and may, by consistent conduct and wise, patient efforts, become the harbingers of peace to a hitherto distracted and trodden-down race. No great result is ever attained without patient, long-continued effort. Deeds of sympathy, consideration and kindness . . . if steadily persisted in, are sure ultimately to exercise a commanding influence. Depend upon it, a kind word or deed is never lost.

"They seem sensible," is Kirk's comment on these instructions, "but the most sensible part is that we are left very much to our own discretion."[2]

Sierra Leone was reached "after a quick passage" on 25

March and Livingstone was impressed by the hygienic reforms effected by the Governor: "what others talked about he did". It struck him as a model colony. They all attended an ordination service in the Cathedral conducted by the bishop, "an energetic good man". On the 30th they took on board twelve Kroomen "who seem good active men". Next day they coaled and watered and stood out again to sea.

Within a month of sailing from England Livingstone found that his wife was in the early stages of pregnancy (she had suffered agonies of sea-sickness besides), and on 9 April, "more than a little startlingly", he noted in his Journal: "This is a great trial to me, for, had she come with us, she might have proved of essential service to the Expedition in cases of sickness and otherwise, but it may all turn out for the best."[3] The apparent callousness of this grunt of annoyance is to some extent offset by his letter to her brother J. S. Moffat on the 16th (then at Beaufort *en route* to Kuruman), requesting him to make arrangements for her comfortable transport from the Cape.

. . . She has been so sick since we left Sierra Leone. . . . I must therefore trouble you to perform a brother's part to her and me by assisting in her journey towards Kuruman. . . . If I attended to the matter myself it would detain the expedition too long and probably lead to a disastrous termination of the whole affair. It is this consideration alone which induces me to presume so far on your kindness. I shall make arrangements at the Cape for Mary to draw the money she will need for the journey.

Thereupon follows, abruptly, a series of questions which bespeak the scientist who is something more than a missionary:

As you wend your way to the north you may be inclined to investigate any point that comes before you. What think you of ascertaining the size of the Cape elephant? Lichtenstein heard that some were 18 feet high! See if you meet a man who measured them? Are ostriches monogamists or polygamists? You will see them; try and count their paces with your watch when at full speed and measure the length of his stride. Any information as to the cause of the migration of springboks, wildebeests—the times, numbers. Try and discover the root and plant by which the Hottentots make their bread to ferment. . . Is there anything really irreligious in the Boguera? Or is it anything more than a political rite?[4]

Concerning this latter question Professor Wallis has written with discernment:

He was by far the most sanely secular, and freest from superstition, of the Victorian missionaries. Robert Moffat had denounced Boguera, the male rites of initiation, as one of the plague-tokens of paganism: Livingstone bids J. S. Moffat give leisure to its investigation in the impartial spirit of ethnological enquiry.[5]

Arrived at Cape Town on the 21st, he was informed by Moffat concerning Mosilikatse and that his Makololo were still at Tete. Two days later at a crowded meeting in the Exchange he was presented with a silver box containing 800 guineas from the colonists by Sir George Grey (perhaps the greatest of all the Cape Governors, and certainly the one for whom he had the greatest admiration). This was followed on the 25th by a grand dinner in the same place at which the Attorney-General presided, "and Maclear's enthusiastic tribute to his friend could hardly be brought to a close". Livingstone says simply, "The Cape people look with much favour on our object, and will vote money for the postal arrangements." Sir George Grey did more, by the formation of lines of communication between the Cape and the Zambesi.

Having gratefully entrusted his wife to the care of her parents, he embarked on the *Pearl* again on 1 May and a week later wrote separately to each of his children and most fully to Agnes:

> Mama was so ill all the way from Sierra Leone that I was obliged to land her at the Cape, but no sooner did I go ashore to book a room for her at the hotel than I heard that Grandpa and Grandma Moffat were there, waiting for us. We were very glad to see them again, as you may be sure, after about six years' separation and now Mama is to go up to Kuruman with them, remain there for some time and then join me by going up through Kolobeng towards the Makololo country. . . . I parted with Mama on the 1st of May and sailed out of Simon's Bay while Mama waved her handkerchief as long as she could see me waving my cap.[6]

To his friend James Young he wrote: "It was a bitter parting with my wife, like tearing the heart out of one. It was so unexpected."

Throughout the whole voyage his attention is given to such natural features as the saline content of the seawater near river-mouths; the structure of the coast, and its vegetation; the flotsam and sea-wrack, the fish, the birds and even the insects alighting on the ship. On the 14th they stood in for the mouth of the Zambesi at what appeared to be the lowest branch of its delta, but proved to be a separate river, thick with pestilential mangrove swamps. "It seemed to me a work of necessity to get out of this region as quickly as possible" and though the day was a Sunday and himself disabled with diarrhoea, he ordered the removal and assembling of the sections of the launch. "People, I hear, blame me for this," he wrote later to Sir George Grey, "but they would have blamed me much more had I lost nearly all the expedition."[7] Taking advantage of the tides, several days were now spent in fruitless attempts to penetrate the labyrinth of shoals, till on 4 June an entrance was effected through a very narrow but deep channel, the Kongone (unknown even to the Portuguese), which proved to be one of the four main arms of the delta and the most navigable.

The fact that at this stage Livingstone abandoned his Journal for a week, and made up some of the gaps from memory, tells more of the arduousness of the task than his bare record. At the very outset he was assailed by misfortune. Gone were all hopes of navigating the *Pearl* on the broad waters of the Zambesi— 300 miles to Tete—in a single trip, and of establishing a base beside the Kafue; the *Pearl* must be released and proceed to Ceylon; the stores transferred to the little *Ma-Robert* which even unladen could scarcely avoid the farther shoals; and the storehouse erected on Nyika or "Expedition Island", a mere forty miles inland and in the midst of a pestiferous swamp. But this was only the beginning of troubles. Two of the staff, his brother and Baines, were already stricken with fever, severe vomiting, and delirium; and another, Bedingfeld, was becoming truculent. He had disputed with the Captain of the *Pearl*, a merchant servant officer, whom he regarded as his social and professional inferior, as well as with the Government surveyor from the Cape on points of navigation. (All the rest of the staff liked and admired Captain Duncan, and Livingstone wrote of Mr. Skead: "With him I would go to the end of the world.") On June 11 Livingstone had been obliged to intervene with a public reprimand. "Captain Bedingfeld, I must have no more of these altercations, and I won't have them." "Then I shall give it you on paper." "Very well; you must do it in a civil way, even on paper." The paper tendered an offer of his resignation, which was accepted but the next day by mutual consent withdrawn. He continued with the precarious navigation of the *Ma-Robert*, towing the freight and piloting the *Pearl*.[8]

Having arrived with great difficulty on 15 June off Mazaro, the junction of the Kongone with the Zambesi, they found a minor war in progress between the Portuguese and the native "rebels". The latter, mistaking them for foes, were preparing a hostile reception, but when Livingstone called out "English!" several of them grounded their weapons and ran to the shore with produce for sale. Livingstone then went ashore to explain his objects and invited them to board the launch. There they were regaled by Bedingfeld with rum: "I resolved never to allow anything of the kind again." The result of conversations ashore, however, was satisfactory. "The shout at our departure contrasted strongly with the suspicious questioning on our approach. Henceforth we were recognized as friends by both parties."

A letter to Sir George Grey of 28 September, describing this incident, begins:

> I return you many thanks for kindness in sending me the numbers of *Punch* and *The Times*. Of the former I am very fond, as they give me a hearty laugh, which in this climate is as good a tonic as one can use. I thank you also for your other services and offers; but, knowing that you prefer information about our progress, I shall commence without preface in the middle of things. . . .[9]

A few days later Livingstone, in company with Bedingfeld and Rae, again put in to Mazaro for fuel, this time during an interlude in a pitched battle, and on landing found himself "in the sickening smell and among the mutilated bodies of the slain". Writing in the third person, he continues:

> He was requested to take the Governor, who was very ill of fever, across to Shupanga, and just as he gave his assent, the rebels renewed the fight and balls began to whistle about in all directions. After trying in vain to get someone to assist the Governor down to the steamer, unwilling to leave him in such danger, as the officer sent to bring our Kroomen did not appear, Dr. Livingstone went into the hut and dragged along his Excellency to the ship. He was a very tall man, and as he swayed hither and thither from weakness, it must have appeared like one drunken man helping another.[10]

Thus much for this incident in the *Narrative*. It is not mentioned in the current Journal. But two years later a fuller account of it is interpolated into the Journal, amplified from notes in Rae's pocket-book.

> I told Bedingfeld that at the request of the Portuguese officers I had agreed to take the Governor over to Shupanga, but could get no one to carry him; "Be so good then as to go down and send up our Kroomen to carry him down." He replied, "O yes", and went off. Waiting some time for the Kroomen and none appearing, but balls whistling overhead, I at last went in and lifted the Governor myself, and when I had got him a few paces from the door a sergeant came and assisted me down to the bank.
>
> When Bedingfeld got back to the boat he said to Mr. Rae, "Let's get out of this as soon as possible." Rae replied, "Some time is necessary to get up steam." B.: "Well get it up immediately." R.: "But the doctor is ashore." B.: "I don't care who is ashore. Let's get out of this; he can get the boat. I will never anchor at this shore again." Rae then took his gun, determined to see what had become of me, and, on coming up the bank, saw me coming with the Governor. On going down again he found that Bedingfeld had put a Krooman outside the cabin door with a gun in his hand and all the rest had guns and fixed bayonets. He seems to have been much too frightened to think of order and would have run away and left me, had not Rae refused to set the engine a-going. . . . He was very pale and agitated and, when R. went ashore, stamped his foot and ordered him aboard.[11]

It is to be noted that Livingstone's subsequent dismissal of Bedingfeld cannot have been influenced by this incident, of which he was not aware until much later. They had little personal contact during the slow passage upstream, Bedingfeld being on the launch and Livingstone on the steamer or ashore; in default of which there ensued a barrage of correspondence between them, both private and official: on the one side fractious and provocative, on the other, reasonable and restrained at first but becoming, after each explosion, sterner and more astringent. Livingstone's acceptance of the first resignation could not, under the circumstances, have been worded more kindly:

> I am sorry to part with you thus, as our personal intercourse has uniformly been of the most amicable kind, but as you kick at the very first instance your overbearance has been curbed, and the success of the expedition depends on the good-tempered obedience of all its members, I feel compelled to do that of which I sincerely lament the necessity.[12]

But the temper of the self-important naval Commander was not improved by the following well-meant advice which he received a fortnight later in reply to another official protest.

A pretty extensive acquaintance with African expeditions enables me to offer a hint for which, if you take it in the same frank and friendly spirit in which it is offered, you will on some future day thank me and smile at the puerilities which now afflict you. With the change of climate there is often a peculiar condition of the bowels which makes the individual imagine all manner of things in others. Now I earnestly and most respectfully recommend you to try a little aperient medicine occasionally and you will find it much more soothing than writing official letters. . . .[13]

That he intended this advice in sober seriousness is apparent from the fact that he actually mentions it in his official despatch to Lord Malmesbury.

Bedingfeld's response to this, somewhat surprisingly, was not another resignation but an offer to resign at the first opportunity of "getting a better man, or one that you like better. In the meantime I will do my best to carry out your wishes as far as I know them, and I trust I shall go home feeling I have done my duty . . ." Livingstone showed this letter to his brother, to Kirk, and to Thornton, requesting them for their views. They were unanimous that Bedingfeld's resignation "was necessary to prevent further disorganization to the Expedition". Not only was he uncongenial to them, but his insubordination had affected the discipline of the Kroomen, who were becoming less and less reliable. Accordingly Livingstone arranged for his departure to Quilimane, there to await the next ship for England. Bedingfeld carried his grievances to the Foreign Office where the Earl of Malmesbury (Clarendon's successor), after full enquiry and consultation with the Admiralty, concluded that "the officer had failed to clear himself" and Livingstone's action was formally approved.

Nevertheless, perusal of the correspondence reveals one point in which Bedingfeld was clearly in the right. "Most of the misunderstandings," he wrote, "would have been avoided and the Expedition benefited, had you treated me as your second-in-command and allowed me to know your plans and see your wishes carried out." This is indeed the main count in the indictment of Livingstone's conduct of the Expedition from first to last, and Professor Wallis's comment is just: "His habitual seclusiveness intensified his difficulties, for, had he been able to communicate his troubles, he would have found loyal and sympathetic co-operation from most of his colleagues."

Bedingfeld's main disqualifications would appear, both from his letters and from the opinion of others, to have been arrogance and irascibility; and there is little doubt that Livingstone, though he cannot be acquitted of want of tact in dealing with him, was justified in his dismissal. One of this officer's least objectionable foibles was strict Sabbatarianism, upon which Livingstone commented: "It is a pity that some people cannot see that the true and honest discharge of the common duties of everyday life is Divine Service." Another was a curious desire that the Expedition's discoveries might include that of the Ten Lost Tribes.

Livingstone felt a grave responsibility in dismissing a naval officer who, though his subordinate, was in receipt of a considerably higher salary than his own; and was sensitive of the repercussions of such action in official circles in England. He was therefore careful to secure the written agreement of others on his staff upon taking it. A letter from his true friend Maclear in Cape Town a few weeks later must have come as some relief to his mind.

> I chanced to be stopping at the Admiralty House when Commr. Bedingfeld arrived. He planted himself beside me at dinner and very soon began nibbling at certain folks of the Expedition. I had received your letter respecting him and a full account from Skead. I was therefore well primed and, the moment he mentioned *Longitude*, I pitched into him without mercy. He winced and I heard nothing more from him about the Expedition. . . .
>
> By the present mail Captain Washington writes to me as follows: "Yours of the 10th November reached me on the 30th December, and I am very glad to have such late intelligence of Dr. Livingstone and that all was going on well. That Commr. Bedingfeld should have left him I do not consider any great loss." . . . Thus you are all right in that quarter.

Maclear gives news of the arrival of the missionary party for Linyanti—"and, I must say, the strangest lot I ever met with". After a deprecatory reference to one of them he continues: "Mr. Moffat said nothing about them, but Mrs. Livingstone was astounded at the *tout ensemble* of the party, and to me expressed a hope that they might not be so located as to hamper you." He gives the political news: the Boers are more than ever on the war-path, claim all the territory as far north as the Zambesi as theirs, and threaten to prohibit Mr. Moffat from going to the Matabele. But he was informed "that Mr. Moffat had resolved to proceed without asking their leave, let the consequences be what they might. He would run no risk, abstaining on his part from any hostile act. So much for the wisdom of our treaties, which virtually arm white barbarians against us."

Whether the Law of Nations acknowledges the right to stop travellers I am unable to say, but I can fancy the fix the Governor will be in if Mr. Moffat, or Moffat and his party, should be detained prisoners. We may augur how the British public would receive the intelligence. What a fuss would be made if a similar occurrence should happen in Europe! To threaten these Scythians is idle without the power of punishing in the event of wrong. At present the route to the Zambesi via Kuruman is in the clouds. I know that the Governor is greatly annoyed by the conduct of the Boers.[14]

Despite Bedingfeld's adverse report on the *Ma-Robert*, Livingstone's own hopes on the success of the little launch were high. On 21 June he had written in glowing and grateful terms to the builder, Sir John Laird "but on second thoughts" (he wrote to Captain Washington) "I did not send it".

The first day was sufficient for getting her into water, and putting her together, by the admirable and simple contrivance your son invented. . . and on the evening of the third day she was ready to act as pilot to the larger vessel. . . . It would be an immense boon if the Government would send out such vessels to run up creeks and rivers, and chase slavers, instead of taking it out of the poor sailors' muscles at the oar . . . She has done exceedingly well, and tows a large launch (pinnace) far better than we expected. [After suggesting some minor improvements.] Now as I am done with criticism, which you may think sufficiently presumptuous, I beg to be most kindly remembered to Mrs. Laird and all your family.[15]

But by the end of August he was exhausting his vocabulary in vituperation of the launch, its builder, and all his works. Very frequent relays were necessary for the little launch to tow a freighted pinnace and whaler back and forth between Expedition Island and Shupanga, and often in dense fog; constant sounding often proved too late to detect a shoal; only the hardest wood (African ebony and *lignum vitae*) could be used for the furnace; to cut it required immense labour and the loss of much time; even then four hours were necessary to raise steam, and half the fuel was consumed in one day; her boiler-tubes were set all on one side and chiefly below the level of the fire, "from which novel arrangement one side remains long cold while the other is hot, like a patient in a palsy"; as for the engines, they were fit "to grind coffee in a shop-window" and the little vessel wheezed so horribly that she was contemptuously re-named the "Asthmatic". She could not even keep pace with the native canoes.

On 31 July Livingstone himself undertook the navigation in which he, or sometimes Kirk in lieu, proved more efficient than the naval officer, "though I would as soon drive a cab in November fogs in London, as be fried alive on a paddle-box in an African sun, but I shall go through it as duty". To his brother-in-law J. S. Moffat he wrote trenchantly:

> Bedingfeld turned out an unmitigated muff, thought we could not move a mile without him and assumed all manner of airs. I mounted the paddle-box and sent him home to nurse his dignity there. . . . His lower jaw felt a weight on it of some cwts. . . . I never met such a fool and a liar, and yet all in combination with extra ostentatious piety.

These difficult cruises back and forth in the lower reaches of the Zambesi for several weeks entailed splitting up the party, and his factual Journal makes it apparent that he was subjected, not only to incessant fatigue, but also to constant anxiety. "I feel fully convinced that it is my duty to press on up the river as quickly as possible to save the health of my companions. Major Sicard urges it strongly." "We shall succeed, but I feel much concerned about our companions down the river. The Lord look in mercy on us all . . ." Yet he is never too busy or too worried to neglect his study of the natural history of the river-side and of the customs of its inhabitants, and his comments on these are the most interesting and informative in his *Narrative*. Baines, one of the pluckiest workers, was frequently ill and was left in charge of the stores; while "young Livingstone and Thornton are not of much use" (wrote Kirk) "when it comes to a hard day's work".[16]

On their first visit to Shupanga, 4 August, they were met by two old friends, Major Sicard and Colonel Nunes, who proved as helpful as ever and placed a large room in the fine old stone-built house near the river at their disposal as a depôt. Among those who were employed for "wooding" here was a youth named Susi, a native of the district, and with him another, Amoda. The House of Shupanga is described in detail by Kirk, and in general as "a very pleasant and comfortable place". For Livingstone it was to be the saddest place on earth.

At length on 8 September, with Kirk and Rae, he reached Tete and went ashore to find the remnant of his faithful Makololo in ecstasies at seeing him. Of the 114 whom he had left there two years ago, thirty had died of smallpox and six been murdered by a suspicious half-caste chief. Despite its promises for their maintenance the Portuguese Government had done nothing for them, but Major Sicard had found them employment and accommodation in a large stone-built house. In consequence they were not elated at the prospect of returning home as yet. Their reception of Livingstone was thus described by Rae:

> The men rushed into the water up to their necks in their eagerness to see their white 'father'. Their joy was perfectly frantic. They seized the boat and nearly upset it and carried the Doctor ashore singing all the time that their 'father' was alive again.[17]

They exclaimed repeatedly: "The Tete people often taunted us by saying, 'Your Englishman will never return'; but we trusted you, and now we shall sleep." Livingstone's own feelings are confided to his Journal:

> They grasped my hands all at once and some began to clasp me round the body, but one called out, "Don't do that! You will soil his clothes." It is not often I have shed a tear, but they came in spite of me, and I said, "I am glad to meet you, but there is no Sekwebu." Then they began to tell me how many they had lost. . . . Poor fellows, how sad I feel when I think on those who have departed from this scene, and I pray, "Free me, O Lord, from blood-guiltiness." The principal men are here. "Grant Lord, that I may be more faithful to them that remain."[18]

On returning downstream he was met by three naval officers of another warship, each of whom volunteered to take Beding-feld's place, but by this time Livingstone was "thoroughly scared of naval officers" and requested the voluntary services instead of a quartermaster, John Walker, and a leading stoker,

William Rowe. It was whilst here again in the Kongone that
he wrote to his brother-in-law J. S. Moffat what is perhaps the
most self-revealing of his letters.

> I sympathize with you in your present position and, though un-
> worthy to give advice, I would say, if I began life again I would certainly
> pay more attention to the will of the Master and less to that of his ser-
> vants. I would seek a more vivid impression of his presence and pray
> more for the leadings of his good Spirit. Ask him for wisdom. He gives
> to all liberally and upbraids not. You need not expect a smooth course,
> but let it always be smooth between your good dear Emily and you.
> Look right on to the end, and, committing your way to the Lord, direc-
> tion will come of course. There's no doubt of it. May the good gracious
> Lord be with Emily and Mary in their time of trial and deliver them.
> Whatever appears duty, bravely follow it.
>
> When I was a piecer the fellows used to try to turn me off from the
> path I had chosen and always began with, "I think you ought, etc.",
> till I snapped them up with a mild "You *think*! I can *think* and *act* for
> myself; don't need anybody to think for me, I assure you." This must,
> according to my experience, be the way all through. I never followed
> another's views in preference to my own judgment—i.e. did a thing out
> of deference to another when I myself thought it wrong—but I had reason
> to repent of it.
>
> And above all things, my dear Emily, cling to your better half and
> support him, if your judgment has not been influenced by the opinions
> of others. There is a good deal of fault-finding in the region to which
> you go. Keep a genuine merry laugh ready for the half of it, and the
> other half lay up as lessons not to be imitated; and it's best to show the
> effect of troublesome advices and injunctions by doing something good-
> naturedly opposite. I don't mean to inculcate rebellion, but we must all
> think and act for ourselves.
>
> I expected snarling after I was gone. I did not seek their praise, nor
> do I much care for their frowns. All came unsought. I have had abuse
> before, and whatever our Father in heaven wills I mean to submit to it
> and learn his lessons. Mary feels these matters more than I do and you
> must remember to soothe her for me. . . .
>
> If I were to begin again as a missionary I should most certainly choose
> to be alone with my wife. I may be differently constituted from you, but I
> never found two agreeing unless one were a cypher. In fact everyone
> has his own way of serving the Master, and he will do better in that way
> than in anyone else's.[19]

"I never found two agreeing unless one were a cypher." The
deliberate cynicism of the words bespeaks no more and no less
than the measure of his uncompromising and inflexible
individualism.

Reassured as to the welfare of his Makololo at Tete, and with his main base established at Shupanga, he could now proceed to his main objective: a survey of the Kebrabasa Rapids and the opening of the Zambesi—"God's highway"—into the heart of Africa. But the idea of blasting the rocks, if necessary, was for the present his own secret. "If we could travel as geographers do, with the legs of a pair of compasses," he wrote to Sir George Grey, "we might have been there long ago."

Leaving the Kongone on 7 October they were off Shupanga again at dusk on the 16th and stayed three days to freight canoes. "Knife given by Lady Franklin stolen by a Portuguese. Feel sorry about it, as I valued it for Lady F.'s sake." On the 16th they were at the confluence of the Shire with the Zambesi, and Livingstone with Kirk and Thornton went ashore to climb half-way up Mount Morambula. "I looked on Morambula with great interest, not simply from its height and beauty, but in relation to its being, even down here, a sanatorium. The Shiré is easily navigable to its very base." With hot sulphur springs at its base and clear chalybeate rills at its summit—"almost anything could be done with it". The main inconvenience is a prodigious number of small mosquitoes in the river.

With the near ending of the dry season the water-level was very low and navigation more difficult than ever; on the 21st they at last reached Sena, with its dilapidated houses, ruined fort and church, and general air of dereliction. "One is sure to take fever in Sena on the second day, if by chance one escapes on the first", Livingstone had remarked on his previous visit. "But no place is entirely bad. Sena has one redeeming feature; it is the native village of the large-hearted and hospitable Senhor H. L. Ferrao."[20] Above Sena the shoals grew very much worse and the Kroomen were often in the water dragging the grounded launch off the sands. "Very trying to their tempers. I thought I saw evidence of them failing at last. I am very sorry to exact such work from them, but I am anxious to get up to Kebrabasa while the water is at its lowest." This gruelling work continued for nine days until they reached the Lupata Gorge. "The Doctor is very good-humoured now that we have passed the shoals" is Kirk's temperate observation; but four days later, 3 November, on arrival at Tete: "The Doctor speaks of remaining only two days at Tete, and going on then to Kebra-basa to see the rapids which he talks of blasting to clear a channel if possible. This, he says, he would spend six months over to say that there was water communication all the way to the Makololo country."[21] Here Major Sicard was again their good host; but the launch needed repairs, and Thornton was ill, and Baines afflicted with sunstroke—"He is to be watched," notes Livingstone, "as it is known he formerly had brain-fever."* Charles L. also preferred to remain in order "to get on with photography". "So far," comments Kirk, "he has only made a mess of it."

On 8 November, therefore, only Kirk, Rae, Walker with the Kroomen and four Makololo volunteers went on with Livingstone; and in a day and a half steaming well over deep water they reached the gorge at the foot of the Kebrabasa Rapids. They drove the *Ma-Robert* as far as she could go, a distance of two miles, till, to save her from being swept round, Livingstone turned the bow towards a rock, with no worse damage than two small dents above the water-line. At this point the Journals of both Livingstone and Kirk expand into some pages of description, mainly geological. Leaving their companions on board they landed on the right bank and essayed what the latter calls a journey of fearful climbing over the quartz rocks, and at length returned for Rae, some of the Kroomen and Makololo, provisions for two days and equipment. With professional care Livingstone measured the width, depth, and rate of the current between the rocks which were "huddled together in indescribable confusion".

> The chief rock is syenite, some portions of which have a beautiful blue tinge *lapis lazuli* diffused through them; others are grey. Blocks of granite also abound, of a pinkish tinge; and these with metamorphic rocks, contorted, twisted, and thrown into every conceivable position, afford a picture of dislocation and unconformability which would gladden a geological lecturer's heart. . . .[22]

But they did not gladden the heart of the explorer. "The Doctor changed his appearance completely from the first time he saw the rocks," wrote Kirk, "and in the shaking of his head we could see that things were not working well." Nevertheless

* Professor Wallis, Baines' biographer, discredits this.

they pushed on up and over the rocks till sunset, then camped and supped on a patch of sand: "the Doctor took a latitude, and we turned in and slept soundly without any covering besides what we wore during the day." Next day they pushed on a little farther, observed more rapids, till fatigued and famished they returned on their tracks. On 13 November they were back at Tete, to find Baines still sick and Thornton very pale and unable to work. ("Herpes myself")—adds Livingstone laconically and in brackets. This irritable skin-disease, he is obliged to confess with obvious self-disgust, incapacitated him for a week. "Things are not going well here," notes Kirk, "between young Livingstone and the others. On the one side they have been sick and are more sensitive on that account; on the other, he is awkward and ungracious."

The tempers of the party were not improved by recurrent and almost incessant fever, and it is here that Livingstone interjects into his *Narrative* a note, significant in anticipation, of its effects on the mind.

> Very curious are the effects of Africa fever on certain minds. Cheerfulness vanishes, and the whole mental horizon is overcast with black clouds of gloom and sadness. The liveliest joke cannot provoke even the semblance of a smile. The countenance is grave, the eyes suffused, and the few utterances are made in the piping voice of a wailing infant. An irritable temper is often the first symptom of approaching fever. At such times a man feels very much like a fool, if he does not act like one. Nothing is right, nothing pleases the fever-stricken victim. He is peevish, prone to find fault and to contradict, and think himself insulted. . . . If a party were all soaked full of malaria at once, the life of the leader of the expedition would be made a burden to him.[23]

And it is here for the first time he publishes the prescription with which he had treated himself and others years ago on his first great journey and concerning which he had written to Maclear from Linyanti: "It is not a strictly scientific combination, but this is a failing of general useful medicines. I have had a great many cases in hand and have not met a single failure."

> *Take of Resin of Jalap and Calomel of each eight grains, Quinine and Rhubarba of each four grains, mix well together and when needed make into pills with spirit of cardamous; dose from ten to twenty grains. The mixture keeps best in powder.*

If the violent symptoms are not relieved in from four to six hours a desert spoonful of Epsom salts may be taken. The Quinine in four or six grain doses completes the cure. It is generally given till the ears sing or deafness is produced. [This last effect he calls *chinconization.*]

Now however, in the Zambesi near the delta, he found this remedy for the first time inefficacious.

Kirk's remarks on the mental effects of fever are more personal:

It is a curious fact that everyone I have met here with the least fever or sickness becomes very irritable. . . . This state is of little consequence with anyone who comes out with it, but becomes a serious inconvenience in such as the Doctor who never says much but often thinks a great deal. . . . As matters look now, if it is impossible to get the launch up, which I believe it to be, I think the Doctŏr will as soon see us all back again and go on alone with his brother.[24]

But not even Kirk, by far the most understanding, level-headed, and brave-hearted of the party, knew that the Doctor who said little but thought much was at this time committing the following entry to his Journal:

Things look dark for our enterprise. This Kebrabasa is what I never expected. No hint of its nature ever reached my ears. The only person who ever saw the river above where we did was Jose St. Anna (Colonel Nunes' nephew) and he describes it as fearful when in flood. This I can well believe. . . . What we shall do if this is to be the end of the navigation I cannot now divine, but here I am, and I am trusting Him who never made ashamed those who did so. I look back on all that has happened to me. The honours heaped on me were not of my seeking. They came unbidden. I could not even answer the letters I got from the great and noble, and I never expected the fame which followed me. It was Thy hand that gave it all, O Thou blessed and Holy One, and it was given for Thy dear Son's sake. It will promote Thy glory if Africa is made a land producing the articles now raised only or chiefly by slave labour. . . .[25]

The early rains had now fallen and, with the speed with which all natural events happen in Africa, the river was already rising to nearly half flood. Livingstone decided on another reconnaisance and this time took all the party, prescribing for them his own remedy against fever and lassitude—hard exercise and perspiration. Leaving Tete again on 22 November they reached the Rapids the following day and disembarked at a lower point for fear of a sudden rise in the river. They had progressed but a little way when they came to a point where the rocks, emerging from the flood, appeared to bar all progress.

Kirk had more than once commented unfavourably on the manners and behaviour of the younger Livingstone. He was irritated by his careful dress, and his "lounging indoors and never exposing himself without an umbrella and felt hat with all the appurtenances of an English gentleman of a well-regulated family. . . . I am afraid most of us are not too particular about appearances when there is hard work doing". Now his criticisms become more scathing.

> Mr. L. has become so tired with the walk as to be fit for little more than sleep. He being too tired to continue the march, we are to remain until tomorrow *in situ.*—Mr. L. is again very tired and scarcely able to walk, so we rest for an hour.—The day is fine and the road good, so we get over some distance, although more than half the time is occupied allowing Mr. L. to have a snooze every half hour or so.[26]

All that Livingstone has to say about his brother at this stage is terse: "One European knocked up by the heat." It seems incredible that he should have thus turned a blind eye to the worthlessness of this brother. Are we to suspect him of misguided loyalty, or sentimental attachment, in being unable to detect—as was apparent to everyone else—who really was the weakest link in the chain?

Leaving the rest of the party beside the Pandazi stream, he progressed with Kirk alone to a mountain which he named Stephanie after the young Queen of Portugal, and returned to find Thornton better but Rae ill and his brother fatigued.

On 1 December he announced that he would go back alone and explore the rapids, "as it had never been my custom, when alone, to leave a matter unfinished". The rest of the party would return to the launch. Upon this Kirk respectfully suggested that such a decision was an insult to those of the party who were still fit to travel; and "Dr. L., reflecting a little, said that, if I chose to volunteer, I might go". In his Journal Livingstone wrote: "Dr. K. thought it would be considered an insult to the Expedition if I went alone, so I gave consent to his forming one of our party—with 4 Makololo." It is possible that even Kirk might have thought twice, had he guessed what exploring with Livingstone would entail.

Despite the fact that villagers came down to their camp the same evening to dissuade Livingstone from a third attempt, urging that no elephant or hippopotamus could tread there (that is, amongst the rocks enclosing an upper waterfall), he prevailed on some reluctant guides to show the way. Starting early on 2 December they scrambled up 1,500 feet and descended 1,000 feet before breakfasting, by which time the sun was scorching the rocks. The Makololo were already dead beat, and their feet were blistered. The guides too refused to stir.

> The Doctor and I went on, accompanied by one of the men, and spent several hours [Livingstone says three] in getting about a mile further on. Such climbing I never had seen. We had to find our way among these gigantic stones, while every step was if we should slip and go down some great crack out of which it would be no easy thing to extricate oneself, even with all the bones entire. [Livingstone: "It was a perpetual sprawl."] It was then a question what was to be done; go on we must; that is we must see the end of this. Dr. L. wished to pass over the hill from where we were. . . . I persuaded him rather to return to the men now and make the attempt again tomorrow. . . . The heat, however, is now like Hell if that place is what I imagine it—you cannot hold on any time by the rocks.[27]

The tale of the next day is best taken up by Livingstone:

> We breakfasted and came to a dead halt, urging everything we could think of to induce the guides to go on and show us the fall which from their description I felt sure existed. They refused steadfastly, though I urged the displeasure of Zandia [their chief], possibly also of Chisaka [paramount chief]. They at last said they would go and die with me. The Makololo declared that they had always believed I had a heart till now, that I had become insane surely, for they shewed me the broken blisters on their feet in vain, and, if they could only speak so as to be understood by the other doctor, they would return with him and let me throw myself away. . . . We went westward. First time we halted they came to a deadlock again, and then the Makololo tried to persuade the doctor by signs to turn back with them. . . .[28] All their efforts of persuasion, however, were lost upon Dr. Kirk, as he had not yet learned their language, and his leader knowing his companion to be equally anxious with himself to solve the problem of the navigability of Kebrabasa, was not at pains to enlighten him.[29]

He thus describes their method of progress "at a pace not exceeding a mile an hour".

The walking was a very different kind of exertion from common travel. It was necessary to leap from rock to rock or clamber and wriggle over and round others, or slide down so as to gain a sure footing. The whole system was shaken and strained to a degree few can conceive. Our shirts were wet. Perspiration ran off the eyebrows and we drank profusely at every bend that led us down to the river. . . .

At last they came to a fisherman mending his net; he gave them a guide.

We very soon were worsted by a perpendicular rock which required to be climbed for 300 feet. The heat was excessive, for the hands could not be held on to the points we were in our ascent fain to grasp. There we were, clambering up the face of a slippery promontory, certain that, if one of the foremost lost his hold, he would knock all the others down who came behind him.[30]

If ever the truth of the maxim "Where there's a will there's a way" was exemplified, it was so on this perilous and truly desperate journey. From the top of the crag they began to descry the waterfall round the corner of a bend in the rapids. "It is named Morumbwa. Both banks consist of high perpendicular slippery Porphyritic rocks. We tried to get nearer but deep furrowed gullies prevented us." He dropped a tape-line over one of these and estimated "fully 80 feet of perpendicular rise" at full flood "which must make a very considerable difference in the appearance of the cataract, if indeed it does not annihilate it altogether . . . It will therefore be necessary" he calmly adds, "to return and examine the whole again when the river is in flood". Forthwith he determined to requisition Government for a stronger vessel and men and materials for blasting the rocks. This would give the Portuguese pause.

At low water a vessel cannot pass. At high water one of 12 or 14 knots power might, but to make it permanently available for commerce the assistance of a powerful Government is necessary, and a company of sappers would soon clear out the channel. This was perhaps the most favourable circumstance connected with the affair, for it would be difficult to induce the Portuguese to give up their pretensions if they could take all the trade into their own hands without [such necessity].[31]

This view he ventilated in a long despatch to Malmesbury on 17 December and showed it to Kirk, who commented: "The Doctor gives a very favourable account of the rapids, much more so than I could do."

They returned over a hill on the north bank covered with

dense bush and scrub, and spent three hours in cutting a way through. It was dark before they reached their sleeping place "and stretched their limbs for the night on the dry and crumpled leaves which formed the first night's bed". With nothing but some biscuit, chocolate, and tea they pushed on the next day "with vigour", jumping from rock to rock and sometimes wading breast-deep in the current, and within four hours met Baines coming to meet them with provisions. "He was sketching," says Livingstone, "as he always does, indefatigably." To Baines they looked "lean and haggard, as if from long illness". Their thick-soled boots were worn through; their clothes can hardly have been in better shape.

If to his loyal native followers it appeared that their leader had taken leave of his senses, it can scarcely have appeared otherwise to his loyal white companion. Kirk does not say so explicitly, but his account would seem to imply as much. This was a signal example of what Dr. Macnair has called Livingstone's "demonic" energy: that inborn stubbornness which would not brook, and refused to admit, defeat. It was the first time in his experience that he had been confronted with an insuperable natural obstacle; and, as it was unprecedented, so to him it was also a thing incredible. Surely it was contrary to God's will; it belied all the indications of God's good providence. And that good providence had never failed him hitherto. And how much depended on the navigability of "God's highway" into the interior! He had staked everything upon it: the opening of Commerce, Civilization, and Christianity into the very heart of Central Africa—with its teeming population. He had *promised* this to the statesmen, merchants, and churchmen in England—and he had never broken a promise yet. Not only his reputation, but his honour, depended on its fulfilment. Is it any wonder that he behaved as one possessed?

He would not "be beat". Leaving instructions to his brother and Baines to explore the upper Rapids the following month at full flood when they would be more easily accessible, and to Thornton to examine the coal-seams to the south, he proceeded with Kirk and without loss of time to the junction of the Shire with the Zambesi, to discover whether another possible waterway into the Interior might be practicable among the "network of rivers" that was said to exist there.

Chapter Nineteen

ZAMBESI EXPEDITION: LAKE NYASA
1859

"So deficient in administrative talent, so remarkable for individual power."

ON 5 December 1858 they rejoined the launch and reached Tete the next day. On the 12th Livingstone, having fever, took 30 grains of quinine and it made him deaf soon after. "Remained so till this morning and am now well (13th)." He adds laconically: "House struck by lightning on night of 11th; went out to render assistance, but none was required. Got wet, which made me worse. House burned down." On the 18th: "I have been troubled with unusual languor several times. Find it difficult to write my despatches."[1] Therefore, since activity was necessary for health, he put them aside to visit Thornton at his coal-seams, and returned to finish them at Sena on Christmas Day. With Kirk he left for the Shire on the 27th and on the 30th they ascended the very steep sides of Mount Morumbala to find it the 4,000 foot escarpment of well-cultivated plateau. "What fools the Portuguese are, not to have a sanatorium here!"

On New Year's Day 1859 they began their cruise up the Shire River against the advice of the Portuguese, who declared it impassable even for a canoe, on account of duckweed. But in fact it was the poisoned arrows of the hostile natives which had deterred the Portuguese. The duckweed, extending for 25 miles, proved no obstacle to the *Ma-Robert* or to any other craft. Livingstone was handicapped by inability to speak a language which was new to him (Chinyanja), and by a "fool of an interpreter" whose terror prevented him from saying what he told him to say. "As we approached the villages, the natives collected in large numbers, armed with bows and poisoned arrows; and some, dodging behind trees, were observed taking aim." "I don't know," says Kirk of one of these,

339

"whether he would have picked off the Doctor or me." On such occasions Livingstone stopped the launch and with deliberate slowness and always unarmed walked ashore, "calling out that we were English and had come neither to fight nor to make slaves". His imperturbability never, or seldom, failed to disarm them.

On the 7th Kirk wounded an elephant "and it instantly turned to us, spread out its enormous ears, curled its proboscis up like a butterfly, and raised its tail in the air like a bull". (Livingstone says merely, "He prepared to charge but a succession of bullets in his face made him desist.") On the way back to the launch, "the Doctor and I were going after a low growl . . . when one of the Makololo called us back". It was a lion hidden in the grass. "We were not twenty yards from him and should never have seen him, till within two or three [yards], for the reeds." (Livingstone does not mention this incident.)[2]

The next day they reached the village of the paramount chief Chibisa, who proved friendly and remarkably shrewd, and informed them of a "small lake" some five days' journey upstream and of a "great lake" farther beyond it; so the day afterwards they proceeded, only to find progress barred by a series of magnificent cataracts "which we called 'The Murchison' after one whose name has already a world-wide fame, and whose generous kindness we can never repay". Livingstone found the latitude to be 15° 55′ S. and waited in vain for nine days for a break in the clouds to obtain a longitude. By the end of the month they were back at Tete.

It was whilst at Tete that he had written on 11 December (when he had fever) a letter on the subject of pacifism to the eminent Quaker, Mr. Joseph W. Sturge, which has been reproduced in full elsewhere. Mr. Sturge had been influential in improving the lot of the slaves in the West Indies and in hastening the date of their final emancipation. Livingstone begins by apologizing for delay in replying to his correspondent's letter which was due to lack of time in England, preventing him from giving "that due attention to the subject as put forward by you which it deserved". He goes on:

> I love peace as much as any mortal man. In fact I go quite beyond you, for I love it so much that I would fight for it. You—who in a land abounding in police and soldiery, ready to clutch every ruffian who would dare

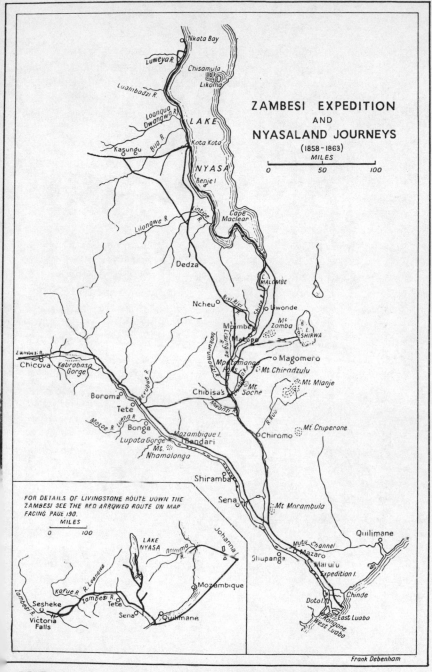

MAP 4   ZAMBESI AND NYASALAND EXPEDITION (1858–1863)

Prepared by Professor Frank Debenham and reproduced from *Zambezi Journals of David Livingstone* by kind permission of the Central African Archives, Salisbury, Southern Rhodesia. Livingstone's routes are indicated by the heavy lines. The inset map shows routes of second visit to Victoria Falls etc. For details of route see arrows on Map 3.

to disturb your pretty dwelling—may think this language too strong; but your principles to be good must abide the test of stretching.

He proceeds to illustrate his point by instancing occurrences in his experience where a display of force, without the use of it, would have prevented a massacre.". . . Had they been armed with revolvers their lives would have been safe. I think so, though it is the most earnest wish and prayer of my heart that I may never be placed in those circumstances in which it may be necessary to take away the life of a fellow man." He explains his own methods of conciliation which have never yet failed in turning foes into friends, and concludes:

> I am widely known as a man of peace. I could quote this were I disposed to accept evidence all on one side, but I know the other side of the question too, and I can never cease wondering why the Friends, who sincerely believe in the power of peace principles, don't test them by going forth to heathen as missionaries of the Cross. I for one would heartily welcome them, from the belief that their conduct would have a good influence, though it would never secure their safety.[3]

During the interludes between his journeys Livingstone, in addition to his long despatches, poured forth a positive spate of letters. The mere enumeration of his correspondents' names, which are noted in his Journal, would fill a printed page. Among those of this period is one of importance (5 February) to Sir Roderick Murchison. He first reports his brother's and Baines' visit to the Kebrabasa Rapids at high flood: though the rocks were covered by the water, the force of its current presented a barrier to canoes and "to this nondescript half-canoe and whole abortion of a vessel". He is therefore requisitioning the Government for one of higher power. Next he briefly adverts to his own and Kirk's exploration of part of the Shire highlands: "it was very pleasant to be away again from all civilization". Then comes the kernel of his letter: the adumbration of his dream—the Christian colonization of Central Africa.

> This brings up a subject which becomes daily more deeply impressed on my mind, but which I have not had courage to speak of to many. It is that the Interior of this country ought to be colonized by our own countrymen. It flitted across my imagination at times after ascertaining the healthiness of these highlands, and the Duke of Argyll said to me, "What a glorious thing it would be for the civilization of Africa if a colony

could be planted in the Interior". I see more in that for the benefit of England and Africa than in any other plan. I give all credit to the efforts of our missionary societies and would not say a word to disparage, but I think twenty or thirty good Christian Scotch families with their minister and elders would produce an impression in ten years that would rejoice the hearts of all lovers of our race. There is no end of totally uncultivated land, and the people are as far as possible from being blood-thirsty, or jealous of strangers. . . . So far from its being considered an intrusion I feel certain it would be esteemed a benefit to have a community ready to trade with them. I have not the taste for trade and never can do more than attempt to develop it for others; but after carefully examining the subject in all its bearings I feel certain, if the proper means are employed, of immense commercial benefits to England. It is rather fortunate that this rapid of Kebrabasa exists, for it will be a barrier to the Portuguese, but with a proper steamer will be none to us. I have authorized Mr. Young to buy one for me if the Government refuses, though it costs more than £2,000. I can spend that without hurting the children, and will do more than that rather than fail.

The Portuguese are as jealous as possible, though they scarcely know the country to which they lay claim. They never explored the Shire and their idea is, after we have examined all, to shut it up as heretofore.* Thanks to the forethought of Lord Clarendon I have a commission to the tribes beyond them which will prevent them from turning me out of the country. Hitherto we have been on the best of terms with them and we mean to avail ourselves of their aid, as soon as the sickly season is over, to examine Manica, the gold country. Very likely we may go up beyond your Falls in April to see what the country and people are like. . . .⁵

This latter project in fact he began to put into effect even earlier, taking with him this time Walker, Rowe, and 14 Makololo as well as Kirk—not without some misgivings on the part of the last.

Rowe pronounced the *Ma-Robert* unsafe, and Rae (the engineer) was left behind. They were to make friendly contact with the fierce Manganja, who regarded them as "evil witches" and held them responsible for a drought. Further, the unhealthy season was approaching. On this matter Kirk wrote:

Bad health and a touch of fever is nothing, were it not for the bad humour it puts anyone in, and sickness is a thing with which the Doctor has no patience, either in himself or anyone else. I have no particular

* [*To Mr. Aspinall Turner, 30 May 1859.*] "A station is to be put up at the mouth of the Shire by way of claiming all our explorations at the north and a custom house is to be erected at the mouth of the Zambesi whose navigability we alone discovered."⁴

wish for a row with the "Manganja Gents", but if the Doctor keeps good health, one can manage them . . . but, if his digestive system don't go all right, he loses his diplomatic power wonderfully.[6]

Livingstone's own private meditations at this time are in another key:

[*3 March*.] If we dedicate ourselves to God unreservedly He will make use of whatever peculiarities of constitution He has imparted for His own glory, and He will in answer to prayer give wisdom to guide. . . . O how far from that hearty devotion to God I read of in others. The Lord have mercy on me a sinner.

[*6 March*.] When employed in active travel my mind becomes inactive and the heart cold and dead; but, after remaining some time quiet, the heart revives and I become more spiritually minded. This is a mercy which I have experienced before, and when I see a matter to be a duty I go on, regardless of my feelings.

I have been more than usually drawn out in earnest prayer of late—the Expedition, the cares for my family, the fear lest Bedingfeld's misrepresentations of my conduct may injure the cause of Christ, the hopes that I may be permitted to open this dark land to the blessed Gospel. I have cast all before my God. Good Lord, have mercy upon me. Leave me not nor forsake me. He has guided well in time past. I commit my way to Him for the future. . . . It is presumptuous not to trust in Him implicitly, and yet this heart is sometimes fearfully guilty of distrust. I am ashamed to think of it. Aye, but He must put the trusting, loving, childlike spirit in by his grace. O Lord, I am thine truly, I am thine. Take me—do what seemeth good in thy sight with me and give me complete resignation to Thy will in all things.[7]

Leaving Tete on the 15th they put in at Sena and on the 20th attended a meeting for the building of a church. "The inhabitants contributed well . . . Rain today after a procession yesterday with an image of Christ. They had tried twice before, and Sr. Ferrao said they now meant to try another image. They always do it at new moon and full, like the rain-makers." The launch went smoothly and well, and the natives were less suspicious and more friendly than before: Livingstone's peaceful demeanour and the spell of his personality had already taken effect.

Collisions often happen from the cowardice of one of the parties. Fear takes possession and imagination says "Strike first—it's your only safety. It will save bloodshed in the end." God grant that I may not come into collision with anyone.[8]

On the 29th they reached Chibisa's again ("Is a jolly person and laughs easily, which is always a good sign")—but lost five days in waiting for guides from another village who came not. On 3 April, a Sunday, Livingstone conducted divine service which the chief attended. Leaving the launch with Walker and Rowe, they went forward on foot, at first with a useless guide, and marched by compass over stony and hilly ground till on the 12th they sighted Mount Zomba (7,000 feet), and on the 18th Livingstone's Journal—which abounds in ethnological notes—has the sudden entry: "Reach Lake Shirwa. For continuation see small note-book."

The existence and whereabouts of this note-book appear to be unknown, but its loss is made good by the description of the Lake in his *Narrative* as well as in his letters, in one of which he says:

> Lake Ngami is a mere pond to it. . . . On wading out half a mile, it got waist deep and had a lot of leeches which made us retreat. . . . We were twenty-two days on foot; slept only two nights in huts. The elevation made it feel cold, but though our beds were always wet with dew at nights . . . we returned in good health.

To sleep on the ground in the open, unprotected by a fire, in a country abounding in lions and other wild beasts, is a thing unthought-of by the boldest traveller. But neither he nor Kirk so much as mentions the risk. For Kirk the discovery was a thrill, but for Livingstone a mere prelude: he had been told of a much greater Lake to the north, called Ninyesse, the "Lake of Stars".

Another account of Lake Shirwa is contained in a long letter to his son Robert, dated 31 May, but the extracts which follow are chosen to show his own view of its discovery in relation to his main purposes, and also his concern for the future of this boy of whom he had seen so little:

> I have been so busy writing despatches of late that I have been unable to write to you, though it has frequently been in my mind that I ought to try. We have had but little intercourse . . . and while I was in England I was so busy that I could not enjoy much the company of my children. I am still as busy and believe that I am doing good service to the cause of Christ on earth. He is pleased to crown my efforts with a sort of success that the world applauds . . . but I long to see the time approaching when the long degraded sons of Africa will stretch out their hands to God. You will understand this if I tell you that we have just returned from the discovery of a magnificent lake called Shirwa. . . .

The discovery is not the chief end in view, though that lies in the way. The great object is the promotion of the welfare of man. . . . We are guilty of keeping up slavery by giving increasing prices for slave-grown cotton and sugar. We are the great supporters of slavery in the world— unwittingly often, but truly. Now I long to see our nation relieved from this guilt and stain, and our Great Father in this fair world has provided ample means for the purpose. We could not only get cotton and sugar in abundance from the region I am opening up, but in doing that by our own people we should be conferring incalculable blessings on our own poor toil-worn fellow-countrymen. As one individual I can do nothing, but God has put it in my heart to try, and He has helped me, and every time He enables me by a discovery or otherwise to bring the subject before men's minds He is helping. Our great duty as His children is to work with Him and for Him. It often seems slow work, aye, and not at all unlikely that I shall lie down and die before my desires for England and Africa are half accomplished. But if I work faithfully He will not be unmindful of the work of faith and labour of love. I thank Him for all He has done for me, and truly He has done much for me.

I wish you to be a thankful, loving child of God. You must give yourself just as you are to Him. Don't try to be anything else but what you are. Never look at others and imagine that to be a servant of Christ you must be like them. Make an entire surrender of your whole nature to God. Give yourself to Him to be what He wills you to be, and look to Jesus and to Him alone as your pattern, your wisdom, your righteousness, your sanctification, your redemption. He has much work to do and He needs people of various capacities and tempers to do it. If you give yourself to Him, He will employ you honourably in life, and in death you will not be unlamented. You must choose some walk in life with a distinct reference to God's glory among men. It is a mistake to suppose that God is best served in the ministry. I serve Him now in command of a steamer. I can ask God's blessing to rest upon me on the paddle-box with as good a conscience as I should were I in other circumstances ascending the pulpit. Choose a path by which you will be able by your exertions to benefit the world, and bend your energies to that, and may the Almighty God grant you His directing aid. . . .

In regard to your personal appearance in company, always try to be natural in everything. Let your smile be pleasant and easy. Seldom show that you are displeased, for very often the displeasure may be a mistake you have made yourself. Work hard at whatever you do   9

On returning to Chibisa's they found Walker very ill with fever, but with medical aid he soon recovered and was well when they reached Shupanga. Thence to the coast for expected mails and stores but, though they waited there a week, no ship arrived. Walker was invalided home and the Kroomen sent back to Sierra Leone. On 23 June Livingstone and Kirk were back in Tete. But it was not a happy return.

We found all well, but there had been a good deal of sickness in our absence and things had not gone smoothly. Poor Baines has many touches and his head seems often to have been quite out of equilibrium; he has done many things which, without this excuse, would have been very difficult of explanation. Thornton has no doubt been sick, but he is now in excellent health and, although he often complains, yet I could not venture to prescribe for his most anomalous symptoms. . . . His geological work has been very limited indeed and he can say very little, even in respect of the coal-fields which it was his especial work to examine minutely. . . . Mr. Rae has been very busy at a hundred little jobs; he has had many touches of his old fever. Mr. Livingstone has had the same; he has made a good collection of birds, of which I am right glad. . . . (*Kirk*.)[10]

Found our companions all well. Baines has been heady for three weeks and made away with Expedition goods to a large amount while so affected. Asked them to put him in confinement. Thornton doing nothing; is inveterably lazy and wants good sense. (*Livingstone*.)[11]

Livingstone at once took summary action, though with evident reluctance. The fact that young Thornton was a protégé of Sir Roderick Murchison made his decision respecting him doubly difficult. But he had ended his letter of 5 February to Murchison on an ominous note:

Your friend Thornton is very clever as far as books go, but you have not made him what you pre-eminently are yourself, a field geologist. He is terribly lazy. I can't get work out of him at all. Kirk discovered fossils in one place, I did in another, and the Portuguese in a third, but Thornton has discovered nothing. I send him where I know coal and matters of interest exist, but he is soon back sleeping. I am in hopes that as he grows more acclimatized, he will work more heartily. I have told him that this is the best chance of distinguishing himself he will ever have, and have not yet given up hopes of him. I mention this because you feel an interest in him, and as much as anyone wish him to get on.[12]

Now, on 27 June, he handed Thornton notice of dismissal. He had "made every allowance for your little illnesses, but could not do so for continued idleness while in perfect health. I am therefore compelled, by your repeated disobedience of orders, to inform you that your salary is stopped from the third day of May, the date at which you retired from one duty and declined beginning another". In his Journal he wrote: "It is absolutely necessary for me to act, for he will go home without any materials and then the blame will come back on me for allowing his salary to run on . . . His is a case of complete collapse. Wished to be invalided by giving Dr. K. many contradictory symptoms. He has several times had hysteria."[13] This fact, corroborated by Kirk, would seem to acquit Livingstone of the charge of undue harshness towards young Thornton. It has been suggested that, instead of dismissing him, he might simply have invalided him home. But neither he nor Kirk could justify themselves on genuine medical grounds for taking such a course. Thornton appears to have accepted his dismissal with good grace and, as will be seen, his subsequent conduct completely redeemed his character from any slur. He first joined Baron von der Decken's expedition to the foothills of Kilimanjaro (a much healthier region), where he acquitted himself well; later he rejoined Livingstone's expedition and ended his short life heroically.

The case of Baines—a man of mature years, an accomplished artist, an experienced traveller—is more complicated. On leaving Tete again for the Kongone on 11 July to pick up stores, Livingstone handed him a severely cautionary letter dated the same day:

> . . . While disposed to overlook the fact of your having given away large quantities of public property by your own confession . . . on the grounds of your head being affected by the fever, a renewal of such conduct will at once incur the stoppage of your salary. It will be imperative on me to invalid you if I find you again go off skylarking with the Portuguese, taking the whaler without authority and very materially damaging the boat, or if you spend Expedition time and materials in painting Portuguese portraits. I shall have no option; however much I should like to favour you, I must do my duty. . . .[14]

He then proceeds (almost unbelievably) to rake up an old complaint of Bedingfeld (of all people) to the effect that "Old Baines knows nothing of storekeeping". He has arranged with Major Sicard to take charge of the stores and Baines can easily examine them every day. Meanwhile he is required to make portraits of natives for the purpose of ethnology as accurately as possible, as well as of birds and animals. He is to waste no more time on portraits of the Portuguese, or on boat-building.

To this Baines made the verbal request that he might stay and work on, though his pay was stopped. But a later entry in Livingstone's Journal on the same day effectually rules out any hope of his being granted even this favour. "I find from Mr. Rae that while Baines made so free with the goods of the Expedition, he took very good care of his own and was both sharp and mean . . . Has a piece of serge in his possession belonging to Rae, gave away some dozens of bottles . . . While I give him the benefit of the doubt as to his sanity while squandering Expedition property, not many would be so indulgent."[15]

When the launch returned to Tete on the 28th, the incriminating piece of missing serge was found in Baines' box. "He gave away the mess wine to the Portuguese whenever they called on him." After, as he says "reflecting on the matter", Livingstone wrote to Baines a letter of dismissal in which he recapitulates the charges against him which can no longer be excused on medical grounds. He may retain the use of the artist's materials and continue to draw rations till his transport home can be arranged, but his salary is stopped from 30 July.[16]

About this time too Kirk notes signs of the impending loss of three sound men:

> Walker is still of a mind to clear out if he can. If he asks to be invalided, I think we can authorize it on a clear conscience as he has had bad health; but the Kroomen are at the bottom of it; they are an insubordinate bad set, and if possible do things to annoy him. . . . The Doctor has done his best. . . . It's even worse however when Rae tells me that Rowe is sick and tired of this also. . . . I thought he was liking it, and he is just the man to suit the Doctor.
>
> Rae is keen to get off. . . . He does not wish to renew the engagement beyond the two years. He will be a loss, as he can do many things and is a fine fellow. I think he may be prevailed upon to remain, if they raise the salary, a thing which none of us would be the worse of, but he is most in need of it.[17]

On 1 August the *Ma-Robert* was dry-docked on a bank in the Kongone and the hull found to be perforated beyond repair. The leaks were partially stopped with clay in canvas bags. Then the funnel threatened to collapse and was patched with sheet iron. The wood available for fuel was rotten and *lignum vitae* too thick to saw. Precarious progress was made upstream, and three palmyra trees kept the engines going for the last three miles till they reached Shupanga. Thereabouts they spent several days "wooding" chiefly with teak, and taking in more clay. On the 16th the bridge of the boiler broke for the fourth time and a day was spent in repairing it. Only by dint of constant baling could they keep the launch afloat, but on the 18th being caught in a current, the boats in tow were swamped, two natives thrown overboard and one was drowned. "This puts a damp upon all our spirits." Kirk wrote: "Dr. L. sick with anxiety and vexation." On the 27th (the day before their arrival at Chibisa's, the only chief they could trust), the native stoker struck work and though admonished became insolent; and as he "seemed inclined to promote a general mutiny, I gave him a beating with a flat piece of wood . . . He did not seem to care for it, so I dismissed him." This appears to be the first time that Livingstone was reduced to employing corporal punishment, and "felt it was very degrading".[18]

At this point Kirk notes that the water was up to the stokehold, and a little later that the engine-room was pumped out eight times in one day, and the leaks were increasing. He wonders whether the launch might not sink while the exploring party were away in the interior, and what would happen then?

> We are amongst those whose monopoly of the river we have broken up, and we cannot expect them to do any act of kindness in the event of a weak party falling into their hands. . . . We shall be guided by circumstances, and the Commander is a much more adventurous person than myself, and in him I have the greatest confidence from his past experience of native character.[19]

Kirk's confidence in his leader was justified, for though the Manganja were more inhospitable and suspicious and much more drunken than the Zambesi tribes, the Livingstone "spell" in securing their goodwill was as potent as ever. One cause of this undoubtedly was his obvious sympathetic interest in their welfare and activities: his *Narrative* abounds in descriptions of their rites and customs, primitive industries and manufactures, instruments, ornaments and so forth. It is filled also with natural history notes, especially of the many varieties of lakeside birds.

The exploring party on this third trip comprised Livingstone and Kirk, Charles L., Rae, Rowe, Hutchins, and 33 Makololo. Leaving Rowe and Hutchins with the launch at Chibisa's the rest of the party struck northwards and made a detour off the route to ascend Mount Zomba which Livingstone correctly estimated at 7,000 feet. On the summit "our native companions complained bitterly of the cold". Pepper was found growing wild there, "an indication of a decidedly humid climate". The slopes were extensively cultivated with cotton. Descending the mountain to the torrid temperature of the Shire valley they reached the southern extremity of Lake Nyasa on 17 September—a limitless sheet of water enclosed like Shirwa in precipitous hills.

In his despatch to Malmesbury, Livingstone is more concerned to define the position of the three main terraces that rise to the east of its southern point than to describe the scenery of this gigantic fissure in the earth's crust. His discovery had, as it happened, forestalled by only two months that made by the unfortunate German traveller, Dr. Albrecht Roscher, who had approached it from the east and was murdered near the Rovuma river on his return. But even more important to Livingstone than the geographical was the human —or rather the inhuman—discovery which he made on the shores of the Lake. For here he found himself in the centre of the Arab slave-trade route from Cazembe's country (Londa) in the far interior (part of which he had traversed in his first great journey) to the Arab port of Kilwa on the east coast, and the Portuguese ports of Ibo and Mozambique.[20] The south end of the Lake was the natural focus of these routes, and there were others too across the fords of the Shire. The agents employed in this hideous traffic were mainly the Ajawa, their brutal instrument being a long forked stick transfixed to the necks of the chained victims. "Seeing that we were English, they evaporated at our approach." Besides this living horror there were other gruesome tokens of the slave-raiders' ravages: burnt-out villages, mouldering skeletons and floating corpses of captives who had died or been butchered on the long march. To Livingstone it seemed a matter of urgency to place an armed launch on the Lake. In default of the Government's response to his former requisition for a vessel to replace the *Ma-Robert* he had written to his friend Young authorizing him to draw £2,000 on his own capital for this purpose, but Young had been disappointingly cautious. So too was Murchison. Livingstone, decisive as ever, resolved to act for himself and placed an order for the immediate construction of the vessel·that he needed, at the cost not of £2,000 but of £6,000, representing half the profits of his book. "She never saw the Lake, but was fated to become only one more of the many burdens under which, in the end, the Expedition foundered."[21]

Remaining only one night by the Lake they reached Chibisa's on 8 October to find the launch still intact and the party left in charge well treated by the villagers, but by this time the effects of their gruelling journey were beginning to tell on the health of all. Kirk wrote: "250 miles at this season and in this country on foot and on strange food is enough for the strongest; and to have no better fare, not even flour or biscuit or decent sugar, on the return, is more than anyone can stand." One after another, singly or in pairs, all the white men were ill: Charles Livingstone for several days "quite worn out" with fatigue and fever, and "horribly disagreeable company" when getting better. But the Doctor himself was "the most serious case", having suffered on the march from intestinal haemorrhage.[22] This condition (the first symptom of the malady that finally killed him) continued on the river-journey. In his Journal for the 14th at the foot of the Murchison Cataract he notes: "Very ill with bleeding. Bled all night. Got up at 1 a.m. to take Latitude. Found by Betelgeuse and Canopus that the Lat. is 15° 55′ S." Comparing this with his observation at the top he calculates "33 (nautical) miles of cataract, but through a comparatively level country".[23] In his Narrative he says merely that they all returned to the launch "in a somewhat exhausted condition" and attributes this to acute indigestion caused either by a fault of the cook or a poisonous kind of cassava. "We were delayed several days in severe suffering."

It is surely to the malignant effects of this physical malady that one must ascribe the morbid irritability that now beset Livingstone. No other circumstance can explain his present procedure and subsequent course of action. Only three days later we find the following startling entries in his Journal:

17 October. Dr. K. and Mr. Rae to proceed overland to Tete to bring away Thornton and Baines and materials to mend bottom of ship at Bar of Kongone. *18th.* Delivered to Dr. Kirk an order to proceed overland to Tete and examine Baines' boxes and take over all public property in his charge. Party left this morning about 10 a.m. with 29 Makololo and two guides from Chibisa's old village.[24]

It is true that Kirk and Rae were the fittest of a very unfit party, as well as the most reliable, and that the march was less than a hundred miles. True also that neither they nor Livingstone could be expected to know that all the watercourses on the route (so plentiful on the outward journey) were dried up and even the grass withered in the savage heat. Kirk, apparently, made no comment on his instructions and has little to record in writing of the journey; but Livingstone's account of it shows that he realized that they came through at the risk of their lives.[25]

Even on the launch, on the 25th, Livingstone wrote: "Sun very hot; almost blistered face, the hot blasts coming as from an oven." On 4 November: "A letter from Mrs. L. says we were blessed with a little daughter on 16 November 1858 at Kuruman—a fine healthy child. The Lord bless and make her his own child in heart and life." The child was christened Anna Mary. (To J. S. Moffat he had written on 15 October: "My wife's letter about her confinement is still behind, so I don't know whether it is male, female, twins or three of them.")

Kirk discharged his repugnant task "in the most gentlemanly and least offensive manner" to Baines, and could find little or nothing in his effects which was not his own property. He then obtained from Major Sicard the statement that he had investigated the charge against Baines and had fully satisfied himself that it was a calumny. Rae also testified to Baines' innocence of any theft. One of the worst counts in the indictment against Baines was his popularity with the Portuguese, who were becoming increasingly resentful of British discoveries in their domains. And though Major Sicard was himself unfailingly courteous and helpful to Livingstone and his expedition, the rest of the Portuguese in Tete now did their best to prevent Kirk from hiring either boat or crew to take Baines down to the Kongone. Baines was again ill on the journey and was a sick man when at length, on 22 November, he rejoined his former colleagues on Expedition Island.

The next day Livingstone called him into the hut and conducted what must be called an inquisition rather than an enquiry, and Baines, says Kirk, "showed no presence of mind in making replies". No doubt he was intimidated by Livingstone's gruff manner, which would be accentuated by his own nervous detestation of the whole proceeding. Livingstone began by saying that he "wished him to explain and clear up the matter. I had no wish to find him guilty. It was a black burning disgrace to the expedition to have to turn out a dishonest member and I wished if possible to avoid it". Then began the cross-examination. There were questions of his having drawn sums of money without authority; of having appropriated a small length of canvas from the ship; of failing to account for the loss of five cases of loaf-sugar; of having damaged the whaler when "skylarking" with Portuguese of low character; of wasting time and materials in painting their portraits after express prohibition; and of inciting their hostility to the Expedition.[26]

Of all these charges Baines could do no more at the time than protest his complete innocence; he demanded a fair hearing in Tete and, when this was denied him, in the nearest British township: "but the Doctor was bent upon taking his Makololo back to their own chief, and would not delay even to allow a fellow-countryman to clear his name of an intolerable slander". Baines therefore wrote his defence at length and sent it to the Foreign Office, rebutting (says Professor Wallis who has examined it) the various accusations with directness and candour, and a magnanimity not always found in his accuser. He has "no wish to hinder or disturb Dr. Livingstone in his work", and imputes no "intentional injustice" to him. "I believe on the contrary that he was grieved to be under the necessity, as he supposed, of dismissing me."[27]

Coupland's open verdict on the whole case deserves consideration. It is one, he says, on which the impartial student must be cautious of committing himself.

Baines, on the one hand, had nothing against him in his previous record on the Australian Expedition or elsewhere; and those who knew him believed him incapable of deliberate theft. Livingstone, on the other hand, clearly had no doubts, and not only is his rectitude unquestionable, but also his kindness of heart. Baines himself admitted that Livingstone's refusal to grant him the regular prosecution he claimed was partly due "to a feeling which, I feel bound to say, he showed in more than one instance during this affair, that he wished to send me home with as little against me as possible". One wonders indeed whether, whatever the truth may have been, those definite charges were really necessary at all. Was not Baines' physical and mental condition the dominant factor in the case? That alone justified his dismissal.[28]

The cases of Thornton and of Baines were referred by the Foreign Office to the Admiralty. Captain Washington adjudged that the former be reinstated without loss of pay if he should return to his post; but the plea of Baines was rejected. He gained much sympathy in other influential quarters, however, and later the Attorney-General was induced to look into his case. Having done so this cautious legal expert expressed himself satisfied on two points: "that Dr. Livingstone's procedure was neither well considered nor well conducted"; but that Mr. Baines, "who had done all that man could do to obtain a full investigation was wasting his time in vain by pursuing the notion of a trial". But Baines pursued it none the less. "For the next seven years he strove, with a persistence which in itself is strongest proof of innocence, to induce Livingstone to do him right."[29] His subsequent career as a traveller, from Walvis Bay to the Victoria Falls, and then from Algoa Bay to Lobengula's country in Mashonaland, places him high among the number of African explorers. As to his defects as store-keeper (a task for which he was totally unfitted) the remark of Kirk, "Baines is a good-natured soul", says much and probably explains everything. And if Livingstone was unjust and untactful in his dealings with him and with other members of his staff, it must be conceded that he was also unlucky.

It is worthy of remark that in the correspondence both of Bedingfeld and Baines there is no hint of any animosity towards Livingstone on personal grounds. Despite their grievances, the one on the score of wounded dignity and the other of injustice, they seem to have still regarded him with respect. If his judgment had erred to their discredit, his own character could not be impugned: there are no counter-aspersions, no recriminations. One could wish that Livingstone on his side had been content to bury the hatchet, but he was not. On the contrary, he never ceased to feel that it was they who had done *him* an injury; his resentment persisted for years and even on his last journey he recurs to it.

In fairness to Livingstone it is only right to put on record a private letter which he wrote later to Murchison, in his capacity as promoter and sponsor of the Expedition.

Private. London, 7 August 1863.

My Dear Sir Roderick,

I understand that Mr. Baines asserts that I dismissed him on a charge of dishonesty without giving him an opportunity of defending himself, and that I was led by the sole evidence of my brother to injure Mr. Baines' character with the public.

These statements are totally opposed to the facts of the case.

My own attention was arrested by an excessive diminution of the eighteen months' supply of provisions after only a few months' consumption, and I at once asked him as store-keeper whither the goods had gone. Mr. Baines replied that he was willing to pay for what was missing. Neither denial nor excuse was offered.

Being very anxious to retain his services, I formed the excuse for him that he might have parted with the goods while his mind was weakened by fever. It was I who made this excuse and not Mr. Baines. I put the remaining stores together and while placing them again in his charge, administered a sharp private rebuke in writing, and Mr. Baines' own opinion of the matter was then expressed to me in an earnest entreaty "to allow him to remain with the expedition without any salary".

This private rebuke which I never intended for anyone but himself was afterwards published by him but never by me.

I was anxious to screen him from blame and to leave other evidence against him out of view, but I had the evidence of my own senses and I had the charge of several lives on which a course of low diet might have fatal results. It was absolutely necessary that I should make a demand for other provisions and give a feasible explanation of the loss we had sustained, and from whom ought such feasible explanation to come but from the store-keeper from whose charge they had gone? I was responsible to my superiors and I felt that some justification was also due to my companions for those privations which we had every reason to anticipate. I therefore stated to Mr. Baines before all those companions that I had no wish to criminate him but a great desire to keep him with the expedition, but I must have some sort of account to render of the loss. His reply given in a sneering manner was that nothing had been lost—all had been regularly expended.

Though I had made an excuse for him I felt that I was to be placed in a very awkward position in the anticipated distress, and had we been left to ourselves for the entire eighteen months for which we had received supplies, and the natural results of coarse or insufficient food allowed, a much more serious charge would have stood against me than any that have been preferred. Fortunately we afterwards received fresh supplies from an unexpected source, but that was then in the unknown future. On receiving therefore an impudent denial that any goods had gone a-missing instead of his own previous admission to myself, I did not feel myself justified in keeping him any longer, but in sending him away I did it in the mode least calculated to injure his future prospects. I *published nothing*, and had Mr. Baines been advised by some of those whom he quotes as friends to follow the same course the whole affair would long ago have been forgotten.

Mr. Baines, I am confident, never saw any evidence of unfriendliness in me, but he became his own accuser by publishing my private rebuke in the Cape papers, and he adopted an unwise course in fishing for sympathy by pretending "to go to meet me in a court of law on the Zambesi", though it was pretty well known everywhere save at the Cape that no court of law existed in the region drained by that river. . . . I am as ready to do a kindness to Mr. Baines as to anyone else, but publicly to withdraw what I never published would be unreasonable, and to admit that I dismissed him on the sole evidence of my brother (though I have every reason to believe that evidence to be unimpeachable) would not be right; and I cannot do it. I have borne Mr. Baines' accusations in silence partly because I have not been within easy distance of the papers he employed, but, while always willing to let everything painful to Mr. Baines' feelings drop into oblivion, there is a limit to forebearance.[30]

It has been remarked of Livingstone at this stage that "he seems to have had a genius for doing the right thing in the wrong way".[31] This is true not only of his dealings with men at close quarters but also with others at long range, whenever he found himself at odds with them. In reply to any letter which he considers an affront or a misrepresentation he resembles a boxer hitting straight from the shoulder, never pulling his punches but never losing his temper. It is this that made him such a formidable antagonist, the more so since he is invariably and unquestionably always in the right. And it is almost with a shiver of apprehension that his biographer uncovers his letters of this period, wondering what mordant sarcasm (all the more devastating because of its studied mildness) they may reveal.

It is a relief to turn from these controversial topics to his letters to his mother, though these are short and not very informative (her faculties were evidently failing); to his sisters, and to his children who were at school, and especially to Robert. These latter, though still somewhat heavily homiletic in tone, are full of affection and fatherly interest in his son's career.

Those to his young brother-in-law J. S. Moffat, then at Inyati, are still the most characteristic, as this of 15 October:

I have been unable to write to you for some time, but my conscience does not accuse me much, seeing never a blessed word comes from you to me. I have received despatches from Government with great regularity . . . but except a few letters from Mary very few have thought us

356

worth their ink. As this is not the first time I have been without letters I care but little, only I hope my good friends will not have got grumpy at my silence notwithstanding. . . .

I am working towards an object which some can see at a glance, others turn up the whites of their eyes at it. But my God may in mercy permit me to benefit both Africa and England on a larger scale than at first sight may appear possible. Some poor noodles place it all to the love of exploration and seeking the glory that cometh from man. Let it stand over to be judged on that day when the secrets of all hearts shall be revealed. In the meantime may the great Power purify my motives and sanctify all my purposes and aims!

How do you get on? You may think now that the missionary field is a queer one. Queer things are said and sung in it, but never mind, my friend. Keep your eyes right on the end, and may our great and good Master come down and dwell with you and yours. "I am with you always, even unto the end of the world." No vain word that. . . .[32]

There is one letter of this period which stands out above the rest. It is to Maclear, and dated 3 November, and headed *Private and Confidential*. It amplifies his previous confidence to Murchison concerning the *reciprocal* benefit of the gospel message, both to the benighted heathen in the as yet uncultivated lands of Central Africa and to those immigrant families of the "honest poor" in England (for whom nothing good is done, though too much is done for the "blackguard poor") who, by settling among them will till the soil and sow the seed —literally as well as metaphorically; and his growing conviction, born of his long experience in Bechuanaland, that missionaries as such, by themselves alone, were "not much good" —or not so good as they might be—unless aided by this reinforcement to their ranks.

He goes on to explain his plan for carrying another steamer in sections up past the Murchison Cataract by engineering a road to the top and launching it on the Lake. "Will you let our good friend, Sir George (Grey), know our plan. He is far-seeing, while I am like a mole."[33]

There speaks the authentic Livingstone, the man whose vision went far beyond that of the most far-seeing of his contemporaries, but whose modesty made him feel himself purblind in comparison with some of them.

Chapter Twenty

ZAMBESI EXPEDITION: LINYANTI
1860

" The Makololo are just such a strange mixture of good and evil as men are everywhere else."

T HE insuperability of the Kebrabasa Rapids to navigation of the Zambesi was an obstacle that Livingstone had tried in vain to minimize, even to himself; but the disappointment was more than allayed by his discovery of the Shire highlands, soon to be known as Nyasaland. As Professor Debenham has emphasized, this discovery proved to be of even greater importance in opening up the continent than that which he had made on his first Great Journey, and is of itself enough to dispose of the view that this expedition was an anticlimax to the other.

The natural resources and productivity of the Shire highlands were after all greater, and the climate healthier, than the Kafue highlands, and in the deflection of his enterprise from the Zambesi to the great Lake, Livingstone saw the good hand of an over-ruling Providence. Here, rather than in the more distant interior, was the true line of advance; for a Christian settlement here would intercept the main slave-routes at their focal points, and an armed launch on the Lake would be a more effective deterrent than "half a dozen warships off the coast".

But he had to wait for its arrival and, though there was much to organize and supervise in the Lower Zambesi meanwhile, he felt that he could no longer defer fulfilling his promise to the Makololo, or rather the remnant of them who still wished to return to their homes. With so much else to exercise his thoughts and energies he had little taste for a prolonged excursion to Linyanti and had earlier in the year even agreed to their own suggestion that his brother should act as his deputy; "but they afterwards thought that it might be construed into disobedience, for Sekeletu had given them orders to return with me".[1]

The first half of the new year was however consumed in a series of vexatious frustrations. The *Ma-Robert* was rapidly disintegrating in all its parts—hull, funnel, engines, boiler, furnace-bridge, cabin—and frequent repairs were necessary to keep it afloat. Mail-bags containing Government despatches were lost in the bar off Quilimane, and he must wait for their recovery or the receipt of others before he could proceed. Meanwhile he improved his acquaintance with the Portuguese, and especially with the new Governor, whose criticisms of his own Government's ineptitude in suppressing a profitless slave-trade provoked Livingstone to a characteristic outburst:

> It is indeed a matter of intense regret that statesmen, known by the laws they have enacted to be enlightened men, should be the means of perpetuating so much misery in this slave-making country, by keeping out other nations, with a pretence to dominion where they have absolutely no power for good. Is it not paying too dearly for a mere swagger in Europe, to have to bear the odium of united Christendom, as the first to begin the modern ocean slave-trade, and the last to abandon it?[2]

When at length he reached Tete on 2 February it was to find that the previous year's crops would not suffice to provision his party and that they must await the new harvest in May. Here he met young Thornton, returned from Kilimanjaro, who requested to be allowed to rejoin the Expedition. This however Livingstone felt bound to refuse and offered him a passage home. Thornton declined this, "stating that he intended to remain some time longer in the country. Says he has no animus against me". Livingstone thereupon gave him the use of some instruments in his charge from the R.G.S. and (presumably) wished him good luck. "He seems buoyed up by the hope of discovering a silver mine long reported as existing at Chicova."[3]

Among his many letters from Tete is one to Sir Roderick, urging again his plan for a steamer on the Lake:

> If Government furnishes the means, all right; if not, I shall spend my book-money on it. I don't need to touch the children's fund, and mine could not be better spent. People who are born rich sometimes become miserable from a fear of becoming poor; but I have the advantage, you see, in not being afraid to die poor. If I live, I must succeed in what I have undertaken; death alone will put a stop to my efforts.[4]

359

Words similar to these last recur in other letters of this period, and they are not mere rhetoric; they are the expression of sober fact, which he proved upon the pulses while he lived with increasing tempo till the last heart-beat.

Going downstream again, they were informed at Sena that the lost mail-bag had been retrieved and was even now on its way up to them in Tete! Renewed sickness now prevailed among the party: first, Rae, then Kirk, then Rowe—"very ill". The two former soon recovered and Rae was as industrious as ever at keeping the launch afloat. Livingstone's Journal dilates on the anomaly he has observed among all African tribes, that whereas they cultivate many kinds of roots and crops (which he particularizes) "none ever took up the idea of spontaneously raising fruit-trees, till individuals had seen this done by foreigners". They are superstitious in Tete about planting either mangoes or coffee: "The native life is one of fear; they are always afraid of something."

Arrived at the Kongone again on 15 March they slept for some weeks in native huts or in a large shed, erected for the use of travellers. Here sleep was rendered impossible by the invasions of mosquitoes, cockroaches, and rats. The antics of the latter would appear both from his Journal, in which he describes their laughter as "most ridiculous", and from his *Narrative*, to have caused Livingstone as much amusement as annoyance.

The rats, or rather large mice closely resembling the *mus pumilio* (Smith) of this region, are quite facetious and, having a great deal of fun in them, often laugh heartily. Again and again they woke us up by scampering over our faces, and then bursting into a loud *He! he! he!* at having performed the feat. Their sense of the ludicrous appears to be exquisite; they screamed with laughter at the attempts which disturbed and angry human nature made in the dark to bring their ill-timed merriment to a close. Unlike their prudent European cousins, which are said to leave a sinking ship, a party of these took up their quarters in our leaky and sinking vessel. Quiet and invisible by day, they emerged at night and cut their funny pranks. No sooner were we all asleep, than they made a sudden dash over the lockers and across our faces for the cabin door, where all broke out into a loud *He! he! he! he! he! he!* showing how keenly they enjoyed the joke. They next went forward with as much delight and scampered over the men. Every night they went fore and aft, rousing with impartial feet every sleeper, and laughing to scorn the aimless blows, growls, and deadly rushes of outraged humanity.

Less diverting but more dangerous were the incursions of other nocturnal pests.

> Scorpions, centipedes, and poisonous spiders also, were not infrequently brought into the ship with the wood, and occasionally found their way into our beds; but in every instance we were fortunate enough to discover and destroy them before they did any harm. . . . Snakes sometimes came in with the wood, but oftener floated down the river to us, climbing on board with ease by the chain-cable, and some poisonous ones were caught in the cabin. A green snake lived with us several weeks, concealing himself behind the casing of the deck-house in the daytime. To be aroused in the dark by five feet of cold green snake gliding over one's face is rather unpleasant, however rapid the movement may be. Myriads of two varieties of cockroaches infested the vessel; they not only ate round the roots of our nails, but even devoured and defiled our food, flannels, and boots; vain were all our efforts to extirpate these destructive pests; if you kill one, say the sailors, a hundred come down to his funeral![5]

On 26 March he left Rae with instructions to board the next home-going vessel in order to superintend the construction of the new launch for Lake Nyasa, and to take home five tin cases of valuable botanical specimens collected by Kirk, meanwhile entrusting them to the care of Col. Nunes. It has often been regretted that Livingstone has little or nothing to say in his *Narrative* in praise of his companions, with the exception of Kirk. (Bedingfeld and Baines are not so much as mentioned by name.) It is with all the more pleasure, therefore, that one can transcribe a part of an enclosure of his seventh despatch in which he gives a high testimonial to this man.

> The services of Mr. Rae, our engineer, being no longer urgently needed in this worn-out steam-launch, it appears to me that . . . he might be of more service to the expedition at home than he can be here, for some time at least. He is thoroughly trustworthy and, besides great nautical experience in his profession, possesses knowledge of that kind of vessel necessary to navigate the rivers and lakes. . . . He has behaved exceedingly well all the time he has been with us and, as he feels so much interest in the undertaking as to offer to invest his savings (£200) in the vessel, his superintendence would secure everything being done in the most workmanlike manner. . . .[6]

The two years' contract of the remaining members of the Expedition was now about to expire and Rae, who was heartily tired of it, would apply for his discharge in any case. Of the original seven there remained now only three: Livingstone, his brother, and Kirk. The Expedition's next immediate obligation was to convey the Makololo back to their homes, but to none of them was this a congenial prospect. Kirk wrote in his diary:

> It seems I can do very little on a tramping excursion of such duration. If the Doctor gives me the hint that I shall be of little service, I shall not apply to go. I wish we were off to Zomba rather than this place. I should work up the Lake region with much pleasure. . . . The Lakes are the Doctor's hobby, too. But for the men, he seems little inclined for this tramp.

And later:

> I should not think of leaving the Doctor alone at this time—that is, if he wishes me. Mr. C.L. is against going up to Sekeletu's; he is for risking nothing in the way of health for these men, although they did bring the Doctor down. . . . But in honour we are forced to undertake a journey which otherwise I should much rather avoid. I see little but fatigue and hardship, perhaps sickness, and all for nothing tangible. . . .

Livingstone had said nothing to Kirk about the termination of his contract, but neither had he given him a hint as to whether he desired the continuance of his services. At length Kirk tackled him with a question as to the probable duration of the journey. Livingstone replied that he thought it might be done in six months there and back. Kirk then, to give him the opportunity of saying whether he wished to dispense with his services afterwards, asked him whether it was intended that the Expedition should remain in being when they returned. "He, however, did not continue the conversation, but only remarked that he was ignorant of the intentions of the Government."[7]

With that astonishing mental energy which cannot but excite our admiration Livingstone was, during these weeks of delay, in addition to all his other activities, compiling a dictionary of the African dialects spoken at Sena and Tete, and—as his correspondence with Portuguese officials shows—improving his knowledge of their language too. He was oppressed by news of the recent war in Italy, and the peace (he wrote to Mr. Braithwaite and others) "engenders more uneasy forebodings than anything I ever heard of". He was alarmed too by Portuguese fraternization with the French and the prospect of their occupation of the territory he had discovered. His eye for country was as observant as ever: on 4 April he notes: "In both Shire and Zambesi the wear of the river is as a general rule on the eastern bank, as if the country were rising on the western side." Upon this Professor Debenham has remarked:

> He was in fact within an ace of discovering that anything moving in the Southern Hemisphere tends to bear to the left, and *vice versa* in the Northern, a phenomenon which played some part in the feature now bothering him [i.e. on his first great journey], that he was on the bank of the Zambesi where it bears against hilly country, but wanted to be on the other bank where the ground was much lower. He noticed the old river terraces, at least three of them, and this no doubt set him thinking of the immeasurable periods of time necessary for the erosion of the great African valleys.[8]

Before leaving the Kongone he received news, as welcome as it was unexpected, in a letter from the Bishop of Cape Town (Robert Gray) dated 31 March that a Mission from the Universities of Oxford and Cambridge would soon be on its way out to join him; and he was requested for information as to the route overland and for any other advice. On re-arrival at Tete he found another letter, previously lost with others, from the same Bishop dated 17 April:

> ... It is intended to send out as soon as the funds are collected both clergy and lay artisans—a small colony.... The Rev. Archdeacon Mackensie is to head the mission as Bishop.... They do not contemplate sailing before the end of the year.... They hope to bring out a medical man. I have urged a small steam-boat....[9]

Livingstone's replies to these and earlier letters are not extant, but a letter to the Bishop of Oxford (Samuel Wilberforce) dated from Sena on 7 April bespeaks his enthusiastic gratitude. "This is the best news we have ever had in Africa." The project was all, and more than all, that he could have desired. He had long since decided that a superintendent with authority was a desideratum for any mission, and the following paragraph in his letter has a significant bearing upon this.

> The late Dr. Philip of the Cape told me that missionaries always did most good by doing things in their own way. I am fully convinced that your way of sending a bishop with your mission is an admirable one. I avoid saying so publicly, as I do not wish to give pain to those with whom I have acted, but I have no doubt that our Bechuana mission would have been more efficient had we possessed an energetic head endowed with

authority. The field is all your own. I think that the church is called upon to put forth her best energies and endeavours to repay somewhat the wrongs we have done to Africa.[10]

Whilst these good tidings must have heartened him for the long journey, his spirits must have been damped somewhat by a conversation with his brother on the very eve of starting. Till this moment he had turned a blind eye, perhaps deliberately, to the defects in Charles which had been crystal-clear to every other member of the Expedition from the outset. Perhaps too it opened his eyes to his own defects as a leader. But only in the privacy of his Journal is there any record of it.

13 *May* 1860. My brother informs me that the members of the Expedition did not get orders what to do, and were always at a loss how to act. . . . All were willing and anxious to help if I only would have told them. He never told me this before. . . . On principle I abstained from multiplying orders, believing that it is more agreeable to men to do their duty in their own way. It is irksome to most men to be in any degree driven as soldiers and sailors are. As he seems to let out in a moment of irritation a long pent-up ill-feeling, I am at a loss how to treat him. As an assistant he has been of no value. Photography very unsatisfactory. Magnetism still more so. Meteorological observations not creditable, and writing the journal in arrears. In going up with us now he is useless, as he knows nothing of Portuguese or the native language. He often expected me to be his assistant instead of acting as mine. . . . He allowed £100 worth of magnetical instruments to be completely destroyed by damp, but must not be blamed.[11]

In his letters and despatches hitherto Livingstone had coupled his brother with Kirk and Rae as "good men and true"! On 9 June we find the entry: "People (i.e. the Makololo) very obstinate since we left Tete, and my brother keeping up his sulks ever since." Two days later his brother returned to the charge, taunting him with the "manners of a cotton-spinner— of the Boers; [says that I] didn't know how to treat men . . . that I cursed him, that I set the devil into him etc. . . . Seemed intent on a row. Would be but a short time in the Expedition; regretted he was on this journey. Would rejoice when he could leave it. So far my brother Charles".

The start of the journey was inauspicious too on account of the Makololo's lack of enthusiasm for their own repatriation. Of the ninety survivors one-third declined to leave Tete, and of those who volunteered several deserted on the march. Four years' contact with a slave-ridden population had infected many of them with a slave mentality, and they preferred the sloth and debauchery of native compounds to the toil of travel. "Their natural affections," says Livingstone, "had become enchained." Persuasion however effected what coercion could not: the best men (eventually only 25) went and the most worthless stayed.

Livingstone's native resilience however had proved equal to absorbing greater shocks than these. His mood of buoyancy is reflected in his last letters from Tete, as thus to J. S. Moffat:

> Our steamer is done—a sham at the best. We leave it on the river at Tete to be swept away by the next flood. . . .
> Got the loan of two donkeys, there being but three in the country. The Portuguese cultivate skin-diseases and drunkenness more than horse-flesh and are asses themselves. Oh, the scamps! But there's a good time coming yet. I am tired of being skipper. I engaged in it only not to be beat. . . .
> We are nearly ready to start. . . . My love to your wife. I have a gold watch-guard made in Tete for her.[12]

They were provided with canoes to the foot of the Kebrabasa Rapids and thence crossed to the north side of the river, winding their way up the rocky bank by slow and short marches to accustom themselves to travel. Besides, Livingstone had at first to allow for the feverish condition of his brother and Kirk. The heat after the rains was now intense, and starting at sunrise they seldom marched for more than 5 or 6 hours in the day and covered no more than $2\frac{1}{2}$ miles (in a straight line) an hour. Livingstone gives reasons for this measured progress:

> To hurry over the ground, abuse and look ferocious at one's native companions, merely for the foolish vanity of boasting how quickly a distance was accomplished, is a combination of silliness with absurdity quite odious.

The country on the north bank was new to him and the magnificence of the scenery inspired him to passages of glowing, even of poetic, description. Indeed his *Narrative* is now invested with something of the leisurely charm and enlivening interest that makes it reminiscent of his earlier *Travels*. Nothing escapes his notice or is too trivial to record: the making and breaking of the night camp; the chaffering and banter of the villagers;

their anecdotes, their names for the stars, moon-blindness, fire-making, water-filtering, game-traps—and much else. The old zest for an open-air life is upon him:

> We have no tent nor covering of any kind except the branches of the tree under which we may happen to lie; and it is a pretty sight to look up and see every branch, leaf, and twig of the tree stand out, reflected against the clear, star-spangled and moon-lit sky.[13]

It would appear from his impersonal account of falling into a game-trap that he was himself the victim of this experience.

> The sensations of one thus instantaneously swallowed up by the earth are peculiar. A momentary suspension of consciousness is followed by the rustling sound of a shower of sand and dry grass, and the half-bewildered thought of where he is and how he came into darkness. Reason awakes to assure him that he must have come down through that small opening of daylight overhead, and that he is now where a hippopotamus ought to have been. The descent of a hippopotamus pitfall is easy, like that of Avernus, but to get out again into the upper air is a work of labour. The sides are smooth and treacherous, and the cross-reeds, which support the covering, break in the attempt to get out by clutching them. A cry from the depths is unheard by those around, and it is only by repeated and most desperate efforts that the buried alive can regain the upper world.[14]

He was as assiduous as ever in his study of the manners and customs of ants: the destructive white, which devoured their beds and blankets; the red-headed white, which bit their flesh; the warrior black, which sacked the tunnels of the white; the minute but voracious red, which attacked their heads and necks and whose mandibles were like forceps; and the even more ferocious reddish driver, advancing across the path in solid inch-wide columns and "never did the pugnacity of either man or beast exceed theirs". He noticed for the first time that, besides the faculty of communication by means of their antennae, "a gift, analogous to that of language, has not been withheld from ants"—it is a clear distinct chirrup twice or thrice repeated—"until then we had not believed in the vocal power of an ant".

The journey was arduous but uneventful. Livingstone was already known in person or by repute to most of the tribes beyond the Kafue, and met with little hostility or obstruction. Soon after he struck into his old route beyond the Chicova

Plain he was greeted as an old friend by the chief Mpende, and a few miles further on another chief apologized for not formerly lending him canoes. He comments upon this: "The sight of our men, now armed with muskets, had a great effect. Without any bullying, firearms command respect." Arrived at Zumbo on 26 June he found the Loangwa too deep to be forded and sent a Makololo across in an inflated waterproof cloak, for three ferrymen on the opposite bank. These arrived half-intoxicated and, receiving no drink by way of payment, presented a loaded musket at the leader of the Makololo.

> In an instant the gun was out of the rascal's hands, a rattling shower of blows fell on his back, and he took an involuntary header into the river. He crawled up the bank a sad and sober man, and all three at once tumbled from the height of saucy swagger to a low depth of slavish abjectness.[15]

They remained for a day by the ruins of Zumbo, "the most charmingly picturesque site in the country", with its view of the confluence of two noble rivers, green fields and undulating forests, backed by a distant magnificent mountain range. He does not pause to meditate, at least in writing, on the crisis that had in this place five years before so nearly terminated his life at the hands of his black fellow-men. Instead he is moved to a lamentation on their present plight, contrasting it with all that might have been if only the teaching of the early Jesuit priests had been perpetuated to posterity. It mattered not to him by whom Christ was preached or in what manner worshipped, whether by Catholic or Protestant, so long as He was preached and worshipped in sincerity. "Those ancient and honourable men who had dared so much for Christianity"— naught remained of their labours now but a broken chapel and a broken bell. Could it be possible that even they, "like many good men formerly among ourselves", had condoned a system of slavery, which inevitably perpetuates barbarism?

> It is an utter ruin now and desolation broods around. . . . The foul hyaena has defiled the sanctuary, and the midnight owl has perched on its crumbling walls, to disgorge the undigested remnant of its prey. One can scarcely look without feelings of sadness on the utter desolation of a place where men have met to worship the Supreme Being, or have united in uttering the magnificent words "Thou art the King of Glory, O Christ!"—and remember that the natives of this part know nothing

of His religion, not even His name; a strange superstition makes them shun this sacred place as men do the pestilence, and they never come near it. . . .[16]

Soon after this, in the Mburuma pass, Kirk was taken seriously ill, becoming suddenly blind and unable to stand. He had been experimenting with various medicines to try their effect. Livingstone was seriously alarmed. "The men, with great alacrity, prepared a grassy bed, on which we laid our companion, with the sad forebodings which only those who have tended the sick in a wild country can realize." He gave him a dose of his "rousers" and on the third day Kirk could ride, and on the sixth could walk. "Moving the patient from place to place is most conducive to the cure," says Livingstone, and adds, "The more pluck a man has, the less likely he is to die."

His pen is now descriptive, more than ever before, of the habits of all the wild life that he saw around him, beasts, birds, and insects. All that region in his day was a vast menagerie, and the wild game less suspicious of man than in ours. This is by far the most fascinating part of his *Narrative*. Once when stooping to pick a wild fruit he was charged by an unseen rhinoceros.

> But she stopped stock-still when less than her own length distant, and gave him time to escape; a branch pulled out his watch as he ran, and turning half round to grasp it, he got a distant glance of her and her calf still standing on the self-same spot, as if arrested in the middle of her charge by an unseen hand. . . . The Doctor usually went unarmed before this, but never afterwards.[17]

He had never outgrown his abhorrence of the indiscriminate slaughter of wild animals, but his power to control his native followers in this respect was slight. It was not in his nature to impose his will on his fellow-men, whether white or black; he could not, nor would he ever try, to enforce obedience. He could really only rule by gentleness; coercion went against the grain in him. The sight of a wounded cow elephant, for instance, in its pathetic efforts to save its young was something that hurt him to the quick; but even when unsuccessful in restraining the blood-lust of his savage followers, he never punished them for disobedience. He was much more severe in his condemnation of the blood-sports of his own countrymen; though he also received the accounts of some of their exploits with a large amount of scepticism.

The writings of Harris and Gordon Cumming contain such full and nauseating details of indiscriminate slaughter of wild animals, that one wonders to see almost every African book since besmeared with feeble imitations of these great hunters' tales. Some tell of escapes from situations which, from our knowledge of the nature of the animals, it requires a painful stretch of charity to believe ever existed.

A grim fact which was to prove the major disillusion of his life was now being borne in upon Livingstone: that all his travelling, undertaken for the promotion of free and honest trade into the heart of Africa, was defeating its own end. His footsteps were dogged by native Portuguese who represented themselves as his "children" and who were bartering vast quantities of ivory in exchange for slaves.

We had long ere this become thoroughly convinced that the Government of Lisbon had been guilty, perhaps unintentionally, of double dealing. Public instructions had been sent from Portugal to all the officials to render us every assistance in their power, but these were to be understood with considerable reservation. . . . We were now fully convinced that, in opening the country through which no Portuguese durst previously pass, we were made the unwilling instruments of extending the slave-trade. . . . It was with bitter sorrow that we saw the good we would have done turned to evil.[18]

Arrived at the Victoria Falls on 8 August they embarked next day in canoes piloted by the famous Tuba Mokoro, the "canoe-smasher", who alone knew the "medicine" to prevent shipwreck. Even so they hit a rock over which white foam flew in their headlong race towards the verge; the canoe half-filled with water, and only his strength and skill averted a complete capsize. "It was not [they were told] the medicine that was at fault; the accident was entirely due to Tuba having started without his breakfast. Need it be said that we never let Tuba go without that meal again?"

They landed safely at Garden Island, to find Livingstone's plantation destroyed by hippo's; with characteristic persistence he planted another with a strong stockaded hedge, but with faint hopes of its survival. To the inscription of his initials on the tree Charles—but not Kirk—gratuitously added his own; but twenty years later there was no sign of either. He measured the depth of the Falls by lowering a line weighted with bullets and a foot of white cloth over the edge, but it was arrested by a projection when paid out 310 feet. This operation became a source of one of the many Livingstone legends: twenty years later when Arnot was there, he was told what a wonderful magician the Nyaka (doctor) had been, for he lowered a line and brought up a white fluttering bird from out of the clouds of spray, and some pearls. When sending Maclear a sketch of the Falls he wrote: "Between ourselves I perpetrated the mad freak of going down the end of the fissure at X, and Dr. K. and my brother followed." (This must have been the precipitous descent to the Gorge which was not then made safe for pedestrians.) He measured the length of the chasm (a difficult feat in itself) from both sides and made it approximately 1,860 yards. This is typical again of his scientific reserve: the length is in fact 1,900 yards. And he has another pen-picture of the scene:

> The whole body of water rolls clear over, quite unbroken; but after a descent of ten or more feet the entire mass becomes like a huge sheet of driven snow. Pieces of water leap off it in the form of comets with tails streaming behind, till the whole snowy sheet becomes myriads of rushing, leaping, aqueous comets. . . .
> In the presence of the strange Mosi-oa-tunya we can sympathize with those who, when the world was young, peopled earth, air, and river with beings not of mortal form. Sacred to what deity would be this awful chasm and that dark grove, over which hovers an ever-abiding "pillar of cloud"?[19]

Before leaving the Falls they were surprised to meet another white man, who was no less surprised—and much more relieved—than they. He was a Mr. Baldwin from Natal. Fired by Livingstone's previous discovery, he had made his way thither by compass alone and while being ferried across the river he had jumped in and swum ashore. For this reason he had been detained and disarmed. "For if," said the ferryman, "he had been devoured by a crocodile the English would have blamed us for his death." When questioned by the natives, he had tried to explain that he had come in Livingstone's footsteps. "The great name had produced an impression, but had not secured his release. And then suddenly out of the blue, Livingstone had arrived in person and all was well."[20]

By him as well as by emissaries from Sesheke, Livingstone

was informed that Sekeletu had for a long time been afflicted with leprosy and urgently desired the Doctor to come to him. Arrived there on 17 August, Livingstone at once went into his hut and spoke with him for a long time. He found that his disease was more like a severe form of eczema (*pemphigus*) than leprosy. Next day he brought in Kirk. "Found that the disease began about the time of (a tribal) disturbance, probably therefore the result of mental anxiety." The young chief was believed, and believed himself, to have been bewitched; several suspects had been executed; and every witch-doctor had given him up except an aged crone. But in conformity with his scrupulous observance of medical etiquette—never to treat a patient unless the native doctor consulted him or abandoned the case—Livingstone agreed to treat Sekeletu only with the consent of "the female physician already employed" and on condition that "she remained in the chief's establishment on full pay".

They applied a poultice of cow-dung to remove scabs and matter caused by her scraping the *bullae* till the flesh was raw. Their treatment after that will be of interest to members of the profession.

> 19*th*. We took the scabs from Sek's legs and bathed with Sulphate of Zinc, 1 grain to the ℥ of water, placing a greased cloth over the sores to prevent sticking. Gave a powder of Rhubarb, Soda and Quinine. This every morning and a pill of 1 grain Calomel, ½ morphia, and ¼ tartar emetic. Touched outside of sores with nitrate of silver to prevent spreading. . . .
>
> 20*th*. Legs seem healthy. Some few spots of new bullae, but nitrate of silver seemed to stop the burrowing. . . . Continue Sulph. Zinc lotion: does not feel sore when touched with nitrate of silver—a bad sign. Takes 2 pills containing quinine, Rhubarb, soda and ginger every morning. Wash 4 times a day; to wash his whole body and clothes. Looks better in the countenance.[21]

The hands of both doctors became infected from contact with their patient, and were cured only by liberal applications of lunar caustic. They could not hope that his improvement would be permanent. Kirk wrote:

> The disease is not known at home, and any treatment of it was experimental; yet it seemed to be quite successful, as at the time of our departure he was quite a changed man, and from a mass of filthy sores had

371

become a respectable member of society. Yet the disease still remained, and I believe will return now we are gone.[22]

Great evils for the tribe followed upon the prolonged sickness of their chief: there was widespread dispersion; crops had failed; sickness was prevalent; they were now an easy prey to invasion. Livingstone counselled the young chief to send a friendly message to Mosilikatse, and told him that it was only cowardice that kept him here in the lowlands. Sekeletu answered pathetically enough: "If the Doctor and his wife would come and live with us, we would remove to the highlands at once; as Mosilikatse would not attack a place where the daughter of his friend, Moffat, was living." He even promised to "cut off a section of his country for the special use of the English". And he had taken a particular liking for the young doctor (Kirk) who was the same age as himself and who had helped so much to cure him. But Livingstone now had commitments in another, and to him more important, sphere than settlement among the Makololo: in the region of the great Lakes, the focus of the slave-trade.

In a broadcast address upon this topic, printed in the *Listener* of 22 September 1955, Mr. Max Gluckman advanced a criticism of Livingstone which must be considered. Why was it, he asks, that the Makololo treated him so liberally, and provided him with men and means to open up trade-routes for them to the coast?

In some part this was due to his character; but in addition he was, at that time, the key figure in Makololo foreign policy.

In his first book, Livingstone described how he went on behalf of the Makololo chief to negotiate what we would call non-aggressive pacts with the chiefs to the north and west of the kingdom—including the chief of the Barotse whom the Makololo had driven out of their homeland. Thus the Makololo chief financed Livingstone as a peace-making ambassador, somewhat outside the ordinary political system, to obtain peace on certain frontiers. He wanted this peace because he hoped to concentrate all his forces on the south-east border to face the militant Matabele. . . .

In this terror of the Matabele, the Makololo chief had seen a hope in Livingstone. Livingstone was a son-in-law of Moffat, who was a favourite of the Matabele king. If Livingstone would settle with the Makololo as missionary, perhaps influence could be brought through his father-in-law to induce the Matabele king to allow the Makololo to return in peace to the uplands. Hence they sent for Livingstone, hence they welcomed him, hence they supported him and financed him loyally; always they kept urging him to become their missionary. They undoubtedly liked and respected him for himself, but it was as Moffat's son-in-law that they wanted him permanently among them. They were not interested at all in the other missionaries who came to settle among them; and these languished, some to death, in the Linyanti swamps. Livingstone held before them this constant promise of peace; and he never fulfilled it. . . .

He had "performed his duty to the Makololo": he had indeed, I would say, done his duty in bringing home those Makololo who had marched with him to the east coast. In the larger duty he had failed to bring them their desired peace and protection. I have said that he did not fulfil his promise to the Makololo; I am tempted to put it more strongly—that he broke faith with them.

Objectively the argument seems uncontrovertible. It is however a generally accepted principle of morality that a promise is not binding when circumstances intervene to prevent its fulfilment; and from Livingstone's point of view such circumstances—namely the unforeseen intrusion of a greater and more pressing obligation, to break the slave-trade—may be said to have arisen. And—though this has no bearing on the moral problem—the fulfilment of his promise would not have produced the desired result. Sekeletu died early in 1864; there followed quarrels about the succession; the tribe, which under Sebituane's rule had become a stable empire, dissolved into factions and soon disappeared. Finally, if Livingstone had consulted his inclinations in preference to what he believed to be his duty, he would without doubt have settled among the Makololo, who were to him "by far the most intelligent and enterprising of the tribes he had met" and by far the most beloved. In letters to J. S. Moffat during this year he wrote:

> I hope to return to the Makololo in time, but having been led, simultaneously with the powerful movement of numbers of pious members of the Universities, to open a field I never contemplated exploring and there found a field which, if diligently cultivated, will bear powerfully on slavery and the slave-trade, I think it a duty to render whatever aid lies in my power.
>
> The Makololo are a noisy set of blackguards, but live in a jolly careless way and have plenty of time and some inclination to be taught, as an amusement. . . . Had Mary come, there would have been a general flitting this year.[23]

He was well aware that his own preference for the Makololo

might not be shared by everybody. He had written at length about their character in his *Travels*, and he saw no reason to revise his cautious estimate of them now.

> I have found it difficult to come to a conclusion on their character. They sometimes perform actions remarkably good, and sometimes as strangely the opposite. I have been unable to ascertain the motive for the good, or account for the callousness of conscience with which they perpetrate the bad. After long observation, I came to the conclusion that they are just such a strange mixture of good and evil as men are everywhere else. [He compares and contrasts some instances of both.] . . . By a selection of cases of either kind, it would not be difficult to make these people appear as excessively good or uncommonly bad.[24]

Mr. Gluckman points to this passage as an example of the balanced judgment, the careful observation and comparison of data, which runs through all Livingstone's writings.

Being desirous to retrieve the medicines left in his old wagon at Linyanti, 120 miles to the south-west, Livingstone borrowed his old horse, now twelve years old, from Sekeletu, and accomplished the journey in three days each way a feat (as Debenham truly remarks) which says much for Livingstone's stamina and even more for the horse. One may add a word of wonder that the animal had not died long since in such a tsetse-infested area.

At Linyanti he found the wagon which he had twice left there still standing (says Coupland) "like some historic monument", and its contents—the medicine-chest, magic-lantern, tools and books—all intact. Two locked volumes of manuscript notes (one on Lake Ngami and the Kalahari Desert, the other on its natural history), which he had handed to Sekeletu's wives with a letter for transmission to Moffat by any English traveller, had been entrusted by them to one of the only two traders who had visited them meanwhile. When he now told them that this man (who is unnamed) had denied having received them, a wife of Sekeletu replied, "He lies, I gave them to him myself." Eventually only one of the two volumes was traced, the lock having been skilfully removed. Livingstone contrasts this trader's untrustworthy conduct with the faithfulness of the Makololo.

Only a few hundred yards from the wagon were the un-marked graves of the members of the Linyanti missionary party who had perished miserably of fever, hunger and thirst, only five months before. He was conducted to the place by the mother of a headman, the other natives standing apart at a respectful distance.

The large party of enthusiastic but totally inexperienced missionaries whose odd appearance had startled Maclear in Cape Town consisted of William Sykes, Morgan Thomas, Holloway Helmore, and Roger Price. All were accompanied by their wives; besides which, the Helmores had a family of four, and the Prices an infant daughter. At Kuruman they separated, the first pair for Inyati and the Matabele to join the younger Moffats there, the second pair for Linyanti and the Makololo where they expected to meet Livingstone. The story of the sufferings of these last has been told by Dr. Edwin Smith in his biography of Roger Price, who, with the two Helmore orphans, alone survived to struggle back to Kuruman. It makes almost unbearable reading. The Makololo were entirely callous to their sufferings, and indifferent to their fate. "Sekeletu robbed them of food, clothing and bedding, riding the while in Helmore's wagon which he had already appropriated. Yet this was the same chief who was still keeping Livingstone's wagon and stores guarded and intact, awaiting their owner's return."[25]

With reference to this wagon, in which Sekeletu had been living ever since in quarantine, Livingstone wrote afterwards in his *Narrative* that if Mr. Moffat (to whom he was writing) considered it to be the property of the orphan children, it ought to be paid for in ivory.

> This the chief readily agreed to; and had it been possible for one with the wisdom, experience, and conciliating manners of Mr. Moffat to have visited the Makololo, he would have found them easily influenced to fairness, and not at all the unreasonable savages they were represented to be.

This belated postscript does but reinforce Moffat's original contention (which he must have expressed to his son-in-law in Cape Town) that no mission, unattended by one or other of them, should ever have been sent.

In accepting without question the Makololo's version of this disaster Livingstone betrays an almost unbelievable credulity. It would appear in the first place that they told him nothing of the fate of any but the Helmores; and in the second, that Sekeletu had taken "most cordially." to Helmore and desired his residence among them. Writing to Tidman on 10 November from Chicova he says:

> On reaching the country of the Makololo in August last, I learned to my very great sorrow that our much esteemed and worthy friends, the Helmores, had been cut off by fever after a very short residence at Linyanti.
>
> Having been unexpectedly detained in the lower parts of this river until May last, my much longed for opportunity of visiting the upper portion was effected only by performing a march on foot of more than 600 miles, and then I was too late to render the aid which I had fondly hoped to afford. . . .
>
> From all I could learn the Makololo took most cordially to Mr. Helmore. They wished to become acquainted with him—a very natural desire—before removing to the Highlands, and hence the delay which ended so fatally. . . . He told the people subsequently to the death of his wife that nothing would prevent him from going and doing his duty whither he had been sent. . . .
>
> The Makololo are quite ready to move, they are perishing themselves, and should they not depart from these Lowlands soon they will break up as a tribe. . . .

To a letter so stilted and even heartless in its tone, so inadequate to deal with the poignancy of its theme, Tidman replied in his usual magniloquent style, pointing out that there was a discrepancy between the Makololo's account of the disaster and that since furnished by the survivors. According to the latter,

> Sekeletu positively refused to allow them to leave his place, or to point out any healthy locality where they might await your arrival. Their settling down therefore in this scene of death was a necessity forced upon them by the will of a despot. . . . The only way in which we can reconcile the statement of your informants with these facts, is by supposing that Sekeletu and his people . . . apprehensive of your resentment, should the truth become known to you, purposely misrepresented the case.[26]

Yet even when, more than a year later, the truth did become known to him, Livingstone could do no better than write thus to his brother-in-law—casting blame for the tragedy on everyone but himself:

> Mr. Farebrother [of the L.M.S.] goes about the country telling at public meetings that I am morally responsible for the loss of the missionaries at Linyanti. A friend of mine, present at one meeting, went and

asked Dr. Tidman why F. did so. "Oh, I am not accountable for what he says", was the reply.—"Why not write to Dr. L. to tell him beforehand of Helmore's movements?"—"I have no official (red tape) connection with Dr. L."—Helmore did not write to me even. I think they wanted to do it all themselves and have it to say that they did not require any aid from me. A precious mull they made of it.[27]

No comment on the fate of the Linyanti mission could be more unjust (to use no stronger word) than those last sentences.

Taking a supply of medicines from the wagon which, as he says, "had been lying only a hundred yards from the spot where the missionaries helplessly perished" Livingstone returned to Sesheke to find Sekeletu much improved both in health and spirits. Lord Clarendon's letter in the Queen's name was formally read and presented to him, and he and his councillors "expressed in a formal manner their great desire to have the English people settled in the Batoka highlands", and with it the wish that their next visit to the Makololo should be made there and not to Sesheke. In the event, however, the recurrence of Sekeletu's malady deferred and then prevented their removal, and three years later the Makololo were broken up and dispersed as a tribe, not from external attack but from internal dissension.

On 17 September Livingstone and his party began their return journey—by the southern route along the Zambesi (see map of first Great Journey)—with an escort led by Pitsane and Leshore to convoy them to Sinamane's village, where they could purchase canoes. Two others of the escort, Moloka and Ramakukanc, were instructed to go on as far as Tete and bring back medicines for Sekeletu. Their route now lay due east over very rough ground as close as possible to the Zambesi, and Livingstone, determined not to miss any important feature of the river this time, made a special detour to the Moamba (or Chimamba) Falls some twenty miles to the south. But after the Victoria Falls he was not impressed. "One Mosi-oa-tunya is quite enough for a continent." Progress along this rough hilly country was difficult and exhausting, and it was at this stage that Charles Livingstone, according to Kirk's diary, "began to get on even his hardened brother's nerves".

At the outset and at intervals throughout the journey, there were protracted and violent quarrels between them. The provocation was, as might be expected, one-sided. Kirk indeed was startled at the violence of the Rev. Charles's language and confesses that, out of charity, he would have liked to share the natives' opinion that he was mad. The worst scene occurred on the return journey when Charles lost his temper and kicked the headman of the Makololo escort provided by Sekeletu for the first stage. "Nothing but the natives' high personal regard for Dr. L. avoided bloodshed in that case. The spear was poised and needed only a stroke of the arm to send it to the heart. . . . For Dr. L.'s sake he held back." It was this incident that prompted David, who had already told his brother that the one mistake of the Expedition had been bringing him with it, to remind him of the accusations he had made against his fellow members. Not content, it appeared, with slandering Baines and Thornton—and possibly, Kirk thinks, himself as well—Charles had actually taunted his brother with allowing Rae to escape with a good character. "Although Dr. L.", Kirk reflects, "may know the truth of his brother's insinuations . . . still they have a powerful influence, as I have more than once observed. For Dr. L., so remarkable for individual power, is deficient in administrative talent". . . . "The character of the two brothers", he concludes, "is in no respect alike. Dr. L. is straight-forward, honest, rather shy—unless engaged in his great scheme for opening up Africa; Mr. C.L." . . . well, perhaps Kirk would have wished this frank opinion to remain buried in the diary.[28]

In view of this, it must have been with more than relief from mere physical exhaustion that Livingstone wrote, when they reached Sinamane's on 6 October: "Never was Sunday more welcome to the weary than this, the last we were to spend with our convoy." Here, according to his invariable rule, he con-ducted divine worship to which the chief—"the ablest and most energetic of the Batoka chiefs we have met"—listened respectfully; and the next chief on the route, Moemba, having heard of it requested that he and his people might be "Sun-dayed" too. Sinamane had sold the party two canoes and had lent three more, manned by his own paddlers, to convey them to Moemba's; but one of his men deserted and returned to him with a tale that the white men had stolen the canoes. There-upon Sinamane armed fifty of his "long spears" and came to Moemba's prepared to retake them by force. He saw at a glance that his man had deceived him, and all was well.

Moemba sold them another canoe and lent them his own two large ones, and in this manner they progressed downstream without incident to the Kariba Rapids. Here Livingstone landed "to have a look at them" first. The current was strong and the water broken here and there; a herd of hippopotami were swimming in the narrows; but the channel was nearly straight and had no cataract, "so we determined to risk it". They were however strongly advised to hire the river-doctor to pray for their safety "or we should all certainly be drowned". Declining this aid, they were followed by the priest and his friends, "who were rather surprised to see us pass down in safety, without the aid of his intercession".[29]

Lower down at the Karivua Rapids he took a more serious risk, attempting to "shoot" them without a previous survey. At once "huge jobbling waves" in mid-current began to fill the three canoes.

> With great presence of mind and without a moment's hesitation, two [Makololo] men lightened each [of two canoes] by jumping overboard; they then ordered a Batoka man to do the same, as "the white men must be saved". "I cannot swim," said the Batoka. "Jump out, then, and hold on to the canoe"; which he instantly did. Swimming alongside, they guided the swamping canoes down the swift current to the rapid, and then ran them ashore to bale them out.

But there was another and a worse rapid below, the current running at six knots. Before descending, the canoes were unloaded. But the stern of the last swung round in the current close to the shore, and all but one man in it leapt overboard for safety.

> He clung to the bow and was swept out into the middle of the stream. Having held on when he ought to have let go, he next put his life in jeopardy by letting go when he ought to have held on; and was in a few seconds swallowed up by a fearful whirlpool. His comrades launched out a canoe below, and caught him as he rose the third time to the surface, and saved him, though much exhausted and very cold.[30]

One would have thought that these experiences would have sufficed to cool Livingstone's ardour for shooting rapids; but when on 12 November they reached the Kebrabasa, by far the greatest and most dangerous of all, in order to save time and avoid the tedious land route and the impending threat of heavy rain he decided again on the canoes, and thereby nearly wrecked his entire company.

First, in crossing to the north bank to examine the position, one canoe was swept into the current; its native paddler leapt to a rock, but the canoe with all its cargo was carried away.

The cook's canoe was abandoned as unsafe and left to float down empty. Then Kirk and his crew (which was the best) led, and succeeded in clearing one dangerous promontory and were about to clear the next, when they saw Livingstone's canoe carried broadside-on towards an island-rock standing off the southern bank, and his brother's canoe making as if to run into it. "We lost a few strokes of the paddles whilst thus looking at the almost inevitable destruction of the others."

> The next thing I saw was the water rushing over our canoe. We were upset and all in the water. The others told me after that we struck with a loud crack. I heard nothing, the thing was instantaneous. Dr. L., occupied with his own danger still, heard the crash and looked up. The thing was over before he could direct his eyes and we were all in the water or clinging on. . . . The water boiled and rushed past, coming up in heavy masses at times and then subsiding. The men behaved admirably. The man at the stern got a hold of the rock; fortunately there was a slight slope where two could hold on. He held the canoe, which was pressed forcibly against the rock, from going down; sometimes it was sucked under. The man at the bow at once jumped into the river, his position was most dangerous, but he held on by the canoe.
>
> I found myself in the water with my body sucked under the canoe which was on its side. I managed to drag myself up and crawl along the canoe to the rock. Having ascertained that the bowman was all right we got a few bundles on the crevice of the rock. By this time Dr. L.'s canoe, which had escaped by a miracle, had come up after landing her goods. We passed what we could catch into her, but most of the things had gone. . . .[31]

Kirk's description of the catastrophe fills several pages of his diary, including a sketch; Livingstone disposes of it in a few sentences.

> . . . A loud crash burst on our ears. Dr. Kirk's canoe was dashed on a projection of the perpendicular rocks, by a sudden and mysterious boiling up of the river, which occurs at irregular intervals. Dr. Kirk was seen resisting the sucking-down action of the water, which must have been fifteen fathoms deep, and raising himself by his arms on to the ledge, while his steersman, holding on to the same rocks, saved the canoe; but nearly all its contents were swept away down the stream. Dr. Livingstone's canoe meanwhile, which had distracted the men's attention was saved by the cavity in the whirlpool filling up as the frightful eddy was reached. . . .[32]

Truly, those who would travel with Livingstone must expect not only hardships but hazards—to say nothing of losses. Kirk's included eight volumes of valuable botanical notes and some hundred drawings, besides his rifle, surgical case, revolver, bedding, clothes, and scientific books. He had saved almost all the Expedition's stores, but his personal possessions now amounted to the clothes which he wore, and they were in rags. But of all his African adventures (says Coupland) this was the one which he was fondest of narrating in after days. "For till the end of his life, when he was eighty-nine, he had never been so near death as that day, when he was only twenty-seven."

Perils by water now gave place to painful toil over hot rocks and burning sand; and the natives, though thoroughly terrified by the rapids, would fain have returned to them and carried the canoes past the most dangerous places and then launched them again. Two large parties of slave-gangs were met with on the way to Zumbo, leading Manganja women with ropes round their necks in one long chain.

There was an occasion recorded by Kirk only, when he and the Doctor, winding their way together through "these execrable rocks" found themselves at nightfall separated from "the others" who were far behind. They were without food and too exhausted to return. Awaking very hungry and faint, the Doctor proposed rejoining the others at a point lower down on the route and farther on, though this involved fording a minor river. They reached the river in the late afternoon of the following day after "a most tedious climb in fearful heat".

> I felt considerably refreshed by sucking the husk of the *motunda* fruit which someone had eaten before us. I went out to hunt but got nothing. On returning, found Dr. L. gone, and, hearing a shot on the other side, crossed to see if he had gone over in search of food. I found the whole party quietly camped some way off the river, but Dr. L. not there. I sent the men to call him. We were both faint in crossing the river. I did so with my stockings on. Dr. L., not doing so, fell from weakness and bruised himself. It seemed now that Mr. C.L., after wandering up to midday, came up to the party, breakfasted, lay for some hours, then took the men off up the hills. They heard our shots calling them, but took no notice.[33]

Kirk makes no further comment, and Livingstone none at all.

They struggled in to Tete on 23 November, within a week of the six months that Livingstone had estimated. It is little wonder that even Kirk felt that he had enough of the Expedition. "I have no desire to be any longer on it," he confided to his diary; and to Sir Roderick Murchison he wrote, "We have kept faith with the Makololo, though we have done nothing else."

The Expedition's "psychological barometer" (says Coupland) had fallen very low when its remnants tramped back into Tete; but there it rose fast and high. A despatch from Lord John Russell, "seen by Lord Palmerston and the Queen", contained great and good news. With no demur whatever it conceded Livingstone's request for a better steamship, and the *Pioneer* was already on the way out. The importance of his discovery of Nyasaland was fully recognized, and his idea of exploring an alternative route to the Lake by the River Rovuma, so as to avoid the approach through Portuguese territory, was warmly approved. Best of all, a well-equipped party from the Universities' Mission with a bishop at its head was coming, with orders to establish a permanent settlement and centre, on Livingstone's advice, in the Shire highlands. ("And all I did to secure this," said Livingstone, "was to make a speech.") He now definitely asked Kirk to stay on. "Dr. L. desires me to remain," says Kirk. "I had intended going home, but at once agreed to stop." But a little later: "Dr. L. seems to intend sending me up the Shire to Nyasa overland, while he will go from the Rovuma and join me in the interior." Then: "I trust that, if I am sent on the overland trip, I may not have C. L. for a companion." On this the Doctor as usual kept his own counsel, but "an accidental word" confirmed Kirk's anxious suspicions. These were heightened by another "outbreak" on the part of Mr. C. L. He had been seen by the native porters to kick a representative of their chief, and here Kirk's diary "boils over". "The Commander should keep him by himself, for he is utterly unsafe . . . I shall wish I had kept my former designs and gone home."[34]

But his personal anxieties were allayed temporarily by a more immediate worry. Contrary to everyone's expectations the *Ma-Robert* had been held together by the attentions of the two sturdy seamen, Rowe and Hutchins, and it was decided to take her as well as the worm-eaten pinnace down the river as far as either could go, "intending to stick to that which swam longest". Leaving Tete on 3 December they kept afloat by dint of plugging the leaks of the *Ma-Robert* continually till on the 21st they grounded on a bank, with the store-rooms full of water and everything in the cabin awash. They worked for two hours, wet to the waist, to get their effects ashore and soon (says Kirk) "the whole vessel went down, showing only the port gunwale, masts, funnel, and upper part of the house above water". He was sent off in a canoe to Sena and the hospitable Senhor Ferrao provided two more. The river rose during the night; the sand-bank on which they had camped was covered; and on the 23rd the masts, funnel, and top of the house were "all that is visible of the infernal ship". On Christmas Eve they spent a damp night in a miserable native hut, and there for several nights there was "no sleep going . . . mosquitoes in thousands". But the New Year found them more comfortably housed in Sena, preparing for the journey to the sea.[35]

A new chapter was about to open in the fortunes of the Expedition.

Chapter Twenty-One

ZAMBESI EXPEDITION: MAGOMERO
1861–1862

*" The awful sacrifice of human life that must be attributed to
this trade of hell."*

CHARLES FREDERICK MACKENSIE, born in 1825 and
brought up in Edinburgh, after a brilliant career as a
student and Fellow of Cambridge, went out as a missionary to the Zulus in Natal and was appointed Archdeacon of that
Diocese by the Bishop of Cape Town (Gray) while still in his
twenties. His *Memoir* written by Dr. Harvey Goodwin, then
Dean of Ely, is a fitting tribute to a noble Christian soul—
gentle, brave, just, and compassionate.

On 1 November 1859 when on a visit home he attended the
"Great Zambesi Meeting" to sponsor Livingstone's undertaking, held in the Senate House in Cambridge. Among the
speakers were the Bishop of Oxford (Wilberforce), Mr. Glad-
stone, Mr. Walpole, and Sir George Grey of Cape Town. He
was asked to preach in Great St. Mary's the same day, but at
the meeting itself he was only a listener and spectator with
some of his friends in the gallery. To one of them he remarked:
"I am afraid of this; most great works of this kind have been
carried on by one or two men in a quieter way, and have had
a more humble beginning." That sentiment would have been
echoed and applauded by Livingstone.

The next day a Conference of the Committee of the Universities' Mission met, at which the Bishop of Oxford presided,
to decide upon measures to establish one or more Stations in
South Central Africa "which may serve as centres of Christianity and civilization, for the promotion of true religion,
agriculture, and lawful commerce, with the ultimate extirpa-
tion of the slave-trade". It is to be noted, first, that the
phrasing of the resolution is virtually Livingstone's, and
secondly, that no ecclesiastical preference is mentioned. As

soon as funds permitted, a body of men was to be sent out, including six clergymen with a bishop at their head, a doctor, artificers in building, experts in husbandry and especially the cultivation of cotton. And finally it was resolved that the Ven. Archdeacon Mackensie be invited to head the Mission, and that the invitation be conveyed to him by the Bishop of Oxford.

Mackensie, believing this to be a call from God, accepted it without hesitation, though with no notion as yet where he was to go. "I suppose it would be where Livingstone first struck the river at Linyanti, but it might not. I fancy our first object would be to find Livingstone, and get his advice." The next year, 1860, was filled with preparations; at the end of it he sailed for the Cape with the first contingent: two clergymen, H. C. Scudamore and L. J. Procter; another not yet ordained, namely Horace Waller; a carpenter and an agricultural labourer. On New Year's Day 1861 he was consecrated in Cape Town as the first Missionary Bishop of the Church of England at the age of thirty-six.[1]

He had been deeply impressed by a letter he had received from Livingstone on the way out. "How excellent," he wrote home, "his way of offering assistance, not as if he were indispensable, but might certainly be of *some* use. This is the way real strength and real knowledge always speaks."[2] Livingstone was at the mouth of the Kongone to meet him on 7 February: "It was a puzzle," he wrote, "to know what to do with so many men." But he and Mackensie took a liking to one another at once, and this despite an immediate disagreement. The young eager-hearted bishop, full of zeal and thirsting for work, wished to get his party on the march and establish the settlement without delay. The *Pioneer* could carry him and his party up the Shire to Chibisa's and leave them there, while Livingstone, who was under orders to explore the Rovuma, could join them there from the north via the Lake. "But there were grave objections to this." Chibisa had removed from his old village to near Tete, and there was no other chief in the Shire country to whose good offices they could safely be entrusted. The Mission would be left without a doctor in an unhealthy region at the beginning of the sickly season of the year. Livingstone says that he "dreaded a repetition of the sorrowful fate which befell the similar non-medical Mission at Linyanti." He proposed instead that Mackensie and one of his staff should join him and Kirk and his brother in exploring the Rovuma, while the rest of the Mission party landed at Johanna, one of the Comoro group of islands between the northern end of Madagascar and the mainland, which was a British naval base.

In the end, but only after long argument, Mackensie yielded. "During the discussion Livingstone continued as friendly and kind as possible, and was most willing to help in carrying out the plan we had thought of, if decided upon. He is an excellent fellow, and I have no fear of any difficulty at any time arising between us."[3] Livingstone further promised that the Rovuma expedition would not delay the settlement of the Mission for more than three months. It proved however abortive on account of the depth in draught of the *Pioneer*. When only thirty miles upstream the river-level suddenly fell and, though Livingstone if alone would have pushed on to the Lake in canoes or afoot, he dared not subject the Mission party to such a venture. He decided therefore to postpone this exploration till next winter and return without delay. Even so it was only by dint of much exertion, to which Livingstone and Kirk were well accustomed, that they got the vessel to the sea in time. "Got immediately aground," says Kirk one day, "getting off only at sunset after much work in which the Bishop, who is a trump of a fellow, distinguished himself."[4]

At the mouth of the Rovuma all the Mission party and crew were laid low with fever, and Livingstone navigated the vessel for the first time across the sea, touching first at Mohilla in the Comoro group, whose mixed inhabitants were Moslems. There is a sentence, quietly and unobtrusively intruded into his *Narrative* at this point, which shows the extent of his liberalism and will come as a shock to the orthodox: "They have mosques and schools, in which we were pleased to see girls as well as boys taught to read the Koran."[5] At Johanna the whole party "benefited by the unbounded hospitality and attention of Mr. Sunley, the British Consul". On 1 May they were again off the Kongone and soon were steaming up the Shire. Mackensie wrote home:

It is very pleasant being on the easy terms we are with Livingstone; and as for Dr. Kirk, we are the greatest possible cronies. . . . . Livingstone is most kind and excellent. He promises to make a tour with us, as soon as we leave the ship, to look out for a site.[6]

"He and the Bishop," wrote Bishop Gray, "get on famously together. The Bishop says they chaff each other all day like two school-boys." But the toil of getting the *Pioneer* up the shallows was severe.

It caused us a great deal of hard and vexatious work, in laying out anchors, and toiling at the capstan to get her off sandbanks. We should not have minded this much, but for the heavy loss of time which might have been more profiably, and infinitely more pleasantly, spent in intercourse with the people. Once we were a fortnight on a bank of soft, yielding sand. . . . In hauling the *Pioneer* over the shallow places, the Bishop, with Horace Waller and Mr. Scudamore, were ever ready and anxious to lend a hand, and worked as hard as any on board.[7]

Only privately to his brother-in-law J. S. Moffat does he enter a qualification. "The bishop is the best of the lot." But later: "The bishop is a very good man but lacking in decision of character."

These arduous days were nevertheless the brightest in the whole story of the Expedition. Livingstone's admiration and genuine affection for Mackensie grew, and not only for him but for his staff. "The missionaries," he wrote to Maclear, "seem a capital lot and very well adapted for their undertaking. The bishop is A.1., and in his readiness to put his hand to anything resembles much my good father-in-law Moffat."[8] Kirk was still his right-hand man. Even his brother was showing signs of usefulness. He had on their former entrance among the tribes on the Shire "very zealously" induced them to take up cotton for cultivation, and his efforts now were meeting with "very gratifying success". Two new species of excellent cotton had been introduced and were being distributed in an area 400 miles in length—"much larger than the cotton-fields of South America." The great want was for Christian agents such as abounded in Sierra Leone and the West Coast generally "where the conduct of England of late years deserves the world's admiration. Her generosity will appear grand in the eyes of posterity".[9]

At long last on 8 July the *Pioneer* cast anchor off Chibisa's village and the party proceeded on foot, and the cheerful young bishop brimming with enthusiasm wrote home:

You would like to see our picturesque appearance on march. Livingstone in his jacket and trousers of blue serge and his blue cloth cap. His
brother, a taller man, in something of the same dress. I with trousers of
Oxford grey and a coat like a shooting-coat, a broad-brimmed wide-
awake with white cover, which Livingstone laughs at, but which all the
same keeps the sun off. *He* is a Salamander. . . .

We were a strange party; Livingstone tramping along with a steady,
heavy tread which kept one in mind that he had walked across Africa.
. . . I had myself in my left hand a loaded gun, in my right the crozier
which they gave me in Cape Town; in front a can of oil, and behind a
bag of seeds. . . .[10]

And yet it was precisely at this stage when their prospects
seemed fairest that Livingstone, looking back afterwards, saw
the turning of the tide and with it the reappearance of the
spectre that was to haunt him and dog his footsteps to the end.
After summarizing the gains of the Expedition hitherto and its
hopeful prospects his *Narrative* strikes a sombre note: "We had
however, as will afterwards be seen, arrived at the turning-
point of our prosperous career, and soon came into contact
with the Portuguese slave-trade."

Arrived at Chibisa's old village on 15 July he was told that
there was war between the fierce Ajawa (Yao) in the district
of Lake Shirwa and the Manganja near Mount Zomba, whom
the former were raiding for slaves; and a number of refugees
from the latter confirmed this. The next day, while resting at
Mbame's (Livingstone being unwell), it was reported that a
large slave-gang was about to pass through his village for sale
to the Portuguese in Tete. "'Shall we interfere?' we inquired
of each other." Livingstone reminded his party that all their
valuable baggage as well as some Government property was in
Tete, and that if they freed the slaves it might be destroyed in
retaliation. On the other hand:

This system of slave-hunters dogging us where previously they durst
not venture, and on pretence of being our "children", setting one tribe
against another, would so inevitably thwart all our efforts, for which we
had the sanction of the Portuguese Government, that we resolved to run
all risks and put a stop, if possible, to the slave-trade which had now
followed on the footsteps of our discoveries.

It was a momentous decision, but one with which all his
party unanimously concurred. They had not long to wait
before putting it to the test. Mackensie with Procter and

Scudamore had meanwhile gone down to a stream to bathe: they heard "a sound of penny trumpets and thought Livingstone had been giving away presents". The actual occurrence is among the most dramatic episodes in the *Narrative*.

> A few minutes after Mbame had spoken to us, the slave party, a long line of manacled men, women and children, came wending their way round the hill and into the valley, on the side of which the village stood. The black drivers, armed with muskets and bedecked with various articles of finery, marched jauntily in the front, middle, and rear of the line; some of them blowing exultant notes out of long tin horns. They seemed to feel that they were doing a very noble thing, and might proudly march with an air of triumph. But the instant the fellows caught a glimpse of the English, they darted off like mad into the forest; so fast indeed, that we caught but a glimpse of their red caps and the soles of their feet. The chief of the party alone remained; and he, from being in front, had his hand tightly grasped by a Makololo.
>
> . . . Knives were soon busy at work cutting the women and children loose. It was more difficult to cut the men adrift, as each had his neck in the fork of a stout stick, six or seven feet long, and kept in by an iron rod which was rivetted at both ends across the throat. With a saw, luckily in the Bishop's baggage, one by one the men were sawn out into freedom. The women, on being told to take the meal they were carrying and cook breakfast for themselves and the children, seemed to consider the news too good to be true; but after a little coaxing went at it with alacrity, and made a capital fire with which to boil their pots with the slave sticks and bonds, their old acquaintances through many a sad night and weary day.

The leader of the gang himself proved to be a former slave of Major Sicard, and for some time Livingstone's own attendant at Tete. While being interrogated "he bolted too". The freed slaves numbered 84, of whom four only had been bought, the rest captured in war. They told their rescuers of horrible atrocities committed on the march. Two women had been shot the previous day for attempting to untie their thongs. One had her infant's brains knocked out, because she could not carry her load and it. A man was despatched with an axe, because he had broken down with fatigue. Self-interest, Livingstone reflected, would have prompted care of their captives rather than murder; "but in this traffic we invariably find self-interest overcome by contempt of human life and by bloodthirstiness". The majority of the captives were women and children; and when all were told that they were free to go or stay, all chose to stay.[11] Among the liberated was a boy named Chuma, and another named Wikatani, both of the Waiyau (Yao) tribe.

When Mackensie returned to the scene a few minutes later it was to find himself presented with a ready-made nucleus for his prospective flock, and he at once, says Livingstone, "wisely attached them to his Mission, to be educated as members of a Christian family", adding that years are usually required for natives to gain the confidence of strangers. Mackensie's approval of what had been done was unhesitating and whole-hearted:

> There had been five or ten minutes' notice of their approach, so that Livingstone had time deliberately to take his course—a course which no one can blame; but surely all will join in blessing God that we have such a fellow-countryman.

And later:

> Livingstone is right to go with loaded gun and free the poor slaves; and we are right, though clergymen and preachers of the Gospel to go with him, and by our presence, and the sight of our guns, and their use if necessary (which may God avert), to strengthen his hands in procuring the liberation of these people. . . . I believe some will blame Livingstone, and more will blame me, but I can only act as I think right. . . .[12]

Next day they went on to Soche's, the liberated men gladly carrying the bishop's goods, and eight more slaves were freed in a hamlet on the way; but a party in charge of some hundred more had already fled. Kirk and four Makololo went off hot-foot in pursuit and spent some days patrolling the river beyond Chibisa's, only to find that by this time the villagers themselves were intimidated and implicated, and some were even hiding the gang till he had passed. Meanwhile Livingstone and Mackensie had freed six more victims on the route and detained two of their guard: "it was of no use to do things by halves". In another village they freed fifty more from a gang whose headman Livingstone recognized as the agent of a merchant in Tete, and who said that he had the Government's licence for all he did. "This we were fully aware of without his stating it."

The question of a site for the Mission had now to be settled, and while they were discussing it a young chief named Chigunda, son of Chiwawa—"the most manly and generous Manganja chief we had met with on our previous journey", who had recently died—came forward with the request that the bishop should live with him at Magomero (some twenty miles west of the south end of Lake Shirwa, and near to the present town of Zomba). "All the chiefs around have fled before the Ajawa," he said. "I only remain; and I will not run away if the English will stay with me." "But," said Livingstone, "there are so many people, and there may be more; and they will want gardens." Chigunda said, "There is plenty of room for them here." The points for and against this proposal were debated very carefully. A situation nearer the Shire would have been preferred, but the Portuguese, though never occupying even its mouth, had now closed it, as well as the Zambesi. There were other objections: it was only 1,000 feet above the sea. At last Livingstone said to the bishop: "If you fall back to Mount Soche, all this densely populated country will go before the Ajawas; if you take your stand here it will be saved." But he thought it advisable first to visit the Ajawa chief and attempt to establish peaceful relationships. They had not long to wait.

Hearing early on 22 July that a raiding party of Ajawa was near they set off with a following of Manganja for a parley, Livingstone as usual unarmed. (On the very day before this he had noted in his Journal: "Very severe attack of haemorrhoids.") The grim tokens of recent ravage were apparent everywhere: burnt villages, devastated crops, destitute fugitives.

> About two o'clock we saw the smoke of burning villages and heard triumphant shouts, mingled with the wail of the Manganja women, lamenting over their slain. The Bishop then engaged us in fervent prayer; and on rising from our knees we saw a long line of Ajawa warriors, with their captives, coming round the hill-side. . . . The Ajawa headman left the path on seeing us, and stood on an ant-hill to obtain a complete view of our party.

Livingstone called out that they had come for an interview only, but at that critical moment the Manganja followers raised defiant shouts which were correctly understood by their adversaries as a challenge, "but they did not strike us at the moment as neutralizing all our assertions of peace".

> The captives threw down their loads and fled; and a large body of armed men came running up from the village, and in a few seconds

they were all around us, though mostly concealed by the projecting rocks and long grass. In vain we protested that we had not come to fight, but to talk with them. They would not listen [but] . . . flushed with recent victory over three villages, and confident of an easy triumph over a mere handful of men, they began to shoot their poisoned arrows, sending them with great force upwards of a hundred yards, and wounding one of our followers through the arm. Our retiring slowly up the ascent from the village only made them more eager to prevent our escape; and in the belief that this retreat was evidence of fear, they closed upon us in bloodthirsty fury. Some came within fifty yards, dancing hideously; others having quite surrounded us, and availing themselves of the rocks and long grass hard by, were intent on cutting us off, while others made off with their women and a large body of slaves. Four were armed with muskets, and we were obliged in self-defence to return their fire and drive them off. When they saw the range of the rifles they very soon desisted, and ran away; but some shouted to us from the hills the consoling intimation, that they would follow and kill us where we slept.

Mackensie's account of the affair is substantially the same as Livingstone's, though he adds: "I had a gun in my hand, but seeing Livingstone without one I asked him to use mine rather than that I should." And Livingstone has one addendum to make, too trivial for insertion in his *Narrative*, but communicated to his son Robert as an item of news that would interest a growing lad. "They rushed at us and shot their poisoned arrows. One fell between the Bishop and me, and another whizzed between another man and me." He concludes his published account with a typical understatement: "We returned to the village which we had left in the morning, after a hungry, fatiguing, and most unpleasant day."

It does not appear that there were any serious casualties on either side in this affray, but it raised very serious consequences. Livingstone, though (as has been seen) in principle strongly anti-pacifist, had invariably in practice behaved as if he were a pacifist; though he firmly believed in a display of force to prevent bloodshed, he had never used it in self-defence; and to this principle and to this practice he consistently adhered. This was the first time in all his experience, as he sadly remarks, that he had ever been attacked by natives or come into collision with them; "though we had always taken it for granted that we might be called upon to act in self-defence". But hitherto, sometimes at the risk of his life in his first great journey, he had avoided this. Mackensie, after earnest thought and discussion

on the matter both at Cape Town and in the field, had independently adopted the same view. "I still think," he had
written, only two days before, "that if by any possibility the
people of this land should attack us, to drive us away or to rob
us, we ought not to kill our own sheep." But now a very different
casus belli had arisen: was it ethically right, was it Christianly
lawful to fight—not in self-defence—but to rescue and liberate
the prisoners from their inhuman captors? In the solution of
this difficult problem the zealous enthusiasm of youth was
countered by the sober judgment and moderation of the man
of much experience.

> The Bishop feeling, as most Englishmen would, the prospect of the
> people now in his charge being swept off into slavery by hordes of men-
> stealers, proposed to go at once to the rescue of the captive Manganja,
> and drive the marauding Ajawa out of the country. All were warmly in
> favour of this, save Dr. Livingstone, who opposed it on the ground that
> it would be better for the Bishop to wait and see the effect of the check
> the slave-hunters had just experienced.

Kirk was not present during this discussion, not having yet
returned from his pursuit of the other slave-gang; but it is
probable that, though loth to disagree with his leader, he would
at first have sided with the majority, since he had written on the
march: "This must be stopped; they must be driven out of the
whole country." Mackensie saw at once the soundness of
Livingstone's arguments against precipitate action, but he had
yet another question to propound.

> On the Bishop enquiring whether, in the event of the Manganja
> again asking aid against the Ajawa, it would be his duty to accede to
> their request: "No," replied Dr. Livingstone, "you will be oppressed
> by their importunities, but do not interfere in native quarrels." This
> advice the good man honourably mentions in his journal.[13]

There was, as will be seen, good reason for this last sentence.
Mackensie's disregard of this wise counsel—though Livingstone
himself was the first to acquit him of all blame—resulted in
disaster to the Mission and in the calumnious assertion of his
successor that "the warlike measures of the Mission were
the consequences of following Dr. Livingstone's advice".

In these circumstances then on 29 July, Livingstone, once
more accompanied by his brother (whom even Mackensie with

his sunny nature had tried to like but failed) and twenty
Makololo carriers, left the Mission party for further exploration
of Lake Nyasa and its possibilities for Christian settlement. He
left them with a large nucleus of prospective native converts, a
capable and energetic administrator, in a peaceful and pleasant
situation and brilliant weather. At Chibisa's he picked up Kirk.
"Never," wrote Kirk, "had a mission a better start." But why,
he asked at this point, was there no doctor on the Mission
staff? An answer may be that Dr. Meller, the medical officer
of the *Pioneer* who accompanied the trio on the first stage of
their journey for some reason not stated, returned to Magomero, and that John Dickinson, the doctor appointed for the
Mission, was expected to arrive by the next contingent.
Further, Horace Waller had himself a good knowledge of
surgery. In default of other information on the point this
explanation, even though inadequate, is suggested.

Livingstone's own impressions of the Mission staff (derived
from his Journal of 10 August and a letter of later date to
J. S. Moffat) reflect the indulgent attitude of a man for whom
ecclesiastical and doctrinal professions are nothing and practical
performance everything:

> The mission is happy in having various temperaments associated
> together. The Bishop is High Church and a strict disciplinarian in theory,
> but liberal and very lax in his control in practice. Waller, the lay mem-
> ber, very careful and somewhat anxious, does not believe in Apostolic
> Succession, Baptismal Regeneration, or any of the High Church tenets;
> argues briskly against them. Procter and Scudamore tend that way
> (High), if any way at all, while parson Rowley is red-hot high church.
> Scudamore and the Bishop work; Rowley writes to fill his purse with the
> fruits of his imagination. . . . They are on the whole a very happily
> constituted family. I think that active labour will work out the High
> Church bigotry which can flourish only in solitude.[14]

At Chibisa's on 6 August Livingstone took from the *Pioneer* a
light four-oared gig and an experienced Irish seaman named
John Neil, and was able without difficulty to hire carriers for
the gig up the Murchison Cataracts from one stage to the next.
He found the drop to be 1,200 feet in forty miles. Within three
weeks they were surmounted and the gig launched on the
upper Shire. The Makololo carriers progressing on foot along
the western shore passed thousands of Manganja who had fled

from the marauding Ajawa. On entering the little Lake Pamalombe (i.e. Malombe) fringed with a dense belt of very tall
papyrus, they could scarcely find an opening to the shore.
"The plants, ten or twelve feet high, grew so closely together
that air was excluded, and so much sulphuretted hydrogen gas
evolved that by one night's exposure the bottom of the boat
was blackened." And here Livingstone lets fall an observation
which is probably the first of its kind ever made. "Myriads of
mosquitoes showed, as they probably always do, the presence
of malaria." But not even he could relate them as cause and
effect.

The land party having been threatened more than once by
the demoralized lake-dwellers, Livingstone went with them on
shore and so continued till on 2 September the gig entered Lake
Nyasa. Pulling along the western shore he took frequent sights
and careful soundings, and named the grand mountain promontory, where he could get no bottom with a lead-line of
35 fathoms, after Maclear. The season was the stormiest in the
year; once they were forced to ride out a sudden southerly gale
for six hours, anchored a mile from shore in seven fathoms.

The waves most dreaded came rolling on in threes, with their crests
driven into spray streaming behind them. A short lull followed each
triple charge. Had one of these white-maned seas struck our frail bark,
nothing could have saved us; for they came on with resistless force;
seaward, inshore, and on either side of us they broke in foam, but we
escaped. For six weary hours we faced those terrible trios, any one of
which might have been carrying the end of our Expedition in its hoary
head. . . . Our black crew became sea-sick and unable to sit up or keep
the boat's head out to the sea. The natives and our land-party stood on
the high cliffs looking at us and exclaiming, as the waves seemed to
swallow up the boat, "They are lost! They are all dead!" When at last
the gale moderated and we got safely ashore, they saluted us warmly,
as after a long absence.[15]

Livingstone acknowledges his debt to the Irish seaman on
such occasions, to whom he now trusted implicitly, and by
whose advice "we often sat cowering on the land for days
together waiting for the surf to go down".

In all his travels he had never seen so dense a population as
on the shores of Lake Nyasa. The natives were at first suspicious
but their curiosity overcame their instinct to be unfriendly.
To them the white men were *chirombo* (wild animals), "but

395

they good-naturedly kept to a line we made on the sand and left us room to dine. Twice they went the length of lifting up the edge of our sail, which we used as a tent, as boys do the curtains of travelling menageries at home". Even more embarrassing was their interest in the white men's ablutions.

They often had to refrain from a proper bath and merely soap the head and upper part of the body because of the crowd of spectators. When his grandson, Dr. Hubert Wilson, was on that coast some fifty years later, he met an old man who had seen Livingstone. His most vivid memory of him was when, with another ten-year-old urchin, he had crept into the reeds to see whether the white man disappeared into the lake whence he had come, as was commonly believed. He did not do that, but he petrified the small boys by "taking something in his hand, dipping it into the water, and rubbing his head till his brains came out!"[16]

Kirk notes in his diary: "Dr. L.'s modesty has driven him to wash in secret." It is a trait worthy of notice in his character that, doctor as he was and "rough tyke" that he considered himself to be, Livingstone had an aversion both to himself appearing naked and to beholding nudity in others. It seemed to him "unnatural", and a thing to be corrected if possible, wherever he found it. Writing to his friend Young from the country of the Baenda Pezi (Go-Nakeds) above the Kariba Rapids on his previous journey, for example, he writes: "Here we are among a people who go stark naked with no more sense of shame than we have with our clothes on . . . They are very hospitable and appreciate our motives; but shame has been unaccountably left out of the question. Can you explain why Adam's first feeling has no trace of existence in his offspring?" Similarly he could never accustom himself to the hideous disfigurement of the filing of the teeth to a point, or to the lip-ring (*pelele*) worn by the women. As to his sensitivity in exposing himself to the curious gaze of the natives, he quaintly apologizes for it thus: "One feels ashamed of the white skin; it seems unnatural, like blanched celery—or white mice." (The present writer, once asking a trusted and intelligent native of Lundazi to say quite frankly how he and his kind appeared in their eyes, or of what object they most reminded him—was answered without hesitation but quite respectfully: "You seem to us, bwana, to resemble peeled bananas.")

By Chitanda's on 16 September, they were robbed in their

sleep of nearly everything they possessed—with the fortunate exception of guns and ammunition, aneroid barometer, and their roll of calico for barter, which Kirk was using as a pillow. "The boat's sail, under which we slept, was open all round, so the feat was easy." They awoke in the morning to find themselves bereft by "these light-handed gentry" of all garments save those which they had slept in—day-clothes of course. "We could not suspect the people of the village," says Livingstone; his suspicions fell on some who had come from the East Coast, but having no evidence "we made no fuss about it, and began to make new clothing". His brother suggested turning back as they were now "destitute", but no notice was taken of this (*Journal* only).

His excursions ashore gave Livingstone the opportunity of filling his note-book with records of various phenomena, natural and human; but it is geography and hydrology that claim his attention most on this journey. It was the season of grass-fires ("smokes") and these sometimes obscured the coast-line of the opposite shore and more than once he mistook another kind of "cloud" for them. This was composed of minute but living particles.

> We sailed through one of these clouds on our side, and discovered that it was neither smoke nor haze, but countless millions of minute midges called *nkungu* (cloud or fog). They filled the air to an immense height, and swarmed upon the water, too light to sink into it. Eyes and mouth had to be kept closed while passing through this living cloud: they struck upon the face like fine drifting snow.

Professor Debenham says that he might have added "the nose also". On Victoria Nyanza the corpses of fishermen had to his own knowledge been found, having been "choked to death by clotted masses of the flies in their noses and mouths". Livingstone continues:

> The people gather these minute insects by night, and boil them into thick cakes to be used as a relish—millions of midges in a cake. One, an inch thick and as large as the blue bonnet of a Scotch ploughman, was offered to us; it was very dark in colour and tasted not unlike caviare, or salted locusts.

The boat journey was no picnic; there was no awning in the open gig. "The sun is now getting to its strength," wrote

Kirk. "It pierces through clothes and makes pains in the joints. Dr. L. is proof against anything and, so long as the boat goes towards the end of the lake, little short of a tempest would discompose him."[17]

The farther northward they progressed the more lawlessness and bloodshed they encountered. The lakeside villages had been despoiled by a recent raid by the Mazitu (i.e. Angoni), and beyond Mankambiri's village the Makololo carriers were afraid to go. Even Kirk now suggested that they should go no further without first securing the alliance of a Mazitu chief. And Charles again proposed turning back, as they were risking the lives of the Makololo by going on. Livingstone remarks merely, "It is evident that personal fears are at work."

Having directed the boat-party to meet him in a bay which was in sight, he again accompanied the Makololo on foot. Two days later he suddenly encountered seven Mazitu armed with spears and shields, their heads fantastically dressed with feathers. Unarmed as usual he went on deliberately to meet them, with Maloka alone, a Makololo who spoke Zulu.

> On Dr. Livingstone approaching them, they ordered him to stop and sit down in the sun, while they sat in the shade. "No, no!" was the reply; "if you sit in the shade, so will we." They then rattled their shields with their clubs, a proceeding which usually inspires terror; but Maloka remarked, "It is not the first time we have heard shields rattled." And all sat down together.

They demanded a present; Livingstone requested them to take him to their chief. He emptied his pockets to show that he had nothing. "The younger men then became boisterous and demanded a goat." This he refused as he had no other provisions, and quietly asked them how many people they had killed that day. "This evidently made them ashamed . . . for on leaving they sped away up the hills like frightened deer."[18] As Debenham observes, the *Narrative* deliberately understates the dangers during those four days of separation; and the notebook merely says, "Cow-itch [the buffalo bean] very annoying" and then, "Met some Mazitu who seemed much afraid but demanded a goat." Was it, asks Debenham, that there was something magnetic in his personality? Or was it that these savage men detected in his clear gaze an utter absence of enmity, yet guessed from his firm chin that provocation could reach a limit?[19]

The boat-party, tempested by storms and with Kirk and the seaman prostrated by fever, had overshot its mark; and for four days Livingstone was "lost". He spent them with little food, fireless nights, and a huddle of terrified natives. Kirk saw that the mountainous coast precluded any descent to the bay he had appointed for their rendezvous. In great anxiety they beat back, and on 6 October found him (with only two Makololo, the rest having fled) in a canoe in the bay. He had reached it after what he called "an excessively tedious and fatiguing march". The studied mildness of his salutation was typical: "What on earth made you run away and leave us?"[20]

By his sight of the mountain masses closing in on both sides of the Lake to the north, Livingstone assumed that they must be near the end of it; and so did Kirk: in fact, they had traversed about five-sevenths of its length. But now shortage of provisions compelled their return; they recorded their last latitudes and put about for "home". It was with a sense of frustration, even of defeat, that they turned back. They had failed not only to survey the whole Lake, but also to find any place on its shores suitable for European settlement. They had missed by only a few hours an Arab *dhow* transporting slaves across it; they had done nothing to save that teeming population from its twofold scourge: northwards the Mazitu, southwards the slave-trade. They could not guess how much, how very much, they had accomplished. For, as Coupland says:

> Within thirty years that coast was to be dotted with the stations of a British Company, trading up and down the Lake "with a steamer on the water", and dotted also with the stations of British missions. And today, on the mountain plateau, about forty miles beyond the point Kirk's little boat had reached, stands the great church of Livingstonia, its lofty tower visible far up and down the Lake, an eternal monument to the faith and works of the man whose name it honours.[21]

And Debenham: "Livingstone does not, either in the *Narrative* or in the private Journal, review the results of the trip, which were immense from a geographical point of view." He does so, however, in a private letter to Sir Roderick Murchison, dated 23 September.

One other fact is worthy of record. The present writer has found among the same papers a scrap of writing, undated and detached, which would seem to entitle Livingstone and Kirk to be called the first, though unwitting, discoverers of the existence of a Great Rift Valley in the earth's crust extending from Palestine through the Red Sea to Lake Nyasa. It reads as follows:

> The birds and animals, shells and fishes collected exhibit many interesting peculiarities. The shells and fishes, for instance, on Lake Nyasa are nearly all new and, taken in connection with those lately brought to me from the Sea of Galilee, lead to the inference that a chain of lakes once existed from Palestine to South Africa.[22]

The return journey was uneventful but both physically and morally exacting; and Kirk, who had once more had his fill of the Expedition, wrote:

> Sitting in the stern of that boat, exposed all day to the sun, has made an impression not easily forgotten. . . . When we land it is to sleep among the reeds or on the sand, frequently with a marsh close to us. . . . The inactivity and pains in the bones and joints from the sun, the gradual emaciation, the fevers and the starvation of that Nyasa journey combine to make it the hardest, most trying, and most disagreeable of all our journeys. It is the only one I have no pleasure in looking back on.[23]

Even Livingstone says: "We reached the ship on the 8th of November in a very weak condition, having suffered more from hunger than on any previous trip." His brother is not mentioned nor is there any record of his feelings; but there must have been some stuff in the younger Livingstone after all to have weathered such an experience.

It was, however, not their own privations, but the pitiable plight of the Nyasa natives that seared the heart and mind and soul of Livingstone as never before. From this time dates his correspondence with Colonel (later Major-General) C. P. Rigby, lately H.M. Consul of Zanzibar, who, according to both Kirk and Waller, did more for the suppression of the slave-trade than any man of his generation.* In a letter describing

*The biography of this remarkable man by his daughter Lilian (the late Mrs. C. E. B. Russell) has not received the recognition which it deserves. It is an indispensable work for any who would study the slave-trade in relation to European, Asiatic, and American policies in the mid-nineteenth century. Rigby was also entrusted by the R.G.S. with the task of conveying Livingstone's body from Southampton to Westminster Abbey in 1874. It

his first visit to the Manganja country two years before, Livingstone had said that the whole population was engaged in the cultivation and working up of cotton, and that he had never seen such wonderful cotton country or such fertile land in his life. But now he found this same country depopulated and the huts full of dead bodies. Where in 1859 there had been villages every two miles or less, there was now a tract of 120 miles devoid of any human being.[24] His *Narrative* on his return journey has little space for observations other than those concerning what he calls "this trade of hell".

> Would that we could give a comprehensive account of the horrors of the Slave Trade with an approximation to the number of lives it yearly destroys! For we feel sure that were even half the truth told and recognized, the feelings of men would be so thoroughly roused that this devilish traffic in human flesh would be put down at all risks, but neither we, nor anyone else, have the statistics necessary for a work of this kind. Let us state what we know of one portion of Africa, then every reader who believes our tale can apply the ratio of the known misery to find out the unknown. We were informed by Colonel Rigby . . . that 19,000 slaves from this Nyasa country alone pass annually through the Custom House of Zanzibar. This is exclusive of course of these sent to Portuguese slave-ports. Let it not be supposed for an instant that this number represents all the victims. [Rigby himself added another 5,000 slaves imported annually by relatives of the Sultan free of tax.] . . . Besides those actually captured, thousands are killed and die of their wounds and famine, driven from their villages by the slave-trade proper. Thousands perish in internecine war waged for slaves with their own clansmen and neighbours, slain by the lust of gain. . . . The many skeletons we have seen, amongst rocks and woods, by the little pools and along the paths of the wilderness, attest the awful sacrifice of human life which must be attributed, directly or indirectly, to this trade of hell. . . . It is our deliberate opinion from what we know and have seen, that not one-fifth of the victims of the slave-trade ever became slaves. Taking the Shire Valley as an average, we should say that not even one-tenth arrive at their destination.[25]

There was however at least one Portuguese gentleman of untarnished honour whom Livingstone was proud and thankful to be able to exempt from complicity in the trade. This was his first, truest, and most constant friend—Major Sicard. Appointed much against his will as Acting-Governor of the

may be added that his daughter was herself a champion of the negro, and in after life was for many years one of Dr. Schweitzer's most valued colleagues in another part of Africa.

slave-port Iboe, he had remonstrated in vain against being "placed over a nest of slave-dealers". He died soon after, but not before he had received the British Government's thanks for his disinterested kindness to the Expedition: "and now that he has gone, as we trust to a better world, we would say never were public thanks accompanied by more fervent private gratitude".

One touch of humour enlivens this sombre story.

> "How far is it to the other end of the lake?" we enquired of an intelligent-looking native at the south part. "The other end of the lake!" he exclaimed, in real or well-feigned astonishment. "Who ever heard of such a thing? Why, if one started when a mere boy to walk to the other end of the lake, he would be an old grey-headed man before he got there."

In descending the Shire they found several huts concealed in the broad papyrus belt beside the lake Pamalombe, occupied by a number of fugitive Manganja families.

> "So thickly did the papyrus grow, that when beat down it supported their small temporary huts, though when they walked from one hut to another it heaved and bent beneath their feet as thin ice does at home."

Near Makena's village on 1 November they slung their frail gig to the branch of a tall shady tree for possible future use, and after a toilsome week's march downstream they reached the *Pioneer* at Chibisa's half-starved and "in a very weak condition". Here on the 13th they were suddenly hailed from a canoe by the Rev. H. de Wint Burrup, a new arrival from Oxford, with the welcome news that another contingent was leaving Cape Town on the *Gorgon*, bringing Mrs. Livingstone, Mrs. Burrup, Miss Mackensie (the Bishop's sister), and Miss Jeannie Lennox. "The bishop," wrote Livingstone, "appeared to be in excellent spirits, and thought that the future promised fair for peace and usefulness"; but privately in his Journal:

> The bishop does not realize his position as he intends leaving his important post at this critical time to bring up his sisters! He seems to lean on them. Most high church people lean on wives or sisters. . . . I hope the bishop will remain at his post; if he doesn't, he is a muff to lean on wife or sister. I would as soon lean on a policeman.[26]

But the tale which Mackensie unfolded was gravely disquieting both to himself and Kirk. Overborne by the appeals of two leading Manganja chiefs he had twice carried war into the Ajawa camp, inflicting casualties, burning their villages, and driving them (at least temporarily) from the country. "The bishop takes a totally different view of the affair from what I do," was Livingstone's first reaction (14 November). His conduct was in direct contravention of his own consistent policy of non-aggression. Henceforth the English would be regarded by one tribe as their open enemies. Nevertheless the thing was done and beyond the fact that, as he puts it, "a friendly disapproval of the bishop's engaging in war was ventured on", there was no dispute or ill-feeling. But later, when the bishop's action was criticized in England and Livingstone himself abused as accessory to it, he publicly threw himself on the side of his friend.

> If the bishop afterwards made mistakes in certain collisions with the slavers, he had the votes of all his party with him, and those who best knew the peculiar circumstances, and the loving disposition of this good-hearted man, will blame him least. . . .
> The question whether a bishop, in the event of his flock being torn from his bosom, may make war to rescue them, requires serious consideration. It seems to narrow itself into whether a Christian man may lawfully use the civil power or the sword at all in defensive war, as police or otherwise. We would do almost anything to avoid a collision with degraded natives; but in case of an invasion—our blood boils at the very thought of our wives, daughters, or sisters being touched—we, as men with human feelings, would unhesitatingly fight to the death, and with all the fury in our power.
> The good bishop was as intensely averse to using arms, before he met the slave-hunters, as any man in England. In the course he pursued he may have made a mistake, but it is a mistake which very few Englishmen, on meeting bands of helpless captives or members of his family in bonds, would have failed to commit likewise.[27]

Such were Livingstone's conclusions on the vexed subject of pacifism, when its theory was put to the touchstone of a practical issue. Nine months later he came to the desolate spot where his friend had died, and wrote to Sir Culling Eardley: "I have just been visiting Bishop Mackensie's grave. At first I thought him wrong in fighting, but don't think so now. He defended his 140 orphan children when there was no human arm besides to invoke."[28]

> Oppressed with the shocking scenes around, we visited the Bishop's grave; and though it matters little where a good Christian's ashes rest,

yet it was with sadness that we thought over the hopes which had clustered round him as he left the classic grounds of Cambridge, all now buried in this wild place. How it would have torn his kindly heart to witness the sights we were now forced to see!

The tragedy of Magomero, like that of Linyanti, has its own place in the annals of heroic but misdirected missionary endeavour. Suffice it that Mackensie and his young, strong, adventurous colleague Burrup, after their brief meeting with Livingstone, returned in good heart to their Mission; and thence with three Makololo started again on foot to Chibisa's in haste to meet their womenfolk on the *Pioneer*. Rain was incessant; they were drenched in fording a river, and again when their canoe capsized. Without food or medicine, fever-stricken and half-starved, on 16 January they crawled to a sodden hut for shelter on an island at the confluence of the Rua with the Shire. On the 31st Mackensie died. Himself utterly exhausted, Burrup with the Makololo's help conveyed the body to the mainland and made the grave and read the Burial Service. He struggled back to Chibisa's and thence was carried in a litter to Magomero, where he too died on 22 February.[29] Constitutionally, Mackensie and Burrup were the strongest men of their whole party. The bishop was a cousin of General Hay of the Mauritius, with whom Livingstone had maintained correspondence, and to him he wrote a letter of condolence if such it can be called.[30]

But this was not the end of sorrows for the Mission. Within a year Scudamore had died; then Rowley and Dickinson were invalided home. Only Waller, the man who of them all "was prepared to give his utmost to the Mission", remained at his post. Worse was to follow.

War, for the Yao were steadily moving on with the certain advance of a strong nation; famine, the result of drought and war; and as a sure consequence, pestilence was slaying its thousands. The Mission therefore decided to leave Magomero and, taking with them (of the released slaves) all the children and such of the grown people as wished to come, they marched in April 1862 to Chibisa's. Here, finding that Dr. Livingstone's Makololo followers had established themselves and grown rich by marauding, the workers separated themselves and built a village on the opposite bank.[31]

Chapter Twenty-Two

ZAMBESI EXPEDITION: THE LAST PHASE
1862–1863

"For the first time in my life I feel willing to die."

WHEN dependent upon any other means than his own powers of locomotion, Livingstone, through no fault of his own, found himself almost invariably "too late". Either through the sickness of his men, or shortage of provisions, or trouble with the boats, or a sudden drop in the river levels, he had been too late to explore the Rovuma upwards from the sea and again too late to reach its supposed exit downwards from the lake. The most exasperating of these delays occurred when he left Mackensie for his rendezvous at the Kongone. The river had dropped and for "five weary weeks" 20 miles below Chibisa's the *Pioneer* was marooned in the shoals. When therefore the *Gorgon* arrived off the Zambesi with his wife and the other ladies on board, there was no one to meet them. Putting to sea again the ship ran into a tornado, from which they had "an all but miraculous" escape. In three weeks they returned, this time to find the *Pioneer* in sight. It happened to be 31 January, the very day—unknown to anyone in either ship —that Bishop Mackensie died.

There followed a duologue typical of the traditions of nautical brevity.

"I have a steamship on the brig", semaphored the captain of the *Gorgon*. "Welcome news", was Livingstone's reply. "Wife on board", was the second message. "Accept my best thanks", came the matter-of-fact answer. "The most interesting conversation I had enjoyed for many a day," was his comment later.

The *Gorgon* had brought not only the steamship which was Livingstone's own purchase and named by him the *Lady Nyasa*, but also the faithful Rae who had supervised the construction of its engines. He had heard from Rae a month after

405

his arrival in London that "he seemed inclined to come out again". And now from James Young: "His whole heart is set on serving you. If one man can be devoted to another, Rae is devoted to you."[1] So then there was still one member of the original Expedition who understood him.

The ship brought also another newcomer in the person of the Rev. Dr. James Stewart of the Free Church of Scotland, who had escorted Mrs. Livingstone from England. Livingstone's first intimation of the proposal to send a deputy from that Church, to confer with him about founding a mission and Scotch settlement in the Shire highlands, had been received in a letter of 2 November 1860 from the Rev. Dr. K. Tweedie of Edinburgh, the Convener. He had replied with enthusiasm and had written to Sir Roderick, who was sceptical: "You will guess my answer. Dr. Kirk is with me in opinion, and if I could only get you out to take a trip up to the plateau of Zomba, and over the uplands which surround Lake Nyasa, you would give in too."[2]

Meanwhile the captain and the surgeon of the *Gorgon*, conducted by Kirk, made arrangements to accompany Miss Mackensie and Mrs. Burrup to the Rua in a gig to pick up, as they hoped, the bishop and his young colleague. They started on 17 February and finding no one at the Rua went on to Chibisa's where they were informed by natives of the unbelievable calamity. Miss Mackensie was by this time almost unconscious with fever; Dr. Ramsey and Mrs. Burrup remained with her at the village; Kirk and Captain Wilson, unprovisioned for a march, went on to Magomero where the sad tidings were confirmed beyond doubt. On 14 March the gig was again alongside the *Pioneer*, the men exhausted and emaciated; the women, prostrated with grief and fever and unable to walk, were carried aboard. The reception of their news by Livingstone was thus described by Dr. Stewart:

It was difficult to say whether he or the unhappy ladies, on whom the blow fell with the most personal weight, were most to be pitied. He felt the responsibility, and saw the widespread dismay which the news would occasion when it reached England, and at the very time when the Mission most needed support. "This will hurt us all", he said, as he sat resting his head on his hand, on the table of the dimly-lighted little cabin of the *Pioneer*.[3]

The same night however he committed to his Journal, and repeated in letters to his friends, the words which have immortalized his memory: "*I will not swerve a hair's breadth from my work while life is spared.*" He little knew when he wrote them how very soon hard fate would deal him a far more devastating blow.

As soon as was possible after the birth of her second daughter in Kuruman, now nearly four years ago, Mary had returned to Scotland to be near her other children. Thomas was being tutored by Dr. Stewart; Robert and Agnes were at school; but Robert was an intractable lad and did not take kindly to education. But she was all the time comfortless and homeless and, though devoted to her children and they to her, she was longing with a passionate intensity to be reunited with her husband. She suffered, we are told, from frequent lapses of faith. Blaikie, who saw the correspondence between them, says: "Her letters to her husband tell of much spiritual darkness; his replies were the very soul of tenderness and Christian earnestness." But perhaps they were not of much comfort to a wife who, after nearly twenty years' marriage, had only lived with her husband in a home for four of them. No doubt he counselled patience; explained why she must wait—until he had fulfilled his promise to the Makololo; until he had explored the Lake; until he had found a healthy site and built a house for them; reminding her with well-meant raillery of other wives who had waited longer for their absent husbands. And he on his part, though he may not have confessed it, was longing for her company almost as much as she for his.

It would appear that she had received some religious help from her companion, Dr. Stewart, on the long voyage out; and this had been strengthened by the practical help she herself could give to the other ladies in the *Gorgon*. But when they reached the Zambesi delta on 8 January there was no one to meet them, so the ship put to sea again and nearly foundered. At last, on 1 February, they returned to discern a puff of smoke close to shore, and soon the white hull of a small paddle-steamer making straight towards them.

There ensued a period of confused activity and heartbreaking frustrations, prolonged to six months; the off-loading and temporary disposal of vast quantities of cargo for the

Mission, most of it superfluous; the transference in its 24 sections of the *Lady Nyasa* to the *Pioneer*, whose engines were now found to be defective and in need of drastic repair, and whose draught could not support the extra weight; journeys back and forth to Shupanga to carry the sections piecemeal; hours grounded in the shoals; hours and days spent in wood-felling; a gale which drove the *Gorgon* out to sea . . .

All this while Livingstone was desperately anxious to get his wife out of the fever-ridden delta on to higher ground. On 23 February we find him writing to J. S. Moffat:

> Mary has, I am happy to say, joined me at last, after a weary and unexpected separation. The missionaries wish her to go up with them and, if she gets fever *up* she must go, though it be ever so much against the grain. But it will be in my company and at some other highland spot than the bishop's place.

Above the words "up she must go" Mary wrote "Do not believe him"—"following this defiance" (says the editor of these letters) "with a swift sketch of her own head in profile, putting the thumb of derision to the nose of scorn".[4]

There was on board the *Gorgon* an amiable and light-hearted assistant-paymaster, W. Cope Devereux, whose impressions of Livingstone, both appreciative and critical, are worth recording.

> The Doctor is very condescending and good-natured. . . . I could not imagine him to be the author of *Travels in South Africa*, but from his appearance I could well imagine him to have accomplished all therein stated. He has the appearance of a practical, hard-working man; he speaks slowly and with some difficulty, not possessing much fluency of speech, perhaps from long residence in Africa. To obtain his attention and see him really at home we must talk of Africa; we are then edified and amused, but this is the case on scarcely any other subject. In fact I call him a persevering, resolute, hard-working pioneer.

But with regard to his abilities as an organizer:

> I never saw such constant vacillations, blunders, delays, and want of common thought and foresight as is displayed on board the *Pioneer*. . . . I have rarely, if ever, seen a man so easily led as Dr. Livingstone. He has been persuaded to disembark a number of the sections to lighten the ship, and without considering the why and wherefore: so at six this morning we drop with the current, giving up the little we have gained at a cost of so much fuel, time, and labour. Again at 9 a.m., when the

ship has been got alongside the bank, and everything in readiness to rear shears, etc., the Doctor is again advised to change his mind, and thinks we had better not get anything out; and finally an hour afterwards, determines to land as much as possible.[5]

Professor Debenham, formerly a member of Scott's last expedition and himself the promoter subsequently of several other polar expeditions, has rejected these strictures on the general ground that a junior officer is incompetent to judge the mind of his leader, and on the special ground that Livingstone's calculations were entirely upset by the arrival of the *Lady Nyasa* in sections, contrary to his own expressed wish. But much the same criticisms are advanced, unfortunately, by an independent observer, namely the shrewd and sober-minded Scot, James Stewart.

> There is a woeful want of arrangement about this same ship (*Pioneer*). Dr. L.'s administrative ability does not seem to extend so far. It was well enough when only an ox-wagon or a number of untutored Makololo were in question; but it seems to fail when brought in upon other minds who will think as well as himself, though not possessing the same determination. . . .
>
> It is not enough that a man in Dr. L.'s position be passively unselfish; he must be actively so; he must see that the selfish of whom there are likely to be many, do not take advantage; that the lazy do their work, and the willing be neither overtasked nor their labours be unrecognized. . . .
>
> Let me say at once that nothing can exceed the perseverance, energy and determination of the leader. This is saying what all the world knows. But these qualities will not always secure the co-operation of others, nor win that success they deserve. . . .[6]

Debenham however is undoubtedly in the right when he concludes:

> Circumstances had forced him into a situation for which he was peculiarly unfitted: the management of affairs for a very dispersed set of parties over whom he had no official authority, but who depended on him for succour, and for whose sins of omission or commission he was saddled with blame.[7]

Again: Devereux, punctilious in Anglican church discipline and its regular observance in naval routine, was puzzled by the apparent laxity of religious worship on the part of the Expedition's personnel:

Sunday on board the *Pioneer* is not observed quite so strictly as I expected; taking into consideration the semi-reverend title and profession of her captain, his former clerical life, missionary professions, etc., I cannot account for it. Whether I am considered uncharitable or not, I think Dr. Livingstone's feelings have undergone a change, and his fame as a traveller has eclipsed that of a missionary.[8]

And again we find corroborative support from Stewart:

I do not feel satisfied with the Sabbaths on board the *Pioneer*. Dr. L. is more faulty on this matter than I supposed. At noon, when we should have had service, he was writing, a despatch or perhaps a letter. . . . I felt wearied, constrained to speak, to take the initiative, but I think it better to wait a little. . . .

I offered to act as chaplain for Dr. L. He made some excuse, but we had worship at night, the first time for a week.[9]*

The memories of an old seaman of the *Gorgon*, which appeared in the *Daily Telegraph* on 19 March 1913, give a very different picture of Livingstone.

Those slave-owners were difficult fellows to handle. They were as slippery as eels and required very careful watching. . . . When he was anywhere about the coast he passed on to us valuable tips as to where our quarry might be found. He was so friendly with the natives, so much beloved by them, and so implicitly trusted that they came to him with information which we used to good purpose. He was a grand man, the Doctor, and was always keen on the advancement of humanity and the stamping out of brutality. . . . It was a great privilege to know him, and to hear him speak. I can see him now, standing alone on deck, gazing dreamily on the African coastline, or engaged in animated conversation with some of the officers. A slim man he was—not very tall. When he came on board or when he was leaving the ship, he shook hands with every one of us, and had a kindly word or two for each. . . . There was something very powerful about him that drew men to him, white and black alike. . . . His eyes were wonderful—keen and with a twinkle of humour about them. And his thin face was deeply tanned. When he spoke to me, or shook hands with me, there came to his eyes an expression that I have never seen so marked in any other eyes. His soul shone through them. . . . And withal he was as gentle as a child. . . .

On Sundays on the quarterdeck he conducted service, addressing the ship's company in simple forceful language, that revealed how deep and universal was his humanity. It was not so much in what he said as in the way he said it that the charm lay. (Reminded that Livingstone broke down in the pulpit when a student.) Well, in that case I warrant it was not a question of nerves, for I don't think he had any. We all recognized in him a man absolutely without fear, as his record shows. It was his

* For Livingstone's private reason see p. 476.

diffidence, no doubt, that broke him down when he first ventured to preach. He was a most retiring man, counting himself among the least, when indeed he was one of the greatest.

There ensued several weeks of strenuous and confused activity, chiefly in transporting the sections of the *Lady Nyasa* on the *Pioneer* for assembly off Shupanga—save when for eighteen days the *Pioneer* was driven out to sea by a gale. At intervals and always after nightfall husband and wife were much in each other's company, as appears from Stewart's Journal, either for walks ashore or aboard the *Gorgon* with the ship's officers. Mary had slight but not serious touches of fever, but on 21 April she suddenly became very ill, and was removed from the *Pioneer* to the House of Shupanga. Her husband never left her side, day or night. The combined attentions of himself and Kirk could do nothing to relieve her; she could no longer retain any medicine. On the evening of Sunday the 27th she sank into a coma, and Livingstone sent a message to Stewart that the end was near.

He was sitting by the side of a rude bed formed of boxes, but covered with a soft mattress, on which lay his dying wife. . . . The man who had faced so many deaths, and braved so many dangers, was now utterly broken down and weeping like a child. I found my own eyes were full before I was aware. He asked me to commit her soul to her Maker by prayer. He, Dr. Kirk and I kneeled down and I prayed as best I could. In less than an hour she was dead.[10]

After a little as they still stood in silence above the bed, Stewart said to Livingstone, "Do you notice any change?" "Yes," he replied without raising his eyes from her face, "the very features and expression of her father."

She was buried next day beneath a large baobab tree in the grounds beside which she had walked with her husband only a few days before. Rae had made a coffin; Stewart, at Livingstone's request, conducted the funeral service. This somewhat introspective soul had been doubtful of Livingstone's attitude and feelings towards him; and in view of the rift that was to come between them later, his Journal entries at this time have a peculiar interest.

27th April. In the morning C.L. read prayers on board ship. It seemed odd to me that he should have done it. But what happened in the evening set my mind at rest. Out of all the ship's company—except Dr. Kirk who was attending all day—I alone was sent for to be with the Dr. in this hour of sorrow and trouble. . . . There were C.L. his brother, and Rae, his companion for four years; there was Waller and Young; but no; I, who was supposed by most on board to be a *nobody*, come in at this trying hour. . . .

1st May. A talk with Dr. Kirk and Dr. L. The first is now my friend. He is a good fellow. . . . He admitted today that he had kept a sort of neutral ground. Dr. L. continues to mourn over his loss. Comes ashore to talk with me at night for a short private walk, and generally is doing his best to be companionable and kind. When walking tonight between the steamer and the house, he said, "There is something I have to do or be; such I take to be the meaning of this dispensation. I wish I could find out."[11]

Their walks and talks were frequent and Stewart might well have numbered the latter as one among (what he elsewhere calls) his most "remarkable conversations" with David Livingstone.

Day after day he poured out his grief in letters: to his children individually; to the Moffats; to Maclear, who was similarly bereaved; to the Murchisons separately; to his mother and sisters, and intimate friends. He never realized how much part of himself she had been, whether present or absent.

[From his Journal.] It is the first heavy stroke I have suffered, and quite takes away my strength. I wept over her who well deserved many tears. I loved her when I married her, and the longer I lived with her I loved her the more. God pity the poor children who were all tenderly attached to her, and I am left alone in the world by one whom I felt to be a part of myself. I hope it may, by divine grace, lead me to realise heaven as my home, and that she has but preceded me in the journey. Oh my Mary, my Mary! how often we have longed for a quiet home, since you and I were cast adrift at Kolobeng; surely the removal by a kind Father who knoweth our frame means that He rewarded you by taking you to the best home, the eternal one in the heavens. . . .

11th May. My dear, dear Mary has been this evening a fortnight in heaven—absent from the body, present with the Lord. . . . For the first time in my life I feel willing to die.—D.L.

19th May. Vividly do I remember my first passage down in 1856, passing Shupanga house without landing, and looking at its red hill and white vales with the impression that it was a beautiful spot. No suspicion glanced across my mind that there my loving wife would be called to give up the ghost six years afterwards. In some other spot I may have looked at, my resting-place may be allotted. I have often wished that it might be in some far-off still deep forest, where I might sleep sweetly till the resurrection morn, when the trump of God will make all start up into the glorious and active second existence.

25th May. Some of the histories of pious people in the last century and previously, tell of clouds of religious gloom, or of paroxysms of opposition and fierce rebellion against God, which found vent in terrible expressions. These were followed by great elevations of faith, and reactions of confiding love, the results of divine influence which carried the soul far above the region of the intellect into that of direct spiritual intuition. This seems to have been the experience of my dear Mary. She had a strong presentiment of death being near. She said that she would never have a house in this country. Taking it to be despondency alone I only joked, and now my heart smites me that I did not talk seriously on that and many things besides.

31st May. The loss of my ever dear Mary lies like a heavy weight on my heart. In our intercourse in private there was more than would be thought by some a decorous amount of merriment and play. I said to her a few days before her fatal illness, "We old bodies ought now to be more sober, and not play so much." "Oh no," said she, "you must always be as playful as you have always been; I would not like you to be as grave as some folks I have seen." This, when I knew her prayer was that she might be spared to be a help and comfort to me in my great work, led me to feel what I have always believed to be the true way, to let the head grow wise, but keep the heart always young and playful. She was ready and anxious to work, but has been called away to serve God in a higher sphere.[12]

[From letters.] Everything else that happened in my career made the mind rise to overcome it, but with this sad stroke I feel crushed and void of strength. I try to bow to the stroke as from the Lord who gave and has taken away, but there are regrets that will follow me to my dying day. If I had only done so and so. . . .

On parting with her dear family and especially the little one whom I have never seen, she seems to have fallen into a gloomy desponding state, but happily the Rev. James Stewart of the Free Church was there and she opened her heart to him. I found a prayer in her handwriting, and another which says bitter things against her own hardness of heart. "Accept me, Lord, as I am and make me such as Thou wouldst have me be." He who taught her to use this prayer did not leave his gracious work unfinished. . . .

. . . I burst into tears and said, "My dearie, my dearie, you are going to leave me. Are you resting on Jesus?" I had to speak loud to make her hear, as her ears were affected by the quinine. I think she understood, for she looked up thoughtfully towards Heaven. . . .

God have mercy on my children, she was so much beloved by them. . . . I feel as if I had lost all heart now. . . . I shall do my duty still, but it is with a darkened horizon that I shall set about it. . . .[13]

Of all the letters of sympathy which he received, probably

the most comforting because the most understanding was that
from Mary's mother:

> I do thank you for the detail you have given me of the circumstances
> of the last days and hours of our lamented and beloved Mary, our first-
> born, over whom our fond hearts first beat with parental affection!
> [She recounts the mercies that were mingled with the trial: though
> Mary could not be called *eminently* pious she had the root of the matter
> in her, and though the voyage of her life had been a trying and a stormy
> one, she had not become a wreck. God had remembered her; had given
> her during her last year the counsels of faithful men . . . and at last, the
> great privilege of dying in the arms of her husband. . . .]
> Now, my dear Livingstone, I must conclude by assuring you of the
> tender interest we shall ever feel in your operations. It is not only as the
> husband of our departed Mary and the father of her children, but as
> one who has laid himself out for the emancipation of this poor wretched
> continent, and for opening new doors of entrance for the heralds of
> salvation. . . . May our gracious God and Father comfort your sorrow-
> ful heart. Believe me ever your affectionate mother, MARY MOFFAT.[14]

There was in the character of those Victorian missionary
pioneers, men and women alike, a sincerity that brooked no
compromise with truth, an intensity of affection unalloyed with
sentiment, and a Christian fortitude impervious to the worst
that fate could do. The cause, the proclamation of the gospel,
transcended any earthly relationships. Though the phrasing of
this letter is conventional of its period, its emotion can be felt;
one can but marvel at the fortitude which could see the greatness of this human bereavement as a necessary price to pay for
her son-in-law's greater work for God in Africa, and of the
truth-loving instinct which could say of her dearly-loved
daughter that she could not be called eminently pious. The
same appraisal is echoed in blunter fashion by Livingstone
himself in a letter to Lord Kinnaird when he says of his wife
that "she was a sincere if somewhat dejected Christian."

The spirit in which he set himself to re-buckle his armour is
reflected in a letter to Horace Waller:

> Thanks for your kind sympathy. In return I say, cherish exalted
> thoughts of the great work you have undertaken. It is work which, if
> faithful, you will look back on with satisfaction while the eternal ages
> roll on their everlasting course. The devil will do all he can to hinder
> you by efforts from without and from within; but remember Him who
> *is* with you, and will be with you alway.[15]

Three valuable months had been wasted in transporting the sections of the *Lady Nyasa* to Shupanga, and two more were needed to assemble them, "the work having been interrupted by fever and dysentery and many other causes". By this time the river was too low for navigation and another whole season had been lost. The Expedition had already passed its time limit and there was little to show for its work. Portuguese hostility was openly growing; the Governors at Mozambique and Tete, flouting directives from Lisbon, were conniving at the slave-trade; the Shire valley was more than ever ravaged by fighting and slave-raiding, pestilence and famine; Chibisa's new village near Tete was destroyed and himself a fugitive. Livingstone sent his brother and Kirk to collect what stores were left in Tete, while he went down again to the Kongone for the remainder. Provisions were running short and could only be supplied from Johanna; so he decided at once on another voyage in the *Pioneer* to that island, again with his brother, Kirk, and Rae.

Kirk had many times decided that he had had enough of the Expedition and all its works. On their return from exploring Lake Nyasa at the end of the previous year he had written in his diary: "My own mind is now fully made up to be off by the very first opportunity." But the disaster at Magomero, the death of Mrs. Livingstone, and urgent necessary tasks in Tete and Shupanga involved him in obvious duties which he could not honourably evade. Nothing but loyalty to the Expedition and its leader had kept him at his post. Letters from home urged "the necessity of returning soon". "I see the force of it," he commented, "as I have for a good while." But now another of these unpredictable journeys with his inscrutable leader was proposed and, what was worse, with his mischief-making brother to whose wagging tongue the Doctor, past all comprehension, still gave credulous heed. "Dr. L., though kind and considerate to me, still is not to be depended on; and any day, if a misunderstanding should take place, all former services would be lost sight of." It is evident that Kirk was becoming distrustful of Livingstone, and not without reason; but once again his loyalty overbore personal considerations. "The deciding factor, as before, was the thought that the Expedition needed him. He stayed."[16]

Livingstone for his part had since his wife's death grown graver, more unapproachable, grimmer and gruffer, and even more secretive than before; yet, as events were to show, more dogged, dauntless and determined than ever, if that were possible. Kirk's diary has an amusing reference to this. The voyage was rough; Charles Livingstone sea-sick; Rae, who had been twice wrecked, fearful; the Doctor more than usually unsociable; Kirk, as ever, observant.

> Dr. L. is uncomfortable at sea and looks so. When the weather gets foul or anything begins to go wrong, it is well to give him a wide berth, most especially when he sings to himself. If it is "The Happy Land"— then look out for squalls and stand clear. If "Scots wha hae"—then there is some grand vision of discovery before his mind. . . . But on all occasions humming of airs is a bad omen.[17]

At Johanna the Consul, Mr. Sunley, "from whom we always received the kindest attentions and assistance", having arranged for an adequate supply of stores "obliged us by parting with six oxen" (for transporting the *Lady Nyasa* up past the Murchison Cataracts); but since nothing could be done on the Shire till the December floods and every day was precious, Livingstone suddenly announced another of those changes of plan which were disconcerting to his colleagues. This was to make a second trial of the Rovuma. None of them but he were in the mood for this adventure, but none could gainsay him.

Having secured the services of a British warship in the harbour to tow the *Pioneer* across the sea, they reached the mouth of that river on 9 September—only to find the water-level much lower than a year ago and now confined to a single channel.

It seemed to Kirk, and no doubt to both his companions, madness to proceed. But the captain of the warship and his officers, with commendable enterprise, lent not only their gig and cutter but themselves also for a two days' reconnoitre; and two other boats were lowered from the *Pioneer*, Kirk and Rae in one and the Livingstone brothers in the other. (It may not have occurred to Kirk that the single narrow channel at least indicated where the depth of water lay, which had been concealed when the shallows were covered.) All went well at first, but "on continuing our voyage we found an intricate maze of sandbanks, across some of which the cutter required to be hauled". Next day they emerged into a fine sheet of water, Lake Chidia, enclosed by hills, and there spent the night, but next morning the naval officers returned taking Rae, who was unwell, with them, and leaving a few of their own men. From now on Kirk began to have grave doubts of Livingstone's sanity.

13 September. The river gets no better; snags and shoals with tortuous windings. . . . Still there is no change in Dr. L.'s plans; he is for going on still, regardless of the return. His determination seems to amount to infatuation. We go where the boat cannot float at many parts and where natives can wade across at almost all points.

16th. The river gets worse as we advance. . . . Dr. L. still carries on, regardless of his return and of the consequences of a long delay.

18th. At noon reach a wide part of the river, very shallow; still Dr. L. means to drag over it. The infatuation which blinds him I cannot comprehend—getting the boats jammed up in a river where they cannot float and where it will be impossible to return. . . . I can come to no other conclusion than that Dr. L. is out of his mind. He is to force the boats through by having natives to assist in hauling them. . . . I spoke to him of the risk of being hauled up high and dry by means of natives and then deserted, and of the further risks attending the probable detention from the falling of the river until the end of November; but he only said that, "if he risked nothing he would gain nothing".[18]

Truly, one who would travel with Livingstone must be prepared not only for strenuous exertions but also for unforeseen excitements, whether from nature or beasts or men. The Rovuma journey was no exception and provided examples of all three. The next day their passage was barred on both banks by a party of natives armed with guns and poisoned arrows. A stiff breeze swept the boats past the first danger point, but the natives took advantage of a bend in the river and reappeared in front. Livingstone laid both boats alongside an island and as usual attempted a parley, but meanwhile another party had stolen up behind.

Wild with excitement they rushed into the water and danced in our rear, with drawn bows, taking aim and making several savage gesticulations. Their leader urged them to get behind some snags and then shoot at us. . . . Notwithstanding these demonstrations we were exceedingly loath to come to blows. We spent a full half-hour exposed at any moment to be struck by a bullet or poisoned arrow.

Livingstone explained that we were better armed than they, "but had no wish to fight, but only to see the river", adding that they were all the children of the same great Father—an argument that always had weight. At length after much persuasion they laid down their arms and waded over to the boats. This was their river, they said; the white men must pay a toll to pass.

It was somewhat humiliating to do so, but it was pay or fight; and rather than fight we submitted to the humiliation of paying for their friendship, and gave them thirty yards of cloth. We then hoisted sail and proceeded, glad that the affair had been so amicably settled. Those on shore walked up to the bend above to look at the boat, as we supposed; but the moment she was abreast of them, they gave us a volley of musket-balls and poisoned arrows, without a word of warning. Fortunately we were so near that all the arrows passed clear over us, but four musket-balls went through the sail just above our heads. All our assailants bolted into the bushes and long grass the instant after firing, save two, one of whom was about to discharge a musket and the other an arrow, when arrested by the fire of the second boat.[19]

Livingstone says "arrested" but Kirk, with a pang of conscience, confesses that he killed one of these two natives and his coxswain the other. " We have been driven to this," he adds, "and have fought in self-defence only. But we must pray God to guide us in future. We have been doing his work in Africa, and trust in his shield . . . Dr. L.'s boat's sail has four bullet-holes through it." Livingstone, as if apologizing for these natives' behaviour, calls them "river-pirates" with a bad name even among their own tribe. They told a neighbouring chief that, had they known, they would not have attacked the English, who can "bite hard". "They offered no molestations on our way down, though we were an hour in passing their village."

For the next five days Kirk's diary is less despairful, despite some heavy dragging of boats over shoals and the feeling that they were still "a tempting bait for savages", but on the 25th after a particularly laborious day with "barely a boat's draught of water" and the hulls endangered with "projecting points" of rock he breaks out again:

Dr. L. is a most unsafe leader. He never thinks of getting back. All he cares for is accomplishing his object at any risk whatever. It is useless making any remark to him.

(*Next day.*) A field of rocks ahead. . . . Yet Dr. L. seems to intend taking up the boats now. If he does, I can only say that his head is not quite of the ordinary construction, but what is termed "cracked".[20]

But the unsafe leader, being now satisfied that the Rovuma was unnavigable and could not proceed out of Lake Nyasa nor be used as a highway to outflank the Portuguese, turned back the next day, and succeeded in descending it without the loss of a man or damage to the boats. Kirk's entry for 9 October is laconic: "Reach ship."

"A miserable and fruitless month" is Coupland's verdict on this journey. But Debenham dissents:

> Miserable it may have been, but it had much to do with the decision of the British missionaries and traders that, after all, the Shire was the only practicable approach to Nyasaland. Much as I hesitate to differ from such an able historian of East Africa, I would go so far as to say that the Nyasaland of today is largely the result of that negative but supremely important journey and that in his uncouth way Livingstone showed finer qualities of leadership in pressing on against the wishes of all his men than in most of the other subsidiary journeys of this period. The eye of discovery is all too likely to be partial, to look upon positive discovery as the supreme aim of geographers, and to neglect those negative results which usually cost more in human misery to attain, but are often the means of guiding future advance in the right direction.[21]

He had indeed against all odds penetrated the mainland to a distance of 114 miles in a straight line (156 miles by actual measurement) to within practicable reach of the Lake by land, and had already decided upon this route along the river-bank for his final journey when he would be alone.

There was to be for Kirk "one more day's experience of that malignant river". Livingstone shared it but would seem to have forgotten it soon after, for he misplaces its occurrence in his *Narrative* as among the events of the upward journey. His only other mention of it appears, curiously enough, in the post-script of a letter to his mother of 21 October from Johanna.

> We went up a few miles after coming back to the ship to get ebony, which grows abundantly on the Rovuma, and when returning I saw a hippopotamus put his head right up in our way in a narrow channel. Several others were a few yards to the left and I said to Dr. Kirk, "That fellow seems waiting for us." The boat went right over him and he put up his head a few yards behind us, then in under us, and lifted a big boat with ten men and about a ton of ebony in it, giving it two tremendous bumps. As the water began to flow in, we ran over to a sandbank with her, to see what damage had been done. The beast followed and Dr. Kirk put a bullet into his ear, which probably gave him the ear-ache. We found that he had tried to bite the boat, but it was too broad and

slipped out of his mouth. The tusks cut some planks like a chisel and made some holes besides.[22]

He had always written regularly to his home-folk in Hamilton and had made provision for their welfare. His letters to his mother are brief, telling her such news of his doings as might be likely to interest her, which was not very much. They cannot be described as very filial, beginning "My dear Mother" and ending "Ever affectionately, David Livingstone". They evince little of the milk of human kindness—as thus (29 November 1861): "I am astonished that none but three letters have come to you. I have written to you by every opportunity except one. I got one from Janet and one from Agnes at the end of three years. They had written none previously because 'they did not expect any sympathy from me'." Those to his sisters are longer but often distinctly tart. Here is a specimen, the beginning and ending of one to Janet (1 January 1862):

> I received your second letter since 1858 a short time ago by one of the missionaries who came up this river [Shire] in a canoe without knowing a word of the language or a bit of the way. [Burrup,] , , ,

> Suffer me to hint that your letter is in a slight degree Miss Grantish. . . . £60 a year will be given if I have it, but how could I know that you could not work when you never wrote to tell me? I think my letters were written in a Christian spirit, but it is questionable if they were thus received. D. Livingstone.

> A happy New Year to you all. Try and write a more loving letter next time, without saying you love me as much as ever. You are utterly inexcusable in not writing. I left orders that in any case of distress you were to be at once relieved. Running into debt by borrowing when you had no prospect of being able to pay was madness. It was never intended that you were to be kept idle on the money intended for mother. . . .[23]

Such letters, however well-meant, can hardly have been perused in the same spirit by the recipient. Those to his children, to whom he always wrote individually, are more frequent. The heavy homiletic note is less pronounced than formerly, and the tone becomes after their mother's death more friendly and familiar, as if he felt drawn into closer and warmer relations with them on that account. This becomes increasingly so in the case of his daughter Agnes. But they never show the least comprehension on his part of the mind and feelings of childhood.

The only one of his children who was giving him cause for anxiety was his eldest, Robert. To him he had written on 26 September 1861, after a lively account of his and the bishop's encounter with the slave-gang, as follows:

How are you doing? I fear from what I have observed of your temperament that you will have to strive against fickleness. Everyone has his besetting fault. That is no disgrace to him, but it is a disgrace if he does not find it out and by God's grace overcome it. Your uncle Robert [Moffat] is very fickle, never overcame it, has had many opportunities of succeeding in life, but wanted steadfastness of purpose, and is now settled down to a poor trader. I am not near to advise you what to do, whatever line of life you choose, resolve to stick to it and serve God therein to the last. Whatever failings you are conscious of, tell them to your heavenly Father, try daily to master them and confess all to him when conscious of having gone astray.

But Robert's wayward disposition showed no signs of improvement and another letter of Livingstone to his sisters (5 May 1862), after Mary's death, shows that it had worried her too.

The poor dear child whom I have never seen was often the subject of her thoughts. . . . But Robert's unsettled state pained her more. It preyed on her mind, and it might have done both good had he come out with her.[24]

And again to his mother from Johanna on 30 August:

I think it may be better for Robert to come out here for a while. I thought education the best legacy I could leave him, but so thought not he, and must rank in life accordingly.

But it was not to his mother or sisters or children that Livingstone confided his deepest thoughts and feelings: it was rather to those whom he felt to be more spiritually akin to him, such as Maclear and Murchison, Sedgwick and Braithwaite. From Johanna he opened his heart to Maclear on 27 October:

Dr. Kirk, I am sorry to say, will soon leave us, and I suppose that I shall die in the uplands, and somebody will carry out the plan I have longed to put into practice. I have been thinking a great deal since the departure of my beloved one about the regions whither she has gone, and imagine from the manner the Bible describes them that we have got too much monkery in our ideas. There will be work there as well as here, and possibly not such a vast difference in our being as is expected.

But a short time there will give more insight than a thousand musings. We shall see Him by whose inexpressible love and mercy we get there, and all whom we loved, and all the lovable. I can sympathize with you now more fully than I did before. I work with as much vigour as I can, and mean to do so till the change comes; but the prospect of a home is all dispelled.[25]

After repairs to the *Pioneer* at the mouth of the Rovuma they put in again to Johanna for their stores, draught-oxen, and some native workers—one of whom was a Moslem named Musa. By the end of November they reached the pestiferous Zambesi delta to find the river lower than usual, and took three weeks of the "old irritating haulage-work" to reach Shupanga. Procter was there and gave a dismal account of the conditions in the Shire valley: whole villages were devastated by famine and war, and the Makololo remnant engaged in systematic plunder. Then the *Pioneer* required more repairs, the rains were late, everyone disgruntled. At last on 11 January 1863 they started with the *Lady Nyasa* in tow, but the *Pioneer* grounded, the *Lady Nyasa* crashed into her, recoiled and grounded on a sandbank. Towing was then abandoned and the two vessels lashed together broadside on. Arrived off the Rua they went ashore to visit Mackensie's grave and Livingstone caused to be erected above it the more permanent cross of which a sketch is shown in his Memoir. On the 25th they were again grounded for a week in Elephant Marsh in the midst of a scene of desolation and horror which Livingstone's pen does not palliate.

Dead bodies floated past us daily, and in the mornings the paddles had to be cleared of corpses caught by the floats during the night. . . . It made the heart ache to see the widespread desolation; the river-banks once so populous, all silent; the villages burned down, and an oppressive stillness reigning where formerly crowds of eager sellers appeared with the various products of their industry. Here and there might be seen on the bank a small dreary deserted shed where had sat, day after day, a starving fisherman, until the rising waters drove the fish from their wonted haunts and left him to die. . . . There were a few wretched survivors in a village above the Rua; but the majority of the population was dead. The sight and smell of dead bodies was every-where. Many skeletons lay beside the path, where in their weakness they had fallen and expired. Ghastly living forms of girls and boys, with dull dead eyes, were crouching beside some of the huts. A few more miserable days of their terrible hunger, and they would be with the dead. . . .

The corpse of a boy floated past the ship; a monstrous crocodile rushed at it with the speed of a greyhound, caught it and shook it as a terrier dog does a rat. Others dashed at the prey, each with his powerful tail causing the water to churn and froth, as he furiously tore off a piece. In a few seconds it was all gone. The sight was frightful to behold.[26]

Passing on from a scene of human woe which they were appalled to witness but powerless to alleviate, they were grounded for another week, and met again by Procter with the news of Scudamore's death. With lowered spirits and aching limbs they crept on towards Chibisa's old village at the rate of half a mile a day. Conditions in the *Pioneer* are described gloomily enough by the missionaries:

> I fear the Expedition is all but "doubled up". The ships are hopelessly fixed in a sandbank fifty miles below us . . . the water is falling, no sign of more rain, fever has laid hold of all the European crew, the officers are all but in rebellion, and the Dr. daily becomes more incapable of self-control. (Rowley.)
> I pity the Dr. more than I can describe; the discontent and murmurs are sickening; it is a ship divided against itself, plank by plank. (Waller.)
> I feel deeply for the Dr., who seems very much depressed by all his trials and difficulties. (Procter)[27]

On 16 March there came an urgent appeal from Waller: Dr. Dickinson was seriously ill and one of the men named Clarke in a state of mania with epileptic fits and dysentery. Livingstone and Kirk set forth without delay but reached the Mission a quarter of an hour too late to see Dickinson alive. Kirk stayed on for ten days till Clarke recovered, and rejoined the party at Chibisa's. Meanwhile young Thornton, who had met them at Shupanga, having been reinstated on the staff with a roving commission, had arrived at the Mission and finding it sorely in need of fresh meat volunteered to go to Tete for sheep and goats. He returned with a considerable flock, but the journey, which had so nearly been the death of Kirk and Rae, overtaxed his strength; he succumbed to fever and dysentery and died on 21 April. Kirk and the younger Livingstone were also seriously ill of the same disease for some days, "and it was deemed advisable that they should go home". So the *Narrative*; but Kirk: "Dr. L. said that his brother had requested to go home and that he had consented, as it would be selfish to keep him any longer; and that as I had desired to go, he would feel the same in my case."[28]

Kirk could have taken leave of Livingstone and the Expedition of his own accord long ere this, had he consulted his own wishes; twice or thrice he had been on the point of doing so, and nothing but his high sense of duty had restrained him. And now on the very eve of his longed-for reprieve, it did so again. For Livingstone himself was at the end of April prostrated with the severest attack of dysentery that had yet afflicted him, and for a month was unable to move. "Dr. Kirk kindly remained in attendance till the worst was past." "Of course we cannot start," says Kirk simply; and then a little later, "I wish I were off, clear of this place, ship, and crew." "The parting took place on the 19th of May," wrote Livingstone—and not a word more. It can have been but little consolation to Kirk to learn that a few weeks later Livingstone named a new mountain-range in his honour; or even to receive this belated word of thanks dated from the Murchison Cataract in June:

> My Dear Kirk—I am sure I wish you every success in your future life. You were always a right hand to me and I never trusted you in vain. God bless and prosper you. Ever yours with sincere affection.
>
> DAVID LIVINGSTONE

As Macnair says: "If these words had been spoken months before they would have saved Kirk many uncomfortable moments, but Livingstone's friends had to take him as they found him."[29] It would be pleasant if one could end on that note, but unfortunately one cannot. On his arrival home Kirk found cause to distrust Livingstone more than ever, as appears from the following letter to Stewart:

> I find that in an underhand way Dr. L. has given me no cause to thank him: he simply said one thing, or rather wrote it, to me and another to the Foreign Office. He is about as ungrateful and slippery a mortal as I ever came into contact with, and—although he would be grievously offended to think that anyone doubted his honesty—I am sorry to say that I do. I think the explanation to be that he is one of those sanguine enthusiasts wrapped up in their own schemes whose reason and better judgement is blinded by headstrong passion. I don't think he would exactly say what he knew was untrue, but for all practical purposes the result is the same, and in him I believe all kindly feelings to be utterly extinct. For the first two years I had great respect for him, and for his energy and force of mind have so still. . . .[30]

Nevertheless there appears no trace in the Foreign Office Papers, which Coupland searched and from which he quotes extensively, of any letter from Livingstone which is adverse to Kirk; and, whatever his faults in other respects, double-dealing of any sort was never one of them. It can only be inferred that Kirk was misinformed. Livingstone's kindly feelings were not extinct, though they were expressed not in words but in securing for Kirk the appointment from the Foreign Office which established his future career.

When in his old age Sir John Kirk was asked what quality in Livingstone impressed him most, he always answered, "His fearlessness—he did not know what fear was." And in an interview with Basil Mathews:

> His absolute lack of any sense of fear amounted almost to a weakness. He would go into the most perilous positions without a tremor or a touch of hesitation. I never knew him blench or show a sign of timorousness in any circumstances whatever.[31]

Livingstone, merciless to himself, had fought off tropical diseases time and again with a defiance that others could admire but not emulate. But this last attack of dysentery incapacitated him for a month, and it may be taken as a symptom that his constitution was already undermined. Meanwhile the bold engineering feat of cutting a track up the side of the Murchison Cataracts had proceeded manfully; but the labour was immense, native aid unobtainable, provisions scant, his men all more or less ill. A Lieutenant of the *Gorgon*, by name Edward D. Young, had retired from the Navy to volunteer his services to the Expedition and was now with the *Pioneer*. On 16 June, within only a month of his recovery, Livingstone entrusted the ship to the temporary command of this officer, and himself with Rae—the last and next to Kirk the staunchest of his original staff—set forth up the rocky forty-mile ascent of the Cataracts to retrieve the gig they had left in a tree two seasons before, in order to obtain provisions from the lake-side and thus be "independent of the South". Young wrote to Stewart: "I think it a rash undertaking, for I never remember having seen a man fail in health and appearance so much in so short a time as the Dr." His observations on the route of native life, fauna and flora, are as lively and informative as ever. Arrived at their destination they found the gig burnt out—by the Ajawa he was asked to believe by the Manganja refugees, but by a forest fire as he deduced after careful inspection and finding the metal work intact. Having returned to the ship on 3 July he opened a despatch from Lord John Russell containing an order which was not unexpected, namely the Recall of the Expedition. He read that:

H.M. Government fully appreciate the zeal and perseverance with which you have applied yourself to the discharge of the duties entrusted to you. They are aware of the difficulties which you must necessarily have met. . . . They cannot however conceal from themselves that the results to which they had looked from the expedition under your superintendence have not been realized. . . .

It is clear that the route by the Zambesi would be attended with serious if not insuperable difficulties, and H.M. Government learn from your last despatches the failure of your attempt to find an independent route by means of the Rovuma.

The motives therefore by which H.M. Government were actuated when they consented to extend the period originally proposed . . . no longer exist. . . . A continuance of the heavy charge which it entails on the public can no longer be justified. . . .[32]

The despatch could not have been more considerately worded; it was desired that arrangements might be effected before the end of July; but if postponement was found necessary, the *Pioneer* should reach the bar while there was water to float her; free passages would be granted to the party; but their salaries could not be continued beyond 31 December. He himself was granted considerable discretion in effecting the withdrawal.

One of his first cares was to write to his brother-in-law in Inyati, confirming the continuance of his personal salary: "Don't be alarmed—I'll stick to you to the last."

To Waller he wrote on 13 August:

I guess that I shall work alone in Africa yet. £100 a year would do to support one. . . . I don't know whether I am to go on the shelf or not. If so, I make the shelf Africa. If *Lady Nyasa* is well sold I shall manage. . . There is a Ruler above and his Providence guides all things. . . . If the work is of God, it will come out all right at last. . . .

A mission without difficulties would be to me like a man without a shadow. Think of Moffat running away from a difficulty—a lion from a turkey-cock—no! no!

There was also news of the arrival of Bishop Tozer, Mackensie's successor, and his colleagues in the Lower Shire at the

426

end of June. It was to them that the Government despatches for Livingstone were entrusted. Livingstone received his Recall with equanimity, but not so the manner in which it was conveyed, and he made no scruple of treating a chief Minister of State to a typically Livingstonian reprimand.

> I take the liberty to complain of the use made of your Ldp.'s despatch before it reached its destination. When Bishop Tozer arrived at the Mission station seven miles below this, the servant sent up hailed the ship's company from shore in strong Surrey dialect: "No more pay for you Pioneer chaps after December—we brings the letter as says it!" . . .
> I have always considered the despatches of a high Officer of State as even more sacred than private correspondence, and as this could not have been degraded to the purposes of gossip with your Ldp.'s sanction, notwithstanding the courteousness of its style, I submit that at second hand my companions and self have been treated with very unmerited humiliation.

He went forthwith to meet the new bishop at the station and was immediately disappointed. The bishop had decided to remove it to the crest of Mount Morambula, to avoid the risk of fever in the lowlands and the hostility of the Ajawa; though "he showed his good sense" in agreeing to take the remnants of Mackensie's freed slaves thither, "otherwise he would have no one to teach". Earl Russell had desired from Livingstone a report concerning the new Mission's plans and his own views thereon, and Livingstone wrote on 17 July:

> Morambula is a detached mountain and the air, on rushing from the east, is rarefied by the ascent and unable to carry as much vapour as it did below. Hence a mass of clouds will rest often and long on the summit. The missionaries will be frequently in a cloud or above it, and great precautions must be taken against cold and damp. But Bishop Tozer is as remarkable for caution as his worthy predecessor was for the want of it in everything where his own safety or comfort was concerned. . . . The bishop does not conceal the fact that the chief attraction of Morambula is its vicinity to the sea and the facility he thereby possesses of withdrawing. . . .[33]

To this depressing news was added that of the withdrawal of James Stewart who, "happening to see the country when the people were nearly all cut off and the land parched with drought", had returned home.

It is among the major ironies of Fate that the Recall of the Expedition, so long deferred by a considerate Government, came in the end just one month too early. For, given only one month's longer grace, Livingstone could have launched his little ship on the Lake and have anticipated by thirty years the suppression of the slave-trade on the East Coast and the British colonization of Nyasaland. . . .

The *Lady Nyasa* had been dismembered for transportation up the Cataracts; he now caused her to be reassembled for return. But as it was impossible to float the *Pioneer* south before the December floods he resolved "in order to improve the time intervening" to carry another little boat up to the Lake, explore its eastern and northern shores, and verify Colonel Rigby's information about the slave-traffic across it. He started with the six oxen and a team of natives along the track already made, with the boat on a wagon; but on 15 July when it ended he recruited some Ajawa and Manganja men from Chibisa's to carry it on their shoulders. A note on their relative capacity appears on the 24th: "Three Manganjas went back this morning—inveterate skulkers, and when told so took their leave. The Ajawa men are far finer specimens and run with the boat." Thus they reached the top of the Cataracts and the Makololo in the party, well accustomed to canoeing, launched the boat on the water. But Fate, always ready with a trick to frustrate Livingstone throughout the whole of this Expedition, trumped his ace again.

> Five Zambesi men . . . were very desirous to show how much better they could manage our boat than the Makololo; three jumped into her when our backs were turned, and two hauled her up a little way; the tide caught her bow, we heard a shout of distress, the rope was out of their hands in a moment, and there she was, bottom upwards; a turn or two in an eddy and away she went, like an arrow, down the Cataracts. . . .
> The five performers in this catastrophe approached with penitential looks. They had nothing to say, nor had we.[34]

His monumental patience with natives is again exemplified; they were after all, he says, only like children; he merely "sentenced" them to go back to the ship as fast as they could for provisions, cloth and beads. Meanwhile he surveyed the Cataracts and found their drop to be 1,200 feet in forty miles.

The men returned on 15 August accompanied by Rae and the ship's steward. (How he and the rest had subsisted meanwhile he does not say.) Two oxen were brought with fresh provisions and one was immediately slaughtered to appease their hunger. Rae reported good progress with the *Lady Nyasa* and "the zealous co-operation of three as fine steady workmen as ever handled tools"; and Livingstone (blind to the good services of others who deserved public recognition) actually records their names, though with an apology to his readers for doing so! Rae returned to continue his supervision and doubt-less expected that his leader would also, for what now could possibly detain him? Twice foiled of attempts to put a boat on the Lake, and under sentence of recall before the year's end, with Kirk away and himself only just recovered from death's door—what was there to keep him any longer in these fatal uplands? The Expedition had been from the very start a cumulative series of disappointments and disasters, due equally to mismanagement and misfortune, and had ended in complete disintegration. Why prolong the already too long drawn-out agony? He had done his best, he had taken risks in doing so—risks not only to himself but to his men; why not confess him-self beaten and be gone?

But that was not Livingstone's way. There were still two months or more of good travelling weather—not to be wasted. He would have one last fling. Since he could not get a boat he would walk; he would go for a walk of 760 miles. One is reminded of Tennyson's Ulysses: ". . . but something ere the end, Some work of noble note may yet be done." And then: "Come, my friends, 'Tis not too late to seek a newer world."

His friends would be his black companions as of old. He would be free again at last—free of authority towards others and of authority from others. He would be alone. But at the last moment someone, probably Rae, reminded him that "all our party had earnestly advised that two Europeans should be associated together on the journey". The ship's steward was weak and anaemic from residence in the lowlands; so "to improve his health" he decided to take this man (whose name he omits to mention) for a "hard march". And he did not regret the choice; neither did the steward. The purpose that he proposed to himself in his Journal was:

> To take the slave-path westwards from the south end of the Lake, to get information of the sources of supply, its connection with the ivory

trade—prices—routes—the situation of the malachite, as this may be the means of inducing merchants to establish lawful trade.

And that prosaic statement is all he has to say on the matter. But his account of this journey, which was comparatively free from incident, occupies three chapters of his book. He achieved his aims, and more. In reading this section one feels transported back into the atmosphere of his earlier *Travels*, though without their travails and tribulations; here is the old Livingstone, in love with his Africans and sympathetic with their pursuits, interested in their religious beliefs and rites, studying the structure of the country, geologizing, botanizing, always taking notes. Again we are impressed with his inimitable way of making friends with local chiefs. Once they were separated from their retinue for three days and fed by villagers who were short of food themselves; once they were mistaken for slave-hunters, but lay down in the presence of their prospective foes and slept undisturbed. The route was not without its horrors. They had already passed "as large a town as ever I saw in Africa —quite deserted—skeletons everywhere", and, before they reached Chinoamba's village, "one dead body lay in our path with a wound in the back; then another, and another, lying in postures assumed in mortal agony, which no painter can reproduce". At Kota-kota, the central slave-depot from across the Lake, he found that he had missed by one day the Arab, Syde ben Habib, whom he had met at Linyanti eight years before (and whom he would meet again).

Thence he struck due westwards and began the stiff ascent to the plateau of 3,500 feet elevation, "somewhat puffed and broken-winded", but the cold pure air was a tonic to the party. He followed at first the main slave-route towards Cazembe's country, but from Mwaza's village (Kasungu) turned W.N.W. towards the upper reaches of the Loangwa. He perceived that he was now on the watershed of the lakes, and heard reports of a considerable river, the Luapula, said to be the main feeder of a lake called Bemba (Bangweolo) and through it of another lake called Mwero; as well as another river, the Lualaba, a main tributary. (He little knew that it was among these same lakes and rivers that he would die.)

Pressing on he reached his farthest point, Chinanga's village, on 27 September, but the piercing winds had affected his men.

"We had lost one, and another poor lad was so ill as to cause us great anxiety." A diet of little but *mapira* meal had brought on a recurrence of his dysentery; provisions for his men were scant; a slave-war was in progress to the north.

> But neither want of food, dysentery, nor slave-wars would have prevented our working our way round the Lake in some other direction, had we had *time*. . . . A month or six weeks would secure a geographical feat. . . . So we decided to return; and though we had afterwards the mortification to find that we were detained two full months at the ship waiting for the flood, the chagrin was lessened by a consciousness of having acted in a fair, honest, above-board manner throughout.

Self-justification could go no further; but it may be doubted whether under the circumstances he could—in a literal sense—have gone any farther himself. Allowing himself and his men three days' rest in this verminous village, he turned back on the 30th by the same route as far as Mwazi's village; thence south-east to cut a corner to the Lake, though it took him through country infested with Maziku (Zulu) raiders. His party being sometimes mistaken for these, villagers were hostile until reassured; and at Bangwe they encountered the raiders who were fully armed. The appearance of a white man however put them to flight, though one of his men was almost in the act of firing. This incident led to a rumour which later reached England that Livingstone had been killed, hearing of which he wrote with sardonic humour to James Young: "Don't go pale on receiving a letter from a dead man." Arrived on 8 October at Molamba by the Lake he had a "delicious bathe". Again on the route south he was saddened by the sight of starving fugitives having "the appearance of human skeletons swathed in brown and wrinkled leather. In passing mile after mile marked with these sad proofs that 'man's inhumanity to man makes countless thousands mourn', one experiences an overpowering sense of helplessness to alleviate human woe, and breathes a silent prayer to the Almighty to hasten the good time coming when 'man and man the world o'er shall brothers be for a' that'." From Chitanda's he struck up over Kirk's Range instead of along the Lake and rested at Chinsamba's stockade in Mosapo. This amiable and intelligent chief, whom he had met at his main village the other side on the outward journey, again befriended him with information and advice as well as food.

We had every reason to be well satisfied with his kindness. A paraffin candle was in his eyes the height of luxury, and the ability to make a light instantaneously by a lucifer match, a marvel that struck him with wonder. He brought all his relatives in different groups to see the strange sights. . . . Our books too were objects of admiration. The idea that enters their minds is that books are our instruments of divination. . . . The sextant and artificial horizon, the weight of the mercury . . . were all pondered over with the same kind of interest that we should take for the first time in any new and wonderful thing.

This was pleasant, but when a few days later he stood leaning against a hedge-wall in another village, listening to the harangue of a slave-trader's agent, "It glanced across our mind that this is a terrible world; the best in it unable, from conscious imperfection, to say to the worst 'Stand by! for I am holier than thou.'"

They reached the ship on 1 November, having been drenched the previous night by the first tropical downpour, but it was first of few. All were well in the ship, and the *Lady Nyasa* ready to float.

The steward, after having performed his part in the march right bravely, rejoined his comrades stronger than he had ever been before. . . . The first fortnight of our return was employed in the delightful process of resting, to appreciate which a man must have gone through great exertions. In our case the muscles of the limbs were as hard as boards, and not an ounce of fat existed on any part of the body.

But still the expected rains held off. "It is of no use to conceal that we waited with much chagrin. . . . We might have visited Lake Bemba; but unavailing regrets are poor employment for the mind, so we banished them to the best of our power." And he had cause for other regrets. In mid-December, while still waiting for the flood, he learned that Bishop Tozer had abandoned the mainland for Zanzibar. Of the freed slaves whom he had agreed to take with him to Mount Morambala six boys were left to the mercies of the Ajawa at Chibisa's, and thirteen women and children to the care of Horace Waller (the only one of Mackensie's original staff who had remained at his post), pending Livingstone's arrival. On that account Waller had been separated from the Mission. With so much at stake Livingstone's first letter to Tozer was diplomatic:

I hope, dear Bishop, you will not deem me guilty of impertinence in thus writing to you with a sore heart. I see that if you go, the last ray of hope for this wretched downtrodden people disappears, and I again from the bottom of my heart entreat you to reconsider the matter, and may the All-wise One guide to that decision which will be most for His glory.[35]

This failing, he again wrote on 18 December with obvious restraint, recalling their joint agreement with regard to the welfare of the natives, merely requesting that the boys be sent to his care, and ending "Believe me, dear Bishop, Yours very faithfully . . ." But to Maclear next day he poured out his heart:

> This I believe to be the first instance in modern times in which missionaries have voluntarily turned tail, but the selection of a detached mountain, considerably higher than Table Mountain and nearly uninhabitable for a mission station, gave rise to a suspicion that the Bishop meant to bolt. I am very sorry to find the suspicion verified; for now the last ray of hope for this down-trodden people vanishes. Had good Bishop Mackensie been spared to us the mission would have been in a very different state; but it is perhaps better to retire than live idly in the clouds. He is a grievous disappointment to me and much more so than our own recall. . . .
>
> I would fain write to your good bishop (Gray) and pour out my distressed feelings to him, but I feel as if I could sit down and cry rather than write.[36]

There is no doubt that, next to the personal shock of his wife's death, this was the severest blow that Livingstone had suffered in Africa. For the U.M.C.A. was his child and his partner; he had sacrificed much to foster and promote its ends: in his own words, he had for these six years "refrained from exploration". Tozer's retirement from the forefront of the battle seemed to him the cowardly betrayal of a sacred trust, a thing incredible. With scathing satire he wrote in his *Narrative*:

> Though representing all that is brave and good and manly in the chief seats of English learning, the Mission, in fleeing from Morambala to an island in the Indian Ocean, acted as St. Augustine would have done had he located himself on one of the Channel Islands, when sent to Christianize the natives of Central England.

Tozer indeed was not Mackensie; his way was the way of expediency, not of adventurous idealism. And yet there is a sense in which discretion is the better part of valour. As Coupland has said with fairness, "He chose Zanzibar not as a goal but as a stepping-stone." His ultimate objective was still the great inland Lakes, but by a yet more northerly route than the

Shire or the Rovuma, and indeed it was attained by his successors eventually—long after Livingstone's day. But the question still remains open: had the Government not recalled Livingstone at that moment, and had the Mission remained at its post, would two decades of misery have been saved to Africa?

The political implications of the Zambesi Expedition have been admirably dealt with by Coupland. Despite its apparent failure he calls it "a landmark in the history of Africa", and again "a landmark in the history of the British Empire". He shows how Livingstone had time and time again bombarded the Foreign Office with warnings of Portuguese intransigence, and how stage by stage Britain, from motives of diplomatic necessity, did nothing, until all the ground was lost. Then France, a much more powerful obstruction than our "old ally", entered the diplomatic field. The warnings of this vehement vagrant missionary-explorer would, if heeded and acted upon, have provoked an international crisis. "It was not that Russell was unmoved by humanitarian ideals." But he was a politician, and as such he must procrastinate. "Meantime Africa would have to wait for Justice."[37]

In the midst of all his labours and sorrows during these last two years, carping tongues and pens were busy in condemnation of Livingstone not only among the Portuguese but among his own countrymen. Privately in Tete and publicly in Lisbon the former expressed their resentment to his criticisms of their administration. This was understandable. In Cape Town the newspapers were denouncing his mismanagement of the Expedition. But he still had good friends in high office there: Maclear, now a knight; Bishop Gray (soon to be Archbishop) who approved most warmly all he had done for the Universities' Mission and deplored his Recall; Sir George Grey, who had secured the maintenance of a monthly overland mail from the Cape to Livingstone's "projected settlement". But the busiest among his detractors in the field and afterwards at home was, sadly enough, James Stewart. The feelings of this man towards Livingstone were throughout peculiar and they have been luminously revealed by the Editor of his Journal in an appraisal which does justice to both.

Inspired by Livingstone's glowing accounts in his *Travels* of the potential resources of Africa, both human and natural, Stewart had prevailed upon the authorities of his Free Kirk to send him out (though partly at his own expense) where Livingstone was and under his direction, to prospect for an industrial mission-station and combine evangelism with native cotton production. He was soon disillusioned both with Livingstone and with his enterprise. His hero was no saint after all, but had feet of clay; he was no director, but a mere improviser of makeshifts; Africa was not the Arcadia that he had depicted in his *Travels* but a land of barbarism and a death-trap. Livingstone was guilty of having suppressed the truth and had deluded him and all the world by false hopes. His rancour was given momentary pause however by Livingstone's sudden startling offer to finance him to the extent of £150 a year from his own pocket if he would stay and start work as a missionary. But instead he continued to listen to the gossip of the disgruntled and even seems to have encouraged it. Captious, frustrated, introverted, his antipathy jaundiced his outlook more and more. In vain did Kirk and Waller point out that Livingstone's account of the country, at the time he wrote it, was not exaggerated; that if Stewart had seen it in the Shire highlands, as they had, before it was devastated and depopulated, he too would have seen it as a land of promise. "The truth is," says Waller, "that he was self-deceived in that he had read Livingstone's travel-story in the light of his own desires." And with regard to his disappointed hopes of help: "Livingstone never grudged or withheld help. He did all, and more than all, that could be reasonably expected." Stewart's Journal of eighteen months in Africa reveals him as the introspective spectator of a tragic scene, preoccupied in soul-dissection and petulant self-grieving. Livingstone's, over a period of six years, is that of a courageous man of action fighting a losing battle at long odds, never a dread and never losing heart. The one stands to the other as a giant to a pigmy.

The following are among the most vehement of Stewart's denunciations:

17 Sept. 1862.—Talk at night. . . . Strong feeling against Livingstone for his mis-statements. His accursed lies have caused much toil, trouble, anxiety and loss of life, as well as money and reputation, and I have been led a dance over half the world to accomplish nothing.

10 Jan. 1863.—I part with Dr. L., and have no wish whatever to meet him again.

Then comes the theatrical climax:

1 Feb. 1863.—In the afternoon I went down the river bank a short way and threw with all my strength into the turbid muddy weed-covered Zambesi my copy of certain *Missionary Travels in South Africa*. The volume was fragrant with odours and memories of the earnestness with which I studied the book in days gone by. How different it appeared now! . . . Thus I disliked the book and sent it to sink or swim in the vaunted Zambesi. So perish all that is false in myself and others.[38]

Yet this was the same man who ten years later, with soberer judgment and truer vision, was to establish the great Scottish industrial mission-station on the shores of Lake Nyasa itself and to name it *Livingstonia*.

Waller (whom Stewart himself describes as "one of the soundest and most unsophisticated Christians I have ever met", and Kirk as "the most sensible and perhaps the only one among those left who really intends doing his utmost") wrote in reply to one of Stewart's effusions when in England, 5 October 1864:

I have not heard a word from the Doctor since he has been home to make me think he is "cool" towards you. With all his grand qualities those who know him make allowances for the unrounded corners of character. . . . His heart's in the right place and he's the bravest man I ever saw or expect to see, which, for one who has longed to have a tithe of his pluck, is a go-and-do-thou-likewise object to gaze on and not pick to pieces. So I always stick up for him though, I confess, with more tact in dealing with his companions he might have made a much greater and more lasting mark.[39]

Chapter Twenty-Three

FROM QUILIMANE TO BOMBAY
1864

"The vessel was so small, that no one noticed our arrival."

THERE remained a serious and embarrassing problem: how to dispose of the *Lady Nyasa*. The Portuguese in Quilimane would have been glad to buy this little vessel, but only—as Livingstone well knew—to employ her as a slave-ship: "but" (as he wrote to Agnes) "I would rather see her go down to the depths of the Indian Ocean than that." He therefore resolved to try and sell her in Zanzibar.

By 19 January the Zambesi had risen sufficiently to float the *Pioneer* and her sister-launch downstream. Anchoring below Mount Morambula, Livingstone took on board two of the Mission staff, 13 liberated women and children, and 25 boys whom the bishop had left there. "We had thus quite a swarm on board." On 13 February they were safely off Quilimane and in the mouth of the Kongone. Here by good fortune they were met by two British cruisers, the *Orestes* (Captain Gardner) and the *Ariel* (Captain Chapman), bound for Mozambique. The former took the *Pioneer* in tow, and the latter the *Lady Nyasa* with Livingstone on board. The sea was rough and Livingstone was invited into the *Ariel* to save him from a buffeting, "but I did not like to leave so long as there was any danger, and accepted the invitation for Mr. Waller who was dreadfully sea-sick". On the 15th they were struck by a cyclone. "The Captain offered to lower a boat if I would come to the *Ariel*, but it would have endangered all in the boat . . . it might have been swamped, and my going away would have taken heart out of those that remained."

Thus to Agnes, but in the *Narrative* he says more:

A hurricane struck the *Ariel* and drove her nearly backwards at the rate of six knots. The towing hawser wound round her screw and stopped her engines. No sooner had she recovered from this shock than she was

437

again taken aback on the other tack, and driven stem-on towards the *Lady Nyasa's* broadside . . . but she glided past our bow and we breathed freely again. We now had an opportunity of witnessing man-of-war seamanship. Captain Chapman, though his engines were disabled, did not think of abandoning us in the heavy gale but crossed our bows again and again, dropping a cask with a line by which to give us another hawser. We might never have picked it up, had not a Krooman jumped overboard and fastened a second line to the cask; and then we drew the hawser on board, and were again in tow. During the whole time of the hurricane the little vessel behaved admirably, and never shipped a single green sea. When the *Ariel* pitched forwards we could see a large part of her bottom, and when her stern went down we could see all her deck. A boat, hung at her stern davits, was stove in by the waves. The officers on board the *Ariel* thought that it was all over with us; we imagined that they were suffering more than we were. What struck us most was the promptitude and skill with which, when we had broken three hawsers, others were passed to us by the rapid evolutions of a big ship round a little one; and the ready appliance of means shown in cutting the hawser off the screw under water with long chisels made for the occasion; a task which it took three days to accomplish.[1]

In the same gale the *Orestes* split eighteen sails, and the *Pioneer*, lightened of some cargo, had her round-house washed away.

At Mozambique the *Pioneer* was handed back to the Navy for despatch under escort of the *Valorous* (Captain Forsyth) to the Cape. With her went Waller and the remnant of the Mission flock. "He continued his generous services to all connected with the Mission, whether white or black; his conduct to them throughout was truly noble and worthy of the highest praise."

Here Livingstone missed by two days the arrival of an old friend, Senhor Canto y Castro, who had been appointed Governor-General: "we believe no better man could have been selected for the office. We trust that his good principles may enable him to withstand the temptations of his position; but we should be sorry to have ours tried in a den of slave-traders with the miserable pittance he receives."

On 16 April he steamed out in the *Lady Nyasa* (her hull having been repaired and repainted) and with favourable currents reached Zanzibar in a week. His hopes of a reasonably good sale were disappointed. "He clung to the hope that she might yet be useful in carrying out his philanthropic schemes." Before finally parting with her he would consult his friend "Sir Paraffin" Young, and the only feasible way of doing so seemed now to take her across the Indian Ocean to Bombay, leave her there for the present, and make a quick run home. Dr. Seward, the Consul, "was very doubtful if we could reach Bombay before the break of the monsoon. It occurs usually between the end of May and the 12th of June". But Livingstone was informed "on what seemed the best authority" that such a voyage could be accomplished in eighteen days, so that there seemed a good margin of time in hand for calm weather. At the last moment another difficulty presented itself.

Three weeks before while in Mozambique, Rae, his invaluable engineer, had received through Captain Forsyth the offer of a partnership in his sugar-business in Johanna, and Livingstone was asked whether he could do without him.

> I replied that I could not stand in the way of his advancement, though I regretted to part with him. Mr. Rae spoke to me, and I replied that in an affair like this which would have an important influence on his whole future life, he ought to decide for himself. He said that he would like to see Sunley himself and have a written agreement, and then go home and bring out a good wife, which I highly approve of as he would be sure to get entangled at Johanna. He has the offer of a situation in Bombay too, but on the whole prefers Johanna. . . . It would be to my advantage if he should come and assist in the sale of the *Lady Nyasa*, but I will not be selfish.[2]

It will be seen that at this date, 8 April, Livingstone was looking no farther than selling the launch in Zanzibar. But Rae went with him to that port, and apparently no more was said till the 28th when Rae engaged six stokers and proposed himself to go to Johanna with the first available man-of-war. Livingstone was so taken aback that he made no reply. He had already expended £53 on coal, oil, rope and canvas. "I have no power to compel," he wrote, "so must comply. We could not go without an engineer." But it was now too late to engage another. He waited one more day and then determined to sail without one, despite the fact that Collyer (the carpenter) was ill, and that Pennell (the seaman) was saying, "There is something wrong with the engines—he knows not what." Rae was in fact "terror-struck" at the thought of such a voyage, and a man with his experience of the sea can hardly be blamed for being so. (Kirk, writing to Stewart on 19 October 1865, reported that Rae had died suddenly of chronic ulcer in the stomach.)[3]

Those who think of Livingstone primarily as a landsman and continental traveller should be reminded that he was familiar with the ocean too, and that he had already been in frequent "perils of the sea". But never was he in greater peril than on this audacious voyage across the Indian Ocean in a river-craft. As Debenham has said: "It was such a remarkable feat that it certainly deserves fuller notice than it has yet had. The *Narrative* deals with it in under two pages." Fortunately his original log is in the possession of his grandson Dr. Hubert Wilson, who has kindly lent it for reproduction here, as well as his Journal in Bombay.

His crew comprised the two white men above-named, and John Reid (stoker); "seven native Zambesians, and two native boys"—Chuma and Wikatani. He was his own navigator and he had no engineer, and no more than fourteen tons of coal, for use only when the wind failed. Would any master-mariner have undertaken such a hazard? And had he known that the voyage timed for eighteen days would lengthen out to forty-five, would even he have done so?

1 *May*.—We went 156 miles and the rating of chronometers having been lost by something done to that taken on shore, I went near enough to Mombasa to ascertain that the rating of Mosambique was still good. Collyer ill.

2nd.—Went 170 miles helped along by the current which at this time of year is very strong.

3rd.—We made only 90 as we were into a bend made by the coast and could see land at Brava. Steamed by day but though we went E. and by it we drifted inland again every night, or rather the land met us again. We had no wind.

We are but three efficient white men as Collyer is useless though getting better. One of the black men has learned to steer and takes my place at the wheel while I superintend him only.

4th.—We steamed out straight but as usual saw land on the morning of the 5th, kept out again, and now the coast trending more to the north we are well away from it.

6th.—The weather more cloudy promises more wind.

7th.—Steamed out but had a calm night and was carried 30 miles West by a current. It ought to have carried us North but seems to set on to the land.

8th.—A little wind and in the right or S.W. direction. During our few days of calm it had been south or S.S.E. Many dolphins about us yesterday and yesterday we passed a great deal of floating weed. . . . We consume about 4 tons of fuel per day of 24 hours. . . .

9th.—A little wind but calm at night—scarcely steerage way. Collyer better.

10th.—Pennell ill of the bilious fever which has troubled us of late months. . . Gave him Rousers—did not operate—took salts but vomited them and on 12th has been vomiting much through the night.

11th.—Very calm through the night—scarcely steerage way, but this morning cloudy with rain and a breeze. We are 1,000 miles from Zanzibar, 100 from the coast and standing out East by N. We go about 80 miles per day, half of which are current—to the North. . . . Found Collyer asleep on watch, and steersman—a black one—going S.E. with sails all aback and flapping. We had much cloud by day but little wind, made seventy miles, only 28 of Lat. and 53 of Long., but the sky is covered over with a striae and we are over the moon's quarter. The moon has a very decided influence on the weather out here. We have not seen a single dhow or ship since we left Zanzibar.

12th.—Had a little wind this morning but it died away and we do not go more than a knot an hour. Striae or cirri with floating cumuli. About midday a squall came from S.E. which tore up our topsail—we caught a little water. Afterwards it fell calm. A small squall after dark. Then dead calm all night afterwards—curious weather this—requiring much patience, but we are in the hands of One who careth for us.

13th.—Calm with a very light breeze from South. Fleecy clouds along over cirri. . . . We go scarcely two knots, yet the clouds above seem going faster—no current—sea light blue. We went yesterday only 40 miles, and today at noon could run her only 63.

14th. Quite calm all night. Pennell ill with a bilious attack like the others, so we can't steam. Sky covered with cirri and glass rising—one stands at 30.1. We will surely get wind soon.

15th.—No wind and no motion as far as easting is concerned for this morning. We still stand Long. 53° 24′ E. Many dolphins go about the vessel and one large shark. A slight breath of wind this morning. Pennell better though still passing much bile—asks for sleeping powder.

Here follow several medical prescriptions, chiefly for the prevention of ague, obtained from Dr. Seward in Zanzibar. Also a transcription of part of an article in the *Quarterly Review* on the humane treatment of London's outcast poor.

16th.—Pennell at work and well. A light breath of wind during night but not enough to move us more than the current which sets N.W. So we are getting up steam intending to get into more windy latitudes than this. Steam 4½ knots.

17th.—Sky covered over with clouds except in some small patches where we have milk-and-water coloured strata or patches of pea-green and dark-blue. Sea dark indigo. Little wind but rain seen falling in S.E. Steaming about 4½ knots. A nice breeze and rain about 3 a.m. It was lighter by sunrise—sky clouded over with cumuli. We creep along at about 2 knots. Barometer 29.95. Small patches of pea-green in sky but covered generally with clouds of milk-and-water hue. Wind in afternoon very light.

18*th*.—Better wind last night and a nice light breeze this morning—going about 3 knots. Wind S.S.W. Bar. 30.05 at 9 a.m. Sky covered with thin stratum and fleecy cumuli float over surface. Went only forty miles in 24 hours—hope for more wind.

Here follows a note from the same periodical on the weight of the African elephant and rhinoceros. Then another on his own account concerning the insincerity of Bishop Tozer's proceedings on Morambala! A little further on comes a paragraph of which the passage on travelling in Africa which begins his Last Journal two years later is a virtual transcript. From now onwards a note of despondency, almost of despair, creeps into his log.

19*th*.—Very light wind all night, but with a swell that shows there has been a breeze in the South. Wind died away during the night.

20*th*.—A very light breeze scarcely keeps us moving in the water. Sky cloudy with a thin stratum and a few fleecy cumuli. A shark following us again. A land bird very like a goose followed us for a while too. No medusae now.

Went only 16 knots in 24 hours, four of these to southward, and this very unusual weather has a very depressing influence on my mind. I feel as if I am to die on this voyage and wish I had sent my accounts to the Government, as also my chart of the Zambesi. Often wish that I may be permitted to do something for the benighted of Africa. I shall have nothing to do at home; by the failure of the Universities' Mission my work seems vain. No fruit likely to come from J. Moffat's mission either. Have I not laboured in vain? Am I to be cut off before I can do anything to effect permanent improvement in Africa? I have been unprofitable enough, but may do something yet, in giving information, if spared. God grant that I may be more faithful than I have been, and may He open the way for me.

21*st*.—Not a breath of wind all night and this morning sea glassy calm with a hot glaring sun and sharks stalking about us. Tell-tale compass damaged by flapping of sail—very hot and all clouds gone—saw a fringe down at horizon. Got up steam at 10 a.m. but no draught. All ill-natured, and in this I am sorry to feel compelled to join.

22*nd*.—The same sad tale to tell of calms all night. This morning however a light, very light breeze gives a little air to us. We passed many small fish and a patch of floating sea-weed. We went N.N.E. yesterday to get further down towards Socotra, where surely we shall have a current if not wind. . . .

23*rd*.—We were enclosed by heavy thunderclouds yesterday and be-calmed. . . . Wind then drew round several ways and raised a chopping sea. . . . Sky all overcast and clouds move not at all—swell from S.W.

A few streaks of pea-green in sky but in general immovable masses of clouds with fleecy ones still beneath.

24th.—At noon yesterday wind gradually rose to a nice breeze and the vessel obeyed her helm. We had gone 4 miles to Eastward and 2½ South so we had gained nothing. Last night wind became light but this morning we are favoured with a light breeze again. Fleecy clouds pass in detached pieces over the sky. A land bird came on board yesterday very tired, sick for it died, purging probably from having drunk salt water. In the evening a squall came over us with some rain. We went fast during its continuance but it chopped round suddenly to S.E. from S.W., and wave meeting wave was very disagreeable and checked our way. About midnight a good breeze sprang up which continued till—.

25th.—Many flying fish came on board through the night. Dolphins played along with us and often leapt out of the water in sport. About 30 pilot-fish were in the hollow between the counter and screw for the sake of the still water there—near the shark—they keep in the still water behind his fins. It is doubtful if they act as pilots to him.

A bird brown in colour with white on rump seems to use his feet in picking up food. He passes along and bounds off the water like an Indian rubber ball. Very many flying fish rise before us. They can fly with great ease 100 yards or more, rising and falling with the swell of the waves. They often rise when pursued by dolphins and do not seem to require to wet their fins as the antients said. The dolphin pursues very swiftly but not so quick as they can fly. The dolphin has very bright colours—rims of brighter green than the rest of the body. This is one of the provisions of nature by which the prey is warned of the approach of the enemy. Incessant activity is a law in obtaining food. If it could be caught with ease and no warning given, races would have the balance turned against them and carnivora alone prevail. The cat shows her shortened tail and so does the rattlesnake shake his to give warning to the prey. The flying fish has large eyes in proportion to other fish, yet flies on board very often at night and kills himself by the concussion.

These remarks recall his invincible belief, confirmed by his study in youth of Dr. Dick's scientific philosophy, that the God of nature and of revelation were one; and by his own experience of the stupor induced by a lion's shake, that it too was among "the merciful provisions of a benevolent Creator". It is but the reflection of the thought of his age which, since Darwin, was striving to reconcile two apparent incompatibles.

The next day marks a crisis in the fortunes of the voyage, involving an irrevocable but most hazardous decision.

26th.—The breeze still continues but I am in great doubts as to the propriety of going on to Bombay. We went 72 miles yesterday. At that rate we should reach our port in 15 days, or one day before the break of the Monsoon. This is running it too close to danger. Then if we go to

Aden we have the wind against us until that change and must go into Maculla for water and provisions. Without that we would require ten days to go there. Then if I am to do aught more for Africa it would be better to keep her at Aden, go home and consult with Mr. Young, then come out and have a passage down in her, going in to examine the rivers Juba, etc., but this would be forestalling the Baron von der Decken and I don't like to appear to run in before him. He may buy the steamer perhaps. This is a case in which one greatly requires the guidance of Him who has been my guide hitherto.

I went up after noon when I found that we had made only 82 miles and put her westwards, but she would steam only at North or South, and by West from S.W., so there is no possibility of our entering the Gulf of Aden. Enquired how much water we had and found it as much as on short allowance will last ten or twelve days. I am shut up to one course, so turned her head E.N.E. for Bombay. May the Almighty be gracious to us all and help us.

27th.—Had a good breeze all night but we made only about 3 knots. Screws and an iron bolt on her bottom hold her back. The barometer is low—29.95—first time we have seen it so. It has always been 30.1 or so. Air cool or rather piercing.

Found that we had made four knots or 96 in 24 hours—breeze promises to keep on with us. It was N.W. and by W. for some time and shifts a little each day.

Here follows a meditation in which, as Blaikie says, "we seem to hear him pacing his little deck and thinking aloud". It shows how far removed his thoughts were from any idea of colonizing Africa in the sense in which Rhodes afterwards conceived it.

The idea of a colony in Africa, as the term colony is usually understood, cannot be entertained. Englishmen cannot compete in manual labour of any kind with the natives, but they can take a leading part in managing the land, improving the quality, increasing the quantity and extending the varieties of the production of the soil; and by taking a lead too in trade and in all public matters, the Englishman would be an unmixed advantage to every one below and around him, for he would fill a place which is now practically vacant. . . .

28th.—Sky all clouded over with a dense still mass and wind lighter. Lightning and thunder in north. Bar. at 9 a.m., 30; was 29.95 at 6 a.m. Wind West, or W. and by it. We passed a red mass yesterday as if a piece of red cloth. See some medusae too.

At noon a dense black cloud came down on us from E. and N.E. and blew a furious gale—tore sails. She, as her wont [is] rolled broadside on to it and nearly rolled quite over—everything hurled hither and thither. It lasted half an hour, then passed with a little rain. It was terrible while it lasted. We had calm after it and sky lightened up. Thank God for His goodness. Calm all night, but barometer is low and we may get a breeze yet. Time of breaking up of the monsoon draws nigh and we are still 840 miles from Bombay, but by the good hand of our God upon us we shall reach it.

29th.—A fine morning but we would prefer a stiff breeze to hasten us on. We go about 1½ or 2 knots just now but even that is better than during the night with sails flapping; had a better breeze through night. Barometer 29.9. Wind S.W., but a heavy cloud in afternoon and in South. Much thunder and lightning ended for us in a squall which turned her to S.E. nearly broadside on to the wind.

30th.—Gentle breeze—clouded over—Bar. at 9 a.m. 30 and the other 30.2. Wind S.W. steady. Light winds through the night. Went 65.

31st.—Wind light and steady—no squalls today. We are still 700 miles from our desired haven. We look to the All Wise and Merciful One for safety and success. Maury says the S.W. backs down gradually towards the East Coast while the N.E. monsoon meets the other face to face when feeling its way into operation. Good breeze all night, clear sky except a few fleecy clouds scattered over it. Bar. at 6 a.m. 29.9. Air feels cool when we are to have a breeze.

The Shupanga men are becoming good sailors, can set sails or trim them, go out to the end of a boom though the sea washes over them. Two can steer.

1 *June.*—We go on slowly though we have a good breeze. A bolt of angle iron intended to strengthen her holds her back and so do the screws. [Sketch.] This angle iron + in front is bent on itself twice. These parts offer resistance in one direction, while the part between the lines marked thus || is bent down on the flat and offers resistance on the others. Bar. at 10 a.m. 29.93 with breeze freshening. Fleecy clouds increasing and haze all around horizon. At 3 p.m. 28,7.

The dolphins go with the ship exactly as a dog does with his master. He careers out from her after flying-fish, then returns and walks alongside till he sees other fish, then off again. He goes very fast but is not a match for the wings, though when the fish gets flurried he may get him; occasionally he gets near enough to stupify his prey which, flying a yard or two, falls in nearly to his jaws as he scuds after it with open mouth, head above water. [Sketch.]

Breeze stiff all night. Barometer low—below 29.9—and at it—according [to] daily variation. Fleecy clouds and haze.

We now find the recurrence of an unhappy note, upon which he had expatiated twice before at greater length on the eve of sailing, interpolated into his log. He could never forget past injuries and this was the injury that rankled most.

2nd.—Breeze still fresh with low Barometer, at 6 a.m., 29.9—fleecy clouds, hazy, 102 miles.

I think that the Oxford and Cambridge missionaries have treated me badly in trying to make me the scapegoat for their own blunders and inefficiency, putting by implication the guilt of idly passing many months without an effort to teach on me by saying that the Makololo had been left to do the best they could, abandoned, though they left us *before* we quitted the country, and had neutralized all their teachings, no instruction having been attempted. But I shall try equitably and gently to make allowances for human weakness though that weakness has caused me *much suffering*.

Barometer at 3 p.m. 29.85—lowest temperature since sailing, 81°. Highest 92°. Breeze still stiff.

3rd.—Stiff breeze all night—wind West—thick murky sky with fleecy clouds skimming quickly past. Sea pretty high. Barometer at 6 a.m. 29.83.

The Barometer being low and sea high I thought it well to prepare for a heavy sea by putting a piece of canvas along the railings which are the only bulwarks in front of the quarter-deck and a wash-board of about 8 inches. The sea was lashing over it. On telling Collyer to bring up the canvas he asked if "I thought he would work all day at that. If he had known he was to be kept that way he would not have come, etc.", bawling out in a most disrespectful manner. I told him he might as well do that as sit sewing on his own account as he does daily. "But that has to be done," said he. As he seemed determined to cause a mutinous uproar I told him I must have none of that, that my authority would be enforced though it might be fatal to him, if we neglected to use precautions for the safety of the ship we might as well jump into the sea at once [*sic*]. The canvas was put on by the Shupanga men. This is very disagreeable but what one always meets, with low men-of-war's men.

Sea very high. A deep bank of cumuli in the South. We are under the influence of a current drawing us to the North-West—110 miles and 50 of northing—though we steered E.–N.E. we had gone N.E. and by E. Put her to East so as to place all our sailing power in that direction while the current draws us to the North. 410 miles from Bombay.

At p.m. Bar. 29.8 [Temp.] 90°.

4th.—Had a good stiff breeze all night—about 4 knots was our speed. The screws hinder as much as if we had another vessel in tow. They make large whirlpools in the water and prevent her ploughing into any wave in front. Barometer at 6 a.m. 29.85.

3 p.m. Bar. 29.8. Temp. of air 87°—wet bulb 82°—diff. 5°. Sky covered over like London fog—breeze fresh.

5th.—Had a very rough night—heavy sea and stiff breeze. This morning sky as if spread over with a London fog and patches of fleecy clouds floating on its face. No sun could be observed either in morning or at noon. Wind W. or W.N.W., but coming round a little more to West. We steer close to it at E.N.E. Barometer at 3 p.m. 29.82—this is a little higher than yesterday. No flying-fish now.

6th.—Sea less last night but this morning sky still covered over with cloud and no sun visible. Barometer at 6 a.m. 29.8, at 9 a.m. 29.86. Wind fallen light N.W. which compels us to sail E. and by it. Several locusts flying about though we are about 100 miles from the nearest land. Corn for Shupanga men done—gave them sago as we have a box of it.

Lord Ravensworth has been trying for twenty years to render the lines in Horace:

"Dulce ridentem Lalagen amabo
Dulce loquentem . . ."

and after trying every conceivable variety of form this is his best:

"The softly speaking Lalage,
The softly smiling still form . . ."

Pity he had nothing better to engage his powers, as for instance the translation of the Bible into some of the languages of the earth!

7th.—No wind all night and now at 9 a.m. sails idly flapping against masts. She does not go more than $3\frac{1}{2}$ in a good fresh breeze. It takes almost a gale to get $4\frac{1}{2}$ out of her. The screws act as if she had a good-sized vessel in tow. How Rae could say that on the trial trip she went between 5 and 6 with two little trysails I don't know. She is a good sea boat however but dreadfully slow. Bar. at 9 a.m. 29.87.

A weary day with only as much wind as ruffles the water but scarcely gives steerage way. A heavy swell from south possibly precedes a breeze—a little rain. Thick surface covered sky—some locusts still about but if they touch the water it is all over with them. Barometer at 3 p.m. 29.8.

No wind all last night but about 3 a.m. a light breeze sprang up from East and veered to E.S.E. Bar. 6 a.m. 29.8.

Was afraid that the east wind of this morning might turn out a N.E. and keep us away from the land, but thanks to a kind Providence it has veered more to the south and we can steer at N.N.E.

Maury makes the change of the Monsoon much later than our Zanzibar friends do. End of May or 12th June is the time of which they spoke positively. Today the sky is clear generally and clouds high. Many night moths have come to us though we are quite 100 miles away from the nearest shore. We are close upon the Andreas bank and 165 miles from Bombay.

Enquire about Jute at Bombay. The Bengal indigo planters drove all others out of the market. Native-made indigo is 30 or 40 per cent. lower in value, from an inveterate tendency to adulterate that and everything.

9th.—Calm all night though Bar. has been 29.76 all yesterday afternoon. This morning a gentle breeze from north—with a good deal of cloud about, one thundering in the south.

He now has a note on Professor Max Muller's observation that the names given in the Hebrew text to Solomon's apes and peacocks, ivory and almond-trees imported from Ophir, were Sanscrit in origin. They must have spread from India to East Africa where they are still in use. The same is true of beads and of a species of millet.

Hitherto his chief enemies had been currents and calms; for'

447

the last few days when almost within sight of land, gales set in—the prelude of the monsoon.

10*th*.—A furious squall came on last night and tore our fore-square sail to ribbons. We had rain with it. Then wind died away—and all morning we were becalmed. About noon a gentle breeze from East sprang up. Then it veered round to W. and by it, increased and in afternoon passed three ships going southwards—one at least an Englishman. Saw two serpents—they are mentioned as often seen on this coast. One was dark olive with light yellow rings round its flattened tail. The other was lighter in colour. They seem to be salt-water animals.

In middle watch a large full-rigged ship passed us on same tack as we were. We saw her light and could see her by the lightning which was much and vivid.

11*th*.—Wet scowling morning—clouds all over and scud flying quickly across face of the great mass—had a good deal of rain. Bar. at 6 a.m. —. It was not so low yesterday evening as during the calm yet we have foul weather now. Mended a portion of sail by sewing the two outside cloths together—the rest was unmendable. Wind N.W.N. which causes too much easting. Rains frequently with thunder in the distance.

A poor weak creature. Permit me to lean on and trust to an all-powerful arm.

12*th*.—The squalls usually come up right against the wind and cast all our sails aback—this makes them so dangerous. Active men are required to trim them to the other side.

We sighted land a little before 12. The high land of Rutnagerish. I thought of going in, but finding that we have 28 hours' steam I changed my mind and push on for Bombay 115 miles distant. We are nearer the land down here than we like, but our N.W. wind has prevented us from making northing. We hope for a little change and possibly may get it nicely. The good Lord of all help us. At 3 p.m. Bar. 29.72. Wind and sea high—very hazy—raining with a strong head wind. At 8 p.m. a heavy squall came off the land on our East. Wind whistled through the rigging loudly and we made but little progress steaming. At 11 p.m. a nice breeze sprang up from East and helped us—about 12. A white patch reported seemed a shoal but none is marked on the chart. Steered a point more out from land. Another white patch passed in middle watch. Sea and wind lower at 3 p.m.·

At daylight we found ourselves abreast high land at least 500 feet above sea level. Wind light and from East, which enables us to use fore and aft trysails; a ground swell on but we are getting along and feel very thankful to Him who has favoured us.

Hills not so beautifully coloured as those in Africa—seem bare and brown, perhaps from the season. Ours are green and covered with trees.

At 10 a.m. were obliged to stop in order to fasten a nut at the bottom of the plunger of the feed-pump. This is the third time it has become loose. The water is discoloured by the freshets in the rivers.

At 11 a.m. Pennell reported that the feed-pump was out of order. It was found that the nut at the bottom of the plunger had come off and the bolt bent; we could do nothing and put it on again. We were opposite Kelsi, 5 miles south of Bancut and 59 from Bombay. Went on intending to go into Rajapur to see if we can get fuel. We must have had a set against us as this is usual when the rivers are in flood.

At 7 p.m. a furious squall came down off the land—could scarcely keep the bonnets on our heads. Pitchy dark except the white curl on the waves which were phosphorescent. Seeing that we could not enter the harbour though we had been near, I stopped and got up the trysails and let Pennell who has been up 30 hours get a sleep.

13th.—We found that we had come North only about 10 miles. We had calm after the squall and this morning sea is as smooth as glass and a thick haze over the land. A scum as of dust on face of water. We are as near as I can guess by the chart about 25 miles from the port of Bombay.

Came to Bhoul rock at midday and latitude agreeing thereto pushed on by N. and by West till we came to Lightship. It was so hazy inland we could see nothing whatever—then took the direction by chart and steered right into Bombay most thankfully, and mention God's good Providence over me and beg that He may accept my spared life for His service.

A great many ships and ample space for them. No one came for a good while, but after we had anchored half an hour a pilot came and asked if we wished a pilot to take us further in. I replied in the negative.

Nothing could be more typical of Livingstone than that last laconic sentence. Having traversed 2,500 miles of ocean in forty-five days with an untrained crew, he had made a perfect landfall, and had made it the day after the threatened break of the monsoon. The feat is dismissed in his published *Narrative* in a couple of pages, mainly devoted to praise of his men, without a word of the intense anxiety that had beset him day and night; and then, whilst waiting unobserved for half an hour in the haze, concluding thus: "The vessel was so small, that no one noticed our arrival."

He went ashore alone to call on the Governor, Sir Bartle Frere, to find him gone away up country; then on Mr. Oliver, the Police Magistrate, to find him busy in Court; having wandered in and heard a few cases, he returned to the ship still unrecognized.

A great deal of cotton lying on the wharves but in a woeful plight. It had been in the rain for some time and some bales lay right in puddles. The sparrows were hauling out portions to build their nests, and the goats were dancing on the bales as if their favourite rocks, defiling the while what is so costly. The slovenly way in which the bales had been put together were a strong contrast to the tidy tight bales of calicoes coming at the same time from England.

Met a great many Europeans coming into business as we were going out. It seems a stirring place where much business is done. Many rich native families were out in carriages taking the air, and people begged from them though not from Europeans. The ladies plastered over with jewels which they seemed anxious to exhibit by lolling out a hand or an arm.

In the ship he found that the Customs officials had called meanwhile with papers for completion, and the request for information to whom he was "consigned". He replied formally but with a touch of humour that except a few bales of calico and a box of beads he had no merchandise, and his crew had nothing but their clothes. "I am consigned to Nobody and I do not know a single soul in the place." The Commissioner then "most politely offered to do anything in his power for me": gave him a note to the harbour-master who sent a pilot to take him round to Massagon, and another to a Parsee merchant for fresh provisions. Two officers, Captain J. Young, C.B., R.N., and Colonel C. Stewart then came aboard with a message from the Governor requesting him to come up to Dapuri. Here he was guest of Sir Bartle and Lady Frere, and was taken to the Free Church Mission School in Poonah, the College, the Roman Catholic Orphanage and was introduced to everyone of note. "Went to church with the Governor. The Archdeacon preached an excellent sermon to an attentive congregation— chiefly of soldiers. Church cool and pleasant." With Frere he discussed at length the whole subject of slavery, and with him formed one of the greatest friendships of his life. "The present Sultan [of Zanzibar] is, for an Arab, likely to do a good deal. He asked if I would undertake to be consul at a settlement, but I think that I have not experience enough for a position of that kind among Europeans. He thought I ought to speak to the Chamber of Commerce. . . ."

Returning to Bombay on 22 June he paid off his men, adding generous gratuities; borrowed money for his passage and John Reid's to England; visited the Scotch Established and Free Church Mission Schools, and entrusted Chuma and Wikatani to the care of Dr. Wilson, superintendent of the latter. He left the *Lady Nyasa* in the charge of Captain Young, and on the 24th embarked with Colonel Stewart for England. Arrived at

Aden on 6 July he was taken by the latter to breakfast and lunch with the Resident, Mr. Merryweather, "a very fine intelligent gentleman and most devoted servant of his Government". Much rain had fallen and the country was greener than when he last saw it: "probably the same effects followed the storms in Egypt at the time of the Exodus". At Suez he saw "a bit of Lessep's Canal" and notes, "The political situation is dark in Europe." At Alexandria: "A great deal of cotton grown; grain imported now from Odessa." Re-embarking there he found the Maharaja Dhuleep Singh on board with his young Princess whom he had married from an English Egyptian School: "he has a number of hooded hawks on board." On the evening of the 23rd he was again in Charing Cross, to be regaled, as Blaikie says, "with what after nearly eight years' absence must have been true music—the roar of the mighty Babylon".

Chapter Twenty-Four

SECOND VISIT HOME·
1864–1865

"I can only remember him as always writing letters."
(Anna Mary.)

LIVINGSTONE reached London on 23 July 1864 and went straight to Sir Roderick and Lady Murchison's, was taken at once to Lord and Lady Palmerston's, and for the next week was warmly received by several of the Lords of the Council and the nobility. "All say very polite things, and all wonderfully considerate." He was evidently surprised and gratified and also somewhat alarmed by this unexpected cordiality. But on the 27th: "Hear the sad news that Robert is in the American army." The unhappy short career of this errant son must be recorded.

In the old days at Kolobeng he was remembered by Oswell as an extremely obstinate little boy, and, according to Livingstone, he had got "a good deal of the vagabond nature from his father". Livingstone's chief desire for all his children was a good education and he had appointed his trustees as their guardians. But since Robert disliked schooling and would not be bid, he arranged with them for his passage to the Cape and thence to Quilimane to join him there. He had written to his son regularly and in a cheerful and by no means censorious manner, but apparently received no replies. He asked Rae, when home in 1860, for a first-hand account of him.

In July 1863 he wrote to Maclear: "Rae, who knows him better than I do, says he is clever but refused to go to College or do anything that the Trustees wanted him to do . . . Bad company, and I fear drink, have been at work on him . . . Rae has a better opinion of him than, from the disclosures at least, I can entertain."[1] Robert's own wish would have been for the Navy but the Trustees (except James Young) "would not hear of it, on the plea that I would disapprove, and never said a

452

word about it to me till all was over . . . But I would not have objected." Both his mother and Rae had thought it best that he should come out to Quilimane and discuss his future with his father.

Accordingly, soon after his mother's death, Robert had sailed from England, arrived at Port Elizabeth in June 1863 and went to Isipingo in Natal, where he hoped first to stay with his uncle Robert Moffat who was on his way thither from Kuruman. But his uncle died suddenly on 6 August when only twenty miles on the way, and it was left to his bereaved aunt to act for a while as a second mother to young Robert. Then came a most pathetic letter of eight pages out of a heart full of motherly affection and anxiety from old Mrs. Moffat to "My beloved Grandson". It is dated 3 October 1863 and ends:

> . . . You are my eldest Grandchild, the firstborn of my own dearest Mary, also my own firstborn, and I cannot but feel the deepest interest in you, more especially as you are now motherless. Do let me know your tastes, your aspirations for this world and for that to come. . . . People say you are shy and reserved, but do, O do open your heart to me. I am now the only mother you have, and I am hoping ere long to join her who was dearer to you than all the world beside. . . .
>
> Old Kuruman is much as you left it. We were long worried with fears of the Boers, but now for three years they have been too busy contending with each other to meddle with us. . . . Mebalwe, whom I think you will remember, is at present with your Uncle John at Matabele. . . . Your Grandfather is still the hale old man—steps out much more lively than some who are only half his age. . . . He joins me in every expression of tender solicitude and affection. Longing to hear from you.[2]

Robert and his younger brothers had received their preparatory schooling under Mr. John Adams, a friend of their father's, at Gilbertfield in Hamilton. The present writer is indebted to his son, Professor W. G. S. Adams, C.H., formerly Warden of All Souls' College, for the following reminiscence communicated at the age of eighty-four.

> Robert had a great deal of his father in him—a dour, determined, impulsive boy. One day my mother said to him: "What are you going to be, Robert?" Looking up from his book he gave a gruff reply, "A traveller like my father." He kept his word. . . . He decided to go to Africa in the hope of finding and joining his father. Arrived in Natal he proceeded up-country, but meeting a party of Americans who told him that there was no white man where they had been, he returned to the

coast intending to try another part of the country by way of the Rovuma river. But he then decided to throw in his lot with the Americans and go and fight in the Civil War. . . .

The next news of Robert comes in an undated letter to his father from himself. The formal manner of address, its startling intelligence, its chivalrous tone and manly directness, lack of all self-pity or expectation of sympathy—are something that, taken together, suffice to acquit the writer of any obloquy.

My dear Sir,—Hearing that you have returned to England I undertake to address a few lines to you, not with any hope that you will be interested in me but simply to explain the position. The agent of Mr. McArthur of Port Natal said that he would write to him and inform him of my position and find me employment till I could find means to reach you. Mr. Rutherfoord, Collector of H.M. Customs at Port Natal, interested himself in me for your sake and treated me with the greatest kindness. I believe that I owe some obligation to Mr. McArthur. All he heard of me was that I was to come out in a certain vessel. Concluding that I had run away he would have nothing to do with me. I should have been very badly off had it not been for the kindness of Mrs. Robert Moffat to whom, besides £1, I owe a great deal, perhaps more than I shall ever be able to repay.

From Port Natal I went to Cape Town where your agent Mr. Rutherfoord advised me to find employment on board a brig which brought me to Boston, America. Here I was kidnapped and one morning, after going to bed on board ship, I found myself enlisted in the U.S. army.

I have been in one battle and two skirmishes, and expect to be in another terrific battle before long. God in His mercy has spared me as yet. I have never hurt anyone knowingly in battle, have always fired high, and in that furious madness which accompanies a bayonet charge and which seems to possess every soldier I controlled my passion and took the man who surrendered prisoner.

The rebels are not likely to hold out much longer as we have nearly all their railroads. My craving for travelling is not yet satisfied, though if I had the chance that I threw away of being educated, I should think myself only too much blessed. I have changed my name, for I am convinced that to bear your name here would lead to further dishonour to it. I am at present in this hospital, exposure and fatigue having given me ague fever.   ROBERT.

Address: Rupert Vincent, N.H. Vols., 10th Army Corps, Virginia.[3]

His father received this letter in October 1864 when at Newstead Abbey and wrote to Sir Roderick Murchison on the 23rd:

The American Minister was here to lunch last week. I spoke to him about my son in America and he promised to do what he could for him.

He is in hospital at Peterburg, ill of ague; says that he has always avoided taking life even in the frenzy of a charge, so I conclude he does not relish his present employment. He adds that his love of travel is as strong as ever. Perhaps something may yet be made of him.[4]

He was wounded near Laurel Hill in Virginia, captured, and died of wounds in a prisoners' camp at Salisbury, North Carolina, on 5 December 1864, at the age of 18.

When this news reached his father at Hamilton on 2 June 1865, his comment shows how this man of one consuming purpose subordinated all earthly ties to the cause for which he had dedicated himself and all that God had given him.

Robert we shall never hear of again in this world, I fear; but the Lord is merciful and just and right in all His ways. He would hear the cry for mercy in the hospital at Salisbury. I have lost my part in that gigantic struggle which the Highest guided to a consummation never contemplated by the southerners when they began; and many others have borne more numerous losses.[5]

Professor W. G. S. Adams writes:

Livingstone had often been concerned about his son's spiritual welfare, but my father told me that when the news came of Robert's death, his father exclaimed: "I am proud of the boy. If I had been there I should have gone to fight for the North myself."

And Stanley recorded that one evening in the last year of his life, "when the tent door was down, and the interior made cheerful by the light of a paraffin candle, the Doctor related to me some incidents respecting the career and death of his eldest son".[6]

Delayed for a week by official functions in London, Livingstone spent the day of his arrival in Glasgow with James Young and his family and next day attended the United Presbyterian Church where he heard "excellent sermons". Then home to Hamilton. "Mother did not know me at first. Anna Mary, a nice sprightly child, told me that she preferred Garibaldi buttons on her dress, as I walked down to Dr. Loudon to thank him for kindness to mother." Agnes, Oswell, and Thomas came next day. He did not recognize Tom, who had grown tall and was also delicate. His little daughter Anna Mary's recollections of him (given to the Christmas number of *Chambers Journal* in

1938) were dim, and not as flattering to him even as his were of her.

It is by no means easy to write of my father. I knew as a child that he was in Africa and, so far as I was concerned, it seemed quite right, if he liked that. I lived with his two sisters at Hamilton, who rarely spoke much about him. I have no idea in what light they regarded his public career.

I was five years old when he came home for the last time, and that was the first time he and I met. I can remember standing beside one of my aunts when she greeted him, and my father looking down at me and saying, "And this is Anna Mary?" He kissed me too, though frankly I did not much like being kissed by anyone with a moustache! He gave me a little later a present of a black doll, which in my heart of hearts I did not admire. I remember feeling, if he was giving me a doll, why not a white one? I played with the black doll in his presence, but once his back was turned I preferred to play with my own white ones.

My father used to take me for walks, but I was very shy of him and did not speak much, and perhaps he was a little shy of me! When on furlough his brother Charles had plenty of time to play with me and tease me, and I thought a great deal of him; whereas my father was absorbed in work, and I can only remember him as always writing letters. . . .

In Glasgow he consulted Professor Syme as to a surgical operation for haemorrhoids and was strongly advised to undergo it; but he finally declined, partly from the delay that it would cause and partly from a horror of the publicity that would ensue. On 17 August he was in Inverary to visit the Duke of Argyll: "the most delightful visit I ever made". Thence to Mull and the islands of Iona, Staffa, and Ulva. There he saw the ruins of his grandfather's croft in a sheltered spot at Uamh, or the Cave, "but none of my family remain, and no one lives there". Returning to Oban on the 24th he met "that famous missionary, Dr. Duff, from India, a tall noble-looking man with a white beard and a twitch in his muscles which shows that the Indian climate had done its work on him". He was delighted with the acclaims that greeted him from the Highlanders wherever he went; "they cheered me as a man and a brother."

Back in Hamilton on 4 September, he worked for three days at the speech he was to deliver on the 19th to the British Association at its annual meeting in Bath, "with coat off and sleeves tucked up. A cold shiver comes over me when I think of it, Ugh!" He took his daughter Agnes with him for company and spent the weekend in the city with friends. The address

David Livingstone
taken at Bath in September 1864
(at the time of addressing the British Association)

was delivered in the Theatre before an audience of 2,500, "but it is a place easily spoken in". His theme was the Portuguese connection with the slave traffic. Nervous at first, as always in public, it was said he gained confidence during delivery. "He spoke under great stress of feeling, with much energy and excitement; and he spoke his mind uncompromisingly." Bishop Colenso of Natal, then under ban by Archbishop Gray for heterodoxy, moved the vote of thanks. This, thought Livingstone, "was a pity, as it looked like taking sides".[7]

On the 23rd he attended the funeral of Captain J. H. Speke, the discoverer with Sir Richard Burton of Lake Tanganyika in 1862. For Speke he had a great respect, but none at all for Burton. He had corresponded with Speke and "anticipated the pleasure of meeting him . . . His sad fate threw a gloom over the whole meeting".[8]

His speech raised a furious storm in Lisbon:

> The Portuguese took great umbrage and were quick to give an official reply. Señor Lacerda, their spokesman, made a most bitter personal attack upon him accusing him of hypocrisy; "of ardour to aggrandize his own nation, and perhaps to do no less honour to himself"; of under the pretext of propagating the Word of God, "exploring for no other purpose than to drive the Portuguese out of Africa"; of "machinations no longer concealed against the indisputable rights of the Portuguese Crown"—and much else in a similar strain. All this pleased rather than disturbed Livingstone. It showed that his shot had got below waterline.[9]
>
> But the facts he had supplied could not be explained away, and Lord Palmerston, as guardian of British foreign policy, openly showed that his sympathies were with the returned explorer's protest against the barbarities of an evil system carried on under the aegis of a European power. Nor was there any hesitation on the part of the churches and of the nation generally in accepting his statement as true, and an agitation at once began for stricter measures to be taken for the patrol of the East African coast.[10]

The repercussions which his speech provoked decided Livingstone forthwith to write another book—a "trumpet blast". This grew in scope as he progressed with it and became his *Narrative* of the Expedition. And the conditions under which it was written turned out to be ideal.

On 8 September when in Hamilton he had received an invitation from the wife of his old friend of Kolobeng days, William Frederick Webb—now of Newstead Abbey—to make their house his home. At first he declined on the plea of separation from his newly-found children, and especially from Agnes. Mrs. Webb countered this by warmly including Agnes in the invitation, and suggesting that the boys should spend part at least of their Christmas holidays there. He still hesitated; this time because of his great wish that Agnes, while with him, should be given good music lessons. Mrs. Webb replied that such a trifle could easily be overcome: Agnes could receive good music lessons with her own daughter, who was of the same age. "At this Dr. Livingstone gave way."

Newstead Abbey, a twelfth-century foundation near Nottingham, was acquired by the Byron family after the dissolution and was their residence for three centuries. It is commemorated by the poet in *Don Juan*. "His character does not shine. It appears to have been horrid", is Livingstone's blunt verdict on the poet. He arrived with Agnes at this ancestral mansion at the end of September and (said Sir Harry Johnston, with truth) "spent there perhaps, all things considered, the eight happiest months of his life". His host, a quiet gentleman of gigantic stature and his junior by sixteen years, shared with him many kindred interests and sentiments as well as happy memories; and he had for him—as for Oswell, Steele, and Vardon—a true and natural affection. He entered eagerly into Webb's plans for bettering the lot of his tenants, and all the pursuits of a responsible landlord. His hostess, an Irish lady of great vivacity and charm, captured his heart at once by her quick perception and the warmth of her welcome to one who felt himself to be, in such a stately home, a shy and inarticulate stranger. And, hardened campaigner as he was, he appreciated the comforts and amenities, the leisured ways and spacious orderliness of such a household. There were four children, all little girls, though the eldest, Alice, was of Agnes' age and her devoted companion. There was a host of servants, and with one and all he could relax and feel at ease. But there was one with whom he felt the mutual bond of a deepening understanding and intimacy. This was his daughter Agnes, child though she was; and this may be said to be his great and most rewarding discovery.

Alice (afterwards Mrs. A. Z. Fraser) in her delightful book of reminiscences, *Livingstone and Newstead*, has remarked upon this:

From the first she seemed fitted to be his natural companion, and to rise superior to her years in this respect. As the weeks passed and they grew to know each other yet more intimately, Agnes became his confidante and friend in a way permitted to few daughters. Circumstances no doubt contributed to this; but, besides all else, there was a certain similarity of character that made them peculiarly responsive to each other. . . . They had the same beautiful simplicity, the same directness of aim, the same same strong sense of faith and duty, the same dislike of many words. Above all, both possessed in a remarkable degree that high courage which perhaps, more than any other quality, is the strongest link between fine natures. . . .

The pride both the two took in each other was touching to witness. . . . They were evidently so much at ease and happy together, that it made it more pathetic to remember how short a time they were permitted to enjoy each other's society. In Livingstone's self-imposed separation from his family, and especially from Agnes, more than in any of the hardships and privations of his African explorations, was to be found the real self-sacrifice and heroism of his life.

She describes his appearance and manner:

He was always extremely neat and careful in his appearance, although there was nothing the least clerical in his manner or dress. I have no doubt this laid him open to criticism. . . . He had rather a peculiar accent in talking, and still more in reading, English. It almost seemed foreign, or as if the language were not quite familiar to him, and did not run from his tongue naturally. . . . Public speaking was always a trial to him, and the only time he was really ill at Newstead arose from the state of nervousness and distress he was thrown into on delivering an address to the Mechanics' Institute at Mansfield in compliance with my father's request. It was a very small affair, and of course it never struck my father that Dr. Livingstone would take it so seriously as he did. . . .

My mother has often told me that during the eight months of his stay at Newstead, he never said one word she could have wished unsaid, or acted on any occasion otherwise than she would have desired, even to the most trifling details. He had naturally the hereditary good breeding of all Highlanders who, although in some cases they may have minor details of etiquette to learn, never have anything essential to unlearn. . . . Every servant in the big household had a peculiar respect and affection for him.

There were several ponds and even some little lakes in the Newstead grounds, and the Doctor was as keenly interested in her father's experiments with birds and fish as if they had been his own: especially in his fond attempts to breed trout from their ova in glass jars. One Sunday morning he and her parents, and her uncle Colonel G. L. Goodlake, V.C. (two clasps), and another old friend were walking home from church, and wandered down to a pond where her father had installed a fish-trap. According to custom and forgetful of the day they drew it up—and in it a remarkably big perch. "It was such a fine specimen, indeed, as to excite them all . . . Dr. Livingstone himself was actually carrying it home in triumph before the full significance of the deed dawned on my mother, and the scandal such a sight was likely to cause in the household." It was suggested that the catch be hidden. "No," said Dr. Livingstone, "if we did this thing, let us not conceal it. There was no harm in it." This episode so impressed the gallant Colonel that he took the other guest aside and exclaimed, "I do respect Livingstone. He is a real good man!"

There were many varieties of duck and other waterfowl in the lakes. In the largest and most remote of these her father had constructed a decoy. He and the Doctor would visit it almost daily. One evening they stayed on till twilight watching for duck, and it was only the fear of being late for dinner that tore them away.

> Both were haunted at night by dreams of the self-same duck, and the following morning my father started out before breakfast to have a look at them. His amusement may be imagined when the first person he came across was Dr. Livingstone, very wet, very muddy, but blissful as a schoolboy, with a couple of fine wild ducks dangling from his hand. He had got up even sooner than my father did to catch the early bird. The risk of being captured by one of the keepers as a poacher—his appearance was disreputable enough for anything—had only added to the zest of the affair.

Her father told him that if he had not been a missionary he would have made a first-class poacher.

She has memories of his reading the daily prayers for the household at her mother's request; of his religious liberality in allowing Agnes to be confirmed into the Church of England, himself a nonconformist; yet of his own strict observance of Sunday as a day of rest; his surprising knowledge of the lives and writings of the Early Fathers, and his admiration for the old monks. Again of his joy in the life of all young things; of his comforting her cold hands on a bitter day with his own big woollen gloves, when the other grown-ups were chiding and impatient; of his spoiling her little sister Ethel (his special pet and playmate) with scones of jam and clotted cream, asserting his medical knowledge of what was good for her against the protests of her nurse; of a good old-fashioned Christmas with charades and songs and dances, and of his suffering himself to be piloted through the figures of a quadrille; and blind man's buff when he was caught, and in his energetic efforts to catch them dashed his head against a sharp corner of the fireplace, and then how the cut was washed and plastered up—in all this and more besides one catches glimpses of a Livingstone who was unknown to his companions on the Zambesi.[11]

They for their part were continuing to "discuss" him, and on 11 February we find Kirk writing to Stewart: "He must have saved a good deal of money, not that I think he sets much value on that. He would give all for a C.B. or better a K.C.B., and there will be a push made in some quarters to get it him." Kirk had met the Speaker of the House of Commons when he wrote this, so that (says the editor of these Papers) "he is reporting what he had heard in responsible society". There is no doubt that Livingstone would have been highly gratified by such a decoration had it been offered him, but it was not: perhaps it would have offended the Portuguese. But there occurred an incident almost at the same time which shows how far removed his mind was from entertaining any such thoughts. At the end of January there arrived at Newstead for a short visit one of Mrs. Webb's many old friends and admirers in the person of Mr. A. Hayward, Q.C. He was also, we are told, the unofficial but regular political agent of Lord Palmerston, who made use of him as an emissary on various important occasions. The Prime Minister had a message for Dr. Livingstone: "Was there anything that he could do for him?" Such a question from such a source can have had only one meaning and, as Macnair remarks, any ordinary man would have sensed that— but not Livingstone. No self-regarding thought was in his mind. His request was that a guarantee, ratified by treaty, be obtained from the Portuguese Government of free access for trade to the Shire highlands. This was in fact secured—but only after his death. Looking back on this offer long afterwards, in 1871, he wrote to Kirk regretfully, "I could only think of my work in Africa. It never occurred to me that it meant aught for myself

or my children till I was out here and Lord Palmerston dead."
(Palmerston died in fact in this same year.)

He had been grievously annoyed by rumours circulated by
Stewart that the Shire highlands were unfit for the cultivation
of cotton, the more so since being informed that these irresponsible criticisms of his chief commercial project had been
reported in the Cape newspapers. Stewart, now hearing that
his indiscretions had reached Livingstone's ears, reopened a
correspondence with him. He strenuously denies the "incredible lie" that he had written to the papers; but he conveniently
omits any mention of his having circulated such rumours by
word of mouth, or by private letters. That he had done so is
apparent in his letters to Kirk, who in reply shows himself a
strong advocate of Livingstone's proposed scheme for the
cotton-fields. Stewart seems at this time to have been the victim
of an almost diseased sensibility, and the mawkish introspective
tone of his letters must have sorely tried the patience of his
correspondent who was busy with matters of much more
important and objective moment. After some pages of self-
exculpation Stewart's first letter, dated from Edinburgh on
5 April 1864, ends:

> Still, I need not say I have faith in you and, though perhaps blindly,
> sympathy and some comprehension of your plans. If I had not this, I do
> not think I would have done what I have, during the last three years.
> Let me hear from you. And if you return to this country let me know
> where I am likely to find you. With all esteem, believe me yours very
> sincerely . . .

Again, in October of the same year:

> Certainly, if you believe all you have heard of me, and I all I have
> heard of your opinion of me, there is nothing both of us should desire so
> much as never to see or to hear of each other again. But I believe we
> have been befooled, and good work in consequence spoiled.

Livingstone's reply to the first of these effusions is lacking in
all but the first few lines: "I am sorry that I was out when you
called, for I did not answer the note with which you kindly
welcomed me home on account of the expectation of soon
seeing you." His reply to the second, in so far as it concerns
their personal relations, is as follows:

> My dear Sir,—My answer to your long letter, as you have conjec-
> tured, must be short. . . . I do not consider myself above having been

deceived, but, unless led to foolish conduct, I do not feel that I have been befooled. Generally I can forgive, and I prefer not to take unkind feelings towards anyone along the path of life. If we carry sunshine in our own bosoms, why should we allow the silly sayings of the past to come back to becloud our joy? . . . [12]

Meanwhile he wrought laboriously at his book which, designed at first as a pamphlet on the slave-traffic, grew into a volume on the story of the Expedition—with the unpleasant features omitted. Thus his visit to Newstead, intended for a few weeks, was prolonged into more than as many months. He called this uncongenial task his daily "lessons", but before it was finished Alice and Agnes and others of the household were co-operating in transcribing the fair copy. Kirk, Rae, and Waller came down severally at his request to advise or where necessary correct. He sent proofs of certain sections to Stewart for the favour of revision, and adopted his suggestions. He used his brother's diary, though it complicated his task, in order to give him the title of joint-authorship and half the share in the profits. He dedicated the book, on Murchison's advice, to Lord Palmerston, "the great Statesman who has ever had at heart the amelioration of the African race".

The *Narrative* has been called flat and dull in comparison with his earlier *Travels*, and so in the main it is. It is the more remarkable for all that it leaves untold: if the story were set forth in its entirety it would provide material for a tragic drama of cumulative intensity. Nevertheless, bald as it is compared with what it might have been, 10,000 copies were sold in five editions.

But there were two old friends to whom Livingstone submitted the final proofs for emendation: one was Professor Owen, the other was Mr. Oswell. With Oswell he had maintained an irregular correspondence ever since old Bechuana days, and they had forgathered frequently on his first visit home. The Webbs had pressed Oswell to come to Newstead while Livingstone was there, but his wife's health prevented him. Instead they exchanged letters every week, and even oftener as the proofs came in, and in reading them one is impressed with a sense of the brightness of a comradeship that age could not weary nor the years condemn.

Oswell to Livingstone

My dear old Friend,—I ought to have written a few lines to you, bad scribe as I am, to welcome you back to England, and I take shame to myself for not doing so long ago; but as I do not feel a bit as if I liked you less, or was one atom the less sincerely happy that it has pleased God to let you return, I hope you will give me credit for all this, and the remembrance of very much more of ancient kindness and pleasant companionship in days gone by, but still very present with *me* at all events. I know your time is taken up with more worthy parties than your old partner . . . and I have but a bit of a cottage, but such as it is I trust you know it is yours as much as mine. . . .

Believe me, Always most affectionately yours—

My wife would beg to be most kindly remembered to you. . . . She knows full well how often and for how long you were her husband's very kind and true friend.

You must have given a very much better account of me than I deserve, so just abuse me a little, as in the event of my being able to go down to Newstead I may only give universal dissatisfaction.

Livingstone to Oswell

. . . If you think I have given you too high a character I am ready to abuse you when we meet, as much as you like, to equalize matters. The Portuguese do the abuse of *me*, so I need no one to lower *my* reputation. With love to Mrs. Oswell.

Don't fear your doing any harm. . . . I think if it [his book] succeeds it will owe more to you than to me. Some passages in the first proofs I don't understand myself, so I blame the printer. . . .

Agnes is delighted with your photo. You look better than ever, thanks to your better half. I am very old and grey, and face wrinkled like a gridiron. A barber offered to dye my hair for 10s. 6d.! I must be very good-tempered, for I did not fight him. . . .

What is the name of the game we used to play by keeping a ball up with the hands? Fives or golf, or what? I am forgetting my English. They throw up a ball by striking against the ground and as it rebounds catch it. With love.

The book would not have been half so good but for you. You are quite right about the Portuguese. Like the reformed Quaker in "Uncle Tom" I feel like "a-cussin' and swerrin' dreadful" when I think on their villainy, and meant to put it clear though mild—*suaviter in modo*, and into them slick. Mollify if you can. . . .

Would the words "It is with sincere gratitude I thank my friends Professor Owen and Mr. Oswell for many valuable hints and other aid in the preparation of the volume" grate on you? Insert them to oblige me. D.L.[13]

The manuscript was finished on 15 April, 1865, to his vast relief, and Agnes had written FINIS when the post was due. "Agnes was transcribing a note to it when we had to bundle it up, and she ran after the letter-carrier."

Among other illustrious guests at Newstead before Christmas had been Sir Roderick Murchison, "tall, stately, and courtly with the elaborate manners of the old school"; and his Lady, tiny, pretty and loquacious—*la spirituelle* as she was called— who with her charmingly indiscreet sallies kept the table in a roar and her husband on tenterhooks. Returning to London, Murchison had written to Livingstone (5 January) with a tentative serious proposal.

> As to *your future*, I am anxious to know what *your own wish is* as respects a renewal of African exploration. Quite irrespective of missionaries or political affairs, there is at this moment a question of intense geographical interest to be settled: namely, the watershed, or watersheds, of South Africa. . . .

Would he care to undertake this "as the completion of your remarkable career"? Proceed by way of the Rovuma and round the south end of Lake Tanganyika, and perhaps reach the sources of the White Nile? "You would bring back an unrivalled reputation, and would have settled all the great disputes now pending."

> If you do not like to undertake *the purely geographical work*, I am of opinion that no one, after yourself, is so fitted to carry it out as Dr. Kirk. . . . I have heard you so often talk of the enjoyment you feel when in Africa, that I cannot believe you now think of anchoring for the rest of your life on the mud and sandbanks of England. Let me know your mind on this subject. . . .

To this Livingstone at once replied:

> I should like the exploration you propose very much, and had already made up my mind to go up the Rovuma, pass by the head of Lake Nyasa, and away west or north-west as might be found practicable. . . .
> What my inclination leads me to prefer is to have intercourse with the people, and do what I can to enlighten them on the slave-trade, and give them some idea of our religion. It may not be much that I can do, but I feel when doing that that I am not travelling in vain. . . . To be debarred from spending most of my time in travelling, in exploration, and continual intercourse with the natives, I always felt to be a severe

privation, and if I can get a few hearty native companions, I shall enjoy myself, and feel that I am doing my duty. As soon as my book is out, I shall start.

"To understand the precise bearing of this proposal, and of Livingstone's reply, it is necessary to say that Sir Roderick had a conviction, which he never concealed, that the missionary enterprise encumbered and impeded the geographical" (Blaikie). He had a special objection to an episcopal mission, holding that by rousing ecclesiastical jealousy it was an additional irritant to the Portuguese. But Livingstone held his own course. Writing to James Young at this time he said: "I would not consent to go simply as a geographer, but as a missionary, and do geography by the way, because I feel I am in the way of duty when trying either to enlighten these poor people, or open their land to lawful commerce."

At the same time a suggestion came verbally from the Foreign Office that he should accept a commission "giving him authority over the chiefs from the Portuguese boundary to Abyssinia and Egypt", but without salary or pension. To this Livingstone replied curtly that "he did not like to be treated like a charwoman"![14]

Campbell attributes this parsimony on the part of the Government to the fact that Livingstone was "somewhat of an embarrassment" to an administration anxious to keep on friendly terms with Portugal. Eventually after some deliberation the Government decided to vote him the sum of £500 for equipment and the R.G.S. an equal sum; but "had it not been for the munificence of his friend James Young, who gave as much as the British Government and the Royal Geographical Society put together for the purposes of the expedition, it is inconceivable that it could have been organized at all."[15]

To add to his annoyance, the grant from the R.G.S. was accompanied by the most detailed directions as to where he was to go and what he was to do, what maps to make and reports to furnish: these however emanated not from the President but, as he told Waller, from two "blockheads" on the Council, and he paid no heed to them. He wrote to Kirk, "I would be delighted if we could go together, but I fear the money won't reach a salary." Couldn't Kirk try to raise it in some other quarter? Failing him, "I would rather go alone than take anyone untried."[16] But Kirk was about to be married and therefore he could not come; besides which, one experience of Livingstone as a travelling companion was probably more than enough. And Livingstone for his part was probably relieved by Kirk's refusal. Instead he solicited the Foreign Office for a government appointment for Kirk as medical officer in Zanzibar, which soon led to his promotion to the important and lucrative post of Consul. With Kirk at the focus of the slave-traffic and himself in the interior at the source of its supply, there was hope that between them they might cut its main artery. At the same time he secured for his brother Charles the Consulship at Fernando Po on the other side of the continent (where Charles died only a year after David). Compared with either of these, the consular position which he accepted for himself—unpaid, obscure and ill-defined, with merely nominal authority, of necessity subject to much toil and many hazards and privations—was humble in the extreme. But after all it would, like his previous appointment, be timed for a term of only two years; then he could come home for good and devote himself to his children. . . .

On 25 April, ten days after the completion of his book, Livingstone and his daughter took leave of their good hosts, and "may God reward them and their family". In London next day he was "horrified by news of President Lincoln's assassination, and the attempt to murder Seward". On the 29th: "Went down to Crystal Palace with Agnes to a Saturday Concert. The music very fine. Met Waller, and lost a train. Came up in hot haste to the dinner of the Royal Academy." There were present the two Archbishops and all the Ministers except Palmerston, who was ill; the Duke of Argyll and Bishops of Oxford and London were within earshot; "Lord Clarendon was close enough to lean back and clap me on the shoulder, and ask me when I was going out." The Master of the Rolls was directly opposite. "The speeches were much above the average. I was not told that I was expected to speak till I got in and this prevented my eating . . . My speech was not reported . . . This non-reporting was much commented on . . . But I did not feel offended."

18 *May*.—Was examined by the Committee [of the House of Commons] on the West Coast; was rather nervous and confused, but let them

know pretty plainly that I did not agree with the aspersions cast on missions.

[To W. F. Webb.] I can stand a good deal of bosh, but to tell me that Christianity makes people worse—ugh! Tell that to the young trouts. You know on what side I am, and I shall stand to my side, Old Pam fashion, through thick and thin, I don't agree with all my side say or do. I won't justify many things, but for the great cause of human progress I am heart and soul, *and so are you*.[17]

On the 23rd he went up by the night train to Scotland again and found his mother "very poorly"; on 2 June "gradually becoming weaker"; on the 5th: "Mother continued very low, and her mind ran on poor Robert. Thought I was his brother and asked me frequently, "Where is your brother? where is that puir laddie?" . . . Sisters most attentive . . . Contrary to expectation she revived, and I went to Oxford. The Vice-Chancellor offered me the theatre to lecture in, but I expected a telegram if any change took place."

Monday, 19 *June*.—A telegram came saying that mother had died the day before. I started at once for Scotland. No change was observed till within an hour and a half of her departure. . . . Seeing the end was near, sister Agnes said, "The Saviour has come for you, mother. You can lippen yourself to him?" She replied, "Oh yes." Little Anna Mary was held up to her. She gave her the last look and said, "Bonnie wee lassie", gave a few long inspirations and all was still, with a look of reverence on her countenance. She had wished William Logan, a good Christian man, to lay her head in the grave if I were not there. When going away in 1858, she said to me that she would have liked one of her laddies to lay her head in the grave. It so happened that I was there to pay the last tribute to a dear good mother.[18]

Before leaving Hamilton he went with Anna Mary to attend the prize-day at Gilbertfield where his boy Oswell was at school. Dr. Loudon, the family's medical friend, had great difficulty in persuading him to go. The thought of a speech terrified him. But he had to go, and of course he had to speak. Of his speech only one sentence was remembered, the last, but it was never forgotten: "Fear God and Work Hard."

At the beginning of August he was back in London with Agnes; on the 8th went to the Zoo with Webb and Kirk; next day parted with the Webbs with considerable emotion; dined at Lady Franklin's with the Queen of Honolulu, "a nice sensible person". On the 11th he said good-bye to the Duchess-Dowager of Sutherland and was shown Garibaldi's rooms: "a good man he was, but followed by a crowd of harpies who used him for their own purposes." He took leave of the Foreign Office the same day: "Mr. Layard very kind." Then to a farewell dinner with his publisher, Mr. Murray, and his last act was to entrust Agnes to the care of Mr. Oswell, who "offered to go over to Paris any time to bring her home, or do anything for her that a father would". He was as good as his word. He called her his "adopted daughter" and she treasured his letters long after, especially this: "If you are within a hundred miles of me let me know, and I will come and shake you by the hand. I will always come even to the end of the earth, if I can be of any use to you, or you want me."[19]

Some ten years later Agnes married Mr. Alexander Low Bruce, of whom Waller wrote to her: "Your husband was a prop and stay to everything which Dr. Livingstone had most at heart." Their son was Colonel Alexander Bruce, D.S.O. Anna Mary, one of the many child-friends of Hans Andersen, was educated by her father's wish at a Quaker school in Kendal, where she met and later married Mr. Frank Wilson, a nephew of her father's life-long Quaker friend Mr. Bevan Braithwaite. Together they worked afloat for the Deep Sea Fishermen Society, and afterwards for the Church Missionary Society in Sierra Leone. Their son was Dr. Hubert Francis Wilson, M.C.

Thomas, who was always delicate, died in Egypt at the age of 26 unmarried. Of Oswell there is more to be told. But it was his daughters rather than his sons who inherited their father's vigour and stamina.

Livingstone had never lost touch with the Protestant French missionaries in Bechuanaland, among them the Rev. M. Frédoux, who was his sister-in-law Ann Moffat's husband; and the Rev. P. Lemue who had married him to Mary, for many years head of the Motito Mission, and whose own wife was devoted to old Mrs. Moffat. They had a niece, Madame Hocédé, who had been governess to the Queen's daughters at Windsor and now kept a school for Protestant English girls in Paris. This was the school he chose for Agnes, and thither he conducted her in mid-August *en route* to Cairo and Bombay. Kirk and Waller came down to Folkestone to see them off. "This is very kind," he notes; "the Lord put it into their hearts to show kindness, and blessed is His name." They never saw him again.[20]

Chapter Twenty-Five

LAST JOURNEYS: BOMBAY AND ZANZIBAR
1865–1866

"In another attempt to open Africa to civilizing influences . . .
I propose to go inland . . ."

THE view has been accepted by some writers in recent years (since Coupland first propounded it) that Livingstone in his last journey was a mystic in quest of a visionary goal, and that he pursued it with a kind of fatalistic obsession to the point of voluntary martyrdom—or suicide. This view is derogatory both to mysticism and to Livingstone. Mysticism in its true sense is not hallucination but heightened perception; it is the clarification and intensification of consciousness into an intuitive awareness of the divine. It is the reverse of "mistiness"; it is the core and kernel of the spiritual life; the most intensive experience of which the soul is capable. Its accent however is on the immanence rather than the transcendence of God.

Livingstone was never a mystic in this sense, either during his last journey or at any time before it. From first to last he was a practical idealist. He felt a beckoning from beyond rather than an illumination from within. He felt himself to be an instrument, however unworthy, in the hand of a transcendent God. Much as he admired the mystical quality in the writings of the Christian Fathers and in the conversation of his Quaker friends, he did so with a certain wistfulness, realizing that their experience was not his but was still something outside his reach. All through his life he was inspired by the sense of a divine vocation, but not sustained by the interior consciousness of a beatific vision. A man who lacks that experience, be it only for a moment in his life, is not a mystic; a man who sets his course towards a geographical goal and plots it with mathematical precision is not a visionary.

Neither did he seek martyrdom. He sought simply to accom-

plish the task which he sincerely believed had been committed
to him, and having done so would return to his children and
await whatever might be the next. To this hope he clung to
the last. It is true that he drove himself to death—but not
deliberately.

He sought for guidance and strength and protection in
prayer; in the promptings of conscience, in dependence upon
that Providence whose directions he believed that he discerned
by manifest "tokens" as he followed them steadily onward.
"I think I am in the way of duty . . . I have never wavered in
the conviction that such is the case." There is a sense in which
such a temper is beyond criticism, a sense in which he too could
say, like his great predecessor in the missionary field: "God
forbid that I should be judged by you or by any man's judgment. Yea rather, I judge not mine own self, but he that
judgeth me is the Lord." Despite his obvious faults of character,
which it would be injustice to him to palliate; despite his
massive common-sense and practical sagacity (except in the
superintendence of others)—his was the other-worldly wisdom
of a dedicated life. That it led him in the end, and others
indirectly, to death and disaster is a fact which constitutes the
paradox of the spiritual life. It may be said to be the apparent
fate of every spiritual adventurer. The pages of history and of
biography alike are blurred with the record of lost causes,
quenched enthusiasms, frustrated purposes, disillusioned hopes.
No facile optimism, no sentimental wishful thinking, can burke
these stark inexorable facts. Livingstone is conspicuous among
many other examples of that antithesis between the spiritual
and the natural which underlies our dual life, and of which the
supreme example for mankind is epitomized in the Life that led
to Calvary.

When Livingstone's last journals and note-books were collected they were found to be complete to the last page, and the
task of editing them was entrusted to his eldest surviving son.
Ill-health and lack of technical experience compelled him to
abandon it, though with a heavy heart; and Agnes (to whose
keeping they were consigned) then approached her father's
oldest friend, W. C. Oswell. But Oswell felt obliged because of
pressing family responsibilities to decline what he would have

esteemed the greatest honour, and could do so with good heart since the publisher Mr. Murray had expressed the view that the Rev. Horace Waller would be the most competent person to undertake the task. And of all Livingstone's associates in Africa it can be safely said that there was none to whom he would more gladly have committed it; for none was more loyal, sensible, sympathetic, or stout-hearted than he.

Arrived at Bombay on 11 September 1865, Livingstone went first to the Governor, Sir Bartle Frere, who (he wrote to Waller) "is a brick, and will do all he can for me". His first care was to recruit native volunteers and at Frere's suggestion enlisted from the Bombay Marine Battalion twelve sepoys with a havildar; then nine negroes from the mission school at Nassick, rescued from slavery; "I have taken every pains to let them know that work, not play, is intended." Also the two Yao boys, Chuma and Wikatani, still in their 'teens, whom he had left in the care of the Rev. Dr. Wilson of the Scottish Free Church Mission and who had acquired a little English: "Chuma is a very sharp fellow; never got into any quarrel at school; I expect his appearance put the fear of death into the Hindoos, but Dr. Wilson thinks it is his goodness."[1]

His next care was to sell the *Lady Nyasa*. He was depending upon this to supplement his totally insufficient means and expected a good price. After several advertisements the launch that he had bought for £6,000 was sold for £2,300; he was advised to invest this in an Indian bank; the bank collapsed in the following year and the whole of his personal expenditure—together with the labour previously expended on transporting the vessel up the Shire for nothing, and then sailing her across the ocean—vanished into air. Meanwhile however he gave an address to the merchants in Bombay suggesting the establishment of a mart on the African coast. Dr. Wilson presided and appealed for a contribution from Bombay equivalent to that granted by the Government and the R.G.S. combined; the result was the promise of £1,000.

Here, as always, he made many friends, and the remarks of two of them deserve mention. The Rev. Dugald C. Boyd wrote: "Livingstone was, though quiet, very communicative . . . He spoke very kindly of Stewart, and seems to hope that he may yet join him in Central Africa." The other, after an excursion with a large party on ponies to the caves in Salsette, is from Mr. Alexander Brown of Liverpool: "Livingstone's almost boyish enjoyment of the whole thing impressed me greatly. The stern, almost impassive man, seemed to unbend and enter most thoroughly into the spirit of the day."[2] During his stay of nearly four months he was for the most part the guest of Sir Bartle Frere, whose impressions (printed as an obituary in the Journal of the R.G.S.) were as follows:

His character it is difficult for those who knew him intimately to speak of without exaggeration. Of his intellectual force and energy he has given proof such as few can afford. His powers of observation and practical sagacity I have never seen exceeded. Both possibly were rendered more acute by the life he led; but he had the quickness of eye, and the power of judging of forces and results which belong only to the great organizer, politician and general. Equally remarkable was his knowledge of character, and penetration. No flattery could blind him, no allurements could lead him aside, while his estimate of men was unfailing. As a whole, the work of his life will surely be held up in ages to come as one of singular nobleness in design, and of unflinching energy and self-sacrifice in execution. . . . I never met a man who fulfilled more completely my idea of a perfect Christian gentleman, actuated in what he thought and said and did by the highest and most chivalrous spirit, modelled on the precepts of his great Master and Exemplar.

The tribute is the more remarkable coming as it does from one who, afterwards Governor of the Cape, has with justice been called "one of the ablest and most high-minded of the British proconsuls of his day". It should perhaps be qualified by saying that Livingstone was an improviser rather than an organizer; and that his judgment of men, though intuitively sound, was by no means infallible.

Before leaving Bombay the double post of Consul and Agency-Surgeon became vacant at Zanzibar, and Livingstone wrote at once to Oswell: "I wish Kirk could get that post; he would be invaluable there." But the Bombay Government preferred one of their own tried officers for the former post and appointed Dr. G. E. Seward. This left the surgeonship open, however, and on New Year's Day 1866 Livingstone wrote to Kirk:

Many happy returns of this day to you, my dear Kirk. The Governor sent for me yesterday. . . . He said that he wished to ask me about you. He knew that I had always spoken very handsomely about you, but there were sometimes private circumstances in a man's character which, unless called upon to reveal, no one would think of mentioning; there may be something (here I put in the word "cranky") yes, something that, though not prominent, might render him an inconvenient public servant. I replied, in terms that I need not repeat, that I knew no defect of character or temper; you got on well with people, but were firm in doing your duty, etc.; and I felt certain that from your hatred of the Slave Trade and knowledge of the whole subject you would be invaluable at Zanzibar. He said that it was a great recommendation that I wished you to be there, and he would have much pleasure in telegraphing to you today.[3]

Kirk, though newly married, had little hesitation in accepting the post which later led to his promotion as Consul, little foreseeing—any more than did Livingstone—the unhappy consequences that would ensue and threaten to sever their friendship. But at the time the situation seemed ideal. As Coupland has said:

Thus, at the core of the growing group of Britons who were sharing in the crusade against the Slave Trade in East Africa . . . a little triple alliance had been formed. Livingstone, its spearhead, penetrating the black veil that still concealed so much of Africa and letting in the light of public knowledge. Kirk, his tried and trusted lieutenant, at his island base. Waller, the closest of all the friends he had made in Africa, in London, with his hand on all the strings of the humanitarian movement.[4]

At the same time he was writing to Waller in affectionate banter:

My dearly beloved Waller . . . Walla means "a fellow" here; buggy-walla, for instance, is a cabby; patiwalla a flunkey. I make no comment. . . .

You may fancy me falling into Tozer's arms (at Zanzibar) and kissing him. He has turned over a new leaf; scrubs the boys with his sleeves tucked up. . . .

You will never be a man till you are wedded. I only wish I had you *in extremis* and a nice girl willing to take you by the hand. Wouldn't I marry you!

Armed with a diplomatic letter of commendation from Frere to the Sultan of Zanzibar, he embarked on 5 January 1866 in a ship of the Chinese fleet, the *Thule* (Captain Brebner), for that monarch's acceptance from the Bombay Government, and reached the island after a passage of twenty-three days. The ship was an "incorrigible roller" and most of the sepoys were sick. He had ordered a set of coloured Scripture slides from an instrument-maker in Bombay to be put in with his magic-lantern; when he opened the box at sea, not one was in it. "The world will never get on," he wrote to James Young, "till we have a few of these instrument-makers hung." The day after his arrival he paid his first official visit to the Palace, and wrote to his daughter:

> His Highness met us at the bottom of the stair, and as he shook hands a brass band which he had got at Bombay blared forth "God Save the Queen"! This was excessively ridiculous, but I maintained sufficient official gravity. After coffee and sherbet we came away, and the wretched band now struck up "The British Grenadiers"—as if the fact of my being only five feet eight, and Brebner about two inches lower, ought not to have suggested "Wee Willie Winkie" as more appropriate. I was ready to explode, but got out of sight before giving way.[5]

He obtained two more audiences, at the first of which he made a set speech, and after the second was presented with the Sultan's *firman* or passport enjoining upon all his subjects the duty of rendering every possible assistance to the bearer. Seeing that a large part of the Sultan's revenue was derived from the customs dues paid by the slavers, the invasion of his dominions by a British subject whose avowed objective was to suppress the Trade must have been an embarrassment, but against it he had to set the value of British friendship. He placed one of his own large houses at Livingstone's disposal during the whole of his stay and showed him every courtesy.

His meeting with Bishop Tozer is not related, but there is nothing to show that they parted otherwise than with mutual goodwill—despite his ribald fling (in an epistolary aside to Waller) at the bishop "holding fast to his crozier and swathed in his muslins".

> Tozer is trying the effect of gaudy dresses, banners and crosses as mission agencies. If he succeeds it will be interesting to find Moham-medans bowing down to red crosses and red flags, not to mention Tozer's red hair, though they think all these are idols.[6]

He must have chuckled long afterwards in Ujiji at Stanley's much more ribald description.

Livingstone's own conception of evangelism to the heathen

was simpler than that of the High Church party, if perhaps cruder. It is expressed in a Journal entry when at sea between Bombay and Zanzibar.

> Issued flannel to all the boys from Nassick; the marines have theirs from Government. The boys sing a couple of hymns every evening, and repeat the Lord's Prayer. I mean to keep this up, and make this a Christian expedition, telling a little about Christ wherever we go. His love in coming down to save men will be our theme. I dislike very much to make my religion distasteful to others. This, with Bedingfeld's hypocritical ostentation, made me have fewer religious services on the Zambesi than would have been desirable, perhaps. . . . Though there is antipathy in the human heart to the Gospel of Christ, yet when Christians make their good works shine all admire them. It is when great disparity exists between profession and practice that we secure the scorn of mankind. The Lord help me to act in all cases in this expedition as a Christian ought.[7]

It must be said with truth (however unpalatable) that since the U.M.C.A. had ceased to be part of the church militant in the front line and had retreated to a "strategic" base, Livingstone had disowned it. He was not himself and never had been a "churchman"; but he would gladly have condoned ecclesiastical frills (much as they irritated him) if only they had been displayed in the field of active service. Reviewing the anomalous situation of a Christian mission in Zanzibar at such a time, he wrote from Lake Nyasa a few months later (24 August) to Professor Sedgwick despondently enough:

> . . . I look at this fine region fast becoming depopulated with feelings of inexpressible sadness. We allow the Zanzibar slave-trade within certain limits, and the effect of this licence is that that insignificant island is a great slave emporium and hundreds of miles of a far finer country is annually swept of crowds of people; our mission there is virtually gagged. The Sultan is all civility and flattery but no missionary progress can be allowed among his bigoted Mahometans, and then about half the missionary strength must always be absent in quest of health. It is almost enough to make Mackensie turn round in his grave to find his mission degraded to a mere chaplaincy to a consulate, and I fear there is no hope of seeing Central Africa occupied by its own Mission in our day. . . . When I see how bigoted and unfriendly the coast tribes are and how friendly the people of the Interior prove themselves, I conclude that Africa must be evangelized from within. . . . But after all I have hopes in the Church yet and cannot believe that all the hopes, prayers, and sympathies which clustered round my poor dear Friend are to go into the air. . . .[8]

His dreams were realized far beyond expectation, but not in his lifetime. In 1873 (the year that Kirk was appointed Consul) within *one month of his death*, Sir Bartle Frere, then Governor of the Cape, was sent to negotiate and conclude a treaty with the Sultan Burghash for the suppression of the Slave Trade in Zanzibar. In 1876 he outlawed the Trade in all his dominions. In the same year the Universities' Mission to Central Africa triumphantly erected the Church, now a magnificent Cathedral, on the ruins of the old slave-market. In the same year the Livingstonia Industrial Mission was established on Lake Nyasa, and the Church of Scotland Industrial Mission at Blantyre, with a Scottish trading station. In 1884 the Shire highlands and all the lakeside territory to the north, once so devastated and depopulated, was flourishing with prosperous settlements; and in 1891 the whole of Nyasaland was declared a British Protectorate. All owed their inspiration and origin to the faith and foresight of one man "who died not having received the promises but who glimpsed them from afar off". By his death he accomplished far more than by his life. Truly it may be said of him, and in more ways than one, that "Nothing in his life became him like the leaving of it".

Meanwhile he was wandering restless and disconsolate through the narrow fetid streets and booths, and into the very heart of the poisonous trade.

It is the old, old way of living—eating, drinking, sleeping; sleeping, drinking, eating. Getting fat; slave-dhows coming and slave-dhows going away; bad smells; and kindly looks from English folks to each other.[9]

The stench arising from a mile and a half or two square miles of exposed sea-beach, which is the general depository of the filth of the town, is quite horrible. At night it is so gross or crass one might cut out a slice and manure a garden with it; it might be called Stinkibar rather than Zanzibar.

On visiting the slave-market I found about 300 slaves exposed for sale, the greater part of whom came from Nyasa and the Shire River; I am so familiar with the peculiar faces and markings or tattooings that I expect them to recognize me. Indeed one woman said that she had heard of our passing up Lake Nyasa in a boat, but she did not see me: others came from Chipeta, S.W. of the Lake. All who have grown up seem ashamed at being hawked about for sale. The teeth are examined, the cloth lifted to examine the lower limbs, and a stick is thrown for the slave to bring, and thus exhibit his paces. Some are dragged through the crowd by the hand, and the price called out incessantly: most of the purchasers were Northern Arabs and Persians.[10]

And in this depressing haunt of wickedness he must wait perforce full seven weeks before the arrival of a warship from the south to take him and his retinue to the mouth of the Rovuma. Meanwhile he could continue to recruit more volunteers, for he would need many. It chanced that three men who had served with him on the Zambesi were now in Zanzibar: Susi and Amoda, from the Shupanga district; and Musa, a Moslem of Johanna, who had served under Lieut. E. D. Young in the *Lady Nyasa* on her voyage up the Shire and had been described by him as a thief and a liar. That indeed was the general reputation of Johanna men. Yet Livingstone engaged nine more, and put Musa in charge of them. Nearly fifty years later Sir Richard Burton described them as "*facile principes* among Eastern impostors . . . as cowardly as they are dishonest. . . . It was not without astonishment," he adds, "that I heard of Dr. Livingstone engaging a party of them for exploration in the African interior." Livingstone was well aware of their general reputation and speaks of them in a letter at this time as "not much to be trusted"; but he had hoped for a picked contingent from Mr. Sunley, the Consul. To him he had written from Hamilton on 2 June 1865 in a letter hitherto unnoticed:

> My dear Sunley,—Can you give me an encouragement to hope for 20 or 25 men if I come to Johanna? I want them as carriers chiefly. . . . I liked the first lot I had from you very much, and blamed the headman most for the second party turning out dishonest. My funds limit my liberality—it is but £2,000 in all. If you give me hope in a letter to Bombay [address follows] I should ask the man-of-war to put me down at Johanna instead of on the coast. . . . I have sent four letters in different directions to you. I had intended taking Belooches [mercenary soldiers], but Col. Rigby so strongly dissuades me that I turn from them to you. I would like them all Johanna men, if I could have two trustworthy headmen and a cook. . . .[11]

For some reason unexplained he received no reply to these various letters and it is very probable, as Coupland suggests, that in default of picked men from Johanna he preferred their compatriots in Zanzibar to the riff-raff of African natives there, morally contaminated, as he believed them to be, with the slave-ships thronging the harbour and the slave-gangs on the clove-plantations. Twenty-four more carriers were engaged from the mainland when he arrived there, so that his total "strength" amounted to sixty: 13 Indian sepoys; 9 "Nassick boys" (so-called but actually emancipated negroes); 10 Johanna men; 2 Shupanga men and 2 Yaos; and 24 negroes from the coast. A mixed assortment certainly, but it is doubtful whether he could have done better. The sepoys were supposed to be disciplined soldiers, and the Nassick boys were supposed to have been "trained", and he had impressed upon them that "work not play" was intended. Himself no disciplinarian he no doubt counted on the havildar and Musa and the headman of the Johanna group to keep them up to the mark; and hoped that the force of moral example and the influence of kindness would take salutary effect. But:

> Livingstone's previous experience in this vital matter had been highly encouraging, but the circumstances had been quite different from what they would be now. The men who had followed him so devotedly across Africa had not been hired at a coastal town. His march had started from Makolololand, and his Makololo porters had been raw tribesmen who, after discussion in the tribal council, had been deputed to accompany the explorer to the coast and back. On the Zambesi the long hauls had been made by water; and most of the few porters needed had again been Makololo. But this time those faithful tribesmen were out of reach, and Livingstone could scarcely hope to find other Africans as simple and unspoiled and as ready to follow him into the unknown.[12]

Moreover, he was a much older man than he was on his transcontinental journey.

His next care was for baggage-animals. He had transported in dhows from Bombay three Indian buffaloes and a calf; in Zanzibar he procured six camels, two mules and four donkeys. What other man than Livingstone, it has been asked, would have encumbered himself with such a menagerie, and for what purpose unless for the benefit of Africa? His purpose was in fact partly experimental: to discover whether tame buffaloes would prove like their wild cousins in Africa immune from the bite of the tsetse; and whether or not the other animals would be infected.

His plan was to go south by sea to the harbour of Mikindani, there disembark, and follow the course of the Rovuma to near its source, cross Lake Nyasa to Kotakota by ferries, and then strike up northwards to the central mart of Ujiji on Lake Tanganyika. Ujiji lay at the head of a well-known Arab trade-route which started at Bagamoyo on the mainland opposite

479

Zanzibar and passed through the Arab trading colony at Unyanyembe. This would be his base for exploration in the interior, and he would "work quietly west" from there. "We were always in too great a hurry last expedition," he had written to Kirk in England. The route inland from Bagamoyo via Unyanyembe would have been much shorter and more direct, but he wanted to see more of Lake Nyasa and he disliked following a slave-route. But by this route he arranged for the despatch of a considerable quantity of stores from the well-known Hindu firm of Ludha Damji in Zanzibar, whose junior manager there was Koorji, and his agent in Ujiji an Arab named Thani bin Suellim. To the latter his stores, consisting of calico and beads for barter, and flour and sugar, tea and coffee for his own use, were consigned. Upon them he depended for subsistence after arrival at Ujiji.

In his Preface to the *Narrative* he had stated the objects of his journey, and its promotion, in the following carefully-worded terms. It is dated from Newstead Abbey on 16 April 1865, the date he sent off the manuscript to his publisher.

> The Government have supported the proposal of the Royal Geographical Society made by my friend Sir Roderick Murchison, and have united with that body to aid me in another attempt to open Africa to civilizing influences, and a valued private friend has given me a thousand pounds for the same object. I propose to go inland, north of the territory which the Portuguese in Europe claim, and endeavour to commence that system on the East which has been so eminently successful on the West Coast; a system combining the repressive efforts of H.M. cruisers with lawful trade and Christian Missions—the moral and material results of which have been so gratifying. I hope to ascend the Rovuma or some other river north of Cape Delagao, and in addition to my other work shall strive, by passing along the northern end of Lake Nyasa and round the southern end of Lake Tanganyika, to ascertain the watershed of that part of Africa. In so doing, I have no wish to unsettle what with so much toil and danger was accomplished by Speke and Grant, but rather to confirm their illustrious discoveries.[13]

After his first great journey he had affirmed that the end of the geographical feat was only the beginning of the missionary enterprise. Now he announced that the geographical feat of discovering the central watershed (and therewith tacitly the sources of the Nile) was again subsidiary to a Christian aim. It was not primarily missionary; it was the exposure of the slave traffic at its centre—with a view to its eventual abolition. This was the chief aim that he set before him on his last journey and which—as is apparent in a letter to his brother John a few months before his death—he pursued steadily to the end. And however some may cavil at Christian missions to the heathen, and others with more justice may criticize some of the methods that have been and still are employed to this end— none can impugn the purely humanitarian purpose with which Livingstone set forth on his last journey. No one who calls himself a human being—whether he be Christian, Jew, Turk or infidel—can deny that Livingstone was right in his undertaking, or assert that in his last journey he was a deluded visionary pursuing a phantasmal quest.

The slave-trade with which Livingstone had made contact hitherto in West and East Africa was that conducted mainly by the Portuguese, by which negroes from the interior were captured and transported to America. But he had been shocked to discover the existence of another Trade of the same kind years ago even among the friendly Makololo: this was conducted by the Arabs for the exportation of human material to India and Persia. There was thus a European and an Asiatic slave-trade. It was the latter with which he was now to become acquainted; and "if the numbers taken were less, the methods were even more cruel".

He put out from Zanzibar on 19 March 1866 with a prayer: "I trust that the Most High may prosper me in this work, granting me influence in the eyes of the heathen, and helping me to make my intercourse beneficial to them." He landed at Mikindani on the 22nd; spent several hours reconnoitring for a route along the left bank of the Rovuma, but to no purpose; and then a day in disembarking the animals "all very much the worse for having been knocked about in the dhow". Then there were saddles to prepare, loads to distribute, the twenty-four extra carriers to engage. On the eve of starting he notes ominously: "A few of the Nassick boys have the slave spirit pretty strongly." Then follows the well-known passage which, "in the light of what was coming, provides in almost every sentence a rare example of dramatic irony" (Coupland).

Now that I am on the point of starting on another trip into Africa I feel quite exhilarated: when one travels with the specific object in view of ameliorating the condition of the natives any act becomes ennobled. Whether exchanging the customary civilities or arriving at a village, accepting a night's lodging, purchasing food for the party, asking for information, or answering polite African inquiries as to our objects in travelling, we begin to spread a knowledge of that people by whose agency their land will yet become enlightened and freed from the slave-trade.

The mere animal pleasure of travelling in a wild unexplored country is very great. When on lands of a couple of thousand feet, brisk exercise imparts elasticity to the muscles, fresh and healthy blood circulates through the brain, the mind works well, the eye is clear, the step is firm, and a day's exertion always makes the evening's repose thoroughly enjoyable.

We have usually the stimulus of remote chances of danger either from beasts or men. Our sympathies are drawn out towards our humble hardy companions by a community of interests and, it may be, of perils, which makes us all friends. Nothing but the most pitiable puerility would lead any manly heart to make their inferiority a theme for self-exaltation; however, that is often done, as if with the vague idea that we can, by magnifying their deficiencies, demonstrate our immaculate perfections.

The effect of travel on a man whose heart is in the right place is that the mind is made more self-reliant: it becomes more confident of its own resources—there is greater presence of mind. The body is soon well-knit; the muscles of the limbs grow as hard as a board and seem to have no fat; the countenance is bronzed, and there is no dyspepsia. Africa is a most wonderful country for appetite, and it is only when one gloats over marrow bones or elephant's feet that indigestion is possible. No doubt much toil is involved, and fatigue of which travellers in the more temperate climes can form but a faint conception; but the sweat of one's brow is no longer a curse when one works for God: it proves a tonic to the system and is actually a blessing. No one can truly appreciate the charm of repose unless he has undergone severe exertion.

"The curtain is up. The tragedy has begun. The hero has made the happy self-confident opening speech which warns the audience of his approaching doom."

Chapter Twenty-Six

LAST JOURNEYS: BEYOND THE LOANGWA
1866

*"No one can truly appreciate the charm of repose unless he
has undergone severe exertion."*

WHEN the *Last Journals* came to Oswell's hands he wrote
to Agnes Livingstone:

I have begun to read the book, and the short curt sentences, full of
pith, bring the dear old Father so vividly before me that I cannot believe
I am never to see him again. The dear old fellow, how quiet and gentle
he has grown in these last journals. I do not mean that he was ever the
contrary, but though his unflinching courage and determination remain
where they ever were, his gentleness seems to have become even more and
more diffused through all he did; he is not only *suaviter in modo* but *in re*
too. I have always said when asked, that the most remarkable trait in
him was quiet unostentatious endurance. I speak of course of his character
as a Man *par excellence*.[1]

It was precisely this gentleness that was his undoing.

On the Zambesi Expedition his policy of issuing general
instructions to his staff, and leaving their execution to the conscience and intelligence of each member, had led to indiscipline; and this despite the fact that these white men were all
predisposed to be loyal. It was a counsel of perfection which
was bred in his bone and which in youth he had found corroborated by so great an authority as Dr. Philip, and even though
experience had taught him to revise it on grounds of expediency
and he had welcomed the coming of a missionary body with a
bishop as its head, nevertheless the original principle "to let
men do things in their own way" was that which he, always an
individualist, continued to adopt himself. In truth he could do
no other. But the same principle applied in the case of semi-
sophisticated black men who had no motive for personal
loyalty, and who expected coercion and not gentleness, was to
prove not only mistaken but disastrous.

Leaving Mikindani on 6 April he struck up along the north bank of the Rovuma, hiring willing villagers to clear a track for the passage of the camels through the low trees, and on 13 May reached the point in the river at which he had turned back in 1862. Continuing up its course to the borders of the Yao country he turned south-west and on 14 July reached Mataka, within 50 miles of Lake Nyasa. "But, long before that first stage of his journey was completed, the note of elation had quite died out from his journal."[2]

It is with dismay, with a shock of personal embarrassment even, that the reader encounters in the pages of his Journal a Livingstone who is prematurely aged. He is powerless to control the behaviour of his own retinue: not only to check their laziness and recalcitrance, but also to prevent their brutal and callous treatment of the baggage-animals. The man who had witnessed with horror the slaughter of wild life in the Bechuana game-traps and described it as "frightful", had condemned the blood-sports of his own countrymen as "itinerant butchery", and had strictly enjoined upon his colleagues the duty of a "sacred regard" for animal life, seems now unable even by a word of rebuke to arrest the calculated cruelty of his men to the domesticated beasts of burden.

7 *April.*—Not understanding camels, I had to trust to the sepoys who overloaded them, and before we had accomplished our march of seven miles they were knocked up.

8 *April.*—I lightened the camels, and had a party of woodcutters to heighten and widen the path in the dense jungle into which we now penetrated.

13 *April.*—Frequently our vision was circumscribed to a few yards till our merry woodcutters made for us the pleasant scene of a long vista fit for camels to pass. . . . The steamy smothering air, and the dank rank luxuriant vegetation made me feel, like it, struggling for existence—and no more capable of taking bearings than if I had been in a hogshead and observing through the bunghole!

17 *April.*—I had to leave the camels in the hands of the sepoys; I ordered them to bring as little luggage as possible, and the Havildar assured me that two buffaloes were amply sufficient to carry all they would bring. I now find that they have more than full loads for two buffaloes, two mules, and two donkeys; but when these animals fall down under them, they assure me with so much positiveness that they are not overloaded, that I have to be silent, or only, as I have several times done before, express the opinion that they will kill these animals. This

observation on my part leads them to hide their things in the packs of the camels, which are also overburdened. I fear that my experiment with the tsetse will be vitiated, but no symptoms yet occur in any of the camels except weariness. The sun is very sharp; it scorches.

23 *April.*—Buffaloes bitten by tsetse again show no bad effects from it; one mule is however dull and out of health; I thought that this might be the effect of the bite till I found that his back was so strained that he could not stoop to drink, and could only eat the tops of the grasses.

24 *April.*—No day was lost by sickness, but we could not march more than a few miles owing to the slowness of the sepoys; they are a heavy drag on us, and of no possible use, except as sentries at night. When we get up at 4 a.m. we cannot get under way before 8 o'clock. Sepoys are a mistake.

26 *April.*—Yesterday I caught a sepoy, Pando, belabouring a camel with a big stick as thick as any part of his arm; the path being narrow, it could not get out of his way; I shouted to him to desist; he did not know I was in sight; today the effect of the bad usage is seen in the animal being quite unable to move its leg; inflammation has set up in the hip-joint. I am afraid that several bruises which have festered on the camels, and were to me unaccountable, have been wilfully bestowed.

30 *April.*—Many ulcers burst forth on the camels; some seem old dhow bruises. They come back from pasture bleeding in a way that no rubbing against a tree would account for. I am sorry to suspect foul play: the buffaloes and mules are badly used but I cannot be always near to prevent it.

Buffaloes again bitten by tsetse, and by another fly exactly like the house-fly but having a straight hard proboscis instead of a soft one; other large flies make the blood run. The tsetse does not disturb the buffaloes, but these others and the smaller flies do. The tsetse seem to like the camel best . . . they do not seem to care for the mules and donkeys.

7 *May.*—A camel died during the night, and the grey buffalo is in convulsions this morning. The cruelty of these sepoys vitiates my experiment, and I quite expect many camels, one buffalo, and one mule to die yet. They sit down and smoke and eat, leaving the animals loaded in the sun. If I am not with them, it is a constant dawdling; they are evidently unwilling to exert themselves, they cannot carry their belts and bags, and their powers of eating and vomiting are astounding. The Makonde villages are remarkably clean, but no sooner do we pass a night in one than the fellows make it filthy. . . .

7 *May.*—Another camel, a very good one, died on the way: its shiverings and convulsions are not at all like what we observed in horses and oxen killed by tsetse; but such may be the cause, however.

8 *May.*—I left the havildar, sepoys, and Nassick boys here [Jponde] in order to make a forced march forward, where no food is to be had, and send either to the south or westwards for supplies, so that after they have rested the animals and themselves five days they may come. One mule

is very ill; one buffalo drowsy and exhausted; one camel a mere skeleton from bad sores; and another has an enormous hole at the point of the pelvis, which sticks out at the side. I suspect that this was done maliciously, for he came from the field bleeding profusely; no tree would have perforated a round hole in this way. I take all the goods and leave only the sepoys' luggage, which is enough for all the animals now.

9 *May.*—I went on with the Johanna men and twenty-four carriers, for it was a pleasure to get away from the sepoys and Nassick boys; the two combined overload the animals. I told them repeatedly that they would kill them, but no sooner had I adjusted the burdens and turned my back than they put on all their things. It was however such a continual vexation to contend with the sneaking spirit, that I gave up annoying myself by seeing matters, though I felt certain that the animals would all be killed.

Two days later the carriers could hardly march for hunger. The Mazitu had "swept the land like a cloud of locusts". "They shake their shields and the people fly like stricken deer." But the villagers were kind and gave them of their penury a little of the sweet reed *sorghum* and sometimes a few fish in exchange for cloth. On the 15th and 16th: "Miserably short marches from hunger, and I sympathize with the poor fellows." Already each day's march became a search for enough food to keep alive. To any other man the situation must have appeared desperate, but the Journal states: "These are the little troubles of travelling, and scarce worth mentioning." Instead it is filled with careful observations of the rocks and plants and of native life. On the 19th he crossed the Rovuma "in two very small canoes", and then the Loendi "which is decidedly the parent stream"; and remained at Matambwe's village on the other side until 4 June. On 20 May he entrusted a Johanna man, Ali, with a despatch, "No. 2 Geographical". On the same day Abraham, one of the Nassick boys, arrived with the report that the sepoys refused to move, even when ordered by their havildar; that a camel and a buffalo were dead, and a mule left behind ill. "I sent a note to be read to the sepoys stating that . . . as soon as I received the havildar's formal evidence, I would send them back." That he should have revoked this decision is extraordinary. But on the 27th the havildar came up and reported that the sepoys "bewailed their folly"; he agreed that they were useless but "they begged to be kept on: I may give them another trial, but at present they are a sad incumbrance".

2 *June*.—The sepoys won't come; they say they cannot—a mere excuse, because they tried to prevail on the Nassick boys to go slowly like them, and wear my patience out. They killed one camel with the butt ends of their muskets, beating it till it died. . . . I thought of going down, disarming them, and taking five or six of the willing ones, but it is more trouble than profit. . . . They offered Ali eight rupees to take them to the coast, thus it has been a regularly organized conspiracy.

3 *June*.—The cow-buffalo fell down foaming at the mouth and expired. The calf has a cut half an inch deep, the camels have had large ulcers, and at last a peculiar smell, which portends death. I feel perplexed, and not at all certain as to the real causes of death.

4 *June*.—Left Ngomano. I was obliged to tell the Nassick boys that they must either work or return; it was absurd to have them eating up our goods, and not even carrying their own things, and I would submit to it no more. . . . Abraham has worked hard all along. . . .

7 *June*.—The havildar and two sepoys came up with Abraham, but Richard, a Nassick boy, is still behind from weakness. I sent three off to help him with the only cordials we could muster. The sepoys sometimes profess inability to come on, but it is unwillingness to encounter hardship; I must move on whether they come or not, for we cannot obtain food here. I sent the sepoys some cloth.

But it was not the worthless sepoys, who should have been dismissed long since, who were the first actually to desert. It was the twenty-four Africans who had worked hardest and suffered most. The Journal for 11 June contains a single entry: "Our carriers refuse to go further, because they say they fear being captured here on our return." The previous day's entry had ended: "An Arab party bolted on hearing of our approach: they don't trust the English, and this conduct increases our importance among the natives. Lat. 11° 18′ 10″ S."

He paid off the carriers next day—one-third of his total "strength"—and was now dependent on hiring whom he could from the villages for short stages. On the 14th: "I am now as much dependent on carriers as if I had never bought a beast of burden—but this is poor stuff to fill a journal with."

On the 18th came the distressing news that the Nassick boy Richard had died, a victim of fever. This troubled him greatly, the more so as he feared that the boy had been made unhappy by the bad influence of the sepoys. Six of these "notorious skulkers" came up the same day and he reprimanded them severely, disrating the naik (corporal) and sentencing the others to carry loads. It is with a feeling of revulsion, almost of incredulity, that we read the entry for the following day:

I gave the sepoys light loads in order to inure them to exercise and strengthen them, and they carried willingly so long as the fright was on them, but when the fear of immediate punishment wore off they began their skulking again. One, Perim, reduced his load of about 20 lbs of tea by throwing away the lead in which it was rolled, and afterwards about 15 lbs. of the tea, thereby diminishing our stock to 5 lb.

Then follows this, without a break: "I lighted on a telegram today: *Your mother died at noon on the 18th June.* This was in 1865; it affected me not a little."

From now on, his troubles with the refractory conduct of his men and their fiendish cruelty to the animals were intensified by gruesome tokens in the track of the slave-route.

19 *June*.—We passed a woman tied by the neck to a tree and dead. . . . We saw others tied up in a similar manner, and one lying in the path shot or stabbed, for she was in a pool of blood.

22 *June*.—A poor little boy with prolapsus ani was carried yesterday by his mother many a weary mile, lying over her right shoulder; an infant at the breast occupied the left arm, and on her head were carried two baskets. The mother's love was seen in binding up the part when we halted, whilst the coarseness of low civilization was evinced in the laugh with which some black brutes looked at the sufferer.

24 *June*.—It is difficult to feel charitably to fellows whose scheme seems to have been to detach the Nassick boys from me first; then, when the animals were all killed, the Johanna men; afterwards they could rule me as they liked, or go back and leave me to perish; but I shall try to feel as charitably as I can in spite of it all, for the mind has a strong tendency to brood over the ills of travel. The havildar . . . thought that they would only be a plague and trouble to me, but he "would go on and die with me".

25 *June*.—A poor little girl was left in one of the huts from being too weak to walk, probably an orphan. The Arab slave-traders flee from the path as soon as they hear of our approach. . . . No food to be had for either love or money.

26 *June*.—We passed a slave-woman shot or stabbed through the body and lying on the path. . . . An Arab who had passed early that morning had done it in anger at losing the price he had given for her, because she was unable to walk any longer.

27 *June*.—Today we came upon a man dead from starvation, as he was very thin. One of our men wandered and found a number of slaves with slave-sticks on, abandoned by their master from want of food; they were too weak to be able to speak or say where they had come from: some were quite young.

28 *June*.—We passed village after village, and gardens all deserted! We were now between two contending parties. . . . We gleaned what

congo beans, bean leaves, and sorghum stalks we could—poor fare enough, but all we could get.

29 June.—One of the Nassick lads came up and reported his bundle, containing 240 yards of calico, had been stolen; he went aside, leaving it on the path (probably fell asleep), and it was gone when he came back. I cannot impress either on them or the sepoys that it is wrong to sleep on the march. . . .

One Johanna man was caught stealing maize, then another, after I had paid for the first. I sent a request to the chief not to make much of a grievance about it, as I was very much ashamed at my men stealing; he replied that he had liked me from the first and I was not to fear, as whatever service he could do he would most willingly in order to save me pain and trouble. . . .

I saw another person bound to a tree and dead. . . . So many slave-sticks lie along our path, that I suspect the people hereabout make a pretence of liberating what slaves they can find abandoned on the march, to sell them again.

Having exchanged the costliest of his means of barter for one meal per day per man, he reached Mtarika's large village on 3 July, and immediately lectured the chief, "a big ugly man with large mouth and receding forehead", on the evil of selling his people. Mtarika wished him "to tell all the other chiefs the same thing"; and provided him with meal, pork, and bean-leaves.

Hearing "very sombre news of the country in front", which was devastated by Maziku raiders, he was obliged at this point to abandon his plan of skirting the Lake Nyasa round its north-east corner and striking directly up to Lake Tanganyika, and instead on 5 July he turned south-west from Mtarika's towards Mataka's where food was said to be plentiful.

His method with slave-dealing chiefs was one of direct attack; his knowledge of their own beliefs concerning supernatural retribution disarmed them. He notes that "they are rather taken aback". The sternness of his admonitions to them markedly contrasts with the mildness of his chastisement of the sepoys: this was all too little and was administered much too late.

7 July.—When the sepoy Perim threw away the tea and the lead lining, I only reproved him and promised him punishment if he committed any other wilful offence, but now he and another skulked behind and gave their loads to a stranger to carry, with a promise to him that I would pay. We waited two hours for them; and as the havildar said that they would not obey him, I gave Perim and the other some smart cuts with a cane, but I felt that I was degrading myself, and resolved not to do the punishment myself again.

8 *July*.—Hard travelling through a depopulated country. . . . Mountain masses are all around us.

9 *July*.—We slept in a wild spot, near Mount Leziro, with many lions roaring about us; one hoarse fellow serenaded us a long time, but did nothing more.

10 *and* 11 *July*.—Nothing to interest but the same weary trudge: our food so scarce that we can only give a handful or half a pound of grain to each person per day. . . . A dead body in a hut by the wayside. . . .

12 *July*.— . . .We set off in the dark, leaving our last food for the havildar and sepoys who had not yet come up. . . . We hurried on as fast as we could. . . . A little rice which had been kept for me I divided.

13 *July*.—A good many stragglers behind, but we push on to get food and send it back to them. . . . We invited volunteers to go on and buy food, and bring it back early next morning; they had to be pressed to do this duty.

14 *July*.—As our volunteers did not come up at 8 a.m. I set off to see the cause, and after an hour of perpetual up and down march, as I descended the steep slope which overlooks the first garden, I saw my friends start up at the apparition—they were comfortably cooking porridge for themselves! I sent men of Mataka back with food to the stragglers behind and came on to his town.

On the route thither he was befriended and liberally provisioned by an Arab, Sef Rupia, in charge of a large slave-gang: this is the first instance of what was to become perhaps the strangest feature of his last journeys—the kindness he received at the hands of the agents of that traffic which, as they well knew, it was his avowed intent to exterminate. "Sef came on with me to Mataka's, and introduced me in due form with discharges of gunpowder. I asked him to come back next morning, and presented three cloths with the request that he would assist the havildar and sepoys, if he met them, with food; this he generously did." Thus, with infinite toil and at the expense of nearly all his means of barter, Livingstone accomplished the first stage of his journey. It had taken nearly three months to travel 350 miles.

Some of Mataka's men, who were Yaos, had lately without his knowledge raided the Lake shore for captives and booty; whereupon Mataka ordered their immediate release and return.

I told him that his decision was the best piece of news I had heard in the country; he was evidently pleased with my approbation and,

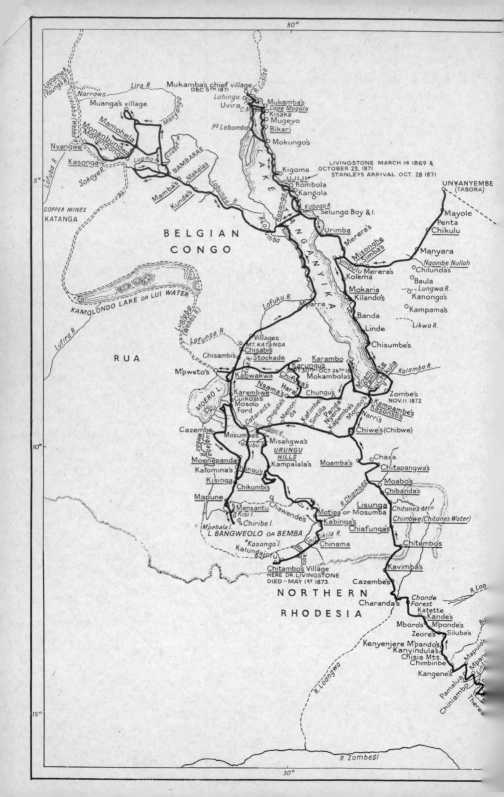

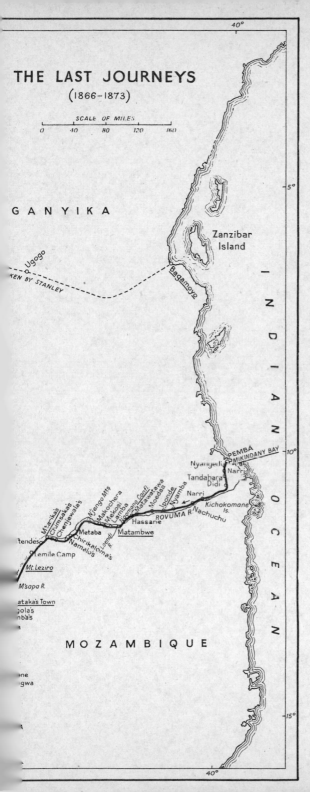

THE LAST JOURNEYS
(1866-1873)

SCALE OF MILES

0   40   80   120   160

40°

GANYIKA

5°

Zanzibar
Island

Ugogo

TAKEN BY STANLEY

Bagamoyo

I
N
D
I
A
N

O
C
E
A
N

10°

PEMBA
MIKINDANY BAY
Nyangelia
Narri
Tandahara
Didi
Njengo Mts
Makochera
Makosi
Lamba
Ngomono Conf.
Matawatawa
Meedaa
Nyamba
Narri
Kichokomane
Is.
ROVUMA R.
Nachuchu
Hassane
Matambwe
Metaba
Chirikalomas R.
Namalos
Chimsaka's
Chenjewala's
Mtarikas
Kendes
Lemile Camp
Mt.Leziro
M'sapa R.
ataka's Town
gola's
nba's

MOZAMBIQUE

15°

40°

MAP 5

LAST JOURNEYS (1866-1873)

This map of Livingstone's last journeys — heavy lines — is based on his own observations and surveys, and was prepared for the edition of his *Last Journals* edited by Horace Waller (Murray 1874). Livingstone warned Waller, in a letter received after his death, that his calculations needed to be checked but that the general features and rivers were trustworthy. (See Map 6.)

turning to his people, repeated my remark. . . . He then scolded them roundly. . . .

I gave Mataka a trinket to be kept in remembrance. . . . He replied that he would always act in a similar manner. As it was a spontaneous act, it was all the more valuable.

He remained a fortnight at Mataka's to recruit the strength of his men and to write a long geological description of his journey up to that point. During its last stages he had lived on nothing but mealie-meal and rice. The result was another attack of dysentery. The sepoys had taken from two to three weeks to straggle along the route which he and the carriers had pioneered in one, and his patience was now exhausted.

The sepoys have become quite intolerable, and if I cannot get rid of them we shall all starve before we accomplish what we wish. . . . Retaining their brutal feelings to the last they killed the donkey which I had lent to the havildar to carry his things, by striking it on the head when in boggy places into which they had senselessly driven it loaded; then the havildar came on (his men pretending they could go no farther from weakness), and killed the young buffalo and ate it when they thought they could hatch up a plausible story. . . .

. . . I resolved to send them back to the coast by the first trader. It is likely that some sympathizers will take their part, but I strove to make them useful. They had had but poor and scanty fare in a part of the way, but all of us suffered alike. . . . I felt inclined to force them on, but it would have been acting from revenge, so I forebore. . . . The havildar begged still to go on with me and I consented, though he is a drag on the party, but he will count in any difficulty.

To ensure their safe return he parted with 66 yards of calico and secured for them the escort of a respectable Arab trader. It was none too soon, since he now learned that they had threatened the Nassick boys with assassination; and even the Johanna men, though of the same faith as the sepoys (Moslems) had declared, "We are ready to do anything for you, but we will do nothing for these Hindis." His retinue was now reduced to 24, out of the original 60.

Leaving Mataka's on 28 July amply provisioned with meat and flour, he began to ascend the mountainous country that encloses the Lake, and was at once absorbed in studying its geology. Arab parties in charge of slave-gangs melted away at his approach. "The fear they feel is altogether the effect of the English name, for we have done nothing to cause their alarm."

On 8 August he arrived at the Lake shore "and felt grateful to that Hand which had protected us thus far on our journey". As though without a care in the world he could write: "It was as if I had come back to an old home I never expected again to see; and pleasant to bathe in the delicious waters again, hear the roar of the sea, and dash in the rollers."

Baulked by the raids of the Mazitu from going north along the Lake, he proposed to ferry across it to Kotakota by one of the Arab dhows which as he knew plied back and forth with slaves or merchandise, confident that the Sultan's letter would secure him passage, but in this he was foiled again. "All the Arabs flee from me," he writes on the 14th; "the English name being in their minds inseparably connected with recapturing slavers, they cannot conceive that I have any other object in view; they cannot read Seyed Majid's letter." Unwilling to accept this check as final he prospected north along the shore to a stream called Loangwa (a common name signifying river) to find that he was cut off not only from access to the interior by the Lake but also from communication with the coast. On the 30th: "The fear the English have inspired in the Arab slave-raiders is rather inconvenient. All flee from me as if I had the plague, and I cannot in consequence transmit letters to the coast, or get across the Lake."

He wrote several letters nevertheless, though seven months elapsed before he could despatch them. Among them was one to Professor Sedgwick (part of which has been quoted in the previous chapter). It begins: "My very Dear Friend, I have taken a sore longing to write to you, though I have not the faintest prospect of being able to send a letter to the sea coast", and continues with an account of his progress thus far. It ends upon a very different topic:

> I have several times recollected a remark made by the Dean of Ely in your house that he might be able to promote the education of my children. I did not think much about it at the time, but it has since struck me that if I had the opportunity I would tell him that I shall esteem it as a great kindness if he in any way remembers them. . . . I have one son at Glasgow College, sixteen years of age; another at a private school in Hamilton about ten years of age. Should the Dean wish any information about them, Professor Andrew Buchanan of Glasgow would supply it, or James Young, another of their guardians—formerly my teacher in chemistry—has made a fortune by Paraffin Oil and is a fine straight-

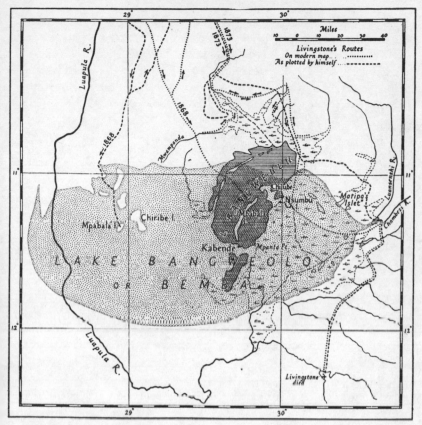

MAP 6   LAKE BANGWEOLO AREA

Livingstone's last days in the Lake Bangweolo area (Northern Rhodesia) are difficult to follow owing to his miscalculations of longitude, etc. Map 6 (reproduced by kind permission of Professor Debenham and the Royal Geographical Society from the Society's Journal for March 1954) shows how far off Livingstone was in his survey of Lake Bangweolo. The dark shaded portion is the lake according to an official 1946 survey. Livingstone's survey is light shaded. His routes (with dates) are plotted for comparison.

"His error was due to a tale of misfortune piling up simultaneously in which cloudy weather, desertion of his followers, accidents to his chronometers and sextants and a steady deterioration in his health were all involved." (Debenham, *R.G.S. Journal*, March 1954, p. 3.)

forward good man. The Dean may have nothing at his disposal, but I do not value his kindly feelings the less, and I am sure you will excuse my asking you to give the above information at your leisure. . . .[3]

Unable to proceed north or west, he resolved to go south to circumvent the Lake. His Journal again becomes filled with various observations, to some of which he would fain have been blind. "It was wearisome to see the skulls and bones scattered about everywhere; one would fain not notice them, but they are so striking as one trudges along the sultry path, that it cannot be avoided." On 13 September he came once again in view, and for the last time, of the well-remembered Shire river. The sight engendered sorrowful reflections:

> Many hopes have been disappointed here. Far down on the right bank of the Zambesi lies the dust of her whose death changed all my future prospects; and now, instead of a check being given to slave-trade by lawful commerce on the Lake, slave-dhows prosper!
> An Arab slave-party fled on hearing of us yesterday. It is impossible not to regret the loss of good bishop Mackensie, who sleeps far down the Shire, and with him all hope of the Gospel being introduced into Central Africa. The silly abandonment of the Shire route by the bishop's successor I shall ever bitterly deplore, but all will come right some day, though I may not live to participate in the joy, or even see the commencement of better times.

He might have crossed the Shire at its confluence with the Lake and thereby cut a corner, but preferred to make a detour south to lecture the chief Mukate on the evil of raiding for slaves. Debenham remarks that his practice never to neglect such opportunities says much for his courage and also for the traditional courtesy of African chiefs. "In fact we may liken the whole of the next seven years, without too much exaggeration, to a man wandering unarmed into the haunts of gangsters in Chicago, telling them they were a bad lot."

Mukate provided him with messengers to ensure his safe passage across Lake Pamalombe in canoes, whence he marched west across the plain between the mountains to Mponda's (not shown on the map) and found a large Arab slave party encamped there.

> Mponda was alarmed lest we should do violence in his town, but I said to him that we went to look only. . . . A crowd went with us, expecting a scene, but I sat down and asked a few questions about the journey in

front. . . . I asked if they had any objections to me looking at the slaves, the owners pointed out the different slaves and said that after feeding them, and accounting for the losses on the way to the coast, they made little by the trip. . . . I said to them it was a bad business altogether. They presented fowls to me in the evening.

Mponda begged him earnestly to stay another day and give medicine to a sick child. He did so with success; and the chief then offered him more food than he could carry. He also desired to accompany him on his journey, but this request was declined. The Journal record of this visit has a laconic interpolation: "A lion killed a woman early yesterday morning, and ate most of her undisturbed." Here too Wikatani, who had been Mackensie's favourite boy among those rescued from the Ajawa, asked leave to remain with his relations. Both he and Chuma were still very young and also lively and lighthearted: "very good boys, but still boys utterly." Describing this farewell in a letter to Waller he adds a typically sardonic comment: "I did not attempt to dissuade him: his excessive levity will perhaps be cooled by marriage." The next day he was deserted at long last by the long-suffering havildar, but with much less regret: "he has never been of the smallest use . . . He has remained behind."

These departures however were trifling compared with the blow that befell him at Marenga's on 25 September. Musa, in charge of the Johanna men, hearing from a passing Arab that the country before them was "full of Mazitu", refused to go further. Livingstone tried persuasion, and when this failed brought him to the chief Marenga, who explained the reason for this rumour, which was false. But Musa's eyes "stood out in terror", and when the march was resumed "all the Johanna men walked off, leaving the goods on the ground". Trying as always to put the best face on his reverses he adds: "They have been such inveterate thieves that I am not sorry to get rid of them . . . though my party is now inconveniently small." It was in fact reduced to eight Nassick boys, besides Susi, Amoda, and Chuma.

The defection of Musa and his fellow-renegades was much less serious to Livingstone in the far interior than its sequel proved to be to his friends in England. Well aware that if its true cause was known they would forfeit their pay and incur severe punishment, on arrival in Zanzibar they went straight to the Consulate with an ingeniously concocted story to the following effect. Their party had reached the northern end of Lake Nyasa, Livingstone as usual leading it, when Musa heard him suddenly call out that the Mazitu were coming. "They came on with a rush, shouting their war-cry and rattling their spears. Livingstone shot two of them down and then, as he was reloading, he fell to a blow from an axe on the back of the neck. Creeping back at sunset they found his body and buried it. The bodies of several of his Nassick boys were lying near. There was no trace of a survivor, or of any of the baggage." The story after close questioning was reluctantly believed by Mr. Seward the Consul, and also by Kirk, and by Mr. Sunley who had recently retired. On the Sultan's palace, on all the Consulates and on the shipping in the harbour, flags were flown at half-mast. When the news reached England, however, it was accepted with a measure of reserve. Sir Roderick Murchison in transmitting a letter from Kirk to *The Times* wrote: "If this cruel intelligence should be substantiated, the civilized world will mourn the loss of as noble and lion-hearted an explorer who ever lived." Kirk wrote personally to Murchison: "You may imagine how I feel, being the first to communicate the sad news regarding my leader, whom I had known, I may say, far more intimately during the Zambesi Expedition than any other member of it . . . I could never wish a better leader." But there were two men who were sceptical: one of them was Waller, who had known Musa and did not trust him. The other was Lieutenant E. D. Young, who had known Musa still better and trusted him even less. He categorically refused to believe a word of the story, and offered to go to Lake Nyasa and prove it false. A small-scale expedition was immediately organized by the R.G.S. and this time amply financed by the Government.

A river-boat similar to the *Lady Nyasa* was constructed in sections and in August 1867 was at the foot of the Murchison Cataracts. It was carried piecemeal up the bank and within three weeks was afloat on the Lake. If he had achieved nothing else by this exploit, Young would at least have demonstrated the practicability of Livingstone's original plan, which some had doubted. It was indeed conclusive proof that if he had been granted but one more month before his recall from the Zambesi

Expedition, its purpose would have been accomplished and many years of toil and fruitless endeavour saved. But Young did more. He at once found evidence in the *south-east* corner of the Lake of the passage of some European traveller—a spoon, a knife, a razor, a cartridge-case, a looking-glass and other trifles which had been given in exchange for food. Then, on the south-west side he met natives who had served the white man as carriers. Next, the chief Marenga produced others, and informed him of the return of the Johanna men through his village soon after Livingstone's departure: they said that they had left him because their term of service was up and the Mazitu were ahead. Lastly he visited the village where Wikatani had made his new home, and interviewed his brother. Young's Expedition returned to the Cape by a warship, and the first news they heard on board confirmed the results of their own investigation. By this time reports of Livingstone, who was then more than 500 miles distant from the farthest point they had reached, had come through to Zanzibar. Musa received the somewhat mild punishment of eight months' imprisonment in irons.[4]

After leaving Marenga's on 26 September, Livingstone and his party were ferried in canoes round the heel of the Lake, and at Katosa's (Kimusa's) village he was greeted by the chief like a long-lost friend, invited to a drinking-bout which he declined, and again loaded with more goods than he could carry. Here he stayed ten days perforce awaiting the arrival of carriers to replace the Johanna men, but when these were not forthcoming he rallied the chief on his lack of authority, and "his strapping wives came to carry loads and shame his people". Thereupon several of the young men turned out and took up the loads, though with evident fear of hostilities ahead.

He now crossed Kirk's Range and found himself on the summit of the Dedza plateau (4,000 feet): a second highland, and as suitable for settlement as the Shire highlands. He was impressed by the fertility of the soil and its capacity for extensive cultivation. The people were primitive Manganja, liberal and friendly, and he was invited by the local chief to preach to them. The scenery was glorious and the delicious air exhilarating. From this point his south-westerly course was determined by his men's fear of encountering the Mazitu, and by his own desire to visit the principal chiefs: his interest in their occupations and their friendly reception are like a breath of old times, and a more buoyant note is apparent in his Journal.

His zig-zag course north-west beyond Chipanga's is explained by the fact that "we had to go in the direction of the villages which were on friendly terms with our guides", and this, though it involved delay, enabled him to extend considerably his knowledge of the geography of the region. On 24 October the party narrowly escaped a raid by marauding Mazitu: "We meant to take our stand on the hill and defend our property . . . and be a defence to the fugitives who crowded up its rocky sides." So near did Musa's fanciful story come to reality. But next day the enemy turned south. As they descended towards the Loangwa valley he dilates upon the native methods of spinning and weaving, smelting and smithying and furnace-making, salutations and ornaments, facial characteristics, comparisons of ancient European customs and history with primitive African. He observes their precautions and vigilance against possible attack and comments: "We have the protection of an all-embracing Providence and trust that He, whose care of his people exceeds all that our utmost self-love can attain, will shield us and make our way prosperous." Botanizing and geologizing as he goes along, he rejoices in the beauty of the scenery and bird-songs, and, greatly as he dislikes this, he shoots big game to feed his men and the villagers: "measuring the animals' height, horns etc., in the approved big-game-hunter fashion, though he never gives details of the actual hunt as they do" (Debenham).

His main difficulty on this stage of the journey (besides short commons) had been shortage of transport and he had sometimes been obliged to relay the loads; but when at Kande's village on 3 December two Yaos, who said that their masters had been killed by the Mazitu, volunteered to join his party as carriers he accepted them—though with some hesitation: "In general, runaway slaves are bad characters, but these two seem good men, and we want them to fill up our complement." It was probably the most disastrous decision he ever made.

On the 6th comes an ominous entry: "Too ill to march", but on the 7th: "Went on." Fear of the Mazitu prevented him from obtaining guides and he followed a game-track due north through a forest to secure meat, till he struck a tributary of the Loangwa and thence turned west towards the main river. This he reached on the 15th and ferried across it and went on northwards, still without guides, through a pathless bush—"a very difficult country, but we held on as well as we could." He forded the Pamazi, sixty yards wide, steeply banked and in flood, "thigh deep on one side and breast deep on the other . . . and found the people on the left bank uncivil; they would not lend a hut, so we soon put up a tent of waterproof cloth and branches". Without guides, and without grain or even herbs, he wandered alone in the bush seeking game; in this he was successful and for some days he and his men lived on meat. On the 23rd: "Hunger sent us on; for a meat diet is far from satisfying; we all felt very weak on it and soon tired on the march . . . between three and four hours is a good day's march." On arrival at Kavimba's they sat down to rest, "and all the force of the village issued to kill us as Mazitu, but when we stood up the mistake was readily perceived, and the arrows were placed again in their quivers." He had acquired four goats, "for whatever kind of food we had, a little milk made all right, and I felt strong and well", but at Kavimba's they were lost, stolen or strayed, and "the loss affected me more. than I could have imagined. A little indigestible porridge, of scarcely any taste, is now my fare, and it makes me dream of butter." Such is the sorry entry for Christmas Day. Kavimba had been suspicious and inhospitable, but hoping for better things the other side of the mountain range that now confronted him he struggled on, and from the summit looked down behind him to the dark green forest and the line of yellowish grass that marked the course of the Loangwa. Here for the exorbitant price of a good cloth he obtained a mess of millet porridge and "tripe" from an elephant's stomach: "it was so good to get a full meal that I would have given him another." At the next village he got nothing but a little more millet, "which grates in the teeth and in the stomach". The people were unhelpful: "they will not answer questions except by misstatements. . . . We are uncertain when we shall come to a village." But still he botanized and geologized, and was cheered by the songs of birds and the sight of flowers. "I shall make this beautiful land better known. It is impossible to describe its rich luxuriance, but most of it is running to waste through the slave-trade and internal wars." On the last day of the year he reached Chitembo's village—to find it deserted; but the old chief was there, working in his garden, "and gave us the choice of all the standing huts; he is much more frank and truthful than our last headman".

Livingstone was now nearer the heart of Central Africa than he had ever been before, but one may wonder what other traveller would voluntarily have endured such hazards and privations to attain it. Imagination, informed by some experience of travel in these regions, is necessary to clothe the bare bones of his Journal record and present the mind with a semblance of the trials, physical and mental, which beset him on this, the first stage of his journey. Yet these are the words with which he sums up his retrospect of the year:

> We now end 1866. It has not been so fruitful or useful as I intended. Will try to do better in 1867, and be better—more gentle and loving; and may the Almighty, to whom I commit my way, bring my desires to pass and prosper me! Let all the sins of '66 be blotted out for Jesus' sake.

Chapter Twenty-Seven

LAST JOURNEYS: HEART OF AFRICA
1867

"I felt as if I had now received the sentence of death."

THE Journal for New Year's Day 1867 opens with the words: "May He who was full of grace and truth impress His character on mine. Grace—eagerness to show favour; truth—truthfulness, sincerity, honour—for His mercy's sake."

Livingstone's chief enemy hitherto had been hunger, and so it continued; to it was now added another no less injurious—rain. These together were sufficient to sap the vitality of the strongest, and he was already far past the prime of life. He was now treading the spongy soil of the fringes of the great central watershed, and the heavy rains had set in—a season when the hardiest traveller in those regions will not venture far abroad, unless for short distances in the intervals of the tropical deluges. He rested a week however in Chitembo's "by the boys' desire, and also because we can get some food"—though the food was a little millet and a creature resembling a rat (*aulocaudatus swindernianus*).

> It is hard fare and scanty; I always feel hungry, and am constantly dreaming of better food when I should be sleeping. Savoury viands of former times come vividly up before the imagination, even in my waking hours; this is rather odd as I am not a dreamer; indeed I scarcely ever dream but when I am going to be ill or actually so.

To this Waller adds that Livingstone could always fall asleep anywhere at the shortest notice, "and this faculty no doubt contributed much to his great powers of endurance".

He left Chitembo's on 6 January "after Service" and entered the forest in a drizzling rain; in descending a deep ravine "two boys fell, and he who carried the chronometers, twice; this was a misfortune, as it altered the rates". Debenham says: "His longitudes for the next few months were twenty miles to the eastward in error, perhaps in consequence of these falls." But still the leafiness of the trees and the young grasses and the bright wild-flowers (which he names) enchanted his eyes, even when plunging through the soggy ooze of the "immense sponges".

9 *January*.—One has to watch carefully in crossing them to avoid plunging into deep water-holes, made by the feet of elephants or buffaloes. . . . There are no people here now in these lovely wild valleys. . . . My stock of meal came to an end today, but Simon gave me some of his. It is not the unpleasantness of eating unpalatable food that teases one, but we are never satisfied; I could brace myself to dispose of a very unsavoury mess, and think no more about it; but this maëre [millet] engenders a craving which plagues day and night incessantly.

10*th*.—In the afternoon an excessively heavy thunderstorm wetted us all to the skin before any shelter could be made. Two of our men wandered, and other two remained behind lost, as our track was washed out by the rains. . . . I am thankful that no one was lost. . . . Simon gave me a little more of his meal this morning, and went without himself; I took up my belt three holes to relieve hunger. . . . At midday reached the village of Chafunga. Famine here too, but some men had killed an elephant and came to sell the dried meat; it was high, and so were their prices.

12*th*.—We bought up all the food we could get; but it did not suffice for the marches we expect to make to get to the Chambezi, where food is said to be abundant; we were therefore obliged again to travel on Sunday. We had prayers before starting; but I always feel that I am not doing right, it lessens the sense of obligation in the minds of my companions; but I have no choice.

On the 15th in fording waist-deep a flooded mile-wide river infested with leeches he lost his little poodle-dog 'Chitane' which had been his companion from the coast. His fierce looks had inspired the village dogs with terror "from their inability to distinguish his head from his tail"; and he had chased them with "unrelenting fury". "He was so useful in keeping all the country curs off our huts, none dare to approach or steal, and he never stole himself. In the march he took charge of the whole party, running to the front and again to the rear, to see that all was right . . . and, poor thing, he perished in what all the boys call Chitane's Water." And so it is named on the map. It is actually, as Professor Debenham observes, the most remote source of the Congo, and it was in the basin of the Congo that Livingstone spent his last years, never sure whether it was the

Congo basin or that of the Nile. "At Chitane's Water in fact he crossed the threshold of his final search, and began the quest which terminated only with his life."[1]

16*th*.—The rain, as usual, made us halt early, and wild fruits helped to induce us to stay. . . . We roast a little grain and boil it, to make believe it is coffee. . . . Ground all sloppy; oozes full and overflowing— feet constantly wet. Rivulets rush strongly with *clear* water, though they are in flood; we can guess which are perennial and which mere torrents.

17*th*.—Detained in an old Babisa slaving encampment by set-in rain till noon, then set off in the midst of it. . . . Rivulets can only be crossed by felling a tree on the bank and letting it fall across.

18*th*.—The headman of Lisunga took our present and gave us nothing in return. . . . This tribe is engaged in the slave-trade, and the evil effects are seen in their depopulated country and utter distrust of every one.

19*th*.—Nothing but famine and famine prices, the people living on mushrooms and leaves [he names and describes the mushrooms]. We get some elephants' meat from the people, but high is no name for its condition. It is very bitter . . . but it prevents the heartburn, which maëre causes when taken alone. I take mushrooms boiled instead; but the meat is never refused when we can purchase it.

On the 20th the worst, and fatal, blow befell him. The two Yao boys whom he had enlisted at Kande's village in the previous month, and "who had been very faithful all the way and took our part in every case", deserted. "Their uniform good conduct made us trust them more than we should have done any others who had been slaves." One of them had that morning exchanged his load with that of a Nassick boy who had charge of the medicine-box "because he was so very careful". The box was packed with five large cloths and all the bearer's clothing and beads.

The forest was so dense and high, there was no chance of getting a glimpse of the fugitives, who took all the dishes, a large box of powder, the flour we had purchased dearly to help us as far as the Chambezi, the tools, two guns, and a cartridge-pouch; but the medicine-chest was the sorest loss of all! I felt as if I had now received the sentence of death, like poor Bishop Mackensie.

The sentence was indeed pronounced, but its execution was stayed for more than six years.

Anyone who has studied the course of Livingstone's arduous career will perceive that it was punctuated by sudden, unexpected, and adverse shocks. Of these the severest perhaps were the letter he received from the L.M.S. after his first Great Journey; the insuperability of the Kebrabasa Rapids; and his wife's death. They occurred in a crescendo series; and this, the loss of his medicines, was that which told hardest of all against the accomplishment of his mission; yet even it was to prove by no means the last. Experience had taught him to be forearmed against disaster, and even to mistrust success; but fate, or however we may name the seemingly malign influence that dogged his footsteps, seldom failed to take him off his guard. Nevertheless, the sublime loyalty of his faith in a divine Providence, under whose guidance all things work together for good, steeled him still to accept every adversity as the Will of God, and even in this shattering blow he strove to discern a beneficent intent.

> All the other goods I had divided in case of loss or desertion, but had never dreamed of losing the precious quinine and other remedies; other losses and annoyances I felt as just parts of that undercurrent of vexations which is not wanting in even the smoothest life, and certainly not worthy of being mourned over in the experience of an explorer anxious to benefit a country and people—but this loss I feel most keenly. Everything of this kind happens by the permission of One who watches over us with most tender care; and this may turn out for the best by taking away a source of suspicion among the more superstitious charm-dreading people further north. I meant it as a source of benefit to my party and the heathen. . . . It is difficult to say from the heart "Thy will be done"; but I shall try.

Yet he did not accept it passively or with inert acquiescence; he returned at once to Lisunga and sent two men still farther back to Chafunga to try and intercept the deserters. He knew that they would only throw away the medicine-box as worthless when they came to examine its contents; still, there was a faint hope that it might be found, despite the fact that the rain had obliterated their footmarks. Meanwhile, and his reflections show the extent to which he was prepared to honour his New Year's resolve, he sought in his mind for every possible reason to exonerate them.

> These Waiyau had few advantages: sold into slavery in early life, they were in the worst possible school for learning to be honest and honourable; they behaved well for a long time; but, having had hard and scanty fare in Lobisa, wet and misery in passing through dripping forests, hungry nights and fatiguing days, their patience must have been worn

out, and they had no sentiments of honour, or at least none so strong as we ought to have; they gave way to the temptation which their good conduct had led us to put in their way. . . .

But in the end his thoughts recur inevitably to the grim reality of his own situation: "True; yet this loss of the medicine-box gnaws at the heart terribly."

Commentators have criticized what they call his "decision" to continue his journey at all under these circumstances; but it was no decision, for it is quite certain that no other idea entered his mind. Campbell: "Unquestionably he ought to have turned back . . . It was folly to persevere." Coupland: "His decision to go on into the unknown without his medicine-chest proved, in the long run, suicidal." But Coupland shows discernment:

> Why then, it has been asked, did he make it? Why did he not return on his tracks to Lake Nyasa whence the main Arab trade-route led to the coast, and send at least for some quinine by Arab agency to Kilwa or by some messenger of his own to Zanzibar? The chances, it is true, were against his getting it unless he went all the way himself; but this, as the sequel shows, he did not fully realize; and in any case, being the sort of man he was, he could not go back, however dire the need, when he had come so far. By point-to-point measure on the map he had walked about 800 miles from Mikindani. He had taken more than nine months over it. And, perhaps, his goal was now not very far ahead. A few more weeks of endurance and he might at last cross the watershed and find a river-system draining not south nor west nor even east, but north—the sources of the Nile! No, nothing would induce him to turn back now. . . .[2]

This is right, even as a practical consideration. And there are others to reinforce it. Livingstone knew that fever when it struck, without the antidote of quinine to check it, would, if it was to prove fatal, strike swiftly. In the case of Mackensie, who had lost his quinine; and in the case of his own wife, who had been unable to retain it when given—death had been swift. On the balance of probabilities, therefore, if he was going to die of fever he would be just as likely to do so on the long journey back to the Lake, or whilst awaiting there the return of a messenger (and at this point there was none that he could safely send), as he would if he continued towards his goal which might now be so near. And, as will be seen, he did take the first possible opportunity of entrusting an Arab, who could travel far more quickly than himself or a messenger, with an order for a fresh supply of medicines from the coast. But when Coupland goes on to say that "he was fortified in his wilful defiance of misfortune and disease by the fatalism which had been steadily growing on him since his wife's death"—we venture to demur. He was not a fatalist. He was a man in holy orders on active service under divine obedience, and as such it is utterly inconceivable that he would allow himself to be deflected from the course of duty by any mischance, even the prospect of imminent death. He had dedicated his life to, and identified himself with, his cause—God's cause. Such a man is not to be judged by conventional standards, because he could never be influenced by prudential motives. His faith in fact was of that very rare quality which is thus described by that eminently sane scientist of the human soul, William Law:

> This faith . . . is that power by which a man gives himself up to anything, seeks, wills, adheres to and unites with it, so that his life lives in it and belongs to it. . . . It is essential to his life and altogether inseparable from it. . . . For faith is as much the one working power of life, as thought is the one working power of the understanding; and the understanding of man may as easily proceed without being led by thought, as the life of man go on without being led by faith; that is, without giving itself up to something or other with which it would be united, and to which it would belong, as its desired good.

A more personal reason for his determination to go on at all hazards is adduced by his friend Oswell in a letter to Agnes dated 8 January 1868:

> Perhaps after all he will return upon his tracks (though I for one fervently hope not). He is so plucky, enduring, and *awfully obstinate* that I'm sure he will not if he can help it. . . . In my opinion he is easily the first of all travellers, alive or dead.[3]

But at the time of writing this Oswell was not aware of the loss of the medicine-chest.

He remained rain-bound at Lisunga for two days. On the 22nd: "We bought all the maëre the chief would sell . . . We were now forced to go on and made for the next village to buy food."

23rd.—Chibanda's stockade, where "no food" was the case, as usual. . . . I sent off the boys to the village of Muasi to buy food. If successful, tomorrow we march for the Chambesi. . . . We all feel weak and easily tired, and an incessant hunger teases us. . . . real biting hunger and faintness.

24th.—The village of Moaba is on the east side of the marshy valley of the Movuhi and very difficult to be approached, as the water is chin-deep in several spots. I decided to make sheds on the west side and sent over for food which, thanks to the Providence which watches over us, we found at last in a good supply of maëre and some ground-nuts.

25th.—Remain and get our maëre ground into flour. . . . Mushroom diet is good only for producing dreams of the roast beef of byegone days. The saliva runs from the mouth in these dreams, and the pillow is wet with it in the mornings. [Then follow ornithological and arboreal notes.]

26th.—I shot a poku, or tsebula, full-grown male. . . . I felt very thankful to the Giver of all good for this meat.

27th.—A set-in rain. . . . In changing my dress this morning I was frightened at my own emaciation.

28th.—The Chambezi was flooded with clear water. . . . The canoe-man was excessively suspicious; when prepayment was acceded to, he asked a piece more . . . kept the last man on the south side as a hostage for this bit of calico; he then ran away. . . .

Went northwards, wading across two miles of flooded flats. . . . Slept in forest without seeing anyone. . . . We observed that the people had a great fear of animals at night and shut the gates carefully. . . . When at Chitapangwa's afterwards, two men were killed by a lion.

29th.—We were shown where lightning had struck; it ran down a gum-copal tree without damaging it.

30th.—Northwards through almost trackless dripping forests and across oozing bogs.

31st.—Through forest, but gardens of larger size than in Lobisa now appear. . . . Chitapangwa sent to enquire if we wanted an audience. "We must take something in our hands the first time we come before so great a man." Being tired from marching, I replied, "Not till the evening", and sent notice at 5 p.m. of my coming. . . . I declined to sit on the ground, and an enormous tusk was brought for me. The chief saluted courteously. He has a fat, jolly face. . . . After talking awhile he came along with us to a group of cows, and pointed out one. "That is yours," said he. The tusk was sent after me too as being mine. He put on my cloth as token of acceptance, and sent two large baskets of sorghum to the hut afterwards, and then sent for one of the boys to pump him after dark.

The day after his arrival at Chitapangwa's he found a small party of Arab slave-traders who were bound for Bagamoyo on the coast opposite Zanzibar on the following day. By payment he prevailed on them to wait another day and spent the whole of 2 February in writing despatches, for the delivery of which to the Consul in Zanzibar they were to receive ten rupees. They were returning by a new and much shorter route, west-south-west, than that which he had followed inland from Mikidani, and he took a careful note of the fifteen villages and three rivers they named. "But not a soul would tell us of this way of coming when we were at Zanzibar . . . It is possible that they did not know of it themselves." In a large packet with the despatches he enclosed all the letters he had written on his journey, and added a postscript to Braithwaite's: ". . . I am excessively lean but take on fat kindly as do some races of pigs."[4] To Dr. Seward the Consul he wrote:

> . . . If you can send anything more to Ujiji at Tanganyika, 50 lb. of coffee, a small box of candles, a stick of sealing-wax, a cheese in tin, a small box of soap, some French preserved meats, half a dozen bottles of port wine, well-packed, and some quinine and calomel and resin of jalap [please do so]. Don't exceed these things, please, for heavy things we cannot carry. Please pay [for] them with what you have in hand. The severest loss I ever sustained was that of my medicines; every grain of them, except a little extract of hyoscyamus. We had plenty of provisions after we left Lake Nyasa, but latterly got into severe hunger. Don't think, please, that I make a moan over nothing but a little sharpness of appetite. I am a mere ruckle of bones. . . . If Dr. Kirk is with you, will you give him all the information with kind regards.[5]

The packet reached its destination, but was not received until 24 January 1868 by Seward's successor, H. A. Churchill, nearly a year later; and Churchill, opining that by that time Livingstone would have long since left Ujiji, waited for further information as to his whereabouts before taking action. In August of that year came two further letters from Livingstone repeating his request for the supplies to be sent to Ujiji, and this time Churchill immediately complied—with what result will appear later.

Livingstone was detained three weeks at Chitapangwa by his refusal to comply with the chief's repeated demands for a tin box and a blanket. The blankets were the property of his Nassick boys; he himself used none. "O great Englishman," said the chief, "you are sorry that you have to give so much for the ox you have eaten. You would not take a smaller, and so I gratified your heart by giving the larger; and why should you not gratify my heart by giving cloth sufficient to cover me, and please me?"

I said that my cloths would cover him and his biggest wife too, all over; he laughed at this, but still held out. . . . I cannot enter into his ideas, or see his point of view; cannot in fact enter into his ignorance, his prejudices, or delusions. . . . One who has no sense of humour cannot understand one who has; this is an equivalent case.

In the end he found that they had been at cross-purposes. Abraham and the Nassick boys had been too terrified of the chief to interpret his replies correctly. Their obsequiousness had put a false construction on nearly everything that was said and had served only to aggravate the chief's suspicions.

He is good-natured, and our intercourse is a laughing one; but the boys betray their terrors in their tone of voice and render my words powerless. . . . This is the great and crowning difficulty of my inter-course. . . . The chief is not so bad, as the boys are so cowardly. They assume a chirping, piping tone of voice in speaking to him, and do not say what at last has to be said, because in their cringing souls they believe they know what should be said better than I do. It does not strike them in the least that I have grown grey amongst these people. . . .

It is hard to be kept waiting here, but all may be for the best; it has always turned out so, and I trust in Him on whom I can cast all my cares. The Lord look on this and help me. Though I have the nine boys, I feel quite alone.

. . . A long misunderstanding would have been avoided, had Abraham told me fully what the chief said at first.

Though Livingstone was at a loss for direct speech in a region which was new to him and where dialects varied among the different tribes, it would appear that in addition to the Chinyanja of the neighbourhood of Lake Nyasa, he was beginning to acquire a knowledge of Swahili, the *lingua franca* of East Africa, which was used also by the Arabs. He had regularly held divine Service every Sunday (according to the Book of Common Prayer) and when in a village had invited the chief or headman and his people to attend; for lack of lantern-slides he had shown them the wood-cuts in Smith's *Dictionary of the Bible* and explained them; these he found that Chita-pangwa "readily understood". But on 17 February the Journal has a brief entry: "Too ill with rheumatic-fever to have Service; this is the first attack of it I ever had—and no medi-cine! but I trust in the Lord who healeth his people." (He had forgotten a severe attack of this illness years ago in the Quango valley.) Yet he was prepared for the road two days later, and only detained by the chief: "and I, being weak and giddy, consented."

> *20th.*—I told the chief before starting that my heart was sore, because he was not sending me away so cordially as I liked. He at once ordered men to start with us, and gave me a brass knife with ivory sheath which he had long worn, as a memorial . . . and came along with us to see that all was right; and so we parted.
>
> *21st.*—The path led us west against my will. I found one going north, but the boys pretended that they did not see my mark, and went west, evidently afraid of incurring Moamba's displeasure by passing him. I found them in an old hut, and made the best of it by saying nothing.
>
> *22nd.*—We met Moamba's people, but declined going to his village, as huts are disagreeable; they often have vermin. . . . Moamba sent a deputation . . . lastly he came himself with about sixty followers. I explained that I had become sick by living in a little hut at Molemba; that I was better in the open air; that the huts contained vermin; that I did not mean to remain any while here, but go on our way. He pressed us to come to his village, and gave us a goat and kid, with a huge calabashful of beer.
>
> *23rd.*—I had a long talk with Moamba, a big, stout, public-house-looking person, with a slight outward cast in his left eye, but intelligent and hearty. I presented him with a cloth; and he gave me as much maëre meal as a man could carry, with a large basket of groundnuts. . . . I showed him some pictures in Smith's *Bible Dictionary* which he readily understood, and I spoke to him about the Bible. He asked me "to come next day and tell him about prayer to God".
>
> He was very anxious to know why we were going to Tanganyika. . . . "What do you wish to buy, if not slaves or ivory?" I replied that the only thing I had seen worth buying was a fine fat chief like him, as a specimen, and a woman feeding him, as he had, with beer. He was tickled at this. . . .

As eventually with Chitapangwa, so with his brother Moamba, Livingstone got on well, though not with his men who were truculent. But neither they nor any other chief could understand or believe that he had no ulterior motive in his journey; therefore, failing to convince them, he turned aside their questions with a jest. By the end of the month he had crossed the Losauswa Range: "the people of the first village shut their gates against us, then came running after us . . . We made our sheds on a height in spite of their protests." In the next village they were treated hospitably. On 10 March:

> I have been ill of fever ever since we left Moamba's; every step I take jars in the chest, and I am very weak; I can scarcely keep up the march,

though formerly I was always first, and had to hold in my pace not to leave the people altogether. I have a constant singing in the ears, and can scarcely hear the loud tick of the chronometers.

Still he went on, making north for Kasonso: "my long-continued fever ill disposes me to enjoy the beautiful landscape." On the 19th he was confronted with an armed band of young men demanding payment for by-passing their village. "After talking a while and threatening to do a deal tomorrow, they left, and through an Almighty Providence nothing was attempted." The next day he reached Kasonso: "he shook hands a long while and seems a frank sort of man." The same night he was attacked in his sleep by a swarm of furiously-biting driver ants. "To describe this attack is utterly impossible. I wakened covered with them; my hair was full of them." But Kasonso was friendly "and gave a grand reception". His son volunteered to accompany them to the Lake, and on 28 March they reached Mombo's village near the ridge. Then—"I was too ill to march through. I offered to go on the 1st, but Kasonso's son objected [on account of his illness]. He went on next day however, and descended the 2,000 foot drop to the level of the Lake (which was called Liemba) at Pambété, not knowing that he had in fact reached the southern end of Lake Tanganyika.

> It seems about eighteen or twenty miles broad, and we could see about thirty miles up to the north. . . . I never saw anything so still and peaceful as it lies all the morning. About noon a gentle breeze springs up, and causes the waves to assume a bluish tinge. . . . The people can tell us nothing about it. They suspect us and we cannot get information, or indeed much of anything else. I feel deeply thankful at having got so far. I am excessively weak—cannot walk without tottering, and have constant singing in the head, but the Highest will lead me further.

He took the latitude and longitude and height above sea-level: "but I only worked out (and my head is out of order) one set of observations. The people won't let me sound the Lake."

There is a gap in his Journal at this point of nearly a month. When he resumes it on 30 April we find a description of the Lake, its geology, the direction of its flow north-westwards, its fauna and flora—and this:

After being a fortnight at this Lake it still appears one of surpassing loveliness. . . .

After I had been a few days here I had a fit of insensibility, which shows the power of fever without medicine. I found myself floundering outside my hut, unable to get in; I tried to lift myself from my back by laying hold of two posts at the entrance, but when I got nearly upright I let them go, and fell heavily on my head on a box. The boys had seen the wretched state I was in, and hung a blanket at the entrance of the hut, that no stranger might see my helplessnes; some hours elapsed before I could recognize where I was.

The above was written from Chikula, the promontory on the south of the Lake shore. Comment upon it is superfluous; on 30 April he was prepared for the march again, up the western side of the Lake "to see whether it narrows or not". (He had written, apparently the day before, "Elephants come all about us. One was breaking trees close by. I fired into his ear without effect; I am too weak to hold the gun steadily.") But he was dissuaded from this project by the headman's "solemn protestations" that the Mazitu were on the war-path and waited a day longer till they were gone; then retraced his steps towards Mombo and slept half-way up the ridge. "I had another fit of insensibility last night; the muscles of the back lose all power, and there is constant singing in the ears, as well as inability to do the simplest sum." Arrived at Mombo's next day: "It is distressingly difficult to elicit accurate information about the Lake and rivers, because the people do not think accurately." He notes that their cotton is of the Pernambuco species, unlike any to be found elsewhere.

Arrived at Moami's on May 11th he was told that an important chief Nsama was at war with the Arabs: "this made us rather anxious to get northwards along the Lake", and he pressed on to Mokambola's at the head of a precipice above it, and thence down the steep descent to Karambo. News of Nsama's war to the north being confirmed by a half-caste Arab, he decided to turn south to Chitimba's where the Arabs had an encampment "and hear from them more certainly".

Thither he now travelled in company with Arabs who were in charge of a slave-gang, having no other resource. Two notes dated 15 and 17 June, at the beginning of this journey are "damning in their very brevity".

A slave tried to break out of his slave-stick last night and actually broke half-inch iron with his fingers, but the broken part stuck in the hole.

A slave in the slave-stick burst out into a loud cry last night, sobbing bitterly—could not say why—a few switches from his master quieted him instantly.

There now began a long period of that close and "startlingly incongruous" association of Livingstone with Arab slave-traders which has puzzled some of his admirers. It is indeed the paradox of his career that, as on his two previous expeditions, the results of his path-finding for legitimate commerce should have been to blaze new trails for this inhuman traffic, so on his last he was forced by circumstances to depend for safety and life itself on the very agents of the men who were perpetrating it. But in stark fact, there was no other course that he could adopt. As Coupland has said: "Always responsive to personal kindness and courtesy, might he not let himself regard these kind and courteous men, steeped though they were in the evil he had made it his life's chief purpose to destroy, as instruments thrown in his path for the furtherance of his immediate aim?"[6] And he was in possession of a potent instrument wherewith to solicit their aid: this was the commendatory letter from the Sultan of Zanzibar who, however ineffectually, was endeavouring to suppress the slave-trade in his dominions; and at last he had found Arabs who could read it.

The principal Arab in Chitimba was one Hamees, who at once made himself responsible for this way-worn and impoverished white traveller. "Hamees has been particularly kind to me in presenting food, bead, cloths, and getting information . . . He is certainly very anxious to secure my safety." His chief concern was that Livingstone should not proceed until peace was restored with Nsama; and this involved a detention at Chitimba's of three months and ten days. He employed the time in writing letters and despatches (none of which was ever delivered); calculating different positions "which have stood over in travelling"; re-reading Smith's *Bible Dictionary*; observing the manners and customs of natives and Arabs; examining the courses of streams, studying the habits of insects and of birds; making frequent but fruitless enquiries about the river-systems to the west and south, and especially about a lake called Moero . . . But he chafed at the long delay: "it is tiresome beyond measure to wait so long." The counsels of the Arabs themselves which way to go, when peace should be restored, were divided, and he had thoughts of going on alone: "I am rather perplexed how to proceed . . . On pondering over the whole subject I see that, tiresome as it is to wait, it is better to do so than go south and then west, for if I should go I shall miss seeing Moero." "Hamees advises patience." Then on 7 July a peace-deputation set forth, "I wished to go too, but Hamees objected, as not being quite sure whether Nsama would be friendly, and he would not like anything to befall me." All turned out for the best however: Hamees concluded peace with Nsama, and the latter when told that an Englishman wished to go past him to Moero replied: "Bring him, and I shall send men to take him thither."

On 6 July he notes in his Journal:

> An earthquake happened at 3.30 p.m. accompanied with a hollow rumbling sound; it made me feel as if afloat, but it lasted only a few seconds. The boys came running to ask me what it was. Nowhere could be safer; the huts will not fall, and there are no high rocks near. Barometer 25.0. Temperature 68° 5'. Heavy cumuli hanging about; no rain afterwards.

This apparently trivial incident was fraught with disastrous consequences. On 2 August he notes: "Chronometer A stopped today without any apparent cause except the earthquake." The previous accident to the box containing these instruments (when he was on his way up from Chitane's Water to Tanganyika) had thrown out his reckoning for longitudes by 20' too far easterly; the earthquake was now responsible for an error in the opposite direction—50' too far to the west: so that "he now had seventy miles more of space on his map than was in fact there, and this affected most seriously his very last journey." But his minute sketch-map of his route to Chikumbi's is so exceedingly detailed and accurate that, says Professor Debenham, the cartographer who compiled the map for the *Last Journals* would have done better to stand by it than to accept his longitudes as correct.[7]

Such were Livingstone's powers of recuperation that the enforced delay at Chitimba, with a normal diet and comparative freedom from mosquitoes, had restored him to partial

513

convalescence, and when he set forth with the motley caravan on 30 August it was with something of his old zest. On the first day they overtook the notorious Tipo Tib, also going westward: he "gave me a fine fat goat". On the third he was deserted by Baraka, the boy who had formerly carried the medicine-chest. Arrived at Nsama's on 9 September, he exchanged presents with that chief and was provided with guides. The next day some people from Ujiji came and reported that his goods had arrived there safely, and he sent back with them a box containing papers, books, and clothes. Returning to Hara he remained there a few days, for, he says briefly, "I was ill". Meanwhile Nsama sent his daughter to Hamees in that village "to be a wife and cementer of peace!" She was carried with due ceremony into Hamees' hut, riding pick-a-back on a man's shoulders. "I had been sitting with Hamees, and now rose up and went away; as I passed him he spoke thus with himself: 'Hamees Wadim Tagh! see to what you have brought yourself!'" Hamees might have spared himself these matrimonial qualms, for on the 20th the bride, seeing preparations being made for a journey and thinking that her father was to be attacked, decamped with her attendants and the guides by night. "Hamees went again to Nsama and got other guides"— but not, it seems, the bride—"to enable us to go off at once."

Progress, commenced on the 22nd, was slow and the highlands waterless; but the Chisera river was a mile wide and choked with papyrus. On 1 October they reached Karunga's. A serious disadvantage for Livingstone of travelling with Arabs was the fact that villagers fled from them, as the Arabs themselves for an opposite reason had done; another that they divined on the Koran for their rate of progress and frequently found authority for delaying "one day more". "Nothing can be more tedious than the Arab way of travelling." Yet for the present, in his still enfeebled condition, he was dependent upon them. On the 20th: "Very ill; I always am so when I have no work—sore bones—much headache; then lost power over the muscles of the back, as at Liemba; no appetite and much thirst." On the 26th they were on the move again, and in three days reached Chifupa's on the river Choma, whence all had fled; then up along the Sanya range. On 3 November they encamped near Kabwakwa where food was plentiful, and showed no disposition to move on. Livingstone has a medical note: "Very many cases of goitre in men and women here: I see no reason for it. This is only 3,350 feet above the sea." Letters came for Hamees with depressing news: the chief Chitimba was dead, and his people fighting for the succession. At this point Livingstone wearying of the delay decided to go on without his Arab escort; and "instead of shaping my course for Ujiji" on the 7th he started for Lake Moero, "convoyed by all the Arabs for some distance: they have been extremely kind". On the next day, passing through Kabwakwa and proceeding south-south-west and then south, he reached the northern shore of the Lake.

It was of course a major geographical discovery and, as Macnair says, sufficient to have made the reputation of any ordinary traveller, but Livingstone records it without elation. Its importance for him was subsidiary to that of the river which flowed through it. This great river was the Chambesi, whose upper reaches he had already crossed; it was said to enter another Lake called Bemba (Bangweolo) to the west, and issue from it as the Luapula which connected it with Lake Moero, thence emerging as the Lualaba it flowed on northwards to another Lake. This chain of Lakes must form the central watershed, but the highest in altitude was undoubtedly Bangweolo. He describes the features of Moero prosaically enough: "it seems of goodly size, and is flanked by ranges of mountains on the east and west." He turned eastward along its shore; the people were suspicious at first, but friendly when reassured. They were mostly fishermen, and he notes the native names of 39 different species of fish.

Having come so far he might as well go further and, turning his back on Ujiji for the second time he went south along the range that flanked the eastern shore, and made for the town of the paramount chief Cazembe where he hoped to obtain more certain information respecting the river-system. On the 12th he crossed the Kalongosi, and on the 18th the stream called Chungu where the Portuguese explorer, Dr. Lacerda, had died seventy years before. This was the European "farthest west" into the heart of Africa, and here he rested till Cazembe should send "one of his counsellors to guide us to his town". Whether these arrived he does not say; but on the 21st he was at the gate of the town when "a number of noisy fellows stopped our party and demanded tribute: I burst through them, and the rest [his retinue of nine men] followed without giving anything." He was met and welcomed by an Arab named Mohamad bin Saleh who provided him with a hut; and then by another, Mohamad Bogharib, who presented a good meal of vermicelli, oil, and honey. He had tasted no sugar for more than a year.

By Cazembe he was accorded a public reception, but he was far from being predisposed in favour of this callous and tyrannical chief: there were too many human skulls at his gate and too many men with cropped ears and lopped hands about his court. Before him pranced his jester, a dwarf, whose uncouth antics elicited from Cazembe his only smile; beside him stood his executioner with a broad sword on his arm and a scissor-like instrument at his neck for cropping ears. When his principal wife came forward with her attendants and two spears in her hand, and a carrier bearing before her two enormous pipes ready charged for smoking, the white man was called upon to salute. "I did so; but she being forty yards off, I involuntarily beckoned her to come nearer: this upset the gravity of all her attendants; all burst into a laugh and ran off." Cazembe sent him plenty of food during his stay, but Mohamad bin Saleh thought him stingy. "But as we cannot consume all he gives, we do not complain."

He employed much of his time at Cazembe in writing letters and a very long despatch to Lord Clarendon, descriptive of the whole geography and vegetable products of his route from Lake Nyasa to Moero. All his other letters entrusted to Arabs for delivery in Zanzibar were destroyed by them, as likely to be too informative about their own evil doings; but the rough draft of his despatch to Clarendon was preserved, with a note stating that it was not copied or sent for lack of paper. It is in some respects more detailed than his Journal, and is of interest for more than one reason. It reveals a knowledge of the earlier ethnic studies of Winwood Reade (whose classic, *The Martyrdom of Man*, was published the year before Livingstone's death) to the effect that the typical negro resembles the ancient Egyptian —a notion, probably erroneous, which Livingstone always held. He disposes of the fallacy of Portuguese geographers that the

Chambesi is the same as the Zambesi; and ridicules another "bold constructor of maps who tacked on 200 miles to the north-west end of Lake Nyasa, a feat which no traveller has ever ventured to imitate. Another has placed a river in the same quarter running 3,000 or 4,000 feet uphill and named it the New Zambesi, because I suppose the old Zambesi runs downhill. I have walked over both these mental abortions, and did not know I was walking on water till I saw them on the maps." There also occurs this personal touch:

> I am so tired of exploration without a word from home or anywhere else for two years, that I must go to Ujiji on Tanganyika for letters before doing anything else. The banks and country to Lake Bangweolo are reported to be very muddy and unhealthy. I have no medicine.

He left Cazembe for the north again on 15 December by the same route, travelling in heavy rain through flooded country: "rain from above, and cold and wet to the waist below" and on the 28th he was no farther on his way than the Kabukwa river. His Journal for the year ends thus:

> We came on to the rivulet Chirongo, and then to the Kabukwa, where I was taken ill. Heavy rains kept the convoy back. I have had nothing but coarsely-ground sorghum meal for some time back, and am weak; I used to be the first in the line of march, and am now the last; Mohamad presented a meal of finely-ground porridge and a fowl, and I immediately felt the difference, though I am not grumbling at my coarse dishes. It is well that I did not go on to Bangweolo Lake, for it is now very unhealthy to the natives, and I fear that without medicine continual wettings by fording rivulets might have knocked me up altogether. As I have mentioned, the people suffer greatly from swelled thyroid gland and Elephantiasis scroti.

Chapter Twenty-Eight

LAST JOURNEYS: GREAT CENTRAL LAKES
1868–1869

"Consciousness of my own defects makes me lenient."

His Journal for 1868 opens with the words:

> Almighty Father, forgive the sins of the past year for Thy Son's sake. Help me to be more profitable during this year. If I am to die this year prepare me for it.

There is a gap after this till 12 January, a day or two after he had resumed the march in company with Mohamad bin Saleh and his slaves. But meanwhile he made several short excursions to Lake Moero and examined its features carefully. From a height from which he viewed it the Rua Mountains were visible to the north-west, but nothing save the lake horizon beyond the island Kirwa to the south and west. He bought some hoes to barter for a goat further on: "one of my goats died and the other dried up. I long for others, for milk is the most strengthening food I can get." By the 12th he had recrossed the Kalongosi and was in Karembwe's village, to find that his enthusiasm for the Lake had infected Tipo Tib and other Arabs who had camped five days beside it. In two days he reached the north-eastern corner of the Lake again, and crossed a plain flooded by the Luao ankle-deep through adhesive black mud—"We had four hours of this"—and then forded the river itself waist-deep. On the 16th he arrived near Kabwabwata and here remained perforce for several weeks. Mohamad was "naturally anxious" to stay a little while with his son; it was the middle of the wet season and the mud was said to be worse near Ujiji. "I am anxious to be off, but chiefly to get news." On the 26th and 27th: "I am ill with fever, as I always am when stationary." But Mohamad, as well as a kind slave-owner, was a good companion: "he cooks small delicacies for me with the little he has, and tries to make me comfortable."

Livingstone beguiled the time with long conversations with this Muslim, who had for twenty-five years been a virtual prisoner at Cazembe's. It appeared that Livingstone's production of the Sultan's letter had considerable effect in securing his release. He had more than once been advised to fight his way out but had always refused. "He seems a man of peace, and unwilling to break the appearance of friendship with the chiefs. . . . He is respected among the Arabs, who pronounce him to be a good man." He confirmed the interesting fact that the Arabs made no attempt to proselytize the natives; the Koran was never translated. This however was not the case with the Swaheli (half caste Arabs) on the coast. Nevertheless Livingstone expresses himself as astonished by the fact that "the establishment of Moslem missions among the heathen is utterly unknown".

Not till 16 March did he set forth again, this time alone with his few men, and then it was to Mpweto, where the Lake empties its waters into the Lualaba, and which he named Webb's river. Here was the house of Syde bin Habib, his old acquaintance in Linyanti, "a very pretty spot among the mountains". Syde was absent, but his agent presented food. The same day he was visited by Mpweto's favourite son: "his father is said to do nothing without consulting him; but he did not seem to be endowed with much wisdom." But Mpweto had taken offence: the white man had gone to his great rival Muabo, before visiting him: he must go away or be driven out. "Mohamad told us previously that it was likely he would refuse to see us. . . . I had no wish to stay or to quarrel with a worthless chief, and resolved to go next day."

The Journal entry for 19 March, his birthday, is: "Grant, Lord, grace to love Thee more and serve Thee better."

At this point a note of uncertainty is apparent in Livingstone's Journal. He is torn by two conflicting desires: one, to go on with the Arabs to Ujiji for long-awaited letters and supplies; the other, which became increasingly the stronger, to discover Lake Bemba (Bangweolo).

25 *March.*—I am thinking of going to Lake Bemba, because at least two months must be passed here still before a passage can be made; but my goods are getting done, and I canot give presents to the chiefs on our way.

11 *April.*—I had a long oration from Mohamad yesterday against going on for Bemba tomorrow. His great argument is the extortionate way of Cazembe. . . . Were my goods not nearly done I would go, and risk the displeasure of Cazembe for the chance of discovering the Lake. . . . I am afraid I must give up this Lake for the present.

12 *April.*—I think of starting tomorrow for Bangweolo, even if Cazembe refuses a passage beyond him: we shall be better there than we are here, for everything at Kabwabwata is scarce and dear. . . . Three of Cazembe's principal men are here and would be a gain to me: they are anxious to go home, but Mohamad detains them, and when I ask his reason he says, "Muabo refuses". but they point to Mohamad's house and say, "It is he who refuses".

The immediate effect of his announcement was a mutiny. This is no wonder; the wonder rather is that his faithful remnant of nine had remained faithful for so long, through such perils and adversities. But again to turn their backs on Ujiji when within only a few marches of Tanganyika, and splash and wade through a watery wilderness once more, was more even than their loyal hearts could bear. "They think that, by refusing to go to Bemba, they will force me to remain with them, and then go to Ujiji . . . The fact is, they are all tired, and Mohamad's opposition encourages them." It now appeared that Mohamad's ulterior motive had been to detach them from Livingstone's service to his own. It is a remarkable testimony to Livingstone's moral strength that the very day after this mutiny six of the nine changed their minds and went with him, even though one of them, Amoda, ran away the day after that—but he too returned subsequently. And of the defection of the rest, which included a few carriers picked up *en route*, it is a very much mellowed Livingstone who could write:

I did not blame them very severely in my own mind for absconding: they were tired of tramping, and so verily am I!

But Mohamad, in encouraging them to escape to him, and talking with a double tongue, cannot be exonerated from blame. Little else can be expected from him; he has lived some thirty-five years in the country, twenty-five being at Cazembe's, and there he had often to live by his wits. Consciousness of my own defects makes me lenient.

He still trusted the Arab well enough to leave the bulk of the luggage with him and, when Amoda ran away, sent that delinquent's bundle back to him. The names of the five who remained with him must be recorded. They were: the ever-reliable Susi, the ebullient Chuma, and three Nassick boys—

Abraham, Gardner and Simon. And all those who deserted will reappear later on in the story.

Though it was now the dry season, the spongy ground between the Lakes was still waterlogged in places: he writes of wading waist-deep through flooded plains, and floundering in black tenacious mud: "this was usually followed by a rush of bubbles to the surface which, bursting, discharged foul air of frightful faecal odour." Again, through grass "so long and tangled that I could scarcely get along"; or, thankful for some shelter, in villages abandoned owing to "the abundance of ferocious wild beasts". In inhabited villages he was sometimes welcomed but more often repulsed, and, uncertain of his reception again at Cazembe's, he sent Abraham in advance from the Mandapala river with a request to Mohamad Bogharib to intercede with that chief for a guide to Chikumbi, near the Bangweolo. The reply from Cazembe was most cordial, and when Livingstone arrived there on 5 May, "I met some old friends, and Mohamad Bogharib cooked a supper, and from this time forward never omitted sharing his victuals with me." Cazembe detained him for more than a month on the pretext of getting good guides; he provided food and promised the white man the freedom of his country to the Lake; he only wondered at his strange desire to see it since it was "only water". The most interesting character in this town was "a sensible old man" named Perembe, with whom Livingstone had conversed before, and who was reputed by the Arabs to be 150 years old. At the time of Pereira's visit in 1796 he was a father; assuming him to be thirty at that time he would now be 102; "and he must be quite that, for when Dr. Lacerda came (in 1799) he had forty children." But as Debenham remarks: "Livingstone was perhaps expecting a little too much when he complains that he could not induce Perembe 'to tell anything of times previous to his own'." Nevertheless he did succeed in eliciting from this ancient a pedigree of the Cazembe chiefs for ten generations with a short biography of the first of them, who had conquered Perembe's ancestor.

Livingstone's estimation of Cazembe improved with acquaintance: he was better than his men; he was poor, but concealed the fact and was generous; he did everything in his power to promote the white man's welfare. Livingstone grew restless and chafed at the long delay; it was not till 11 June that he was fairly started, but then it was with the chief's goodwill and' recommendation to his brother Moenempanda. The latter gave him a public reception as Cazembe had done; but was less helpful: "he promised a man to guide me to Chikumbi, and then refused." Here Livingstone stayed for a week, and set forth again on 22 June across a grassy plain to Luongo, which was crossed by a bridge. In a letter to Waller he shows that he had seldom been more affected by the sufferings of slaves than at this time, and his Journal entry for 24 June affords a poignant illustration of this.

> Six slaves were singing as if they did not feel the weight and degradation of the slave-sticks. I asked the cause of their mirth, and was told that they rejoiced at the idea "of coming back after death and haunting and killing those who had sold them". . . . Then all joined in the chorus, which was the name of each vendor. It told, not of fun, but of the bitterness and tears of such as were oppressed. . . .

Still more moving is the often-quoted passage which occurs two days later, reflecting as it does the mood of melancholy evoked by these scenes:

> We came to a grave in the forest; it was a little rounded mound as if the occupant sat in it in the usual native way; it was strewed over with flour, and a number of large blue beads put on it; a little path showed that it had visitors. This is the sort of grave I should prefer: to lie in the still, still forest, and no hand ever disturb my bones. The graves at home always seemed to me miserable, especially those in the cold damp clay, and without elbow-room; but I have nothing to do but wait till He who is over all decides where I have to lay me down and die.

After wading for hours on end through floods beyond the Chando he reached Chikumbi on 1 July. This chief made him welcome and suggested a wait of two days only for the choice of a good guide. The next day Livingstone wrote again to Dr. Seward for supplies, adding to the list sundries such as shoes, beads, stationery, and the new Nautical Almanac. "I borrowed some paper from Mohamad Bogharib to write home by some Arabs going to the coast. I will announce my discovery to Lord Clarendon; but I reserve the parts of the Lualaba and Tanganyika for future confirmation. I have doubts on the subject. . . ." He was more intent than ever with questions to natives about the direction of the drainage of the central rivers.

Macnair presents a convincing picture of Livingstone at this stage:

> In general he was respectfully treated by the tribes, but he must have been in their eyes a strange enigma. This emaciated old man who wandered about for no understandable purpose, with complete disregard of rain and storm; always moving patiently on, asking innumerable questions, and writing everything in a book; gentle to everyone and doing no harm; speaking of a God whose name was new to them and praying a great deal. Probably, in their eyes, he was more or less mad, and therefore to be respected![1]

At the end of ten days Chikumbi said that the Mazitu were raiding the country and he feared to send a guide lest he should be blamed for inciting them to attack his village. Livingstone secured a guide from another tribe and departed. The country became more populous as he neared the Lake, though many villages and gardens were deserted through fear of the Mazitu. On 13 July he was threatened by a drunken rabble who mistook his party for these marauders: "poising their spears at us, taking aim with their bows and arrows, and making as if about to strike with their axes." He was calmly walking on into the midst of them when one of their number came to him and, addressing the others, said, "This is only your *pombe* [drunkenness]. White man, do not stand among them, but go away."

> Then he placed himself between me and a portion of the assailants, about thirty of whom were making their warlike antics. While walking quietly away with my good friend they ran in front and behind bushes and trees, took aim with bow and arrow, but none shot; the younger men ran away with our three goats. When we had gone a quarter of a mile my friend told me to wait and he would bring the goats, which he did. I could not feel the inebriates to be enemies; but in that state they are the worst one can encounter, for they have no fear as they have when sober. One snatched away a fowl from our guide; that too was restored by our friend, I did not load my gun; for any accidental discharge would have inflamed them to rashness. We got away without shedding blood, and were thankful.

Two days later a similar incident occurred. Arrived at a village on the Mpanda, the headman began to shut his gates against him "with frantic gesticulations". But others of his people, equally drunk, insisted on detaining him. "I sat down a little, but seeing that the chief was still alarmed I said to his people, 'The chief objects and I can't stay.' They saw the reasonableness of this, but I could not get my cowardly attendants to come on. . . . So I went on through the forest, and in an hour and a half came to a sponge where, being joined by my attendants, we passed the night." Next day he came to another "sponge" and here, by way of contrast, some young men came forward and offered to carry him across; "but I had got off my shoes and was in the water, and they came along with me, showing the shallower parts." Then yet another—"with 150 paces of deep water . . . The water in these spongy oozes felt very cold, though only 60° in the mornings, and 65° at midday." The people beyond it invited him to their village; "but the forest, unless infested with leopards or lions, is always preferable, for one is free from vermin and free from curiosity-gazers . . ." On the 18th he reached the north shore of Lake Bangweolo, "thankful that I had come safely hither". Waller comments: "It is extraordinary to notice the total absence of all pride and enthusiasm, as—almost parenthetically—he records the fact."

He told the chief Mapuni that his goods were all expended, and that he had nothing to offer for the hire of guides but a fathom of cloth. The chief was satisfied with this, and at once gave him a public reception. He explained his object in coming so far: to see and measure the Lake; make friends with the people—"we were all children of one Father"—and make them better known to the outside world. He told them about cotton-growing in the Zambesi district, and how it had been thwarted only by the slave-traffic: "they were pleased with this." He showed them his watch, compass, burning-glass, and Bible, telling them a little of its contents, and was "loudly drummed home". It is clear that the magnetism of his personality with untutored savages had lost nothing of its power.

Next day he went down to Masantu's and was detained there for nearly a week by strong winds and high waves, and then, though the water was still very rough, prevailed on five stalwart canoe-men to paddle him across to the islands in a large and long canoe: "we could not go to Kisi because, as the canoe-men told us, they had stolen their canoe thence." His observations are various and minute: the prevailing winds south-easterly; fish, grass, rushes, flowers; a hammerhead's nest; one shell; a graveyard. He correctly surmised that the Lake was shallow (its greatest depth is only 30 feet). He persuaded the paddlers against their inclinations to go on before dark and sleep in Mpabala, which was well populated.

> Here we cooked a little porridge and ate it, then I lay down on one side [of a large shed] with the canoe-men and my attendants at the fire in the middle, and was soon asleep, and dreamed that I had apartments in Milvart's Hotel. This made me feel much amused next day, for I never dream unless I am ill; . . . a freak of fancy surely, for I was not at all discontented with my fare, or apartment; I was only afraid of getting a stock of vermin from my associates.

His great desire was to cross over to Chirubi, the largest and most populous of the islands, and thence to the uninhabited islet Kasango (the tops of whose trees he could just discern); and thence to the southern shore of the Lake; but the paddlers, fearful of retribution from Kisi, would stay at Mpabala only two nights.

> I thought of seizing their paddles, and appealing to the headmen of the island, but . . . resolved to bear with meekness, though groaning inwardly, the loss of two of the four days for which I had paid them. I had only my coverlet to hire another canoe, and it was now very cold; the few beads left would all be required to buy food on the way back; I might have got food by shooting buffaloes, but that on foot, and through grass with stalks as thick as a goose-quill, is dreadfully hard work. I had thus to return to Masantu's.

Six pages of Livingstone's note-book are filled with lunar and stellar observations for longitude sights from Mpabala; and he must have spent many hours in questioning the more intelligent of the natives concerning the main features of the Lake and its affluents. Their knowledge of the latter proved surprisingly accurate; but their definition of the lake area to the south and south-east was vitiated by an unfortunate misunderstanding in the use of place names, so that Livingstone construed a term meaning "sandy place" into "mainland"—and this mistake grievously threw out his bearings on his last journey.

Professor Debenham made a very thorough survey of the Lake in 1952, and carefully compared its actual outline with that which Livingstone deduced both on this and on his last journey. Not only so, but he elucidates the causes of Livingstone's mistakes. He remarks that the refusal of the paddlers to take him farther than Mpabala "was most unfortunate for Livingstone, for it stopped him just short of a point at which he would have solved the riddle of the lake". Had they taken him two hours farther he would have recognized that "most of his 'lake' was a vast swamp of reeds", and the confusion of place-names is partly responsible for his making the lake area "a long east-west oval, whereas really it is as broad as it is long". The fault in his chronometers would further elongate Livingstone's map of the Lake by twenty miles in a westerly direction. These apparently minor accidents of fortune, he says, "acquired a major importance on his last journey to the swamps four years later".[2]

On his return northward from the Lake he wrote what Waller calls "an elaborate treatise" on the climate of this region with reference to the periodical floods on the rivers which drain the enormous cistern-lakes of Central Africa. It certainly shows no diminution of his mental powers; indeed, considering his lack both of time and of resources, it must be reckoned as perhaps the most remarkable of all his contri-butions to science. The variety, range, and minuteness of his observations are amazing: the quantity and seasons of the annual rainfall; the positions and heights of the lichens and orchids on the trees, and ferns in the crevices of rocks; the opposing directions of upper and lower wind-currents observ-able from double sheets of clouds and from the smoke of burning grass; the sandy bottoms of the sponges (of which he had crossed, often thigh-deep and with many a painful jolt, no less than 29); the presence of oxide of iron in some of them from outcrops of brown haematite—these are among the indications which he notices, and which might serve to eluci-date the problem of excessive inundation. His tentative deductions therefrom would be intelligible only to a trained geologist; but with scientific caution he propounds no theory, concluding this admirably written document with "Thanks to that all-embracing Providence which has watched over and enabled me to discover what I have done. There is still much to do, and if health and protection be granted I shall make a complete thing of it."

Debenham describes the scientific result of "this bold dash" to the Lake with only four men as a "geographical masterpiece" and adds that it could hardly be improved upon even now. And Coupland: "Weary though he was and fever-ridden, it was the old self-reliant Livingstone that struck back on his tracks, alone, with only four 'faithfuls'. . . . It was an exploit in the old style." Alas, that it was to prove the last of them.

Of the letters that he wrote home at this time very few reached their destination. There is one which he wrote to Moffat from near Lake Moero in March, despairing of his hopes of reaching Bangweolo on account of the floods and long delays through the strifes of the Arabs and natives. Another to his daughter Agnes, after he had reached the Bangweolo, also dwells much on his past difficulties but has a touch of his old sardonic humour:

> I broke my teeth tearing maize and other hard food, and they are coming out. One front tooth is out, and I have such an awful mouth! If you expect a kiss from me, you must take it through a speaking-trumpet.[3]

Another to his friend Oswell explaining in technical language the part of the river-system he had traversed and that which he intended to examine; and ridiculing those two officious "blockhead busybodies" of the R.G.S. who had required him to send "copies if not the originals" of all his memoranda. The letter ends on a wistful note.

> I hope you are playing with your children instead of being bothered by idiots. In looking back to Kolobeng I have one regret, and that is that I did not feel it my duty to play with my children as much as to teach the Bakwains. I worked very hard at that, and was tired out at night. Now I have none to play with. So, my good friend, play while you may. They will soon be no longer bairns. My kind love to their Mother and them.[4]

On 30 July, having noticed no single case either of goitre or of elephantiasis anywhere near the Lake, he commenced his march back northwards "eager to get to Chikumbi's in case Mohamad should go thence to Katanga" (that is, a trading centre for copper far to the west, now centred round Elizabethville in the Belgian Congo. It was evidently the report of rivers, especially the Lufira, in that region that drew him thither). But when near Kisinga he was met by Mohamad bin Saleh who was about to go north to Manyuema: "this is all in my favour; it is the way I want to go to see the Lualaba and Lufira to Chowambe. The way seems opening up before me, and I am thankful." When Syde bin Omar arrived from the Luapula soon afterwards, however, with news of Mazitu wars in that territory, the Arabs agreed to unite their forces to beat a safe retreat. "They objected very strongly to my going away down the right bank of the Luapula with my small party, though it was in sight, so I resolved to remain till all went." But the delay appears to have been too much for his patience, since on 15 August he started off alone with his small party for Cazembe. He got no further than to Kisinga: "some people were killed in my path." He writes: "Feeling my way. . . . Rumours of wars perpetual and near." Then on 1 September: "Two men come from Cazembe—I am reported killed." From this point his Journal entries, which had been intermittent, cease and are not resumed till 7 October (when he had reached the Kalungosi) with a brief recapitulation of intervening events. These relate chiefly to the fortunes of war among the confusedly contending parties; tribal, Mazitu, and Arab. Waller summarizes the situation: "All was turmoil and panic, and his life appears to have been in imminent danger." He mentions one such occasion himself:

> . . . I was surrounded by a party of furious Imbozhwa. A crowd stood within fifteen or twenty yards with spears poised and arrows set in the bowstrings, and some took aim at me: they took us for plunderers. . . . One good soul helped us away—a blessing be on him and his. Another chief man took us for Mazitu! In this state of confusion Cazembe heard that my party had been cut off; he called in Moenempanda and took the field in person. . . .

Not until 23 September, when the Arab forces were united, did he continue the march from Kisinga, and then struck up with them by another route almost due north, mapping it with his usual precision as he went, and noting the rocks, runnels, birds, and flora. At the Papusi on 6 October "we were met by about 400 of Kabanda's men, as if they had come to dispute our passage at the ford; I went over; all were civil; but had we shown any weakness they would no doubt have taken advantage of it." Next day they reached the Kalongosi where it flowed

528

over five cataracts, and on the 12th came to a ford which he measured by pacing it thigh-deep in the water.

> It ran so strongly that it was with difficulty I could keep my feet. Here 500 at least of Nsama's people stood on the opposite shore to know what we wanted. Two fathoms of calico were sent over, and then I and thirty guns went over to protect the people in the ford: as we approached they retired. I went to them, and told them that I had been to Nsama's, and he gave me a goat and food, and we were good friends; some had seen me there, and they now crowded to look till the Arabs thought it unsafe for me to be among them: if I had come with bared skin they would have fled. All became friendly: an elephant was killed, and we remained two days buying food.

He was now on his old route between the mountains and Lake Moero and on the 22nd reached Kabwabwata, where Syde bin Habib was expected to join the company. "He has an enormous number of tusks and bars of copper" (from the Katanga mines). There too was Mohamad Bogharib, ready to start early in November. But on the very eve of their departure fresh wars broke out, this time between the Arabs and the local tribes over several runaway slaves of whom some had been recaptured, and Mohamad would not stir. On the 13th Livingstone's own "runaways" returned to him: the remnant of the unreliable Nassick boys. He took them all back, finding excuses for their behaviour, and adding with one of those touches of self-criticism which characterize his Last Journeys: "I have faults myself."

His impatience also finds frequent expression:

> 8 *November.*—Ill of fever two days. Better and thankful.
>
> 13*th.*—I was on the point of starting without Mohamad Bogharib, but he begged me not to go till he had settled some weighty matter about a wife. . . . We must have a new moon, which will appear in three days. . . .
>
> 16*th.*—I am tired out by waiting after finishing the Journal, and will go off tomorrow north. . . .
>
> 19*th.*—I am prepared to start today, but Mohamad Bogharib has been very kind, and indeed cooked meals for me. . . . He now begged of me not to go for three days, and then he would come along with me! Mpamari [i.e. Mohamad bin Saleh] also entreated. I would not have minded him, but they have influence with the canoe-men on Tanganyika.
>
> 20*th.*—Mohamad Bogharib purposed to attack two villages near to this, from an idea that the people there concealed his runaway slaves;

by remaining I think that I have put a stop to this, as he did not like to pillage while I was in company. Mpamari also turned round towards peace. . . . We go on the 22nd.

But on that same day their encampment was furiously attacked at dawn by the Babemba and other local tribes. They had no stockade but kept their assailants at bay with guns whilst others felled trees for a line of defence. The attack lasted for seven hours: Livingstone admired the gallantry of the attackers, who rescued their wounded in the face of whistling bullets; and of the defenders had far more praise for the native African bowmen than for the half-caste Arab gunmen.

It was quite evident to me that the Swaheli Arabs were quite taken aback by the attitude of the natives; they expected them to flee as soon as they heard a gun fired in anger, but instead of this we were very nearly being cut off, and should have been but for our Banyamwezi allies. . . .

Had it not been for the Banyamwezi, who shot vigorously with their arrows, and occasionally chased the Imbozhwa [Babemba], we should have been routed.

As for himself, he did not go near the fighting, but remained in what he called "my house" to defend his "luggage" if necessary.

He judged that the guilt of this savagery lay neither with the native attackers nor the native attacked, but that it was solely the Arab slave-raiding which had precipitated it. Though the defenders had fenced themselves in with a stockade, the attack continued for two more days, and on the last Livingstone was the horrified witness of a murder in cold blood.

A fine young man was caught and brought in by the Banyamwezi; one stabbed him from behind, another cut his forehead with an axe. I called in vain to them not to kill him. . . . They killed him. It was horrible: I protested loudly against any repetition of this wickedness, and the more sensible agreed that prisoners ought not to be killed. . . .

Next day "I told Mohamad Bogharib that the war was undoubtedly his work. . . . He does not like this; but it is true." Neither would the Arab agree at first to Livingstone's proposal that he should send back the captured slaves, to show that he disapproved of the act and was willing to make peace: "this was too humiliating". But when, a few days later, Mohamad asked his advice because he did not know what to do, "I took care not to give him any" beyond repeating that which he had disregarded. In the end six captives were returned. Mohamad Bogharib had a conscience, and for this reason Livingstone liked him better than his associates, Mohamad bin Saleh or Syde bin Habib.

All this while he was chafing at the prolonged detention: "it is excessively vexatious to me." More than once he had thought of marching off with his few attendants and risking attack, but was prevented either by Mohamad Bogharib's entreaties or by lack of food. He beguiled the interval by writing a paper on the sources of the Nile, the subject which from now on and above all others engrossed his thoughts. Among speculators of old time he mentions Sesostris, Alexander the Great, Julius Caesar, his centurion Nero, and the geographer Ptolemy: and pays tribute to "the patient toil and laborious perseverance" of modern British explorers: Speke, Grant, Burton, Baker, and especially the Dutch lady, Miss Tinné.

> Old Nile played the theorists a pretty prank by having his springs 500 miles south of them all! I call mine a contribution, because it is just a hundred years (1769) since Bruce, a greater traveller than any of us, visited Abyssinia, and having discovered the sources of the Blue Nile, he thought he had then solved the ancient problem.

He signed this paper "David Livingstone".

He was of course completely mistaken, but his mistake was not unreasonable. In 1858 (the year before he himself discovered Nyasa) Speke and Burton had discovered Tanganyika at Ujiji. Speke then discovered the Victoria Nyanza. Returning down the Nile he met Baker who had discovered Lake Albert, calling it the "second source" of the Nile. Livingstone's information, derived from "various reliable sources" (Arabs), was that it rose between 9° and 10° south latitude, namely some 400 or 500 miles south of the Victoria Nyanza; whilst Tanganyika "is declared to send its water through north into Baker's Lake. If this does not prove false, then Tanganyika is an expansion of the Nile." Tanganyika is in fact 500 feet higher than Lake Albert and therefore, as Debenham points out, the Arabs were not declaring an impossibility. He continues: "The strange thing is that probably this did happen at one time, before the Mufumbiro volcanoes erupted and reversed the drainage back into Lake Tanganyika, whence it had to find an exit to the west into the Congo system."[5]

At length and at last in company with "a motley group, composed of Mohamad and his friends, a gang of Unyamwezi hangers-on, and strings of wretched slaves", he took the Ujiji road. Several slaves escaped from time to time, but no efforts were made to recapture them. On the 16th he wrote: "I had made up my mind to leave the whole party"; but was dissuaded by Syde bin Habib who averred that the headman Chisabi was not to be trusted, which indeed proved to be the case. In crossing the Lofunsa on the 22nd two men were drowned, and two were rescued by good swimmers, among whom was Susi. On Christmas Day, past mount Katanga, "We can buy nothing but the very coarsest food, while Syde, having plenty of copper, can get all the luxuries." The way was hard and the journey delayed by some of the party falling sick. But as Livingstone wades through the rivers and rivulets, his eyes are as alert as ever to observe and note every natural feature. His Journal for 31 December ends with the words, "Scenery very lovely."

The Journal entry for New Year's Day 1869 omits the usual prayer, and opens thus:

> I have been wet times without number, but the wetting of yesterday was once too often: I felt very ill, but fearing that the Lofuko might flood I resolved to cross it. Cold up to the waist, which made me worse, but I went on for 2½ hours E.
>
> *3rd.*—I marched for one hour but found I was too ill to go further. . . . I had a pain in the chest, and rust of iron sputa: my lungs, my strongest part, were thus affected. . . . Lost count of the days. . . . Very ill all over.
>
> *About 7th.*—Cannot walk: pneumonia of right lung, and I cough all day and all night: sputa rust of iron and bloody: distressing weakness. Ideas flow through the mind with great rapidity and vividness, in groups of twos and threes: if I look at any piece of wood, the bark seems covered with figures and faces of men, and they remain, though I look away and turn to the same spot again. I saw myself lying dead in the way to Ujiji, and all the letters I expected there useless. . . .

His thoughts were with his children and friends, and the lines of a verse rang through his head perpetually, "I shall look into your faces. . . ." At this stage Mohamad Bogharib overtook him and undoubtedly saved his life. "I am so weak that

I can scarcely speak." His feet were sore and swollen, and continual coughing prevented sleep. Mohamad contrived a litter and he was carried in it up and down steep ravines for the rest of the journey. Having lost track of dates he calculates them by the days of the lunar month. He continues to note the geological features of the country.

> Mohamad Bogharib is very kind to me in my extreme weakness, but carriage is painful; head down and feet up alternates with feet down and head up; jolted up and down and sideways—changing shoulders involves a toss from one side to the other of the kitanda. The sun is vertical, blistering any part of the skin exposed, and I try to shelter my face and head as well as I can with a bunch of leaves, but it is dreadfully fatiguing in my weakness.
>
> I had a severe relapse after a very hot day. Mohamad gave me some medicines. . . .

On 14 February they reached the confluence of the river Lofuko with the Lake, where Syde bin Habib had large canoes. "I sent to Syde to say that all the Arabs had served me except himself." Since Thani bin Suellim at Ujiji had promised a canoe on his arrival, the only favour he desired of Syde was to inform Thani, by one of his canoes, "that I was here very ill, and that if I did not get to Ujiji for proper food and medicine I should die." This message had the desired effect; Syde at once sent flour and two fowls, and the promise of help with canoes. The next day he wrote in his Journal:

> The cough and chest pain diminished, and I feel thankful. My body is greatly emaciated. Syde came today, and is favourable to sending me up to Ujiji. Thanks to the Great Father in Heaven.

No doubt the prospect—now in sight—of adequate medicines and other creature comforts, and above all news from home, had something to do with his recovery from this, the gravest illness he had ever suffered. But incessant motion under tropical heat by day, with a pronounced drop in the temperature by night; recumbent in a slung hammock with no back-rest, and with nothing to eat but gruel; these are factors not at all conducive to recovery from pneumonia; and his survival from such an ordeal must, from a medical point of view, be regarded as almost miraculous.

He was still seriously ill when, nearly a fortnight later, he embarked in a canoe; the weather was rough and the waves high; the crew put in to several islets for shelter. He kept anxious count of the hours' paddling every day. On 8 March he wrote from the Kasanga islet:

> Patience was never more needed than now; I am near Ujiji, but the slaves who paddle are tired, and no wonder; they keep up a roaring song all through their work, night and day. I expect to get medicine, food, and milk at Ujiji, but dawdle and do nothing. I have a good appetite, and sleep well: these are favourable symptoms; but am dreadfully thin, bowels irregular, and I have no medicine. Sputa increases; hope to hold out to Ujiji. Cough worse. Hope to go tomorrow.

Three days later they went on the Kibize islet near by, and there waited for a fair wind to cross the Lake. Next day they crossed it in ten hours. Only a few days more of pain and weariness, and the long desired haven of his hopes would be reached: medicines to cure his sickness, food to restore his health, means of barter to secure provisions, letters to cheer his heart. On 14 March he reached his goal, to find—no medicines, no letters, no food, no milk; nothing but a little tea and coffee and sugar. He bought some butter and some flannel. "I found great benefit from the tea and coffee, and still more from flannel to the skin."

Chapter Twenty-Nine

LAST JOURNEYS: GREAT RIVER SOURCES
1869–1871

"I read the whole Bible through four times whilst I was in Manyuema."

"THERE were many disappointments in Livingstone's life," says Coupland, "but none more bitter than that which met him at Ujiji." This is however an overstatement. The disappointment, shattering as it was, was no worse than some he had suffered in the past, and not nearly so severe as he would suffer on his next visit to Ujiji. Moreover, the shock of this blow is not so noteworthy as the resilience with which he countered it.

On checking his losses he found only a quarter, or less, of the cloth ordered from Zanzibar, and much of it useless for barter. Packing-stuff had been fraudulently substituted for calico. The bulk of it, and the best of his beads, had been stolen. "Medicine, wine, and cheese had been left at Unyanyembe, thirteen days east of this." (The actual distance is 150 miles. Speke and Burton, travelling in the opposite direction in May 1858, had taken twenty-four days. Now, in 1869, the route was blocked by Mazitu wars.) Milk, his best restorative, was unprocurable at Ujiji because the cows had not calved. Of luxuries he had only tea, coffee, and sugar; of necessities virtually none. Of food for the mind there was nothing: no letters, no newspapers; and of such he had been starved for three years.

The man sent in charge of these goods proved to be "a genuine specimen of the ill-conditioned, English-hating Arab". He demanded extortionate payment for his journey, and when asked "to go a mile every second day for milk", he refused. "I had to expel him from the house." Another "respectable Arab" supplied the milk which, together with the flannel, probably hastened Livingstone's recovery, for on 28 March he could write, "my cough has ceased, and I walk half a mile." On

535

13 April he was writing to the Governor of Unyanyembe "to make enquiries about the theft of my goods", and to Thani bin Suellim in the same place for a boat and crew to go down the Tanganyika. His old acquaintance Syde bin Habib was turning into an enemy and not without reason: "he refused to allow his men to carry my letters to the coast; as he suspected that I would write about his doings in Rua." By the 27th he had written no less than forty-two, "which in some measure will make up for my long silence", but no traveller from Ujiji would carry them; all offered excuses, "but I suspect they fear my exposure of their ways more than anything else". After this there is a gap in his Journal for three weeks. On 17 May is an entry: "I wish I were away, now that I am getting stronger." Meanwhile he wrote a well-considered reply to critics of the wholesale emancipation of negroes in the West Indies and America, which however a fuller knowledge of the complex problems involved might have caused him to modify.

On the 20th his agent Thani bin Suellim arrived from Unyanyembe, by whom he was by no means favourably impressed. "He is a slave who has risen to freedom and influence." He brought two light boxes with him and charged for their carriage, though this had been prepaid. "When I paid him he tried to steal . . . I gave him two cloths and a double blanket as a present." He returned the cloths as they were injured by rain on the way, and demanded coffee. When this was given he asked for more. More being refused, "in revenge he sends round to warn all Ujijians against taking my letters to the coast." On 29 May a caravan was setting forth for Unyanyembe.

> I took my packet of letters to Thani, and gave two cloths and four bunches of beads to the man who was to take them to Unyanyembe; an hour afterwards, letters, cloths and beads were returned; Thani said he was afraid of English letters; he did not know what was inside. I had sewed them up in a piece of canvas; that was suspicious, and he would call all the great men of Ujiji and ask them if it would be safe to take them; if they assented he would call for the letters, if not he would not send them. I told Mohamad bin Saleh, and he said to Thani that he and I were men of the Government, and orders had come from Syed Majid to treat me with all respect; was this conduct respectful? Thani then sent for the packet, but whether it will reach Zanzibar I am doubtful.

He may well have been doubtful; none of these letters were

delivered and they must have been deliberately destroyed. And the suspicions of the Ujijians would have been confirmed had they known what Livingstone was writing in his Journal at this time:

> This is a den of the worst kind of slave-traders; those whom I met in Urunga and Itawa were gentlemen slavers: the Ujiji slavers, like the Kilwa and Portuguese, are the vilest of the vile. It is not a trade, but a system of consecutive murders; they go to plunder and kidnap, and every trading trip is nothing but a foray. . . . They are nearly all miserable Swaheli at Ujiji, and have neither the manners nor the sense of Arabs.

Mohamad bin Saleh did him a further service. Some houses becoming untenanted by the exodus of the caravan, Livingstone wished to obtain the rent of one of them as he had been living in a lean-to; "two headmen tried to secure the rent for themselves, and were defeated by Mohamad bin Saleh."

Although his packet of forty-two letters was destroyed, two other letters which he wrote at this time somehow slipped through. One was to the Sultan of Zanzibar. In it he expresses cordial thanks for the benefit of the Sultan's letter of recommendation, and the great kindness of the Arabs, especially Mohamad Bogharib who had certainly saved his life. He then complains of the theft of his goods and "begs the assistance of your authority to prevent a fresh stock of goods, for which I now send to Zanzibar, being plundered in the same way." He requests the escort of one or two guards of good character to ensure their safe transit; and adds that he wishes to hire twelve or fifteen good freemen to act as canoe-men or porters. He gives precise details of his intended route: first "down" Tanganyika to the Luanda country; then back to Ujiji; then to visit Manyuema and Rua; "and then return to Zanzibar, when I hope to see your Highness in the enjoyment of health and happiness."

The other letter is to Kirk, dated 30 May. In it he refers to the probability of his packet of letters never reaching the coast. He then enumerates his needs and continues:

> I have written to Seyd Majid begging two of his guard to see to the safety of the goods here into Thani bin Suellim's hands or into those of Mohamad bin Saleh. As to the work to be done by me, it is only to connect the sources which I have discovered from 500 to 700 miles south of Speke and Baker's with the Nile. The volume of water which flows

north from latitude 12° south is so large, I suspect I have been working on the sources of the Congo as well as of the Nile. I have to go down the eastern line of drainage to Baker's turning-point: Tanganyika, Uziga, Chowambe (Baker's) are one water, and the head of it is 300 miles south of this. The western and central lines of drainage converge into an unvisited lake, west or south-west of this. The outflow of this, whether to Congo or Nile, I have to ascertain. The people west of this, called Manyema, are cannibals if Arabs speak truly, I may have to go there first, and down Tanganyika, if I come out uneaten, and find my new squad from Zanzibar. I earnestly hope that you will do what you can to help me with the goods and men.[1]

Two days later he wrote in his Journal: "I am thankful to feel getting stronger again, and wish to go down Tanganyika, but cannot get men: two months must elapse ere we can face the long grass and superabundant water in the way to Manyuema." Close observation of the drift of the green scum (*confervae*) on the surface of the water during this, the dry season, proved the presence of a northward current; and this convinced Livingstone that the outflow from the Lake must lie in its northern extremity. The Ujiji Arabs seemed to confirm this by asserting that "Tanganyika, Usige water, and Loanda are one and the same piece of river"; but therein they were only masking their ignorance, since Usige and Ruanda are districts, not rivers; and the only river at the north end of the Lake, the Lusize, flows into it and not out of it. Livingstone had in fact unwittingly passed the river which is the true outlet from the Lake, when ill in the canoe passing up along its west shore—namely the Lukuga which, flowing westward to join the Lualaba, becomes one of the sources of Congo. But the canoe passed by it and, as Debenham says, "had he chanced to camp within the bay leading to it he would almost certainly have heard of it and investigated." As things were however, both by observation of the northward set of the current from where he was and by the erroneous information of the Arabs who had never even been to the north end of the Lake, he convinced himself that the Lake must be itself a kind of vast "river" flowing north into the known Nile; and also that the Lualaba might be another, western, arm of the same great river—unless indeed of the Congo: a possibility which he never ignored, and which is indeed the fact.

Meanwhile he was assiduous in making enquiries as to ways

and means. On 7 June, "Mohamad Bogharib goes in a month to Manyuema, but if matters turn out as I wish, I may explore this Tanganyika line first." But on the 22nd, "After listening to a great deal of talk . . . I have come to the conclusion that it will be better for me to go to Manyuema about a fortnight hence, and if possible trace down the western arm of the Nile to the north—if this arm is indeed that of the Nile, and not of the Congo. Nobody here knows anything about it, or indeed about the eastern or Tanganyika line either. . . . A great chief is reported as living on a large river flowing northwards; I hope to make my way to him, and feel exhilarated at the thought of getting among people not spoiled by Arab traders." He judged that by the time he returned his "new squad" and fresh supplies would have arrived at Ujiji, and then his future course would be clear. "And may the Highest direct me, so that I may finish creditably the work I have undertaken. I propose to start for Manyuema on the 3rd July."

At last "after a great deal of delay and trouble about a canoe" they pulled out of Ujiji on 12 July soon after midnight, under a full moon, and reached the Kabogo well after nightfall the next day. Here Livingstone sounded in dark water offshore, but his line broke at 326 fathoms. After pulling all night on the 15th they landed at the islets off the west shore, where they were joined by Mohamad Bogharib, and prepared food for the journey. "The cookery is of the very best, and I always get a share; I tell them that I like the cookery, but not the prayers, and it is taken in good part." Not till 3 August was the mainland journey begun, from a point only fifteen or twenty miles north of the real (but unknown) outlet from the Lake, the Lukuga river—another of those unlucky accidents which, as Debenham remarks when noticing it, dogged Livingstone's footsteps to the end of his last journey.

He had reckoned on no more than four or five months for this journey; but it was more than two years before he returned to Ujiji. As always he underrated difficulties and overrated his physical powers. He would not recognize that his constitution was too deeply undermined for permanent recovery; "and when disease recurred, as it was bound to do, it left him each time less capable . . . of breaking through by force of will the series of obstacles that thwarted and delayed him." His Journal

entries are briefer than usual and, though his eyes were as alert
as ever for any object or circumstance worthy of note, they tell
their own tale. At the end of the first day's march over undulating country he is obliged to record that only 3½ hours
proved "very fatiguing in my weakness".

> 10 *August*.—Any ascent, though gentle, makes me blow since the
> attack of pneumonia; if it is inclined to an angle of 45°, 100 or 150 yards
> make me stop to pant in distress.
> 25 *August*.—We rest because all are tired; travelling at this season is
> excessively fatiguing. It is very hot at even 10 a.m. and 2½ or 3 hours
> tires the strongest—carriers especially so.
> 2 *September*.—We remained at Katamaba to hunt buffaloes and rest
> as I am still weak.

Yet on arrival at Bambarre, on the 21st, he can note characteristically: "My strength increased as I persevered." He
had been impressed on the way by the magnificence of the
mountain scenery in this unknown land, "surpassingly beautiful"; the mountain heights crowned with waving palms, the
slopes with forest trees of enormous size hung with huge thick
climbers, the abundance of large wild fruits and of strange
birds, the fertility of the soil, the many well-ordered villages
with square leaf-thatched huts and walls of hardened clay.
He suffered more than ever the discomfort of being made a
gazing-stock (this was an embarrassment to which he never
became inured in all his travels); but succeeded in avoiding
dwellings infested by bugs and human ticks, introduced by the
Swaheli Arabs but formerly unknown to the natives. Having a
touch of fever, he at once set himself to the task of writing letters
which, by their length and colloquialism, make up for the
brevity of his Journal. Of these, one of the longest and most
interesting is to his son Tom, whose state of health was giving
him cause for anxiety. It is quoted verbatim by Blaikie in four
pages of closely printed type.

> I sometimes feel greatly distressed about you, and if I could be of any
> use I would leave my work unfinished to aid you. But you will have
> every medical assistance that can be rendered, and I cease not to beg
> the Lord to be gracious to your infirmity. . . .

He reverts to the compulsory abolition of slavery in America:

> War brought freedom to 4,000,000 of the most hopeless and helpless
> slaves. The world never saw such fiendishness as that with which the

Southern slaveocracy clung to slavery. . . . Their cotton was King. . . . War has elevated and purified the Yankees, and now they have the gigantic task laid at their doors to elevate and purify 4,000,000 of slaves. I earnestly hope that the Northerners may not be found wanting in their portion of the superhuman work. The day for Africa is yet to come. . . .

With regard to his own exploration of the Nile sources:

I had to feel every step of the way, and generally was groping in the dark. . . . I gradually gained more light on the country, and slowly and surely saw the problems of the fountains of the Nile developing before my eyes. The vast volume of water draining away to the north made me conjecture that I had been working at the sources of the Congo too. . . .

I am thankful that a kind Providence has enabled me to do what will reflect honour on my children. . . . None of you must become mean, craven-hearted, untruthful or dishonest, for if you do you don't inherit it from me. . . . I shall not live long, and it would not be well to rely on my influence. . . . I could help you a little while living, but have little else than what people call a great name to bequeath afterwards. I am nearly toothless, and in my second childhood. . . .[2]

He describes how he had extracted his front teeth, loosened by biting "hard tack" (maize corn-cobs), by jerking them out with string: "I shall need a whole set of artificials."

He continues his series of long letters to his friend Oswell on the probable sources of the Nile:

I have not the faintest prospect of being able to send a letter for many months to come, but I want to be partially prepared for the time when the bustle of putting up a parcel may arrive. I don't feel it right on these occasions to give my friends a hurried scrawl. . . . I shall try and give you now what may be of permanent interest if, as usual, it be viewed through the indulgent medium of your friendship.

The great size of the Lualaba had made him "fear that it was the Congo". But now he is led "as yet only to conjecture" that it is really a "lacustrine lake" and the arm of one of the Nile sources, of which Tanganyika is another. These may be in fact "the two arms into which Ptolemy makes the head waters collect . . . and all we moderns can fairly claim is the *re-discovery* of what had sunk into oblivion". He goes on to try and show, from our knowledge of Egyptian and Ethiopian records, that Ptolemy was a reliable geographer. "I am dreaming of finding the lost city of Meroe at the confluence of the two head

branches." But Ptolemy knew only of two lines of drainage—
northwards. There is another which is the source of the Kafue,
and so of the Zambesi, which he proposes to name after Oswell
in anticipation. It was known to Herodotus by report when in
Sais. The letter ends: "I long sorely to retire."[3]

He wrote also to Sir Thomas Maclear: "I have to go down
and see where the two arms unite—the lost city Meroe ought
to be there—then get back to Ujiji to get a supply of goods . . .
and finish up by going round outside the south of all the
sources . . . I have still a seriously long task before me." Upon
this Blaikie comments that, though weaker in health than he
had ever been, and much poorer in means than he expected to
be, he was actually enlarging his plan of exploration.

On 1 November, "Being now well rested, I resolved to go
west to Lualaba and buy a canoe for its exploration." The fact
that it was now the commencement of the rainy season did not
deter him. He went by the southern route and crossed the
Luela five times "in a dense dripping forest". The villagers
refused to accompany him from one hamlet to the next "for
fear of being killed and eaten". In the large villages he was
"variously treated"; but in one of them the door of his hut
was pushed off while he was resting, as if he had been "a wild
beast in a cage". The reason for this hostility was yet another
of those "unlucky accidents" that befell Livingstone on his
last journeys, and it is thus succinctly explained by Coupland:

> . . . His exploration of Manyuema coincided with its first commercial
> penetration by the Arabs. . . . Bamberre had hitherto been their "far-
> thest west"; but while Livingstone was on his way thither he met, as it
> chanced, the first exploiter of the virgin field beyond, one Hassani Du-
> gumbe, who was returning towards Ujiji with no less than 18,000 pounds
> of ivory, obtained at much less than the normal price. And, unhappily,
> he and his slaves had pursued their lucrative trade with needless violence.
> The natives had been insulted, plundered, and in some villages done to
> death. Naturally, therefore, when Livingstone appeared not many weeks
> later he was met with fierce suspicion.[4]

He succeeded in reaching the Luamo and crossing it within
only some ten miles from its confluence with the Lualaba; but
found it useless to try and buy a canoe, "for all were our
enemies".

> The worst they did, after trying to get up a war in vain, was to collect
> as we went by in force fully armed with their large spears and huge

wooden shields, and show us out of their districts. All are kind except those who have been abused by the Arab slavers. . . . I was very glad that no collision had taken place. We returned to Bambarre 19 December 1869.

Thus ended his first attempt to reach the Lualaba—in failure. He says not a word about his return journey, but his map shows that he took a northerly route. Next day he wrote:

While we were away a large horde of Ujijians came to Bambarre, all eager to reach the cheap ivory, of which a rumour had spread far and wide; they numbered 500 guns, and invited Mohamad [Bogharib] to go with them, but he preferred waiting for my return from the west. We now resolved to go due north; he to buy ivory, and I to reach another part of the Lualaba and buy a canoe.

25 *December*.—We start immediately after Christmas. I must try with all my might to finish my exploration before next Christmas.

The next day he was off again, despite severe fever, "as I have always found that moving is the best remedy", through slippery forest ways and drenching rain; and on New Year's Day 1870 is the prayer: "May the Almighty help me to finish the work in hand, and retire through the Basango before the year is out. Thanks for all last year's lovingkindness."

This time it was not men who were the enemies, but nature and his own debility. He mapped the route with his customary care, but only rarely does he name the villages in his Journal. Three days' events are more than once collated into a single entry. The entries begin to read distressingly more like a bulletin of ill-health than a travel-diary. For the first time he took the precaution of boiling his water for drinking—a simple prophylactic which, had he but known it earlier, might have prevented dysentery. This time Mohamad Bogharib was with him, a good companion, but of little help.

5, 6 *and* 7 *January*.—Wettings by rain and grass overhanging our paths, with bad water, brought on choleraic symptoms; and opium from Mohamad had no effect in stopping it: he, too, had rheumatism. On suspecting the water as the cause, I had all I used boiled, and this was effectual, but I was greatly reduced in flesh, and so were many of our party.

12*th*.—It is too trying to travel during the rains.

15*th*.—Choleraic purging again came on till all the water used was boiled, but I was laid up by sheer weakness near the hill Chanza.

27, 28, *and* 30 *January*.—Rest from sickness in camp. The country is indescribable from rank jungle of grass . . . reeds clog the feet, and the leaves rub sorely on the face and eyes. . . .

I had ere this come to the conclusion that I ought not to risk myself further in the rains in my present weakness, for it may result in something worse.

By this time, having struggled due north and then due west and then north-west, he had reached the source of the Manyango—"fine sweet water"—and thrust aside that thought. On 2 February he was climbing over "the bold hills Bininango" with the resolution "I propose to cross it" (i.e. the Lualaba) "and buy an exploring canoe, because I am recovering my strength"; but decides to turn south-west towards the Arab chief Katomba (Mamohela) "to take counsel" first, since he knows more than anyone else about the country. Next day:

Caught in a drenching rain which made me fain to sit, exhausted as I was, under an umbrella for an hour trying to keep the trunk dry. As I sat in the rain a little tree-frog, about half an inch long, leaped on to a grassy leaf, and began a tune as loud as that of many birds, and very sweet; it was surprising to hear so much music out of so small a musician. I drank some rain-water as I felt faint. . . .

As Coupland pertinently asks, could any man but Livingstone, so ill and in such discomfort, have written such a passage at such a time?

Then he went on, waist-deep in liquid mud and holed deeper by the tread of elephants; next, tripping and stumbling over intertwined reeds; till he reached a hut to (partially) dry his clothes and rub his legs with oil, and—"in the morning had a delicious breakfast of sour goat's milk and porridge". Two days later the drenching was repeated, from the clouds above and streams below: "I lay on an enormous boulder under a Muabe palm and slept during the worst of the pelting." On 7 February he reached Katomba's camp at Mamohela "quite knocked up and exhausted".

Yet on the same day he could write: "Rest, shelter, boiled water, and above all the new species of potato called *nyumbo* . . . soon put me all to rights." He was even proposing to start again, this time north-west; but on the 13th had to confess "I was too ill to go through mud waist deep". Instead he took to his old recreation in sickness—letter-writing. One, to his brother John in Canada, is no longer extant but is summarized by Blaikie.

He contrasts the lucid reasonable problem set him by Sir Roderick, which quite fascinated him, with the absurd instructions of officious members of the R.G.S. He had traversed the watershed in every direction, but at a cost wearing both to mind and body. He is sad about the fate of the U.M.C.A., but cannot forbear a jibe at the new bishop, "strutting about with his crozier at Zanzibar, and on a fine clear day getting a distant view through a telescope of the continent of which he claimed to be bishop". He denounces the vile policy of the Portuguese, and laments the indecision of some influential persons in England who virtually uphold it. The Government's "generous offer to him of a small salary when he should settle somewhere" consorts queerly with handsome salaries given to men who risk nothing in its service; but rather than sacrifice the welfare of Africa, he "would spend every penny of his private means". He seems surrounded by a whole sea of difficulties, but to persevere in the line of duty is his only conceivable course. He holds as firmly as ever to his old anchor: "All will come right at last."[5]

His time-table was lengthening out far beyond anticipation, but he must wait for the rain to cease. May 1st: "Rains continued; and mud and mire in the clayey soil of Manyuema too awful to be attempted." Other factors contributed to threaten his further progress. On the 24th: "A party of Thani's people came south and said that they had killed forty Manyuema, and lost four of their own number: nine villages were burned—and all this about a single string of beads which a man tried to steal!" Again early in June, a second party was hired by a local chief for ten goats and a tusk to avenge his brother's death, with the result that 40 Manyuema were killed, 31 captured, and 60 goats seized. When at last the rains ceased, after a fall of 58 inches, and he prepared to march once more, his carriers deserted. 26 June: "Now my people failed me; so with only three attendants, Susi, Chuma, and Gardner, I started off to the north-west for the Lualaba."

The paths were clogged with thick adhesive mud, and he crossed fourteen rivulets in one day—some thigh deep. But the people were friendly and, passing through the nine burnt villages, he pressed on to a village near Nasangwa's where some trading Arabs were camped, and reached it on 30 June. While he was himself "sleeping peacefully" there, an Arab was murdered in his sleep at Nasangwa's. Livingstone arrived there in time to forestall a massacre, though "death to all Manyuemas glared from the eyes of half-castes and slaves." Then by good hap Mohamad Bogharib appeared on the scene and "he joined in enforcing peace". The traders departed but not without telling Susi and the rest "what I knew long before, that they hated having a spy in me on their deeds". Mohamad's arrival was fortunate in another way, for his men could inform Livingstone that the Lualaba lay, not north-west, but west-south-west from Mamohela, and that the route he was pursuing was almost impassable. And now another malady rendered retreat inevitable.

> For the first time in my life my feet failed me, and now having but three attendants it would have been unwise to go further in that direction. Instead of healing quietly as heretofore, when torn by hard travel, irritable-eating ulcers fastened on both feet; and I limped back to Bambarre.

At Mamohela he was "welcomed by the Arabs, who all approved of my turning back". Katomba, who had always been "very kind", gave him abundant provisions for the rest of his journey. These hard unscrupulous traders had nothing to gain and much to lose by thus befriending him, and one can only suppose that they were impelled to do so by nothing but involuntary admiration for his almost superhuman fortitude. He limped back to Bambarre on 22 July—and there remained perforce for eight months.

> If the foot were put to the ground a discharge of bloody ichor flowed, and the same discharge happened every night with considerable pain that prevented sleep; the wailing of the slaves tortured with these sores is one of the night sounds of a slave-camp; they eat through everything— muscle, tendon, and bone, and often lame permanently if they do not kill the poor things. . . . The vicinity was hot, and the pain increased with the size of the wound.
>
> 18 *August.*—Patience is all I can exercise: these irritable ulcers hedge me in now . . . but all will be for the best, for it is in Providence and not in me.
>
> 24 *August.*—The severe pneumonia in Marunga, the choleraic complaint in Manyuema, and now irritable ulcers warn me to retire while life lasts.

(The present writer, who contracted merely superficial tropical ulcers on the feet in Africa some thirty-five years ago, bears the scars of them to this day.)

"I read the whole Bible through four times whilst I was in Manyuema." So he wrote much later in a single Journal entry on 3 October 1871; and, as Macnair has pointed out, the much-soiled pages of the little pocket Old Testament up to the Book of Proverbs and including the metrical version of the Psalms, which he carried for "emergency reading", and a pocket Bible for "more deliberate occasions", unconsciously reveal the tenor of his inner life. The Gospels and Epistles were so deeply engrained in his mind that for refreshment's sake he had only to consult his memory, and the same is true of the Psalms; but of the latter the pages most thumbed and marked are those containing the 40th to 43rd, and 95th to 113th; the 46th is almost too grimy to be read, so too the 90th; while the 23rd and 121st were obviously frequently read in the metrical version familiar to his childhood. Somewhat surprisingly the Book of Proverbs is also much thumbed; but the Book of Job, so pertinent to his own condition, does not seem to have interested him. Of the historical books it is obvious that the Pentateuch most fascinated him, and especially Exodus. [6]

More and more as he lay a prisoner in the rude shelter of his lonely hut and pondered the story of Moses, the idea—fantastic though it was—of this "man of transcendent genius" having reached the Nile sources and so "having visited these parts", grew in his imagination until it became what he called a "waking dream", or what others would call an obsession.

25 *August.*—One of my waking dreams is that the legendary tales [preserved by Josephus] about Moses coming up into Inner Ethiopia with Merr his foster-mother, and founding a city which he called in her honour 'Meroe', may have a substratum of fact. . . .

I dream of discovering some monumental relics of Meroe, and if anything confirmatory of sacred history does remain, I pray to be guided thereunto. If the sacred chronology would thereby be confirmed, I would not grudge the toil and hardships, hunger and pain, I have endured.

Livingstone knew, because Bishop Gray had told him in a private letter from Cape Town in 1864, of the intended deposition of Bishop Colenso of Natal for his critical study of the historical accuracy of the Pentateuch (which shattered the credulity of many biblical literalists); and he must have known too that the deposition had been annulled by the Privy Council in the following year. At the time he had expressed himself as not willing to "take sides" in the controversy; but whether this indicates a desire to suspend judgment it is impossible to say. If, however, his discovery of the Nile sources would corroborate the biblical record, this would be great gain, and Blaikie is right in saying: "His reverence for the Bible gave that river a sacred character, and to throw light on its origin seemed a kind of religious act."

> 25 *October.*—In this journey I have endeavoured to follow with unswerving fidelity to the line of duty. My course has been an even one, turning neither to the right hand nor to the left, though my route has been tortuous enough. All the hardships, danger, and toil were met with the full conviction that I was right in persevering to make a complete work of the exploration of the sources of the Nile. Mine has been a calm, hopeful endeavour to do the work that has been given me to do, whether I succeed or whether I fail. The prospect of death in pursuing what I knew to be right did not make me veer to one side or the other. I had a strong presentiment during the first three years that I should never live through the enterprise, but it weakened as I came near to the end of the journey, and an eager desire to discover any evidence of the great Moses having visited these parts bound me—spellbound me, I may say—for if I could bring to light anything to confirm the Sacred Oracles, I should not grudge one whit all the labour expended.
>
> 2 *November.*—I long with intense desire to move on and finish my work; I have also an excessive wish to find anything that may exist proving the visit of the great Moses and the ancient kingdom of Tirhaka; but I pray, give me just what pleases Thee, my Lord, and make me submissive to Thy will in all things.

He must go down the central Lualaba or Webb's Lake River to its junction with its western arm or "Young's Lake River" and thence up to the Katanga head waters, "and then retire". He adds, "I pray that it may be to my native home."

Memory, or more probably the transcript of a passage from another writer of antiquity which he had kept, now seemed to reinforce his speculation. Herodotus had recorded a story told to him by the Scribe of Minerva in the City of Sais concerning two hills with conical tops, Crophi and Mophi, between Syene and Elephantine [near the modern Luxor and Assouan], between which flowed the sources of the Nile. It is true that the "Father of History", usually somewhat credulous, was himself sceptical of this information: "To me this man seemed not to be speaking seriously"; but when on 18 August two Arab traders arrived at Bambarre with a tale of a lake twelve days distant from the Katanga copper-mine, and of four rivers rising from fountains not far from thence, and of a mound between them "the most remarkable in Africa"—Livingstone's mind leapt to a connection between these features and those described by the Scribe at Sais. Might not they too have "a substratum of truth"? He proceeds to elaborate an ingenious theory to give the supposition plausibility, if only to himself, and then characteristically to asperse the findings of his predecessors.

> I am a little thankful to old Nile for so hiding his head that all "theoretical discoverers" are left out in the cold. With all real explorers I have a hearty sympathy, and I have some regret at being obliged, in a manner compelled, to speak somewhat disparagingly of the opinions formed by my predecessors. The work of Speke and Grant is part of the history of this region, and since the discovery of the sources of the Nile was asserted so positively it seems necessary to explain, not offensively I hope, wherein their mistake lay, in making a somewhat similar claim. My opinions may yet be shown to be mistaken too, but at present I cannot conceive how.

They were of course delusions, and to a later generation made wise after the event with the knowledge that Speke and Grant were the true discoverers of the sources of the Nile, and Livingstone himself the unwitting discoverer of those of the Congo, they have seemed like the hallucinations of a mind bemused. But if we put ourselves in his position, with no other knowledge of Egyptology than that which was current in his day, and the apparent evidence of a great river and a great lake—both far south of the Victoria Nyanza—with a northward flow, we may feel that his hypothesis though not yet verified was not entirely without justification.

But though his archaeological speculations were at fault, he had at this time the good fortune to make an important contribution to zoology. This was his description of the appearance and habits of a rare ape allied to the chimpanzee, called by the natives *soko* but not even yet scientifically identified. Though not carnivorous it attacks men and animals (even leopards) by seizing a forearm and biting off the fingers, which it then spits out. It is hunted and eaten by the Manyuema with such eagerness, and so human is its behaviour, as to suggest this as "their first stage towards cannibalism". Livingstone's account of this strange beast is among his most vivid pieces of writing, although "the bandy-legged, pot-bellied, low-looking villain . . . takes away my appetite by his disgusting bestiality of appearance". To his son Tom he wrote: "The sight of a soko nauseates me. He is so hideously ugly. I can conceive no other use for him than sitting for a portrait of Satan."

On 26 September he is able to report "the ulcers healing", though it will take a long time for the tissues to be replaced. But he must still await the arrival of Syde bin Habib and Dugumbe, who may have letters from the coast and men for the journey. He now has reason to fear that his packet for Zanzibar "may have fared badly" and that his box and guns will never be sent. He wrote a despatch to the Earl of Derby which was received at the Foreign Office a few weeks before his death. In it he expresses his wish to name the lakes and rivers he had discovered after Lord Palmerston, President Lincoln, Bartle Frere, James Young, Oswell and Webb. He recalls his early friendship with the last three.

'Paraffin' Young, one of my teachers in chemistry, raised himself to be a merchant prince by his science and art, and has shed pure white light in many lowly cottages, and in some rich palaces. . . . I too have shed light of another kind, and am fain to believe that I have performed a small part of the grand revolution which our Maker has been for ages carrying on, by multitudes of conscious and many unconscious agents, all over the world. Young's friendship never faltered.

Oswell and Webb were fellow-travellers, and mighty hunters. Too much engrossed with mission-work myself to hunt, except for the children's larder, I relished the sight of fair stand-up fights by my friends with the large denizens of the forest, and admired the true Nimrod class for their great courage, truthfulness and honour. Being a warm lover of natural history, the entire butcher tribe bent only on making 'a bag', without regard to animal suffering, have not a single kindly word from me.

On 10 October he emerged from his hut, having been confined to it for eighty days, during the last twenty of which "I suffered from fever which reduced my strength, taking away my voice and purging me . . . It was choleraic"; and many Manyuema had died of it. But now, with only one ulcer open and the rains coming, "I am thankful to feel myself well." And yet—"I feel the want of medicine strongly, almost as much as the want of men." Again: "I am in agony for news from home;

all I feel sure of now is that my friends will all wish me to complete my task."

His Journal becomes a soliloquy interspersed with such news as reaches him from the outside world, and this is chiefly of rapine, violence, and murder. The Swaheli Arabs were playing havoc in the Manyuema villages: "they are the most cruel and bloodthirsty missionaries (*sic*, meaning "of superior education") in existence, and withal so impure in talk and acts, spreading disease everywhere." He writes of the many deaths which occur through sheer brokenheartedness among free men who have been captured and enslaved, and quotes with grim appropriateness Ecclesiastes iv, 1. And yet, for brutality and barbarism, there was little to choose between oppressors and oppressed:

> The evils inflicted by these Arabs are enormous, but probably no greater than the people inflict on each other. . . . Cold-blooded murders are frightfully common here. . . . The Manyuema are the most bloody, callous savages I know; one puts a scarlet feather from a parrot's tail on the ground, and challenges those near to stick it in the hair. He who does so must kill a man or woman!
>
> Their cannibalism is doubtful, but my observations raise grave suspicions.

A week after he wrote that sentence James, one of the three Nassick boys who had deserted and were now hoping that he would take them back, was killed by an arrow; and Susi and Chuma long afterwards gave Waller indisputable proof that his body had been eaten.

But soon there were reprisals, when the Manyuema found that their spears and arrows were a match for the Swaheli guns. "The next thing they will learn will be to grapple at close quarters in the forest . . . It will follow too, that no one will be able to pass through this country." A respectable Arab said to him: "If a man goes with a good-natured civil tongue, he may pass through the worst people in Africa unharmed." This had always been his own policy and he had proved it true, but he adds that time is also required to let them become well acquainted with one. As the weary weeks draw on towards December and then into January he desponds:

> I groan and am in bitterness at the delay, but thus it is: I pray for help to do what is right, but sorely am I perplexed and grieved and mourn. I cannot give up making a complete work of the exploration.

I am grievously tired of living here. Mohamad [Bogharib] is as kind as he can be, but to sit idle or give up before I finish my work are both intolerable; I cannot bear either, yet I am forced to remain by want of people. . . .

When Syde and Dugumbe come, I hope to get men and a canoe to finish my work among those who have not been abused by Ujijians and still retain their natural kindliness of disposition. None of the people are ferocious without cause. . . .

The education of the world is a terrible one, and it has come down with relentless vigour on Africa from the most remote times! What the African will become after this awfully hard lesson is learned, is among the future developments of Providence. . . .

Oh for Dugumbe or Syde to come! . . . but this delay may be all for the best. . . .

I am sorely let and hindered in this Manyuema. Rain every day and often at night; I could not travel now, even if I had men; but I could make some progress; this is the sorest delay I ever had. I look above for help and mercy.

On New Year's Day 1871 he exclaims: "O Father! help me to finish this work to Thy honour." And with it is the yearning for his children, home, and friends. (To Maclear)—"I have an intense and sore longing to finish and retire, and trust that the Almighty may permit me to go home." To his daughter Agnes:

I commit myself to the Almighty Disposer of events, and if I fall, will do so doing my duty, like one of His stout-hearted servants. I am delighted to hear you say that, much as you wish me home, you would rather hear of me finishing my work to my own satisfaction than merely to gratify you. That is a noble sentence. . . . I hope to present to my young countrymen an example of manly perseverance. I shall not hide from you that I am made by it very old and shaky . . . almost toothless—a few teeth that remain out of their line, so that a smile is that of a he-hippopotamus—a dreadful old fogie, and you must tell Sir Roderick that it is an utter impossibility for me to appear in public, and even then the less I am seen the better.

At long last, on 22 January, "A party is reported to be on the way hither. This is likely enough, but reports are often so false that doubts arise." This one however proved true. On the 27th: "Caravan reported to be near, and my men and goods at Ujiji." The next day it arrived, led by Hassani and Ebed, with news of great mortality from cholera spreading inland from Zanzibar where no less than 70,000 had succumbed "and my 'brother', whom I conjecture to be Dr. Kirk, has fallen." The men sent by Kirk would remain at Ujiji till informed "of my whereabouts"; then they would come on to Bambarre "and bring my much longed-for letters and goods". On 4 February: "Ten of my men from the coast have come near to Bambarre, and will arrive today. I am extremely thankful to hear it, for it assures me that my packet of letters was not destroyed; they know at home by this time what has detained me, and the end to which I strain." The same day the men arrived—with no goods, and only one letter: it was from Kirk, proving him to be alive. As for the goods: "Their two headmen, Shereef and Awathe, refused to come past Ujiji and are revelling on my goods there."

Chapter Thirty

LAST JOURNEYS: FARTHEST WEST
1871

" The sights I have seen on this journey make my blood turn cold, and I am not sentimental."

"I FEEL the want of medicines strongly, almost as much as the want of men." So he had written a few days before, and now, though once again deprived of medicines or creature-comforts of any kind, at least the men had come and he could march. And though the men were "Banians"—the term is properly applied to Indian merchants on the coast, but Livingstone extends it to include their negro slaves who were like them Mohammedans and the most worthless types of such —they were surely better than none at all and could carry loads. So at first he was full of gratitude and wrote to Waller: "Ten men have come from Kirk who, like the good fellow that he is, worked unweariedly to get them and the goods off in the midst of disease and death".[1] And in his Journal: "Great havoc was made by cholera, and in the midst of it my friend exerted himself greatly to get men off to me with goods." But now these men (only seven of whom were from Zanzibar, three having been picked up *en route*) averred that they had Kirk's instructions to bring him back to Zanzibar and not to follow him further west; so positively indeed that he scrutinized Kirk's letter again for confirmation, and finding none gave them orders to proceed. They then struck for higher wages in advance, which perforce he granted—"double free-man's pay at Zanzibar. But for Mohamad Bogharib and fear of pistol-shot they would gain their own and their Banian masters' end to baffle me completely." There were further delays: one was too ill to start at once; the assassin who had misled James to his death was found, and crowds collected to eat him, but were disappointed; the remaining two of the Nassick boys who had defaulted hovered about the camp "and impudently followed me. I told them to be off."

Mohamad would not allow the deserters to remain among his people, nor would I. It would only be to imbue the minds of my men with their want of respect for all English, and total disregard of honesty and honour; they came after me with inimitable effrontery, believing that though I said I would not take them, they were so valuable, I was only saying what I knew to be false.

With this rabble from Zanzibar and his three "faithfuls", Susu, Chuma, and Gardner, the start was made on 16 February, along the old route to a ford over the Lulwa: "the grass and mud are grievous, but my men lift me over the waters". On the 24th he reached Mamohela again, "where we were welcomed by all the Arabs, and I got a letter from Dr. Kirk, and another from the Sultan, and from Mohamad bin Nassib who was going to Karangwe: all anxious to be kind. Katomba gave flour, nuts, fowls, and goat." He also gave him a baby *soko* as a pet, and Livingstone, always at his best and happiest in describing the behaviour of animals, expands on this in a letter to Agnes and in his Journal:

She is the least mischevious of all the monkey tribe I have seen, and seems to know that in me she has a friend, and sits quietly on the mat beside me. In walking, the first thing observed is that she does not tread on the palms of her hands, but on the backs of the second line of bones of the hands; in doing this the nails do not touch the ground, nor do the knuckles; she uses the arms thus supported crutch-fashion, and hitches herself along between them; occasionally one hand is put down before the other, and alternates with the feet, or she walks upright and holds up a hand to anyone to carry her. If refused, she turns her face down, and makes grimaces of the most bitter human weeping, wringing her hands, and sometimes adding a fourth hand or foot to make the appeal more touching. Grass or leaves she draws around her to make a nest, and resents anyone meddling with her property. She is a most friendly little beast, and came up to me at once, making her chirrup of welcome, smelled my clothing, and held out her hand to be shaken. I slapped her palm without offence, though she winced. She began to untie the cord with which she was afterwards bound, with fingers and thumbs in quite a systematic way, and on being interfered with by a man looked daggers, and screaming tried to beat him with her hands: she was afraid of his stick, and faced him putting her back to me as a friend. She holds out her hand for people to lift her up and carry her, quite like a spoiled child; then bursts into a passionate cry, somewhat like that of a kite, wrings her hands quite naturally, as if in despair. She eats everything, covers herself with a mat to sleep, and makes a nest of grass or leaves, and wipes her face with a leaf.

I presented my double-barrelled gun which is at Ujiji to Katomba, as he has been very kind when away from Ujiji; I pay him thus for all his services. He gave me the soko and will carry it to Ujiji for me; I have tried to refund all that the Arabs expended on me.

His scrupulosity in this respect earned him a good name not only among the Arabs but the natives: "I overhear the Manyuema telling each other that I am the 'good one'." To Agnes he gave a descriptive account of these people, and with it a glimpse of the trials to which his popularity with them subjected him.

I have to submit to be a gazing-stock . . . but try to get over it good-naturedly, get into the most shady spot of the village and leisurely look at all my admirers. When the first crowd begins to go away, I go into my lodgings to take what food might be prepared. . . . The door is shut, all save a space to admit light. . . . Eager heads sometimes crowd the open space, and crash goes the thin door, landing a Manyuema beauty on the floor. . . . To avoid darkness or being half-smothered, I often eat in public, draw a line on the ground, then "toe the line", and keep them out of the circle. To see me eating with knife, fork and spoon is wonderful. . . .

But the continuance of the inhuman traffic amongst them makes him "sick at heart".

Many of the Manyuema women are very pretty. . . .The men are handsome. Compared with them the Zanzibar slaves are like London door-knockers. . . . The way in which they murder the men and seize the women and children makes me sick at heart. It is not slave-trade. It is murdering free people to make slaves. It is perfectly indescribable. Kirk has been working hard to get this murdersome system put a stop to. Heaven prosper his noble efforts! . . .
I am grieved to hear of the departure of good Lady Murchison. Had I known that she kindly remembered me in her prayers, it would have been great encouragement.

By this time he had taken the measure of his "Banian" escort:

The men sent by Dr. Kirk are Mohammedans, that is, unmitigated liars. . . . The two headmen remained at Ujiji, to feast on my goods and get pay without work. Seven came to Bambarre, and in true Moslem style swore that they were sent by Dr. Kirk to bring me back, not to go with me if the country were bad or dangerous. Forward they would not go. I read Dr. Kirk's words to them to follow wheresoever I led. . . . After a superabundance of falsehood, it turned out that it all meant an advance of pay, though they had double the Zanzibar wages. I gave it, but had to threaten on the word of an Englishman to shoot the ring-leaders before I got them to go. . . .

Then follows an extremely interesting generalization, retrospective of his experience among Bantu races—the more so when one remembers that his first impression of the semi-civilized Bechuanas had been unfavourable, and that in his journeys into the interior he had sought in vain for the noble savage.

> I have travelled more than most people, and with all sorts of followers. The Christians of Kuruman and Kolobeng were out of sight the best I ever had. The Makololo, who were very partially Christianized, were next best—honest, truthful, and brave. Heathen Africans are much superior to the Mohammedans, who are the most worthless one can have.[2]

(By Mohammedans he intends the riff-raff of the coast and Zanzibar of that persuasion; not the superior type of Arab such as he met in Mohamad Bogharib and his friends.)

On 2 March he pursued his journey by a new route south-westwards through dense forest and on the 4th reached Mona-ngongo, thrilled by the beauty of the scenes through which he passed.

> The villages are very pretty, standing on slopes. The main street generally lies east and west, to allow the bright sun to stream his clear hot rays from one end to the other, and lick up quickly the moisture from the frequent showers which is not drained off by the slopes. A little verandah is often made in front of the door, and here at dawn the family gathers round a fire and, while enjoying the heat needed in the cold that always accompanies the first darting of the light or sun's rays across the atmosphere, inhale the delicious air and talk over their little domestic affairs. The various shaped leaves of the forest all round their village are bespangled with myriads of dewdrops. . . .

His eyes linger lovingly on the cocks that strut and ogle; the kids that gambol and leap on the backs of their dams quietly chewing the cud; the thrifty wives baking their new clay pots over a fire of grass-roots, and extracting salt from the ashes of last night's burning.

> Infancy gilds the fairy picture with its own lines and it is probably never forgotten, for the young taken up from slavers and treated with all philanthropic missionary care and kindness, still revert to the period of infancy as the finest and fairest they have known. They would go back to freedom and enjoyment as fast as would our own sons of toil, and be heedless to the charms of hard work and no play, which we think so much better for them, if not for us.

But such idyllic scenes were the exception, not the rule. As he went on he became more and more oppressed by the feeling that he was following or crossing trails of blood. "Some men followed us as if to fight, but we got them to turn peaceably; we don't know who are enemies, so many have been maltreated and had relatives killed." "In some cases we found the villages deserted; the people had fled at our approach in dread of repetitions of the outrages of the Arab slavers. The doors were all shut." Yet there was this consolation: "Many have found out that I am not one of their number . . . they stand up and call loudly, 'Bolongo! Bolongo!' (Friendship!) They sell their fine iron bracelets eagerly for a few beads."

The next day he heard that Mohamad Bogharib's party had passed him on the west; this was a sore disappointment, briefly noticed: "I thus lose twenty copper rings I was to take from them, and all the notes they were to make for me of the rivers they crossed."

On 9 March, having crossed two streams called Sokoye he came near Kabongo, Kasonga's village, and learned that he was within six miles of the Lualaba (though for some days he had been following its course at that distance). But Kasonga had no canoes, and it would take five or six more days' trudging to procure one. Next day:

> I had a long fierce oration from Amur, in which I was told again and again that I should be killed and eaten—the people wanted "a white one" to eat! I needed 200 guns, and "must not go and die". . . . I left this noisy demagogue, after saying I thanked him for his warnings, but saw he knew not what he was saying. The traders from Ujiji are simply marauders, and their people worse than themselves; they thirst for blood more than for ivory. . . . The prospect of getting slaves overpowers all else, and blood flows in horrid streams. The Lord look on it!

News of rapine and slaughter continued daily, and on 20 March is the single entry: "I am heartsore, and sick of human blood." Cold rains and sickness now delayed his march, and when on the 28th almost within sight of his goal the Banian slaves again attempted mutiny, there was wrung from him a veritable heart-cry: "It is excessively trying, and so many difficulties have been put in my way I doubt whether the Divine favour and will is on my side."

This is the first, as it is indeed the last, expressed utterance of such a doubt arising in the mind of David Livingstone, but it must have been the ejaculation of a feeling pent-up within him for many a weary month. Six months before, he had written whilst in passive durance vile at Bambarre (as if in vindication before God of the rectitude of his course and in childlike trust) the passage beginning: "In this journey I have endeavoured to follow with unswerving fidelity the line of duty . . ." Now when once again in the flush of activity and on the very eve of what he hoped would prove to be his greatest discovery, this doubt as to whether it really was the Will of God arises and the fact gives to its utterance an intenser poignancy. It is all the more moving for its restraint. "So many difficulties" is an understatement of all the toils, hardships, and frustrations he had suffered hitherto; and they were but the prelude of others which he must have known that he might yet have to undergo.

Perhaps it is a doubt that must beset every spiritual adventurer nearing the end of his quest, whatever the quest may be. For all geographical or scientific discovery is but the symbol of an inner quest. Livingstone's doubt in fact poses a religious problem: it is the fundamental problem which ultimately confronts every dedicated life. Starkly stated it amounts to this. Is the Power that animates and informs the universe friendly? Or is it indifferent, or callous, or inimical to our noblest endeavours? Is the Divine Personality really there?— are all things working together for good according to the counsel of His Will? Or are these guidings which I take to be the intimations of his Providence merely delusive, and are all my prayers and aspirations nothing more than the echoes of my own thoughts and desires coming back to me? Are we the instruments of His hand and the objects of His care, or are we the puppets of blind circumstance and the playthings of an inscrutable remorseless fate? In so far as these sceptical questions bear upon the life of Livingstone, we must look to the end. He had not yet reached bed-rock.

The next day, 29 March, he reached the Lualaba at Nya-ngwe's village—farther west than any European had ever penetrated—and records the fact without a trace of elation. One crumb of consolation however awaited him there: "Abed said that my words against bloodshedding had stuck into him, and he had given orders to his people to give presents to the chiefs, and never fight unless actually attacked."

At Mamohela he had been informed that the Lualaba "made a great bend west-south-west". If this proved true it would nullify all his hopes that it was the Nile, but he would go on nevertheless and verify it for himself. "I had to suspend my judgment, so as to be prepared to find it after all perhaps the Congo." At Kasonga's he was partly reassured: "It makes a second great sweep to the west and there are at least 30° of southing; but now it comes rolling majestically to the north, and again even makes easting." Now at Nyangwe all doubts about its true direction were dispersed.

> I went down to take a good look at the Lualaba here. It is narrower than it is higher up, but still a mighty river, at least 3,000 yards broad and always deep. . . . The current is about two miles an hour away to the north.

Debenham observes that he must have restarted his chronometers, which had run down during his illness with pneumonia, when he arrived at Ujiji in March 1869, since the longitude of that place was well known. Now at Nyangwe they had again gone "dead" and he contrived an ingenious method for restarting one of them and for estimating his longitude. "I took distances and altitudes alternately with a bullet for a weight on the key of the chronometer, taking successive altitudes of the sun and distances of the moon. Possibly the first and last altitudes may give the rate of going, and the frequent distances between may give approximate longitude." In the result it was found to be only a few miles in error.[3]

He was getting to the end of his writing-paper and economized by writing some of his letters on the backs of old cheques, and some pages of his Journal across the sheets of old newspapers. His ink had also run out and he used a substitute from the seeds of a plant called by the Arabs *zugifare*; it is of reddish hue and was mistaken by some correspondents for his blood. He says that he sent his men "over to the other side" to cut wood and build a house of grass walls for free ventilation. The sense of this seems obscure, for he never crossed the river, and his grass-walled house was erected in the village.

His main preoccupation now was to procure canoes, or at

least a canoe, but though protestations of help were frequent, none was forthcoming. "They all think that my buying a canoe means carrying war to the left bank", and the worthless "Banian slaves" encouraged this infamous rumour. It was in this predicament that he wrote the first of three letters to Kirk, begun on the way to Nyangwe since it is dated 25 March, but continued in that village since it is addressed from the Lualaba. It is written minutely on a proof-sheet of the Proceedings of the R.G.S. recording a meeting in November 1869, at which his own letter from "near Lake Bangweolo" had been read. The informal friendliness of its tone, and the moderation of its criticism of these same "Banian slaves" who were wrecking all his purposes, are noteworthy.

I very thankfully received your letter of 28 Feb. '69 . . . containing a welcome one from Agnes to you. By it I first learned that you had taken unto yourself a wife who has presented you with a daughter. Blessings on them both. . . . I have but one regret in looking back on my stationary missionary life and that is that I did not play more with my children but I worked so hard physically and mentally that in the evening there was seldom any fun left in me. I thankfully accept your invitation to lodge with you at Zanzibar, but I feel so woefully far away and am going still farther away in order to make a complete work of the exploration of the sources of the Nile. I have been sorely let and hindered in Manyuema and, reaction against the bloody Ujijian slaving having set in, I went off not without apprehension, and until I get beyond the region of bloodshed I cannot feel safe. . . .

I find great difficulty in getting a canoe. . . . All flee from us. Your men seem as eager for bloodshed as others. All long to be able to brag of bloodshed. That Shereef Bosher has put me to great inconvenience by refusing to send me my own beads and other things while he stops to feast at my expense. . . .

I feel extremely thankful for all you did for me in the most trying circumstances a man could be placed in. I send a cheque for Rs. 4000 by Mohamad Bogharib. . . .

If you write to Seward remember me kindly to him and to his wife. Take good care of your better half and child. Move about as often as you can. Good people are scarce. I am thankful to hear you say that my words have had some little effect at home. I have often said with a sore heart, I have laboured in vain and spent my strength for naught and in vain. Yet surely my work is with the Lord and my judgment with my God. The cheery prospect of stopping the East Coast slave trade belongs to you, and therein I do greatly rejoice. . . .[4]

At the same time he was writing to his brother John:

As soon as I ascertain where the western arm joins the eastern I shall return and pray that the Almighty may lead me safely home. . . . Had I known all the toil, hunger and hardship and time involved in getting a clear idea of the drainage, I might have preferred a strait-waistcoat and head shaven and a blister on it, to undertaking this task.[5]

Meanwhile the weeks dragged on. He beguiled the time by watching the busy native life that thronged round him, so full of colour and animation; counting the people who passed his door (700 one market-day); watching the river flowing by, sounding its depth and marking its fall almost daily; listening eagerly to accounts of its flooding, of its colour further down, of its fish—and comparing them with those of the Nile. More than all he loved to frequent the market-place and listen to the chaffer and the haggling over wares: cassava, palm-oil, fish, salt, pepper, cocks, pigs, earthen pots.

With market-women it seems to be a pleasure of life to haggle and joke and laugh and cheat; many come eagerly and retire with careworn faces; many are beautiful, and many old; all carry very heavy loads. . . .

At least 3,000 people at market today, and my going among them has taken away the fear engendered by the slanders of slavers and traders, for all are pleased to tell me the names of fishes, and other things. . . . There is quite a roar of voices in the multitude. It was pleasant to be among them. . . .

The market is a busy scene—everyone is in dead earnest—little time is lost in friendly greetings. . . . Each is intensely eager to barter food for relishes . . . the sweat stands in beads on their faces . . . cocks crow briskly and pigs squeal. . . . The men flaunt about in gaily-coloured *lambas* of many folded kilts—the women work hardest—the potters slap and ring their earthenware all round to show that there is not a single flaw in them.

It is a scene of the finest acting imaginable. The eagerness with which all sorts of assertions are made . . . and then the intense surprise and withering scorn cast on those who despise their goods. Little girls run about selling cups of water to the half-exhausted wordy combatants. To me it was an amusing scene. I could not understand the words that flowed off their glib tongues, but the gestures were too expressive to need interpretation.

A stranger in the market had ten human under jaw-bones hung by a string over his shoulder; on enquiry he professed to have killed and eaten the owners, and showed with his knife how he cut up his victim. When I expressed disgust, he and others laughed. . . .

I see new faces every market day. Two nice girls were trying to sell their venture which was roasted white ants, called *gumbe*.

The tedium of delay was punctuated by gleams of hope, but

it was always hope deferred: canoes were promised, but none came. There were three principal Arab traders in Nyangwe: Abed, Hassani, and another not named. "There is no love lost among them," says Livingstone. Of the three, all were kind, Abed was the most friendly. "He sends cooked food every day." In return Livingstone taught him to make a mosquito-net from calico. On 12 April his new house was ready: "a great comfort, for the other was foul and full of vermin: bugs, that follow wherever Arabs go, made me miserable, but the Arabs are insensible to them; Abed alone had a mosquito-curtain and he never could praise it enough." The "Banian slaves" continued their calumnious tales against him in order to try and force him to return, and again attempted mutiny, and "Hassani harboured them till I told him that if an English officer harboured an Arab slave, he would be compelled by the Consul to refund the price, and I certainly would not let him escape; this frightened him." At last on 16 May, "Abed overheard them plotting my destruction . . . and advised me strongly not to trust myself to them any more, as they would be sure to cause my death. He was all along a sincere friend, and I could not but take his words as well meant and true."

It was at this point that he wrote his second letter to Kirk, with, be it noted, not a word of reproach, but enclosing a note of their dismissal. "I am glad to get rid of them by their own desire."⁰ Two days later, however, he wrote in his Journal:

> I was on the point of disarming my slaves and driving them away, when they relented and professed to be willing to go anywhere; so, being eager to finish my geographical work, I said I would run the risk of their desertion, and gave beads to buy provisions for a start north. I cannot state how much I was worried by those wretched slaves, who did much to annoy me, with the sympathy of all the slaving crew. When baffled by untoward circumstances the bowels plague me too, and discharges of blood relieve the headache and are as safety-valves to the system

It would appear that he still clung with a desperate hope to purchasing a canoe, and was willing to risk anything, possibly life itself, on the chance. Time and time again Abed had tried to negotiate this on his behalf, but in vain. By the tragic irony of fate this white man who had come among the natives of Central Africa with the avowed intent of delivering them from slavery was regarded by them as a potential foe. And even when his peaceful demeanour reassured them—as when he secured the release of a captive woman who fled to him from the Arab traders—they feared each other too much to give him aid. The Arabs themselves, by *force majeure*, had no difficulty whatever in obtaining canoes for their nefarious purposes. On 24 June "Hassani got nine canoes and put sixty-three persons in three; I cannot get one."

This incident had a curious sequel. After four days' journey downstream the leading canoe was wrecked in the narrows of the river and five lives were lost; the rest returned. The event seemed to him directly providential: "We don't always know the dangers that we are guided past." He mentions this briefly in his third letter to Kirk two days later, recalling his friend's similar catastrophe on the Zambesi, and announcing a change of plan. The same basaltic dyke which cuts the Lualaba further down is likely to run across the country and cut Lomame, and this would render the ascent of the Lomame impossible; therefore he must cross the Lualaba from where he now is and proceed overland to the Katanga region. "I go due west on foot on the 2nd day of the new moon, about 9th July." Though the "Banian slaves" had mutinied twice he does not so much as mention this, and is still full of gratitude for Kirk's exertions on his behalf: the large supply of goods has anyhow got through to Ujiji.

> On this page I intended to put an Arabic dismissal to the ringleaders. I use it now to say, please do not be offended with palavers. I am really reduced to beggary notwithstanding all the bountiful provision you with immense difficulty made for me, and that too almost entirely by the villainy of the unmitigated drunken scoundrel Shereef. His Banian owner is in part to blame; for he must have known his habits and his brandy when he imposed them on us. . . .[7]

And now indeed there seemed good hope of accomplishment. Dugumbe, the wealthiest and most influential of all the Arab traders, who had befriended him before, arrived from the coast with a large retinue and 500 guns, and at once presented Livingstone with a large store of beads.

> All know that my goods are unrighteously detained by Shereef and they show me kindness, which I return by some fine calico which I have.

Among the first words Dugumbe said to me were, "Why, your own slaves are your greatest enemies: I will buy you a canoe, but the Banian slaves' slanders have put all the Manyuema against you". I knew that this was true, and that they were conscious of the sympathy of the Ujijian traders, who hate to have me here.

A week later, at the first opportunity, he explained to Dugumbe his plans:

To go west with his men to Lomame, then by his aid buy a canoe and go up Lake Lincoln to Katanga and the fountains, examine the inhabited caves, and return here, if he would let his people bring my goods from Ujiji. He again referred to all the people being poisoned in mind against me, but was ready to do everything in his power for my success.

On 5 July he offered Dugumbe £400 for ten men to replace the "Banian slaves"—"to go up the Lomame" (a reversal of his altered plan) and thence back "up by Tanganyika to Ujiji"—adding that he would give all his goods in store at Ujiji besides: in other words, all that he possessed. But Dugumbe "took a few days to consult with his associates". Two days later: "Dugumbe advised my explaining my plan of procedure to the slaves, and he evidently thinks that I wish to carry it towards them with a high hand. I did explain all the exploration I intended to do. . . . When pressed on the point, they say they will only go with Dugumbe's men to the Lomame, and then return." A week later they reiterated to Dugumbe their refusal: "he spoke long to them, but they will not consent to go further. When told that they would thereby lose all their pay, they replied, 'Yes, but not our lives', and they walked off from him muttering, which is insulting to one of his rank." Livingstone then made one more, and (as it proved) the last, appeal to Dugumbe.

"I have goods at Ujiji; I don't know how many but they are considerable; take them all, and give me men to finish my work; if not enough, I will add to them; only do not let me be forced to return now that I am so near the end of my undertaking." He said he would make a plan in conjunction with his associates, and report to me.

The day after (14 July) there is a single entry in the Journal: "I am distressed and perplexed what to do so as not to be foiled, but all seems against me."

Whether or not this "bold and prosperous Arab" would

have proved a true friend, and whether Livingstone would by his aid have reached Katanga and the fountains which he supposed would prove to be the sources of the Nile, cannot be known. It is probable that Dugumbe, like Abed, was genuinely desirous to further his plans, but that their colleagues were more reluctant. There is point too in Coupland's suggestion that even Dugumbe felt somewhat dubious about this white man's invasion of those virgin fields which he meant to exploit himself, and "he may well have shared in some degree the Ujijians' belief that Livingstone was not as harmless as he looked". This would account for his procrastination. But unforeseen and malignant fate intervened to forestall any decision.

The Manyuema people must have now become quite familiar with this old tired stranger who came and went among them, with his white skin and lank hair, his friendly questionings and curious interest in their concerns. His ways were gentle—he had no slaves; even the Arabs respected him. Thus they were as little prepared as he was for the appalling shock which, on 15 July, "wiped out every hope he had cherished, every plan he had made at Nyangwe, and, almost with the force of a physical blow, sent him staggering back along the path to Ujiji".[8]

It was a hot, sultry day, and when I went into the market I saw Adie and Manilla, and three of the men who had lately come with Dugumbe. I was surprised to see the three with their guns, and felt inclined to reprove them, as one of my men did, for bringing weapons into the market, but I attributed it to their ignorance, and, it being very hot, I was walking away to go out of the market, when I saw one of the fellows haggling about a fowl, and seizing hold of it. Before I had got thirty yards out, the discharge of two guns in the middle of the crowd told me that slaughter had begun: crowds dashed off from the place, and threw down their wares in confusion, and ran. At the same time that the three opened fire on the mass of people near the upper end of the market-place volleys were discharged from a party down near the creek on the panic-stricken women, who dashed at the canoes. These, some fifty or more, were jammed in the creek and the men forgot their paddles in the terror that seized all. The canoes were not to be got out, for the creek was too small for so many; men and women, wounded by the balls, poured into them, and leaped and scrambled into the water shrieking. A long line of heads in the river showed that great numbers struck out for an island a full mile off: in going towards it they had to put the left shoulder to a current of about two miles an hour; if they had struck away diagonally to the opposite bank, the current would have aided them, and, though nearly three miles off, some would have gained land: as it was, the heads above water showed the long lines of those that would inevitably perish.

Shot after shot continued to be fired on the helpless and perishing. Some of the long line of heads disappeared quietly; whilst other poor creatures threw their arms high, as if appealing to the great Father above, and sank. One canoe took in as many as it could hold, and all paddled with hands and arms: three canoes, got out in haste, picked up sinking friends, till all went down together, and disappeared. One man in a long canoe, which could have held forty or fifty, had clearly lost his head; he had been out in the stream before the massacre began, and now paddled up the river nowhere, and never looked to the drowning.

By-and-by all the heads disappeared; some had turned down stream towards the bank, and escaped. Dugumbe put people into one of the deserted vessels to save those in the water and saved twenty-one, but one woman refused to be taken on board from thinking that she was to be made a slave of; she preferred the chance of life by swimming, to the lot of a slave; the Bagenya women are expert in the water, as they are accustomed to dive for oysters, and those who went down stream may have escaped, but the Arabs themselves estimated the loss of life at between 330 and 400 souls. The shooting-party near the canoes were so reckless, they killed two of their own people; and a Banyamwezi follower, who got into a deserted canoe to plunder, fell into the water, went down, then came up again, and down to rise no more.

My first impulse was to pistol the murderers, but Dugumbe protested against my getting into a blood-feud, and I was thankful afterwards that I took his advice. Two wretched Moslems asserted "that the firing was done by the people of the English"; I asked one of them why he lied so, and he could utter no excuse: no other falsehood came to his aid as he stood abashed before me, and so telling him not to tell palpable falsehoods, I left him gaping.

After the terrible affair in the water, the party of Tagamoio, who was the chief perpetrator, continued to fire on the people there and fire their villages. As I write I hear the loud wails on the left bank over those who are there slain, ignorant of their many friends who are now in the depths of the Lualaba. Oh, let Thy kingdom come! No one will ever know the exact loss on this bright sultry summer morning. It gave me the impression of being in Hell.

Livingstone's second impulse was to send his consular Union Jack into the village to cause a cease-fire and was thus able to save more than thirty survivors. At his urgent request Dugumbe sent men across the river to stop the carnage and arson there, but this Arab was either too late or his authority too weak to prevent the destruction of twenty-seven villages. Though he was not directly responsible for the atrocity and "is the best of the whole horde" Livingstone could not exonerate him from complicity. He did indeed of his own accord save twenty-one of the fugitives and liberate them; but when Livingstone demanded that he should "catch the murderers and hang them up in the market-place as our protest against the bloody deeds", his reply was evasive. Had the massacre been committed by Manilla (a notorious slave-raider) he said that he would have done so; but it was done by Tagamoio's party, that is, of his own. But he confessed that "he had committed a great error, and speedily got the chiefs who had come over to me to meet him at his house and forthwith mix blood".

The motive of the crime was obscurely explained as an act intended "to punish the friends made by Manilla who, being a slave, had no right to make war and burn villages; that could only be done by free men. Manilla confesses to me privately that he did wrong in that." But as Livingstone saw it, it was an act of sheer terrorism for which all the Arabs were directly or indirectly responsible, and he could no longer abide their company. Even the appeal of the Manyuema chiefs, who now fled to him for protection, could not move him.

> Many of the headmen . . . came over to me and begged me to come back with them and appoint new localities . . . but I told them I was so ashamed of the company I found myself in that I could scarcely look the Manyuema in the face. They had believed that I wished to kill them— what did they think now? I could not remain among bloody companions and would flee away, I said; but they begged me hard not to leave them until they were again settled.
>
> The open murder perpetrated on hundreds of unsuspecting women fills me with unspeakable horror; I cannot think of going anywhere with the Tagamoio crew; I must either go down or up Lualaba, whichever the Banian slaves choose.

He could not remain to see to their protection, but could only appeal to Dugumbe to cement friendship with them and "to restrain to some extent his infamous underlings". Dugumbe answered: "I shall do my utmost to get all the captives, but must make friends now, in order that the market may not be given up." As to the "Banian slaves", "they would like to go with Tagamoio and share in his rapine and get slaves". Livingstone would now have had little difficulty in getting canoes, "but with bloodhounds it is out of the question. I see nothing for it but to go back to Ujiji for other men." Yet he evidently debated the point with himself before finally making up his mind. It was abandoning a great chance.

16 *July.*—At last I said that I would start for Ujiji in three days, on foot. I wished to speak with Tagamoio about the captive relations of the chiefs, but he always ran away when he saw me coming.

17 *July.*—All the rest of Dugumbe's party offered me a share in every kind of goods they had, and pressed me not to be ashamed to tell them what I needed. I declined everything save a little gunpowder, but they all made presents of beads, and I was glad to return equivalents in cloth.

18 *July.*—The terrible scenes of man's inhumanity to man brought on severe headache, which might have been serious had it not been relieved by a copious discharge of blood; I was laid up all yesterday afternoon with the depression the bloodshed made—it filled me with unspeakable horror. "Don't go away", say the Manyuema chiefs to me; but I cannot stay here in agony.

19 *July.*—Dugumbe sent me a fine goat, a maneh of gunpowder, a maneh of fine blue beads, and 230 cowries, to buy provision in the way . . . two very fine large Manyuema swords and two equally fine spears, and said that I must not leave anything; he would buy others with his own goods and divide them equally with me; he is very friendly.

The same day a few market people reappeared, some 200, where "formerly they had come in crowds"; and seven canoes instead of fifty: "but they have great tenacity and hopefulness, an old established custom has great charms for them, and the market will again be attended if no fresh outrage is committed". It is certain that nothing but an insuperable difficulty would have caused Livingstone to abandon his westward exploration now, seeing that he would be helped and no longer hindered by the Manyuema chiefs. But the unreliability, to say the least, of his so-called Banian slaves rendered any prospect of success nugatory. He must return to Ujiji and recruit sound men, replenish himself with means for travel and with medicines, even though this would involve a backward tramp of 95 days—then back to the Lualaba again. Yet this is actually what he had in mind.

The hideous massacre at Nyangwe was not without salutary effects.

It was recorded in a despatch of great length to the Foreign Secretary, and indeed it became one of the chief causes of the appointment of a Royal Commission to investigate the subject of the African slave-trade, and of the mission of Sir Bartle Frere to concert measures for bringing it to an end.[9]

Livingstone started on his journey to Ujiji on 20 July: "All Dugumbe's people came to say good-bye, and convoy me a little way." The "Banian slaves" delayed the start by malingering but Dugumbe provided the necessary spur, adding good advice: "Do not delay for anyone, but travel in a compact body, as stragglers now are sure to be cut off." To travel at all was to invite danger, for the white man and his party were certain to be taken for marauders; and though indeed his reception in the villages was at first friendly, the route was strewn with gruesome signs of depredation. "Men are worse than beasts of prey." At Kasongo's: "I had to scold and threaten them, and set men to watch their deeds." Here three of his men decamped, but were replaced by Kasongo. Then on through miles of gutted villages, and across the Sokoye streams to another village—"ill and almost every step in pain". Here hostility was active: stones were thrown and murder attempted. "We sleep uncomfortably, the natives watching us all round." Next day: "They would come to no parley." Livingstone was aware that ambushes were being laid and sent men in advance to reconnoitre; but that same day, 8 August, was nearly his last.

> In passing along the narrow path with a wall of dense vegetation touching either hand, we came to a point where an ambush had been placed, and trees cut down to obstruct us while they speared us; but for some reason it was abandoned. Nothing could be detected; but stooping down to the earth and peering upwards towards the sun, a dark shade could sometimes be seen; this was was an infuriated savage, and a slight rustle in the dense vegetation meant a spear. A large spear from my right lunged past and almost grazed my back, and stuck firmly in the soil. The two men from whom it came appeared in an opening in the forest only ten yards off and bolted, one looking back over his shoulder as he ran. As they are expert with the spear I don't know how it missed, except that he was too sure of his aim and the good hand of God was upon me.

He was last in the file of his retinue and all were allowed to pass the ambuscade before him; but he was mistaken for their Arab leader, since he was wearing a type of red jacket worn by Mohamad and others who had sponsored raids against them.

> Another spear was thrown at me by an unseen assailant, and it missed me by about a foot in front. Guns were fired into the dense mass of

forest but with no effect, for nothing could be seen; but we heard the men jeering and denouncing us close by: two of our party were slain.

We had five hours of running the gauntlet, waylaid by spearmen, who all felt that if they killed me they would be revenging the death of relations. From each hole in the tangled mass we looked for a spear; and each moment expected to hear the rustle which told of deadly weapons hurled at us. I became weary with the constant strain of danger and, as I suppose happens with soldiers on the field of battle, not courageous, but perfectly indifferent whether I were killed or not.

Nor were these deliverances from the hand of man his only escapes from sudden death in a single day.

Coming to a part of the forest cleared for cultivation I noticed a gigantic tree, made still taller by growing on an anthill 20 feet high; it had fire applied near its roots; I heard a crack which told that the fire had done its work, but felt no alarm till I saw it come straight towards me; I ran a few paces back and down it came to the ground one yard behind me, and breaking into several lengths it covered me with a cloud of dust. Had the branches not previously been rotted off, I could scarcely have escaped.

My attendants, who were scattered in all directions came running back to me, calling out "Peace! peace! You will finish all your work in spite of all these people, and in spite of everything." Like them I took it as an omen of good success to crown me yet, thanks to the Almighty Preserver of men.

His losses included, besides three milch goats, all his remaining calico, a telescope, umbrella, and five spears, dropped by a bearer in precipitate flight. On at last emerging from the forest, near the villages of Monanbundwa, they rested for awhile and soon saw the chief "walking up in a stately manner unarmed to meet us". He had heard the gun-fire and came to ask the cause. When it was explained as due to a mistake on the part of the attackers, he conducted Livingstone to his village, and presented him with ten goats, and then proposed that he and his people should join forces with Livingstone's party and carry war in retaliation into the enemies' country. "I again explained that the attack was made by a mistake . . . that I had no wish to kill men; to join in his old feud would only make matters worse. This he could perfectly understand." He accompanied the party a long way, and at one point said, "Here we killed a man of Moezia and ate his body."

Here Livingstone breaks off to discuss the custom of cannibalism, which cannot be accounted for on the score of hunger, since the country abounds in nutritious food of every variety, and he specifies all the ingredients. "They seem to eat their foes to inspire courage, or in revenge"—but not till the corpse has been buried and become putrid. "The only feasible reason I can discover is a depraved appetite, giving an extraordinary craving for meat which we call high." They also smear the fat of lions on the tails of oxen as a preventive to the tsetse-fly: "When I heard of this I thought that lion's fat would be as difficult of collection as gnat's brains or mosquito tongues; but I was assured that many lions are killed and are extremely fat." His humour had not deserted him.

After a long march across plains and water-courses next day, "I rested half a day, as I am ill. I do most devoutly thank the Lord for sparing my life three times in one day. The Lord is good, a stronghold in the day of trouble, and He knows them that trust in Him." But the brevity of his notes for the rest of the journey and the frequency of such jottings as "Rest from weakness"—"Ill all night"—tell their own tale. Blaikie states without authority but what is likely enough to have been the fact that, even before starting on this return journey, "the intestinal canal had given way, subjecting him to severe internal haemorrhage with excruciating pain". He was prostrated for ten days at Bambarre, then "better and thankful", resumed the march, only to succumb again for two days more. Still he struggled on, tramping when he could, resting when he must. Weak as he was, he would suffer no indiscipline; and when near Makala's some of his former renegades "came impudently into the village, I had to drive them out".

When beyond Kunde's on the Katambe he met an Arab caravan and heard of the death of the Sultan Seyed Majid in Darasalam: "he was a true and warm friend to me. . . . Seyd Burghash succeeds him; this change causes anxiety." On 23 September he wrote:

> I was sorely knocked up by this march from Nyangwe back to Ujiji. In the later part of it I felt as if dying on my feet. Almost every step was in pain, the appetite failed, and a little bit of meat caused violent diarrhoea, whilst the mind, sorely depressed, reacted on the body. All the traders were returning successful: I alone had failed and experienced worry, thwarting, baffling, when almost within sight of the end towards which I strained.

To add to his torment, angular fragments of quartz on the path cut into his feet which were cramped into ill-fitting shoes —his last pair; and the dust of the march caused ophthalmia: "my first touch of it in Africa". But he must have been buoyed up on these last marches by the thought of the medicines and all the other comforts which awaited him at Ujiji, which in desperation he had been prompted to offer to Dugumbe weeks ago in exchange for a few men to cross the Lualaba. Now at least he could use them to recuperate his strength.

He reached the shore of Tanganyika on 9 October and was delayed six days on the islet Kasenge for a canoe; three days more for another to make the crossing; and on the 18th was ferried over by night. His Journal notes are intermittent and fragmentary. But on the 23rd he wrote from Ujiji:

> Welcomed by all the Arabs, particularly by Moenyeghere. I was now reduced to a skeleton, but the market being held daily and all kinds of native food brought to it, I hoped that food and rest would soon restore me; but in the evening my people came and told me that Shereef had sold off all my goods, and Moenyeghere confirmed it saying, "We protested, but he did not leave a single yard of calico out of 3,000, nor a string of beads out of 700 lbs." This was distressing.
>
> I had made up my mind, if I could not get people at Ujiji, to wait till men should come from the coast, but to wait in beggary was not what I ever contemplated, and I now felt miserable. Shereef was evidently a moral idiot, for he came without shame to shake hands with me, and when I refused, assumed an air of displeasure, as having been badly treated; and afterwards came with his good-luck salutation twice a day, and on leaving said, "I am going to pray", till I told him that were I an Arab, his hand and both ears would be cut off for thieving, as he knew, and I wanted no salutations from him. In my distress it was annoying to see Shereef's friends passing from the market with all the good things that my goods had bought.

This was the nadir of Livingstone's misfortunes. He was utterly destitute not only of the bare necessities of life, but of all hope of procuring any. Never in his life had he been so near complete disaster. But even in this extremity he would maintain his independence—at least temporarily.

> 24 *October.*—My property had been sold to Shereef's friends at merely nominal prices. Syed bin Mahid, a good man, proposed that they should be returned and the ivory be taken from Shereef; but they would not restore stolen property, though they knew it to be stolen. Christians would have acted differently, even those of the lowest classes. I felt in

my destitution as if I were the man who went down from Jerusalem to Jericho and fell among thieves; but I could not hope for Priest, Levite, or good Samaritan to come by on either side; but one morning Syed bin Mahid said to me, "Now this is the first time we have been alone together; I have no goods, but I have ivory; let me, I pray you, sell some ivory and give the goods to you." This was encouraging; but I said, "Not yet, but by-and-by." I had still a few barter goods left, which I had taken the precaution to deposit with Mohamad bin Saleh before going to Manyuema, in case of returning in extreme need.

Thus far in his Journal. But on the back of an old envelope are brief notes written in an unsteady hand:

25th.—Call Shereef and demand my goods. Said Ludha (a Banian merchant) had ordered him to stay a month and then leave. Had divined on Koran, found I was dead. Then sold all.

26th.—News from Garangenza. Many Arabs killed. Road shut up. One Englishman there.[10]

Dazed and bewildered, dismayed and helpless, he sat down to consider what was best to be done, but no clear way out of his plight suggested itself. Then after four days, as if by a miracle and from a totally unexpected source, came deliverance.

But when my spirits were at their lowest ebb the good Samaritan was close at hand, for one morning Susi came running at the top of his speed and gasped out, "An Englishman! I see him!" and off he darted to meet him. The American flag at the head of the caravan told of the nationality of the stranger. Bales of goods, baths of tin, huge kettles, cooking-pots, tents, etc., made me think, "This must be a luxurious traveller, and not one at his wits' end like me" (28 October).

Chapter Thirty-One

LAST JOURNEYS: WITH STANLEY
1871–1872

"Never was I more hard pressed; never was help more welcome."

STANLEY'S meeting with Livingstone is among the most dramatic episodes in all the annals of exploration. It is remarkable for its coincidence in time: their arrival at Ujiji, after long journeys from opposite directions and both at great hazard, was practically simultaneous; it is remarkable too because of their almost incongruous dissimilarity in character. The fact that both were exceptionally well-seasoned campaigners is their single point of comparison; had they met in other circumstances it is probable that Livingstone would have regarded Stanley in a very different light. Yet their five months' intimate companionship was passed, not only without a jarring note but in increasing harmony: on Livingstone's side, unbounded gratitude; on Stanley's, a sincere and wondering respect that grew into positive veneration.

Stanley must be reckoned among the hardest travellers and boldest adventurers who have ever lived. At the age of thirty he had to his credit a record of adventure enough to satisfy most men for a lifetime, and his greatest exploits were yet to come. His career, both past and future, has its own place in the history of travel; but his discovery of Livingstone marks the turning-point of his fortunes: at one bound he leapt into fame. There have been no greater or more dauntless travellers in Africa than these two, yet there is this difference between them: Stanley never experienced a tithe of the privations that Livingstone voluntarily endured; nor were his journeys subsidiary as Livingstone's were to humanitarian ends. Stanley was a good companion; but he was no Oswell or Steele or Webb, no English sportsman of gentle birth.

His lot from boyhood had been a hard and unhappy one.

575

Orphaned in infancy and subjected later for ten years to the savage brutality of a Welsh workhouse, he was flung adrift on the world at fifteen to fight his way in America. There he found precarious employment in several trades, but no security till, after exciting vicissitudes by land and sea, he turned journalist and joined the staff of the *New York Herald*. In that capacity he served as a war-correspondent in the Abyssinian campaign with conspicuous success, and established a reputation for audacity and foresight. After a roving commission through the Mediterranean islands to Spain he was instructed, late in 1868, to go to Aden for news of Livingstone who was rumoured to have found the Nile sources and to be on his way down the river. The rumour proving false, he was recalled to London and sent again to Spain, where at considerable risk he witnessed and reported upon the revolutionary war. Meanwhile the mystery of Livingstone's whereabouts was deepening, and the manager of the *New York Herald*, Mr. James Gordon Bennett, decided on another attempt to "feature" the lost explorer. He summoned Stanley to Paris by a telegram. Reaching Paris late on 17 October 1869, Stanley went at once to the Grand Hotel and found his chief in bed.

"Where do you think Livingstone is?"—"I really do not know, sir."—"Do you think he is alive?"—"He may be or he may not be."—"Well, I think he is alive and that he can be found, and I am going to send you to find him."

The proposition took even Stanley aback. He knew nothing of Central Africa, and he himself believed that Livingstone was dead. The search, he ventured to suggest, would be very costly—perhaps £2,500. Mr. Bennett replied:

"Draw a thousand pounds now, and when you have gone through that draw another thousand, and when that is spent draw another thousand, and when you have finished that draw another thousand, and so on; but FIND LIVINGSTONE!"

Then he added, thoughtfully and deliberately, "The old man may be in want; take enough with you to help him, should he require it."

But this was not to be Stanley's immediate objective. He was to go first for "copy" to the inauguration of the Suez Canal; then up the Nile; then to Jerusalem, Constantinople; the Crimea; over the Caucasus to the Caspian Sea; thence through Persia to India; Persepolis, Baghdad, the Euphrates Valley.

"Probably you will hear by that time that Livingstone is on his way to Zanzibar; but if not, go into the interior and find him if alive. Get what news of his discoveries you can; and if you find he is dead, bring all possible proofs of his being dead. That is all. Good-night, and God be with you."

This extensive programme was duly executed with Stanley's usual skill and daring. On 7 January 1871 he was in Zanzibar and his first care was to interview the Consul, Livingstone's former colleague on the Zambesi. The two men took an instant dislike to one another. Stanley's manner appears, even from his own account, to have been designedly insolent, and Kirk regarded him with "a broad stare". He concealed from Kirk his real motive for seeking men and means to enter the interior, but threw out the casual question as to how Livingstone "would conduct himself towards me, supposing I might possibly stumble across him in my travels?" Kirk, no doubt wishing to shield Livingstone from such a contingency, was betrayed by the adroit Welshman into making some rather indiscreet remarks upon Livingstone's habitual seclusiveness, remarks upon which the latter afterwards put a slanderous misconstruction. Stanley had developed, besides his natural high qualities of courage and determination, a vein of hard, ruthless, arrogant, and even brutal egotism. Mrs. Fraser, when he was the guest of her parents at Newstead Abbey on his return to England, wrote of him:

> He was the typical American journalist, almost aggressively so both in accent and behaviour. His eyes were like small pools of grey fire, but the least provocation turned them into grey lightning. They seemed to scorch and shrivel up all he looked at. His whole personality gave the impression of overwhelming and concentrated force—a human explosive.[1]

This impression is certainly confirmed by a reading of his book *How I Found Livingstone*. Its very title—so curiously anticipative of the modern literary vogue—betrays his incurable, insufferable self-consciousness. Miss Florence Nightingale's comment upon it was severe: "The worst possible book upon the best possible subject". He tells his journey with journalistic gusto, and though the telling of it jars, it is nevertheless a tale of undoubted heroism and its author a man of the bravest calibre.

Stanley left Zanzibar for Bagamoyo on 4 February; the prevailing cholera lost him six weeks in recruiting his personnel. While there he again met Kirk, who had come over to expedite the despatch of 35 loads which he had consigned to Livingstone on 2 November 1870—one hundred days before. This procrastination confirmed Stanley in the belief that Kirk was quite indifferent to Livingstone's fate. He found the carriers "living in clover, thoughtless of their errand and indulging their own vicious propensities". But on the evening of Kirk's arrival, "they started in a fright, with but four of their escort".

With two tough white men named Farquhar and Shaw, 23 mercenary soldiers and a small army of carriers and cooks, besides some pack animals, Stanley set out from Bagamoyo on 21 March. His equipment, which included much ammunition, many guns, and some collapsible boats, weighed six tons. He took the direct caravan route due west to Unyanyembe and, as Coupland says, whereas Livingstone "trudged across Africa, Stanley strode". He dragooned his black retinue with the whip, and his white colleagues with his fists. Before he reached the Arab settlement at Unyanyembe (in four months) Farquhar was dead, and Shaw becoming a wreck. Here he found a sealed packet of letters for Livingstone registered on 1 November of the previous year, and the caravan from Kirk which had preceded him, and promptly took charge of both. But now his real difficulties began. An armed native force barred the way to Ujiji, defying further Arab intrusions; the Arabs on their part were preparing an offensive. Stanley decided to aid them if only to clear the road. Before they were ready to attack he fell sick of fever and lay semi-conscious for a week. Recovering, he joined forces with the attackers. They were routed, and fled in panic, leaving him and his party to their fate. He effected a retreat to Unyanyembe, and prepared to defend the place alone with his handful of men, several of whom had been killed and many more had deserted. During a lull he wrote in his diary: "My position is most serious. I have a good excuse for returning to the coast, but my conscience will not permit me. . . . In fact, I feel I must die sooner than return."

For four days he was besieged; then the attackers withdrew.

Supplementing his reduced following as best he might, he began his second march on 20 September with only 54 men; setting his course south-west to by-pass the native forces. He was obliged to leave Livingstone's stores behind, but compelled a letter-carrier, Kaif-Halek, to come on to Ujiji with his mail-bag. When only a week out, Shaw—who had once tried to assassinate him in his tent, but whom he had nursed assiduously all the way—left him with four bearers, only to perish soon after in the bush. Ten days later he was faced with mutiny—and murder. Only his presence of mind and intrepidity saved him; he forced the two ringleaders to ground their guns, soundly rated them and then pardoned them. By mid-October he was steering north-west, and when within eight days' march of Ujiji was informed of the arrival there of a white man with a grey beard who was sick. This, he could scarcely doubt, was Livingstone. But now he had to circumvent an area ruled by predatory chiefs who exacted so much *hongo* that at last he decided to "run the blockade" by moonlight through the jungle. Once the party were detected and a hue and cry raised; they escaped into dense undergrowth, but a woman screamed and Stanley could only silence her with the whip and a gag. After so many dangers—of which the foregoing is a bare summary—he reached Ujiji on 10 November; Livingstone, who logged it as 28 October, being thirteen days out in his reckoning.

When within 300 yards of the town and in a dense throng of its people, Stanley was greeted by a respectful voice in English, "Good-morning, sir!" Turning sharply he saw a man "with the blackest of faces, but animated and joyous", capped with a turban and clad in a long white shirt; and asked, "Who the mischief are you?" "I am Susi, the servant of Dr. Livingstone." Then another voice, "Good-morning, sir!" "Well, what is your name?" "I am Chuma, sir." "Is the Doctor well?" "Not very well, sir." "Now, you, Susi, run and tell the Doctor I am coming." "Yes, sir", and off he darted like a madman. Stanley says that his heart beat fast, and that his emotion was well-nigh uncontrollable.

> . . . So I did that which I thought was most dignified. I pushed back the crowds and, passing from the rear, walked down a living avenue of people, until I came in front of the semi-circle of Arabs, in front of which stood the white man with the grey beard. As I advanced slowly towards

him I noticed he was pale, looked wearied, wore a bluish cap with a faded gold band, had on a red-sleeved waistcoat, and a pair of grey tweed trousers. . . . I walked deliberately to him, took off my hat, and said, "Dr. Livingstone, I presume?" "Yes," said he with a kind smile, lifting his cap slightly. "I thank God, Doctor, I have been permitted to see you." He answered, "I feel thankful that I am here to welcome you."[2]

Salutations are exchanged with the Arabs, whom the Doctor introduces by name. He points to his seat under the verandah: a straw mat covered with a goatskin, and another skin nailed to the wall behind it: "I protest against taking this seat, which so much more befits him than me, but the Doctor will not yield; I must take it."

Stanley was too absorbed in conning the features of "the wonderful man at whose side I now sat in Central Africa" to take notes of their first conversation. "Every hair of his head and beard, every wrinkle of his face, the wanness of his features —were all imparting intelligence to me." More than a thousand natives were gazing at them as they talked, but presently the Arabs "with a delicacy I approved" rose up, and the crowds dispersed. Stanley called Kaif-Halek and handed Livingstone his long-overdue mail-bag.

The Doctor kept it on his knee, then presently opened it and read one or two of his children's letters, his face in the meanwhile lighting up. He asked me first to tell him the news. "No, Doctor," said I, "read your letters first, which I am sure you must be impatient to read." "Ah," said he, "I have waited years for letters, and I have been taught patience. I can surely afford to wait a few hours longer. No, tell me the general news; how is the world getting along?"

So he was told of "tidings from Europe that made my whole frame thrill"; of the Pacific Railroad; of the opening of the Suez Canal; of the trans-Atlantic cables; of the election of General Grant; of the fate of Schleswig-Holstein, and then of that of France—and much else—till noon wore on to evening and with it a feast of good things, and Livingstone kept repeating, "You have brought me new life!" Still they talked on into the darkness, with the thunder of Tanganyika's surf below them and the chorus of night insects around, till Stanley said, "Doctor, you had better read your letters. I will not keep you up any longer." "Yes," he answered, "it is getting late; and I will go and read my friends' letters. Good-night, and God bless you." "Good-night, my dear Doctor; and let me hope that your news will be such as you desire."

Livingstone sat late over his budget, but was up before Stanley in the morning. "Hulloa, Doctor! You up already? I hope you have slept well?" "Good-morning, Mr. Stanley! I am glad to see you. Hope you rested well. . . . You have brought me good and bad news. But sit down." There was good news about Agnes and Oswald, but sad news about Tom; sad news in "the death of good Lord Clarendon—my constant friend", but relief in "the proof that the Government had not entirely forgotten me in voting £1,000 for supplies". Then Stanley, still gazing at him intently to assure himself that "the man was not an apparition", said, "Now Doctor, you are probably wondering why I am here?"

"It is true," said he, "I have been wondering. I thought you at first an emissary of the French Government . . . until I saw the American flag; and I was rather glad it was so, because I could not have talked to him in French; and if he did not know English, we had been a pretty pair of white men in Ujiji! I did not like to ask you yesterday, because it was none of my business."

If the old explorer's verbal response to the younger's jubilant disclosure of his sole purpose in coming thus far into Central Africa—namely, to "FIND YOU"—at Mr. Bennett's behest— seemed to the latter somewhat lacking in warmth, he does not say so but contents himself with recording it faithfully.

Well, indeed! I am very much obliged to him; and it makes me feel proud to think that you Americans think so much of me. You have just come in the proper time; for I was beginning to think that I should have to beg from the Arabs. . . . I wish I could embody my thanks to Mr. Bennett in suitable words; but if I fail to do so, do not, I beg of you, believe me the less grateful.

Always more articulate on paper than in speech, he wrote in his Journal:

I am not of a demonstrative turn, as cold indeed as we islanders are usually reputed to be; but this disinterested kindness of Mr. Bennett, so nobly carried into effect by Mr. Stanley, was simply overwhelming. I really do feel extremely grateful, and at the same time a little ashamed at not being more worthy of the generosity. Mr. Stanley has done his part with untiring energy; good judgment in the teeth of very serious obstacles.

He was well enough versed in the ways of the world to be aware that the press magnate's motive cannot have been entirely philanthropic, but that could not lessen the personal debt that he felt he owed to him. Concerning Stanley he wrote later to Waller:

> He behaved as a son to a father—truly overflowing in kindness. The good Lord remember and be gracious unto him in life and in death. Oswell [his son] was told by Kirk that Stanley would make his fortune out of me; if so he is heartily welcome, for it is a great deal more than I could ever make out of myself.[3]

And to Agnes:

> He laid all he had at my service, divided his clothes into two heaps and pressed one heap upon me; then his medicine-chest; then his goods and everything he had; and to coax my appetite often cooked dainty dishes with his own hand.
>
> He came with the true American generosity. The tears often started into my eyes on each proof of kindness. My appetite returned and I ate three or four times a day, instead of scanty meals. I soon felt strong, and never wearied with the strange news of Europe and America he told. The tumble-down of the French Empire was like a dream. . . .[4]

And again: "Never was I more hard pressed; never was help more welcome."

Though Stanley must have been temperamentally incapable of comprehending the true Livingstone, it is nevertheless to him that we owe the most vivid and authentic—indeed, almost the only—pen-portrait of Livingstone that exists, and which is the more valuable as having been made in the last year of his life. Though suffused with the aureole of hero-worship, its veracity is unmistakable.

> I defy any one to be in his society long without thoroughly fathoming him, for in him there is no guile, and what is apparent on the surface is the thing that is in him. . . . Dr. Livingstone is about sixty years old, though after he was restored to health he looked like a man who has not passed his fiftieth year. His hair has a brownish colour yet, but is here and there streaked with grey lines over the temples; his beard and moustaches are very grey. His eyes, which are hazel, are remarkably bright; he has a sight keen as a hawk's. His teeth alone indicate the weakness of age; the hard fare of Lunda has made havoc in their lines. His form, which soon assumed a stoutish appearance, is a little over the ordinary height, with the slightest possible bow in the shoulders. When walking he has a firm but heavy tread, like that of an overworked

or fatigued man. He is accustomed to wear a naval cap with a semicircular peak, by which he has been identified throughout Africa. His dress, when first I saw him, exhibited traces of patching and repairing, but was scrupulously clean.

I was led to believe that Livingstone possessed a splenetic, misanthropic temper; some have said that he is garrulous; that he is demented; that he has utterly changed from the David Livingstone whom people knew as the reverend missionary. . . .

I grant he is not an angel; but he approaches to that being as near as the nature of a living man will allow. I never saw any spleen or misanthropy in him: as for being garrulous, Dr. Livingstone is quite the reverse; he is reserved, if anything; and to the man who says Dr. Livingstone is changed, all I can say is, that he never could have known him, for it is notorious that the Doctor has a fund of quiet humour, which he exhibits at all times when he is among friends. . . .

His gentleness never forsakes him; his hopefulness never deserts him. No harassing anxieties, distraction of mind, long separation from home and kindred, can make him complain. He thinks "all will come out right at last"; he has such faith in the goodness of Providence. The sport of adverse circumstances, the plaything of the miserable beings sent to him from Zanzibar—he has been baffled and worried, even almost to the grave, yet he will not desert the charge imposed upon him by his friend Sir Roderick Murchison. To the stern dictates of duty, alone, has he sacrificed his home and ease, the pleasures, refinements, and luxuries of civilized life. His is the Spartan heroism, the inflexibility of the Roman, the enduring resolution of the Anglo-Saxon—never to relinquish his work, though his heart yearns for home; never to surrender his obligations until he can write FINIS to his work.

There is a good-natured *abandon* about Livingstone which was not lost on me. Whenever he began to laugh, there was a contagion about it that compelled me to imitate him. It was such a laugh as Teufelsdröch's—a laugh of the whole man from head to heel. If he told a story, he related it in such a way as to convince one of its truthfulness; his face was so lit up by the sly fun it contained that I was sure the story was worth relating, and worth listening to.

Another thing that specially attracted my attention was his wonderfully retentive memory. If we remember the many years he has spent in Africa deprived of books, we may well think it an uncommon memory that can recite whole poems from Byron, Burns, Tennyson, Longfellow, Whittier, and Lowell. . . .

His religion is not of the theoretical kind, but is a constant, earnest, sincere practice. It is neither demonstrative nor loud, but manifests itself in a quiet practical way, and is always at work. It is not aggressive, which sometimes is troublesome, if not impertinent. In him religion exhibits its loveliest features; it governs his conduct not only towards his servants but towards the natives, the bigoted Mohammedans, and all who come in contact with him. Without it Livingstone, with his ardent temperament, his enthusiasm, his high spirit and courage, must have become uncompaniable, and a hard master. Religion has tamed him, and made him a Christian gentleman ; the crude and wilful have been refined and subdued; religion has made him the most companiable of men and indulgent of masters—a man whose society is pleasurable to a degree. . . .

From being thwarted and hated in every possible way by the Arabs and half-castes upon his first arrival at Ujiji he has, through his uniform kindness and mild pleasant temper, won all hearts. I observed that universal respect was paid to him. Even the Mohammedans never passed his house without calling to say, "The blessing of God rest on you!". Each Sunday morning he gathers his little flock around him, and reads prayers and a chapter from the Bible in a natural, unaffected, and sincere tone; and afterwards delivers a short address in the Ki-swaheli language about the subject read to them, which is listened to with evident interest and attention.[5]

If it cannot be said that intercourse with Livingstone effected what may be called "conversion" in Stanley, it caused him seriously to reflect and set his thoughts in a new direction— especially to what he called "the doctrine of forbearance", and he ever after looked back on this experience as the most important in his life. The tone of his eulogium is obviously intended as a counterblast to what he conceived, though quite unjustifiably, to have been Kirk's estimate of Livingstone.

Livingstone recommences his Journal on 16 November with the words:

As Tanganyika explorations are said by Mr. Stanley to be an object of interest to Sir Roderick, we go at his expense and by his men to the north of the Lake.

He had told Stanley that he regarded this line as second in importance to the central line of drainage, the Lualaba, flowing north from latitude 11° (i.e. from the north shore of Bangwe-olo); and that the Chambesi, its most southern extremity, swung round to meet it from well south of Tanganyika. The connection between Tanganyika and the Albert Nyanza was therefore secondary, but by no means to be neglected. In his autobiography Stanley explains that no bribe would have induced his men to extend their term of service to the period which would have been necessary to explore the Lualaba; and, of the several alternatives which he proposed, Livingstone accepted the last, namely that after their cruise to the north end of Tanganyika, he should return with him to Unyanye-mbe, and there await the new contingent of porters whom he would despatch with all speed from the coast. They embarked on Lake Tanganyika the same day in a large canoe provided by Seyd bin Mahid, with sixteen paddlers, four of Stanley's picked men, Susi, Chuma, Gardner, Amoda and his wife Halimah, a good cook although (said Livingstone), "she can never tell the difference between tea and coffee". The voyage, it was hoped, would complete his convalescence, which was already marked by his eagerness to be up and doing.

Two pages suffice for Livingstone's account of this cruise, a whole chapter for Stanley's. Some incidents in it are worthy of note. Landing at Makungo's on the fifth day, *hongo* was truculently demanded, and "the Doctor being the elder and more experienced of the party, the charge of satisfying all such demands was left to him . . . and I was quite curious to see how the great traveller would perform the work." Livingstone met it calmly and smilingly with the counter-demand of a sheep—one little sheep—because they were hungry. The chief "was rather taken aback at this", but soon produced a lamb and a large pot of *pombe*, of which Susi and Bombay (Stanley's headman), imbibed too freely, whereby Livingstone's sounding-line, his entire stock of white sugar, a sack of flour, and much of Stanley's ammunition, were lost to the party during the night. On putting out next morning stones were thrown at the canoe, but (says Livingstone), "we slipped off quietly; they called after us, as men baulked of their prey". Off Bikari they were stoned again. "As one came within a foot of my arm, I suggested that a bullet be sent in return in close proximity to their feet; but Livingstone, though he said nothing, yet showed plainly enough that he did not quite approve of this." A day or two later, in a deserted spot where they were about to land, the assaults were again attempted and when they pulled out:

"Neatly done," cried the Doctor, as we were shooting through the water, leaving the discomfited would-be robbers behind us. Here again my hand was stayed from planting a couple of good shots, as a warning to them in future from molesting strangers, by the mere presence of the Doctor who, as I thought, if it were actually necessary, would not hesitate to give the word.

In other circumstances, Stanley was never the man to brook

interference with his designs, as his career well shows; but in company with Livingstone, silent disapproval was a sufficient deterrent.

On the seventh day they reached the friendly country and magnificent scenery of Cape Magala. Accounts of the flow of the Lusize River were contradictory, but while Livingstone was still optimistic in believing that it must flow out of the Lake, Stanley "was more inclined to doubt". They pulled on to Mukamba's and here, on 26 November, Livingstone notes briefly: "Mr. Stanley has severe fever". Stanley says:

> During the intervals of agony and unconsciousness I saw, or fancied I saw, Livingstone's form moving towards me, and felt, or fancied I felt, Livingstone's hand tenderly feeling my hot head and limbs. I had suffered several fevers between Bagamoyo and Unyanyembe, without anything or anybody to relieve me of the tedious racking headache and pain. . . . But though this fever was more severe than usual, I did not much regret its occurrence, since I became the recipient of the very tender and fatherly kindness of the good man whose companion I now found myself.

During a night at Mukamba's. Stanley was awakened by "several sharp, crack-like sounds", and found they were caused by slaps of chastisement administered by the Doctor upon the thick hide of Susi, who was again overcome by excessive potations and this time sound asleep in his master's bed. The slaps were accompanied by admonitions: "Get up, Susi, will you? You are in my bed. How dare you, sir, get drunk in this way? . . ." And so forth. At length Susi awoke, crestfallen and contrite. Stanley, who would have used much sterner measures himself, was both amused and impressed by the incident.

On the 27th at dusk they pulled across the Lake and in nine hours reached Lohinga. The day after they cruised in the delta of the Lusize, and here all doubts were set at rest. The river flowed into the Lake and not out of it. Livingstone took the disappointment philosophically. "The outlet of the Lake," he wrote, "is probably by the Logumba River into Lualaba as the Luamo, but this as yet must be set down as a 'theoretical discovery'." In fact, it is perfectly correct. Lohinga and Mukamba (whom they visited at his principal village on 5 December), were the frankest, most intelligent and hospitable chiefs they met with on this journey.

Their return along the western shore was without incident

till, when in sight of Cape Lebomba, to avoid a storm, they beached in a cove near a village. Stanley was taking an afternoon nap from which he was roused by one of his men. "Master! Get up quick. Here is a fight going to begin!" He snatched his revolver and went out to find his men sheltered behind the canoe, with guns pointed at a passionate mob approaching. Stanley's first question was, "Where is the Doctor?" He had gone over a hill with his compass and with Susi and Chuma. Stanley had hardly despatched a messenger when the Doctor and his two men appeared on the brow of the hill "looking down in a most complacent manner upon the serio-comic scene". Meanwhile the chief and his son were fighting drunk, the latter performing maniacal antics in a state of nature. Livingstone approached and calmly asked what was the matter. He was told that no Arab could remain for an instant on their soil. Baring his arm he showed that he was a white man, none of whom ever did injury to the black, and induced them to sit down and talk quietly. He listened patiently to their loud protestations against Arab cruelty and was continuing to talk to them "in a mild paternal way", when the chief suddenly arose and slashed himself with his spear, exclaiming that the Wangwana had wounded him! An uproar ensued, but Livingstone intervened with the offer of a present, and soon the chief and his son "were sent on their way rejoicing". Stanley relates the whole episode very dramatically; Livingstone says merely: "Some men here were drunk and troublesome; we gave them a present and left them."

The same day, 9 December, they pulled back across the Lake to Mokungo's and on the 13th were again in Ujiji, Stanley having been again stricken with fever, from which he suffered a relapse before Christmas Day. It was his fourth attack since his arrival at Ujiji but he recovered quickly, and lectured his cook on the importance of the day for white men and the necessity of preparing a sumptuous repast. But the roast was spoiled and the pies and custard burned. "That the fat-brained rascal escaped a thrashing was due only to my inability to lift my hands for punishment." Livingstone says simply: "Had but a sorry Christmas yesterday".

Almost at once, after their return, Livingstone had "rushed to his paper" and had written his letter of thanks to Mr.

Bennett of the *New York Herald* and many other letters to "his numerous friends"; then to his Journal to make up the arrears from his field-notes. It was whilst he was thus employed that Stanley (an amateur draughtsman) made the sketch of him sitting on the floor of their verandah which, improved by an artist in England, is reproduced in Stanley's book. "By this I am enabled to restore him to the reader's view exactly as I saw him"; and the impression, with its rapt look and oblivion of discomfort in his posture, is valuable in preserving his appearance only eighteen months before his death. On 7 January 1872 they left in canoes for Urimba "luxuriously furnished", the bulk of the caravan with pack-animals following the shore route.

On New Year's Day Livingstone had committed to his Journal the prayer: "May the Almighty help me to finish my work this year for Christ's sake!"

They stayed three days at Urimba awaiting the land-party, during which Stanley added a zebra to their larder and was again fever-stricken. Soon after starting (7 January) on the eastward route he secured a buffalo and thus the whole party were well provisioned. The country being trackless they depended on the compass, Stanley leading; rains were heavy and frequent, and Livingstone's feet sore and cramped. By the 18th the party was nearly exhausted as well as famished (the men having improvidently guzzled all the dried meat) and Stanley wrote: "It was a most desperate march. . . . The Doctor's feet were very sore and bleeding from the weary position certainly." But the next day he brought down two fine zebras and they halted for a day's rest.

Stanley has constant praise for Livingstone as the ideal travelling companion, always helpful, unruffled and enduring; who knew so well how to console a young hunter for bad luck and to make the most of any success; he taught him how to harden his leaden balls with melted zinc. And he had a fund of anecdotes to enliven their wayside halts, illustrative of all he had witnessed of African nature and aptitudes. "I conclude from the importance he attaches to these, that he is more interested in ethnology than in topographical geography. Though the Nile problem and the central line of drainage are frequently on his lips, they are second to the humanities observed on his wanderings." But when he related the massacre at Nyangwe "there is real passion in his language and an angry glitter in his eyes".

But Livingstone was not always communicative. The impression that clung to Stanley closest was of his "regarding me with eyes so trustful, and face so grave and sad". . . . "There was an earnest gravity in it—a composure settled, calm, and trustful."

> Even my presence was impotent to break him from his habit of abstraction. I might have taken a book to read, and was silent. If I looked up a few minutes later, I discovered him deeply involved in his own meditations, right forefinger bent, timing his thoughts, his eyes gazing far away into indefinite distance, brows puckered closely, face set and resolute, now and then lips moving, silently framing words.
>
> "What can he be thinking about?" I used to wonder, and once I ventured to break the silence with, "A penny for your thoughts, Doctor."
>
> "They are not worth it, my young friend, and let me suggest that, if I had any, possibly I should wish to keep them."
>
> After which I invariably let him alone when in this mood.
>
> Sometimes these thoughts were humorous and, his face wearing a smile, he would impart the reason with some comic story or adventure. I have met few so quickly responsive to gaiety and the lighter moods, none who was more sociable, genial, tolerant, and humorous. You must think of him as a contented soul. . . .[6]

But sometimes Livingstone's cogitations were the reverse of this. Stanley was embarrassed when they dwelt upon old grievances that ought long since to have been buried—against Bedingfeld, Baines, and Bishop Tozer. It does credit to the scruples of the younger man that he did not encourage these reminiscences, but yet they recurred.

Stanley had bought a riding-donkey for Livingstone in order to save his tortured feet, but Livingstone (probably to prevent the severe pains of haemorrhoids) insisted upon walking. On the 27th, when nearing Misonghi, the party was attacked by a swarm of wild bees, "three or four of which", says Stanley, "settled on my face and stung me frightfully. We raced madly for about half a mile, behaving in as wild a manner as the poor be-stung animals." Livingstone fared worse.

> A swarm of bees attacked a donkey Mr. Stanley bought for me, and instead of galloping off, as did the other, the fool of a beast rolled down and over and over. I did the same, then ran, dashed into a bush like an ostrich pursued. They gave me a sore head and face, the donkey was

completely knocked up by the stings and died in two days in consequence. We slept at Misonghi.

But Stanley (as Debenham remarks) tells the whole truth, not only a part of it.

As this was an unusually long march I doubted if the Doctor could march it, because his feet were so sore, so I determined to send four men back with the *kitanda*; but the stout old hero refused to be carried, and walked all the way to camp after a march of eighteen miles. He had been stung dreadfully in the head and in the face; the bees had settled in handfuls in his hair; but, after partaking of a cup of warm tea and some food, he was as cheerful as if he had never travelled a mile.[7]

From the Ngombe Lakes on 7 February, Stanley despatched a bearer to Unyanyembe for the letters and medicines that he expected from Zanzibar. He was himself by this time the victim of recurrent fever: on 4 February Livingstone had noted: "Mr. Stanley so ill that we carried him in a cot . . . for three hours about north-east, and at last found a path which was a great help." Next day: "Mr. Stanley a little better, but still carried." There is no mention of this in Stanley's record; but the day before their arrival at Chikulu he tells a tale against himself with ingenuous candour. His cook Ulimengo had omitted to clean the coffee-pots, which were poisonously dirty.

Being half-mad with huge doses of quinine, and distressingly weak, I sharply scolded him . . . and violently asked him if he meant to poison us. . . .

He turned to me with astounding insolence and sneeringly asked if I was any better than the "big master", and said that what was good for him was good for me—the "little master".

I clouted him at once, not only for his insolent question, but because I recognized a disposition to fight. Ulimengo stood up and laid hold of me. On freeing myself I searched for some handy instrument; but at this juncture Livingstone came out of the tent, and cried out to Ulimengo, "Poli-poli-hapo!" (Gently, gently, there!) "What is the matter, Mr. Stanley?" Almost breathless, between passion and quinine, I spluttered out my explanations. Then, lifting his hand with the curved forefinger, he said, "I will settle this." I stood quieted; but, what with unsatisfied rage and shameful weakness, the tears rolled down as copiously as when a child.

I heard him say, "Now, Ulimengo, you are a big fool, a big thick-headed fellow. I believe you are a very wicked man. Your head is full of lying ideas. Understand me now, and open your ears. . . . Everything in the camp is my friend's. The food I eat, the clothes on my back, the shirt I wear, all are his. . . . He came only to help me, as you would help your brother or your father. I am only the 'big master' because I am older. . . . Try and get all that into that thick skull of yours. Don't you see that he is very ill, you rascal? Now, go and ask his pardon. Go on."

And Ulimengo said he was very sorry, and wanted to kiss my feet, but I would not let him. Then Livingstone took me by the arm to the tent, saying, "Come now, you must not mind him. He is only a half-savage, and does not know any better". . . .

Little by little I softened down, and before night I had shaken hands with Ulimengo. It is the memory of several small events which, though not worth recounting singly, muster in evidence and strike a lasting impression. . . .[8]

"You bad fellow. You very wicked fellow. You blockhead. You fool of a man"—were the strongest terms he employed, where others would have clubbed or clouted, or banned and blasted. His manner was that of a cool, wise old man, who felt offended and looked grave.

The letters and medicines were duly received at Chikulu. The packet contained a letter from Kirk dated 25 September, requesting Stanley to take charge of Livingstone's goods and do his best to forward them; adding some "wild advice" about a route, but the tone of the letter, says the recipient with apparent surprise, was "good-natured and hearty". Livingstone was at first too engrossed with his own letters to pay any heed to this information, but the caustic manner in which it was conveyed must have registered unconsciously. On 18 February, the fifty-third day from Ujiji, Stanley proudly conducted the Doctor arm-in-arm to his old quarters in Unyanyembe, and said, "Doctor, we are at last at Home!"

He again used all his powers of persuasion to try and persuade Livingstone to return with him.

18 *February.*—Mr. Stanley used some very strong arguments in favour of my going home, recruiting my strength, getting artificial teeth, and then returning to finish my task; but my judgment said, "All your friends will wish you to make a complete work of the exploration of the sources of the Nile before you retire." My daughter Agnes says, "Much as I wish you to come home, I would rather that you finished your work to your own satisfaction than return merely to gratify me." Rightly and nobly said, my darling Nannie. Vanity whispers pretty loudly, "She is a chip of the old block."

When Livingstone's stores that had lain there for a year were examined, they were found to contain little of value: the ravages of white ants had accounted for much, and those of

Arab traders for more. But "to his great joy" he found four flannel shirts from Agnes, and two pairs of "fine English boots most considerately sent" by Waller. Stanley's store-room had also been broken into and several of its contents rifled. Even so with consistent generosity he deprived himself of the bulk of his supplies, including some that he might have needed for his own journey to the coast—enough, he says, to equip Livingstone for four years. He remained at Unyanyembe for nearly a month dividing and packing the stores, and organizing all the details for his journey and that of his "illustrious companion"; whilst Livingstone wrote thirty long letters and made up his Journal for transmission to Zanzibar. He also wrote an outline of his proposed route:

> I propose to go from Unyanyembe to Fipa; then round the south end of Tanganyika; then across the Chambesi, and round south of Lake Bangweolo, and due west to the ancient fountains; leaving the underground excavations till after visiting Katanga. This route will serve to certify that no other sources of the Nile can come from the south without being seen by me. No one will cut me out after this exploration is accomplished; and may the good Lord of all help me to show myself one of His stout-hearted servants, an honour to my children, and perhaps to my country and race.

He was proceeding on the assumption that the Lualaba was an arm of the Nile, and the Chambesi, running through the Lake, its remotest tributary. Exploration of the south shore of the Lake would confirm that there was no other inlet. (Fipa was a district west of the south of Tanganyika; but it will be seen that he actually struck the shore of this Lake much higher up in order to complete a survey of its whole western shore.)

During this time Stanley renewed his persuasions that Livingstone should accompany him home, but was always met with the same reply: "I must finish my task". He also took occasion to study his companion's character more closely: "he is a strong man in every way, with an individual tenacity of character". But there was one feature in it which distressed him.

> 3 *March.*—Livingstone reverted again to his charges against the missionaries on the Zambesi and some of his naval officers on the expedition. I have had some intrusive suspicious thoughts that he was not of such an angelic temper as I believed him to be during my first month with him;

but for the last month I have been driving them steadily from my mind.
. . . Livingstone, with all his frankness, does not unfold himself at once;
and what he leaves untold may be just as vital to a righteous understanding of these disputes as what he has said. . . .

When however, he reiterated his complaints against this man and the
other, I felt the faintest fear that his strong nature was opposed to for-
giveness and that he was not so perfect as at the first blush of friendship
I thought him. I grew shy of the recurrent theme, lest I should find my
fear confirmed.[9]

But he goes on to reproach himself with having unwittingly
elicited these animadversions from Livingstone by "pestering
him with questions upon this topic and that"; and concludes
that they count for nothing when contrasted with "his daily
method of life, his pious habits, in the boat, the tent, and the
house". His final appraisal of Livingstone, too long to quote in
full, is even more eulogistic than that made during his first
month with him.

He preached no sermon, by word of mouth, while I was in company
with him; but each day witnessed a sermon acted. The Divine instructions, given of old on the Sacred Mount, were closely followed, whether
he rested in the jungle-camp, or bided in the traders' town, or in the
savage hamlet. Lowly of spirit, meek in speech, merciful of heart, pure in
mind and peaceful in act, suspected by the Arabs to be an informer and
therefore calumniated, often offended at evils committed by his own
servants, but ever forgiving, often robbed and thwarted, yet bearing no
ill-will, cursed by the marauders, yet physicking their infirmities, most
despitefully used, yet praying daily for all manner and condition of men!
Narrow indeed was the way of eternal life that he elected to follow, and
few are those who choose it. . . .

His conversation was serious, his demeanour grave and earnest. Morn
and eve he worshipped and, at the end of every march, he thanked the
Lord for His watchful Providence. On Sundays he conducted Divine
Service and praised the glory of the Creator, the True God, to his dark
followers. . . . Nothing in the scale of humanity can be conceived lower
than the tribes of Manyuema with whom he daily conversed as a friend.
. . . In regions beyond ken of the most learned geographers in Europe,
he imitated the humility of the Founder of his religion, and spoke in
fervent strains of the heavenly message of peace and goodwill. . . .

Had there been anything of the Pharisee or the hypocrite in him, or
had I but traced a grain of meanness or guile in him, I had surely turned
away a sceptic. But my every-day study of him, during health or sickness,
deepened my reverence, and increased my esteem. He was, in short,
consistently noble, upright, pious, and manly, all the days of my companionship with him. . . .[10]

He records too a conversation after Sunday Service on 4

March in which the veteran asked the younger man his opinion as to how missions to the heathen should be best conducted, and found that their views nearly corresponded. Livingstone's own comments, almost a soliloquy, deserve reproduction, especially as revealing his attitude towards his last geographical discoveries in relation to his main purpose and vocation.

I feel sometimes as if I were the beginner for attacking Central Africa, and that others will shortly come; and after those, there will come the thousand workers that you speak of. It is very dark and dreary, but the promise is, "Commit thy way to the Lord, trust in Him, and He shall bring it to pass". I may fall by the way, being unworthy to see the dawning. I thought I had seen it when the Zambesia mission came out, but the darkness has settled again, darker than ever. It will come though, it must come, and I do not despair of the day, one bit. The earth, that is the whole earth, shall be filled with the knowledge of the Lord, as the waters cover the sea.

Loneliness is a terrible thing, especially when I think of my children. I have lost a great deal of happiness, I know, by these wanderings. It is as if I had been born to exile; but it is God's doing, and He will do what seemeth good in His own eyes. But when my children and home are not in my mind, I feel as though appointed to this work and no other. I am away from the perpetual hurry of civilization, and I think I see far and clear into what is to come; and then I seem to understand why I was led away, here and there, and crossed and baffled over and over again, to wear out my years and strength.

Why was it, but to be a witness of the full horror of this slave-trade? . . . My business is to publish what I see, to rouse up those who have power to stop it, once and for all. That is the beginning, but in the end, they will also send proper teachers of the Gospel, some here and some there, and what you think ought to be done will be done in the Lord's good time. . . .[11]

By 13 March the preparations for Stanley's homeward march and for the resumption of Livingstone's eastward were completed. The arrangement was that Stanley, as soon as he reached Zanzibar, should enlist fifty freemen armed with guns and hatchets and loads of ammunition, to act as carriers wherever Livingstone would go. It was their last night together. "My days," wrote Stanley, "seem to have been spent in an Elysian field." One fragment of their conversation which he preserved is worth repeating.

"Tomorrow night, Doctor, you will be alone."

"Yes; the house will look as though a death had taken place. You had better stop until the rains, which are now near, are over."

"I would to God I could, my dear Doctor; but every day I stop here keeps you from your work and home."

"I know; but consider your health; you are not fit to travel. What is it? Only a few weeks longer. You will travel just as quickly when the rains are over as you will by going now. The plains will be inundated between here and the coast."

"You think so; but I will reach the coast in forty days; if not in forty, I will in fifty—certain. The thought that I am doing you an important service will spur me on."[12]

In his published book Stanley says that he noted down all that Livingstone said to him that night; "but the reader shall not share it with me—it is mine!" But in his Autobiography, edited by his wife after his death (and from which much in this' chapter has been taken), the following excerpt from his diary of that night is transcribed:

> I have received the thanks that he had repressed all these months in the secrecy of his heart, uttered with no mincing phrases, but poured out, as it were, at the last moment, until I was so affected that I sobbed, as one only can in uncommon grief. The hour of night and the crisis . . . his sudden outburst of gratitude . . . all had their influence; and, for a time, I was as sensitive as a child of eight or so, and yielded to such bursts of tears as only a scene such as this could have forced.[13]

The next morning: "We had a sad breakfast together. I could not eat, my heart was too full; neither did my companion seem to have an appetite." Stanley suggested leaving two men behind for a day or two in case anything was forgotten, and "I will halt a day at Tura for your last word, your last wish. And now we must part—there is no help for it. Good-bye." But Livingstone said: "Oh, I am coming with you a little way. I must see you off on the road." As they walked together the carriers broke into song. "I took long looks at Livingstone, to impress his features thoroughly on my memory." He elicited from Livingstone an outline of his plans: to strike south round the extremity of Tanganyika; then south-west to Chikumbi's* on the Luapula; cross it and go due west to the copper-mines of Katanga; eight days south of Katanga to the fountains; thence by Katanga to the underground houses of Rua, and

---

* This appears to be a misunderstanding. Livingstone's intention, from which he never wavered, was to go round the south shore of Lake Bangweolo first, and then enter the Luapula for a river-journey north.

ten days on the Lufira north-east in Stanley's collapsible boat to Lake Kamolondo, and on to "Lake Lincoln". Thence north by the Lualaba to the "fourth lake". He calculated eighteen months for the entire journey. Stanley suggested a two years' contract with the men he would enlist, to date from their arrival at Unyanyembe. Livingstone: "Yes, that will do excellently well." Stanley: "Now, my dear Doctor, the best of friends must part. You have come far enough; let me beg of you to turn back." Livingstone: "Well, I will say this to you: you have done what few men could do—far better than some great travellers I know. And I am grateful to you for what you have done for me."[14]

The last farewells were made and repeated; Stanley unable to restrain his emotion, Livingstone calm and steady. The contrast of temperament is reflected in their Journals: Stanley's is dramatic to a degree; Livingstone wrote merely: "Mr. Stanley leaves. I commit to his care my journal sealed with five seals." For him this interlude had been a gleam of light against a sombre background; now he must return into the shadows. But for Stanley it had been the supreme experience of his life, and was to prove the spring-board of his adventurous career. So they parted, these two greatest among African travellers, so incongruously different in character and in their life's purposes—the one to a lonely death in the jungle swamps of Bangweolo, the other to fame, fortune, and the founding of the Congo State.

Chapter Thirty-Two

LAST JOURNEYS: JOURNEY'S END
1872–1873
"I must finish my work."

WOULD that Stanley's parting with Livingstone had ended on that high heroic note! But he had not only found and rescued Livingstone; he had also, as Coupland says, in a sense "appropriated" him and all the credit of befriending him—and this too to the discredit of one of his truest friends, John Kirk.

For a clear understanding of the temporary rift between them it is necessary to revert to some previous correspondence. It will be remembered that Livingstone had written to Kirk from the Lualaba three letters in grateful acknowledgment of his having sent "with immense difficulty" seven Banian slave porters—even though they proved so intractable that in his third letter he said he was on the point of dismissing them. It should be noted that his gratitude was both premature and out of all proportion to the benefit received, and this fact reflects his own natural generosity, good sense, and willingness to make the best of a bad job. But when he arrived back at Ujiji half dead with hunger and illness to find that all his goods had been looted by the two Banian headmen who had remained there in charge of them, having refused to go on to him with their men—he wrote again, this time in justifiable remonstrance. The letter is official and begins formally—"Sir", but its tone, considering the circumstances, is remarkably moderate. In it he recounts in detail the misdeeds of Shereef and Awethe in plundering his goods. This letter must clearly have been written before Stanley's arrival, and the date he gives to it (30 October) must, according to his mistaken reckoning, be two or three days late. For it is followed by an important postscript which is correctly dated 16 November, that is two days after Stanley's arrival. In it he refers to information "just received"

both verbally and by letter of the prolonged delay at Bagamoyo of the second contingent of Banian slaves whom Kirk
had sent, and this "makes the matter doubly serious". The
postscript ends:

> I feel inclined to relinquish the hope of ever getting help from Zanzibar
> to finish the little work I have still to do. . . . I want men not slaves,
> and freemen are abundant in Zanzibar; but if the matter is committed
> to Ludha [the Hindu agent whom he had himself employed] instead of
> an energetic Arab, with some little superintendence by your dragoman
> or others, I may wait twenty years and your slaves feast and fail.[1]

It needed but this factor to confirm his opinion that Kirk
had been dilatory and lethargic. And he wrote to Waller:

> By some strange hallucination our friend Kirk placed some £500 of
> goods in the hands of slaves with a drunken half-caste tailor as leader.
> . . . It is simply infamous to employ slaves when any number of freemen
> may be hired!
> Tell Kirk not to believe every Banian's tale. It makes him a gape
> and not a disciple of David Livingstone.[2]

The latter half of this was added as a postscript from Unyanyembe. And with it there went two other letters to be
delivered by Stanley in Zanzibar. One was that which he had
already written to Kirk from Ujiji.

The other began, "My dear Kirk"—but its tone was very
explicit:

> As I am sending by Mr. Stanley for fifty freemen from Zanzibar to
> enable me to finish my work, I beg you to favour me with your influence
> with the Sultan, that he may give me an able headman to lead them
> quickly here, and continue with me till I have finished what I have still
> to do. . . . His duty, as you very properly told others, is to do what he
> is ordered, and see that those under him do the same, without reference
> to the customs or practices of any other caravan. I wish you to hand over
> to Mr. Henry M. Stanley the sum of £500 out of the money placed in
> your hands for my use by H.M. Government, to be laid out by him, and
> you will receive his receipt as a sufficient acknowledgment from me.
> He knows the kind of men and necessaries I need, and I am sure your
> consular influence will be used to help him to get all I require, and a
> speedy departure of the party inland. If you received two letters written
> hastily on the 28th of October 1871, as soon as I reached Ujiji, one for
> you and the other for Lord Clarendon, you may have been led to employ
> Banian or other slaves again instead of free men. Do not hesitate; please
> at once to discharge them, no matter what expense may have been
> incurred. . . .

There was also an instruction to Stanley dated 14 March:

> I have been subjected to so much loss by the employment of slaves in caravans sent to me by H.M. Consul that, if Mr. Stanley meets another party of the sort, I beg of him to turn them back, but use his discretion in the whole matter.[3]

The tone of asperity is understandable considering the situation in which Livingstone had found himself before Stanley's arrival, and might find himself again after Stanley's departure. The only sting to be detected is in the tail of the postscript: "I may wait twenty years and your slaves feast and fail", and even this, in view of what must have seemed to him sheer negligence on Kirk's part, is pardonable. There is no reason to suppose and no evidence whatever to show that Livingstone was influenced in giving vent to these strictures by Stanley's sour prejudice against Kirk. He was basing them on simple facts, and the main fact was that Stanley had succeeded where Kirk had failed. His need was so great and urgent for men and means to finish his work that he could no longer pay heed to good intentions, or any explanations or excuses for their non-fulfilment; deeds alone must prove their worth. Stanley had not only furnished him with men and means in the interim, he had *brought* them to him—and that in the teeth of every obstacle of cholera, wars, sickness, and floods. He had proved himself the ideal executant. To him therefore the selection, enlistment and despatch of carriers could be more safely entrusted than to Kirk. Let Kirk now act as the authority and leave to Stanley the execution.

But meanwhile, unknown to him, help was coming from another quarter. In December 1871 (Sir Roderick, optimistic to the last about Livingstone's welfare, having died on 22 October) the R.G.S. became alarmed by news that all communication between Ujiji and Unyanyembe was blocked by native wars. By public subscription the Society immediately launched an expedition for his relief, to be led by two naval officers, Lieutenants L. S. Dawson and W. Henn, and a third volunteer—none other than the explorer's youngest son, Oswell.

Reaching Zanzibar on 17 March they were joined by a Methodist minister, the Rev. Charles New, and the four were lodged together by Kirk in the Consulate. With his aid they soon acquired a vast quantity of stores and recruited 20 askari and 6 Nassick boys. The three men then crossed to Bagamoyo to enlist porters, leaving Oswell to follow later. But hardly had they arrived there when they were met by some of Stanley's men, sent in advance with cables for the *Herald*. Whereupon Dawson, satisfied that Livingstone was safe and well and that the objects of the expedition had been "forestalled", returned to Zanzibar and resigned his command. On 7 May Stanley himself arrived.

The difficulties and dangers of his return had been almost as great as those of his outgoing journey, but again he had won through with Livingstone's Journal and letters intact. He made no attempt to dissuade Henn from proceeding but agreed with him that this was now unnecessary. In the event, both Henn and New resigned as the result of a dispute as to which should take command. There remained young Oswell Livingstone, and Stanley's impression of him is interesting.

> A tall, slight, young gentlemanly man, with light complexion, light hair, dark lustrous eyes. . . . There was an air of quiet resolution about him, and in the greeting which he gave me he exhibited rather a reticent character . . . composed, even to a little sternness . . . but with flashing eyes that vivified an otherwise immobile expression.[4]

Of the two, Henn and young Livingstone, he thought "the latter would have been the fittest leader. . . . He seemed able by nature to support the burden of responsibility." And he strongly advised him to take charge of the party which he was himself about to engage and go on and join his father. Oswell said, "Oh, I mean to go." He crossed to Bagamoyo, took charge of Stanley's caravan and began to prepare alone to lead the march. But he was ill with malaria and dysentery; there were reports too of floods and swamps, and this was the height of the rainy season. He returned to Zanzibar to consult Kirk, who wisely forbade the journey, but Stanley still told Oswell that it was his duty to go to his father. Oswell took Kirk's advice and returned to England with Stanley and New. When Livingstone himself heard of his son's projected journey he was much distressed and, though unaware of his illness or of the unusual floods, wrote to the Foreign Office of "the natural anxiety I feel for the safety of my son Oswell coming through the feverish districts between this cold highland and the coast".

But the contents, and still more of the tone, of a letter from his son caused him to put a very different construction on that young man's behaviour. In his Journal for 27 June 1872 he notes: "Received a letter from Oswell yesterday, dated Bagamoyo 14 May, which awakened thankfulness, anxiety, and deep sorrow." The cause for "deep sorrow" is explained in a very private letter to his sister Janet six months later from the south side of Lake Bangweolo. Oswell's declared purpose had been to induce his father to return with him, give him money to complete his education, and recognize his responsibility towards "his forgotten family". But since having heard that the Government was considering the award to his father of a grant of £2,500 and that a further £2,000 might become available from public subscription, he had decided to return to England and attempt to draw the money for this purpose. Livingstone's reception of this intelligence is so mordantly scathing that it is best buried in oblivion.[5]

The Search Expedition thus proved abortive, but Stanley's vituperation of Kirk unfortunately did not. On his return to England he carried out a deliberate campaign of slander against him both in public speeches and in the press. In one of the former he was reported to have said that "he had a mission from Livingstone to describe Kirk as a traitor". Though in a subsequent conversation with Waller he denied this, he did not retract it publicly. He was also reported to have quoted Livingstone as having said: "I don't think he will be Consul any longer after this." Newspapers in England and in India made the most of this unsavoury copy, and Kirk's friends with one accord rallied to his defence. His predecessor Churchill wrote to the *Telegraph*:

> If there has been any neglect at Zanzibar in communicating with Dr. Livingstone, I, as the political agent and Her Majesty's Consul there during the last five years, must share with Dr. Kirk the blame.

He enumerated the caravans which they had despatched at intervals and explained the difficulties that had obstructed their path, and added that since no news had come through from Livingstone for nearly two years and his whereabouts were unknown, it was believed that he was dead. Oswell Livingstone wrote to the same paper confessing his dismay at the "erroneous opinions" which his father had apparently conceived of Kirk during Stanley's stay with him.

> Let me state at once that Dr. Kirk is totally unworthy of the accusations which are daily reaching the public, and can have but one source. I may add that nothing could exceed the kindness that we, the members of the Search Expedition, experienced from him and Mrs. Kirk during the whole time we were in Zanzibar.[6]

But no one was more horrified than Waller, for (as Coupland says), he saw that more than personal considerations were at stake. This calumny would not only wreck Kirk's reputation; it would break up their "triple alliance", it would imperil the fight against the slave-trade. It had been repeated in the *Bombay Gazette* by a vindictive correspondent, an ex-naval officer with a shady record. Waller wrote at once to that paper, rebutting the charges against Kirk and showing that they emanated from one who had much to lose from the suppression of the slave-trade. He also wrote to Livingstone a long and passionate letter of protest which, however, the latter never received, happily indeed, for "if Waller had been aware of Livingstone's disavowal of any intention to censure Kirk, he would of course have been wholly reassured". But Livingstone had fortunately received intelligence from another source of the wounding effects upon Kirk of his letters to him, namely from his son Oswell when in Zanzibar, and he then wrote to the Foreign Office:

> I regret very much to hear incidentally that Dr. Kirk viewed my formal complaint against Banians as a covert attack upon himself. If I had foreseen this, I should certainly have borne my losses in silence. I never had any difference with him, though we were together for years, and I had no intention to give offence now. But the public interest taken in this expedition enforces publicity as to the obstacles that prevented its work being accomplished long ago.[7]

And to Kirk himself:

> My dear Kirk, I am sorry to hear by a note from Oswell that you had taken my formal complaint against certain Banians and Arabs as a covert attack upon yourself; this grieves me deeply, for it is a result I never intended to produce. . . . It looked to me as if a band of dishonest persons had conspired to hoodwink you and me.[8]

The letter continues to tell in a friendly spirit of his plans for the future and final return to the coast. But he never lived to know the repercussions of Stanley's slanderous onslaughts against Kirk in England. These were such as to cause perturbation in the Foreign Office. A slur had been cast on the character of a well-known member of its diplomatic staff, and the whole matter must be fully investigated. The man entrusted with this task was Sir Bartle Frere. In due course, after a very thorough examination of all the official and unofficial documents, he submitted his report. In it he made the following points:

1. Dr. Livingstone's complaints were well founded. The things sent to him by Dr. Kirk did not reach him; those taken by Mr. Stanley did.

2. It was possible, but not certain, that this was due to the different types of porters employed. Dr. Kirk's agency was the largest and most influential Hindu house in Zanzibar, which was always employed by the English Consulate for such work and was usually most successful. Mr. Stanley's was a newer house employed by the American Consulate. In any case Mr. Stanley's own convoy would have failed to reach Ujiji but for his presence with it and the extraordinary energy with which he pressed it forward.

3. Dr. Kirk was in no way to blame for the delays of his convoys. He had done what anyone on the spot, *not judging after the event*, would have said was for the best. A public officer who, I can affirm from personal observation, is conspicuous for the careful, conscientious, laborious and most efficient discharge of every duty connected with the important offices he holds, is not likely to have failed in what to him was a labour of love and a duty of long and uninterrupted friendship; and I cannot conclude this memorandum without expressing my conviction that Dr. Livingstone never had a truer or warmer friend than Dr. Kirk; and in saying this I confidently believe that I am only saying what Dr. Livingstone himself would say, if he were here to give us his deliberate testimony.[9]

The above summary of this unpleasant episode is drawn partly from a series of letters printed without comment as an Appendix to Stanley's book, the insertion of which is tantamount to a somewhat ungracious withdrawal of his accusations, and partly from several long sections in Coupland's book, *Livingstone's Last Journey*, which was written with the main purpose of completely exonerating Kirk. The author writes as an advocate rather than as a judge, and though his vindication may be deemed somewhat too emphatic in certain respects, it is nevertheless successful in the main.

The R.G.S., still unsatisfied as to the welfare of the great explorer, now organized two other expeditions in search of him. Assuming that he had discovered the source of the Congo and not of the Nile and would probably follow its course to the sea, they sent the first—financed by James Young with the munificent gift of £2,000, and led by Lieutenant W. J. Granby, R.N.—to Loanda. He reached that port in January 1873, but it was not till October that he succeeded after great difficulties in striking the Congo near Lukangu, where he was delayed for six months. Then came news of Livingstone's death and soon afterwards the order of recall.

The second attempt was a revival of the Search Expedition of the previous year, and Lieutenant V. L. Cameron, R.N., was chosen to lead it. He reached Zanzibar in January 1873 and was joined by two other officers and a volunteer—none other than Livingstone's nephew, Robert Moffat, who had sold his sugar plantation in Natal in the hope of being accepted. The party, after several weeks' delay in securing porters, left Bagamoyo for Unyanyembe at the end of March. All four were repeatedly fever-stricken and at the end of May Moffat had died. The survivors struggled on and reached Unyanyembe in August. Here they were again held up for several weeks, not only for lack of porters but also because of prostration from malaria, which was causing two of them partial blindness. When a note was brought to Cameron on 20 October he could not read it, so sent for the bearer. The bearer was Chuma. He said that his master was dead, and that he and his companions were carrying his body to the coast.[10]

Meanwhile Livingstone, ignorant alike of the deplorable controversy raging between his friends at home and of the gallant sacrifices that were being made for his relief, was waiting "wearily, wearily!" for the arrival of the caravan from Zanzibar. The fifth day after Stanley's departure was his birthday and he commemorates it in his Journal with this single heart-cry:

19 *March.*—Birthday. My Jesus, my King, my Life, my All; I again dedicate my whole self to Thee. Accept me and grant, O Gracious Father, that ere this year is gone I may finish my task. In Jesus' name I ask it. Amen, so let it be. David Livingstone.

As the weeks went by his loneliness deepened. The torrential rains, which were drenching Stanley homeward-bound, fell round him in his *tembe* day and night, and accentuated his sense of isolation. He read books: Baker's *Albert Nyanza*— "artistic and clever"; Mungo Park's *Travels*—"they look so truthful"; and E. D. Young's *Search after Livingstone* (of 1867) which had just reached him—"thankful for many kind words about me; he writes like a gentleman". And he contrives to be busy: he makes a sounding-line out of lint and tars the tent left by Stanley, and makes cheeses; converts fresh-ground rice into flour; puzzles over the nomenclature in Ptolemy's geography, and finds the derivation of native name-places; visits the Arabs to keep in touch with the latest local news and records it, and doctors them when sick; a chill from bathing gives him a touch of fever and prompts him to buy milch cows and calves; discusses sympathetically but critically some aspects of primitive belief, such as that of survival; describes in detail how a cat kills a snake, and the spawning of trout; prepares a map of Lake Tanganyika for Maclear (which is reproduced by Debenham)—and much else.

Though the accomplishment of the task to which he looked forward as his ultimate goal was always his central thought, it grew in his mind as the symbol of a greater achievement. As in his early days he had regarded "the geographical feat" as no more than "the beginning of the missionary enterprise", so now, his discovery of the Nile sources was not to be an end in itself but the means towards the abolition of the slave-trade, without which the missionary enterprise itself could not begin. He had written to Maclear only a few days ago, and Stanley had taken the letter: "If indeed my disclosures should lead to the suppression of the East Coast slave-trade, I should esteem that as a far greater feat than the discovery of all the sources together." And in his Journal:

> To overdraw its evils is a simple impossibility. The sights I have seen, though common incidents of the traffic, are so nauseous that I always strive to drive them from memory. . . . The slaving scenes come back unbidden, and make me start up at dead of night, horrified by their vividness.

On 1 May he notes: "Finished a letter for the *New York Herald*, trying to enlist American zeal to stop the East Coast slave-trade. I pray for a blessing on it from the All-Gracious."

That prayer was answered, for the immortal words with which this letter concludes are those engraved above his tomb in Westminster Abbey:

All I can say in my solitude is, may Heaven's rich blessing come down on every one—American, English, Turk—who will help to heal this Open Sore of the World.

It was noticed, some time after these words were chosen for his most fitting memorial, that they were written exactly one year before his death.

On 13 May he committed to his Journal the words:

He will keep His word, the gracious One full of grace and truth—no doubt of it. He said, *He that cometh unto Me I will in no wise cast out, and Whatsoever ye shall ask in my name I will do it.* He WILL keep his word; then I can come and humbly present my petition, and it will be all right. Doubt here is inadmissible, surely. D.L.

But coincidently with his yearning to fulfil the *end* of his life's purpose there grows in him also a haunting doubt as to the *means*. The caution of the trained scientist forbids absolute certainty that the four fountains beyond Katanga are really the sources of the Nile; his dream may yet prove to be a delusion.

21 *May.*—I wish I had some of the assurance possessed by others, but I am oppressed with the apprehension that after all it may turn out that I have been following the Congo; and who would risk being put into a cannibal pot, and converted into black man for it?

31 *May.*—In reference to this Nile source I have been kept in perpetual doubt and perplexity. I know too much to be positive.

24 *June.*—The medical education has led me to a continual tendency to suspend the judgment. . . . I am even now not at all "cocksure" that I have not been following down what may after all be the Congo.

Though this period of waiting was pain and weariness to him, his Journal contains some of the most moving and memorable passages he ever wrote. The following, for example, is instinct with the ardour of his earlier days, but gains force from the gathered experience of his maturity.

I would say to missionaries, Come on, brethren, to the real heathen. You have no idea how brave you are till you try. Leaving the coast tribes and devoting yourselves heartily to the savages, as they are called, you will find, with some drawbacks and wickedness, a very great deal to admire and love. Many statements made about them require confirmation. You will never see women selling their infants; the Arabs never did, nor have I.

—And also some of the most charming. He is fascinated by the behaviour of the wagtail, the bird as common in native villages as is the sparrow in our farmyards and the one which (as the present writer has observed) is never molested.

A wagtail dam refused its young a caterpillar till it had been killed—she ran away from it, but then gave it when ready to be swallowed. The first smile of an infant with its toothless gums is one of the pleasantest sights in nature. It is innocence claiming kinship, and asking to be loved in its helplessness.
. . . The wagtail has shaken her young quite off, and has a new nest. She warbles prettily, very much like a canary, and is extremely active in catching flies, but eats crumbs of bread-and-milk too.
Sun-birds visit the pomegranate flowers and eat insects therein, too, as well as nectar.

But most of all it is the nesting of the whydah bird that enchants him.

A family of ten whydah birds (*Vidua purpurea*) come to the pomegranate trees in our yard. The eight young ones, full-fledged, are fed by the dam as young pigeons are. The food is brought up from the crop without the bowing and bending of the pigeon. They chirrup briskly for food; the dam gives most, while the redbreasted cock gives one or two, and then knocks the rest away. . . .
Another pair of the kind had ten chickens, also builds afresh. The red cock-bird feeds all the brood. Each little one puts his head on one side as he inserts his bill, chirruping briskly, and bothering him. The young ones lift up a feather as a child would a doll, and invite others to do the same, in play. So, too, with another pair. The cock skips from side to side with a feather in his bill, and the hen is pleased. Nature is full of enjoyment. . . .
Cock Whydah bird died in the night. The brood came and chirruped to it for food, and tried to make it feed them as if not knowing death! . . .
Whydahs, though full-fledged, still gladly take a feed from their dam, putting down the breast to the ground and cocking up the bill and chirruping in the most engaging manner and winning way they know. She still gives them a little, but administers a friendly shove-off too. They all pick up feathers or grass, and hop from side to side of their mates as if saying, "Come, let us play at making little houses". . . . The young crouch closely together at night for heat. They look like a woolly ball on a branch. By day they engage in pairing and coaxing each other. They come to the same twig every night. Like children they try and lift heavy weights of feathers above their strength.

—And also some of the most vividly descriptive. He loved to watch the women—three at a time—pounding unhusked rice with heavy pestles in a huge wooden mortar. To how many who have often watched the same scene will his words evoke an instant memory of it, but to how few will it have occurred to depict it so minutely!

> Each jerks up her body as she lifts the pestle and strikes it into the mortar with all her might, lightening the labour with some wild ditty the while, though one hears by the strained voice that she is nearly out of breath. When the husks are pretty well loosened, the grain is put into a large, plate-shaped basket and tossed so as to bring the chaff to one side; the vessel is then heaved downwards and a little horizontal motion given to it which throws the refuse out; the partially cleared grain is now returned to the mortar, again pounded and cleared of husks, and a semicircular toss of the vessel sends all the remaining unhusked grain to one side, which is lifted out by the hand, leaving the chief part quite clean: they certainly work hard and well.
>
> The maize requires more labour by far: it is first pounded to remove the outer scales from the grain, then steeped for three days in water, then pounded, the scales again separated by the shallow-basket tossings, then pounded fine, and the fine white flour separated by the basket from certain hard rounded particles, which are cooked as a sort of granular porridge—*mytelle*.

The same observant and approving eye takes note of the behaviour of children who were always for him, white or black, a special object of attraction.

> In many parts one is struck by the fact of the children having so few games. Life is a serious business, and amusement is derived from imitating the vocations of the parents—hut-building, making little gardens, bows and arrows, shields and spears. Elsewhere boys are very ingenious little fellows, and have several games; they also shoot birds with bows, and teach captured linnets to sing. They are expert in making guns and traps for small birds, and in making and using bird-lime. They make play-guns of reed, which go off with a trigger and spring, with a cloud of ashes for smoke. Sometimes they make double-barrelled guns of clay, and have cotton-fluff as smoke. The boys shoot locusts with small toy-guns very cleverly.

Early in August he notes the first appearance of swallows, and then describes with extraordinary minuteness the method by which sun-birds pick out the young spiders from their webs.

Abrupt transitions from one theme to another are frequent in Livingstone's Journal; but suddenly at this point (5 August) occurs an interpolation so unexpected that his editor, Waller, enclosed it within asterisks:

What is the atonement of Christ? It is Himself; it is the inherent and everlasting mercy of God made apparent to human eyes and ears. The everlasting love was disclosed by our Lord's life and death. It showed that God forgives, because He loves to forgive. He works by smiles if possible, if not by frowns; pain is only a means of enforcing love.

Here he lifts the cardinal tenet of the Christian faith from the incomprehensibility of a doctrinal formula to the certitude of personal relationship, and shows that this faith is not conceptual but experiential and is based, not on the shifting sands of theological speculation, but on the rock of conscious experience. The only one of his biographers previously to comment upon it was Campbell, himself a theologian, who said that "the man capable of writing these words and believing them must rank with the foremost of spiritual seers", and that they are the more remarkable since the evangelicalism to which Livingstone owed his religious training was not in the habit of thus expressing itself at that period.[11]

He was also writing in graphic detail of hippopotamus hunting on the Zambesi—"the bravest thing I ever saw"; of the feasibility of mission-work anywhere within a hundred miles of the East Coast and the best means of conducting it; of the Moslem faith—good and bad; of evidences of ancient primitive civilization in Africa; and quite a treatise on geological epochs in the southern half of the continent.

These literary excursions were a source of recreation at intervals in the tedium of long weeks of suspense. On 1 June he begins to count the days and calculates that 15 July should be the latest date for the arrival of the caravan; (Stanley should be near Malta on 14 June. On 22nd he would be 100 days gone; "he must be in London now".) On 13 June a runner arrives hot-foot and reports that the caravan is already at Ugogo, half-way from the coast; so it will arrive "before the end of this (sic) month. . . . I do most fervently thank the good Lord of all for His kindness to me through these gentlemen" (Stanley and the American Consul). But when June passes into July his impatience increases. On 3 July come letters and with them the news of Sir Roderick's death.

. . . The best friend I ever had—true, warm, and abiding—he loved me more than I deserved; he looks down on me still. I must feel resigned to the loss by the Divine Will, but still I regret and mourn.

Wearisome waiting this; and yet the men cannot be here before the middle or end of this month. I have been sore let and hindered in this journey, but it may have been all for the best. I will trust in Him to whom I commit my way.

5*th.*—Weary! weary!

7*th.*—Waiting wearily here, and hoping that the good and loving Father of all may favour me, and help me to finish my work quickly and well.

July draws to its end: "Weary waiting this, and the best time for travelling passes over unused." But next day he has news that an Arab caravan is twelve days off, and that his own had gone by another route. "Thankful for even this in my wearisome waiting." On 4 August: "Wearisome waiting"— the sun is now "rainy at midday" and the heat increasing— "but this delay may be all for the best". On the 6th: "I can think of nothing but 'when will these men come'." Then at last on the 9th three men appeared in advance of the main body.

I do most devoutly thank the Lord for His goodness in bringing my men near to this. Three came today, and how thankful I am I cannot express. It is well—the men who went with Mr. Stanley came again to me. "Bless the Lord, O my soul, and all that is within me bless His holy name." Amen.

15*th.*—The men came yesterday (14th) having been seventy-four days from Bagamoyo. Most thankful to the Giver of all good I am. I have to give them a rest of a few days, and then start.

On the same day he wrote to Agnes:

No one can estimate the amount of God-pleasing good that will be done, if by Divine favour this awful slave-trade, into the midst of which I have come, be abolished. This will be something to have lived for, and the conviction has grown in my mind that it was *for this end* I have been detained so long.

It is certain that no other caravan, unled by a European or an Arab, would of its own volition have made such a journey or with such despatch. It was propelled by the dynamic of Stanley's personality from behind, and attracted by the magnetism of Livingstone's in front. The one had given them the spur, the other would give them rein. The party numbered fifty-seven, among them some of Stanley's old followers, and the new recruits included a few Nassick boys who had been enlisted from Bombay for the abortive Search Expedition. Among these were two brothers, John and Jacob Wainwright, the latter well above his fellows in education. To them were added Livingstone's own last five "faithfuls"—Susi, Chuma (now married), Amoda (and his wife Halimah), Mabruki, and Gardner.

Ten days were spent in weighing and packing the loads and on the 25th they were off. The Nassick boys were in charge of the cattle—ten kine, some goats, and two donkeys—and on the second day they lost the best milch cow. On the third they lost them all, but these were recovered except one. The "Nassickers" were punished: "Susi gave them ten cuts with a switch". On 2 September two carriers made off with twenty-four lengths of calico, and a day was lost in fruitless pursuit of them. The heat was now intense and many of the men tired and sick; the caravan was rested "as we shall have to make forced marches on account of the tsetse fly". But now Livingstone's old enemy was upon him. On 18th at Merera's they halted to prepare food, and next day: "Ditto, ditto, because I am ill with bowels, having eaten nothing for eight days". They went on to Simba's, but on 21st: "Rest here, as the complaint does not yield to medicine or time." He observes a kite in a lofty tree and examines its nest and eggs. After two days he went on, and on 24th can report: "Recovering and thankful, but weak", and next day, "I am getting better slowly". Two days later: "Am getting well again, thanks". The heat intensified on lower ground as they approached Tanganyika.

From Tumbulu they struck southward on 3 October over a range of hills. Sheer exhaustion now forced him to mount a donkey, but he dismounted to save it up and down the steep hills, "very sore on legs and lungs". Once scenting water it bolted with him; "The saddle was loose but I stuck on". On 8 October they sighted Tanganyika far away below them, but were obliged to rest "because all are tired, and several sick. ... Inwardly I feel tired too." On the 14th they reached Mokaria, fifty feet above the Lake: "at sunset the red glare on the surface made the water look like a sea of reddish gold".

By this time Livingstone must have known that his dysentery was chronic, but the idea of yielding to it or of admitting it even to himself seems never (as Coupland remarks) to have

611

crossed his mind. They killed an ox at Mokaria and rested for a day: "I am right glad of the rest, but keep on as constantly as I can." The villagers burned their camp when they started, and next day "two lions growled savagely as we passed". On 1 November the early rains fell during intervals of scorching heat. The going was easier as they progressed towards the foot of the Lake, but food harder to obtain. On the 9th: "Men sent off to search for a village return empty-handed, and we must halt. I am ill and losing much blood." He sent off others to try elsewhere, and yet others to find a path away from the mountain villagers, "for they will kill us all". While waiting he writes a note on the flocks of swifts and migratory swallows over the Lake, and the early budding of the flowers and trees before the rains.

> Though this is the hottest time of the year and all the plants are burnt off or quite dried, the flowers persist in bursting out of the hot dry surface, generally without leaves. A purple ginger, with two yellow patches inside, is very lovely to behold, and it is alternated by one of a bright canary yellow; many trees, too, put on their blossoms.
>
> The sun makes the soil so hot that the radiation is as if it came from a furnace. It burns the feet of the people, and knocks them up. Subcutaneous inflammation is frequent in the legs, and makes some of my most hardy men useless. We have been compelled to slowness very much against my will. I too was ill, and became better only by marching on foot.

Then comes this note:

> The spirit of missions is the spirit of our Master, the very genius of His religion. A diffusive philanthropy is Christianity itself. It requires perpetual propagation to attest its genuineness.

On the 8th his large riding-donkey became ill, but next day "began to eat, to my great joy". On the 10th "the donkey is recovering". His Journal entry of this day begins: "Out from the Lake Mountains, and along high ridges of sandstone and dolomite." The lake-shore valleys had become too formidable for transport. Here Professor Debenham has an interesting comment:

> For this reason they crossed the Kalambo river some 1,500 feet above the lake and some miles upstream of the falls. It seems a needless shaft of ill fortune that caused him to miss so narrowly the discovery of the highest falls in Africa, having already discovered the broadest.[12]

On the 16th the donkey died, "evidently from tsetse and bad usage; it is a great loss to me". The villagers had been on the whole unfriendly, but on the 19th having skirted the foot of the Lake they reached Kampamba's: "he is still as agreeable as he was before, when he went with us to Liemba".

Livingstone was now striking south along the track he had followed upwards from the Chambesi early in 1867 during the dry season; now the rains were beginning, but he had taught himself long since to defy the elements. He lightened the loads of his carriers, "which pleased them much". And he gave to all except defaulters presents of calico and beads, but only half to the "two Nassickers" who had lost the cows. Kasonso's successor gave him a sheep—"a welcome present, for I was out of flesh four days". He reached the river Lofu on 28 November to find it spanned by a single rotten pole and guarded by a man who demanded a fee. To this he agreed if the man re-made the bridge; if not, and he did so himself, then the toll-man should give him a goat. "He slunk away, and we laid large trees across." Equally characteristic of his attitude to native recalcitrance was his reaction next day when the chief Chiwe (Chibwe) presented a small goat with crooked legs and some millet flour, but grumbled at the exchange token of a fathom of cloth. "I offered another fathom and a bundle of needles, but he grumbled at this too and sent it back. On this I returned his goat and marched."

But he marched, crossing his old track, west towards the Lualaba instead of south to the Chambesi. In his Journal for 3 December he says: "A stupid or perverse guide took us away today N.W. or W.N.W. . . . 'If you go S.W. you will be five days without food or people'. We crossed the Kangomba, fifteen yards wide and knee deep. Here our guide disappeared, and so did the path." Nevertheless he continued to march west. In a letter to Maclear from Lake Bangweolo later he explains this.

> I was at the mercy of guides who did not know their own country, and when I insisted on following the compass they threatened, "no food for five or ten days in that line". They brought us down to the back or north side of Bangweolo, while I wanted to cross the Chambesi and go round its southern side. So back again south-eastwards we had to bend.[13]

Debenham however points out that the guides were probably

right, for a S.W. course would have led him into an area which even now is sparsely populated and rather densely forested.

Two days before this he had crossed a rivulet where was a nutmeg-tree in full bearing, a wild species similar to that found in Angola. The naturalist's curiosity was excited. In two places he says: "Who planted the nutmeg-tree on the Katanta?"

His westward journey was without incident save for heavy rain and sometimes shortage of food. "Always too cloudy and rainy for observations of stars." "No food for either love or money." But his men were not above making free with anything they could get if they could get it with a little bluff.

> The pugnacious spirit is one of the necessities of life. When people have little or none of it they are subjected to indignity and loss. My own men walk into houses and steal cassava without shame. I have to threaten and thrash to keep them honest, while, if we are at a village where the natives are a little pugnacious they are as meek as sucking doves. The peace plan involves indignity and wrong.

But he was better served by these men than he had ever been since his first great journey. To Maclear he wrote that "they have behaved as well as Makololo. I cannot award them higher praise, though they have not the courage of that brave, kind-hearted people." And to Stanley, when nearing the end: "I am perpetually reminded that I owe a great deal to you for the men you sent. With one exception the party is working like a machine. I give my orders to Manwa Sera, and never have to repeat them."

It was at this time that he wrote to his brother John in Canada a letter which is remarkable not only for the significance of its contents, but also because it is addressed to a member of his family whom he had not seen for more than thirty years. In it he makes clear that his last geographical achievement is to be merely the instrument of a nobler purpose, his personal renown no more than a lever to set it in motion and bring it to pass. As in his younger days he had acknowledged that motives, even the best of them, are mixed—the altruistic with the ambitious, so now: the means could only be justified by the end.

> If the good Lord permits me to put a stop to the enormous evils of the inland slave-trade, I shall not grudge my hunger and toils. I shall bless

His name with all my heart. The Nile sources are valuable to me only as a means of enabling me to open my mouth with power among men. It is this power I hope to apply to remedy an enormous evil, and join my poor little helping hand in the enormous revolution that in His all-embracing Providence He has been carrying on for ages, and is now actually helping forward. Men may think I covet fame, but I make it a rule never to read aught written in my praise.[14]

That he himself was ailing is apparent, not from anything he says, but from his handwriting. Of his Journal entry for 13 December Waller comments that "scarce one pencilled word tallies with its neighbour in form or distinctness", but that "with the same painstaking determination as of old" the names of the three rivers crossed that day, hours of marching and direction, are all entered in his note-book. On the 18th he reached the Kolongosi at a point higher upstream than he had previously touched, but: "so cloudy and wet that no observations for latitude and longitude can be taken at this real geographical point. . . . We crossed it in very small canoes, and swamped one twice, but no one was lost."—"A wet bed last night, for it was in a canoe that was upset. It was so rainy that there was no drying it." For a month past he had been constantly drenched in rain and drizzle and flooded streams. He turned south from the Kolongosi and on Christmas Day was across the Mopoposi.

I thank the good Lord for the good gift of His Son Jesus Christ our Lord. Slaughtered an ox and gave a fundo and a half to each of the party. This is our great day, so we rest. It is cold and wet, day and night. The headman is gracious and generous. . . .

There follows a scientific note on the White and Blue Nile.

The weather became still wetter and colder, and one of his men died after being carried some distance: "he was a quiet good man". On "29th or 1st January" he notes: "I am wrong two days", but rectifies the date two days later. His customary prayer for New Year's Day 1873 is omitted. On the 3rd "our last cow died of injuries received in crossing the Lofubu. People buy it for food, so it is not an entire loss." But it was only milk that could keep him alive and a supply of goats was now more than ever a necessity.

Once over the ridge of the Urungu hills they were plunging ever deeper into the wide waterlogged fringe that surrounds the shallow basin of the Lake proper, where the soggy sticky "sponges" were pocked with hidden pot-holes of some wandering elephant's feet and intersected by the swirl of a current that alone betrayed a river's course. As Waller says, "had Dr. Livingstone been at the head of a hundred picked Europeans, every man would have been down within a fortnight", and his native followers "must have been under the most thorough control to endure these marches at all, for nothing cows the African so much as rain". Only his engrained sense of duty which was as habitual with him as most men's habits are; only his native obstinacy which had the strength of an obsession, and his rugged determination "not to be beat"—drove him and them along. His Journal is mainly descriptive of the behaviour of the people in whose villages they camped, and only interspersed with records of the weather.

> 6 *January*.—My men broke into a chorus as they were pitching my tent. Cold, cloudy, and drizzling.
> *7th*.—A cold, rainy day keeps us in a poor village very unwillingly.
> *8th*.—Got off in the afternoon in a drizzle. . . . A sluggish rivulet 100 yards broad with broad sponges on either bank waist-deep, and many leeches.
> *9th*.—[Many rills and deep sponges.]
> *11th*.—Cold and rainy weather, never saw the like.
> *13th*.—Storm-stayed by rain and cold. . . . Never was such a spell of cold rainy weather except on going to Loanda in 1853.

Then on the next day, in the midst of all this misery, after praising the skill and industry of the villagers in cultivating their crops, comes the following note:

> There are many flowers in the forest: marigolds, a white jonquil-looking flower without smell, many orchids, white, yellow, and pink asclepias, with bunches of French-white flowers, clematis—*methonica gloriosa*, gladiolus, and blue and deep purple polygalas, grasses with white starry seed-vessels, and spikelets of brownish red and yellow. Besides these are beautiful blue flowering bulbs, and new flowers of pretty delicate form and but little scent. To this list may be added balsams, compositae of blood-red colour and of purple; other flowers of liver colour; bright canary yellow, pink orchids on spikes thickly covered all round, and of three inches in length; spiderworts of fine blue or yellow or even pink. Different coloured asclepedials, beautiful yellow and red umbelliferous flowering plants, dill and wild parsnips, pretty flowery aloes, yellow and red, in one whorl of blossoms, peas, and many other flowering plants which I do not know.

The words, occurring in such a context, set like gems in the drabbest frame, are such as to cause the reader to catch his breath.

Troubles thickened as they went on. Guides went astray, detours were made, canoes were difficult to get, villagers fled from them in terror.

> 17*th*.—By waiting patiently yesterday we drew about twenty canoes towards us this morning, but all too small for the donkey, so we had to turn away back north-west to the bridge over Chungu's. If we had tried to swim the donkey across alongside a canoe it would have been terribly strained. . . .
>
> 18*th*.—We lost a week by going to Chungu (a worthless, terrified headman). . . .
>
> 19*th*.—Some 400 yards of most fatiguing, plunging, deep sponge. . . . Many leeches plagued us.
>
> 20*th*.—Tried to observe lunars in vain; clouded all over, thick and muggy. Came on disappointed. . . .

He was now too enfeebled to splash through these sponges, and from time to time had to be carried pick-a-back. Unable to take observations he had lost sense of direction.

> 23*rd*.—I don't know where we are, and the people are deceitful in their statements; unaccountably so, though we deal fairly and kindly. Rain, rain, rain, as if it never tired on this watershed. . . .Must plod on without guides.
>
> 24*th*.—Was neck-deep for fifty yards and the water cold. We plunged in elephants' footprints 1½ hours. . . . Carrying me across the broad sedgy rivers is really a very difficult task. . . . The main stream came up to Susi's mouth, and wetted my seat and legs. . . . Each time I was lifted off bodily and put on another pair of stout willing shoulders, and fifty yards put them out of breath: no wonder! . . . The water was cold, and so was the wind. . . . The Lake is near, but we are not sure of provisions. Our progress is distressingly slow. Wet, wet, wet; sloppy weather truly, and no observations. . . .
>
> 25*th*.—Kept in by rain.
>
> 26*th*.—The women are collecting mushrooms. . . . The sick people compelled us to make an early halt.
>
> 27*th*.—On again through streams, over sponges and rivulets thigh-deep. . . . I lose much blood, but it is a safety-valve for me, and I have no fever or other ailments.
>
> 28*th*.—A dreary wet morning, and no food we know of near. It is drop, drop, drop, and drizzling from the north-east. We killed our last calf but one last night, to give each a mouthful. . . .
>
> 29*th*.—No rain in the night, for a wonder. . . . The music of the singing-birds, the music of the turtle-doves, the screaming of the frankolin proclaim man to be near.

30th.—Remain waiting for the scouts. . . . Wet evening.

1 *February.*—Waiting for scouts. They return unsuccessful—forced to do so by hunger. . . . Killed our last calf and turn back for four days' hard travel to Chitunkwe's.

2nd.—March smartly back to our camp of 28th ult. . . .

3rd.—Return march to our bridge on the Lofu. . . .

4th.—Camp among deserted gardens. . . . Welcome supply of cassava and sweet potatoes.

5th.—Arrived at Chitunkwe's . . . more civil than we expected . . . he would give us guides. . . . We returned over these forty-one miles in 15 hours. . . . We have lost a month by this wandering.

8th.—The chief dawdles, although he promised great things yesterday. He places the blame on his people. . . . The guides came at last.

9th.—Slept in a most unwholesome ruined village. Rank vegetation had run over all and the soil smelled offensively.

10th.—Back again to our old camp on the Lofu . . . all wetted, but we have food.

11th.—A drizzly night was followed by a morning of cold wet fog, but in three hours we reached our old camp on the Lofu.

The circuitous route from Chunga's and back is shown roughly on the map. A most valuable commentary upon it is provided by Debenham who traversed this region in the dry season of 1953, and who with the authority of a specialist explains in great detail the causes that led Livingstone into this disastrous maze. He was misled partly by the original error in his longitudes and the impossibility of rectifying them in the rains into the belief that he was much nearer the Chambesi than he was, partly by the silvering of the reflector in his sextant, and partly by a local confusion in native names (Lovu and Lufupu). In spite of his ignorance of his true position, however, Debenham shows that his mapping by compass-bearings of his route is as accurate as ever.[15]

On 13 February "we came within sight of the Luena (estuary) and Lake", but Debenham says this cannot have been the open water, from which he must have still been some six miles distant. From there he sent Susi and another man "to the first villages of Matipa for large canoes to navigate the Lake, or give us a guide to go east to the Chambesi, to go round on foot". He adds: "I remain because of an excessive haemorrhagic discharge."

> If the good Lord gives me favour and permits me to finish my work, I shall thank and bless Him, though it has cost me untold toil, pain, and travail; this trip has made my hair all grey.

Two days later the messengers returned with the news that "Matipa is on Chirube islet . . . but far off from this". Debenham has explained elsewhere in great detail Livingstone's mistake in the position of this islet and indeed of the whole contour of the Lake. It is, he says, the sorriest trick that fortune ever played on the great geographer. He illustrates it by superimposing a modern map upon Livingstone's which shows that "Matipa's island is *not* at the eastern end of the swamps, but only four miles from Chilubi Island and near the western end"—in fact, "just round the corner" from where Livingstone then was.[16] It is little wonder therefore that the messengers took a fortnight to find Matipa and return to camp. During their absence Livingstone, as if he had not enough discomforts to endure, was attacked at midnight by an army of red ants.

> I lighted a candle . . . and lay still. The first came on my foot quietly, then some began to bite between the toes, then the larger ones swarmed over the foot and bit furiously, and made the blood start out. I then went out of the tent, and my whole person was instantly covered as close as small-pox (not confluent) on a patient. Grass fires were lighted, and my men picked some off my limbs and tried to save me. After battling for an hour or two they took me into a hut not yet invaded, and I rested till they came and routed me out there too! Then came a steady pour of rain, as if trying to make us miserable. At 9 a.m. I got back into my tent.

It was scarcely an occasion, as Coupland observes, for scientific observation; yet Livingstone recorded minutely their order of battle and the way in which they insert their sharp mandibles curved like sickles into the skin, using their six legs as a lever to push them home. "Their appearance sets every cockroach in a flurry, and all ants, white and black, get into a panic."—"They took all my fat," he adds simply.

It must have been during this enforced delay that he wrote or continued the writing of his last letters. It is clear that he had no presentiment of death, but was looking forward to the completion of his task. Soon the rainy season would be over; the south shore of Bangweolo would be the limit of his southern journey and he was now nearly there; then he would be waterborne down the Luapula; only "eight days" overland thence south of Katanga to the fountains of the western arm; then back to the Lualaba and down it to the central lakes; then home. In imagination he saw himself almost within sight of his goal.

[To James Young.] *Opere peracto ludemus*—the work being finished we will play—you remember in your Latin rudiments lang syne. It is true for you and I rejoice to think it is now your portion, after working nobly, to play. May you have a long spell of it! I am differently situated; I shall never be able to play. [He quotes Proverbs 24: 11.] . . . Though hard work is still to be my lot, I look genially on others more favoured . . . I love to see and think of others enjoying life.

During a large part of this journey I had a strong presentiment that I should never live to finish it. It is weakened now, as I seem to see the end to which I have been striving looming in the distance. This presentiment did not interfere with the performance of any duty; it only made me think a great deal more about the future state of being.[17]

[To Waller.] I hope you will yet be a missionary bishop of Bembatouk Bay or elsewhere, and I shall give you *osculum pacis* with a smack that will make the rafters ring, and girls all giggle, and Mrs. Waller jealous. . . .

Will you speak to a dentist about a speedy fitting of artificial teeth? And will you secure some lodgings—say, anywhere near Regent's Park; comfortable and decent, but not excessively dear? Agnes will come up, and will need accommodation at the same place; one sitting-room will do for both.[18]

[To Thompson.] Your note and pamphlets kindly sent in July 1866 came to hand in Unyanyembe in August 1872. . . . Thanks for the notices of your family. I can recollect them only as children and would pass them on the street unwittingly. Ralph was a lithe blithe boy— Jessie had smiles and tears in perfect control. . . . Your friends paid a graceful tribute to you in franking you home and back again, and conferred honour on themselves. May they long flourish in doing similar deeds. . . . Remember me to Saul Solomon, and Rutherfoord.[19]

He had written early in the previous year from Tanganyika his last of many letters to Oswell; and also at some time during this journey to the Webbs of Newstead Abbey—a letter so sad that they destroyed it. He was now some 15 miles only from the mouth of the Chambesi and was there marooned from 13 February to 1 March. On the 15th "we killed our last goat" —and with it his only source of milk. Three separate fruitless attempts were made to reach Matipa, "while we wait hungry and cold". On the 19th, "after a cold wet morning in this uncomfortable spot" he got into a small canoe and was paddled near enough to the Lake to hear it "bellowing" (with waves): only a large canoe could survive it in windy weather; and without canoes of some kind "no movement can be made in any direction; for it is water everywhere, water above and water below". On the 22nd: "I was ill all yesterday, but escape fever by haemorrhage." On the 26th Susi and Chuma with a guide had succeeded in reaching Matipa, who promised canoes for the price of five bundles of wire. "I am devoutly thankful to the Giver of all for favouring me so far, and hope that He may continue His kind aid." But only a few of the promised canoes came, so "I propose to go near him tomorrow, some in canoes and some on foot. The good Lord help me." He slept that night "on a miserably dirty fishy island; all are damp"—and was more than ever impressed by the immensity of the watery wilderness surrounding him.

Next day he landed on Matipa's island. But here he was again detained for no less than three weeks more by the chief's procrastination. Matipa was "an old man and self-possessed", but his village swarmed with mice and was close and fetid. On 6 March Livingstone moved his camp to the low summit of the island "where we can see around us and have a fresh breeze from the Lake". After ten days, "Matipa says, 'Wait'. . . . Time is of no value to him." Livingstone made bread by a process of his own invention, using the ferment of *pombe* to leaven it. On the 16th: "Sunday.—Service. I spoke sharply to Matipa for his duplicity. He promises everything and does nothing. . . . Ill all day with my old complaint." Next day: "The delay is most trying." Then, as if ashamed of grumbling, he adds: "So many detentions have occurred that they ought to have made me of a patient spirit." The 19th was his sixtieth birthday —his last, and he committed to his Journal a thanksgiving and a prayer.

19 *March.*—Thanks to the Almighty Preserver of men for sparing me thus far on the journey of life. Can I hope for ultimate success? So many obstacles have arisen. Let not Satan prevail over me, Oh! my good Lord Jesus!

When that evening Matipa proved recalcitrant, only one canoe having come, he could stand it no longer. "I made a demonstration by taking quiet possession of his village and house: fired a pistol through the roof and called my men, ten being left to guard the camp; Matipa fled to another village."

Next day Matipa sent presents of food and desired him to

remain till the floods diminished, but "I gave him a coil of thick brass wire and his wife a string of large neck beads, and explained my hurry to be off. He is now all fair, and promises largely. . . . I am glad I had to do nothing but make a show of force." He had sent Susi in advance across the Chambesi to Kabinga's, but that chief was mourning for his son killed by an elephant and would do nothing. The situation on Matipa's island was as cheerless as elsewhere; "It is flood as far as the eye can reach. . . . One does not know where land ends and Lake begins." On the 24th, having given Matipa a parting present, he started with all his goods for Kabinga's in four canoes.

> *24th.*—We punted six hours to a little islet without a tree, and no sooner did we land than a pitiless pelting rain came on. We turned up a canoe to get shelter. We shall reach the Chambesi tomorrow. The wind tore the tent out of our hands, and damaged it too; the loads were all soaked, and with the cold it was bitterly uncomfortable. A man put my bed into the bilge . . . so I was safe for a wet night. . . .

Then next day, with a last defiance to outrageous fortune:

> Nothing earthly will make me give up my work in despair. I encourage myself in the Lord my God and go forward.

Another six hours' punting, and he studied the caterpillars and spiders and fish in the reeds. "Fish abound and ant-hills alone lift up their heads. . . . The wind on the rushes makes a sound like the waves of the sea." They were caught in a stream of the Chambesi, one canoe capsized and a girl was drowned. Two guns and three boxes of ammunition were retrieved from the shallows, but the donkey's saddle lost. A pad was made for it instead. There were further mishaps to the party on shore. Next day they crossed the Chambesi and camped beyond it; canoes were sent back to Matipa's for the rest of the men. On the 30th; "Sunday: A lion roars mightily. The fish-hawk utters his weird voice in the morning, as if to a friend at a great distance." But now the donkey broke a large canoe, and another return must be made to Matipa's to pay for it. On 3 April: "Very heavy rain last night; six inches fell in a short time. The men at last have come from Matipa's." On the 5th the journey was resumed from Kabinga's, the luggage in canoes, the men on land. "We pulled and punted for six or seven hours S.W. in great difficulty. . . . The amount of water spread over the country constantly excites my wonder; it is prodigious. . . . Pitiless pelting showers wetted everything. . . One canoe sank. . . ." Next day: "A lion had wandered into this world of water and ant-hills, and roared night and morning as if very much disgusted; we could sympathize with him!" They lost touch with the land-party, and that night took refuge on an ant-hill. Most of next day was spent in hauling the heaviest canoe through reeds and mud, whilst searching for their fellows. "All hands could move her only a few feet. Putting all their strength to her, she stopped at every haul with a jerk, as if in a bank of adhesive plaster." He measured the crown and stalk of a papyrus plant, and recorded the behaviour of hundreds of large, hairy caterpillars. On the 9th, having crossed the Muana kazi, he landed to overtake the land-party; and then came the beginning of the end. . .

10 *April.* . . . I am pale, bloodless, and weak from bleeding profusely ever since the 31st of March last; an artery gives off a copious stream, and takes away my strength. Oh, how I long to be permitted by the Over Power to finish my work.

12*th.*—Great loss of blood made me so weak I could hardly walk, but tottered along nearly two hours and then lay down quite done. Cooked coffee—our last—and went on, but in an hour I was compelled to lie down. Very unwilling to be carried, but on being pressed I allowed the men to help me along by relays to Chinama, where there is much cultivation.

13*th.*—Fish and other food are abundant, and the people civil and reasonable. . . . The sky is clearing, and the S.E. wind is the lower stratum now. It is the dry season well begun.

But it was too late. Even in this extremity he finds strength to produce a page and more of natural history observations: on different species of aquatic vegetation; on the young fish that bob in and out from the leaves and feed on the soft moss which adheres to them; on one species of fish whose lower jaw turns down into a hook enabling it to cling to the plant and suck in the soft pulp. His language is as minutely descriptive and economical as ever. He notes also that with the south-east aerial current has come sultriness; a blanket is scarcely needed till the early morning "when the turtle-doves and cocks give out their warning calls" and then "the fish-eagle lifts up his remarkable voice. . . . Once heard his weird unearthly voice can never be forgotten. . . . It seems as if it were calling to some one in another world." That is his last comment upon Nature.

> 15*th.*—Cross Lolotikila again. . . . I, being very weak, had to be carried part of the way. Am glad of resting; blood flow copiously last night.
>
> 17*th.*—A tremendous rain after dark burst all our now rotten tents to shreds. Went on at 6.35 a.m. for three hours and I, who was suffering severely all night, had to rest. . . .
>
> 19*th.*—I am excessively weak, and but for the donkey could not move a hundred yards. It is not all pleasure, this exploration. The Lavusi hills are a relief to the eye in this flat upland. Their form shows an igneous origin. . . . No observations now . . . I can scarcely hold the pencil, and my stick is a burden.

The next day, a Sunday, after Service they crossed a sponge and then a river, the Lokulu (Molikolu) in a canoe. The day after, Livingstone tried to ride the donkey, but fell to the ground. Susi undid his belt; Chuma ran ahead to stop the march and returned. Livingstone said: "Chuma, I have lost so much blood there is no more strength left in my legs; you must carry me." He was carried back to the village he had left, and sent a note to the chief Muanazawamba requesting a guide for next day when he hoped to have recovered. The reply was friendly and kind. Meanwhile his men were making a hammock, seven feet long crossed with three-foot rails a hand-breadth apart, covered with grass and a blanket, slung on a long pole overhead with another blanket to protect him from the sun. His last Journal entries are as follows:

> 21*st.*—Tried to ride, but was forced to lie down and they carried me back to the vil. exhausted.
>
> 22*nd.*—Carried in *kitanda* over sponge S.W. 2¼ (hours).
>
> 23*rd.*—Do. 1½.
>
> 24*th.*—Do. 1.
>
> 25*th.*—Do. 1.
>
> 26*th.*—Do. 2¼. To Kalunganjofu's, total 33 = 8¼.
>
> 27*th.*—Knocked up quite and remain: recover, sent to buy milch goats. We are on the banks of the R. Molilamo.

With these words, as Campbell has said, David Livingstone unconsciously addressed his farewell to the world.

Some points call for remark. It will be noticed that he does not mention that he had fallen or slipped from his mount.

The river Lulimala is misspelt Molilamo in his diary, but spelt nearly correctly in his map—Lilimala. He multiplies the hours by four to give the mileage covered: it was an over-estimate, the distance between the Lukulu and Lulimala being no more than twenty miles.

The details which he omitted perforce from his diary were supplied verbally months later by Susi and Chuma in reply to questions by the Rev. Horace Waller in England. On the 22nd (Tuesday) he suffered excruciating pain and they were thankful to reach another village, though the people fled at their approach. On hearing their drums he exclaimed, "Ah, now we are near!" On Wednesday they pushed on through the same expanse of flooded treeless waste. Another deserted village afforded a night's shelter. On Thursday his pain was so great that frequent halts were necessary; Chuma had to lift and support him when he got out of the *kitanda*; they halted for the day and night among some huts. On Friday after a short march they reached a village, partly inhabited. Here, lying in the shade on his *kitanda* while a hut was being prepared, he asked that a villager be brought to him since the headman had disappeared. Several came and drew near to him, curious and friendly. They were asked: "Did they know of a hill on which four fountains took their rise?" The spokesman answered: "No. They were not travellers, and all those who used to go on trading expeditions were now dead." (Fortune, which had never been kind to Livingstone, was cruel to the last.) After a while he dismissed them, explaining that he was too ill to continue talking. On Saturday they came to Kalunganjofu's on the Lulimala.

Here he summoned Susi and instructed him to count over the bags of beads that still remained in stock and, when informed that there were twelve, told him on the first opportunity to buy with them two large tusks to exchange *when they got to Ujiji* for cloth which they would need on their way back to the coast. (The prospect of death was one that had often engaged his thoughts since the eve of his first great Journey— "Am I on my way to die in Sebituane's country?"—but now that it was imminent no thought was farther from his mind. He was actually making arrangements for his homeward journey.)

The next day, Sunday April 27, when he made his last

Journal entry, he seemed to be dying. Two attempts were made to procure goats, on that and the day following, but in vain. The chief however sent him the present of a kid and some ground-nuts; and he asked that some mapira corn be pounded with the nuts, but when this was brought he was unable to eat. On Tuesday the chief, with most of his people, came early to the village, and promised not only to provide canoes but to superintend their passage across the river. "Everything should be done for his friend." But now Livingstone was unable to stand, and asked that the wall of the hut where he was should be broken to admit of his being carried through it to the *kitanda* outside. "This was done, and he was gently placed upon it and borne out of the village." His bed was laid in the bottom of the largest canoe and an attempt made to lift him on to it. But now he could not bear the pressure of a hand under his back. (Autopsy, subsequently performed by Farijala, disclosed a clot of blood "the size of a fist" in the lower intestine.) "Beckoning to Chuma, in a faint voice he asked him to stoop down over him as low as possible, so that he might clasp his hands together behind his head; directing him at the same time how to avoid any pressure on the lumbar region of the back. In this way he was deposited in the bottom of the canoe and quickly ferried across." The same precautions were used for disembarking on the other side, and while Susi ran ahead to Chitambo's to arrange for the building of a new hut, Chuma remained as one of the bearers. On this day Livingstone's sufferings were most intense. The bearers were frequently implored to stop and let him rest on the ground. When one of them was called to him he could not speak. When near the village he again entreated to be left motionless, and so remained for an hour in some gardens outside it.

On that day, 29 April 1873, in Chitambo's old village in the district of Ilala on the south shore of Lake Bangweolo, the Pathfinder came to his last halt. They laid him under the broad eaves of a native hut while the large new one, of branches, reeds and grass, and banked with earth, was being prepared in a drizzle of rain. By nightfall it was ready, the bales and boxes placed inside, the bed raised from the floor with sticks and grass, and the old traveller gently lifted in. Early next morning Chitambo came to pay his respects, but Livingstone was obliged to ask him to come next day when he hoped to have recovered strength to talk. In the afternoon he asked Susi to bring his watch and showed him how to hold it while he slowly wound the key. That night some of his men silently went to their huts, whilst others stayed watching by their camp-fire. Inside the hut sat the boy Majwara, to call Susi or Chuma if their master woke or wanted anything. About 11 p.m. there was sound of distant shouting and Susi was called. Livingstone said, "Are our men making that noise?" "No," replied Susi, "I can hear from the cries that the people are scaring away a buffalo from their dura fields." Silence. Then he said slowly, "Is this the Luapula?" "No, master, we are in Chitambo's village near the Lulilama." Again silence for a while. Then, speaking in Swahili, he said, "*Sikun'gapi kuenda Luapula?*" (How many days to the Luapula?) Susi replied, "*Na zani zikutatu, bwana*" (I think three days, master.) A few seconds after, as if in great pain, Livingstone sighed, "Oh dear, dear!" and then dozed off into sleep.

About an hour later Susi was called again. Livingstone told him to boil some water, and when this was brought, to hold his medicine-chest and a candle near him. With great difficulty he then selected some calomel, and directing Susi to pour a little water into a cup and leave another empty one beside it, he said in a low feeble voice, "All right; you can go out now." About 4 a.m. Majwara called Susi again. "Come, I am afraid." The lad's evident alarm made Susi rouse Chuma and three other men. They entered the doorway and looked towards the bed. Livingstone was not lying in it but appeared to be kneeling beside it. They instinctively drew backwards. Majwara said that he himself had been to sleep some time ago (how long he could not say), and woke to find the *bwana* in the same position as before he had closed his eyes. Approaching nearer they could see by the dim light of the candle stuck to the top of a box the moveless figure of their master kneeling by the bedside, his body stretched forward, his head buried in his hands upon the pillow.

They watched for a little, but the figure did not stir.

The death was at first concealed from Chitambo from fear of his imposing the customary death-fine due to a chief from travellers, but when the secret was divulged he reassured them: they were good men, and he had been a "traveller" too; he would assist them in everything and arrange for funeral honours forthwith. When told that, come what might, the body should be borne to Zanzibar, he objected that this would be an impossible task, and with native good sense and good nature, said, "Why not bury him here?" But Susi replied, "No, no—very big man."

The heart and viscera were removed and deposited in a dug hole beneath a large *mvula* tree, on the trunk of which the name LIVINGSTONE was deeply carved by Jacob Wainwright; the body was embalmed with raw salt, swathed in calico and bark and sail-cloth and lashed to a pole, and the procession of sixty men started on their eight months' journey. It holds its own place among the finest exploits in the whole history of travel. But the belief that Susi and his companions were consciously actuated in their heroic undertaking by the unalloyed sentiment of devotion to their master, or propelled thereto by the dynamic of his own indomitable spirit outlasting death, is unfortunately one which overrates the sensibility of the primitive negro. A simpler and more prosaic explanation is probable. They knew in what high honour he was held by his own people, and the responsibility that lay upon themselves to preserve intact his writings and instruments and especially his mortal remains. The production of his body was necessary evidence that they had not deserted him. At all costs and in their own interests it must be delivered to the authorities in Zanzibar. Even when after incredible toil and hardship, to which were added sudden battle and bloodshed, they staggered into Unyanyembe, they were again strongly urged, this time by another white man, to abandon their burden, but they steadily adhered to their purpose and went on— to encounter and surmount difficulties and losses almost as great as those they had already endured. And so they bore his body to the sea, to be buried in his own land among his own folk as a great chief should, and there in the temple of Britain's great ones it rests; but they laid his heart beneath the soil of Africa and there, dust unto dust, it mingles with the mould of the land he loved and gave his life for.

EPILOGUE

WHEN one looks closely into life, as most people are bound to do before they get to the end of it, there is one reflection above all which presses upon the mind with increasingly disturbing force: that life promises more than it fulfils, that it suggests a good which it somehow fails to impart. The pages of history and of biography alike are blurred with the record of lost causes, quenched enthusiasms, unrealized ideals, frustrated hopes. Livingstone's life is no exception; rather, it is a conspicuous example of that stark inexorable truth. The verdict of the great apostle, whom he in many ways closely resembles, is borne out in his own experience: "If in this life only we have hope in Christ, we are of all men most miserable."

If during his last hours of consciousness there was given to him an interval of lucid perception in which to realize that this was journey's end for him, and therewith to review the incidents of his career—with all its achievements and mischances, all his successes and disappointments, laid up together for good or ill in the hand of his God, and with them the greatest disappointment of all, the crown of his life's work unaccomplished —it must have seemed that all he had striven for had been failure; that over it all might be written one word: Disillusion. In everything he had failed: he had failed as a husband; he had failed as a father; he had failed as a missionary; he had failed as a geographer; he had failed most of all as a liberator. It was through his fault that his wife had died untimely; through his neglect that his children were orphaned; through his misdirected zeal that the Bakwena and Makololo were left unshepherded; through his misfortune that his last discovery had gone by default, and with it all hope for the liberation of the negro. There was nothing worth-while to show for it all.

It is true that he accomplished far more by his death than by his life. One can point to the host of markets and of missions (his own Universities' Mission among them) that, fired by the inspiration of his example, established themselves on the mainland of East Africa within less than a decade of his death; and one can say that his apparent failure was more than made good by an aftermath that far exceeded his greatest hopes. But this leaves the fundamental question unanswered. For in the first place, it is a principle of moral philosophy that the worth of action is to be judged, not by its success in consequences or results, but solely by the quality of the motive and the integrity of the agent. In the second place, if one takes results as the criterion and looks beyond a decade to the lapse of nearly a century, one sees the consummation of Livingstone's life-purposes largely nullified: Commerce corrupted by exploitation, Civilization polluted by depravity, Christianity distraught by rival policies within and hostile policies without, and the whole future of Africa imperilled in the turmoil of racial conflict.

The truth is that Livingstone's life poses a problem. It is crucial because it is essentially religious, and therefore of universal significance. It may be expressed thus: What is the meaning and purpose of our fugitive existence here—in a world where much is doubtful and obscure, and more is incomprehensible?

Setting aside any consideration of self-regarding aims, personal desires and inclinations, which have no end beyond their own satisfaction and perish with fulfilment because their directive impulse is nothing but a kind of rationalized instinct; and assuming the magnetic attraction of an ultimate objective of more enduring value, namely to do the Will of God—how may we know with any certitude what it is? That is the fundamental problem which the life of Livingstone poses. Throughout it, from first to last, he had sincerely sought to know and do the Will of God. Had he really merged his will in God's Will, or had he mistaken it for his own?

The psychologist, seeking ulterior motives and rational explanations for human behaviour, and sceptical of an intuitive moral sense transcending reason, would doubtless say that Livingstone was the victim of self-delusion and that what he took for landscape was only a mirage. But this is to reduce all the noblest human aspirations to a fiasco. Further, it fails to explain the conflict of duties in Livingstone, and the fact that when confronted with alternative courses of action he deliberately and consistently chose the harder.

The religious thinker on the other hand would say that conscience, not rationalized instinct or even the theoretical reason itself, is the only guide to our knowledge of what is right, and obedience to its dictates the only norm towards the fulfilment of the purpose for which we were created; so that in the last resort it is not reason but conscience which is the true organ of spiritual understanding, and like the needle of a compass points to the lodestone with which it has an integral affinity. According to this view the will of man, informed by that inward monitor, is identical with the Will of God.

For a true comprehension of the significance of Livingstone's life we must look deeper than psychological analysis and envisage it against the background of eternal values. Whatever his faults of temperament and defects of character he stands before us, as Campbell has well said, as one of the moral giants of our race. For he is to be numbered in the roll of those men of faith of whom the world was not worthy; concerning whom it is written that "they died, not having received the promises, but having glimpsed them from afar off were persuaded of them and embraced them, and confessed that they were strangers and pilgrims upon earth. . . . And truly, if they had been mindful of that country from whence they came out, they might have had opportunity to have returned. But now they desire a better country, that is, an heavenly. . . ."

MEMORABILIA FROM LIVINGSTONE

My views of what is missionary duty are not so contracted as those whose ideal is a dumpy sort of man with a Bible under his arm.

I read the whole Bible through four times whilst I was in Manyuema. . . . The Bible gathers wonderful interest from the circumstances in which it is read.

It is something to be a follower, however feeble, in the wake of the great Teacher and only model missionary that ever appeared among men.

Forbid it that we should ever consider the holding of a commission from the King of Kings a sacrifice, so long as men esteem the service of an earthly sovereign an honour.

I still prefer poverty and mission-service to riches and ease. It's my choice.

The spirit of missions is the spirit of our Master; the very genius of his religion.

I am a missionary, heart and soul. God had an only Son, and He was a missionary and a physician. A poor, poor imitation I am or wish to be. In this service I hope to live, in it I wish to die.

I never made a sacrifice. Of this we ought not to talk when we remember the great sacrifice which He made who left His Father's throne on high to give Himself for us.

A hard bed might be a greater sacrifice to one than sleeping on the ground to another.

I had a great objection to school-keeping, but I find in that, as in almost everything else that I set myself to as a matter of duty, I soon became enamoured of it.

Some of the brethren do not hesitate to tell the natives that my object is to obtain the applause of men. This bothers me, for I sometimes suspect my own motives.

On the other hand I am conscious that though there is much impurity in my motives, they are in the main for the glory of Him to whom I have dedicated my all.

Man is a complex being and we greatly need our motives to be purified from all that is evil.

I think you are not quite clear upon the indications of Providence, my dear brother. I don't think we ought to wait for them. Our duty is to go forward and look for the indications. In general I have observed that people who have sat long waiting have sat long enough before they saw any indication to go.

Cautious reverence is required in ascribing human movements to the influence of divine Providence.

We don't know how bad some people are until they are tried, nor how good others are till put to the test.

I like to hear that some abuse me now, and say that I am no Christian. Many good things were said of me which I did not deserve, and I feared to read them. I shall read every word I can on the other side and that will prove a sedative.

I have always found that the art of successful travel consisted in taking as few impedimenta as possible, and not forgetting to carry my wits about me.

We have neither sugar nor salt; it is hard fare and scanty. In the evening I shot a full-grown male nsevula. I felt very thankful to the Giver of all good for this meat.

I notice that the mongoose gets lean on a diet of cockroaches. This would be invaluable to fat young ladies at home.

The new-fangled coal-scuttle helmets serve chiefly for the frightening away of game when you want them to stand.

She had a profusion of iron rings on her ankles, to which were attached little pieces of sheet-iron, to enable her to make a tinkling as she walked in her mincing African style. The same thing is thought pretty by our own dragoons in walking jauntily.

The first smile of an infant with its toothless gums is one of the pleasantest sights in nature. It is innocence claiming kinship, and asking to be loved in its helplessness. . . . . Nature is full of enjoyment.

I think I am in the line of duty . . . I have never wavered in my conviction that this is the case.

I can be rich without money.

The day of Africa is yet to come.

A life of selfishness is one of misery.

Be manly Christians and never do a mean thing.

Depend upon it, a kind word or deed is never lost.

There is never a bad but it might have been worse.

Let us appear just what we are.

Never too old to learn.

There's a good time coming.

All will come right at last.

BIBLIOGRAPHY

BOOKS SELECTED

Agar-Hamilton, J. A. I., *The Native Policy of the Voortrekkers* (Maskew Miller, Cape Town, 1928).

Anderson-Moreshead, A. E. M., *History of the U.M.C.A.* (1909).

Blaikie, W. G., D.D., *Autobiography* (Hodder & Stoughton, 1901).

—— *Life of David Livingstone* (Murray, 6th Edn., 1910).

Cameron, V. L., *Across Africa* (London, 1877).

Campbell, R. J., D.D., *Livingstone* (Benn, 1929).

Chamberlin, D., *Some Letters from Livingstone* (O.U.P., 1940).

Cochrane, W., D.D., *Memoir of Walter Inglis* (Ontario, 1887).

Coupland, Sir R., *Kirk on the Zambesi* (O.U.P., 1928).

—— *Livingstone's Last Journey* (Collins, 1945).

Debenham, F., O.B E., D.Sc., *The Way to Ilala* (Longmans, 1955).

Devereux, W. C., *Cruise in the* Gorgon (Bell & Daldy, 1869).

Elliott, W. A., *Nyaka* (L.M.S., 1908).

Fraser, Mrs. A. K., *Livingstone and Newstead* (Murray, 1913).

Goodwin, H., D.D., *Memoir of Bishop Mackensie* (Deighton, Bell, 1865).

Hughes, T., Q.C., *David Livingstone* (Macmillan, 1906).

Johnston, Sir H. H., *Livingstone and the Exploration of Central Africa* (Philip, 1891).

Journal of the Royal Geographical Society.

Kruger, Paul, *Memoirs*, ed. A. Schowalter (Unwin, 1902).

Livingstone, D., *Missionary Travels, etc.* (Murray, 1857), 1st Edn.

—— *Narrative of Expedition to the Zambesi* (Murray, 1865), 1st Edn.

—— *Last Journals*, ed. H. Waller (Murray, 1874), 1st Edn.

—— *Cambridge Lectures*, ed. W. Monk (Deighton, Bell, 1860).

—— *Zambesi Expedition, Journals, etc.*, ed. J. P. R. Wallis (Oppenheimer Series, Chatto and Windus, 1956).

Lovett, R., *History of the L.M.S.*, 1795–1895 (Froude, 1899).

Macnair, J. I., D.D., *Livingstone the Liberator* (Collins, 1940).

—— *Livingstone's Travels*, ed. (Dent, 1954).

Mathews, B., *Livingstone the Pathfinder* (O.U.P., 1932).

Moffat, J. S., *Lives of Robert and Mary Moffat* (T. Fisher Unwin, 1885).

Northcott, Cecil, *Livingstone in Africa* (Lutterworth, 1957).

Oswell, W. E., *William Cotton Oswell* (Heinemann, 1900).

Russell, Mrs. C. E. B., *General Rigby* (Allen & Unwin, 1935).

Schapera, I., *Apprentice at Kuruman* (Oppenheimer Series, 1951).

Simmons, J., *Livingstone and Africa* (E.U.P., 1955).

Smith, E. W., D.D., *Robert Moffat* (S.C.M., 1925).
—— *Great Lion of Bechuanaland* (Independent Press, 1957).
Stanley, Sir H. M., *How I Found Livingstone* (Sampson Low, 1872).
—— *Autobiography* (Sampson Low, 1909).
Theal, G. Mc., D.Litt., LL.D., *History of South Africa since September* 1795 (Swan Sonnenschein, 1908).
Wallis, J. P. R., *Thomas Baines* (Cape, 1941).
—— *The Matabele Journals of Robert Moffat* (Oppenheimer Series, 1945).
—— *The Matabele Mission* (Oppenheimer Series, 1945).
—— *The Zambesi Journals of James Stewart* (Oppenheimer Series, 1952).
Willoughby, W. C., *The Soul of the Bantu* (S.C.M., 1928).

MANUSCRIPTS IN ARCHIVES

LONDON MISSIONARY SOCIETY, *Westminster*.

ROYAL GEOGRAPHICAL SOCIETY, *Kensington*.

RHODES-LIVINGSTONE MUSEUM, *Livingstone*.

CENTRAL AFRICAN ARCHIVES, *Salisbury*.

LIVINGSTONE MEMORIAL, *Blantyre*.

BODLEIAN LIBRARY, *Oxford* (*Clarendon Correspondence*).

RHODES HOUSE, *Oxford* (*Waller Papers*).
    also
FAMILY LETTERS (*in possession of his grandson*).

REFERENCES

Note: Where extracts from manuscripts have already appeared in print, the reference is to the publication rather than to the archives in which the manuscript is preserved.

In the case of the last chapters, references to Livingstone's *Last Journals* are not given, since the many quotations from them are in chronological sequence and can be found without difficulty.

Chapter 1

1. Macnair, 33
2. Blaikie, 9

Chapter 2

1. L.M.S. Archives
2. Campbell, 58
3. Cochrane, 221
4. Blaikie, 20
5. Blaikie, 27
6. Chamberlin, no. 2
7. Blaikie, 23
8. Blaikie, 27
9. Campbell, 61
10. Blaikie, 25
11. Moffat, 229
12. Blaikie, 19
13. Blaikie, 26
14. Blaikie, 27
15. Blaikie, 24
16. *Travels,* 7
17. *Travels,* 7

Chapter 3

1. Chamberlin, nos. 3–6
2. L.M.S. Archives
3. L.M.S. Archives
4. Blaikie, 43
5. Smith, 205
6. Moffat, 63
7. L.M.S. Archives
8. Blaikie, 222
9. L.M.S. Archives
10. Johnston, 64–69
11. Chamberlin, no, 7
12. Chamberlin, no. 9
13. Chamberlin, no. 8
14. L.M.S. Archives
15. L.M.S. Archives
16. Chamberlin, no. 10
17. L.M.S. Archives

Chapter 4

1. L.M.S. Archives
2. L.M.S. Archives
3. Blaikie, 37
4. Chamberlin, no. 11
5. L.M.S. Archives
6. Blaikie, 39
7. *Travels,* 10
8. Chamberlin, no. 11
9. Chamberlin, no. 12
10. L.M.S. Archives
11. Hughes, 21
12. Chamberlin, no. 12
13. Chamberlin, no. 14
14. Chamberlin, no. 31
15. Chamberlin, no. 14
16. Chamberlin, no. 15
17. *Travels,* 51
18. Chamberlin no. 15
19. L.M.S. Archives
20. Blaikie, 52
21. Blaikie, 54
22. Chamberlin, 39

Chapter 5

1. Chamberlin, no. 14
2. Chamberlin, no. 13
3. L.M.S. Archives
4. Blaikie, 47
5. Hughes, 22
6. Roxborough, 33
7. Hughes, 23
8. Smith, 106
9. Chamberlin, no. 18
10. L.M.S. Archives
11. Macnair, 86
12. *Travels,* 13
13. Campbell, 102
14. Chamberlin, no. 19
15. Blaikie, 56
16. Family Letters

Chapter 6

1. Blaikie, 57
2. *Travels*, 230
3. L.M.S. Archives
4. Blantyre Archives
5. Chamberlin, no. 21
6. Blaikie, 61
7. Blaikie, 58
8. Blaikie, 60
9. Macnair, 86
10. Chamberlin, no. 22
11. Willoughby, 206
12. Chamberlin, no. 22
13. L.M.S. Archives
14. L.M.S. Archives
15. Chamberlin, no. 27
16. L.M.S. Archives
17. Chamberlin, no. 27
18. L.M.S. Archives
19. Chamberlin, no. 27
20. L.M.S. Archives
21. Blaikie, 69
22. Blaikie, 68
23. Chamberlin, no. 25
24. Chamberlin, no. 30
25. Chamberlin, no. 31

Chapter 7

1. L.M.S. Archives
2. Blaikie, 71
3. R.G.S. Archives
4. Chamberlin, no. 29
5. Chamberlin, no. 29
6. Blaikie, 64
7. Chamberlin, no. 30
8. Blaikie, 77
9. Journal R.G.S., XXXVII, 356
10. Blaikie, 75
11. Blaikie, 79
12. Macnair, 112
13. Central African Archives
14. L.M.S. Archives

Chapter 8

1. Oswell, i, 106
2. Oswell, i, 108
3. Journal R.G.S., XX, 31
4. *Travels*, 69
5. Blantyre Mem. Archives
6. Blaikie, 86
7. Macnair, 30
8. Blaikie, 229, 301
9. Oswell, ii, 19, 130

Chapter 9

1. *Travels*, 74
2. Chamberlin, 138
3. Chamberlin, 139
4. Chamberlin, no. 35
5. Blaikie, 89
6. Blaikie, 89
7. Smith, 206
8. Blaikie, 95
9. Chamberlin, no. 38
10. L.M.S. Archives
11. Chamberlin, no. 36
12. Family Letters
13. *Travels*, 79
14. Oswell, i, 241
15. *Travels*, 89
16. Oswell, i, 247

Chapter 10

1. Blaikie, *Autobiog.*, 289
2. *Travels*, 91
3. Oswell, i, 254
4. Oswell, i, 255–6
5. Blaikie, *Autobiog.*, 290
6. Blaikie, 98
7. Chamberlin, no. 37
8. Chamberlin, no. 38
9. Fraser, 19
10. Oswell, i, 258
11. Chamberlin, no. 39
12. Blaikie, 109
13. L.M.S. Archives
14. L.M.S. Archives
15. Chamberlin, no. 46
16. Blaikie, 108

Chapter 11

1. *Travels*, 94
2. Chamberlin, no. 41
3. Chamberlin, no. 42
4. Chamberlin, no. 43
5. Macnair, ed. T., 408
6. Campbell, 162
7. Blaikie, 111
8. L.M.S. Archives
9. Chamberlin, no. 44
10. Chamberlin, no. 46
11. L.M.S. Archives
12. *Travels*, 99
13. *Travels*, 119
14. Sillery, 116–17
15. Theal, 335
16. Schowalter, i, 44
17. Macnair, 141
18. *Travels*, 121
19. Chamberlin, no. 45
20. Chamberlin, no. 46
21. *Travels*, 95
22. *Travels*, 119

Chapter 12

1. Rhodes–Livingstone Archives
2. *Travels*, 122–61
3. Chamberlin, no. 48
4. Blaikie, 115
5. Campbell, 155
6. *Travels*, 166–77
7. Blaikie, 115–16
8. *Travels*, 179
9. *Travels*, 195
10. *Travels*, 182
11. Chamberlin, no. 50
12. *Travels*, 190
13. Chamberlin, no. 50
14. *Travels*, 192
15. *Travels*, 187
16. Blaikie, 118–19
17. Macnair, 149
18. *Travels*, 199
19. Blaikie, 118
20. *Travels*, 203–26
21. Blaikie, 121
22. Chamberlin, no. 50
23. Blaikie, 122–7

Chapter 13

1. *Travels*, 230
2. Elliott, 31
3. Johnston, 149
4. Blaikie, 129
5. Chamberlin, 163
6. Blaikie, 134
7. Johnston, 160
8. Chamberlin, no. 54

Chapter 14

1. Mathews, 93
2. Chamberlin, no. 54
3. Blaikie, 155
4. Blaikie, 136
5. L.M.S. Archives
6. Campbell, 198
7. Chamberlin, no. 55
8. Blaikie, 138
9. *Travels*, 430
10. L.M.S. Archives
11. Central African Archives
12. *Travels*, 441
13. Central African Archives
14. L.M.S. Archives
15. Central African Archives

Chapter 15

1. Matabele Journals, 188–316
2. L.M.S. Archives
3. Chamberlin, no. 58

4. Chamberlin, nos. 57, 58
5. Chamberlin, no. 59
6. Debenham, 113
7. Debenham, 120
8. Central African Archives
9. Central African Archives
10. Central African Archives
11. Central African Archives
12. *Travels*, 673

Chapter 16

1. Central African Archives
2. Family Letters
3. L.M.S. Archives
4. Wallis: Z.J., xvi
5. Central African Archives
6. Chamberlin, no. 62
7. Chamberlin, no. 63
8. L.M.S. Archives
9. Campbell, 234
10. *Travels*, 677
11. L.M.S. Archives
12. L.M.S. Archives
13. Blaikie, 166
14. L.M.S. Archives
15. Blaikie, 168
16. Cape Town Newspaper
17. Blaikie, 176
18. Journal R.G.S.
19. L.M.S. Archives
20. Blaikie, 174
21. Simmons, 73
22. Blaikie, 181
23. Blaikie, 178
24. Blaikie, 178
25. The Nonconformist
26. Blaikie, 182
27. Blaikie, 182–9
28. Campbell, 239
29. Cambridge Lectures
30. Blaikie, 192
31. Campbell, 230
32. Blaikie, 198
33. Journal R.G.S.

Chapter 17

1. L.M.S. Archives
2. Campbell, 243
3. Clarendon Corresp.
4. Blaikie, 195
5. Simmons, 77
6. Coupland: K. on Z., 76, 81
7. Clarendon Corresp.
8. Coupland: K. on Z., 84–94
9. Blaikie, 193
10. Smith: G.L.B.

11. Wallis: M.M., xii
12. Wallis: M.M., no. 1
13. Wallis: M.M., no. 3
14. Wallis: M.M., no. 6
15. L.M.S. Archives
16. Lovett, i, 619
17. Blaikie, 231
18. Campbell, 270
19. Smith: G.L.B.
20. Campbell, 266
21. L.M.S. Archives
22. Blaikie, 202
23. Blaikie, 368

Chapter 18

1. Coupland: K. on Z., 41
2. Coupland: K. on Z., 102
3. Wallis: Z.J., 3
4. Wallis: M.M., no. 23
5. Wallis: M.M., xi
6. Wallis: Z.J., xxxii
7. Cambridge Letters, no. 2
8. Wallis: Z.J., 12
9. L.M.S. Archives
10. Narrative, 27
11. Wallis: Z.J., 153
12. Wallis: Z.J., 15
13. Wallis: Z.J., 18
14. Central African Archives
15. Cambridge Letters, no. 1
16. Coupland: K. on Z., 120
17. Macnair, 222
18. Wallis: Z.J., 42
19. Wallis: M.M., no. 23
20. Narrative, 35
21. Coupland: K. on Z., 129
22. Narrative, 54
23. Narrative, 72
24. Coupland: K. on Z., 132
25. Wallis: Z.J., 63
26. Coupland: K. on Z., 133
27. Coupland: K. on Z., 135
28. Wallis: Z.J., 69
29. Narrative. 60
30. Wallis: Z.J., 70
31. Wallis: Z.J., 70

Chapter 19

1. Wallis: Z.J., 73
2. Coupland: K. on Z., 138
3. Chamberlin, no. 66
4. Cambridge Letters, no. 13
5. Central African Archives
6. Coupland: K. on Z., 139
7. Wallis: Z.J., 84
8. Wallis: Z.J., 89

9. L.M.S. Archives
10. Coupland: K. on Z., 144
11. Wallis: Z.J., 109
12. Central African Archives
13. Wallis: Z.J., 115
14. Wallis: Z.J., 115
15. Wallis: Z.J., 116
16. Wallis: Z.J., 118
17. Coupland: K. on Z., 146
18. Wallis: Z.J., 125
19. Coupland: K. on Z., 152
20. Narrative, 125
21. Macnair, 231
22. Coupland: K. on Z., 159
23. Wallis: Z.J., 125
24. Wallis: Z.J., 126
25. Narrative, 132
26. Wallis: Z.J., 132
27. Wallis: Baines, 180
28. Coupland: K. on Z., 161
29. Wallis: Baines, 181
30. Central African Archives
31. Debenham, 155
32. Wallis: M.M., no. 45
33. Central African Archives

Chapter 20

1. Wallis: Z.J., 82
2. Narrative, 138
3. Wallis, Z.J., 150
4. Blaikie, 226
5. Narrative, 151
6. Wallis: Z.J., 347
7. Coupland: K. on Z., 168
8. Debenham, 110
9. Central African Archives
10. Central African Archives
11. Wallis: Z.J., 163
12. Wallis: M.M., no. 47
13. Narrative, 156
14. Narrative, 187
15. Narrative, 201
16. Narrative, 203
17. Narrative, 215
18. Narrative, 241
19. Narrative, 258
20. Coupland: K. on Z., 175
21. Wallis: Z.J., 260
22. Coupland: K. on Z., 175
23. Wallis: M.M., nos. 47, 60
24. Travels, 510
25. Campbell, 269
26. L.M.S. Archives
27. Wallis: M.M., no. 73
28. Coupland: K. on Z., 181
29. Narrative, 324
30. Narrative, 329
31. Coupland: K. on Z., 178

32. *Narrative*, 334
33. Coupland: K. on Z., 180
34. Coupland: K. on Z., 183
35. Coupland, K. on Z., 184

Chapter 21

1. Goodwin, 187
2. Coupland, K. on Z., 188.
3. Goodwin, 254
4. Coupland: K. on Z., 189
5. *Narrative*, 351
6. Goodwin, 262, 265
7. *Narrative*, 352
8. Central African Archives
9. *Narrative*, 354
10. Goodwin, 275
11. *Narrative*, 355
12. Goodwin, 285
13. *Narrative*, 363
14. Wallis: M.M., no. 76
15. *Narrative*, 370
16. Debenham, 191
17. Coupland: K. on Z., 206
18. *Narrative*, 284
19. Debenham, 193
20. Coupland: K. on Z., 208
21. Coupland: K. on Z., 210
22. Central African Archives
23. Coupland: K. on Z., 210
24. Russell, 129
25. *Narrative*, 391
26. Wallis: Z.J., 213
27. *Narrative*, 364, 416
28. Goodwin, 317
29. Goodwin, chap. xii
30. Goodwin, 371
31. Moreshead, 37

Chapter 22

1. Central African Archives
2. Central African Archives
3. Blaikie, 248
4. Wallis: M.M., no. 76
5. Devereux, 219, 229
6. Stewart Papers, 12, 44
7. Debenham, 197
8. Devereux, 229
9. Stewart Papers, 18, 25
10. Blaikie, 251
11. Stewart Papers, 57, 59
12. Blaikie, 252-4
13. Central African Archives
14. Blaikie, 257
15. Blaikie, 258
16. Coupland: K. on Z., 239
17. Coupland: K. on Z., 240
18. Coupland: K. on Z., 241-2

19. *Narrative*, 435-8
20. Coupland: K. on Z., 244
21. Debenham, 201
22. Wallis: Z.J., 216
23. Central African Archives
24. Central African Archives
25. Wallis: Z.J., 376
26. *Narrative*, 449-52
27. Stewart Papers, no 27
28. Coupland: K. on Z., 252
29. Macnair, 273
30. Stewart Papers, no. 18
31. Campbell, 345
32. Wallis: Z.J., 379-82
33. Central African Archives
34. *Narrative*, 478
35. Blaikie, 270
36. Central African Archives
37. Coupland: K. on Z., 260-78
38. Stewart Papers, 190
39. Stewart Papers, no. 23

Chapter 23

1. *Narrative*, 578-9
2. Rhodes-Livingstone Archives
3. Stewart Papers, 241

Chapter 24

1. Central African Archives
2. Blantyre Memorial Archives
3. Central African Archives
4. Central African Archives
5. Blaikie, 299
6. Stanley: How I Found L., 601
7. Blaikie, 289
8. L.M.S. Archives
9. Macnair, 287
10. Campbell, 295
11. Fraser, *passim*
12. Stewart Papers, 228, 232
13. Oswell, ii, 77-89
14. Blaikie, 293-6
15. Campbell, 299
16. Coupland: L.L.J., 26
17. Blaikie, 298
18. Blaikie, 299
19. Fraser, 165
20. Coupland: L.L.J., 26

Chapter 25

1. Waller Papers
2. Blaikie, 305
3. Coupland: L.L.J., 31
4. Coupland: L.L.J., 32
5. Blaikie, 311
6. Campbell, 288
7. Blaikie, 309

8. Rhodes-Livingstone Archives
9. Blaikie, 311
10. *Last Journals*, 6
11. Rhodes-Livingstone Archives
12. Coupland: L.L.J., 28
13. *Narrative*, vi

Chapter 26

1. Oswell, ii, 133
2. Coupland, L.L.J., 45
3. L.M.S. Archives
4. Coupland: L.L.J., 60–7

Chapter 27

1. Debenham, 236
2. Coupland, L.L.J., 53
3. Oswell, ii, 99
4. Rhodes-Livingstone Archives
5. Coupland: L.L.J., 54
6. Coupland: L.L.J., 57
7. Debenham, 251

Chapter 28

1. Macnair, 318
2. Debenham, 256
3. Blaikie, 329
4. Oswell, ii, 101
5. Debenham, 246

Chapter 29

1. Coupland, L.L.J., 75
2. Blaikie, 331–5
3. Oswell, ii, 108
4. Coupland, L.L.J., 78
5. Blaikie, 337
6. Macnair, 368

Chapter 30

1. Coupland: L.L.J., 91
2. Blaikie, 342–3
3. Debenham, 269, 274

4. Coupland: L.L.J., 109–14
5. Macnair, 330
6. Coupland: L.L.J., 115–16
7. Coupland: L.L.J., 116–17
8. Coupland: L.L.J., 120
9. Blaikie, 346
10. Macnair, 334

Chapter 31

1. Fraser, 194
2. Stanley: How I Found L., 411
3. Waller Papers
4. Blaikie, 358
5. Stanley: How I Found L., 428–34
6. Stanley: Autobiog., 284
7. Stanley: How I Found L., 595
8. Stanley: Autobiog., 276
9. Stanley: Autobiog., 274
10. Stanley: Autobiog., 281
11. Stanley: Autobiog., 277
12. Stanley: How I Found L., 624
13. Stanley: Autobiog., 279
14. Stanley: How I Found L., 626

Chapter 32

1. Stanley: How I Found L., 704
2. Waller Papers
3. Stanley: How I Found L., 663
4. Stanley: How I Found L., 655
5. Family Letters
6. Coupland: L.L.J., 199
7. Stanley: How I Found L., 713
8. Coupland: L.L.J., 107
9. Coupland: L.L.J., 213
10. Cameron, i–ix
11. Campbell, 351
12. Debenham, 296
13. Blaikie, 372
14. Blaikie, 374
15. Debenham, 308
16. Debenham, 316
17. Blaikie, 373
18. Waller Papers
19. Chamberlin, no. 68

Index

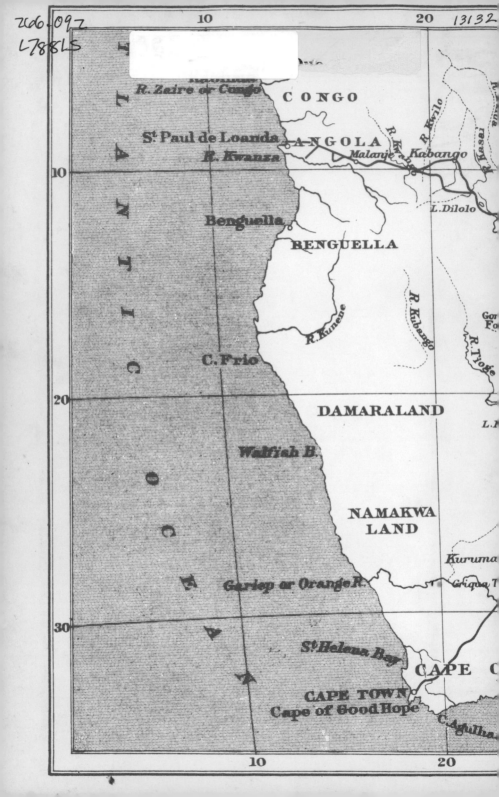